THE ESSENTIAL
HAYIM GREENBERG

THE ESSENTIAL
HAYIM GREENBERG

Essays and Addresses
on Jewish Culture, Socialism, and Zionism

Edited by MARK A. RAIDER

Foreword by PAUL MENDES-FLOHR

The University of Alabama Press

Tuscaloosa

The University of Alabama Press
Tuscaloosa, Alabama 35487-0380
uapress.ua.edu

Publication has been made possible in part through generous assistance from the Posen Foundation as well as the Brandeis-Genesis Institute for Russian Jewry, with the support of the Genesis Philanthropy Group.

Typeface: Garamond

Manufactured in the United States of America
Cover image: Hayim Greenberg, detail from sketch by Saul Raskin of dignitaries at a Jewish National Workers' Alliance banquet honoring Chaim Weizmann, *Der Tog*, c. 1942
Cover design: Michele Myatt Quinn

∞

The paper on which this book is printed meets the minimum requirements of American National Standard for Information Sciences—Permanence of Paper for Printed Library Materials, ANSI Z39.48-1984.

Cataloging-in-Publication data is available from the Library of Congress.
ISBN: 978-0-8173-1935-9
E-ISBN: 978-0-8173-9069-3

To my father David H. Raider and father-in-law Walter Roth,
whose Labor Zionist values are a source of pride and inspiration

Do you know what shocks me most in you? . . . You think like an intellectual, you speak like a freethinker, and you have theories which reek of radicalism. . . . Yield to my prayers, renounce your mad ideas; become good, simple, innocent, and happy once more.

—Anatole France, *The Revolt of the Angels* (1914)

Contents

Illustrations

Foreword

My initial encounter with the intellectual legacy of Hayim Greenberg (1885–1953) was as a graduate student at Brandeis University. Ben Halpern (1912–90), my principal mentor and dissertation adviser, had often spoken of Greenberg with palpable admiration, indeed, affection. He had drawn close to Greenberg when he joined the editorial staff of *Jewish Frontier*, the intellectual monthly of the American Labor Zionist movement, founded by Greenberg in 1934. The *spiritus rector* of Labor Zionism in North America, Greenberg was Halpern's intellectual alter ego. Halpern's indebtedness to Greenberg came to expression not only in his frequent reference to articles Greenberg had written (in English, Hebrew, and Yiddish) but also, indeed primarily, in his evocation of the cultural and ethical commitments of his beloved teacher and friend. Greenberg represented for Halpern the embodiment of a secular Jewish ethos that wedded intellectual integrity, inflected by universal values, with an unyielding concern for the well-being and dignity of the Jewish people.

Greenberg was a public intellectual, one who paradoxically finds oneself a social outsider and yet also bound to the *Lebenswelt* of one's birth by a sense of passionate fidelity and thus responsibility. By dint of their learning and reflexive imagination, public intellectuals stand critically apart from society and its institutions and at the same time deem it their obligation to address the concerns of that society. Intellectuals of this ilk are torn between their private, inner life and their public commitments.[1] How Greenberg managed to balance the pull of the private and the demands of the public he sought to serve, we do not know. For as Mark A. Raider notes in his introduction to this volume, Greenberg's personal papers are lost. That it was a struggle we know from his friends and colleagues. His close associate Marie Syrkin (1900–89) poignantly observed that he was at heart "a nineteenth-century Romantic born too late into a brutal time with which he was always at odds."[2] He was apparently inwardly and essentially a shy person who despite his predilection for meditative scholarship yielded to the calling of a public intellectual. This posture was attested by the very first sentence of the editorial of the inaugural issue of *Jewish Frontier*: "The thoughtful Jew can no longer escape the conviction that he must take a definite stand in regard to the pressing Jewish problems of our time. . . . He has to realize that the business of being a Jew may be either a blessing or a curse, but that apathy is impossible."[3]

Greenberg brought to the public discourse on Jewish affairs a cosmopolitan sensibility honed by the multilingual scope of his education and learning. Born in Bessarabia (now Moldova), which since the 1812 Peace of Bucharest was incorporated into tsarist Russia, he was at home in Yiddish, Russian, and presumably Romanian and Ukrainian. He also acquired a sovereign command of Hebrew. Indeed, in the wake of the October Revolution of 1917 he moved to Kiev, the capital of Ukraine, in order to edit—together with David Koigen (1879–1933) and Fischel Schneerson (1888–1958)—a Hebrew literary journal.[4] Obliged to flee the Soviet Union in 1921, he continued his activity as a Hebrew publicist in Berlin, where he edited *Haolam* (The World), the official weekly of the World Zionist Organization, and the Zionist monthly *Atidenu* (Our Future). Upon immigrating to the United States in 1924, he assumed the editorship of the Labor Zionist Yiddish weekly, *Der yidisher kemfer* (The Jewish Fighter). Commenting on Greenberg's quadrilingual existence—English, Hebrew, Russian,[5] and Yiddish—Marie Syrkin noted that he was at home in each of these languages and their respective cultural universes. "No link in his [multilingual inheritance] had ever been wholly severed, and the tentacles of feeling reached nostalgically to several and sometimes contradictory areas of thought and tradition."[6]

The multiple and diverse skeins of Greenberg's cultural inheritance lend his writings and thought an intellectual elasticity and thus instinctual resistance to the doctrinaire ideological positions that tended to characterize his Zionist and socialist contemporaries. His non-dogmatic Zionism and socialism are richly documented in this comprehensive anthology of his writings meticulously edited by Raider. In addition to his learned annotations alerting the reader to what are now arcane references and forgotten personalities, Raider's introduction places Greenberg within the Zionist discourse of his day and thereby also illuminates his role as a uniquely independent thinker within the ranks of Labor Zionism.[7] He sought to steer Zionist discourse not only from sinking amidst the shoals of doctrinaire postures but also from the shallow sentiments of nationalism and the politically myopic reflexes that it engenders. Greenberg's steady intellectual guidance is as urgent today as it was in his day. This is all the more reason to commend Raider's judicious selection of his writings.

Paul Mendes-Flohr

Acknowledgments

> On my way from New York to Philadelphia, I was reading a book by T. S. Eliot, a rather intriguing book on the definition of culture, and when I arrived at Penn Station, I came to the conclusion that I knew less than I knew yesterday.
>
> —Hayim Greenberg, June 15, 1949

The process of editing, researching, and constructing this anthology has taken nearly two decades. Until my sabbatical year in 2013–14, a variety of personal and professional obligations intervened to slow my progress. Yet my interest in the project never wavered and with each step my appreciation for Hayim Greenberg's intellectual talents and political labors grew and deepened. Having reached the end of my journey, I recognize how much there is yet to learn to fully appreciate the stunning achievement that is Greenberg's *oeuvre*.

This anthology project would not have been possible without the generous support of many colleagues, associates, and friends. Here at last I have the opportunity to thank them for their time, patience, and energies.

For their scholarly expertise and gracious collegiality, I am indebted to Allan Arkush, Shlomo Avineri, Jonathan Beecher, Dan Ben-Amos, Deborah Bernstein, Mark L. Blum, Ronald Bosco, Marc Zvi Brettler, Angela Brintlinger, Martin Ceadel, J. Eugene Clay, Mitchell Cohen, Peter Conn, Christopher B. Daly, the late Moshe Davis, Irene Delic, Glenn Dynner, Bartow J. Elmore, Stefan Fiol, Martin Francis, the late Lloyd P. Gartner, Ted Gilman, Daniel J. Goldhagen, Aryeh Goren, Arthur Green, Gildas Hamel, Sigrun Haude, Jeffrey Haus, Andrew Heinze, Elie Holzer, Cecelia Klein, Gerd Korman, Eli Lederhendler, Louis D. Levine, Daniel Markovic, Michael A. Meyer, Yehudah Mirsky, W. David Nelson, Avraham Novershtern, Shailaja Paik, Yaron Peleg, Monty Penkower, Yohanan Petrovsky-Shtern, Benjamin Ravid, Benjamin C. Ray, Dwight Reynolds, Rebecca Rossen, Ovadia Shapiro, Yaacov Shavit, Gideon Shimoni, Jeffrey Shoulson, Paul Spickard, Willard Sunderland, Ettie Taft, D. A. Jeremy Telman, Melvin I. Urofsky, Christian Wiese, Irvin Wise, Luke Whitmore, Mira Yungman, Jeffrey Zalar, and Sergei Zhuk.

From start to finish, this project benefited from the research assistance of a handful of remarkable and resourceful students. My thanks to Shmarya Gershon, Shawn Halstead, Aaron Levy, Morris Levy, and Neil Tevebaugh-Kenwryck for their detective work and technical assistance. Debra K. Burgess combed through a penultimate draft of the manuscript, fixed numerous errors, and helped ready the project for publication.

During my years at the University at Albany, where I began this project, I enjoyed the support of the Center for Jewish Studies, including its first-rate assistant director Yoel Hirschfeld and exceptional advisory board led by Peter Elitzer, Alan P. Goldberg, and Carl H. Rosner. At the University of Cincinnati, I am privileged to work with superb colleagues who make the history department an intellectually stimulating and convivial environment. I am deeply grateful to the department (under the past and present leadership of, respectively, Willard Sunderland and Christopher Phillips) for welcoming me into its ranks. The university's Center for Studies in Jewish Education and Culture, directed by my wife Miriam B. Raider-Roth, is my second academic home and an unparalleled platform for excellence in teaching, learning, and research. Both the department and the center have been crucial to my endeavors as a scholar.

For his indefatigable encouragement, I owe a special debt of thanks to my friend and colleague Gary P. Zola, executive director the Jacob Rader Marcus Center for the American Jewish Archives, located on the Cincinnati campus of the Hebrew Union College–Jewish Institute of Religion. Kevin Proffitt, Lisa B. Frankel, Dana Herman, Al Simandl, and the other talented AJA staff members have been generous and helpful in myriad ways. Phillip Reekers provided expert assistance with the book's digital images.

I am also deeply grateful to the following research librarians who fielded numerous inquiries and offered critical assistance: Phoebe Acheson (Public Library of Cincinnati and Hamilton County), Liangyu Fu (University of Michigan Libraries), Leo Greenbaum, Lyudmila Sholokhova, and Yeshaya Metal (YIVO Institute for Jewish Research), Gail Malmgreen (Robert F. Wagner Labor Archives), and Sally Moffitt (University of Cincinnati Libraries).

From 2006 to 2013 the Posen Foundation's college and teacher education projects in the United States and Canada provided an especially generative and hospitable environment for my work in modern Jewish history. I wish to thank my partners in the foundation's academic advisory council—David Biale, Laura Levitt, Andrea Lieber, Naomi Seidman, Susan Shapiro, and James Young—for their camaraderie and outstanding academic leadership. A special word of appreciation is also due to Felix Posen, the foundation's visionary founder, and his son Daniel Posen. Their steadfast commitment to the study of secular Jewish culture is instrumental to the field of Jewish studies and the academy, and I will always be grateful for their warm friendship and generosity.

Life takes unexpected turns and my transition to the University of Cincinnati was not uncomplicated. Many caring and honorable people stepped forward to assist me during this difficult period. I would especially like to acknowledge Charles J. Faruki, Martin A. Foos, Gary L. Greenberg, Jack C. Rubenstein, and Joel M. Sweet. As well, I deeply appreciate the support of Myrna Baron, Diane Berger and Matthew A. Cahn, the late Theodore Bikel and the late Tamara Brooks, Arthur and Nanette Brenner, Jill Egar, Zohar Egar, Beth and Peter Elitzer, Barbara and Dan Elman, Gonen Haklay, Lewis Kamrass, Richard and Mona Kerstine, Robert L. Kuykendal, Janet and Dennis Mendel, Michelle Mendelowitz and Dani Yuval, Orit Netter, the Posen family, Robert S. Rifkind, Anna and Jon Rosen, Carl H. Rosner, Gloria and Al Shapiro, Michael H. Steinhardt, the late S. Arthur Spiegel, and Beatrice Winkler and the late Henry R. Winkler. I am grateful for the efforts of Mary Brydon-Miller, Steven DeLue, Claire Goldstein, Charlotte Newman Goldy, Annette Hemmings, Anna Klosowska, Marc A. Levitt, Michael A. Meyer, Haim O. Rechnitzer, and Sven-Erik Rose. My profound thanks for the public support of Robert Alter, Judith R. Baskin, David Biale, Sharon Feiman-Nemser, Evyatar Friesel, Carol Gilligan, Robert Kegan, Daniel C. Levy, Sara Lawrence-Lightfoot, Shulamit Reinharz, Jonathan Rosen, Jonathan D. Sarna, Robert M. Seltzer, Anita Shapira, James Young, and Steven J. Zipperstein.

It would be difficult to overstate the role of several key figures and sponsors in helping to bring this book project to fruition. Kenneth Bob, president of Ameinu, the successor organization of the American Labor Zionist movement and the Jewish Frontier Association, granted permission to reprint much of the material in this volume. At the University of Alabama Press, editor-in-chief Dan Waterman shepherded the manuscript through the acquisitions, vetting, and production process. Mark Bauman and Adam Mendelsohn, coeditors of the series Jews and Judaism: History and Culture, and the anonymous peer reviewers offered constructive criticism and valuable suggestions that improved the undertaking as a whole. Jon Berry, Bonny McLaughlin, Vanessa Rusch, Eric Schramm, and Blanche Sarratt contributed expert technical assistance. The Brandeis-Genesis Institute for Russian Jewry, with the support of the Genesis Philanthropy Group, the Charles Phelps Taft Research Center at the University of Cincinnati, the Posen Foundation, and the University at Albany Faculty Awards Program provided generous funding for my research and the book's publication.

I am very fortunate to have a circle of academic peers whose scholarly work and interests dovetail with my own: Ofer Shiff, Zohar Segev, and Matthew Silver—comrades-in-arms at the intersection of American Jewish and Zionist history—are a wellspring of imaginative talent and warm friendship. Haim O. Rechnitzer, my Cincinnati *hevruta*, is a learned confrere and invaluable sounding board. Daniel J. Tichenor is an exemplary scholar, a loyal friend, and a darn good squash partner.

Over the years, I have been blessed with extraordinary teachers and mentors. Leon A. Jick (1924–2005) and Lawrence H. Fuchs (1927–2013) gave unstintingly of their time, knowledge, and friendship to encourage my graduate studies. Mishael M. Caspi (1932–2013) was like a father to me and his imprint remains on all I strive to accomplish. Muki Tsur continues to inspire and spur my interest in the history of Labor Zionism and the kibbutz movement. Murray Baumgarten, David Biale, and Paul Mendes-Flohr are generous friends and trusted advisers. No words can adequately express my abiding gratitude to Jehuda Reinharz, Jonathan D. Sarna, Robert M. Seltzer, and Stephen J. Whitfield for their unflagging support, friendship, wisdom, and counsel.

As I neared completion of this book project, I lost my cherished grandfather Alfred (Avram Berl) Raider and uncle Philip W. Raider. I treasure their memories and miss them both dearly. Special thanks to my parents David and Elizabeth Raider and my in-laws Walter and Chaya Roth for being such wonderful and loving role models. My siblings, siblings-in-law, and nephews and nieces are a terrific clan and they too deserve a shout-out: Elana Raider; Daniel, Shari, Elias, and Yael Raider; Ari Roth, Kate Schecter, Isabel and Sophie Roth; and Stephen Zeldes, Judy Roth, Miko and Tema Zeldes-Roth. To Miriam, my best friend and beloved, and my children Jonah, Ezzie, and Talia, thank you for everything—you keep me grounded, renew each day, and make my world whole.

Mark A. Raider, Cincinnati, Ohio, July 2015

Editor's Note

This volume is organized chronologically and reflects the course of historical events that shaped the Jewish public arena during Hayim Greenberg's lifetime (1885–1953). It has been intentionally designed to complement scholarly works that survey modern and American Jewish history from the late nineteenth to mid-twentieth centuries. The essays are accompanied by detailed annotations that seek to situate and explain each document in its specific cultural, political, and historical context. Though the book might have included many more items, my aim from the outset has been to produce an anthology that highlights Greenberg's wide-ranging intellectual, philosophical, cultural, and political interests. The essays presented here were selected to provide the reader with a representative and substantive sample of Greenberg's most important writings.

A brief explanation is in order concerning the organizational structure of this volume. In general, I have attempted to make the collection as accessible and useful as possible to students, researchers, and interested lay readers alike. Each essay is accompanied by a series of head notes and cross-referenced annotations. In cases where Greenberg mentions well-known persons (e.g., Aristotle, Theodore Roosevelt) and major historical events (e.g., the American Civil War, World War I), the notes tend to be brief. Where a fuller explanation seems warranted owing to Greenberg's discussion of particular persons, issues, or developments, I have included pertinent discursive material. In a handful of instances Greenberg refers to seemingly obscure sources and it has not been possible to provide detailed or precise information with certainty; this, too, is duly noted. A glossary is included to assist readers unfamiliar with Hebrew and Yiddish terminology used frequently in Greenberg's essays. Information that appears infrequently has been inserted directly into the body of the main text.

Throughout the volume, I have endeavored to refer readers to English-language materials and contemporary scholarship concerning specific texts, themes, and concepts rather than routinely citing original sources (e.g., the Hebrew Bible, premodern rabbinic texts, works by Spinoza, Hegel, Freud, Yiddish and Hebrew literature). My purpose in this regard is to help guide students to materials that will support further study and independent investigation. That said, I have also determined that in many instances the elucidation of given moments in the text is best served by identifying and explicating the original source of non-English language references.

Lastly, I have retained most of Greenberg's specific Jewish, Palestinian, and Zionist locutions because of their cultural and historic value. Accordingly, in various essays one will note the use of terms such as Mandatory Palestine, Yishuv, and so on. In many instances, common English spellings have been retained and/or inserted for the sake of ease and readability (e.g., Judah, Nablus, Jaffa). In general, I have deployed a simplified orthography and transliteration of Hebrew, Aramaic, and Yiddish terms to give English-speaking readers as clear a phonetic equivalent as possible without introducing complex diacritical marks and special linguistic values. Exceptions in this regard are terms and names for which a common usage is highly familiar (e.g., *kibbutz*, *yiddishkeit*). The volume also uses standard abbreviations for classical and premodern Jewish sources, such as "Gen." (Genesis), "Exod." (Exodus), "1 Kgs." (First Kings). Citations for the Talmud are indicated by the letters "B." (Babylonian Talmud) and "J." (Talmud of the Land of Israel, also known as the Jerusalem Talmud), followed by the names of specific tractates and folio numbers. Unless otherwise noted, all translated terms are from Hebrew and all emphases in the essays have been retained from the original texts. Wherever necessary, minor emendations and stylistic adjustments were made to the essays in order to unify and enhance the volume overall. Square brackets within quotations indicate additions intended to clarify the meaning of the original text.

THE ESSENTIAL
HAYIM GREENBERG

Introduction

Free Associations—An Intellectual and Political Profile of Hayim Greenberg

Mark A. Raider

Hayim Greenberg (1885–1953) was a remarkable secular Jewish public intellectual and political activist who stood at the center of revolutionary trends that transformed Europe, America, and Palestine at the dawn of the twentieth century. A talented writer and speaker who mastered four languages—Yiddish, Hebrew, Russian, and English—he distinguished himself as an essayist and polemicist in an era awash with competing ideas of traditionalism, radicalism, liberalism, socialism, and Zionism. By the eve of World War I he emerged as an important voice in Russian, Hebraist, and Yiddish political and literary circles.[1] His intellectual and cultural labors in eastern and central Europe, a veritable proving ground of modern Jewish politics, sharpened his editorial sensibility and elevated his visibility in the Jewish public arena. In 1924, he journeyed to the United States on a cultural mission sponsored by the Zionist Organization, where he also took up his New World post as editor of *Farn folk* (For the People), a leftist Zionist weekly modeled on a Belorussian publication of the same name. With the 1932 union of American Poalei Zion (Workers of Zion), a branch of the Russian socialist Zionist party, and Zeirei Zion Hitahdut (United Young Zionists), an offshoot of the non-Marxist branch of socialist Zionism that flourished in eastern Europe, Palestine, and Yiddish-speaking immigrant quarters in the West, he next assumed the editorship of *Der yidisher kemfer* (The Jewish Fighter) and, shortly thereafter, *Jewish Frontier*, the publications of the Labor Zionist movement in the United States. During World War II, as a member (and for a brief period acting chairman) of the American Zionist Emergency Council executive and subsequently as a member of the Jewish Agency executive and the first director of the Department for Education and Culture in the Diaspora, he was a central figure in world Zionist affairs.[2] He is also credited with playing a key role in winning the Latin American delegations' crucial support for the United Nations resolution establishing the State of Israel in 1948.[3]

On March 16, 1953 thousands of mourners, including Israeli cabinet ministers Golda Meir, Dov Yosef, and Peretz Bernstein, attended Greenberg's funeral at New York City's Bnai Jeshurun Congregation. The street outside the synagogue held an overflow crowd. A lengthy obituary in the *New York Times* noted Greenberg was a "leading personage" of the Zionist movement and "an intimate of the ranking officials of the State of Israel."[4] A statement issued by Greenberg's "close friends" Israeli prime minister David Ben-Gurion and president Yitzhak Ben-Zvi called him "a man of the rarest quality" who was "steadfast in the struggle for the establishment of Israel and the renaissance of the Jewish people."[5] The Jewish Telegraphic Agency described him as "a leading philosopher of labor Zionism" and "one of the outstanding intellectual figures of the contemporary Zionist movement."[6] These and other depictions of Greenberg as one of "the foremost Zionist leaders in the world"—his devoted admirers idealized him as a "*rebbe*," "sage," and "prophet"—underscore his transnational significance as a Jewish and Zionist leader.[7] Even Greenberg's erstwhile ideological and political rivals respected his intellectual talents and labors on behalf of the Jewish people.[8] In 1953, together with former President Harry Truman and Yosef Sprinzak, the Speaker of the Israel's Knesset, Greenberg posthumously received the Stephen S. Wise award from the American Jewish Congress for outstanding leadership.[9] As well, several Jewish and Zionist institutions in the United States, Israel, and Argentina were named in Greenberg's honor following his death, including the World Zionist Organization's Institute for Youth Leaders from Abroad, the Jewish Agency's Hayim Greenberg Teachers Institute in Jerusalem, a Jewish cultural center in Buenos Aires, and various Jewish-sponsored literary prizes.

And yet half a century later, the acclaim and renown Greenberg once enjoyed as "a revered and beloved leader" has all but vanished from Jewish public consciousness.[10] Indeed, as historian Stephen J. Whitfield observes, Greenberg's legacy seems "cursed by oblivion."[11] The question must be asked: Why has Greenberg slipped down the proverbial memory hole? The answer, I would suggest, can be broken into four parts: (a) the epochal changes to the Jewish public arena since the 1950s have yielded a kind of collective American Jewish amnesia about the community's earlier history; (b) Greenberg's personal disposition was at odds with the Weberian model of "charismatic authority" that burnished the legacies of Chaim Weizmann, Louis D. Brandeis, David Ben-Gurion, and other well-known twentieth-century Jewish political figures; (c) the unusual character of Greenberg's multilingual *oeuvre* and the prevailing biases of modern scholars have mitigated against his inclusion in the canon of Jewish history and thought; and (d) the ongoing cultural gap between American and Israeli Jewry, including ambivalence to the notion of a symbiotic Israel-diaspora relationship, has rendered Greenberg's voice mute.

To begin, it would be difficult to overstress the profound structural and social transformation of American Jewry since the end of World War II—and the community's collective amnesia about its past. Historians have documented the sweeping intellectual, economic, cultural, and political changes that have moved

1. "Lives of Our Times: Hayim Greenberg" (1948); courtesy of the Jewish Telegraphic Agency.

Jews from the margins to the mainstream of American society in the latter half of the twentieth century. The once-thriving Yiddish-speaking immigrant milieu of the late nineteenth and early twentieth centuries has passed from the scene. In the space of two generations, American Jewry has emerged as a largely unified countrywide English-speaking ethnic minority as much at home in the New World as any time in American history. In tandem, the waning of left-wing Jewish ideologies and movements in the West—a loose coalition of socialist and communist parties, trade unions, workers groups, and immigrant societies so prominent in Jewish life before World War II—the development of a secure and prosperous American Jewish community mindful of its ethnic clout, and the meteoric rise of Israel as a sovereign state have caused a sea change in modern Jewish politics.[12] The metamorphosis of American and world Jewry since Greenberg's day—a tumultuous period when he stood out as a key interlocutor between the Zionist movement, European Jewry, the Yishuv, and American Jews—is nothing short of astonishing. In today's American Jewish community—the strongest and wealthiest diaspora Jewish society in history—liberal and bourgeois values prevail, Israel ranks as a top priority, and a wide array of robust organizations sustain the social, religious, and political landscape.

Second, Greenberg's unusual profile as a leader is noteworthy. He did not fit the mold of Jewish cultural or political leadership typical of his day, nor did he identify unconditionally with any Jewish, Zionist, or socialist camp. Unlike many strong-willed contemporaries he did not actively seek the limelight or strive for higher political office. He was by temperament modest, self-effacing, and somewhat aloof, and though widely admired he never sought to cultivate a personal following or political base.[13] A son of the Russian Jewish intelligentsia, his perceptive and sensitive diagnoses of western Jewry's acculturationist and assimilationist tendencies did not undermine his faith in diaspora Jewish culture's vitality. Likewise, he refused to dilute his synergistic commitments to Judaism, Zionism, and socialism or sublimate his attachments to Europe, Palestine, and America. He sustained a vigorous non-Marxian socialist vision, decrying the excesses of Soviet Communism while advancing a voluntaristic social democratic agenda as humanity's best hope for creating a just, equitable, and secure future. He vigorously asserted a non-doctrinaire Jewish nationalist worldview at odds with Zionism's prevailing forces, including his own Labor Zionist movement—the left-wing social democratic coalition that dominated Zionist affairs, the Yishuv, and later the State of Israel from 1934 to 1977. He was, according to Irving Howe, the literary critic and appreciative observer of eastern European Jewish culture, "probably the most gifted of the Yiddish intellectuals [in the United States] . . . at once enthusiast and skeptic, public man and private intelligence, a creature of multiple moods and personae." "What matter[ed] most about his work," Howe asserted, was "the variety of his tone, the cut of his argument, the insight along the way."[14] In sum, Greenberg was a fiercely independent thinker whose "free associations" made him something of a gadfly and an outsider among the very circles that prized his humane and articulate leadership.[15]

Third, the seeming indifference of modern Jewish studies to Greenberg and other ignored figures—dubbed "un-persons" by historian Lloyd P. Gartner—bears scrutiny. The "un-person," according to Gartner, is one of those individuals "who occupied prominent positions, or were even at the center of great affairs, and have been obliterated from the place in historical writing which they should reasonably be given."[16] If Greenberg's legacy suffers, in part, from the tendency of scholars to privilege the body of literature produced by elite theologians, philosophers, and scholars, it may also be due to the fact that his *oeuvre*, though ample and partially anthologized, is unconcentrated and diffuse.[17] In contrast to Leo Strauss, Mordecai M. Kaplan, Hannah Arendt, Kurt Lewin, Abraham Joshua Heschel, and other significant (and well-researched) twentieth-century Jewish intellectuals, Greenberg never produced a unified comprehensive or definitive theological, philosophical, political, or artistic work.[18] The lack thereof, it may be posited, reflects his lifelong commitment to balancing intellectual pursuits with practical tasks, including demands imposed on his leadership by the exigent circumstances that rocked the globe and threatened Jewish survival in the pre-state era.

Fourth, taking the full measure of Greenberg's significance requires sensitivity to the place of performance-oriented oral literature in modern Jewish history.

Because spoken artistry (sometimes but not always transcribed) constituted a sizable quotient of Greenberg's creative body of work, scholarly appreciation in this regard is critical to evaluating his effectiveness and impact. Ironically, however, whereas oral literatures have always been fundamental to the subfields of ancient, classical, and medieval Jewish studies, modern Jewish studies is "more at ease with the written word" and ambivalent about the value of spoken texts.[19] This attitude has contributed to the deemphasis of Greenberg and other figures—consider, for example, Ray Frank, Zvi Hirsch Masliansky, Meyer London, and Emil Hirsch, to name but a few—whose public speaking, preaching, and oratory is critical to the record of American Jewish history. The literary scholar and Zionist polemicist Marie Syrkin, who was close to Greenberg personally,[20] recounted his distinctive talent as an orator. She described him as "the master of a lost art—conversation," who radiated a quiet charisma, inclusive warmth, and possessed the ability to enrapture audiences large and small. "Nobody could tell a story like Greenberg," she said, "and by story I do not mean an anecdote or joke but a reminiscence which in the telling became a finished product. . . . His hearers learned to recognize the premonitory signs. A moment of silence, a flick of the cigarette, and another one of a thousand-and-one adventures of the spirit would begin."[21] In a word, the act of expression was itself an event in which Greenberg's discourse combined form and function to attain rhetorical efficacy. From a myriad of such experiences, Greenberg generated a vast paper trail that includes transcribed speeches and public utterances as well as fully developed prose, articles, and other writings.[22] Such an admixture, the folklore scholar Dwight Reynolds observes, is typical of groups that live a "cosmopolitan and international lifestyle that is enmeshed with the consumption of written texts and various forms of mass media."[23]

Finally, it is hard to escape the conclusion that Greenberg—who lived in the United States for most of his adult life but also spent extended periods in the Yishuv—has been shelved for what are essentially ideological reasons. On the one hand, in the words of Hadassah leader Rose L. Halprin, he provided transcendent "moral" leadership. He was "never servile to the great, nor condescending to the humble," she noted, "his Zionism did not negate the diaspora, but envisioned great creativity for it in the future no less than in the past."[24] On the other, Greenberg's distinctive position as a key Zionist interlocutor made him, voluntarily, something of an outsider in both American Jewish life and Palestine/Israel—a relationship he described as "a choice between two loves, one which transcends the other."[25] On a few occasions, he seriously considered personal immigration to Palestine/Israel. In 1949, for example, he was asked to succeed Zalman (Rubashow) Shazar (later Israel's third president) as editor of *Davar* (The Word), the country's venerable Labor movement daily. Like Abba Hillel Silver, the eminent Cleveland rabbi and Zionist leader, Israeli colleagues considered Greenberg to be one of the few "American" leaders with crossover potential in the fledgling Jewish state.[26] He mulled over the possibility but declined the movement's request. Anecdotal evidence suggests Greenberg, a lifelong smoker, was by this time ailing and required medical attention not yet available in Palestine. As well, his wife, Leah, and son, Emanuel, wished to remain in the United States.[27] Whatever the mix of personal and family reasons, many of his Israeli contemporaries viewed his decision not to go on *aliyah* as a sign of weakness and failure.[28] Yet for Greenberg, the prism of *shlilat hagolah* (negation of the exile) was far more complex than simply a matter of domicile or residence. Challenging the organized Zionist movement's "fruitless dogmatism" and reductionist efforts "to create monistic wholeness by decree," he offered an erudite and compelling vision of the duality of diaspora Jewish life and the modern Jewish state. Rather than mutually exclusive propositions, he argued, "all Jewish roads sooner or later . . . lead to the same destination: to *Erez Israel*."[29]

In an era that placed a premium on "normalizing" Jewish life, Greenberg—prized for his incisive, nuanced, and generative worldview—stood above the fray. He rejected the philosophical and ideological certitude required of the communal and political standard bearers of his day. Meanwhile, he used his perch as a "marginal man" (a term coined by sociologist Robert E. Park to describe a cultural hybrid "on the margin of two cultures and two societies") to full cultural and political advantage.[30] Together with those whom the cohort literary scholar Carole S. Kessner has dubbed the "other Jewish intellectuals," including Horace M. Kallen, Simon Rawidowicz, Milton Steinberg, and Trude Weiss-Rosmarin, Greenberg remained unapologetically committed to the twin aims of preserving and building up modern Jewish life in all its variety.[31]

Greenberg's writings and utterances constitute a systematic corpus that illuminates a wide array of topics, questions, and themes central to the Jewish encounter with modernity. Moreover, despite a paucity of archival resources concerning his personal life and organizational work, the sheer volume of Greenberg's literary output warrants scholarly attention.[32] Viewed as an aggregate, one is immediately struck by the range and depth of his intellectual, cultural, and political grasp. His essays—frequently organized like talmudic discussions stretching across time and space—draw on everything from classical Jewish texts to Russian and Hebrew folklore and literature, to European and American political philosophy, to European, Middle Eastern, and Asian cultural and political developments of the 1920s, 1930s, and 1940s, to conversations with Jewish pioneers in Palestine and taxi drivers, street vendors, and cooks in America's cities. A polymath of the first order, his distinctive talents are also evident in his searching essays on prayer, death, Jesus' crucifixion, Martin Luther, church and state, Fyodor Dostoyevsky, Vladimir Lenin, Freudian psychoanalysis, the French thinker Henri Bergson, Mark Twain, Gandhi, the Bengali writer Rabindranath Tagore, the

Japanese philosopher Toyohiko Kagawa, and much more.[33] It is hoped the present critical edition will introduce a new generation of readers and researchers to Greenberg's *oeuvre* and restore him to his rightful place in Jewish and Zionist history.

Formative Years

Born on December 31, 1885, in Chișinău (Kishinev), Bessarabia, Hayim Greenberg grew up in the twilight of the Romanov dynasty. He was raised in the Pale of Settlement's traditionalist Yiddish-speaking milieu, but although he apparently "attracted attention as a *Wunderkind*" (prodigy), little is known about his upbringing.[34] By his own admission, he never received any advanced religious training. Nor for that matter did he have much of a formal secular education before studying for his doctorate as young man. He did, however, possess a passion for learning, and he taught himself to read and write in Yiddish, Hebrew, and Russian (as well as German and English in his adult years). His autodidactic proclivity and voracious intellectual appetite resulted in a broadly based Jewish and general education.

Greenberg broke early on with traditional Judaism as a religious system and in its place he adopted the secular nontheistic revolutionary ethos that stamped much of his generation.[35] In the early 1900s he became involved in Russia's clandestine Zionist youth circles and earned a reputation as a persuasive speaker. In 1905, he coauthored a proclamation that was widely circulated by Russian Zeirei-Zion following the Kishinev pogrom.[36] At age twenty-one, he made his debut as one of the youngest Russian Zionist delegates to the 1906 Helsingfors Conference, which adopted resolutions favoring the program known as *Gegenwartsarbeit* (a German term connoting Zionist work in the diaspora) as well as equal rights for Jews and other nationalities in the Russian empire.[37] Prior to the outbreak of World War I, he was among the youthful editors in St. Petersburg of the Zionist Organization of Russia's weekly *Razsvet* (The Dawn), a liberal Russian Jewish journal with a large readership. After the Kerensky revolution of 1917 (also known as the February revolution), he found employment as a lecturer in medieval Jewish literature and Greek drama at the University of Kharkov. He apparently studied for his doctorate at this juncture, but it is unclear if he was permitted to complete the course work. He also met at this interval his future wife, Leah Rabinowitz (1892–1979), with whom he shared a passion for Russian literature, especially (as later noted in his ethical will of April 18, 1949) the Romantic poetry of Mikhail Lermontov. They were married in Moscow on March 13, 1918. Meanwhile, Greenberg's translations of the Zionist thinker Ahad Haam's essays from Hebrew into Russian "earned him a high reputation" among educated Jewish circles, "where many people who were interested could not read Ahad

Haam in the original."[38] Next, he relocated to Kiev where he coedited the Hebrew literary journal *Kadimah* (Onward) with David Koigen and Fishl Schneerson and became a leading proponent of Tarbut (Culture), a Zionist cultural organization dedicated to promoting Hebrew language and literature that was later proscribed by the Bolshevik authorities.[39] In the uncertain and turbulent period that followed the Bolshevik revolution, Greenberg remained faithful to a combination of Zionist and socialist ideals. He did so, however, at enormous political and personal risk. His last stand in Russia was in defense of Habimah (The Stage), Moscow's reputable Hebrew theatre. Recognizing the threat of Bolshevism's growing excesses, Greenberg composed a well-known manifesto in defense of Habimah and persuaded the Russian intellectuals Maxim Gorky, Anatoly Lunacharsky, and Vyacheslav Ivanov to sign it. Later, he tried to enlist the support of Romain Rolland and Anatole France in support of the Hebraist cause.[40]

The efforts to save Habimah failed and following this episode Greenberg, like many other Zionist activists, was arrested on several occasions by hostile Soviet authorities.[41] The majority of Russian radicals, particularly the Bolshevik leadership, viewed Jewish nationalist sentiment contemptuously. They considered Zionism, in the words of Leon Trotsky, to be nothing more than the "hysterical sobbings" of self-delusory Jewish particularists.[42] At the same time, the Soviet regime's increasingly repressive and totalitarian policies dealt a devastating blow to the Russian Jewish radical movements. Inevitably, Greenberg, like tens of thousands of others, had no recourse except emigration. After a brief stay in Kishinev, with the intervention of Maxim Gorky he was permitted to leave the Soviet Union along with a group of Russian Jewish writers and scholars.

In 1921, Greenberg journeyed to Berlin, joining other eastern European Jewish émigrés in this important center of Hebraist and Zionist activity.[43] For a brief period he coedited *Haolam* (The World), the Zionist Organization's Hebrew weekly, with the Hebraist journalists Moshe Kleinman and Shmuel Perlman. He also coedited the Zionist monthly *Atideinu* (Our Future) with Zvi Woyslawski and continued his cultural work with Tarbut.

In Berlin, Greenberg carved out a niche for himself as a Jewish public intellectual, while he and Leah started a family—their son Emanuel was born on March 7, 1923 (d. 1986). In contrast to other Jewish radicals who became anarchists or Communists, he never rejected his past or his cultural inheritance. His non-Marxist and voluntaristic brand of socialist Zionism was deeply rooted in eastern European Jewish life. He prized the riches of Yiddish literature alongside modern Hebrew, and his profound respect and appreciation of Judaism's spiritual and homiletic traditions were integral to his *Weltanschauung*. "Those powers that build a Jewish personality," he would later assert, must be "nourished from sources which are regarded, at least formally, as religious."[44] The purportedly agnostic Greenberg was strongly influenced by the strains of religious neo-

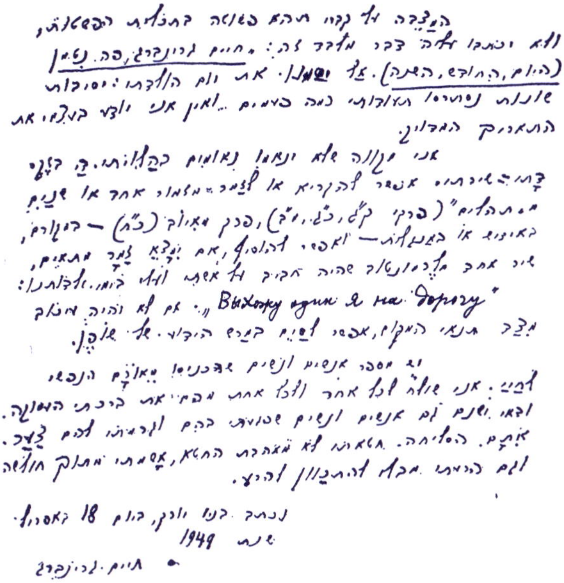

Translation: The tombstone on my grave should be as plain as can be, and nothing should be inscribed on it but the following: "Here rests Hayim Greenberg (the day, the month, the year)." Do not mark my date of birth; for various reasons my birth certificates were corrupted several times, and I myself do not know the exact date.

I hope that there will be no speeches at my funeral. A religious musical service will be enough. One or two psalms may be recited or sung (Psalms 203, 23, 42) and a chapter from Job (28) may be read in the original, in Yiddish, or in English. If a fitting singer should be available, a song by Lermontov, dear to my wife and me in our youth ("I Go Out on the Road Alone") could be sung. If the facilities of the place permit, the well-known march of Chopin could be played in conclusion.

There are a number of men and women who brought the light of their souls into my life. To each of them I send my deep blessing. There are also no doubt men and women whom I hurt and to whom I caused sorrow. Of them I ask forgiveness. I sinned not out of love of sin; I was guilty out of weakness, and I did wrong without the intent to do so.

2. From Hayim Greenberg's Ethical Will (written in New York, April 18, 1949); courtesy of Ameinu.

Judaism propounded by Hermann Cohen in the prewar era and later developed by Martin Buber and Franz Rosenzweig.[45] Buber's monthly *Der Jude* (The Jew), one of the most important organs of Jewish thought in central Europe, as well as the latter's seminal philosophical work *Ich und Du* (I and Thou) (1923), resonated with Greenberg's meditative nature, evoking his nascent existentialism. Like Buber, Greenberg possessed a rich appreciation of the poetic, philosophical, and mystical elements of rabbinic Judaism and Hasidism. However, where Buber saw the inscrutable hand of God at work in Jewish modernity, Greenberg (like his close friend Haim Nahman Bialik) perceived organic and dynamic social and historical forces. He considered theological notions of redemption to be powerfully constitutive folk myths that bolstered the Jewish people's integrity and survival across time and space.[46] In 1923, for example, Greenberg offered the following assessment of the relationship between Jewry's centuries-old tribal belief in its election and its temporal reality: "Our dream of redemption, preserved in us only by the strength of the messianic spirit that imbued it, and that even now may be kept alive only by reflections of the messianic splendor, can be solved and realized only by non-messianic means."[47] Modern Jewish life, Greenberg thus argued, required both continued faith—a sense of mission—and a pragmatic constructivist view of Zionism.

Greenberg's eclectic views put him at odds with the rising young leadership of German Zionism. This is amply illustrated by the case of Kurt Blumenfeld, the influential second-generation German Zionist leader and one of the best-known Jewish figures of the day. Blumenfeld, a native German Jew, came from a highly assimilated, middle-class background. In part, Blumenfeld's Zionist conversion stemmed from the romanticization of Germany's *Ostjuden* (eastern European Jewish immigrants) and their presumed Jewish authenticity. He viewed Zionism as "the modern way to Judaism" for German Jews like himself who were estranged from their heritage and religious tradition.[48] The only way of resuscitating German Jewry, he believed, was by instilling in native-born Jews an ardor for Jewish identity and culture akin to that of eastern European Jewry. In order to avoid the pitfalls of assimilation in central European society, he reasoned, the Jews must immigrate to Palestine, where they could live wholly Jewish lives. Unlike Greenberg, Blumenfeld considered Jewish life in the diaspora untenable and espoused an anti-diaspora doctrine.[49] Despite their divergent philosophies, Blumenfeld's ideas resonated with Greenberg and he adopted Blumenfeld's concept of "Palestinocentrism," albeit in a modified undogmatic form.

With respect to the amalgamation of Greenberg's Zionist and socialist views, he was closest to Chaim Arlosoroff, a Russian émigré like himself, who completed his formal education in Berlin. Arlosoroff, a cofounder of the German branch of Zeirei Zion affiliated with Hapoel Hazair (The Young Worker) in Palestine, emerged in this period as a brilliant economist and a rising star of European Zionist politics. Despite the fact that Greenberg was fourteen years Arlosoroff's senior, the two men developed a warm relationship that transcended the gap in their ages. "Although they were different," the Mapai leader Yosef Sprinzak later recalled, "they possessed a commonality of spirit and essence. . . . They were both poets and dreamers."[50] Sprinzak's intriguing description underscores the *mentalité*, or common generational impulse, of Greenberg, Arlosoroff, and other secular Jewish activists who identified with the Second and Third Aliyah pioneers of the Yishuv. They were profoundly inspired by A. D. Gordon's cosmic vision of *kibush haavodah* (the conquest of labor)—a pioneering Jewish variation on the Tolstoyan philosophy of physical toil and national redemption.[51] This concept, with its layers of historically unfolding meaning—*avodah*, the Hebrew word for labor, is also the classical term for worship—symbolized the transformation of Jewish life in toto, both in its traditional and modern forms. Grafted to this philosophical trunk was the strategy of the Labor Palestine; pioneering, colonization, and socialism provided the essential links between Zionist ideology and praxis.[52]

While Arlosoroff drew on Gordon's romantic philosophy, his Zionist thinking was also shaped by the scientific rigor of the German academy. Out of this admixture, he developed an original synthesis of populist socialism and pragmatic Zionism, a program with which Greenberg and other diaspora members of Zeirei Zion strongly identified. In contrast to Gordon's vague political views and Russian Poalei Zion's doctrinaire Marxist Zionism, Arlosoroff promoted what came to be known as a "constructivist Zionist" program. He maintained that pioneering settlement and the gradual development of Palestine's Jewish socioeconomic infrastructure would eventually enable the Zionists to stake a claim for a Jewish state.[53] Consequently, Arlosoroff supported Chaim Weizmann's conciliatory policies toward the British authorities and the latter's emphasis on "economic and social initiatives within the political conditions created by the Mandate."[54]

Against the background of Buber's neo-Hasidism, Gordon's Russian-style romanticism and populism, and Arlosoroff's Zionist constructivism, Greenberg sharpened his own understanding of Jewish life and modern society. In a 1923 *Haolam* article, he stated: "We [Zionists] have neither sufficiently clarified nor explained . . . that *Erez Israel* will not suddenly be acquired at a historically propitious moment, but that it will rather be built stone upon stone and layer upon layer. . . . The success and victory of our political labors, those which we have achieved and those which are yet to be achieved, are meaningless unless accomplished on the basis of positive substance as well as sensible economic and cultural values that were and are created by ourselves."[55]

Greenberg's Labor Zionism, an amalgam of political, economic, spiritual, and ethical positions, proved attractive to thoughtful secular and national-minded Jews. He was wary of doctrine, whether religious- or scientific-based. He drank deeply from the wellspring of Russian populism, with its moral revulsion for the mass suffering of the Russian people caused by absolutism and capitalism. He considered Jewish social regeneration to be a matter of this-worldly redemption rather than an elusive goal to be pursued irrespective of contemporary needs and concerns. He refused to sublimate the importance of the individual to abstract conceptions of God, a future classless society, or even a Jewish state in the making. On the one hand, he supported the notion of an open society with an economic infrastructure designed to provide for the common welfare of its members. On the other, he rejected all forms of social experimentation that required the individual's physical or spiritual repression. In this way, he forged an original and nuanced assessment of socialist Zionism. He retained a firm belief in the need to create a socially just world, the importance of a Jewish national home in *Erez Israel*, the vitality of Judaism in its myriad forms, and the moral imperative of individual freedom.

The Spectrum of Jewish Leadership

In the 1920s there arose a generation of American born-and-bred immigrant sons and daughters who came to maturity in the wake of the Great War's global upheaval and sweeping changes in Jewish life.[56] The new postwar reality, which included British control of Mandatory Palestine, transformed the nature of Zionist politics. The predominance of the Berlin Zionists came to an end with the defeat of the Central powers, and the eastern European Zionists were rendered ineffectual by war-torn Russia's ongoing civil strife. Now, British and American Zionists, whose power stemmed from their territorial federations in the victorious Allied nations, provided the Zionist organization's new leadership. The struggle between British and American Zionist leaders for political control of the world movement was contentious. Chaim Weizmann, whose programmatic orientation did not differ significantly from that of Louis D. Brandeis, emerged as the movement's undisputed leader. In a related development, Weizmann's American supporters, led by the journalist Louis Lipsky, deposed the so-called "Brandeis group" and assumed the leadership in American Zionism.[57] In large measure, the change represented the ascendance of the American movement's growing lower- and middle-class ranks and an acknowledgment of London's centrality in Zionist politics.[58]

On February 10, 1924, Greenberg arrived in the United States as the leader of a WZO-sponsored Tarbut fundraising mission. Though he initially possessed a modest awareness of the American scene, he rapidly found his footing in New York City's Lower East Side owing to the transnational nature of eastern European Jewish émigré milieu. As well, he immediately filled the vacuum in socialist Zionist leadership created by the absence of the once-formidable wartime triumvirate of Ber Borochov (who returned to Russia after World War I and died shortly thereafter), Chaim Zhitlowsky (who joined Poalei Zion at the height World War I but later abandoned the party), and Nahman Syrkin (who died unexpectedly on September 6, 1924). These men had played critical roles in the American Jewish Congress of 1918 and the postwar American Jewish scene. In fact, Syrkin participated in the Jewish delegation that accompanied President Woodrow Wilson to the Versailles Peace Conference.[59] By the winter of

1924, however, the movement's leadership had devolved upon a group of party functionaries among whom the political activist Baruch Zuckerman and writer David Pinsky were notable exceptions. The arrival of Greenberg, who possessed a reputation as a sophisticated and accomplished Zionist spokesman, lecturer, and literary figure, brought fresh energy and vigor to the American branch of Labor Zionism. As he took up the movement's mantle in the United States, his visibility was bolstered by his perch as editor of *Der yidisher kemfer* (The Jewish Fighter), a high-minded Yiddish weekly that published the work of many of the best Yiddish poets, writers, and political thinkers of the day.

Though Greenberg would become known in the United States as a keen observer of Zionist affairs, the elite leaders of the Zionist Organization of America (ZOA) and United Palestine Appeal (UPA) at first regarded him as an interloper and something of a threat. In fact, they initially shunned him. Arlosoroff, who spent extended time in the United States as a *shaliah* (emissary) between 1926 and 1929, described the prevailing attitude of the ZOA and UPA leaders as "keeping the stranger out":

> A stranger in the sense of this program is everybody who does not belong (to the particular set of people in office . . .). Keeping out, in the sense of this program, means preventing anything that might lead to a regular cooperation and, in consequence, perhaps to share in the publicity which such cooperation entails. . . . [A] striking case is Mr. Hayim Greenberg. . . . Mr. Greenberg, though a [Zeirei Zion] Hitahdut member, is not only a man of rare gifts and character, but he has also come to enjoy, in the Yiddish speaking quarters of American Jewry, a high reputation as one of the most excellent speakers, writers, and lecturers in the country. He repeatedly offered his volunteer services both to the UPA and the ZOA, in the beginning of several successive seasons. The result of it all, to make a long story short, was that he has not, so far, been called upon *even once* to do the slightest thing for the UPA [headquarters]. In much the same way, not one of the Zionist periodicals has taken cognizance of the remarkable editorials which, for years, he has contributed bi-weekly to *Farn folk*. No other consideration can have brought about this but the fear lest a different attitude would give credit and publicity both to Mr. Greenberg and to *Farn folk*, whereas publicity should be used as a political weapon to the exclusive benefit of those who "belong."[60]

Greenberg's mistreatment at the hands of the ZOA and UPA leadership was arguably a missed opportunity from Arlosoroff's perspective. But it was also ironic insofar as Greenberg professed a nationalist agenda akin to the Brandeis's Progressive vision of American Zionism. Like Brandeis, Greenberg embraced the theme of American exceptionalism and viewed the prospect of Jewish sovereignty as crucial to modern Jewry's survival and a means to the larger goal of humanity's elevation. Nor did he shrink from the charge of dual loyalty. In 1915 Brandeis had famously declared "multiple loyalties" to be "objectionable only if they are inconsistent." "Every American Jew who aids in advancing the Jewish settlement in Palestine," Brandeis asserted, "though he feels that neither he nor his descendants will ever live there . . . [will be] a better American for doing so."[61] Now, in the 1920s Greenberg picked up where Brandeis (by then ensconced as a US Supreme Court justice and out of public view) left off. In numerous Yiddish- and English-speaking venues, he advanced a synthesis of Zionism and Jewish pluralism that harmonized American Jewry's attachments to the United States and the fledgling Jewish national home. Democracy and diversity, he asserted, were fundamental to the Jewish future, and modern Jewish existence should not be reduced to a clash of irreconcilable choices or a default position of "spurious universalism."[62]

Despite the hostility of the ZOA and UPA leaders, Greenberg performed a sizable quotient of organizational and political work from the time of his arrival in the United States. Hebraist and Zionist groups across the country eagerly sought his services as a public speaker.[63] Following in the footsteps of other popular Jewish and Zionist speakers, he embarked on regular lecture tours. Usually, he would visit a string of metropolitan centers where the Labor Zionist movement or its fraternal order, the Jewish National Workers' Alliance (also known in Yiddish as the Farband), was strong, stopping for a couple of days to meet with the local Zionist leadership, address a movement gathering, and promote the Labor Zionist program in lectures to various Jewish constituencies including the Labor Zionist Pioneer Women's organization (affiliated with Moezet Hapoalot, the women's division of the Histadrut in Palestine), regional Yiddish-speaking groups and clubs, and *landsmanshaftn* (mutual aid societies).

A fiercely independent interpreter of Jewish and world affairs, Greenberg did not shrink from challenging his audience's preconceptions and ideological beliefs. His attitude to his socialist Zionist comrades in this regard is especially revealing. Though he generally respected the movement's strategy and agenda (despite "endless difficulties with the movement leadership"), it was clear he expected reciprocal treatment and autonomy when it came to issues of philosophical import.[64] The only official party positions he ever held were as editor of *Farn folk*, *Der yidisher kemfer*, and *Jewish Frontier*. Like the party's secretary general, the Poalei Zion-Zeirei Zion (PZ-ZZ) national convention elected the journals' editors. In theory, this meant Greenberg was accountable to the national membership. In practice, however, it guaranteed him considerable freedom and an unrestrained platform for expressing his personal views.

Greenberg's political approach and public statements were generally accepted by the membership, who in turn acclaimed them as their own.[65] Yet even so there were instances when he expressed opinions or endorsed policies at odds with the party as a whole. On such occasions, he aroused the ire of PZ-ZZ's executive bodies, and a few attempts were made to censure him. Such instances proved to be litmus tests not only of Greenberg's personal forbearance, but also his special stature. The historian Ben Halpern, who witnessed some of these episodes, later recalled:

> The procedure was almost traditionally fixed. Strong-minded, self-willed men who loved and knew well how to shine in the limelight, arose one after another and thundered, remonstrated, reproved with a brave display of rhetoric. . . . At last Greenberg arose. . . . In stern simple words, he told them of the basic distinctions between black and white, of the liberty of conscience which gave life to the role of editor. . . . He never denied the interests of the party . . . but insisted that it was his duty, not any other's, to judge what was due to each. . . . The lions rampant couched like lambs—and one could see how in their submission they felt themselves uplifted, ennobled, flattered in their self-esteem that they could maintain such a relationship to so gentle a shepherd, testifying to their own higher qualities as well as to his.[66]

It should be noted that such treatment differed markedly from that of the celebrated figures Borochov, Syrkin, and Zhitlowsky in previous decades. For example, when Borochov modified and liberalized his Marxist approach, he was virtually ostracized by the party faithful.[67] Likewise, Syrkin's advocacy of Jewish participation in World War I on the side of the Allies prompted calls for his expulsion from Poalei Zion and eventually caused him to resign from the party's central committee.[68] And when Zhitlowsky broke with the party he not only became *persona non grata* but was regarded as a traitor.[69] As a result of their supposed transgressions, Borochov, Syrkin, and Zhitlowsky, originally revered as demigods, became heretics.[70] Greenberg, on the other hand, was alternately the "*ben yakar*" (darling) and high priest of the movement. His talent for unpacking modern life's mysteries in meaningful Jewish terms made him, in the eyes of his followers, an indispensable translator.[71] As mentor, teacher, publicist, philosopher, and political leader, Greenberg sustained the evolution of Labor Zionist commitment in the fluid American setting. Like Berl Katznelson, who, as historian Anita Shapira points out, was unrivaled in the scope of his influence in the Yishuv, the source of Greenberg's authority was not political but rather stemmed from his capacity to articulate the moral and ethical basis of the Zionist enterprise as a whole.[72] Colleagues and friends, Greenberg and Katznelson were woven of the same cloth. Their leadership transcended the Labor Zionist orbit and they came to be regarded as the Zionist left's foremost spiritual guides. Both generally abstained from serving in official party positions with the exception of editing movement publications; Katznelson edited *Davar* from its founding in 1925 until his death in 1944.

The 1930s provided Greenberg with the scope and inducement to emerge as an important mediator among Zionism's various factions and supporters. His mix of idealism and pragmatism, including his tolerant cultural and political orientation, resonated with a broad segment of the American Jewish public, especially Jewish liberals and leftists who were proud of their eastern European ethnic identity. He also garnered a devoted following among American Zionists, particularly socialist Zionists, who responded positively to his non-doctrinaire constructivist brand of Labor Zionism. Furthermore, his personal contact with the socialist Zionist movement in the Yishuv provided an important point of contact between Jewish communal and political leaders in the United States and Palestine.

The parallel between Greenberg and Brandeis has already been noted. It is also useful to consider Greenberg in comparison to other American Jewish and Zionist leaders of the pre-state era. Consider, for example, the investment banker Felix Warburg, labor leader David Dubinsky, and Abba Hillel Silver, strong-willed, self-assured, and imperious men, each of whom was regarded as (and considered himself to be) politically influential. They marshaled American Jewry's growing ethnic political power—in different areas of American life—and devoted their energies and talents to leveraging their communal authority to the greatest extent possible in their dealings with American power brokers, policymakers, and elected officials.[73] By contrast, Greenberg's authority did not stem from a religious base. Nor was he was a privileged entrepreneurial figure who amassed independent wealth and political clout. He did not command the unquestioned allegiance of a political party, trade union, or workers' association. Rather, he labored in the interstices of the American Jewish scene. Put somewhat differently, unlike Warburg, Dubinsky, and Silver (or his previously mentioned predecessors Borochov, Syrkin, and Zhitlowsky), Greenberg never attempted to impose his political agenda or direct Zionist policy. Rather, in an Americanized version of Katznelson's approach, his guidance took the shape of an unflagging, passionate, and self-reflective critique on behalf of the collective—the voice of loyal opposition from within, oftentimes ahead of the curve. Golda Meyerson (later Meir), who served as a Jewish Agency official and Histadrut *shlihah* (emissary) in the 1930s and 1940s, later described Greenberg's station in the following terms: "It was important to know what Greenberg thought on this or that matter. It was a natural thing. In the same way, thousands of people in Jewish Palestine . . . longed to know what Berl Katznelson thought—did he approve or not? Hayim Greenberg was of this type . . . diffusing purity over his surroundings; whoever had a moral stain did not feel particularly comfortable in his presence. . . . I never felt that if you did something unworthy and did not tell Hayim Greenberg about it you could sit in his company and he would not know about it. There was always the feeling that he saw and knew."[74]

In an era when Jewish powerlessness characterized Jewish life everywhere, Greenberg's significance is best understood in relation to the common tensions embedded in the Jewish public arena, and his impact is most visible in the way he influenced other American Jewish and Zionist leaders. Given the spectrum of early twentieth-century American Jewish leadership, Greenberg clearly fits the paradigm of a leader who was committed to an ideological worldview and who exercised both "active" and "passive" influence over his "fellow Jews," including other leaders.[75]

Forging a New Labor Zionism

If Greenberg's political capital in Zionist circles rose with the fortunes of the Palestine labor movement, which in the early 1930s achieved a dominant position in the Yishuv, his authority in the United States was linked to his incisive appreciation of American Jewry's changing spiritual, cultural, and political needs. He believed Labor Zionism, while primarily a blueprint for advancing Jewish national interests in Palestine, could also serve as a strategy for elevating American Jewish life. He understood the Yishuv's success depended upon the concurrent development of many spheres including agriculture, education, industry, social welfare, trade unionism, urban centers, housing, and immigrant absorption.[76] He championed the efforts of Jewish Agency, WZO, and Palestine labor movement and strove to engage American Jews in "an informed, alert public" discussion about the Yishuv as a model of intentional and renascent Jewish culture. In terms that echoed both Brandeis's Progressive vision and Katznelson's socialist orientation, Greenberg asserted American Jewish engagement with the Zionist project would "strengthen the dynamic influence of labor Palestine on Jewish life in America." The "new values created in Palestine," he stated, "the rapture of pioneering, the ennobling of human labor, the heroic attempt to elevate social relationships, are beginning to stimulate Jewish life everywhere."[77] Greenberg's views also aligned with the Zionist technocrat Arthur Ruppin, who emphasized the importance of building bridges between "*haluziut* (pioneering) and *baalebatiut* (bourgeois values), between the pioneering principle and the economic principle."[78] "The peculiarity of our task," Ruppin asserted, "lies in the fact that the Jews of Palestine cannot, like the Jews of the *galut*, concentrate on commerce. . . . Our reconstruction work may be compared to the advance of an army; no single arm of the service can advance by itself. It can proceed only in cooperation with other arms. . . . Our artillery is agriculture."[79]

While Greenberg challenged American Jews to view themselves as partners in building the Yishuv, he recognized that reality in the United States propelled Jewish life in a very different direction from that in Palestine. In the United States Jews encountered a highly developed social and economic infrastructure that offered choices unavailable to Palestine's Jewish immigrants; they also faced a very different set of limitations. The acculturation of America's eastern European Jews gave rise to an English-speaking Jewish middle class concentrated in the nation's major cities. The Old World ethnic-national sensibility that colored the Yiddish-speaking milieu at the turn of the nineteenth and twentieth centuries was gradually replaced by a left-leaning American Jewish liberal identity. In time, the Jewish community as a whole became less tribal and more enmeshed with the mainstream of American society, a process that rapidly accelerated during the Roosevelt era of 1930s and 1940s.[80] Against this dynamic backdrop, Greenberg argued that Labor Zionism's strength in the United States depended upon the movement's commitment to specific ideas and values—in addition to increased membership numbers and fundraising efforts. He also sought to take advantage of America's meteoric growth in educational attainment and literacy, technological innovations in the publishing industry, including new efficiencies in production, marketing, and distribution, the country's thriving immigrant labor press, and the swift development of the magazine industry.[81] To this end, he deployed *Jewish Frontier*, a monthly English-language journal created in 1934 by the American Labor Zionist movement. Breaking out of the Yiddish-speaking milieu, he swiftly positioned *Jewish Frontier* as a lively hub of Jewish culture and politics for a diverse readership scattered across the country. His broad interests and growing acquaintance with many leading American intellectuals, including Reinhold Niebuhr, Maurice Samuel, Hannah Arendt, Kurt Lewin, Will Herberg, and Ludwig Lewisohn, made the journal a stimulating forum of intellectual debate. Additionally, *Jewish Frontier* translated and published articles written in Hebrew that were previously unavailable to the English-reading public. It regularly featured Palestinian personalities such as David Ben-Gurion, Berl Katznelson, Yitzhak Ben-Zvi, and Zalman Rubashow (later Shazar). The journal also took special pride in presenting literary translations, such as the poetry of Haim Nahman Bialik, Rahel Blaustein, and Nathan Alterman as well as prose by Shlomo Zemah and Hayim Hazaz. In short, *Jewish Frontier*'s totality of purpose distinguished it from the *Menorah Journal*, *New Palestine*, *Liberal Judaism*, and the *Reconstructionist*, the other major Anglo-Jewish periodicals of importance during the interwar period.[82] As a result, historian Aaron Berman observes, Greenberg's emphasis on "substantive and thoughtful articles attracted the attention of many American Jews" who never joined a Zionist group.[83]

In voicing Labor Zionism's commitment to the Jewish public beyond the ranks of the party faithful, Greenberg articulated a new vision of the movement as a whole.[84] He explained his agenda in *Jewish Frontier*'s premier issue: "We consider the creation of a Jewish labor society in Palestine as the chief task of our generation. . . . Because we are 'Palestinocentric,' we cannot ignore the diaspora. We cannot be indifferent to the problems of world Jewry in general or American Jewry in particular because the diaspora is the reservoir from which the Jewish homeland must be fed. . . . We represent that synthesis in Jewish thought, which is nationalist without being chauvinist, and which stands for fundamental economic reconstruction without being communist."[85] Greenberg's statement, which affirmed the durability and vitality of Jewish communal life in the United States, represented a dramatic shift in cherished movement doctrine. Reversing the stringent Marxist-inspired canon declaimed by Borochov two decades earlier ("Our ultimate aim, our maximum program is socialism. . . . Our immediate aim, our minimum program is Zionism"),[86] he echoed the Zionist philosopher Ahad Haam's notion of strengthening Jewish life in the diaspora "by the creation of a fixed center for our national life in the land of its birth."[87] He also rejected the dogmatic imperative of immigration to *Erez Israel*. "There is no place for an *ipso facto* solution of the Jewish question," he maintained. Focusing instead on autonomous will as the yardstick of Jewish behavior, he insisted on the primacy of the Yishuv as a "source of national inspiration" and the "chief channel for the flow of Jewish energy."[88]

To be sure, Greenberg often used poetic imagery to describe the Zionist project as a whole. He was similar in this regard to an array of Zionist figures—activists, writers, and politicians—for whom traditional Judaism and the Hebrew Bible's potent symbols, themes, and motifs invested modern Jewish nationalism and the Palestine labor movement with an air of sacred purpose and mission.[89] What set Greenberg apart from other American and European movement leaders was his personal familiarity with and close ideological proximity to various Palestinian Zionist groups, parties, and settlement frameworks. His language reflected a deep and rich understanding of Jewish sources, but his affinity for Zionism and the Yishuv stemmed neither from religious conviction nor belief in historical inevitability. No matter the ideational overlay of one's Zionism, he argued, the fulfillment and happiness of the individual held the key to the movement's success. "There are no transitional generations in history," he asserted, challenging the determinist views of his Zionist and socialist comrades.[90] He took this argument to Labor Zionism's base camps, too, asserting the primacy of *hagshamah azmit* (self-actualization) and voluntaristic socialism. "I would be an opponent of [Zionist] pioneering in Palestine," he stated at a workers gathering during a 1935 visit to Palestine, "if the hardships entailed in the rebuilding of a long neglected country were imposed on Jewish youth from above and against its will, if the pioneers of Palestine were considered as manure on the fields of the country so that a future generation might enjoy its roses. But pioneering in Palestine is a voluntary task assumed after free deliberation by those inclined to do so and finds personal satisfaction in following its call."[91] As this statement illustrates, Greenberg did not shy away from challenging the party faithful and voicing his dissent publicly. Following in the footsteps of Gordon and Syrkin, he professed an undogmatic view of *haluziut* and called upon Jews from all walks of life to see in the labor enterprise the *summum bonum* of modern Jewish life.[92] He promoted the view that Zionist colonization in Palestine depended on the will of the Jewish masses and would succeed only if the new Yishuv was erected on a socially just foundation.[93]

Greenberg's emphasis on Zionism's universalistic ethical responsibility included his insistence on the equitable treatment of Palestine's indigenous Arab population. Like Hugo Bergmann, Martin Buber, Hans Kohn, Judah L. Magnes, Henrietta Szold, and others who gravitated to Brit Shalom's idealistic bi-national agenda, he insisted on mutuality and respect for the cultural and national needs of both peoples. Greenberg parted ways with such figures, however, in his belief that Jewish political sovereignty need not be reduced to a zero-sum proposition and that Zionism's duty necessarily involved erecting safeguards to protect the rights of the Arab minority in the Yishuv and a future Jewish state. The contest between Jew and Arab in Palestine, he cautioned, was akin to the biblical struggle between Jacob and Esau, and the "Esau problem is not simple." The "full tragedy of being Esau," he noted, was revealed by the Austrian Jewish poet Richard Beer-Hofmann in *Jacob's Dream* (1915), in which Esau, suffering desperately from hunger, is prepared, as in the story told in Genesis, to forfeit his birthright for a pot of lentils. "But after the mess of pottage has been eaten," Esau's hunger is "stilled" and (unlike the biblical account) he is "a man again." "I want my birthright, too," Esau now declares.[94] Comparing this dilemma to the Yishuv's success vis-à-vis the rising economic situation of the local Arab population, Greenberg stated: "One can prove to an Arab in Palestine that he has lost nothing through Jewish colonization. One can show him all the advantages that have accrued to him; one can persuade him that in the future he will profit more from Jewish immigration. He will understand and agree, but the Esau-worm will, nevertheless, gnaw at his heart. The mess of pottage is conceded, but where is the birthright? . . . Perhaps the problem of Jewish-Arab relations belongs to the realm of psychology rather than economics or politics. We must have good economists and diplomats in Palestine. Our life with the Arabs, however, demands the presence of competent social physicians. The labor movement, above all, must discover the therapeutic measures which will heal the sore spots in the relations between Jew and Arab."[95]

The foregoing discussion is characteristic of Greenberg's philosophical and literary style. His attachments and commitments are evident in his description of the "Esau problem." He draws on traditional Jewish sources and Western literature to establish the broad contours of his analysis. Next, he squarely analyzes the dilemma at hand with an eye to the merits of the Arab position without devaluing the justice of the Zionist enterprise. The solution to addressing the dissonance between competing Jewish and Arab claims, he asserts, is not the superiority of one camp over the other but rather a structural rapprochement between them, born of both pragmatic necessity and genuine regard for the enduring cultural-political needs of both peoples.[96] To this end, Greenberg argued, the hard work of building meaningful and constructive relationships between Jews and Arabs in Palestine begins at the grassroots level—in the realm of everyday interactions between Jewish colonies and Arab villages—and is thus a political and moral imperative for Palestine's labor movement.

In making the case for human rights and the value of the individual as an intrinsic aspect of Zionism's struggle, Greenberg invariably found himself engaged in philosophical battles on several fronts in Palestine, America, and Europe. Internally, he fought against Zionism's susceptibility to romantic chauvinism including that of Labor Zionism's party leaders and Marxist hardliners. Toughness was critical for them and they decried efforts to give priority to moderation and humanitarian concerns as weakness. Meanwhile, externally he confronted a broad spectrum of anti-Zionists, Communists, and right-wing Zionist political opponents who derided socialist Zionism's vision of the future Jewish state as a utopian chimera.[97]

Revisionism and Communism

When Revisionist Zionists sought to establish a foothold in the United States, a campaign initiated by Vladimir Jabotinsky in 1920 and reinvigorated by his supporters in the early 1930s, Greenberg sought to expose what he considered to be right-wing Zionism's fanatic tendencies.[98] In *Jewish Frontier*, he published numerous editorials and articles analyzing Revisionism and its leaders.[99] He also used specific events such as incriminating Revisionist testimony drawn from the controversial Arlosoroff murder trial (April–July 1934)[100] and hate-mongering speeches from Betar youth conferences as occasions to underscore "the threat of Revisionist irresponsibility."[101] A visit by Jabotinsky to the United States in 1935, for example, prompted Greenberg to insist that "all serious Zionists" must demand of Jabotinsky "not only his usual brilliant oratory, but also a sober and reasonable explanation of his relations with, and his position in, the sinister movement of frank Fascist hooliganism."[102] Through such pieces, Greenberg emphasized the contrast between Labor Zionism and Revisionism and, at least implicitly, American Jewish liberalism and right-wing Palestine-based Jewish extremism.

In 1935, a debate led by Ben-Gurion and Jabotinsky over the Zionist Organization's immediate political objectives and strategy caused a rift between the Labor Zionist and Revisionist movements. At the heart of the disagreement was a simmering dispute between, on the one hand, the Palestine labor movement's pragmatic and cooperative nation-building strategy and, on the other, the Revisionists' insistence on a maximalist political and territorial strategy. As a result of this clash, Jabotinsky resigned from the Zionist Organization's executive committee and founded the alternative New Zionist Organization. The struggle between the Labor and Revisionist wings of the Zionist movement was protracted, bitter, and sporadically erupted in violence among partisans in Palestine. It also found echoes in the American Jewish setting among followers of both camps. (Eventually, Ben-Gurion and Jabotinsky effected a political reconciliation, and in 1946 the New Zionist Organization rejoined the Zionist Organization.)[103] Greenberg explained the clash to his American audience in the following terms:

> From the very start a chasm was formed between Labor Zionism and Revisionism. It was primarily the chasm between realism and adventurism. . . . Revisionism, which at first asserted that is was merely radically Zionist, that it did not want a separate economic program either for the diaspora or for the building up of Palestine, and that it was not oriented toward any particular class in Jewry, began, as if in revenge for its failure to effect an alliance with Labor, to be more and more hostile to labor. This hostility to Labor, which is today a cruel fact in Jewish life, began to feed on ideologies and political tendencies which had sprung from the soil of other nations. It began ever more to absorb elements of Fascism. The naive among us believed that, no matter what happened in the gentile world, it was absolutely impossible for a reactionary movement to arise in Jewish life. Fascism, they thought, was a purely non-Jewish malady with which Jews, on account of their historic immunity, could not possibly be infected. Unfortunately it turned out that we were not at all immune, and that the Fascist bacteria found a fertile soil for multiplication in Revisionist circles.
>
> The first and most significant trait of Fascism and Revisionism is the hatred it bears toward internationalism, toward every form of friendly cooperation between one nation and another. Not for nothing does the Revisionist leader and teacher, Vladimir Jabotinsky, quote so often the old Latin proverb, *Homo homini lupus* (man is to man as a wolf). Not for nothing do the Revisionists hold that wolfish relations exist and will and should exist between nations. This is no libel upon Revisionism. When we read in the Revisionist press that to help the Austrian Socialists in their struggle for liberty is treason against Jewry and Zionism; that only two courses are left to the Arab, either back to the desert or into the depths of the sea; that we should not in the least be concerned with the problems of other nations; that we have but one task for the next few generations, namely, to build the Jewish State, and that only after we have attained this goal,

> and provided we have spare time, shall we be able to worry "about dogs and cats, about Chinamen and Arabs"—when we read this, we see in it a pathological expression of national egotism which is not only immoral, but essentially stupid, against the real interests and beneath the dignity of Jewry and Zionism. It is impossible, from a purely practical point of view, to build a Jewish National Home or a Jewish state in Palestine without a minimum of cooperation with other nations or at least with certain progressive elements of other nations.[104]

Greenberg's anti-Revisionist remarks can be productively compared to the views of Rabbi Stephen S. Wise, American Jewry's premier communal leader in this period. Unlike Greenberg, Wise had long been an ally of Jabotinsky. He was particularly admiring of Jabotinsky's successful efforts during World War I to establish the Jewish Legion, a Jewish volunteer regiment that served as part of the British military, and his vigorous insistence that Britain's postwar mandatory regime fulfill its obligations to the Yishuv.[105] Now, however, with Hitler's rise and the new urgency of the Zionist project, Wise concluded that Revisionism's "major policies," including its "pianissimo" in the United States and "fortissimo" in eastern Europe, had become "immeasurably imperiling" and "unmistakably endangering." Calling Revisionism "a species of Fascism" and a "dangerously reactionary movement," he argued that "all that is best in Jewish life is permanently and indissolubly allied with the social and democratic ideals of our day." He excoriated Jabotinsky's movement for its implication, "as Fascism declares, that the state is all and the individual is nothing" as well as for its "war in Palestine against the Jewish workers." Opposing Jabotinsky's maximalist policies, he asserted that "an Arab-less Palestine would be as grievous a moral disaster as a Jew-less Palestine." "The solution of the Arab question in Palestine," Wise declared, "will be the ultimate test of the Jewish people, even as the attitude of Christendom towards the Jew is the test of Christianity." Lastly, Wise deplored Revisionism's elevation of militarism as a virtue in itself. "The worst of assimilationism," he said, "is not to be found in the vulgar Jew but in Jews who choose a way of life that is basically evil and who gladly and proudly proclaim their adherence to that way of life as if it were good. . . . A decent self-defense is our duty. An aggressive bristling Fascistic, militaristic disregard and provocation of others it is our holiest duty to avoid."[106]

Greenberg's and Wise's perspectives reveal some intriguing overlapping elements. They both argued that Jabotinsky's flirtation with fascism was dangerous and even anathema to Jewish and social democratic values. They decried Revisionism's anti-labor posture as a threat to the stability of Palestine's new Jewish society in the making. They also warned that Jewish extremism and disregard for Palestine's Arab inhabitants undermined Zionism's moral basis, while chauvinist Jewish nationalism threatened to turn the Yishuv into a pariah society. In characterizing Revisionism as a "pathological expression of national egotism" that was "against the real interests and beneath the dignity of Jewry and Zionism," Greenberg deployed a humanist and history-minded yardstick by which to evaluate right-wing Zionism's implications. Wise's denunciation of Jabotinsky's "aggressive bristling fascistic, militaristic disregard and provocation of others" as the "worst of assimilationism" was itself a kind of history lesson, amplified by the rabbinic pronouncement that it was among Jewry's "holiest" duties to reject such "evil." In sum, Greenberg and Wise both responded to Revisionism by employing a shared discourse of complementary secular and religious liberal sensibilities. They cast Revisionism as beyond the pale by invoking meta-historical themes that fused realpolitik with their respective views of modern Jewry's and American society's election.

Another theme to which Greenberg devoted attention in *Jewish Frontier* was the distinction between Communism and democratic socialism. Beginning in the early 1930s, while many intellectuals were still enchanted with the Russian Revolution, Greenberg published a series of penetrating analyses of Communism. In a letter addressed to a fictional "Communist friend," he delineated the danger of Communism's authoritarian tendencies: "Ends and means in politics are analogous to form and content in art. Form in art is not merely technique; means in politics are not merely instruments. The content must be felt in the form. The means must contain the basic elements of the end. When this minimal harmony between means and ends is lacking, we get the stake at which the holy inquisition burns unbelievers to save their souls. I cannot subscribe to Niechaev's famous slogan: 'Full speed ahead, right through the mud.'"[107]

In his unwavering humanism, Greenberg insisted that the socialist program maintain the sanctity of individual liberty and strive to preserve the integrity of diverse ethnic, social, and religious groups. He categorically rejected Marxism's "deification of society," noting that "there is no social substitute for individual life; personality refuses to live by proxy."[108] Such assertions reflect the abiding influence of Gordon on Greenberg, especially the notion that "human nature as a whole cannot be regenerated unless the individual has undergone the process himself."[109] Greenberg maintained that the strength of the working class was a function of its inner vigor and the creative process by which it realized its goals. Consequently, he refuted Communism's prevailing theory of revolutionary stages. "What is the sense of dictatorship—that very dictatorship which is first called the dictatorship of the peasantry and the proletariat, then merely of the proletariat, then of the Party, then of a wing of the Party, till it finally becomes the dictatorship of one man? I know all the arguments. The dictatorship is temporary, the political slavery that you have introduced is a sad necessity. These will disappear in the future, when the final goal of socialism will have been realized. But how can one transform a man into something worthless in order to endow him with worth? How can we introduce slavery for the sake of freedom, an epidemic in the interests of sanitation?"[110] Greenberg summed up his disenchantment with Soviet Communism by declaiming the security, happiness, and fulfillment of the current generation to be legitimate ends in themselves. The litmus test of all social and political movements, he believed, was whether they sought to deny individual liberties in their quest to transform the world. For Greenberg, Communism, precisely because it was prepared to sacrifice current generations on the altar of political expediency, was a desecration of socialism's humanist vision.

In considering Greenberg's views on Revisionism and Communism, it is important to stress the extent to which the exigent conditions of the 1930s shaped his thinking. The urgent and dire nature of economic and political developments—the Great Depression, the vulnerability of European Jewry, the rise of the Hitler regime, and the precariousness of the Yishuv—weighed heavily on him. His response to the complex global environment was bound up with a primary belief that social democratic values offered the greatest hope for the future of Western democracy and the Jewish people.

The Holocaust and World War II

In the wake of Hitler's rise to power in Germany and the Palestine Arab riots of 1936–39, Greenberg's pacifism gradually yielded to a reassessment of the principled use of armed force for self-defense.[111] Not unlike Nahman Syrkin's support of Woodrow Wilson's call to arms during World War I or the Palestine labor movement's decision to protect the Yishuv, Greenberg's change of heart stemmed from his anguish over European Jewry's worsening plight, increasing disillusionment with the attitudes of American, European, and Asian pacifist leaders to Jewish suffering, and growing realization of the need for Jewish self-defense against Arab violence. His disaffection with pacifism occasioned a public exchange of views with the Indian leader Mahatma Gandhi, who conducted a similar discourse with Martin Buber, Judah L. Magnes, and others. Though Greenberg admired Gandhi as a spiritual "brother," he was dismayed by his indifference to rising antisemitism among Muslims in India and his failure to speak out against the Nazi persecution of European Jewry.[112] Gandhi explained his views in an article entitled "Death Has No Terror":

> Why should [the Jews] not, like other peoples of the earth, make that country their home where they were born and where they earn their livelihood? Palestine belongs to the Arabs in the same sense that England belongs to the English or France to the French. It is wrong and inhuman to

> impose the Jews on the Arabs. What is going on in Palestine today cannot be justified by any moral code of conduct. . . . If I were a Jew and were born in Germany and earned my livelihood there, I would claim Germany as my home even as the tallest gentile may, and challenge him to shoot me or cast me in the dungeon; I would refuse to be expelled or to submit to discriminating treatment. And for doing this, I should not wait for fellow Jews to join me in civil resistance but would have confidence that in the end the rest were bound to follow my example.[113]

Though Greenberg considered Gandhi's anti-Zionist pronouncement a betrayal of his humanitarian worldview, he did not simply criticize the Indian leader's insensitive remarks. He instead used the opportunity to stimulate public debate and draw attention to the perils facing the Jewish people. He squarely tackled the proposition that Jews should, at all costs, accommodate themselves to their host countries and avoid the supposed evils of nationalism. Contra Gandhi's suggestion that German Jewry practice non-resistance against the Nazis, Greenberg titled his reply "We Are Treated as Subhumans—We Are Asked to Be Superhuman":

> If Gandhi demands that we practice superheroism in Germany, he requests that in Palestine we should renounce the most elementary rights which every people may and should claim. When he asks why we do not 'like other peoples of the earth' make our home in the lands where we were born and where we earn our livelihood, he indicates that he has not pondered the unusual drama of the paradoxical Jewish history. . . . Gandhi's question rings like a veiled accusation; it sounds as if we have purposely refused to become rooted in any country but Palestine. . . . It is regrettable that Gandhi approached our problem without that fundamental earnestness and passionate search for truth which are so characteristic of his usual treatment of problems. . . . He therefore failed to grasp the unequalled tragedy of Jewish existence.[114]

In taking aim at the moral and philosophical inconsistencies of Gandhi's argument, Greenberg crossed the Rubicon. He defected from the pacifist camp and adopted the Ciceronian proposition of the "ever-present and ongoing tension between respect for law and the resort to violence," a concept to which many American Christian pacifists would gravitate after the bombing of Pearl Harbor in December 1941.[115] Already Greenberg's rebuff in the mid-1930s of the War Resisters League, with its radical Gandhian agenda, signaled his commitment to pragmatic political strategies centered on the responsible use of armed force.[116] In early 1939, however, while the American media showed keen interest in the

Indian leader's anti-Zionist statement, outside of the Anglo-Jewish press Greenberg's views garnered little notice. The disappointing result taught Greenberg an important lesson about the American media's selectivity and the American public's general inattentiveness and indifference to Jewish suffering in Europe.[117]

After the outbreak of World War II, Greenberg determined to use *Jewish Frontier* as a lightning rod for news and statements about the Jewish condition in Palestine and Europe, as well as a channel for information that might not otherwise reach the American public. In February 1941, for example, he publicized a letter smuggled out of Palestine that "managed to slip past the censors." Stressing the British Mandatory administration's "severe repressive measures," he condemned the occupying regime as "'colonial' in the worst sense." "The administration has muzzled the press with a most stringent censorship. Any serious criticism of the government has become impossible, as if the country were occupied by a hostile army." He also noted British hostility to the Zionist enterprise generally and "the incredibly brutal treatment—reminiscent of [tsarist] Russian police methods—which the administration has seen fit to mete out to the so-called 'illegal' immigrants in order to insure that the White Paper remain inviolate."[118] "There can be no other interpretation of this policy when we learn that the sick, naked, barefoot refugees were led at night from the camps, where they had been interned, to ships ready to deport them; that their bare bodies were beaten to the point of blood and wounds if they refused to go; that some were beaten till they fell unconscious. . . . There is apparently no cruelty and no folly which the Palestine administration is not capable of in order to demonstrate . . . that the White Paper has not been abolished, and will not be abolished in the future."[119]

The publication of such information was valuable in the Zionist Organization's wartime strategy of pressuring Britain to relax restrictions on the Yishuv. In fact, in preparation for a March 1941 meeting between Chaim Weizmann and Lord Moyne, the British resident minister in Palestine later assassinated by the extremist right-wing Jewish group known as the Stern Gang, Weizmann forwarded a copy of Greenberg's "Palestine Administration Indicted" to Lord Moyne. Next, Weizmann, who noted that "Greenberg is a responsible person and has considerable influence in American labor circles," subsequently embarked on a three-month trip to the United States "at the request of the British government, which was concerned at the extent of anti-British propaganda then rife in America."[120]

During the following year, rumors of the Nazi campaign to exterminate European Jewry reached the West and reports of the so-called "Final Solution" became too well known to be dismissed as mere propaganda. In the summer of 1942, a Yiddish document chronicling the murder of several hundred thousand Polish Jews was smuggled out of eastern Europe by members of the Bund, the Polish Jewish labor movement, and delivered to Greenberg. However, as Marie Syrkin later lamented, even Greenberg and the editorial boards of *Der yidisher kemfer* and *Jewish Frontier* who had been struggling since the early 1940s to digest and publicize news of European Jewry's plight did not grasp the magnitude of the Nazi atrocities.[121] In September 1942, however, *Jewish Frontier* ran a complete English translation of the document under the heading "Murder in Poland." Next, Greenberg, whom the Chicago reporter, playwright, and Hollywood screenwriter Ben Hecht described as "one of the best informed people in New York on the massacre of the Jews," received independent confirmation of the extermination of European Jewry from underground sources and eyewitnesses via Switzerland.[122] He decided to skip the October publication of *Jewish Frontier* and instead to devote the entire November issue to publicizing the information smuggled out of Europe. Framed by a bold black border, the latter was titled "Jews under the Axis, 1939–1942" and contained detailed accounts of the plight of Jews in Poland, Germany, Romania, Lithuania, Czechoslovakia, Yugoslavia, France, and Holland. The lead editorial grimly declared: "In the occupied countries of Europe a policy is now being put into effect, whose avowed object is the extermination of a whole people. It is a policy of systematic murder of innocent civilians which in its dimensions, its ferocity and its organization is unique in the history of mankind. . . . The annals of mankind hold no similar record of organized murder as a calculated policy of state. We publish this somber record to acquaint the free world with these facts and call on the governments of the Allied nations to do whatever may be done to prevent the fulfillment of this horror which broods over the blood-engulfed continent of Europe."[123]

Jewish Frontier had the grievous distinction of being the first English-language publication to print full accounts of the Nazi genocide. Meanwhile, Greenberg broke ranks with the American Jewish establishment, including Stephen S. Wise, Bernard Baruch, Felix Frankfurter, Henry Morgenthau, Jr., Henry Monsky, Joseph Proskauer, and others who, despite growing awareness of the tragedy's full scope, were reluctant to appear at odds with the Roosevelt administration.[124] In the turmoil of this fraught and politically complicated environment, Greenberg, who was a staunch proponent of the Allied war effort and supporter of FDR, felt duty-bound as a Jewish and Zionist leader to publicly decry the Nazi regime's murderous agenda and the catastrophic tragedy that would eventually become known as the Holocaust. Greenberg's *cri de coeur* in *Jewish Frontier* set off tremors in American Jewish circles and helped to electrify the Jewish and non-Jewish press. A month later, the US State Department officially confirmed the incoming reports of Nazi atrocities.

In late 1942 Greenberg collaborated with Hecht, among the American media's most influential Jewish figures, to reach as large an American audience as possible.[125] Though affiliated with rival Zionist camps—Hecht aligned himself with the "Bergson Group," a Revisionist cohort that included Hillel Kook (known as Peter Bergson in the United States), Eri Jabotinsky, and other right-wing activists—both men appreciated one another and they found common cause in breaking news of the Holocaust. In February 1943, Hecht shrewdly published a full account (based on Greenberg's sources) of the massacre of Europe's Jews in the *American Mercury* and an abridged version in *Reader's Digest*.[126] The following month Democratic congressman George M. Grant of Alabama read the *Reader's Digest* piece into the *Congressional Record*.[127]

Unlike the Bergson group, which relied on antagonistic and even incendiary public relations tactics, Greenberg did not frame his public outcry as a universal condemnation of the Roosevelt administration or Jewish and Zionist leaders. Nor did he believe it "ethical to attack a whole race—even the race of Germans."[128] His anguish, however, was no less acute—as revealed by a Madison Square Garden address titled "Bankrupt!" delivered on February 12, 1943:

> The time has come, perhaps, when the few Jewish communities remaining in the world which are still free to make their voices heard and to pray in public should proclaim a day of fasting and prayer for American Jews. . . . They deserve to be prayed for. They are not even aware what a misfortune has befallen them, and if they were to look at themselves with seeing eyes they would realize with shock how intolerable this misfortune is. . . . At a time when the American Jewish community is the largest in the world, at a time when the eyes of millions of Jews in Europe who are daily threatened with the most terrible and degrading forms of physical extermination are primarily turned to American Jewry, this American Jewish community has fallen lower than perhaps any other in recent times, and displays an unbelievable amount of highly suspect clinical "health" and "evenness of temper." If moral bankruptcy deserves pity, and if this pity is seven-fold for one who is not even aware how shocking his bankruptcy is, then no Jewish community in the world today (not even the Jews who are now in the claws of the Nazi devourer) deserves more compassion from heaven than does American Jewry.[129]

Dubbed the "*J'Accuse*" of wartime Jewry, Greenberg's blistering critique of the American Jewish condition caused considerable controversy.[130] The statement also reflected his personal journey from pacifism to the principled use of force for self-defense. In larger terms, however, it was a compelling elucidation of an argument that would prove to be standard fare in the campaign for Jewish statehood, namely that American society's values and interests were coextensive with alleviating Jewish suffering and championing postwar Jewish national reconstruction. Greenberg's synthesis of realpolitik and idealism, which reflected a major recalibration of left-wing Jewish and Zionist attitudes in this period, starkly contrasted with the pacifism of contemporary American spokesmen like

Charles Clayton Morrison, editor of the *Christian Century* and author of *The Outlawry of War* (1927), and A. J. Muste, the Quaker minister-cum-radical labor leader *Time* magazine called the "Number One US Pacifist." That is, unlike western Christian leaders who could afford to be purists, Greenberg represented a minority whose European kith and kin faced unprecedented victimization and brutality at the hands of the Nazi regime.[131] Keenly aware of the dangerous potential of widespread Christian misperceptions of the Jews—from the taint of the centuries-old allegation of the Pharisaic betrayal of Christ, to vulgar American literary characters like Meyer Wolfsheim in F. Scott Fitzgerald's *Great Gatsby* (1925) and Budd Schulberg's Sammy Glick in *What Makes Sammy Run*? (1941), to grotesque political caricatures of Jews as masters of capitalism, socialism, internationalism, or radicalism—Greenberg was impelled to come to the defense of the Jewish people, most immediately of American Jewry as it navigated the uncertain terrain of the 1940s. This herculean task was complicated by the fact that even late in the war "most Americans were neither deeply touched nor troubled by the news about Jews coming out of Europe" and a majority "believed Nazi persecution of the German Jews was either partly or entirely the Jews' own fault."[132]

The stark tragedy of World War II and the Holocaust would become evident in due course. To this day, the debate over American Jewry's response to events in Europe continues to elicit vociferous and passionate controversy. For the purposes of this study, however, it is sufficient to emphasize that Greenberg, like other American Jewish and Zionist leaders, could do little to affect the outcome of international developments or shape the Allied Powers' wartime priorities. This does not mean he did not try or was lacking in will, but rather the overwhelming nature of historical events dictated his minor role in determining the fate of European Jewry. During World War II Greenberg reached the apex of his political influence when Stephen S. Wise and Abba Hillel Silver clashed over the direction of the American Zionist Emergency Council (AZEC) and resigned from their co-leadership positions. At this juncture, Greenberg stepped up to serve as AZEC's acting head. He also played a key role at the Biltmore Conference in New York City (1942) and the American Jewish Conference in Pittsburgh (1943). Only after the defeat of Nazi Germany did it become possible—in both political and strategic terms—for American Jewry to fully mobilize in support of postwar reconstruction and the campaign for Jewish statehood.[133]

America and Israel

World events in the late 1940s made it clear that modern Jewry could not rely on the old understandings and rules of engagement that defined Jewish life for much of the nineteenth and twentieth centuries. Just what postwar Jewish reconstruction required, however, including the extent of American Jews' responsibility for "render[ing] the direct help . . . required of them as kinsmen and coreligionists," was a matter of debate and controversy.[134] Greenberg, devoid of the rigidity that characterized many Jewish political and communal leaders of his generation, was well equipped to meet the crisis with perspicacity and imagination. He had already established himself as an eloquent spokesman for Jewish nationalism; he also explicitly emphasized the importance of diaspora Jewry and the issue of Arab national rights in Palestine. In the heyday of the Communist left, he decried Bolshevism's excesses while offering a compelling defense of democratic socialism. In the wake of the Hitler regime and the Holocaust, he transformed from a pacifist into an articulate defender of the principled use of force. A confidant of the Jewish Agency's and Labor Palestine's leading personalities, he was also a Jewish public intellectual whose intimate contact with Asian leaders, Latin American diplomats, and European and American Christian artists, writers, and philosophers proved to be an invaluable conduit to constituencies with whom American Jewry and the Zionist movement had otherwise strikingly little connection.[135] In sum, Greenberg's cultural, political, and intellectual capital helped to stand Zionism and American Jewry in good stead.[136]

With the establishment of the State of Israel in 1948, world Jewry confronted a new reality for which there was no historical precedent. The fledgling Jewish state, faced with the immediate tasks of refugee absorption, immigration from the Arab lands, social and economic infrastructure development, and securing its territorial integrity, shouldered immense tasks that shaped its development and challenged its ability to survive.[137] Where unstable lines of attachment and alliance had previously connected the Yishuv and American Jewry, there now arose a vital partnership based on a mixture of mutuality, necessity, and a shared sense of common destiny.[138] In practical terms, Israel's emergence as a sovereign country also required the transfer of the Vaad Leumi's (pre-state Israeli society's national assembly) and Jewish Agency's internationally recognized political, diplomatic, and economic functions to the state's new governmental authority.[139] Nahum Goldmann, Abba Hillel Silver, Rose L. Halprin, and other significant Zionist leaders in the United States whose clout derived from their proximity to American power and ability to mobilize American Jewish political support now found themselves displaced by Israel's elected officials.[140] Individually, they remained important communal figures and leaders in the Zionist movement's volunteer orbit. On the whole, however, as US-Israel relations became a matter of formal intergovernmental contact they were increasingly marginalized.

Nonetheless, even after 1948 Greenberg (like several American Zionist leaders) continued to perform a sizable quotient of communal, organizational, and political work. His impact in this regard may be difficult to gauge, but it is clear that he, at least as much as Goldmann, Silver, Halprin, and others, figured prominently in the Jewish public arena and American ethnic politics.[141] His official role as head of the Jewish Agency's new Department of Culture and Education, a task for which he was eminently qualified, made him something of an ambassador at large to diaspora Jewry. He also remained visible in the American political landscape, as when he and other American Jewish leaders met President Harry S. Truman in November 1950 to discuss US financial aid to Israel, support for Iraqi Jewish emigration to Israel, and rising Mideast tensions over Egypt's blockade of the Suez Canal.[142]

And yet it must be stressed while Greenberg appeared to have access to political power—or, more precisely, given his distinctive position in the Labor Zionist movement, to Israel's Mapai-dominated government—essentially, his only real tool was the power of moral suasion. That he understood as much is evidenced by the time and energy he continued to invest in *Jewish Frontier's* "high-grade journalism."[143] One of a small number of mid-twentieth century American Jewish publications that "played a central role in and made crucial contributions to American letters," *Jewish Frontier* reached its apex in the early 1950s—each monthly issue often running fifty pages in length or more (including commercial advertisements), with a circulation of roughly 20,000 and a regular audience that likely averaged 90,000 to 100,000 readers.[144] Like other magazines directed at distinct "cultural minorities," *Jewish Frontier's* impact cannot "be measured by [its] circulation figures" alone. Rather it should be considered in light of its capacity to reach a broad audience beyond dues-paying members of the Labor Zionist movement including "the well educated" and "intellectuals."[145] It was also no doubt buoyed by the fact that American labor in the early 1950s "stood at a historic high-water mark." "One out of every three working people in the US was a union member," it has been observed, "and all these union members received labor papers" from a variety of sources.[146]

Jewish Frontier's thought-provoking and generative content, ranging from literary and cultural analyses to treatments of contemporary social, economic, and political matters, reflected the "high order" of Greenberg's influence and broad outlook.[147] Under his watch, the first English translations of Hebrew and Yiddish literary works by Shmuel Yosef Agnon, Haim Hazaz, and Sholem Asch mingled alongside exposés by well-known journalists Dorothy Thompson and Norman Angell, scholarly treatments by Charles A. Beard and Sidney Hook, essays on Israel and the Middle East by David Ben-Gurion, Moshe Sharett, Abba Eban, and other prominent Israeli politicians, and probing analyses of American Jewish life and culture by Ben Halpern, Max Lerner, Marie Syrkin, and others who later became distinguished academicians. Equally significant, especially considering McCarthyism, the Red Scare of the 1950s, and the rising Cold War era, was Greenberg's determination that *Jewish Frontier* should remain a flagship of democratic socialism. The journal consistently promoted a leftist vision of civil rights and social justice in America through editorials and articles focused on income inequality, the scourge of Jim Crow, the repeal of the Taft-Hartley Act (1947) and the McCarran-Walter Act (1952), the defense of Julius and Ethel Rosenberg, and other key issues of the day. In parallel, it championed a progressive Zionist outlook that minimized American conceptions of capitalist competition and celebrated the cooperative agenda of Israel's robust coalition of socialist forces (e.g., the Mapai party, the Histadrut, the *kibbutz* and *moshav* movements).

Beyond *Jewish Frontier's* orbit, Greenberg was widely recognized as a distinguished public intellectual with a keen understanding of Jewish modernity and Israel-diaspora relations in the post-state era. When Hebrew Union College–Jewish Institute of Religion awarded Greenberg an honorary doctorate it valorized his commitment to "the high ideals of the Jewish tradition and the noble aims of Jeffersonian Americanism," his unique contribution to "the integration of contemporary thought with Jewish aspirations," and his profound interpretations of "the religious genius of Jewry."[148] An eloquent voice that probed the fundamental issues freedom and security, liberalism and social justice, and political sovereignty, Greenberg also cautioned against the idolatry of Jewish statehood and the dangers of ideological reductionism.[149] The philosopher Simon Rawidowicz similarly warned against making a cult of Jewish autonomy and ignoring the Jewish moral spirit. The comparison between Rawidowicz and Greenberg is particularly instructive inasmuch as their innate skepticism made them incapable of accepting traditional Judaism's sacred premises, while their agnostic *yiddishkeit* drew strength from an appreciation of the abiding role of such notions in Jewish culture and history.[150] In 1949, for example, Greenberg explained the relationship between religion and culture as follows:

> Religion with every people in the world is . . . a manifestation of a searching human mind. . . . [It] constitutes a very essential part of every national culture in the world, even of those cultures which may boast in our day of advocating for abolishing religion. . . . Even they are consciously or subconsciously imbued with certain traditional religious elements which entered into whatever culture they possess and whatever language they speak.
>
> As to whether specifically in the Jewish context religion constitutes part of Jewish culture . . . historically, up to the last two or three generations, before the emergence of a secular trend, there was no Jewish culture but religious culture. Jewish philosophy was religious. Jewish literature, until the eighteenth or nineteenth century, was predominantly religious. . . .
>
> Jewish culture is a stream, a stream of spiritual life, and that stream of Jewish spiritual life has its main currents, its minor currents, its oppositional currents to the main current, which are just as essential as the main current. It has its doubts, its gropings, its conflicts, its hopes, its ethics, and its aesthetics.

> . . . Jewish culture, in addition to the spirit of the bible and the spirit of the Talmud, is based on Kabbalah, on mystical insights. It is based on the Jewish medieval philosophy, on Jewish rationalism. It is based on Hasidism. It is based on lore. It is based on the music of the simple folk. It is based on Haskalah. It is based on the Enlightenment. It is based on the Jewish revolutionary spirit which became manifest in the nineteenth and twentieth centuries. It is based on the *haluziut* movement. It is based on the *kibbutzim* and the *moshavim* in Palestine. It is based on new values which, in turn, get their nourishment from very ancient and classical Jewish values being applied to modern times, to our modern conscience and to our modern consciousness. This is a long stream. . . . It is not static. It is dynamic.[151]

Equally illuminating is the tension between Greenberg's position and that generally espoused by American Jewish thinkers who professed a firm belief in God. Where, for example, his friend Mordecai M. Kaplan, the founder of Reconstructionism, perceived "ethical ideals that make God manifest in the world" and considered God "the apotheosis of the interrelated unity of all reality," Greenberg saw this-worldly strategies derived from Jewry's historical past and existential needs.[152] In a world lacking ethical and moral certitude, he reasoned, the Jewish people developed a mythos that sustained and buttressed its collective survival across time and space. He articulated this theme in a 1951 speech to the New York Board of Rabbis:

> However one evaluates the concept of chosenness from an objective historical or from a psychological standpoint, the fact remains that this concept was accepted as a great subjective truth in the consciousness of the people during many generations, and a subjective truth is always historically more dynamic than an objective truth which has failed to penetrate the consciousness of the people. During many centuries Jews were aware that, in addition to being a people like any other, a collective physical entity, they were also . . . a group of "conspirators" against the forces of darkness and uncleanness in the world, and that this "conspiracy" was part of Providence's plan leading to the "end of days," which would come about sooner or later—time was not a factor and it was not desirable to hasten the end. Perhaps we should paraphrase this belief in chosenness and instead of saying "Thou hast chosen us," we should say, "I have chosen You."[153]

Greenberg also elaborated on his non-doctrinaire view of modern Jewish culture in response to Israeli leaders who in the years immediately following the establishment of the Jewish state called on young American Jews to make *aliyah*.

"The recruitment of American Jewish youth for agricultural pioneering in Israel," David Ben-Gurion and other government officials insisted, "should become the primary function of the Zionist movement in the US."[154] Ben-Gurion's statements led to a public dispute with Jacob Blaustein, president of the American Jewish Committee, which was ostensibly resolved in the "Blaustein-Ben-Gurion Agreement" (1952). The latter formality held that "*aliyah* rests with the free discretion of the American Jew himself: it is entirely a matter of his own volition."[155] But the Blaustein–Ben-Gurion Agreement did not quell the underlying cause of the debate. The Zionist leadership in Israel continued to declaim the principle of *shlilat hagolah* (negation of the exile), arguing that diaspora Jewish life was ultimately futile and authentic Jewish life was only possible in the Land of Israel. No stranger to controversy, Greenberg entered the fray and challenged the Zionist movement and American Jews to rethink the nature of the relationship between Israel and America and to reconceptualize the place of the Jewish state in modern Jewish life.[156] To drive home his point, he deliberately addressed the Twenty-third Zionist Congress (1951) in Yiddish rather than Hebrew—an ironic twist given his Hebraist credentials and role as head of the Jewish Agency's Department of Education and Culture.[157]

> Should we be ashamed of the exile? I am proud of it, and if *galut* was a calamity (who can pretend it was not?), I am proud of what we were able to perform in that calamity. Let others be ashamed of what they did to us in exile. We have every reason to consider our exilic past with heads proudly lifted. . . . True, the *galut* in which Jews live today is no longer that in which they lived so many generations in the past. The Jewish capacity for living creatively as a people in the sphere of time alone has been sadly depleted. . . . But we know—and this is one of the most important elements of the Zionist idea—that not only our political and socioeconomic position in many countries of the diaspora, but also our spiritual and cultural situation everywhere demand that we resume national life in the sphere of space, of territorial rootedness, and of political independence. . . .
>
> I would be less than honest with you if I failed to note in a few words a new spiritual danger which may arise from the accentuation—or rather, the hyper-emphasis—of our new orientation toward space. In some circles one no longer talks of *Jewish culture* but of *Israeli culture*. . . . But the best of states, even the ideal one, has no power to produce an original or characteristic culture of its own in a few years' time. Least of all does it possess this power if it regards itself as an end in itself, if it apotheosizes itself and cuts itself off from the spiritual history of its people, from its past, and from the values created in the past. . . . There will be no culture of tomorrow without a culture of yesterday and of the remoter past, unless we want to

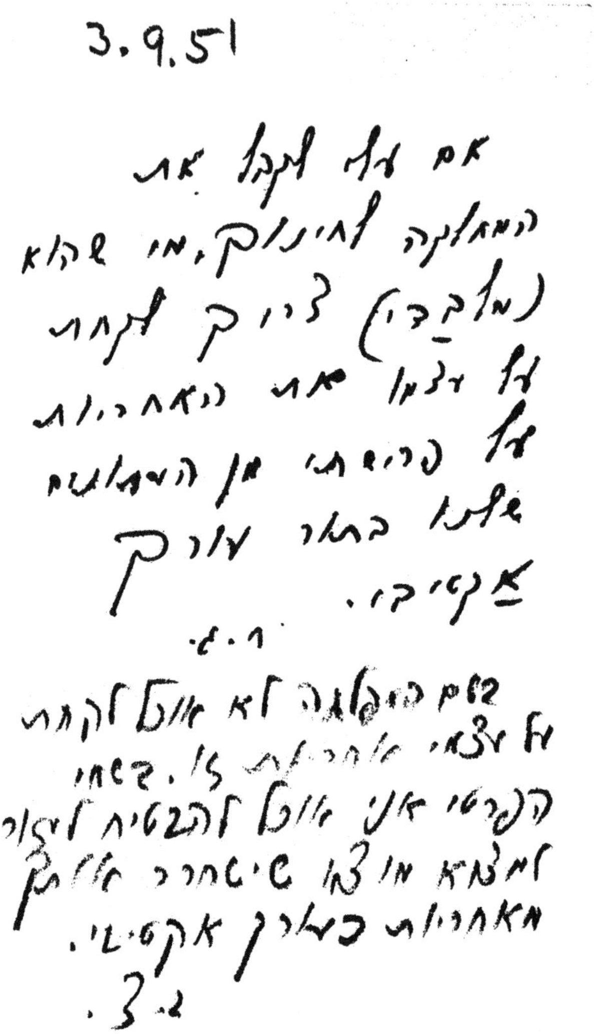

3.9.51

אם עלי לקבל את
המחלקה לחינוך, מי שהוא
(מלבדי) צריך לקחת
על עצמו את האחריות
על פרישתי מן העתונים
שלנו בתור עורך
אקטיבי.
ח. ג.

בשם המפלגה לא אוכל לקחת
על עצמי אחריות זו. בשמי
הפרטי אני יכול להבטיח לעזור
למצוא מוצא שישחרר אותך
מאחריות כעורך אקטיבי.
ב. צ.

Translation: If I am to receive the [Jewish Agency's] Department of Education, someone (apart from myself) must take responsibility for freeing me from our periodicals and the role of active editor. H. G.

In terms of the party, I cannot take this responsibility on myself. Speaking for myself, however, I can promise to help find a way to release you from the responsibility of serving as active editor. B. Z.

3. Note from Hayim Greenberg to Baruch Zuckerman (September 3, 1951); courtesy of the Central Zionist Archives, Jerusalem, Israel.

> reconcile ourselves to a shallow pseudo-cultural style attuned to the local ethnography and narrow horizons of a small irritably nationalistic state.[158]

Next, Greenberg addressed the core problematic of Zionist doctrine as espoused by Ben-Gurion and others. "Wherever Jews live as a minority," he conceded, "where they are not politically or socially independent, and are subject to the everyday pressures of its civilization and mode of life, but rely on the good graces of the non-Jewish majority, such a place is *galut*." But while Jews have been "compelled" throughout history to flee many host societies, he explained, "no one drives them out of any part of America. If, in a general sense, exile may be conceived symbolically as night, then there are some exiles of pitch black night, and some where the night is moonlit."[159] The foregoing statement captures Greenberg's considered, sensitive, and poetic amalgam of the ideas of election, exile, and diaspora. American society offered, he believed, a singularly favorable environment for Jews to champion individual freedom while pressing their ethnic and cultural interests.[160] Yet he challenged the idea American Jews could sustain a secure profile in a vacuum—detached from Israel and other diaspora Jewish communities. In contrast to the American Jewish Committee's non-Zionist rejection of "the notion, from whatever source it emanates, that American Jews are in any sense 'exiled,'" Greenberg offered a nuanced albeit metahistorical view of the Jewish experience. "All Jewish roads," he asserted, "sooner or later, directly or indirectly, with landmarks or without them, lead to the same destination: to *Erez Israel*."[161]

Deeply engaged in a variety of Jewish cultural and political activities over the course of five decades, Greenberg deployed a distinctive *Weltanschauung* that combined radicalism, liberalism, and cosmopolitanism with a profound love of modern Jewish life and culture in all its variety. He viewed diaspora Jewish culture, including that of the American Jewish diaspora, as inextricably bound up with Zionism, Jewish statehood, and the quest to secure the future survival of the Jewish people. He stressed the need to educate future generations not only about Zionism but the totality of the Jewish experience. "Without such education," he said, "Zionism may be a doctrine, a convincing theory, a program, a plan, an undertaking of desperate urgency, an appeal to sentiment, a noble humanitarian enterprise, but not a profound creative experience."[162] There was for him no unbridgeable chasm between these elements of his position. He was an agnostic with profound attachments to traditional Judaism, a socialist who aligned with progressive causes, an eastern European radical who believed in the promise of America, and a Zionist who believed in the vitality of the diaspora and fought for the creation of the Jewish state. His commitment to *klal yisrael* (Jewish peoplehood) anchored his readiness to take intellectual and political risks without fear of embarrassment or rejection.

Greenberg's ideas about Judaism, Zionism, and socialism emerged against the backdrop of the early twentieth century when dynamic historical conditions dramatically reshaped Jewish life and the globe. Where many other Jewish thinkers failed to articulate a durable vision of the future, Greenberg offered a nuanced alternative that joined abstraction with reality. He professed a principled, reasoned, and humanitarian realpolitik without resorting to sectarian partisanship masquerading as tough-minded savvy. His contributions to the public arena were forthright, resolute, and incisive—and predicated on the value of open, tolerant, and responsible discourse. He sustained robust intellectual, cultural, and political ties with a wide array of kindred spirits and ideological opponents alike. Not all American Jews pursued the paths espoused by Greenberg, but a sizable swath of the American Jewish community (including the Zionist movement) did embrace his guiding vision of modern Jewish life—a *mélange* of secular and spiritual themes, this-worldly and existential commitments, and liberal and nationalist principles. The extent to which he correctly anticipated American Jewry's future profile and the complex diaspora-Israel relationship characteristic of our day underscores the singular importance of both his intellectual and political leadership.

1

The Meaning of Zionism

(1922)

Hayim Greenberg lived in Berlin from 1921 to 1924. In this period, he developed close relationships with several key Jewish and Zionist leaders, writers, and intellectuals. He also worked as a coeditor of the weekly sponsored by the World Zionist Organization, Haolam *(The World), and the monthly* Atideinu *(Our Future). He composed the following essay—an extended argument for Zionism—against the backdrop of postwar reconstruction of Jewish life in eastern Europe, civil war in Russia, Arab riots in Jerusalem (1920) and in Jaffa (1921), and the Twelfth Zionist Congress (1921).*

I

Is nationality an absolute value, or does it have a meaning for us exclusively as connected with or applied to specific phenomena of social life? Hitherto we have been receiving two answers to this basic question of the national problem that are different and contradictory. The answers to this question are essentially to be found in close dependence on the general tendency of the worldview and the character of the world outlook of those ideologists who are preoccupied by the question.

If we were to reduce all the spiritual tendencies of mankind during the course of world history to two focal and contradictory trends, then it might not be paradoxical to say that the spiritual life of mankind—the strivings of peoples, social groupings, and individuals—revolves around one of the following two factors, understood in their broadest and most generalized sense: around utilitarianism and around erotism [life energy].

By utilitarianism we mean every kind of spiritual tendency that acknowledges as the sole criterion of the value of any human action the point of view of usefulness exclusively, independently of what we mean by usefulness. It is possible to bring into this conception of utilitarianism even that kind of spiritual tendency that advises mankind to abstain from a whole series of material benefits and empirical advantages—from everything that in day-to-day life we call "useful" or "agreeable." For many utilitarians propose, instead of this-worldly usefulness, a usefulness of a different nature, such as, for instance, ethical usefulness. Those representatives of ethics and of the spiritual principle of life who advise mankind to free itself once and for all from everything that agitates and occupies it in everyday life and to set itself as the sole aim of its existence the realization of certain ethical principles (i.e., justice or love) are, fundamentally, also utilitarians, with the sole difference that they disagree with utilitarians of the materialist tendency as to what is the highest "usefulness" and human good.

By erotism we understand an order of human thoughts and emotions that recognizes as the most precious thing in our lives not those goals that we consciously strive toward, out of a logical consideration of their usefulness, whether material or ethical, but solely the satisfaction of those inclinations, sometimes "aimless" and often "inexplicable," inherent in man, of that erotic spirit that often forces us to strive for specific objects whose internal value either completely refuses to yield to rationalization, or yields to it only to a highly relative degree. In this absence of calculation that underlies every such aspiration, and that frees it from any kind of material or spiritual "profit," in this consciousness of the right and the obligation to strive toward certain objects not because their "usefulness" is clear to us, or their superiority to other objects, but because there is an indefinable though profoundly real and intimate connection between the aspirants and the object of their aspiration—it is this that constitutes the fundamental factor of what we call erotism.

Against the background of history these two tendencies of human thought have carried on an intense struggle, now with one overcoming the other, now with both existing simultaneously and alongside each other in one and the same society but advancing within its boundaries different elements that are the bearers of one or the other principle. And in the present instance, too, it depends on one or the other tendency of human thought—utilitarianism or erotism—which of two contradictory answers is given to the question we asked: Is nationality an absolute or merely a relative value?

In its very nature, utilitarianism is inclined to belittle the element of nationality. A utilitarian like Diogenes[1] naturally could not accept it. Not for nothing did this Greek Cynic,[2] who belittled everything beautiful, everything that had style and art, in a word, everything "erotic" in life, and reduced everything of positive value solely to the realization of a certain number of abstract principles, maintain that the absence of a fatherland was an authentic good. Not for nothing did he call himself "Apolis," a man outside the state, outside a homeland and a nation. Nor was it accidental that the last of the Greek Cynics preached the idea of a "single flock" and of "world citizenship," while the followers of the Stoic[3] school with their applied morality were the most zealous advocates of pure cosmopolitanism. The first fathers of the Christian church, who were confronted by such a general and overriding utilitarian-ethical task as the introduction of the "kingdom of God on earth," who were striving as it were to drain away a man's blood, and deprive him of his whole individual style, of just those factors that make him an "erotic" being, were also bound to have a negative attitude toward the national factor from the very beginning. Like Diogenes, they too were utilitarians, people who contemplated the whole of life from the point of view of a certain kind of "usefulness," of a special usefulness, to be sure, that did not promise worldly material benefits but the highest spiritual good, which they valued above everything else. Nor was it for nothing that a moralist like [Leo] Tolstoy,[4] who throughout the course of the literary activity of his last period, strove, just as had his spiritual ancestors, the fathers and founders of the Christian church, to make men colorless and to deprive them of just that emotional sphere that makes them the bearers of erotic aspirations, also had a negative attitude toward the national factor.[5] In the last analysis he was also a utilitarian, and insofar as he was such, the erotic nature of nationalism was alien to him.

Utilitarians of the other, non-ethical, materialist tendency (I mean primarily the ideologists of the socialist movement) were also bound to have a negative attitude toward the national factor, at least during the first period of their evolution. For those who, like the Church Fathers, like Tolstoy, like Diogenes, also preached the definite point of view of usefulness, and considered the entire value of life to consist in the satisfaction of a specific group of material needs, the factor of nationality was bound to be unacceptable for a long time, for fundamentally it conceals within itself the authorization of a certain area of erotic aspirations. And it is just this utilitarianism that explains the profoundly negative attitude toward the national question of the founders of the socialist movement in Europe; this explains their neglect of the question of national culture and even of the question of the political independence of the small nations. Later on, to be sure, life compelled the representatives of socialism, too, to review their attitude toward the national question; many of them were then obliged to acknowledge nationalism as one of the most important factors in the history of mankind. But even today the majority of the socialist ideologists, in their recognition of the importance of the national question, start out primarily from the necessity of disencumbering the class struggle from everything that might prevent its free and unhindered evolution, from the desirability of freeing the struggle of the rising class against the ruling class from those national frictions that have often interfered with that struggle, obscuring class-consciousness and preventing the idea of a struggle for the creation of new conditions of human life from crystallizing with sufficient distinctness. Because of this they were ready to solve a whole series of acute national questions not for the sake of realizing one national idea or another that constituted an absolute value, but solely because they saw in the solution of these questions a means of lightening the process of the class struggle.

The second consideration taken at the present time as a point of departure by the majority of the ideologists of socialism, in their acknowledgment of the importance of the national question, simply rests on the abstract principle of human freedom. As long as there still exist certain groups that feel they have specific national individualities, the representatives of the socialist movement do not regard themselves as morally or politically justified in sanctioning the political oppression these nationalities are subjected to. In any given case they have the same neutral attitude toward nationalism as they have toward questions of religion and faith. As long as people have certain religious needs, then, independently of our own attitude toward those needs, the state must ensure the possibility of satisfying them.

This negative attitude on the part of the socialist movement toward nationalism completely corresponds to the spirit of a movement in which a class that at the present time is climbing up the social ladder is taking part. Every rising social group that still has to conquer a place for itself and to win a certain terrain beneath its feet is perforce condemned in the first period of its development to a utilitarian-rationalistic turn of mind. The need to struggle and to concentrate one's will on one single point, the necessity for eliminating from one's path everything that might distract attention and energy from the performance of the central task confronting such a social group, inevitably forces it and its ideologists, during the first period of its activity and struggle, to disregard everything that does not fit into the sharply defined framework of the task that confronts it.

But in the course of time the rising social group, constantly fortifying its own position in social life, winning ever more firm ground beneath its feet, and even beginning to rest a little from the first stages of its bitter and all-encompassing struggle, becomes more and more receptive to an understanding of the value of the factors that it had completely disregarded during the first period of its evolution. The firmer and the more stable the social position of the rising class becomes, the more it can allow itself material and spiritual "luxury," the more powerful it becomes and consequently the richer it becomes spiritually, identifying itself with those cultural advantages that beforehand had been inaccessible to it, the more cultured and hence the more individualistic it becomes—the base broadens on which various aspirations of an erotic character begin to evolve in its midst, too. And the larger the place occupied in the life of the rising class by this sort of aspiration, the more receptive it becomes to the national idea in its pure, absolute form.

The same thing must also occur with that rising class whose development we are at the present time witnessing. During the past few years we have already been witnessing symptoms of a fundamental shift in the attitude of the socialist movement toward the national problem. It is enough to recall such eminent ideologists of western socialism as [Jules] Ferry[6] and [Engelbert] Pernerstorfer,[7] who have already begun reminding their fellow-thinkers that collectivism demands a higher development of mankind, and that since mankind lives in national forms, collectivism, naturally, must favor the existence of free, independent, and self-conscious nations. These symptoms were displayed with particular clarity in one of the speeches of the late [Jean] Jaurès,[8] in which he indicated that personalities with their characteristic traits and their singularity would not only not fuse together and not be annihilated in the future socialist organization, but that these personalities—collective as well as individual, in the form of nationalities and peoples—would simply have to acquire a broad arena for their own individual development in the future social order. This prognosis led this apostle of socialism to conclude that "our duty in the present era is to preserve for that happy time all those collective individualities now in existence, so that later on they would receive the possibility of a full and mighty development."[9]

Thus, with the strengthening of the individual and, so to speak, "erotic" demands of mankind, a positive attitude toward nationality will have to be established as an absolute value. The consciousness of the great value of the national ego will have to be made more profound.

II

What does this national ego consist of?

On this question, too, we meet with two different mutually contradictory answers which give rise to two different views of nationalism.

One interpretation regards the national ego as something established and fixed once and for all. This view, which basically goes back to [Georg Wilhelm Friedrich] Hegel,[10] regards the national spirit as something constant, existing for itself and in itself, independently of any historic changes or stratifications. The representatives of this view have raised the national spirit, the national ego, to the level of a metaphysical entity independent of our empirical life. It is with this same spiritualistic interpretation of the concept of the national ego that we meet in many Russian Slavophiles who are under the influence of Hegelianism and are striving to fix the essence of the Russian national ego and to reduce it to a definite, eternal, unshakable scheme of traits and peculiarities. The best Slavophiles have tried to prove that there exists a whole series of cultural values that are completely incapable of evolving on Russian soil, being organically contrary to the Russian ego, and that, on the other hand, the Russian national ego contains within itself a spiritual essence that cannot be borrowed by any other Western people.[11] This metaphysical view, which considers the cultural destiny of every nation foreordained, attempts to confine the national spirit of every people within the framework of a single specific formula, in the belief that such a formula is really capable of laying down boundaries that the national ego will not overstep.

In Jewish literature the reflections of this view of the essence of the national ego are displayed most graphically in some of the works of Ahad Haam,[12] who tried to reduce the Jewish national ego to a specific sum of philosophical truths, and to establish that outside the religion and outside the existence of these truths there was no Jewish nationality, and that if the contemporary concrete Jewry abandons one or another of these truths it deprives itself by that alone of its Jewish character.[13]

This view, unconditionally conservative in tendency, considers that a people has created a definite character for its national culture at a certain period of its historic development, and that that character has become, as it were, untouchable, and that it cannot and even should not be changed throughout all the further processes of the historical development of the people. The representatives of this view are joined by the metaphysical ideologists who have tried and are trying to lay down a principle of the division of labor between different nationalities, in the sense that each nationality is a sort of "specialist" in a specific domain of material or spiritual culture, and that any given nation, predestined for its "specialty," is even quite incapable of the organic possibility of displaying its creativity in any of the other domains of culture that are the specialties of other peoples. It is these ideologists who have attempted to assign to the Romans a talent for statesmanship, to Greeks purely plastic gifts, to the Jews a feeling for justice, to the Germans the capacity for harmoniously logical philosophical thought and so on, condemning each nation to a specific "mission," which it is not free to abstain from, and theoretically depriving every people of the possibility of penetrating into a domain that does not "belong" to it.

As a counterweight to these spiritually enslaving theories there is another view that has been crystallizing more and more with a full feeling for reality and in accordance with the authentic process of historical development. According to this view, a nation is not a group of people with a cultural and psychological physiognomy that is congealed once and for all, but a living social organism that is in a process of uninterrupted *becoming*.[14] The character of this becoming is always determined to a greater or lesser extent by the total sum of cultural and psychological accumulations that have occurred in the nation during its historical past. According to this view, the national ego does not allow of a precise logical formulation. Contemporary science does not yet know of the social or psychological chemistry with whose help we might succeed in analyzing the national psyche into its constituent elements and subject it to a quantitative analysis. What we call the national spirit or the national ego is something that cannot be formulated, something that cannot be grasped in all its living reality. However much we strive to define the character of one people or another, by means of any complicated or simplified formula, we will never succeed. There is, for instance, a conception of the German people as a nation of dreamers and philosophers; this conception is founded on the fact that this people produced the most powerful thinkers in Europe and the "dreamiest" of the romantic poets. But does such a definition correspond to a whole series of other impressions given us by the immediate activities of the German people, in which we can observe just as vivid a display of the practical and utilitarian spirit, which for a time has obscured for us the tendency of the Germans toward daydreaming and abstractions?

There exists a conception of the English people as a nation with clearly expressed utilitarian traits, but this same ultra-practical people contains a multitude of religious sects which we encounter in scarcely any other people in Europe.[15] The English people is considered to be a nation of conquerors, a people of explorers, tamers of the sea, emigrants, tourists, and colonizers. It is customary to consider it the most mobile of peoples, completely unattached to its own land and country. Yet in no other people in the world do we see such dedicated love for and profound piety toward the family hearth as we observe in the average Englishman.

Whatever description we apply to one people or another, we always risk colliding with a variety of internal contradictions and contrasts. We can never be in a position to contrive a formula that would clearly, and more or less precisely, lay down the psychological boundaries between one nation and another. Nevertheless these boundaries—intangible, inexpressible, and not subject to fixation—are real, like the life of these peoples itself, like the incontestable "difference" that exists between them. Everything we call national peculiarities, national spirit, or the national ego is nothing constant, which is defined for all historical life; precisely the same elements can be constituents of the psychology of any people, but the combinations, the compositions of these elements, the proportional interrelationship between them, the degree of contradictoriness and discordance of these same elements in the national psyche—it is these nuances and intangible shadings that create what we call the national soul and the national ego.

The national ego is thus a definite *system* of such elements, which in themselves are common to all men, universal and, so to speak, "neutral" as far as nations are concerned. At the same time, this system can itself change considerably in the process of the historical evolution of a people, absorbing new elements, accentuating or obscuring within itself now one principle, now another. But in all its changes—however essential—this system, under certain conditions, can conserve the whole of its national singularity. In this interpretation of the national ego, the only one that is acceptable, what rises above the *results* of the historical life of a nation is its limitless and indefinable *potential*. Normal national life is the discharge of these potentialities, while the actual national ideals are nothing but a striving for a freeing of the process of discharge from everything capable of hindering it. It is the presence and the role of the potential principle in the nature of nationality that serves as the basis underlying the uninterrupted national *becoming*, which we counterpose to the so-called national being. And if it is still possible to talk about the formulation of this *being* with respect to a nation that has already definitively exhausted all its potentialities, that is, that has already finished its existence, it is quite irrational to draw any obligatory conclusions from the national "substance" of a living people, whose potentialities conceal so much that is new and contradictory, so much that is unknown and unexpected for itself. In this sense the truth is accommodated far more by that Jewish tendency that, as a counterweight to Ahad Haamism, is embodied in different variations in the works of [Micah Yosef] Berdichevsky,[16] on the one hand, and of [Martin] Buber[17] on the other. Just as Berdichevsky saw nothing fundamentally unharmonious in the transfer to Jewish soil of Nietzschean morality, so Buber intuitively understood the elements of "underground" Judaism in our past culture that substantially contradicted the official, canonical Judaism that Ahad Haam considered the basis of Jewish nationalism. For neither of them will the Jewish national ego fit into any system.

For both of them the Jewish national ego is that force that lends its Jewish stamp to every act of Jewish life and to every factor of cultural borrowing. At the same time, the essence and the content of the cultural life, the ideals, the standards, the principles, the ethical, philosophical, and religious values can change in the historical process of the life of the people without in the least destroying the Jewish national ego. What is particularly convincing in this connection is the difference established by Berdichevsky between the epoch of the First Temple and the epoch of the Second Temple.[18]

On the basis of a comparison between these two epochs, Berdichevsky asks the question: What is more typical and characteristic of the Jewish national ego? Is it the spacious, picturesque, earthy life we see in the epoch of the First Temple, with the almost pagan way of life of Palestinian Jewry, or is it the asceticism that evolved in Jewry during the last period of its life in Palestine, in the epoch of the Second Temple? Where can we seek the authentic manifestation of the Jewish national ego? In the beauties of the [Hebrew] Bible with its harmony and rhythm, happily joined in it with the flame of the loftiest emotions of the human soul, or in the Talmud, which extinguished the flame of the Jewish heart and laid down the principle of its servitude?[19]

Without going into the fundamental differences that exist between the cultures of these two most remarkable epochs of Jewish history, Berdichevsky rightly thinks that the Jewish national ego was expressed in the spiritual life of both epochs equally. For the "spirit" of any nation is defined not by essence and content, but by the characteristic form in which the nation invests its cultural experiences and creativity. A nation is a color-producing organism, and in creating its own life—when that is not violated by the will of another people—even when it borrows foreign cultural values, it does not thereby lose its own individuality, but on the contrary, enriches it still more. For in borrowing the elements of a foreign culture, a free nation imbues them with its own characteristic stamp, harmonizing them with its own peculiarities and lending them the character of its own national singularity. There can be no doubt that if the encounter in antiquity between Jewish culture and Hellenism had taken place under different political conditions, if Hellenism had not been thrust upon Palestinian Jewry by the force of arms of the Syrio-Greek population, if Jewish culture had encountered Hellenism in a peaceful competition, then Palestinian Jewry would have absorbed a great deal of value from the ancient Hellenic culture, which would later have dissolved in Jewish culture and been given a national character. It is precisely in this that the fundamental essence of a nation is to be found—that it is not an essence, but a form, a coloring, and a style. The content gravitates rather toward the universal, the form toward the national, similar to the way in which logic gravitates toward the pan-human, psychology toward the national, science toward the general, art toward the individual. Hence we are right in calling national everything displayed by a nation in its life's activity when unhampered by any outside will.

And it is this interpretation of the "national" that gives rise to a completely different interpretation of nationalism, which in contrast to the moribund, completely reactionary nationalism that is wholly based on the fixed summing up of national culture, sets no bounds at all to the further evolution of a people, and leaves to a people the right to react immediately to the whole of the surrounding world, while borrowing any cultural values it likes from any other people it likes, and to respond with a living heart to all the manifestations and tendencies of universal life.

It is just this liberating nationalism, which opens up a boundlessly large field for the evolution of the people, and does not force its spirit into one frame or another—whether philosophical, religious, or ethical—that, as we shall see further on, underlies the Zionist movement. From this point of view we would have the right to formulate the essence of Zionism in this form: Zionism strives for the transformation of the Jewish people into a free, collective individuality that nothing and no one can hamper in its manifestations or evolution. For Zionism does not strive for the conservation of Jewry in the form in which it congealed at a specific point in its evolution, but toward the free discharge in the process of its further evolution of its potential forces, which are inexhaustible and not subject to fixation.

III

In recent years, Zionism has been confronted by a rival national movement within Jewry which, like Zionism, promises to transform Jewry into a free individuality but without one condition Zionism regards as indispensable—without a territorial concentration. That is the autonomist movement in Jewry,[20] which in the past few years has already broken up into a whole series of tendencies that, for the most part, are based on the principle of personal autonomy. And now, in order to analyze the value of this principle, we must proceed to an explanation of the extent to which national and personal autonomy are really capable of solving the national problem of a minority in the broad sense in which we have been discussing it so far.

The fundamental mistake made by the partisans of national-personal autonomy is that that they confuse the sociological question with the question of public law. Fundamentally, the principle of personal autonomy is nothing more nor less than a declaration in its own way by the state, which asserts that it has nothing against a free development of the broadest kind of one or another nationality that is part of it and that it is ready—insofar as that depends on the organs of administration—to leave to each nation the juridical possibility of manifesting its ego. But this factor of public law, which has its own very protracted history, especially in the political evolution of Austria-Hungary, completely fails to solve the sociological problem confronting us. The state cannot, need not, and is not obliged to ensure the possibility of evolution to every individual nationality; the state is merely obligated and able to eliminate from the path of every nation those obstacles to its evolution that derive from the oppression of the state apparatus. And if we put the question that interests us not on juridical but on sociological grounds, we are bound to see at once the thoroughgoing futility of a national theory that is founded exclusively on the principle of individual autonomy.

Just what is social life? If we wanted to reduce to one common denominator all the forces that are active in social life and that give it its shape, we should have to come to the conclusion that the character of each example of social life is the result of a social compromise continuously being manifested in the daily life of the organized population by a process of reciprocal imitation. No more or less normally organized society could even exist without such a reciprocal compromise, without each individual's surrender of certain traits of his ego, and without his imitating a whole series of other individuals within the boundaries of the society he lives in.

This compromise does not, of course, go on in accordance with a conscious mutual agreement, but by virtue of the unconscious, instinctive human striving for a common life. It is in this striving that the causes of the constant, and for the most part unconscious, reciprocal imitation are rooted. And it is this all-embracing instinct of reciprocal imitation that is also bound to absorb a minority settled in the midst of the national majority. It forms a maelstrom of individual traits and qualities, likes and dislikes, tastes and inclinations, repulsions and attractions, that make up the electric currents vibrating among people living in the same territory, separating and reuniting them, and being resolved in the establishment of a certain resultant harmony. And it is just this maelstrom that constitutes the process of a continuously renewed creation of social life, in which the majority of the members of organized society take part, and which is bound to absorb the national minority embedded in the midst of the territorial majority. A national minority living in a foreign country participates in this social compromise to a comparatively negligible degree only when it is condemned to an isolated, enslaved life, when it is deprived of elementary human rights, when it is shut off from a whole series of areas of labor and economic activity. But a national minority that is not isolated from the majority by artificial legal boundaries, and that has the real possibility of participating in the life of the whole society living on a certain territory, must perforce become a participant in the above-mentioned process of reciprocal imitation. As it participates in this continuous, reciprocal compromise that is renewed day after day, the national minority, it is obvious, introduces into this process of social life elements of its own individuality, but these last, if only because of their quantitative insignificance, are condemned to spontaneous suppression through the quantitatively numerous elements introduced by the territorial majority.

[Gabriel de] Tarde[21] is right in considering social man as a somnambulist, a being subject to the ineluctable mesmerism of the surrounding majority. Outside this hypnotic force that exists in and around us, that the whole atmosphere of social life is imbued with, the creation of any kind of human society would be unthinkable. And it is this reciprocal hypnotism, which daily gives shape to social life, that must perforce lead to the depersonalization of the national ego of the territorial minority. The more weighty the majority, and the more insignificant the minority, the more the latter is exposed to assimilation; for the greater the flow of mesmerizing factors from the life of the majority, the more profoundly do these factors develop within the national minority a capacity and a readiness to submit to the mesmerizing forces of the majority.

Often, in its struggle against the assimilating influence of the majority, the minority attempts to draw strength from the reservoir of the hypnotic influences of its own past. Every people has definite deposits of the hypnotic influences of the past, ancient deposits contained in its language, its way of life, its culture, traditions, and memories. A substantial part of these deposits is also preserved in the reservoir of its instincts, in a whole series of purely biological peculiarities that conserve within themselves psychological elements. A people may really counterpose these forces of the past to the hypnosis that proceeds from the depths of the majority. And it goes without saying that the richer the reservoir of hypnotic influences of the past in a given people, the longer the historical road traversed by that people, the more vital and the richer the store of its memories, the easier it is for it to resist the mesmerizing influence of the majority and the more slowly it will yield to denationalization and depersonalization. But in the last analysis the hypnotic influences flowing from the immediate life of the majority with which the minority come into daily contact are bound to paralyze the force of the hypnotic influences that are nourished primarily by the heritage of the past and that the minority counterposes to the majority. However rich the past of a national minority, whatever force of resistance that past may give it, it offers no more than the possibility of stretching out over a greater or lesser period of time the process of its own denationalization, and in the last analysis this inherited store is never capable of equaling through its own power the vital fountain of mesmerizing forces daily imposing their influence on the national minority that finds itself in direct physical, material, spiritual, vocal, and optical contact with the territorial majority. Hence the national profile of the minority is bound to become more and more effaced to the extent that it expands its participation in all the domains of social life, whose character and tone are determined and dictated by the majority of the population. Instead of the normal discharge of the national creative potential, what inevitably takes place is its stifling, suppression, and gradual atrophying.

In order to be able to say about any people that it is really utilizing everything inherent in its national ego, that people must be given the opportunity freely to display its own singularity in the independent resolution of all those vital problems that beset mankind. But if a national minority with equal rights takes part in the resolution of those vital problems in close collaboration with the territorial majority, there can be no chance for such independence, since the tastes and the style of the majority, in the broadest sense of these terms, its criteria of beauty and ugliness, satisfaction and discontent, justice and injustice, will authoritatively impose its sociologically unavoidable hegemony in the conduct of life, a hegemony that will inevitably suppress the willpower, the tastes, the inclinations and the style of the national minority.

When we speak of "imitativeness," the word is associated by us for the most part with a certain striving, or a readiness to consider oneself below others; we see in imitation only slavery and aping. Such a one-sided view of the character and the origins of imitativeness will not sustain criticism, for imitativeness very often is but a striving for harmony, for the establishment of harmonious interrelationships between the separate individuals and separate groups that make up a human society concentrated on a specific territory. By virtue of this natural and wholesome striving toward the greatest possible diminution of the number of psychological frictions and discords in social life, we are constantly involving ourselves in the process of imitation, consciously or unconsciously, whether we notice it or not, whether we want to or not. In that process each of us is both the subject and the object of imitation: at one and the same time each of us is both the hypnotist and the medium. By virtue of the striving, not to be eradicated from human nature, toward the establishment of a harmonious principle in social life, the national minority is obliged to imitate the territorial majority specifically in the domains of activity, thought and feeling, creativity, and the forms of its self-manifestation.

It is customary to think that it is only the weak who imitate the strong, the slaves the slave driver, but we completely forget that by virtue of this same ineradicable human striving for harmony the oppressor very often imitates the oppressed, the master his slaves, the national minority that invades a foreign territory as its enslaving element the oppressed national majority. The Franks in Gaul[22] were quickly Latinized in spite of their having been conquerors; they quickly adopted the Roman language, Roman customs, and the whole of Roman culture. The same thing happened with the Normans,[23] who appeared in England as conquerors; the same thing happened with the Varangians,[24] and to some extent with the Tartars[25] who came to Russia as imperious conquerors. Here the hypnotizing and assimilating force naturally was on the side of the majority, which dissolved within itself the ruling national minority. In the striving for the harmonizing of life, there disappeared the national singularity of the element that by virtue of its scanty numbers had to adapt itself to the general resultant social level.

People's inclination to walk in step, with the same gait, was displayed long before it was forcibly introduced into contemporary European armies. In this connection it may be worth recalling a series of curious measurements, carried out by the representatives of the French psychological school, that showed that people living in the same city for a long time have approximately the same gait and the same average walking speed, even though there is no external authority that would force them into such a mutual adaptation.[26] Here again there manifests itself the force we were discussing before—a striving for rhythm and harmony that consciously, unconsciously, and subconsciously overflows into imitation. It goes without saying that wherever there is any mutual imitation there is a quicker and easier depersonalization of that social element whose members, because of their scanty numbers, are to a great degree "mediums," if one may express it in this way, rather than "hypnotists."

Some psychologists have tried to establish definite differences between the logic of different peoples; they have tried to prove that each people has its own methods of logical thought. Even without agreeing with the extreme conclusions drawn in this connection by Gustave Le Bon,[27] who maintained, for instance, that the English think deductively and the French inductively, we cannot nevertheless deny that even though there exists one single logic with its universal laws, common to all mankind, none of us thinks in accordance with the full strictness and precision of those laws, and each of us displays certain deviations from the theoretically binding logical standards. In these deviations there is a countless multitude of the most variegated shadings and nuances that distinguish not only separate individuals but also such collective individualities as nationalities. But the joint sojourn of two nationalities on the same territory, which forces them to come into direct daily contact and to solve jointly all social problems, also forces them to become as far as possible understandable to each other, and to reduce to the smallest possible minimum the number of ideas and devices to express them that are the property of only tightly knit, intimate circles.

But the impossibility of establishing the most homogeneous possible methods of logical thought and the expression of thought and feeling, always forces the national minority to adapt itself to the logical bent and to the logical deviations that characterize the national majority, until in the course of time the national minority divests itself of its own peculiar habits, ways, and methods of logical thought. The minority is held powerless to conserve its singularity and the important elements of its individuality, in the process of the socially compulsory adaptation. And this need for mutual understanding for all those who make up a normally organized society also leads the national minority to other paths of adaptation and denationalization.

In the interests of mutual understanding and social collaboration, the national minority is compelled to learn the language of the surrounding majority. At the same time, the majority usually takes advantage of its right not to know the language of the minority in its midst. The mass acquisition of the language of the surrounding majority is an absolutely inescapable phenomenon in a progressive society in which the minority is drawn into close collaboration with the majority of the population in all the domains of social life. It makes the minority particularly receptive to assimilatory influences.

The inner life of the majority, which naturally attracts the representatives of the national minority (for it feels that it is precisely here that the threads are woven that make up the complicated network of the social life of the whole country) spreads out broadly before the minority that has acquired the foreign tongue; there is a gradual deepening in it of the striving to enter into that life and fuse with it.

For a people living on its own territory and forming the majority of the population, there is no danger of entering to any degree into the inner life of any other people, for it assimilates everything it borrows from a foreign culture. While adapting itself to various of its elements, it at the same time adapts them to itself, melting them down in its own crucible and fusing them with its own spiritual substance. But for a people living as a minority in a foreign country, there is a real danger from the foreign culture, for it finds itself in intimate intercourse with the living exponents of that culture, and together with its basic elements it gradually also acquires from the immediate objects of imitation methods of perceiving those elements. Thus it loses what is the most precious and vital thing in the nature of a nationality—its specific *feeling for the world.*

We look for national Jewish elements in the creative activity of assimilated Jews; we rejoice when we sense echoes of Jewish influence in the works of [Heinrich] Heine[28] and [Ludwig] Boerne;[29] it flatters us when someone discloses to us remote reflections of prophetic ideals in the works of [Mark] Antokolsky,[30] or a refraction of the messianic longings of ancient Jewry in [Karl] Marx[31] and [Ferdinand] Lassalle,[32] and reflections of "typical Jewish *Weltschmerz*" [German for "melancholy"][33] in [Isaac I.] Levitan.[34] We see in all this a consoling proof of the ineradicability of our national ego. But in doing so we forget that in our national culture, which is carried on in the name of national Jewry, denationalization and psychologically assimilatory elements are already manifesting their effects. For the most part we completely fail to notice that in contemporary Jewish *belles lettres,* for instance, there is a predominance of the Russian landscape we are familiar with from [Ivan] Turgenev,[35] [Maxim] Gorky,[36] [Anton] Chekhov,[37] and [Ivan Alekseyvich] Bunin,[38] in almost the same forms of perception we encounter in them. While unconsciously preserving in our conscious assimilation certain traits of our national ego, and while remaining in Jewry for the sake of Jewry, we lose elements of our national individuality without noticing it ourselves. More and more we subject our own perception of the world to the perception of those who "fill the earth" and impregnate with themselves, their spirit, their influences and their teachings the whole atmosphere of life that we breathe and cannot help but breathe together with them. Every country is its own kind of "vessel," into which there flows the specific content of the national spirit, which pervades the entire life of the country and is materialized in it. But the striving of a national minority to lodge its own spirit in a vessel that is already filled comes up against lively resistance, thanks to which it grows weaker and weaker and becomes more and more vulnerable, yielding, and anemic. And however powerful that striving might be at given moments of its manifestation, it is always weaker than the law of harmony that social life cannot help but submit to.

In the life of every national minority, in the light of what was said above, two different and contradictory forces are active—a centrifugal and a centripetal. The need for the harmonization of life, on the one hand, forces the national minority to strive for a fusion with the surrounding majority; on the other hand, the reservoir of instincts and historical accumulations, which continues to nourish its will to existence, forces it to mark itself off consciously from the majority, to hold aloof from it, to set up special boundaries and dikes that would prevent the national majority from engulfing it. Reflections of its own national way of life struggle, now overtly, now covertly, against the bright light of the foreign, but authentically alive, full-bodied national way of life; the past struggles with the present and with the embryos of the future concealed in it; dead ancestors contend as it were with the foreign, but physically close, living, contemporaries.

A struggle goes on between these two objectively unequal, but stubbornly unyielding forces: each of them embraces a definite period in the historical life of the people, and sometimes they are also active at the same time, in the same epoch, manifesting themselves in the reciprocally enfeebling tendencies and inclinations of different elements of the people. It is in this struggle between two mutually exclusive principles that the inner life of the national minority takes place. Attracted by two magnets, eternally torn not only by the distance between the striving and its realization, but also by the profound contradictions in its very aspirations and mutually irreconcilable inclinations, this life is deprived of that stability and balance that are so important for normal cultural accumulations, for the growth and the evolution of the great social masses.

The national feeling of a minority nation tends now toward atrophy, now toward hypertrophy. In one case as in the other this is bound up with an immense tension of the will, of consciousness, of attentiveness. Intellectual and emotional energy is expended not on immediate, positive creation, but on a whole series of *acts of resistance*—now on resistance to the assimilatory influences, now on subduing one's willpower for the reaffirmation of one's own ego. The creatively most precious domains of the unconscious and the subconscious are thus condemned to a systematic impoverishment in favor of an ever more refined, sterile consciousness, whose breath dries up the juices of the creative imagination. Neither the anaesthesia of the national feeling nor its hyperaesthesia, neither of these two diametrically opposed processes toward which the life of the minority nation gravitates, goes on with impunity for the latter.

Thanks to the constant control of the ever vigilant consciousness, which comes to the aid of the self-maintaining, conservative nationalism and of the assimilatory process of penetrating into the life of a foreign nation, elements of the "unaccountable" disappear from the life of the national minority more and more. The latter becomes decreasingly "naïve" and "sincere," less and less original, and creative. The ineluctable destiny of history hovers over the future of national minorities: however powerful the authority of the ghosts which command their descendants to go on living the lives of those who preceded them, the authority of the living must sooner or later take what belongs to it by natural, inalienable right. The brow of a minority nation is "marked"; its life is a prolonged fading away that cannot help but have the same end that every dying away must have in our world.

In this national agony individual bright sparks may of course flare up from time to time; a feverish clinging to the life that is slipping away may at times light up the eyes of the condemned nation with a special, deceptively promising luster that has an undeniable charm. But however bright at individual moments these sunset illuminations of the national life, they can do no more than postpone the hour of demise, and never prevent it altogether. Such is the inevitable fate of every minority people, however favorable the general social conditions of its existence and however broad the personal, autonomous rights it may enjoy: sociological inevitability is always more powerful than the broadest juridical opportunities.

IV

In the light of the aforesaid, it becomes understandable why Zionism arose in our own era, and not in the medieval ghetto or in the pre-Emancipation epoch of modern history, which was still completely imbued with the spirit of the ghetto.

The ghetto was incapable of giving birth to the Zionist movement, for by the very fact of its existence it screened off the most fundamental aspects of the *galut* [exile]. The crystallization of every social ideal demands the most extensive possible unmasking of the negative sides of "what is," to which the ideal counterposes its "what should be." What was indispensable for the crystallization of the Zionist ideal was the unmasking of the *galut,* whereas the ghetto obscured the *galut* and toned down as it were its ugliest features in its mysterious veils. Despite its humiliation, the Jewry of the ghetto in a certain sense felt itself to be an independent nation. The ghetto was a substitute for a territory, one might even say a substitute for Jewish statehood, and its inhabitants, who had scarcely any contact with the surrounding non-Jewish world, were bound to form an illusory idea of their national independence. Religion, which set its stamp on the Jewish way of life and the whole life of the ghetto, was something more than a religion, if by the latter is meant merely a number of dogmas and the rites symbolizing them. The Jewish religion in the medieval ghetto, which regulated almost all aspects and facets of the internal national life, was the basis of an integral national existence. By taking advantage of its exclusive authority and by dictating the forms of existence of Jewish social and individual welfare, it set up *de facto* boundaries around Jewry just as a territory or a state does with respect to other peoples. Thanks to it Jewry was united inwardly not only and not so much by a common world outlook as by a common feeling about the world, by common forms of perception of the whole surrounding world.

In such a state of affairs the Jewry of the ghetto could not have a desire for national emancipation; that could only arise later, when the abysses of the *galut,* so menacing to national existence, became apparent. For the ghetto really was, in certain respects (as a certain Western Jewish writer[39] perspicaciously expressed it), a separate state maintaining a "vassal" relationship to the surrounding peoples and states. Between the Jews and the non-Jewish population there existed certain relationships on the grounds of a peculiar coordination in the resolution of a series of economic tasks, but in their nature these relations approximated what we are accustomed to call "international relations."

Living exclusively among its own people and speaking predominantly if not a language of its own then for the most part a language distinct from that of the surrounding population, standing out sharply through its own way of life, having its own rabbis and magistrates who were not merely clerics but also executors of civil and even judicial functions, Jewry, which was deprived by virtue of its juridical and general social position of any points of contact with the culture and manner of living of the peoples surrounding it, and left to imitate almost exclusively its own social milieu, was bound to feel itself behind the gates of the ghetto completely insulated and isolated, and thus also armored by its social organism against external destructive influences. As a "spiritual territory" the ghetto shielded Jewry from the danger of national depersonalization; called forth by the instinct of self-preservation, it lulled to sleep the volitional creative principle in Jewry; it soothed its national hurt, comforted it with a substitute and thus paralyzed those spiritually revolutionary forces within it that were the only ones capable of creating a movement like Zionism.

We should be sinning against truth were we not to indicate at once another important factor that helped preserve Jewish national individuality in the ghetto, that protected the people from assimilation and because of that held up for many long centuries the development of an active movement of national emancipation. We have in mind that Stoic principle which, appearing in world history in countless different forms, has always hampered creative forces and suppressed the questings of individuals and of great social masses. The renunciation of "worldly vanity" was, in the Jewish ghetto, too, one of the most important means of reaffirming the national ego. From its very inception the ghetto was rooted in the principle of individual and social asceticism.

In it was forbidden everything that even in the remotest way might have threatened Jewry with the blurring of its national profile. Personal inclinations and quests, curiosity and mere inquisitiveness, anything that might give pleasure to the eye or gladden the ear, anything capable of enlarging the arena of human activity and creativity and enriching the personality with new elements and carrying it forward to a new path of struggle and achievement—all this was sacrificed in the ghetto to the one law it lived by, the law of national self-preservation and self-conservation. In this connection Shakespeare's Shylock[40] must be taken as extraordinarily typical. When sounds of music ring forth in the Venetian street, bubbling with gaiety, Shylock, who knows that the Christian youth is preparing itself at this time for its revelries, brimming over with the ravishing spirit of the Italian Renaissance, turns to Jessica[41] and says: "Shut all the doors and windows, that the base voice of the Christians may not burst into my dwelling."[42] In the deep and secret recesses of his heart Shylock knew that in the world that extended so spaciously beyond the gates of the ghetto there was much that was rich, picturesque, vital, and alluring. But he also knew that the world was full of poison for Jewry, and for the sake of preserving his own people he sacrificed his own secret longings, his desires and his passions, and was ready to sacrifice the youth of the being most precious to him, his own daughter.

The autonomization of Jewish life is only thinkable on the basis of renunciation and ascetic self-limitation, on the basis of a collective self-enclosement and suppression of one's own personality—such is the internal logic and philosophy of the ghetto. The instinct of self-preservation suggested to the people that a normal life, and even the mere striving for it, were fatal to its existence, and freedom of individual thought and development concealed within itself a threat to the national integrity, which was rooted in the spiritual values and standards obligatory for the whole people. By virtue of that instinct it intentionally, as it were, "unnormalized" its life and confined the Jewish personality in heavy spiritual fetters.

Nor should one forget that for the Jews of the Middle Ages neither the Christians nor the Moslems (to say nothing of pagans) were beings of equal value from the point of view of religion and ethics. With all the power and might of the sovereign non-Jewish world, with all the juridical and social servitude of the Jews, the medieval Jew regarded himself as a being immeasurably higher than the highest and most heroic representative of Christian or Muslim society. Imbued with the consciousness of its chosenness, its exclusive religious and ethical loftiness, its more intimate and filial closeness to God, the enslaved Jewry of the ghetto possessed a sort of special profoundly rooted pride; it regarded itself as the highest aristocracy, the authentic nobility of mankind—true, a nobility that was persecuted and for the time being still not recognized by the nations, but to make up for that, long since recognized by providence, which was leading its own people along thorny paths to heights of glory and greatness. For the masses of medieval Jewry, down to the very eve of the Emancipation epoch, assimilation necessarily seemed to be a self-degradation to a lower rank, a desecration of the family arms. [Heinrich] Heine's symbolic dog, which on the Sabbath reverted to princely state, must be interpreted as meaning that throughout the week it had merely seemed to be a dog, whereas subjectively it was aware of its lofty descent even on ordinary days.[43]

Thus we see that the ghetto was far from being a foreign country in the specific sense of the word as we now use it. We call a country foreign in which we live in the midst of a surrounding foreign majority, in immediate contact with that majority in the process of social life, rotating in its orbit, meanwhile being aware of and sensing its, as well as our, national independence and the social discords flowing from all this. But the ghetto, unfamiliar with such intimate intercourse with the surrounding world, was therefore not a foreign country, but a Jewish island in the midst of a non-Jewish sea, a peculiar Jewish oasis in the wilderness of the *umot haolam* (nations of the world). [Haim Nahman] Bialik[44] with his subtle artistic flair grasped this point more penetratingly than anyone else. In his *Scroll of Fire* the Jewish boys and girls taken out of Judea by the enemy wander about not in a foreign land but in "the unhealthy island immemorially cursed by baldness."[45] It is only after a clear-eyed boy falls down from a height into the arms of the Abaddon River chasm[46] that the waters carry him to "a distant land, unknown, a land whose name is stranger."[47] Only then are the tragic outlines disclosed to him of a really foreign country, in which he is condemned either to horrifying solitude or to the overcoming of his own solitude by penetrating into the depths of the alien soil.

On that island oasis represented by the ghetto, Jewry felt itself to be spiritually sovereign, and if it did not go on forging its own future destiny there and creating new values, nevertheless it was able stalwartly to husband the heritage brought there and carefully to preserve every little mark stamped by history into the soul of the people.

The Jewry of the ghetto, by virtue of the conditions described above, was not subject in any more or less discernible degree to the action of those sociological laws that the life of a minority nation is subject to. There was therefore no room in its life for the rise of effective Zionism in any form.

V

The asceticism of the ghetto naturally had to be softened by something. The ineradicable human striving for as free, active, and many-sided a life as possible had to find an outlet in Jewry, too. Jewry, which in the course of many centuries had lived only on the proceeds of its past creative life, had to take cognizance of the fate of those potentialities of life that it had systematically smothered in itself, but which, having withdrawn into the underground of spiritual life, were nevertheless waiting in a half-slumber for a chance to discharge themselves. And Jewry, of course, took cognizance of this: it deliberately removed the discharge of its own potentialities to the far-off future. It found compensation for its self-restriction, its self-enclosure, its individual and social asceticism, in its faith in a messianic era that was going to reconcile all the contradictions of life, solve all the tormenting questions, give freedom to all enslaved forces, remove prohibitions, and snap the fetters off the whole people as well as off the individual Jew.

Without this profound faith in the coming messiah, the millennial ascetic life which Jewry had voluntarily condemned itself to would have been unthinkable. Jewry associated with the image of the messiah a "legalization" of those feelings, experiences, actions, and behavior over which the yoke of prohibition hung so heavy. The element of revolt and rebellion against themselves in the name of the emancipation of their own human and national ego was, as it were, softened and submissively thawed out under the caressing rays of this secret faith in the promised deliverance.

But as always happens with feelings that are driven underground, here too these were bound to flare up from time to time with a bright flame of protest against their subjugation. Critical occasions were bound to occur in the life of the ghetto when the mute dissatisfaction with its own fate that had been accumulated day by day could not help but find an active and effective outlet. From time to time, the hidden daydreams and longings were bound to burst out to the surface of life in savage, demented torrents. And as a matter of fact the volcano of the ghetto, which had been congealed in slumberous daydreams, had its eruptions—such were the numerous messianic movements that so often shattered the moderate course of life in the quiescent ghetto.[48] Irreconcilable elements of Jewry counterposed to the principle of compromise underlying the ghetto their own revolutionary words and actions. In proclaiming the principle of deliverance from the *galut* these elements headed by their messianic leaders anticipated the consequences that were bound to be brought about by the realization of Israel's dreams.

Once we found ourselves on the road to Zion, the boundaries we had set ourselves in the name of our self-preservation lost all sense and value. Such was the inner logic of nearly all those pseudo-messianic movements that for the most part failed to acknowledge all the ballast of prohibitions with which Jewry of the ghetto had burdened itself and in which the pseudo-messiahs saw the embodiment of *galut* asceticism. Since the rebirth of Jewry in Palestine that was bound up with the coming of the messiah was associated in the popular imagination with emancipation from all spiritual fetters, the hopes that flared up for an imminent return to the mother country could not but be accompanied by that "bursting of the dams" that characterizes almost all messianic movements. Nor is there any occasion for astonishment here that the majority of these movements led to a falling away of a more or less important part of those elements of Jewry they had seized on. Since the messianic movements recruited their followers among the most irreconcilable elements of the people, distinguished by a heightened eagerness for spiritual emancipation and the normalization of life, it was extremely difficult for the Jews who had already tasted of the breath and riches of the "messianic age" to return to the broken trough of the ghetto after the revelation of the bankruptcy of the mystically liberating "great march."[49] This "either-or" philosophy that underlay medieval messianism, with its extreme, excessive switches from the consolidation of Jewry on the principles of a national restoration to a complete exodus from Judaism altogether, concealed an instinctive prognosis of the future destinies of Jewry, which sooner or later would be confronted by the dilemma of a definitive disappearance or a radical renovation.

The outbursts of the messianic movements were the threatening harbingers of the further destruction of the ghetto. With all its solidarity the ghetto was bound slowly to outlive itself and to collapse from its own internal decomposition. Every volitional tension has its own natural limits; sooner or later the ascetic principle by which ghetto Jewry lived was also bound to come up against these limits. During the long ages of its existence the ghetto had been preparing its own contradictions; in fact it had already begun decomposing long before the Christian peoples flung its gates wide open. Even before the Emancipation, which put an end in the West to the juridical ghetto, breaches had begun to appear in its walls. They were made by the individual Jew, who for many centuries had been languishing in the spiritual bondage of the ghetto and was avid for space and freedom for his thoughts and feelings, for his life, his activity, struggles and achievements. The spiritual courage and decisiveness of Baruch Spinoza,[50] the mental travail of Uriel Acosta,[51] the tragic confusion of the misunderstood and to this day unappreciated "gambling rabbi" Leon de Modena[52]—these are the graphic manifestations of that muted and initially subterranean, but later open and distinct fermentation that was going on in the ghetto even before the Emancipation.

The Emancipation, which appeared in the ghetto with its blinding, consuming light, found ready there a cluster of moths drawn toward the deceptive flame. The terrain it found there was ready, for the thirst for deliverance that had not been able to find any quenching in the messianic movements was seeking fresh water not only beyond the age-old walls of the ghetto, but also beyond the limits of Judaism in general. The Emancipation did not create assimilationism; it was simply the godmother of all the assimilatory tendencies engendered in the ghetto itself, which had exhausted its own internal energies. It simply provided a formula and a slogan for what was already simmering in the spirit but still had no name. The individual Jew saw in the Emancipation and in assimilation the possibility of his own liberation, his own long-awaited *tikun* (redemption).

At this time it would be a misplaced surrender to that narrow partisan dogmatism and the polemical and apologetic spirit alive among us were we to repeat the old claim that the assimilationist movement was a manifestation of servile tendencies on the part of the cowardly, conciliationist, shamefully opportunistic elements of Jewry. The more objectively and dispassionately we study the most recent history of the Jewish people, the more appreciation we gain for what the last generations of Jewry have gone through, the clearer it becomes to us that the early intellectual assimilationist movement was, in terms of its internal tendency, an authentic, spiritually emancipating movement.

It was far from the worst elements of Jewry who were seized by assimilationism. In the orbit of the assimilationist movement we find the most vital and the brightest forces at the disposal of Jewry. And if, in our retrospective enquiry into the assimilationist movement, we now see so many negative elements of artificial adaptation and imitation, we must not forget that approximately the same kind of process was also to be observed in the unquestionably non-opportunistic messianic movements. The difference between the elements that took part in the messianic movements and those that were overcome by assimilationist influences consisted in that the former imitated the imagined type of the normalized Jew, whereas the latter imitated the immediately observed type of the normal Christian. A measure of the artificiality we find so distasteful existed in messianism just as it did in assimilationism. It was only the ghetto that remained "natural"; only those conservative elements of Jewry who constituted the opposition to Sabbatai Zevi[53] and Moses Mendelsohn,[54] and called for a reconciliation with the *galut* and the ghetto, were natural. Every radical renovation is bound up with a break, with a renunciation of routine, with destructive acts and with a violent, compulsive, artificial forcing of the existing "I" nearer to the image of the ideal ego.

Such were the messianic movements, and such, too, was the assimilationist movement, which only prejudice and a superstitious historical apprehensiveness prevent many from realizing that it contained elements of a unique kind of messianism.

The assimilationist idea was not realized. Aside from a whole series of external highly complex sociohistorical reasons, the failure of the Jewish assimilationist idea to be realized is explained by the fact that the will to a national way of life proved to be more profound in Jewry than it had seemed to the apostles of national suicide. True, there also appeared a powerful resistance from the isolationist tendencies that were and are still rooted in the life of the majority of the European peoples—tendencies nourished by racist prejudices, the religious factor, and a whole series of transitory but for the time being extremely powerful economic conditions. But there can be no doubt that the above-mentioned resistance gained special force and irresistible impetus from Jewry itself, in which the assimilationist leanings collided with an insurmountable obstacle of an internal, subjective character.

Jewry had such deep organic roots that no assimilationist passion was capable of eating them away without leaving a trace. The history of sincere, intellectual assimilationism may be thought of as the history of a quest for the locus of the national spirit. But this quest led to nothing: it remained just as fruitless as the quest for the soul in philosophy. The entire organism of the Jewish people had already been so imbued from time immemorial with national elements rooted in it and cherished for centuries, that no operations, however bold and decisive, could free the people from these elements all at once. Jewish assimilationism was inclined to regard itself as a catastrophe, as a revolution—which is just what constituted its primordial strength and its messianic significance—but reality unfolded before it a long road of complex and burdensome evolution, with numerous stages, transitory phases, and gradual growth. In order to attain the "vineyards and fig trees" [Deut. 8:8] of the assimilationist Canaan, "forty years of wandering in the wilderness" [Josh. 5:6] of evolution were also needed, and it was just these forty years that also killed the soul, the *elan*, and the passion of assimilationism.

The idea of a catastrophic Jewish assimilation was not realized. It produced in Jewry a whole series of ravages and shifts without providing the "way out"[55] it had been straining for in the person of its most demanding and irreconcilable elements. But regardless of the destructive role it played in Jewish life and history, it should be looked upon nevertheless as a purifying storm which swept over the gloomy fields of *galut* Jewry. While destroying and ravaging, it at the same time created and fertilized, and however paradoxical it may sound, one must agree that it was the very movement of assimilation in Jewry that prepared the ground for the idea of Zionism.

The ghetto was incapable of producing an effective Zionism; assimilationism produced it. It was not merely that assimilation, which familiarized Jewry with new domains of culture and with contemporary European civilization, placed in its hands weapons of struggle and creativity it could not have had before; it was not merely that it reinforced the active principle in Jewry and heightened its capacity for a vital conduct of life. What was far more important was another service assimilation rendered the new, national Jewry: it led Jewry precisely to what we referred to above as "the unmasking of the *galut*."

Assimilationism deprived Jewry of its island; it deprived the Jews of the oasis they had planted for themselves in the wilderness of the diaspora. Thanks to the emancipationist tendencies in the life of the Christian peoples, the Jews were reinstated in their own natural rights; thanks to assimilationism the Jews began to accept the surrounding non-Jewish world as an element of equal value. The emancipated Jews, for their part, "bestowed," if one may express it in this way, "equality of rights" on the Christian world. The arena of mutual intercourse grew substantially broader. Jews began to participate in general social activities and to enter into ever more intimate contact with the non-Jewish world and to be subject to the effects of the sociological laws shared with that world.

Assimilation annihilated that social and personal asceticism that the isolated and armored world of the ghetto had clung to, and—what was even more important—it cut Jewry off from any road back into the world of the ascetic ghetto. It gave form and expression to those demands that had been leading an underground life in the ghetto; it increased the number of those demands and heightened their acuteness. It opened up to Jewry all the variety, the vitality, and the brightness of the inner life of other peoples, showed it all the squalor of its own life, held up before it a mirror in which it could see the full distortion of its national countenance. The new universally human requirements that assimilation nourished in Jewry later became, in the East just as in the West, an organic part of its national requirements. And since the immensely magnified and heightened national requirements, unknown to ghetto Jewry whose demands were so meager, could not find satisfaction in the conditions of the *galut* existence, Jewry was compelled to seek paths for their satisfaction beyond the boundaries of the ghetto—in the creation of its own territorial center, in *Zionism*.

Jewry could feel itself to be a minority nation only when its national consciousness was aroused after the destruction of the assimilationist movement. It was only then that it began to come up against the national majority in the process of a life led in common, and to convince itself of the impossibility of discharging the potentialities slumbering in it under the pressure of an alien, powerful national ego. It was only after the Emancipation and the assimilationist movement accompanying it that it became possible to apprehend the *galut* as a category that was negative in its very essence. The ghetto perceived the *galut* as a certain sum of negative phenomena, flowing from the malevolence of the dominant peoples, from their conscious, intentional oppressiveness. But for the new, post-Emancipation, and post-assimilationist Jewry[56] the *galut* appeared in all its organically negative essence, with all its enduring and ineffaceable aspects that were beyond good or ill will. For this Jewry realized how altogether impossible it was to delimit the sphere of influence of two self-affirming national egos within the limits of the identical socio-territorial organism. Thus the *galut* proved that it was completely self-sufficient. And it was only this image of a self-sufficient *galut* and the spectacle of the gulfs unfolding within it that were capable of evoking in Jewry an effective striving for a radical national renovation—Zionism.

Assimilation radicalized the tendencies of Jewish nationalism. It educated individual Jews and through them a significant part of the people as well, to readiness for Zionism.

Thus Zionism is a manifestation of the volitional pressure of the national potentialities of the Jewish people that were stirred up by the promise of assimilation. It is a product of the sharpened sense of the insurmountability of the distance that in the conditions of *galut* life separates Jewry's will to life and creativity from the possibility of its realization. Zionism is the struggle for Jewish individuality—a struggle not for the conservation and fruitless preservation of one or another fixed trait of that individuality, but for the creation of a free background for its uninterruptedly renewed becoming, for its free and (to take a term from [Henri] Bergson)[57] "cinematographic" evolution. The searchlight of history has illuminated for the new Jewry the tortuous paths leading the Jewish individuality past a gradual depersonalization into a national Nirvana—and Zionism was born, which combined the self-affirmation of Jewish contemporaneity with a struggle for the birth and the way of life of the countless ranks of generations to come. Zionism is struggle with historical fate: a bright, joyous shining of a new and distant sun struggles against its background with the melancholy reflections of a sunset. It has transformed Ahasuerus[58] into Prometheus.[59]

2

Policy and Labor

(1923)

In November 1917, following strenuous efforts by Chaim Weizmann who was then president of the British Zionist Federation, Great Britain issued the Balfour Declaration recognizing the "establishment in Palestine of a national home for the Jewish people." The declaration raised Jewish hopes of attaining political sovereignty in Palestine and energized the Zionist movement worldwide. Shortly after World War I, however, Arab riots broke out in Palestine in 1920 and 1921. The British government attempted to pacify the situation by issuing the Churchill White Paper of 1922, which restricted Jewish settlement to one part of mandatory Palestine, set new limits on Jewish immigration in accordance with the country's "economic absorptive capacity," and precluded the possibility of Jewish self-governance. Dismayed by the modification of British policy and gravely concerned about eastern European Jewry's precarious postwar position, many Zionists called for the White Paper's annulment and the renewal of a maximal program of Jewish colonization and settlement. Reflecting on what he considered to be the "messianic political mood" of the times, Hayim Greenberg counseled moderation and argued that only "non-messianic" and practical labors would bring about Zionism's realization in Palestine.

Sometimes it seems that if the fate of Zionism depended on one sweeping action, one decisive step, the mutual exertion of the people's power and the concentration of its will for the sake of one historical act, full of uplifting courage, then our national dilemma would have been solved in full a long time ago. If we were given the chance to execute our dream of national redemption one day, we would have found the courage of spirit and the dedication of soul within us necessary for it. The redemptive longings that stir in the depths of the people's heart and hid in the innermost recesses of those who wandered far from us and who consciously pretend not to know us, the messianic dream that took deep root in our soul and occasionally burst to the fore in revolutionary tendencies of *tikun olam* [repairing the world], the thankful prayer we say to God for the miracles he performed for us,[1] and which trembles not only on our lips but in our blood and all the organs of our national body, all of these might release in us forces that have long been tied down by historical chains.

But the special reality in which we find ourselves dictates different ways of redemption than the ones our soul longs for so deeply. We cannot attain our dreams all at once, in one decisive hour. This may be the biggest paradox of our national life: our dream of redemption, preserved in us only by the strength of the messianic spirit that imbued it, and that even now may be kept alive only by reflections of the messianic splendor, can be solved and realized only by non-messianic means. We cannot enjoy completely even one hour of satisfaction, and time is on our side only relatively and meagerly.

We committed a grave sin against ourselves, and still do so, by not acknowledging this dramatic paradox in our new national life, and by not arriving at the necessary conclusions. Sometimes, the sublime tendencies of one's soul, which in themselves may bring honor to their harbingers and to humanity at large, and which under certain conditions we should acknowledge and accept, must be suppressed in less opportune times. Our tendency toward messianic catastrophe may be praiseworthy, but within the historical reality on which our existence and future depend, the blessings of messianism became a debilitating disease. Our misfortune and our fault is that we did not recognize this paradox and did not harden our hearts in order to free ourselves completely from those false signs, that spring from the messianism that forms the basis of our redemptive hopes. This element is alive within us, it controls our thoughts and the wishes of our heart, our work, the way we fight, and the language we use when we speak to our people. Rather than eradicate this controlling element from our midst, we contributed to its development in us and in the people, by design and unbeknownst to us. Our sin becomes doubly great, if we remember and admit to ourselves, that for a momentary victory we sometimes used this messianic element to conjure up instant redemption, which is so easy to call up from the depths of peoples' hearts. And so now, when we are called upon to begin a series of real and non-messianic actions, whose weight and magnitude will advance us toward our goal after years of work and an uncommon and incessant ability to overcome many expected and unexpected obstacles, now comes reality and avenges our sin which we committed during the twenty-five years of political Zionism. This sin of ours, which we nourished, even though we should have relegated it to storage for future generations in the fires of the nation's soul, is perhaps the very reason for the mental crisis that grips the movement now, and for the bitter taste of unfulfilled hopes, which descended of late upon us and is spreading before our eyes to the rest of the people, who must support and aid us, and who are a vital and nourishing source for our national construction work.

The unnecessary and exaggerated emphasis on the political element of Zionism, which occupied most of us and which was no doubt useful to a certain degree (after all, it was very opportune at times and formed the basis for national political victories), also caused the movement many losses, and its accursed outcome casts a shadow on our entire situation now. By overemphasizing the political element, and by the great and many hopes we had for it and which we made known to the people as well, we helped the messianic element and the belief in miracles to take over the people and capture even those fires of thought and sentiment, that we ought to have filled with other things.

It is not our intention to downgrade in any way the value of political work, that which was already done, that which is being done, or which will be done in the future. After the Balfour Declaration, the [British] Mandate, and all other political victories, that elevated the entire nation and made it into a national political entity in the international arena,[2] is there a need to elaborate on the practical and moral value of this work, to prove what is already known? The negative political element of Zionism that always existed and still does is not the political work itself, but the exaggerated value we gave it; that special emphasis which distracted the attention of the masses from the main and most important purpose of Zionism. The Zionist propaganda, that served as an unsuccessful surrogate for Zionist education, blurred our sense of responsibility and took off some of the burden of us and of the people as well, because it distracted the people's attention from the real meaning and fundamental ways Zionism could be realized along with its politics; it distracted attention from what is central and crucial to what is secondary and auxiliary. "The time has come, if you desire, to attain your goal!" This kind of messianic political mood may not have been expressed directly, but could be gleaned from the special tone of our discourse by the more eager and impressionable among the people. We did not explain or emphasize enough, that the Land of Israel cannot be had in one fortuitous historical moment, but must be built layer by layer. We did not know or sense how much our preference for buying over building [the land] was detrimental to the people's willingness to act. We were too eager to convince the people immediately, we took our difficult task to lightly, and instead of being pedagogues we fell into the trap of demagoguery.

When we spoke to the people, we used weak and relative historical analogues. We sounded the approaching "pangs of the messiah" [B. Sanhedrin 98b] to the masses, and by doing all these things we aided and abetted the popular thirst for miracles, which metamorphosed from the belief in [Theodor] Herzl's[3] charter[4] to the romantic belief in the goodwill of history to bestow on us new "favors of Cyrus,"[5] as it did to our fathers in the past. We did all of these things and unfortunately succeeded in aiming at one of the greatest deficiencies that life in exile has inflicted on our people—the weakening of its will and talent for orderly and determined construction, the fruits of which can only be reaped after many years of concentrated toil.

This deficiency of an unproductive people, who has no existence save for that in the world to come, and whose life is but a series of "lucky" moments, is the most entrenched and dangerous internal enemy that stands between us and our national revival. From the very beginning of the Zionist movement we should have fought against our incapacity for productive work, that seeps through all our limbs like poison, and which sometimes appears like false signs of prophecy. But we failed to fight against these debilitating tendencies, and even helped them take control of the redemptive aspirations, which can only be realized through a deliberate and moral redirection. This is how the Zionist worldview became "platonic," full of "*agadic*" pleasure (if it is possible to use [Haim Nahman] Bialik's[6] term here),[7] and full of passive daydreaming.

And now? Let us not try and light the people's soul into "great fires," that have no place in our time and in our world, and which always "die" and are extinguished shortly after they ignite. Instead of great fires let there be an "eternal candle," the same one that spreads its light and fire sparingly, and without which no continuous construction work is possible. We may have had use for such great fires if it were possible to attain our goal all at once. But now that our goal can only be attained by the sweat of our brow, we must develop and cultivate within us another power—the power of diligence and the stubborn silence of those who are busy at work.

3
East and West
(1925)

Against the backdrop of mass waves of eastern European immigration to the United States, which abruptly halted in 1924, and the Fourth Aliyah, the cohort of largely urban middle-class Polish Jewish families that immigrated to Palestine between 1924 and 1932, Hayim Greenberg contributed to the vigorous discussion in the Jewish public arena concerning the nature of modern Jewish identity and culture. In this period, roughly two-thirds of the global Jewish population lived in Europe (over ten million total) and nearly one-quarter (slightly under four million) lived in North and South America. Asia, Africa, and Australasia combined accounted for less than 8 percent of the global Jewish population. In the following essay, Greenberg surveys the historical and cultural relationship of the Jews to the Eastern and Western worlds. Though profoundly enchanted by the interconnection of the Jews with the East (he uses the term "Orient," the accepted nomenclature of the time), he argues Jewish life became, over time, "a basic link in the spiritual organism of Europe": "If it is inevitable that we must be 'attached' to either Europe or Asia . . . we are [today] much more Westerners than Easterners." Greenberg's Eurocentric view of Jewish history is characteristic of the Zionist movement in this period.

Are we Jews an Oriental or a Western people? Are we *still* an Oriental people, as we once were, or have we become a Western people? To whom are we most nearly related? To the nations of the West or to those of Asia?

This is not an anthropological problem. Nor is it a question of what we are racially. Ethnic descent and national consciousness sometimes go hand in hand, and at other times their ways part and the two have little effect on each other. One can very easily imagine a people of Semitic descent whose spiritual orientation is European. Finns, Latvians, Estonians, and Magyars[1] are non-European peoples anthropologically. Racially they belong to the Asian Mongol branch of the human race. But which Finn or Magyar remembers this or bears it in mind? They are spiritually closer to French, English, Germans, and Russians than to

Turks or Tartars,[2] Kalmyks[3] or Kirghizians.[4] Their cultures are European and their entire spiritual outlook is European.

What are we, then, if we disregard our genealogy and consider only our real "essence" that lives and expresses itself within us? Are we Asians or Europeans, if we disregard our past and think in terms of our present and of the future as we would want it to be? Are we perhaps neither, or both half-Europeans and half-Asians, an amalgam, a people with a psyche made up of differing scraps, or perhaps an enviable and highly refined synthesis of both Asia and Europe?

The old debate between "Easterners" and "Westerners" that has raged among the Russian *intelligentsia* is recently showing signs of a compromise solution: that Russia is neither of Asia nor of Europe, but a unique organism which should be defined by a new and synthetic appellation—Eurasian. Are we, Jews, like the Russians, also Eurasians?

Were this a purely academic question concerned with national psychologies and historical metaphysics, we could safely leave the entire matter to specialists in this field—if there is such a thing as a "specialist" in this area. Let them argue it as long as they like until they come up with some definite information, and we, ordinary people, will accept the definition that had been ready made for us. Isn't this what we do in nearly all instances of more or less complicated scientific questions? But when this question is being brought down from the realms of abstraction to a practical level, and some even lend edge to it by imposing political significance on it, then it is time that even ordinary Jews take an interest in it and decide what they think on this subject, or what they should think about it.

In recent years, the more radical elements of the Jewish *intelligentsia* in Palestine have been debating this question of East and West. There this question is naturally more immediate than it is in our own midst, because it concerns some very real and political problems, because there it is closely linked not only with the general question of Jewish relations with the East as a whole, but much more immediately with the relations with the physical representatives of the world of the East, with our nearest neighbors, the Arabs.

In Palestine there exists an important group, important because it numbers in its ranks some outstanding personalities—which claims to have discovered in itself a veritable well of genuine "Eastern" attitudes and tries to transform these into an Oriental *Weltanschauung*;[5] it also advocates an eastern-Oriental orientation for Jewish national politics. We must, they say, come to *Erez Israel* as "Easterners," as people who genuinely wish to help the Asian nations to liberate themselves from the yoke of Europe, to develop their unique culture, to counteract the cultural influences of the West. This is not an altogether new sentiment. Years ago Yizhak Epstein[6] "discovered" that the *fellaheen* [Arab peasants] in Palestine were our blood brothers and that we must come to the country to uplift them from their low estate. Menahem Ussishkin[7] at one time earnestly suggested that it was our mission to revive the entire Orient, and that it was the function of Zionism to redeem Asia, and especially the Muslim-Semitic world. For many years a pious adventurist (the late [Yehiel] Mikhael Halpern)[8] imbued with medieval-messianic notions appeared in various circles in *Erez Israel* and advocated an exotic plan of a new mission for the Jewish people to organize the peoples of the East against Europe. Martin Buber,[9] too, indulged in some metaphysical speculations regarding the Jews as the "one hundred percent" Orientals, and thus subject to a burden of commandments and special duties partaking of the character of an Oriental mission. In more recent years, it is quite easy to indulge in such thinking. Here and there throughout the extensive East events are taking place which demonstrate that the East is awakening and that the somnolent Asian peoples are developing a lively will to power and independence. Events in Egypt, in French and Spanish Morocco, in Syria and in other Arab countries, the resurgence of Turkey, despite its defeat in the Great War,[10] the liberation movement in India,[11] the unrest in China,[12] the Bolshevist "liberation policy" throughout Asia and Africa,[13] Oswald Spengler's[14] sensational "prophecy" regarding the imminent demise of the West despite its culture, civilization and economic power—all of these facilitate psychological skepticism about Europe and mystical attraction to the Orient.

However, as long as we deal only with ideas, with fantasies, with moods, with platonic sympathies, prophecies and predictions, these are neither better nor worse than scores of other similar theoretical exercises. But when we are faced with practical political conclusions to be drawn from such mental exercises, we must be much more cautious, strict, and consistent with ourselves.

First of all, we must ask ourselves not whether we *are* (in the abstract sense of "being," which has little relationship to our existence as concrete living human beings) but whether we actually *feel* as an Oriental people. If we do not feel so, then we are not it; and if we are not an Oriental people, then our orientation cannot be on the East—*unless*—unless we set up an entirely new policy according to which we must betimes analyze the future course of development of the various peoples and races in the world political "stock market," and line up on the side of tomorrow's victors. But we could have an honest and sincere orientation on the East only if in our deepest feeling, in our innermost character, wishes and tastes, we felt more "at home" in the spiritual atmosphere of Asia, and more alien and excluded in the atmosphere of Europe—and this feeling must totally disregard the classification assigned to us by anthropologists and historians.

What is the case? Do we feel more "at home" among Eastern peoples? Is an Iranian more understandable to us than a Russian? Is a Druze[15] closer to us than a Pole? Is a Bedouin more "transparent" to us than a German? Is a Chinese or a Hindu spiritually closer to us than an Englishman? Is Mohammed more accessible to us than St. Francis of Assisi?[16] And even [Rabindranath] Tagore,[17] is he more understandable to us than [Maurice] Maeterlinck?[18] Do we "fear" the Oriental less than we fear the average European or American?

It should be self-evident that when I say "we" I do not have in mind the entire one hundred percent of the Jewish people, but only its majority. It is quite possible that among our brothers in the Arab countries, in North Africa, and also among some of the *Sephardim* in Europe, the West is much more alien, incomprehensible, spiritually repulsive or at least less attractive and international than those parts of the East where they live. But it is *we,* European, *Ashkenazi* Jews who are the majority of the Jewish people, with all our merits and shortcomings, with all our originality as well as our spiritual enslavement. And it is evident that the choice of orientation between East and West, depends largely, if not exclusively, on us. And should a catastrophe occur that would suddenly remove us from the scene, it is quite possible that there would not remain in the world a political-cultural "entity" capable of adopting any kind of orientation at all.

And so, do we *Ashkenazi* Jews truly feel we are more an Eastern than a Western people? Would the perspective of the hegemony of the Eastern peoples be more acceptable to us than the hegemony of the Western peoples (were we to be confronted with the alternative of only one or the other having the upper hand)?

Should we answer this question in the affirmative, it would be necessary, first of all, to renounce our understanding of our own history at least during the past century. We would then have to say to ourselves that our history during the past century was a mere episode, an accident that had little to do with our inner being. During the past century we gave to German literature [Ludwig] Boerne,[19] [Heinrich] Heine,[20] [Berthold] Auerbach,[21] [Arthur] Schnitzler,[22] [August von] Wasserman,[23] [Otto] Weininger[24]—but this was merely some kind of misunderstanding. We enriched European philosophy, through the medium of the French, with [Henri] Bergson[25]—but this was a mere accident. We contributed to Europe the wide-ranging critic and literary historian Georg Brandes[26]—but this has nothing to do with our essence. Beaconsfield [Benjamin Disraeli][27] in England, [Léon] Gambetta[28] in France, [Walter] Rathenau[29] in Germany, [Leon] Trotsky[30] in Russia—it was a mere accident that we "sent" a few Jews to meddle in European politics. Two Jews have created the theory and practice of the European socialist movement—we bear no responsibility for this.[31] Jewish temperament gave impetus to all the European revolutions and Jewish blood was shed in them—this does not concern us. [Mark] Antokolsky,[32] [Isaac] Levitan,[33] Joseph Israels,[34] Max Liebermann[35]—they are only incidentally European artists. [Felix] Mendelsohn[36] and [Arthur] Rubenstein,[37] only incidentally are they European composers. That a substantial part of the European press was developed by Jews, that many Jews hold positions of authority in European political parties, that it would be impossible to introduce a *numerus clausus* [Latin for "closed number"][38] on the European and American stage (even if someone should want to do so)—

this too is a mere accident. And the fact that we Europeanized our modern Hebrew and Yiddish literatures—this too is only an episode. This is how we would have to regard our history during the past century.

But such a remarkably large number of "accidents," "misunderstandings," and "episodes" that occur in such a short time cannot be either accidents or misunderstandings or episodes. Here we are confronted with a system, with a remarkable creative tendency that is perhaps the best proof that fundamentally the spiritual milieu of Europe was not simply a climate into which we had wandered and from which we have to escape. Without love, without dedication, without spiritual affinity, without a conscious awareness (or unconsciously, if one prefers it that way) that we were a not insignificant part of Europe, it would have been impossible to achieve the things we have achieved, it would have been unthinkable that we contribute daily not only to the economic life but to the very *sanctum sanctorum* [Latin for "Holy of Holies"] of the spiritual life of the European nations. We were, after all, not merely craftsmen in European culture, but creators; not only assistants, but teachers and instructors; not only helpers, but at times prophets and seers of new spiritual values in Europe. Should we try to remove from European culture that part which we have contributed to it—who would permit it? Our share has become a basic link in the spiritual organism of Europe which has also enriched us; and for this we pay back with interest—some among ourselves, as well as outside us, even maintain at times that we pay too high an interest.

But what was our family relationship with the East during the past few generations, or even centuries? What did the East offer us, and what did we take from it? For that matter, what did we give the East and what has it accepted from us? And where are the real, living, not artificially concocted symptoms of our tendency to become Orientalized—aside from our geographical orientation on the East because *Erez Israel* is located in the Near East? And to the extent that in recent years we feel a greater interest in the spiritual essence of the East (perhaps because the entire West has begun to take a deeper interest in the East), our cultural appetite and philosophical curiosity are much more strongly aroused by remote India,[39] with which we Jews hardly ever had any contact in the past, than by the Arab Muslim-Semitic world which is so much closer to us geographically, historically, and anthropologically.

If it is inevitable that we must be "attached" either to Europe or to Asia, to the East or to the West, then, though we are not full-blooded Europeans, we are at least ten times more European than Asian; we are much more Westerners than we are Easterners. It would be altogether too theatrical, we would be guilty of too much false makeup were we suddenly to pretend to be Turks and put on Oriental masks.

Uncounted threads bind us to Europe's spirit, its past and its present. No matter how much we are driven from Europe, we are driven as "one's own" and not as strangers; and no matter how much we may run to the East, the West runs with us and within us. It is almost impossible to imagine that our marriage to Europe took place only during the last couple of generations. The results of this match are too numerous and too important to have taken place in such a short time. Frequently it seems that the time of our official emancipation in western Europe is merely an official date which marks the moment when the marriage between us and Europe was legalized, but that before this, before even the "engagement" was announced, we had for centuries carried on an illicit love affair with the West. There are times when one thinks that the greatest cultural service which the Arab world performed for us was precisely this—that it introduced us in the Middle Ages to the West and thus caused us to fall in love with it. This may sound paradoxical, but it is a fact nevertheless. When we encountered the Arab conquerors of Spain, we both believed that here a marriage was being contracted between two sister cultures, the Jewish and the Arab. But only later it became apparent that the Arab culture in Spain was merely a matchmaker between us and Europe. The matchmaker did her job and returned home. But we remained in and with Europe. And when now we are beginning to return to the geographic East, the West follows us there.

And should it prove true that the West is tired and exhausted, that it is entering, historically speaking, into its last agonies of dying, then this will strongly influence also us and our spiritual destiny. For, consciously or unconsciously, our destiny has long been closely bound up with the fate of Europe's spirit—with its peaks as well as with its abysses.

4

Sabbatai Zevi: The Messiah as Apostate

(1926)

Hayim Greenberg's view of Jewish culture was anchored by a rich and profound appreciation of traditional religious impulses in Jewish history, including the phenomena of Jewish mysticism and messianism. In the following essay, Greenberg explores the case of Sabbatai Zevi (1626–76), a Sephardic rabbi and kabbalist born in Izmir (Smyrna), Turkey, who in 1648 proclaimed he heard a "heavenly voice" and declared himself to be the messiah. In a synthesis that mixes psychological insights with an analysis of Jewish thought and medieval Jewish history, Greenberg asserts that the false messiah's trajectory, which ended in forced conversion to Islam, reflected medieval Jewry's "revulsion against continued passive waiting for redemption" and "the stubborn refusal to be reconciled to the hobbled reality of Jewish life." In the final analysis, he argues, Zevi's apostasy was "the tragic act of revenge of a fallen hero."

I

Why did Sabbatai Zevi[1] become an apostate? How did it come about that the man who considered himself the redeemer of his people, the messiah, the messenger of God announcing the salvation of the world, bowed his head before the [Ottoman] sultan's court *mufti*,[2] donned a Turkish turban, and adopted the Muslim name Mohammed?

For many years his followers and disciples sought an answer to this riddle. The opponents of the "false messiah" assiduously exploited Sabbatai Zevi's conversion to the Muslim faith to prove to the aroused and messianically exalted public that their hero, upon whom they had pinned such high hopes, was a mere charlatan, a "destroyer of Israel," and an apostate. But Sabbatai Zevi also had many followers who found it difficult, or altogether impossible, to renounce their messianic dream, and who therefore spared no effort to defend Sabbatai Zevi's good name to themselves and before the Jewish people as a whole. The ordinary, unsophisticated public which had for so long adored Sabbatai Zevi and literally counted the minutes until he would display his divine power almost at once created a legend to account for what happened and to refute all doubts. According to this legend, Sabbatai Zevi did not become an apostate at all. One of the greatest miracles occurred in the sultan's palace—a kind of emanation, a ghostly reflection separated itself from Sabbatai Zevi, and it was this image that adopted the [Muslim] faith. Sabbatai Zevi himself vanished from the palace unnoticed and an angel bore him on his wings to heaven. There was also no lack of rationalists among the people who did not deny the fact of Sabbatai Zevi's apostasy, but interpreted it in their own fashion. Since Sabbatai Zevi would soon become the king of a free *Erez Israel*, they said, he intentionally, though only superficially, adopted the Muslim faith in order to become a welcome visitor in the sultan's palace and thus have an opportunity to observe at leisure the ways of royalty and to study the art of war.[3]

But among Sabbatai Zevi's disciples there were also some who knew and believed that it was the real Sabbatai Zevi who had adopted [Islam], and who could not stomach the rationalist and all too prosaic and earthy explanation that he betrayed his God in a make-believe gesture only in order to worm his way into the sultan's palace. It is precisely the ones who were closest to him who had to reject such a realistic political interpretation, because for them Sabbatai Zevi was not a politician, nor a national hero in the secular-political sense of the term, but, above all, he was the great prophet, the messiah anointed by God who came into the world to uproot evil and to liberate all mankind from its contradictions. Sabbatai Zevi's closest disciples and associates were deeply imbued with the visions and moods of the "applied kabbalah"[4] of [the] Ari[5] and Hayim Vital,[6] and they had perforce to seek mystical interpretations for Sabbatai Zevi's act which appears to have come as an unexpected surprise also for them. This led to a series of sophist, paradoxical interpretations which, in their unique form, reflected the moods of that mysticism-ridden time—the tragic conflicts of those passionately messiah-anticipating times.

Sabbatai Zevi's closest "armor bearer," Nathan of Gaza,[7] did not lose heart even when he realized that his "King of Judah" was now called Mohammed. So far as he was concerned, Sabbatai Zevi remained the same "Our Lord the Messiah" that he had been before. He sent letters to all the communities which had accepted Sabbatai Zevi in which he explained that Sabbatai Zevi's act was the fulfillment of the ancient prophecy that the messiah would appear in the world as "a poor man riding on an ass" [Zech. 9:9]. The [Hebrew] term *ani*, a poor man, Nathan explained, should be understood allegorically and not literally: the messiah must for a time be in a state of spiritual poverty and deprivation. He cannot fulfill his mission until he will have been tormented by impurity for a time. He cannot display his true messianic power until he will, for a time, deprive himself of the fulfillment of the commandments and deny himself good deeds. This, Nathan believed, explained Sabbatai Zevi's adoption of [Islam]. The messiah must suffer, and through his suffering be purified and strengthened; and now that he was in the bosom of the ruling church, he experienced the greatest possible suffering. Moreover, the greater his grief, the more profound his spiritual "poverty," the nearer we will be to redemption.

Nathan of Gaza also cited the *Zohar*[8] according to which the messiah must have his hours of being "internal" rather than "external," and this prophecy of the *Zohar,* he maintained, was fulfilled now that Sabbatai Zevi's external being was most unattractive as a result of his having become an official "Ishmaelite"[9] wearing a Turkish turban on his head. Sabbatai Zevi, Nathan of Gaza explained, was at the moment experiencing what Queen Esther had experienced once before him. She merited becoming the savior of her people only after undergoing the degradations of Ahasuerus' harem.[10] And somewhat later Nathan of Gaza declared that Sabbatai Zevi entered the Muslim world in order to "redeem" the sparks of holiness that lie hidden within the depths of impurity, since the elements of good and evil, of sanctity and profanity are not sharply dissociated and redemption can come to the world only after they are totally separated one from the other. The messiah must therefore descend to the lowest depths of depravity in order to elevate from its abysses the individual sparks of sanctity which suffer there and plead to be redeemed from their "exile."[11] Looked at in this light, Sabbatai Zevi did not at all capitulate before a ruler of flesh and blood by becoming a Muslim. On the contrary, his apostasy was one of the greatest works which the messiah must perform on earth, and his entry into [Islam] was really a declaration of war against evil, and a glad tiding for the scattered sparks of holiness lost in the deserts of uncleanness and yearning for liberation. The patriarch Abraham took Hagar for a wife [Gen. 16:2–4]. Jacob married the daughters of Laban the Aramite [Gen. 29:1–30].[12] Moses descended to the uncleanness of an idolatrous priest and took his daughter for a wife [Exod. 2:15–22].[13] And now "Our Lord the Messiah" descended into the murky abysses of the Muslim world. But the aim of all of them was to rescue the "sparks."

Among Sabbatai Zevi's followers there were also some who felt no need to resort to the sanction of quotations from sacred books or to rationalizations of a historical nature. For these it was obvious and understandable that it was providence that led Sabbatai Zevi on the road to apostasy in order that the cup of his suffering be filled and that he be made ready for his great mission. During the seventeenth century many *anusim* [forced converts] from Spain, Portugal, and from the Italian districts ruled by the Vatican wandered about. Many of these had already been brought up on the dogmas and images of the Catholic Church, and considerable numbers had already been born Catholics. It was therefore natural that even after they shook off their enforced Catholicism and returned to Judaism they should retain elements of Christian mysticism. These forced converts, who were brought up in the Christian dogma of the mystery of the "suffering God,"[14] felt less doubt than anyone else at the sight of the fall of the messiah. Sabbatai Zevi was being mocked. Jews and non-Jews insulted and humiliated him. They taunted him and jeered: "Messiah, where is your divine power?" But the same was done by Jews and Romans to Jesus before his crucifixion.[15] His mockers placed a crown of thorns on Jesus' head,[16] and Sabbatai Zevi permitted to be placed on his head a Turkish turban which was a still greater humiliation for him and pained him even more than thorns might. In the minds of these former Catholics, the Christian "passion of the Lord"[17] and the Jewish "agonies of the messiah" (*hevlei mashiakh*) [B. Sanhedrin 98b][18] became so inextricably intertwined that to some of them it seemed that had the misfortune of Sabbatai Zevi's apostasy not taken place, this would have been the most convincing proof that he was indeed a false messiah. The kabbalist Abraham Miguel Cardozo,[19] who had himself been a forced convert to Catholicism and had returned to Judaism, suggested in his famous letter on Sabbatai Zevi's apostasy that "final redemption" would not come until all Jews first became victims of apostasy, and from the depth of their degradation—like the lost sparks of sanctity embedded in evil—they cried out to God to send them their redeemer.[20]

Such were the lines along which Sabbatai Zevi's devotees tried to rehabilitate their messiah. It is not inconceivable that among them some were not entirely sincere, and repeated these excuses not because they truly believed them, but in order to sustain the messianic movement with which they did not want to break for one reason or another. What is clear is that in an environment that was intoxicated with kabbalistic concepts and images, in a community which regarded the *Zohar,* and even lesser mystical works, as more holy than the [Hebrew] Bible or the Talmud, the interpretations described above appeared so natural, understandable and obvious, that no effort was required to accept them.

Naturally, Sabbatai Zevi's enemies, and also those of his former disciples who in time succeeded in ridding themselves of the fumes of their former messianic intoxication, reacted altogether differently and began to abuse their deceiver who had first enflamed within them such high hopes and then so cruelly and bitterly disappointed them. To these it was clear proof that by adopting [Islam] Sabbatai Zevi demonstrated that he had been no more than a "scoundrelly swindler" all along.[21] Their most common accusation was that Sabbatai Zevi from the very start had no other aim than to seduce Jews from the path of righteousness and that he intentionally misused the trust of the people for his personal power ambitions, and at the first moment that real danger threatened him from the Turkish power, he saved his own skin by embracing [Islam] without giving the matter a second thought. But even some of these opponents found some justification for Sabbatai Zevi and tried to be impartial in this situation. These pointed to Maimonides[22] and cited his famous "Letter to Yemen"[23] in which Maimonides declared that it was the duty of a Jew to practice *kidush hashem,* to sacrifice his life for the sanctification of God, when compelled to worship idols, but that this commandment did not apply in the case of forced conversion [to Islam], because the pure monotheistic concepts of Islam brought it close to Judaism.

In this connection it is interesting to point out that Rabbi Jacob Emden,[24] who had devoted much energy and passion to eradicating all organizational and psychological traces of the Sabbatai Zevi movement, was nevertheless inclined to find some justification for the false messiah. In his famous work *Torat hakenaot* (The Doctrine of Zealotry) [1752][25] he subtly suggests that Sabbatai Zevi resolved to convert [to Islam] only after the sultan's personal physician, Guidon,[26] himself an apostate, called his attention to the danger that threatened all the Jews in the Turkish empire should he, Sabbatai Zevi, as the chief culprit, refuse to pass to the dominant Muslim faith. But Jacob Emden hinted at this thought so subtly (perhaps because of his extreme caution about everything he said on this subject, considering that he was the chief opponent of all the after-effects of the Sabbatai Zevi movement) that recent Jewish students of that period who depended so heavily on *Torat hakenaot* hardly noticed Emden's hint. [Heinrich] Graetz,[27] too, felt no need to examine carefully the chief motives that dominated the life and career of Sabbatai Zevi. Graetz maintained with almost unquestioned certainty that Sabbatai Zevi accepted the Muslim faith just as soon as Guidon informed him that if he remained stubborn, "burning torches would be tied to his body, he would be dragged through the streets and flogged with rods." Graetz even doubted whether "Sabbatai Zevi experienced an inner struggle before he decided to accept the advice of the apostate doctor."[28] In [Simon] Dubnow,[29] too, we find a similar approach to the subject. "Guidon," Dubnow says, "frightened him so with threats of torture, with the humiliation and degradation of the death penalty, that he [Sabbatai Zevi] lost his head altogether. The instinct of self-preservation suggested to the false messiah that he must decide to adopt the Muslim faith."[30]

Even modern Jewish historians were not sufficiently unhampered in their researches to probe the tragic and conflict-ridden world of Sabbatai Zevi's inner life with original methods or with intuition. Unconsciously, perhaps, they painted the portrait of Sabbatai Zevi using the same harsh colors employed long ago by Sabbatai Zevi's rabbinical opponents. They oversimplified his personality and refused to note the complex and dramatic elements in his character.[31]

II

No psychologically convincing explanation of Sabbatai Zevi's abandonment of Judaism was thus provided either by his disciples or by his opponents. The former introduced too much mystical speculation in their apologies; the latter resorted to oversimplified rationalizations.

We will naturally disregard Sabbatai Zevi's unsophisticated followers from among the common people who resorted to the easiest way out: they simply refused to believe the entire story; they denied the facts; it was not Sabbatai Zevi who embraced Islam, only his apparition, and thus he made fools of the Sultan, his courtiers, and his clerics.

But we must seriously consider the more earnest explanations offered by Sabbatai Zevi's more refined and mystically minded disciples and associates. Their interpretations are characteristic of an environment that was saturated with kabbalistic mysticism which endowed them with a capacity for unique thought and imagination. But from the documents they left us, it is evident that all their interpretations cannot explain the objective nor even the subjective causes of Sabbatai Zevi's apostasy.

It is no accident that all during his life, until the moment when he stepped over the borderline into Islam, Sabbatai Zevi never so much as hinted of such a possible eventuality—assuming another faith in order to "redeem" the "sparks of sanctity" that lead an existence of enslavement within the realm of "uncleanness." It is also suspicious that neither Nathan of Gaza nor [Abraham Miguel] Cardozo, in all their letters defending Sabbatai Zevi, even hinted that he had ever suggested the possibility of such an intentional "descent" as a precondition for a subsequent "rise," despite the fact that such a statement—even a forged one—would have served the purpose of their letters: to save the public from melancholy, disappointment, and despair.

Sabbatai Zevi's action appears to have come as a total surprise also to his closest followers, even to his Judas Iscariot[32] (the Polish kabbalist Rabbi Nehemiah Kohen)[33] with whom Sabbatai Zevi maintained a relationship of the closest confidence till the last moment. Had Sabbatai Zevi confided his intended apostasy to the Polish kabbalist, who first made a pilgrimage to him in Turkey and only later lost faith in him, one of two results would have followed: either Rabbi Nehemiah Kohen would have truly believed that the impending apostasy was planned for kabbalistic reasons and his faith in Sabbatai Zevi's messianic mission would have been strengthened. (Such an explanation would have readily appealed to Nehemiah Kohen, for he, too, temporarily embraced [Islam] for the sake of general Jewish interests.) Or, having decided to expose Sabbatai Zevi as a swindler, he would have widely publicized his plan of "redeeming the sparks of sanctity" and warned the Jews not to trust in the integrity of the false prophet's statements. The fact that some time *after* his apostasy Sabbatai Zevi hinted at his mission of redeeming the sacred from among the unclean proves nothing. The defeated hypnotist might himself have become a "medium" for the hypnosis which he induced in his disciples.

On the other hand, there are no grounds for doubting that had Sabbatai Zevi harbored the idea of embracing [Islam] for mystical reasons—the same kind of reasons that his disciples later advanced in his justification—he would have done so earlier and not under duress; he would not have postponed such a crucial act to a time of such unfavorable circumstances that his apostasy could be interpreted as a result of cowardice and incapacity for *kidush hashem*. All his preparations for his encounter with the sultan, his dividing the earth into twenty-six kingdoms corresponding to the number of his nearest associates, his conversations with his visitors when he was already imprisoned in the Gallipoli fortress—from all the details that are known to us regarding the last days preceding his apostasy, it is evident that he regarded his impending audience with the sultan as the great moment that would reveal to the entire world his divine mission and supernatural might, and that he did not at that time foresee that his visit to the royal palace would merely mark the beginning of a difficult and painful stage on the road of his mission.

It is still more difficult to agree with the oversimplified explanations of his opponents. It is impossible to conceive that a mere "swindler," a dishonest and conscienceless careerist, could successfully become the leader and the psychological focus of such a grandiose and overwhelming movement which seized upon a large part of the Jews in all the countries of the Jewish dispersion of that time—from Gaza and Jerusalem to Amsterdam and Venice. Suffice it to recall the effect which Sabbatai Zevi produced on the Jews of *Erez Israel* when he was anointed in the Gaza synagogue as messiah in a ceremony of exalted veneration,[34] or the enthusiasm of the entire Jewish community in Smyrna when he was there proclaimed as messiah. Special prayers and hymns were composed and sung in his honor in many European and Asian synagogues and houses of prayer. A veritable tide of pilgrims streamed with irresistible impetus from remote countries to the Turkish fortress where he was imprisoned. The diplomatic reports of the English ambassador in Turkey to his government told of Sabbatai Zevi's great influence on Balkan Jewry. And even such a sober and disciplined mind as Baruch Spinoza's[35] was impressed by the Sabbatai Zevi movement. Taking into consideration all these factors, it becomes evident why the rationalizations and all too smug simplifications of Sabbatai Zevi's opponents have such an unconvincing ring.

Sabbatai Zevi possessed one great talent—the talent of sincere and profound faith in the reality of his mission and the actuality of his dreams. When scores of thousands of Jews obeyed him when he ordered them to transform ancient and historically sanctified fast days into occasions of orgiastic celebration; when in the synagogues of hundreds of cities prayers on behalf of "our Lord the Messiah" were intoned; when many Jews decided to abandon all their earthly possessions, to leave their old established homes and go to *Erez Israel*; when hundreds of the most pious rabbis, scholars, kabbalists, and community leaders expressed their enthusiasm for Sabbatai Zevi and his mission, we must naturally explain this, first of all, as a result of the fevered moods and mystical yearnings of that tragic time. But there also can be no doubt that Sabbatai Zevi's personality was largely instrumental in uncovering these secret yearnings for a messiah and transforming them from a potential to a real force. In this regard he could become effective only as a result of his special talent—his sincere and profound faith in himself, in his vision, and in his hallucinations. The mass man of that time needed a hero, a focal personality that would reflect and crystallize his yearnings and challenges, and this hero had to possess, above all, sincerity and faith. Had Sabbatai Zevi lacked these qualifications, the "mob" of that time would have been compelled and able to produce for itself a "genuine messiah" instead of the false one. In times like those, when the mass rises above itself, when it transcends its daily routine rhythms, when its senses react with passionate intensity, it becomes productive and gifted and capable of "producing" an additional couple of prophets and messiahs. It is therefore instructive that in Sabbatai Zevi's day it never even occurred to anyone to compete against him. No one felt able to satisfy better and more intensively the messianic thirst of the time than Sabbatai Zevi. In such times one "swindler" gives rise to a competing one; one pretender evokes another. But the fact that Sabbatai Zevi had no competitors within the area of the messianic movement is perhaps the most convincing proof that he was *subjectively* the true messiah, and that his mission was one inspired "by God."

III

How then are we to explain Sabbatai Zevi's abandonment of Judaism?

We have no choice but to assume that this was an instance of one of those sudden crises that are characteristic of the lives of particularly exalted natures whose passionate feelings and experiences lead them to states of extreme hysteria. Sabbatai Zevi's adoption of the Muslim faith was no doubt completely unexpected by himself as well as by his followers. It is quite possible that even half an hour before his appearance before the sultan, or before his talk with the court physician, Guidon, he would have regarded the *fatal* step which he made with such terrifyingly silent determination as absolutely out of the question.

At that moment there seemed to have occurred in Sabbatai Zevi's life one of those "accidents" which lie dormant in a kind of embryonic state below the level of consciousness and await, in a manner of speaking, a suitable occasion when they break through with catastrophic force. They are "accidents" only in relation to the conscious awareness of the person; but for the subconscious, for the underground existence of the personality, such "excesses" are thoroughly motivated, well prepared and "illegally" nurtured. Spontaneous decisions, such as Sabbatai Zevi's, occur either in moments of highest elation, when the individual is especially confirmed in the strength of his ego, or in moments of deepest depression, when all one's hopes and dreams suddenly disintegrate within one. In either case we are confronted with illogical decisions which feed on deep, internal, "unconscious logic."

Such logic characterized Sabbatai Zevi's fatal decision. His mystically heroic striving to bring about an absolute transformation in Jewish life was from the very start pregnant (if one may use such a simile) with a determination to depart from Judaism. His messianic mission which was fundamentally a mighty affirmation of Judaism, was, on its reverse side, a striving for the total negation of Judaism and its future existence. His messianism was an expression of a despairing will not to be reconciled to the ordinary, prevailing mode of Jewish existence, which admitted of only two alternatives: the supreme summits of courage and strength, or the lowest depths with their demonic fascination of extinction and death. The absolute negation of the *galut* and all its manifestations, the revulsion against continued passive waiting for redemption, the stubborn refusal to be reconciled to the hobbled reality of Jewish life—these were fundamentally the psychological factors which at that time gave rise to messianic yearnings and that, more than anything else, determined the life pattern of Sabbatai Zevi. To *galut* he declared in no uncertain terms: "I reject you." He challenged Jewish destiny to combat, and this declaration of war contained the logical conclusion never to revert to existing conditions. He must either rise above this fate, or descend below it, but under no circumstances would he remain face to face with it. *Galut* must be destroyed either by means of the complete liberation of Jewry or as a result of its total extinction. This was the unconscious but deeply rooted "logic" of Sabbatai Zevi's messianic career.

The Sabbatai Zevi movement was one of the mightiest protests in Jewish history against the traditional Jewish submission, against the accepted sense of duty to tolerate patiently and to wait passively, against the necessity to suppress vital needs and always to adjust to alien conditions of life. When we also consider the great and hitherto unappreciated role which the forced converts played in this movement, it becomes clearly understandable why this explicitly negative attitude toward *galut* inevitably led to excesses such as Sabbatai Zevi's apostasy, which served as a signal for an extensive wave of apostasy among many of his followers.

The *anusim,* the forced converts, introduced into the movement a particularly potent drive. Their yearning for the liberation of the Jewish people was naturally much more intense and profound than among the rest of Jewry, not only because they had suffered more than other Jews, but also on account of other no less compelling psychological reasons. Their life as forced converts who led a secret Jewish existence developed within them a morbid yearning after publicly professed Jewishness on one hand, and on the other hand it sharpened their striving for a more normal and free existence in general. Though their professed Christianity was insincere and had been foisted upon them by force, we must bear in mind that as official Christians they had for some time lived in close relationship with more normal and happier peoples, and it was natural that in the course of these relations there should awaken within them long suppressed human urges. When many of these forced converts to Catholicism flocked to Turkey, where they could resume their Judaism openly, they nevertheless, in a certain sense, continued to regard the Jewish ghetto and its mode of life from the viewpoint of their erstwhile Christian coreligionists. The Jewish *galut* revealed itself to them as something loathsome and deformed. Uriel Acosta,[36] who broke the chains of the Catholic Inquisition and returned to Judaism, also felt impelled to break the bonds of *galut,* of the ghetto, of the confining rabbinical discipline, after he had lived in the Amsterdam ghetto for a time. This revulsion against the ghetto explains the phenomenon which at first glance appears incomprehensible, that many former forced converts to Christianity who returned to Judaism after much suffering and effort later returned to Christianity, and this time of their own free will. And it was precisely among such forced converts that Sabbatai Zevi found his most exalted devotees who, on their part, strengthened in their leader a negative attitude toward *galut* which he already felt strongly. Characteristic in this regard was the prophecy of the above mentioned kabbalist Cardozo that the final redemption would come only after all the Jews adopted another faith.[37] This prophecy reflected extreme anti-*galut* sentiments which filled the hearts of the *anusim* and which communicated themselves to other Jewish circles and strengthened in the "hero" of that time, in Sabbatai Zevi, the determination to put an end to the *galut,* if not by means of total redemption, then at least by means of an act of desperation which would lead to the extinction of Jewry in general.

For years Sabbatai Zevi prepared himself for an "exodus from *galut*." He believed that there existed a supernatural exit from *galut*, and all his mystical preparations tended toward a single aim: finding the keys to this exit. But when it became absolutely clear to him that the supernatural exit was irrevocably sealed and that all his preparatory steps had been in vain, that the keys could not be found, he turned to the subterranean exit, to the redeeming abyss of national self-destruction. At the moment when Sabbatai Zevi donned the Turkish turban on his head, he fiercely "attacked" the *galut* just as he had stormed it before when he underwent the rites of "practical kabbalah"[38] which he believed would place upon his head the crown of the "King of Judah."

Only a total despairing in his own strength, only a profound conviction of the full inner bankruptcy of his spiritual existence, could have made Sabbatai Zevi put on the Turkish turban. And when Rabbi Jacob Emden suggested that Sabbatai Zevi decided to adopt [Islam] in order to save the Jews of Turkey from the danger which loomed over them on his account, this too is an indication that when Sabbatai Zevi stood before the sultan he had already lost his faith in his messianic mission. Had he at that moment still retained his messianic exaltation, had he continued to believe that he was still the bearer of supernatural powers that would enable him to open for Jewry a supernatural exit from *galut*, he would not have felt humbled also when the Turkish authorities threatened him and when Guidon warned him. His exalted imagination would have come to his aid at that moment and suggested some way out of the danger, and he would not have surrendered.

Why and how he lost his faith in himself and in his mission and in the power of practical kabbalah is a psychological riddle to which the meager documents and information of the Sabbatai Zevi movement do not provide a convincing answer. It is quite possible that Rabbi Nehemiah Kohen, who was himself an informed practitioner of practical kabbalah, had feverishly and daily awaited the coming of the messiah, and had undertaken the arduous journey from Poland to Turkey in order to meet Sabbatai Zevi, and later declared that he did not believe in Sabbatai Zevi's mission, served to undermine Sabbatai Zevi's confidence in himself. We do not know the substance of the long conversation which Nehemiah Kohen had with Sabbatai Zevi when the latter was already imprisoned in the fortress some days before his appearance in the sultan's palace. We know but one thing of this conversation which was supposed to have lasted three days and three nights—that Nehemiah Kohen offered Sabbatai Zevi numerous proofs that he was not the messiah and thus caused him unheard of anguish. It is possible that this conversation aroused grave doubts in Sabbatai Zevi and finally altogether destroyed his faith in his mission. Sabbatai Zevi had awaited Nehemiah Kohen's arrival from Poland with great impatience. He had pinned great hopes on this kabbalist, and to his close disciples he said that Nehemiah Kohen had been sent by providence itself to precede him and to clear the way for his great triumph. And then this Nehemiah Kohen turned out to be the one to declare courageously—in an environment which was literally aflame with faith and enthusiasm for Sabbatai Zevi—that he did not believe at all in Sabbatai Zevi's mission.

There are thus grounds for assuming that Nehemiah Kohen played an important role in the bankruptcy of Sabbatai Zevi's faith in his mission. But whether for this or for other reasons, it is clear that Sabbatai Zevi experienced a critical moment before his abandonment of his Judaism—a moment when he suddenly awoke from the intoxication of the dreams and visions which had held him in their power for many years. He experienced a moment of sobering and he suddenly beheld the gray expanse of the tedious reality of the world, with its merciless physical and material laws which formerly he was neither able nor willing to see. Instead of his own private reality, he suddenly became aware of the actual reality. He looked into the face of this reality which now confronted him and at once sensed his total powerlessness and the complete impossibility of transcending this reality for which he had striven all his life. He saw before himself two alternatives: the dreary, sad, and endless road of the *galut*, and the other road which led directly to the yawning mouth of the abyss. Which of the two could he choose? Which did he have to choose? Long ago he had vowed, silently, never to return to the way of the *galut*—he now chose the other way.

There is a possible element of truth in one detail of a popular legend of that time. According to this legend the Turks in the palace did not see what actually happened. The Turkish courtiers in Adrianople[39] merely saw a frightened and broken man who bowed his head before the sultan and his learned *mufti*. They were not aware that what was taking place before their eyes was the tragic act of revenge of a fallen hero. Sabbatai Zevi may have thought of Rabbi Joseph della Reyna,[40] and he donned the Turkish turban and accepted the name Mohammed not out of fear of the Ottoman king of flesh and blood, but as a protest against the "King of Kings," against the merciless God of Israel.

5
Our Stand
(1934)

4. Portrait of Hayim Greenberg (c. 1935); courtesy of Ameinu.

In 1933 the American Labor Zionist movement launched the journal Jewish Frontier. *Under Hayim Greenberg's editorial leadership,* Jewish Frontier *became a significant forum of liberal Jewish, socialist, and Zionist intellectual discourse in the 1930s, 1940s, and 1950s and included in-depth analysis of events in Palestine/Israel. Greenberg's statement below, issued against the backdrop of Adolf Hitler's rise to power as chancellor of Germany, calls attention to the dramatic countrywide escalation of public and state-sponsored manifestations of antisemitism, including daily attacks in the German press on Jews, intimidation, violence, and pogroms perpetrated by the Nazi S.A.*

*(*Sturmabteilung*) or Brownshirts (*Braunhemden*), new laws passed forbidding Jews to serve as government officials and prohibiting the ritual slaughtering of meat (April 1933), and public burnings of books by Jews and anti-Nazi authors. These and other events presaged the promulgation by the Nazi government of the Nuremberg Laws of 1935, which completed the process of stripping Jews of their rights as German citizens and opened the door to the Holocaust.*

The thoughtful Jew can no longer escape the conviction that he must take a definite stand in regard to the pressing Jewish problems of our time. Assimilation as a conscious program has long become an anachronism; indifference has replaced the assimilationist viewpoint among fairly large Jewish circles. This indifference, essentially a masked form of assimilation, though still widespread, has lately begun to yield to an increasing sense of unease. Recent economic and political developments, together with the social neuroses that followed in their wake, have brought the Jew again sharply face to face with the eternal Jewish question. He has to realize that the business of being a Jew may be either a blessing or a curse, but that apathy is impossible.

The catastrophic events in Germany have profoundly agitated every Jew. Unless one indulges in Germanophobia on principle and believes in the inherent barbarism and wickedness of the German soul, one must ask whether such paroxysms are not possible in other civilized countries under given conditions of national stress. Those who are not in the habit of thinking in terms of "saintly-nations" and "sinner-nations" see in the German happenings manifestations of subconscious forces which lead an independent life under a thin layer of rationalism, and break out into the open at the first favorable opportunity. Such a realization causes a sharpened sense of personal insecurity and isolation in whatever environment the Jewish minority finds itself.

Naturally enough, many modern Jews find themselves glancing hopefully at the antithesis of the German tragedy—the communist experiment in Soviet Russia. Even non-communists have ample reason for considering the eventful October revolution of 1917[1] as the most significant milestone in the history of a new world. The modern Jew has a specific psychic impulse toward a country where radical change in social-economic conditions goes hand in hand with a vigorous fight for racial and national equality and where every vestige of antisemitism is staunchly repressed. However, a closer examination of the formulated and unformulated problems of Soviet Jewry leads one to the melancholy discovery that there is no place for an *ipso facto* solution of the Jewish question even in the land of social revolution.

It is true that Jews are becoming an organic part of the Soviet economic structure in increasing numbers. A considerable number of Jews have been settled on the land.[2] An even larger number have been absorbed by industry and by many branches of government service. Insofar as the concrete economic problems of Soviet Russia are being solved in general, they are also being solved for Russian Jewry. Provided there are no unexpected upheavals one may hope that in time there will remain no "declassed" Jews, but that all will be "re-classed" into the economic structure of the huge workers' country. This process of economic integration, however, is accompanied by national disintegration. National individuality, the cultural entity of a group which draws its vital sap from its own sources, is lost. For this no one is to blame. Within the limitations of the Soviet regime (thanks to these limitations Zionism is persecuted, Hebrew is taboo, and the religious expressions of national feeling are barely tolerated) the Jewish population enjoys all legal rights for the development of its individuality. Theoretically, Jews enjoy a wide cultural autonomy: Jewish courts, a Yiddish-speaking state[-sponsored] school, a Jewish theatre subsidized by the state, and Jewish publishing houses which are maintained by government funds.[3] But legal rights are merely the fig leaf to cover the collective impotence of a group which seeks to retain its own spiritual culture without its own economic structure. The Jewish courts do not function; a steadily decreasing minority of Jewish children study in the Jewish schools; Yiddish is being increasingly supplanted not only by Russian but by Ukrainian and White Russian. It is an open secret that an intensive process of "Red assimilation" is going on in Russia.[4] From the standpoint of the national will to live, it makes little difference to the Jew whether he is molten in the liberal or in the socialist melting pot.

The threat of national destruction is an actual one for Soviet Jewry. A new *galut* feeling is developing which explains in great measure the awakened interest in Birobidzhan as a Jewish national territory.[5] The very existence of the Birobidzhan experiment supports our thesis that social revolution as such is incapable of solving the Jewish problem in its full scope. Birobidzhan is a Soviet edition of Zionism, Russian Jewry's confession of homelessness. It is a new expression of the old idea that no general social changes can automatically solve the Jewish problem.

In the light of these new experiences—the nightmare of the German calamity and the danger of the Russian "idyll"—*Jewish Frontier*[6] will fight for the concentration of Jewish energy on Palestine so as to create a home for those millions of Jews who feel themselves economically, politically, or spiritually homeless in various countries of the world.

We give preference to Palestine as a potential Jewish territory, first of all because of its rich historic and traditional associations—"imponderabilia" which furnish immense treasuries of creative energy. Besides this sentimental motive, which even the most realistic calculations cannot ignore as a source of national inspiration, we insist on the primacy of Palestine on more tangible grounds. The energy displayed by the pioneering elements of our peoples over the space of nearly half a century represents national capital which must be increased. The pioneering spirit of Jewish workers has already created the necessary foundation for an extensive agricultural and industrial mass colonization. More Jews are entering into Palestine today than into any other country in the world.[7] An annual immigration of forty or fifty thousand Jews is no longer utopian. It is fast becoming an established fact. The results already achieved in Palestine are in themselves a sufficient stimulus for investing still more national energy. They are ample warrant for considering Palestine the chief channel for the flow of Jewish energy.

At the same time we must give ourselves a strict accounting of the dangers which threaten the reconstruction work in Palestine. We are considering now not so much the outer, purely political, dangers as the inner ones. It would be the greatest calamity (as well as folly) if Palestine were transformed merely into a refuge for Jewish capital without Jewish labor; if the Jews of Palestine were to figure primarily as employers while labor would be recruited from other national groups. Such a Jewish society would have neither a firm moral nor material base. It would become a national shame. A country belongs to those who labor on it and not to those who hold the "title." We will therefore struggle with all our might against the narrow selfishness of those Jewish elements, in and out of Palestine, who would be guilty of national treason because of petty class interests. These groups are hindering Jewish labor in its effort to become an organic part of the economic structure of the country and are undermining the foundations of the national renaissance. Therefore in all fundamental reconstruction problems we will support the Histadrut Haovdim—the organization of 50,000 Jewish workers whose aim is to create a homeland based on cooperative principles and founded on social justice. We see in the Histadrut not a party organization, not a sect which canonized dogmas, but the most vital instrument of national responsibility. This body of Jewish labor will keep the Jewish homeland from being transformed into a new [Belgian] Congo or a new Liberia.[8] The struggle of the Histadrut for Jewish labor, for the dignity of labor in general and for the dignity of Jewish labor on Jewish soil in particular; its formation of independent economic cells in agriculture and industry which will serve as the beginnings of a future cooperative society in Palestine—will receive our active assistance.

We consider the creation of a land of Jewish workers in Palestine as the chief task of our generation. This does not mean, however, that we will disregard the tormenting problems of Jews in the diaspora countries. We consider it our function to mirror the Jewish struggle for existence in the difficult transition period which whole countries and continents are now experiencing. Because we are "Palestinocentric," we cannot ignore the diaspora. We cannot be indifferent to the problems of world Jewry in general or American Jewry in particular because the diaspora is the reservoir from which the Jewish homeland must be fed, and because we feel that the anguished problems of Jews the world over must be examined in the light of our analysis. Heartened by the social and cultural rejuvenation of the Jewish worker in Palestine, we will conscientiously seek means of reconstructing our local Jewish life on the basis of productive labor and a more individualized cultural life.

We believe that the new values created in Palestine—the rapture of pioneering, the ennobling of human labor, the heroic attempt to elevate social relationships—are beginning to stimulate Jewish life everywhere. We seek to strengthen the dynamic influence of labor Palestine on Jewish life in America by means of an informed, alert public opinion. Particularly today, when reaction and suicidal cupidity threaten to invalidate all that has been achieved in Palestine, we feel that there must be a publication which will interpret contemporary events in Palestine and take its stand on the frontiers of Jewish life throughout the world. We represent that synthesis in Jewish thought, which is nationalist without being chauvinist, and which stands for fundamental economic reconstruction without being communist. Only such a synthesis, represented by labor Palestine can answer the need of the disorientated modern Jew.

6

Jew and Arab

(1934)

Hayim Greenberg showed special concern for the issue of Jewish-Arab relations earlier than most other Zionist leaders in the United States. In the following essay, written after one of Greenberg's frequent trips to Palestine, he examines the place of the Arabs in the country's emerging Jewish economy. The rising standard of living, he explains, has generally benefitted the Arabs, but meanwhile the Yishuv's rapid development threatens to undermine the dignity of the Arab community. The solution to the problem, he asserts, is not the superiority of one people over the other. Rather, Zionism must address the competing Jewish and Arab claims in a forthright and honest manner and seek both a structural and psychological rapprochement with Palestine's Arab inhabitants.

In Palestine I asked myself many times: Have I told the truth about Palestine? Was I justified in claiming for years that we have not harmed the Arabs economically; that the Arabs were better off with us than without us?[1]

I made no scholarly study of the question. For that I had neither the time nor the specialist's knowledge. However, while traveling about the country—visiting towns and villages, houses and hovels, observing women and children—I came to an inescapable, no longer theoretical, conclusion: the closer an Arab settlement lay to the zone of Jewish colonization, the better fed and better housed were the inhabitants. The houses were cleaner and larger; the trees were more numerous. The stores were more elaborate. The children were friendlier; Arab boys on bicycles and Arab-owned automobiles were seen more frequently. The reverse was also true. The farther the village was situated from a center of Jewish colonization, the more dirt and mud were visible; the larger the number of blind wrecks—men in rags and women in tatters. The hungry, barefoot children suffered from sick, inflamed eyes; their camels were scrawny, the donkeys undersized—desert creatures without the romance of the desert.

I discussed the subject with Jews, Englishmen, and working-class Arabs with whom I had occasion to chat several times. The Jews confirmed my observation.

The Englishmen brought dozens of other examples. The Arabs made no denials whenever questions of fact and not diplomacy were involved. Jews who had lived in the country almost half a century and had a romantic weakness for the Arabs agreed with me. They agreed that the general well-being of the Arab had been increased, even though they were profoundly shocked to hear that friends had reproved me for driving with an Arab chauffeur from Haifa to Tel Aviv, or that a little Jewish boy in Jerusalem had called out "*Aravi asur*" [the Arab is forbidden], when I was about to get a shoe shine from an Arab bootblack.

Today the Arabs have more and better-paid work; they have easier and humaner working conditions. No such change would have been possible without Jewish colonization. English officials, outwardly ultra-courteous, furnished me with handfuls of material which demonstrated how influential Jewish colonization had been in raising the economic standard of the Arab. However, to discourage me, they would say evasively: "But that's not the problem; that's not the difficulty in Arab-Jewish relations." When I finally urged one such Englishman to speak up, he took out a fresh cigar, muttered what might have been "you know" or "I'll tell you," and proceeded to tell me of his family troubles. His mother and elder brother lived somewhere in Australia. Their only income was a meager pension from the English government, not enough to keep body and soul together. He, the Jerusalem official, had to support both because the older brother was a ne'er-do-well who spent his days at tennis. Two years ago he had passed a bad check. If not for the help of the Jerusalem brother, he would have been jailed. "And can you imagine," said the English official, "that he never so much as sends me a card! Furthermore, this only brother of mine is my bitterest enemy and would be happy to hear that a Bedouin's knife had dispatched me. He eats my bread but the good-for-nothing doesn't wish to be beholden to me. Marxists, they tell me, believe only in economic motives. How idiotic! The lowest of the low seeks dignity above all else. If he doesn't get it, he is prepared to destroy the whole world. I have told you a story. You can deduce the moral."

True enough, an old story with an old moral. Cain and Abel [Gen. 4][2]—economically equal! Had they been what Englishmen called "Marxists" they could have lived in peace—the one with his sheep, the other with his fields. But Cain also wanted his "dignity"—that God should smile when he laid his sacrifice on the altar. An old story—Joseph and his brethren [Gen. 37]; Isaac and Ishmael [Gen. 25:1–17]; Jacob and Esau [Gen. 25:19–34]. The Esau problem is not simple. Richard Beer-Hofmann[3] in his dramatic poem *Jacob's Dream* [1915][4] has revealed the full tragedy of being Esau.[5] "Give me a pot of lentils. I am hungry. Take the birthright for the pottage." But after the mess of pottage has been eaten, the hunger stilled, one is a man again. "I want my birthright, too."[6] Jacob seeks to persuade Esau that he does not need the birthright; that the difference between Jacob and Esau is not the difference between greater and lower, but merely a difference in kind. But Esau is not persuaded—he wants what the Englishman calls "dignity"—the birthright for himself and for his children.

Is this the crux of the Arab-Jewish problem? My Englishman's knowledge of [Friedrich] Nietzsche[7] is slight; he has probably never heard of Alfred Adler,[8] but I feel he is right. Intuitively, he has grasped the essentials of the question. There are probably no absolute Jacob natures or Esau natures. The "Nordic" theoreticians are pathologically obsessed with the notion of superiority. Probably one is cast for the role of Jacob or Esau not so much because of spiritual differences as because of historic conditions. Nevertheless, the time comes when Esau rebels against his state. If he cannot have the birthright, he does not want Jacob to have it either—or else, let Jacob have it at a distance so that Esau's eyes will not grow sick with envy.

[Vladimir] Lenin[9] understood this when in the years of military communism, he bestowed a sense of superiority on the wretched Russian worker. The Russian proletarian was hungry and cold. Instead of a pot of lentils, Lenin gave him a vision of a pot of meat in times to come. For years the worker's chief gratification came from the new aristocratic rank he had secured during the revolution. [Adolf] Hitler,[10] too, understands the secret. He intoxicated all German youth with a sense of superiority to erase the Esau stigma. Germany may have to forgo the pot of lentils for years, but as long as the young men can march along the streets and believe they are not inferior to France and that Europe is terrified, all is well.

One can prove to an Arab in Palestine that he has lost nothing through Jewish colonization. One can show him all the advantages that have accrued to him; one can persuade him that in the future he will profit more from Jewish immigration. He will understand and agree, but the Esau-worm will, nevertheless, gnaw at his heart. The mess of pottage is conceded, but where is the birthright? "Jacob says that he will not lord it over me. I believe him; I believe that he will not wish to lord it, that he will respect my rights—but his very existence is a violation of me, because Jacob reminds me, even through his benefactions, that he is Jacob and I am Esau—at any rate, Esau for the time being."

Perhaps the problem of Jewish-Arab relations belongs to the realm of psychology rather than economics or politics. We must have good economists and diplomats in Palestine. Our life with the Arabs, however, demands the presence of competent social physicians. The labor movement, above all, must discover the therapeutic measures which will heal the sore spots in the relations between Jew and Arab.

7
Revisionism
(1934)

The Revisionist Zionist party (also known as the Union of Zionist Revisionists) was founded in 1925 by Vladimir (Zeev) Jabotinsky. It originally advocated a revision of the Zionist Executive's generally conciliatory policy to the British mandatory regime and stepping up the pace of Jewish settlement in Palestine. Jabotinsky, a brilliant orator, writer, and polemicist, considered himself to be the true heir of Theodor Herzl's legacy of classical Zionism. He was a staunch opponent of Labor Zionism and placed a premium on the notions of military strength, armed resistance against the British, and retaliation by Jews in Palestine against Arab attackers. Hayim Greenberg, an outspoken critic of Jabotinsky and the Revisionists, composed the remarks below in the weeks following the assassination of Chaim Arlosoroff (1899–1933), a prominent Jewish Agency official and Labor Zionist leader presumed murdered by right-wing Zionist extremists, and the subsequent Eighteenth Zionist Congress (1933) at which the labor movement emerged as Zionism's dominant political faction.

It is impossible to understand the rise of Revisionism without taking into consideration a number of factors in the general history of the Zionist movement. Some features of the battle now being waged between us and Revisionism actually existed, although in other forms and under other names, more than twenty-five years ago.

Many of us still remember the conflict between what used to be known in Zionism as "small colonization" and "large colonization."[1] The devotees of large colonization deprecated all possibilities of Jewish economic development in Palestine so long as we did not have the fullest political guarantee for a large and autonomous Jewish center or for a Jewish state. The efforts to create Jewish economic positions in Palestine and to carry on colonization work under the conditions then existing under the Turkish regime[2] were contemptuously branded by the proponents of large colonization as Hibat Zion [Love of Zion].[3] *Hovevei Zion* [Lovers of Zion],[4] they contended, and those who were under the influence of Hovevei Zion psychology, were thrilled by such gains as "one more goat in Palestine" (a famous remark by [Moshe Leib] Lilienblum).[5] In their circles [Theodor] Herzl's formula was often quoted: "We are going to create in Palestine 'not things but conditions.'"[6] They failed to understand at that time that certain things, however small and insignificant, can themselves begin to play the role of conditions. They also failed to understand that those who wanted to carry on what was called small colonization wished to do it not because their horizons were narrow, not because they were satisfied with small gains, not because they did not entertain any maximum ideal of Zionism, but because they believed that small-scale colonization, that is, concrete work and gradual extension and strengthening of the Jewish settlement in Palestine was in itself a real way to future maximum gains.

The same psychology of the former so-called "maximalists,"[7] and of those who put too much faith in political and too little faith in organic work, led later on in the postwar years [after 1918] to the rise of the Revisionist trend in Zionism. Reality continually fed fresh food to their psychology. Bloody occurrences in Palestine, which could have been avoided if the British government had set more store by its obligations;[8] the severance of Transjordania[9] and the reduction of the base of Jewish colonization; constant political obstacles to Jewish immigration and colonization on the part of the British administration; the formation of such a group as Brit Shalom [Covenant of Peace],[10] which gave unmistakable evidence of liquidation, of renouncing the true content and aims of Zionism—as this gave rise in certain Zionist circles to a feeling that the heritage bequeathed by Herzl was going under, and that Zionism was again becoming a puny Hovevei Zion affair. Hence they maintained, with a certain measure of subjective justice, that they were the only surviving adherents of genuine Zionism—of *great* Zionism.

There were times when the leaders of the Revisionist faction tried to establish friendly contacts with the labor movement.[11] If the workers, they argued, were really as radical as they professed to be, and if they possessed real revolutionary energy, they should logically adopt the Revisionist slogans and fight against any attempt to minify Zionism. But the workers paid no attention whatever to these overtures on the part of the Revisionists. This was not because the Jewish labor movement of Palestine had embarked upon a course of liquidation or semi-liquidation of Zionism, but because it felt to an enormous extent responsible for the fate of Zionism, and because common sense and experience had developed in it a realistic view of the concrete tasks of Zionism.

Labor Zionism does not renounce even for one moment the maximum aims of the Zionist movement. Whether or not there is to be a Jewish state is of little concern to it, but it has never given up the thought of creating a large Jewish national center in Palestine with political autonomy for millions of Jews. Its realism consists in this, however, that it bears in mind the limits of political action, that it does not believe in the magic potency of maximum slogans, and that it is convinced that the more Jews penetrate into Palestine, and the stronger their social and economic positions in the land, the more solid ground will be created for maximum political demands.

From a certain point of view it may be said that the Labor Zionist movement has forced upon itself a kind of political asceticism. If it wanted blindly to follow its national instincts, it might perhaps be working for an armed uprising against the foreign political factors which lord it over Palestine. If it wanted blindly to follow its socialist entitlements, its energies might perhaps find expression in a desperate attempt at social revolution. However, it takes account of reality. It knows that we are not now in an era of decisive battles, but in a period of the gradual building of Jewish positions in the land; that many years and perhaps decades will have to pass until conditions favorable to national or social maximalism are created in Palestine.

Herein we find an explanation of the so-called political opportunism of the labor movement in Palestine.[12] It is opportunism not in the sense of anti-radicalism, but of anti-adventurism. We know and feel that we must have a number of years of comparatively peaceful constructive work in Palestine, and for the sake of these constructive efforts we are ready to renounce maximalist gestures and cries which can only complicate our position and hinder our work. In this sense we may be called political ascetics, but also political realists. On account of this Naziritism,[13] which is a product of its realism, labor, with its sound instinct and no less sound logic, rejected anti-Revisionist watchwords which it regarded, and still regards, as ineffectual phrase-mongering.

Hence, from the very start a chasm was formed between Labor Zionism and Revisionism. It was primarily the chasm between realism and adventurism. As a result there ensued a conflict between the Revisionist groups and that force in Zionism which in recent years has become the most significant factor in the movement, namely, the Labor wing.[14] Revisionism, which at first asserted that is was merely radically Zionist, that it did not want a separate economic program either for the diaspora or for the building up of Palestine, and that it was not oriented toward any particular class in Jewry, began, as if in revenge for its failure to effect an alliance with Labor, to be more and more hostile to labor. This hostility to Labor, which is today a cruel fact in Jewish life, began to feed on ideologies and political tendencies which had sprung from the soil of other nations. It began ever more to absorb elements of fascism.[15] The naive among us believed that, no matter what happened in the gentile world, it was absolutely impossible for a reactionary movement to arise in Jewish life. Fascism, they thought, was a purely non-Jewish malady with which Jews, on account of their historic immunity, could not possibly be infected. Unfortunately it turned out that we were not at all immune, and that the fascist bacteria found a fertile soil for multiplication in Revisionist circles.

The first and most significant trait of fascism and Revisionism is the hatred it bears toward internationalism, toward every form of friendly cooperation between one nation and another. Not for nothing does the Revisionist leader and teacher, Vladimir Jabotinsky,[16] quote so often the old Latin proverb, "*Homo homini lupus*" ("Man is to man as a wolf").[17] Not for nothing do the Revisionists hold that wolfish relations exist and will and should exist between nations. This is no libel upon Revisionism. When we read in the Revisionist press[18] that to help the Austrian Socialists[19] in their struggle for liberty is treason against Jewry and Zionism; that only two courses are left to the Arab, either back to the desert or into the depths of the sea; that we should not in the least be concerned with the problems of other nations; that we have but one task for the next few generations, namely, to build the Jewish state, and that only after we have attained this goal, and provided we have spare time, shall we be able to worry "about dogs and cats, about Chinamen and Arabs,"[20]—when we read this, we see in it a pathological expression of national egotism which is not only immoral, but essentially stupid, against the real interests and beneath the dignity of Jewry and Zionism. It is impossible, from a purely practical point of Jew, to build a Jewish national home or a Jewish state in Palestine without a minimum of cooperation with other nations or at least with certain progressive elements of other nations.

If in the near future we are to witness nothing but national selfishness in the world, nothing but isolation between the nations, war of one against all and of all against one, and along with that universal antisemitism; if we are to abandon our faith that there are at least some parts of the nations which are not infected with national hate and are ready or may be ready to assist us in the building of a Jewish Palestine, then we may as well give up our hope for the Zionist solution of our problems. If this be a true picture of the future, if no other picture be possible, the Jewish question cannot be solved at all. In such a world of absolute evil, the weakest of the cultural nations cannot attain what the Revisionists term the "Kingdom of the House of David."[21]

The second salient trait of fascism and Revisionism is its inclination to imperialism. For several years now the Revisionist press has propagated in all languages the old jingoistic idea that there are certain specific creatures in the world which are called colonial peoples, that such peoples are not worthy to become nationally and politically independent, that they must be ruled by the stronger and more civilized European nations, and there is only one language they understand—the language of the lash. They advocate this not only with regard to the workers of Palestine, where they would like to institute a colonial regime on the old English or French model, but also with regard to India and the African colonies. It is often both painful and ridiculous to read how the Revisionists reprove the English people, declaring that the English are beginning to degenerate because they no longer display that appetite for ruling other people for which they were once so distinguished. It is as though they were saying to the English, "If we Jews are pacific, it is because we cannot help it: we have as yet no army and no navy, we are not yet able to oppress other people. But you who have everything that is necessary for it, why have you permitted yourselves to be weakened by the sentimental pacifistic propaganda?"

The third fascist trait in the Revisionist psychology is faith in the unlimited power of militarism. Everything on earth can be solved and gained by military force. This Jewish militarism, which is a mixture of small-town faith in the magic potency of a military uniform, postwar madness, and adventurism, has begun to express itself both in the training of Revisionist youth, and in the formation of military cells, especially in Poland and in Palestine.[22] The Revisionists are waiting and praying and hoping for a new world war.

The Revisionist press not only points out the fact that there is not explosive material in the world for a new world war, but it frankly and shamelessly advocates the need and great benefits of a new bloodbath. If they were asked point blank: Since you are preparing for war and since you are already forming military cells for this purpose, perhaps you can tell us, from the point of view of the Jewish interests in Palestine, upon whom are you preparing to make war? Upon whom and with whom? They would not be able to give a clear answer. Even if we accept for a moment their militaristic premise, it is evident that they possess no definite political orientation whatever. They are against England, they are against the Arabs within Palestine and without, they are against Soviet Russia. Who, then, are our potential friends? To this there is no answer. This we do not know, they will answer. If there is a world war, we shall decide then to whom it will be more advantageous for us to throw our support, or, to put it more vulgarly, who will pay us more for our support by furthering the creation of a Jewish state in Palestine.

It is obvious that they are merely preparing cannon fodder for governments which will make use of Jewish military cells for their own benefit. The stamp of adventurism is all over this business. Then comes the lying fascist cry of absolute national unity in which class considerations do not play or are not allowed to play any part—the hatred for Marxism and the class struggle.[23]

Unfortunately, Revisionism has succeeded in contaminating also a few general Zionist circles with this quasi-national ideology. Revisionism has already become a point of support for all those who wish to disguise their class interests with a hundred percent Jewish patriotism.

What, in point of fact, does the labor policy of the Revisionists consist in? They have formed a new labor organization in Palestine[24] as a rival to the Histadrut, and the thing is beginning to smack too much of what is known in America as "company unions,"[25] "contract labor,"[26] and [the] "sweatshop system."[27] It is their contention that in order to build a Jewish national center in Palestine we must have private capital, and, above all, wide opportunities for profit. In Palestine, they assert, there should be no labor movement that champions the class interests of the workers. The unfortunate thing about it is that there are also honest Zionists who persuade themselves that it stands to reason there ought to be no labor movement in Palestine like the one we have created there. In taking this view they overlook one slight distinction between capital in a country like Palestine, a land of colonization, and capital in the so-called colonial countries, in, for example, Belgian Congo[28] or British Uganda.[29]

The Belgian capitalist, when he comes to the Congo, is not concerned that the country be developed for millions of Belgians who are yet to come there. He deals there, not with his people, but with the so-called "colored natives," for whom he has no respect or love or pity. He comes there with definite and brutal aim: he is to produce there, by means of cheap and semi-slave labor, as much merchandise as possible, and this merchandise is to be disposed of, not in the Congo in order to satisfy the economic needs of the native population, but in the anonymous world market. The dearer he can sell the Congo raw materials, and the cheaper he can pay the Africans for their labor, the more profitable his business. He is not operating in his homeland, but abroad; and if as a result of his economic management in the colonial country part of the natives perish of semi-starvation and unsanitary conditions, it does not trouble him in the least. Imperialist capital in a colonial land is not interested in the land per se. Its intentions are strictly exploitative [in relation to] the maximum predatory utilization of the natural wealth and physical strength the native population possesses. What will happen in the coming ten or fifteen years after his exploitative invasion is no concern of his. The same may be said of British capital in a colonial country like Uganda. Palestine, however, is no Belgian Congo, no British Uganda, no Dutch Java.[30] It is not a colonial country at all, but a land of colonization. The Jewish capital which today comes to Palestine must reckon with the existence of from fifty to sixty thousand [Jewish] wage workers, who are not mere material for temporary exploitation, but part of the rising new Jewish settlement. Unbridled exploitation of the workers is thus not only against the class interests of the workers as workers but also against the national interests of the whole Jewish people. Jewish capital, if it would really be constructive in Palestine and help in the building of a Jewish national home, must therefore regard the worker not only as a producer, but also as a consumer. If the wage earner of Palestine does not receive sufficient purchasing power, a normal domestic market cannot be created in the country whether for farm or industrial products. In the final analysis it must not only hinder labor, but the capitalist class itself, which will have to think of its production in terms of export only.

In this sense it is not a question of a particular class or stratum of the population, but a general, national question. Whoever is opposed to the building of a Jewish economy on the basis of adequate purchasing power for the working people of Palestine is by that very fact opposed to Zionism in general.

If the Palestinian worker is not assured of a minimum purchasing power, the whole economic endeavor in Palestine will be of no real value. It is, therefore, the task of the Histadrut to create sound working conditions in line with general national interests. The so-called class interests coincide in this case with general national interests. This alone is reason enough why we should combat Revisionism in all its forms with every honorable weapon at our command.

It is not our fault if differences of opinion are turned into hatred. We cannot help it if a political battle which could be waged in legal forms is turned into a civil war. It is not our fault if the worst and ugliest class struggle imaginable is now going on in Palestine, a struggle between two wings of one and the same working class. We did not kindle the fires of discord in Palestine. We were ready to negotiate, to find a way of cooperation and peaceful relations.[31] We did not succeed. The fascist temperament of Revisionism is forcing battles upon us which we do not relish. We shall, however, be compelled to continue our fight not only in the interests of the labor movement, but for the sake of Zionism and all Jewry.

8

Notes on Marxism

(1935)

Hayim Greenberg gravitated to socialism as a youth and thereafter never wavered in his idealistic striving to create an egalitarian, democratic, and socially just world. He also possessed a penetrating and clear-eyed view of the potentiality and limitations of Marxist philosophy, and he proved unsparing in his criticism of Marxism's "deification of society" and its tendency to "reduce" human life to "the zone of social relationships." In the following essay, written against the backdrop of Labor Zionism's emergence as a dominant political force in Zionist affairs, Communist leader Joseph Stalin's elimination of Russian political opposition, and Chinese leader Mao Zedong's consolidation of control of the Chinese Community Party, Greenberg explores Marxism's relationship to the broad spectrum of Western philosophical thought. He also ponders socialism's capacity to elevate the human condition and solve the enigmatic puzzle of "I and the cosmos."

Marxian Messianism

All is lawful or unlawful, good or evil, constructive or destructive, depending on the period or the stage of development in which it occurs. This was the dialectical yardstick used by Karl Marx[1] for his historical and sociological studies. The genealogy of this measuring rod is well known. Beginning with Heraclitus,[2] this method had periodic reincarnations and eclipses till it reached [Georg] Hegel[3] and his doctrine of "panlogism"—the theory that the whole must be interpreted in terms of logic. The fact that the young Marx later ridiculed Hegel's metaphysics and exchanged panlogism for paneconomism is unimportant. Marx never denied Hegel's fundamental teaching that "antithesis is the root of all motion and life; each thing moves, grows and displays activity only insofar as it carries its antithesis within itself."[4] If one follows this method to its logical conclusion one must assume that just as capitalism and primitive communism were historically justified for their periods (Marx not only admitted but stressed this point) so might socialism become outmoded when—to use a Hegelian term—"negation of negation"[5] sets in. All that comes into being has been dialectically determined and hence justified. But destruction and death are also dialectically determined and *ipso facto* justified.

> " . . . *alles, was entsteht,*
> *Ist wert, dass es zugrunde geht.*"[6]

The Russian [Alexander] Herzen,[7] a feebler thinker but a man of greater intellectual courage, foresaw a revolution (revolution, not counter-revolution) against a future socialist order, several hundred years after the establishment of the socialist system. He visualized a revolutionary minority which would burst out in passionate protest against the stratification, slavery, and Philistine boredom of a socialism grown reactionary. He could not foretell the slogans of this minority, what its concrete social ideal would be—[perhaps] anarchism? He did not believe, however, that social development would end with socialism. Though preaching socialism he at the same time opposed a fetishistic conception of the socialist ideal. Marx, on the other hand, despite his cold logic, daring objectivity, and iron dialectic, chose to be unaware of the Hegelian thesis that the absolute manifests itself in relatives. He conceived as absolute that which is historically relative, and introduced a mystical strain of eschatology into his monumental scholarly structure.

One does not have to be an orthodox historical materialist to accept Marx's thesis that the friction of class interests in the course of centuries generated the heat needed to turn the wheels of history. Everyone concedes the validity of this idea. Only scholastics cannot grasp it; dogmatic theologians do not want to. But Marx never gave a clear answer to another question. The economic struggle which runs like a scarlet thread through world history gave rise to a flood of human energy. How will that energy be utilized "in the last days," in a ripe, fully established socialist society? Will it atrophy, or will it have to seek new channels and new modes of struggle? If this spiritual tension is doomed to slacken, then history will give way to dull contentment and degeneration. If it remains quick and eager, there must be conflicts to feed it. What conflicts does the as-yet-unformed, infinitely blissful "socialist society" hold in store for us? Marx never wished to admit the possibility of such conflicts. He viewed social revolution in terms of "a leap from the kingdom of necessity into the kingdom of freedom."[8] He regarded socialism as the last step in economic evolution, as the happy epilogue to the spectacle which we call human history. But what happens after the epilogue? Should the curtain rise again, will we have a new drama with new passions and conflicts, new victors and victims?

In this respect, the creator of scientific socialism remained the greatest of utopians. The conception of a socialist regime which would satisfy all human desires and appease all conflicts is not a scientific one. It is a naive messianism, a new version of the Cinderella tale.

[George] Bernard Shaw[9] has said that "the man with a toothache thinks everyone happy whose teeth are sound."[10] The Eskimo is certain that heaven consists of quiet waters on whose surface swim numerous fat fish. The Eskimo need not blush before the [Muslim] who transforms his paradise into well-watered gardens where sit the righteous, clad in green silks, drinking sherbets, and transfixed by the gazelle-like glance of some young girl; nor need the Muslim quail before the Jewish conception of the *shor habor* [wild bull],[11] Leviathan,[12] and "preserved wine" to be served in the hereafter as the reward of righteousness.[13] All these conceptions are the justifiable expressions of primitive optimism.

Marxian philosophy is a modern relapse into this primitive optimism; it represents the naiveté of the human race scientifically decked out. If socialism claims to be able to solve all human problems and to banish human suffering; if after [Fyodor] Dostoyevsky,[14] [Eduard von] Hartmann,[15] and [Friedrich Wilhelm] Nietzsche,[16] after the abysses of the human soul uncovered by modern psychology, socialism should still claim to be a panacea, it would have to be viewed as one of those patent medicines which are good for all human ills ranging from a cold to progressive paralysis. Actually Marxism is the application of a quantitative criterion to qualitative phenomena, the attempt to use an objective yardstick for subjective concepts like contentment, joy, or suffering. Eduard von Hartmann's bitter witticism—that the earnest philosophic pessimist should support the socialist movement because only in a fully developed, well-fed socialist society would man at last free himself of all childish illusions and upon perceiving reality in its true nakedness, the eternal unavoidable character of suffering, would therefore seek a way for cosmic suicide (the destruction of the world)—might well be called a hysterical excess of thought; but this witticism has a deeper understanding of, and respect for, the human soul than has Marxian optimism. However, Hartmann did not wish to realize that the redemptive quality of socialism lay not in its capacity to abolish suffering, but in its ability to free man from degrading suffering, from suffering that is zoological rather than human. That is probably the significance of the *midrash* which ascribes to Job the characteristic outburst: "Lord of the world, I will endure all suffering, except the suffering of poverty."[17] Leprosy and the loss of sons and daughters are not lesser griefs than poverty, but poverty places man on a par with beasts. It is not "God-sent" like more intense forms of suffering, but comes from man and the social system, and is therefore avoidable. In this sense, the task of socialism is not to bring happiness (happiness is not the total sum of many individual pleasures, just as wisdom is not the sum of detailed truths) but dignity. It cannot give more. No matter how high the socialist tower of Babel[18] should rise, it will not reach infinity.

Marxian optimism is an attempt to arrest man's capacity for suffering; the human race will always revolt against such an effort. Man does not wish to stop suffering—he wishes to suffer on a nobler plane.

Schopenhauer and Marx

Had [Arthur] Schopenhauer[19] known Marx he surely would have described him as the most striking modern embodiment of what he characterized as "vulgar optimism."[20] His philosophical antisemitism would have classified Marx as typically "Old Testament," as both pre-evangelical and anti-Buddhist in his attempt to be at home on the earth and to find ease in this "vale of tears."[21] Schopenhauer viewed man as essentially homeless, whereas Marx, geocentric in outlook, considered this planet our true dwelling, provided the social system received a thorough renovation. Marx wanted to create a paradise for man; Schopenhauer would have viewed the Marxian dream as

> "Organized charity, scrimped and iced,
> In the name of a cautious, statistical Christ."[22]

He was sure that there was no paradise from which man would not seek to flee, even though there was no refuge for his flight.

Marx knew that a life not overburdened with joyless work, free from economic insecurity and perhaps attended by intellectual enjoyment, would meet all man's requirements and longings. To Schopenhauer, on the other hand, it was clear that the greatest abundance of comforts, even when attended by a deeper sense of human solidarity, might turn into an inward emptiness, which in the long run would prove just as unbearable as present economic slavery and social conflicts. He knew that man's grasp will always be greater than his reach, and that whatever the amount of wealth, there is always some "ill'th"[23]—to employ an expression coined by [John] Ruskin[24]—inherent in life which can be neither eradicated nor reduced by means of social reconstruction.

The Individual and Nirvana

Is there any logical or organic connection between atheism and socialism? The Greek Sophists[25] five centuries before our era were all atheists "in the name of knowledge," yet who among them was a socialist? During past ages socialist thought was based on religious conceptions; those medieval "free thinkers" who successfully circulated the notorious atheistic diatribe *De Tribus Impostoribus* [Latin for "*The Three Impostors*"] (i.e., Moses, Jesus, and Mohammed)[26] were politically and socially more reactionary than the pious non-conformist sects. Till the eighteenth century, socialism welled from religious sources only. What inspired the communist movements of the Middle Ages was not the "scientific truth" that there is no purposeful, directing mind behind the world's great drama, but the religious belief that servitude was introduced by the oppressors against the will of God, that "if the Creator had willed it, He would have created both lord and serf,"[27] and that communism was God-ordained. Even in the nineteenth century neither Moses Hess[28] nor [Ferdinand] Lassalle[29] saw any contradiction between their socialist credo and their belief in God and the immortality of the soul. They could see no logical interdependence between the conception of a purely mechanical universe where only simple particles move aimlessly, without guidance or design, and an ideal aiming at a planned and harmonious society. Marx was the first to try to establish a philosophical connection between socialism and atheistic materialism. He was not aware that his hostility to religion was conditioned psychologically, an emotionally colored reaction to a concrete state of affairs.

Nineteenth-century socialism was confronted with the reactionary influence and police power of the Roman Catholic Church; with the papal [encyclical] *Rerum Novarum*[30] based on the idea that it is God's will that the human race be divided into rich and poor; with the social cynicism of the Protestant Church authorities; with the Byzantine despotism of the Greek Orthodox Church. It was but natural for the young, persecuted movement to consider a degenerated and thoroughly corrupt religious institutionalism the enemy of the oppressed, and its spiritual atmosphere "opium for the people."[31] Thereupon Marx conceived the exploiters' role of contemporary religious institutions as the natural and permanent function of organized religion. He mistook religious institutionalism for religion itself, and petrified forms of historically conditioned religions for the essence of religious mood. Our modern view that religion as such contains not a literal, but a symbolic representation of truth and life, and that therefore it should be valued "artistically" rather than intellectually, was foreign to Marx's mind. He confused changing theologies with the persistent religious impulses which gave them birth. It was as though the purchaser of a poor electrical appliance were on that account to oppose electricity. From this point of view, the connection between modern socialism and militant atheism was accidental. But Marx wished to build this accidental relationship into a permanent, indestructible identity. He strove to change socialism into an independent, self-contained, all-embracing *Weltanschauung*. The old truth that man is a social animal was for the first time fully appreciated and grossly exaggerated in Marxism. Marxism detached the problem of life entirely from the cosmic problem; it reduced the problem to the zone of social relationships—a process which finally culminated in a type of deification of society.

[Baruch] Spinoza[32] viewed the individual man as a mode of God-substance; Marx also viewed the individual not as an entity in himself, but as a mode of *his* substance—society. Once you grant that society is the only substance and that the individual's problems and cravings are purely of a social nature—Isn't he a social and only a social animal?—there can be no God and no extra-social religion. Human society takes the place of God, and devotion to the common well-being, the place of worship. This trend of thought runs from Auguste Comte's[33] positivist theology and [Ludwig] Feuerbach's[34] thesis, *Homo homini Deus est* [Latin for "Man is God to man"][35] through Marx's cult of collectivism, to that pseudomentality which finds rhetorical expression in [William] Blake's[36] "Thou art a man, God is no more. Thine own humanity learn to adore."[37]

Marx knew that while social problems could be solved through human effort and will, the specifically individual problems (those which are primary and most tormenting) have no rational solution. To escape this difficulty he "killed" the individual by declaring him non-existent—the illusion of a delirious social organism. When the organism will recover (after the social revolution), its cells will lose the sick consciousness of individuality: a finger does not know it has a separate life until it hurts.

Society, the sole substance and reality, can have no problem of destiny. Its problems are historical, not metaphysical. Questions of whence, whither, and wherefore are alien to society as such. Its aim is adjustment, not salvation, and the only knowledge which it requires is pragmatic, utilitarian in character. It can solve its peculiar problems without God, freedom of will or immortality. It does not have to grasp the inner meaning of cosmic existence. It can "afford" to be irreligious. Because the Marxian man of the future, the happy citizen of the socialist state, will be a sound cell in a normal social organism, he will not suffer from a morbid individual consciousness. All metaphysical desires and cravings will be eliminated or, to quote Marx, "all which is mysterious, all which leads theory to mysticism, finds its rational solution in human practice,"[38] in the practice of a normal social organism.

Thus Marx endowed future economic relationships with magic potency. Man is confined entirely to his own circle; the world at large is to be considered merely the physical environment of human life; human life is reduced to the sphere of omnipotent social relations, and, according to [Anatoly] Lunacharsky[39] (the one-time neo-Marxian theologist) the individual's craving for "eternity" will find its normal satisfaction in the blissful dissolution of his ego in the collectivized society. The individual's salvation is *Nirvana* in the bosom of the social cosmos.

Marxian philosophy became a peculiar brand of westernized Buddhism.

Marx and Nietzsche

Nietzsche was also an atheist, but there was a sharp difference between his atheistic despair and Marx's atheistic mirth. Marx knew that there was no God; Nietzsche knew that "God had died," that "we had slain Him long ago."[40] In a mood of trivial intellectualism he greeted God's "death" with enthusiasm as a charter of deliverance, but at bottom he never ceased to feel helplessly entangled in the inexorable meshes of natural law which knows nothing of the insatiable yearnings of the individual. God's "death" was Nietzsche's nemesis, his catastrophe.

No European was as bitterly opposed to the discouraging fiction of the individual existing only as a cell of the social organism as Nietzsche. Whether or not he was familiar with Marx's work is unimportant. Nietzsche represented the most passionate protest against the Marxian tendency in European thought. He viewed the individual as the primary and final reality. He knew before [William] James[41] that individuality is founded in feeling, and that the recesses of individual feeling, the darker, blinder strata of character, are the only places in which we catch real fact in the making, and directly perceive how events happen. He knew before [Sigmund] Freud[42] that the impulses of the human soul are more varied and profound than we are aware of and that the source of those impulses is the individual. There is no social substitute for individual life; personality refuses to live by proxy. How could Nietzsche accept a teaching based on an all-devouring collectivism? The individual's indestructible will to live offered, through Nietzsche's personality, the fiercest revolt against Marx's "homicidal" intentions. If the individual is merely a "mode," there can be no substance: then community, society, humanity is just a multiplication of "modes," and billions of zeros are still zero. God was dethroned. Should he enthrone society? Nietzsche was too much the "realist" to sing Hallelujah to statistics.

Hence, in contrast to Marx's optimistic "at-homeness," Nietzsche's desperate sense of homelessness! "Where is my home? For it do I ask and seek, and have sought, but have not found it. O eternal everywhere, O eternal nowhere, O eternal in vain."[43] A godless world is no home for the individual. There is no power in such a world to shelter or to rescue the human "I." While Marx, the collectivist, envisaged a life wholly protected and fenced in, Nietzsche, the individualist, anticipated eternal struggle and infinite tragedy. Socialism? It is a solution to the problem "society and I," but it does not solve the enigma "I and the cosmos." It will solve the problem of economics, but whenever a new Zarathustra[44] descends from his meditative mountain to preach to the crowd, human beings, even "socialized" ones, will hear him. The prophet's words will be: "Live dangerously! Erect your cities beside Vesuvius,[45] send out your ships to unexplored seas!"[46] The crowd will listen and—cease to be a crowd. It will become transfigured into a tragic chorus and rediscover the never dying "hero" of human tragedy.

That is the vision of the Nietzschean man, who preceded and survived the philosopher Friedrich Nietzsche. The Nietzschean man is still alive. He may be a socialist; he cannot be a Marxist.

9

To a Communist Friend

(1936)

It is not possible to understand Hayim Greenberg's brand of democratic socialism without considering his attitude to Marxist theory generally as well as his ethical and practical opposition to Soviet Russia's prevailing Bolshevik sensibility in the 1930s and 1940s. Greenberg wrote the following essay, presented as an "open letter" to a fictional friend, on the eve of the Moscow purge trials (1936–38), a series of public trials that showcased the alleged guilt of Soviet leader Joseph Stalin's opponents who were accused of conspiring to assassinate Stalin, dismantle the new Soviet state, and replace Communism with Western-style capitalism. The trials, which generated worldwide attention and consolidated Stalin's autocratic rule, resulted in a series of forced confessions, the unlawful imprisonment and exile of many suspects, the execution of dozens of wrongfully convicted defendants, and a general purge of the Communist Party and the Red Army. In this remarkably predictive exposition, Greenberg surveys the philosophical underpinnings of socialism, exposes the distortions and abuses of Marxism under the Bolshevik regime, and explains "why I am a socialist but not a Communist."

In your letter you ask me to return to Russia. "You will never take root in another land. After fifteen years of exile, it is time to come home, time to realize that your opposition to communism springs from 'intelligentsia complexes' from which you can still free yourself," you say.

Let us examine what you call my liberal "intellectual complexes." I am a pacifist and a socialist. I am an opponent of force and a believer in democracy. I state the case baldly and simply at the outset because I know how outdated and remote these terms now sound—a sentimental hangover from the idealistic intoxication of the nineteenth century. Our age is made of sterner stuff with little tolerance for what it conceives to be roseate unrealities. That is why I feel the need to redefine my position, to tell you why I cannot return to the Russia that is "building socialism." I want, if possible, to have you understand why I am a socialist but not a Communist. And I also want you to know that I write with a profound sense of the greatness of the undertaking in the Soviet Union, as well as with a profound grief for what I consider its failure.

In the fifteen years since I left Russia, my opposition to the prevailing capitalist system has become more passionate and determined, but at the same time the attempted solution of tangled historical reckonings through physical force arouses in me a revulsion as strong as that I felt in the unforgettable years of the Russian Civil War.[1] I suppose at this point I could close my letter with good wishes to you and yours. The implications are clear, but we have not seen each other so long, and the doors of Russia are barred to me. I have a great longing to speak to you of things which have become alien and unreal to you.

Do you remember our college janitor Fyodor, whom the professor of biology nicknamed "Darwin's assistant"? When we asked him once whether he had really stopped going to church he had answered, "Yes; yes, it's already two months since I've adopted the atheistic faith." Fyodor apparently had no undue qualms. But I cannot accept the "atheistic faith," nor has [Yemelyan] Yaroslavsky,[2] the Soviet Savonarola[3] of atheism who peddles crumbs from [François-Marie Arouet de] Voltaire's[4] bourgeois rationalist banquet, been able to convert me. You know my attitude to the church and to organized religion in general. And you also know that no one in Russia gave a more scathing criticism of organized religion than the most religious Russian of the twentieth century, Leo Tolstoy.[5] I have not forgotten the reactionary part played by the church in Russian history, nor the crippling effect of organized religion in various periods of world history. There is good reason for a religious man to fight the dogmatism and corruption of religious institutions. But official communism has declared war not only on the church and the synagogue, but against every honest effort toward a religious orientation in the universe. Waldo Frank,[6] for instance, an American communist sympathizer who has a notion that [Karl] Marx[7] is not enough because he is godless and that our only salvation lies in a synthesis of Marxism and Spinozistic "God-intoxication,"[8] would not be able to get his articles past the Russian censorship. Fyodor was right. You are not only atheists, but you have also accepted the "atheistic faith." You have become a church, created a dogma, and established a Vatican. True, you do not burn heretics—the Catholic Church has not burned any for some centuries either—but you view the "heretic" as a character low intellectually and morally, and suspect politically. To join the Communist ranks would therefore mean to enroll myself in a "congregation," to subscribe to primitive superstitions draped in scientific veils. Perhaps my ancestors were Marranos.[9] I do not wish to be one. I still cannot understand why I must deny God in order to transform the world into "God's kingdom." I cannot understand why I must deny reason or plan in the cosmos, in order to introduce reason and plan into the social system, or why I must not believe in the independent existence of spirit, in order to free the world of capitalist unspirituality. If a materialistic viewpoint were really the first prerequisite of a social revolution, then the former French bourgeoisie (whose philosophic superstitions you have inherited) should have been the vanguard of the Communist movement.

True, the socialist movement also gropes in the same close cellar of dogmatic materialism. But socialism makes no pretenses to being a church; it does not drive its adherents to intellectual dishonesty. It is not concerned with my "heresies." It is not one of my obligations as a socialist to believe that since there is no soul, and since what we call "soul" is merely a "reflex of the brain," all psychic processes must be explained in terms of matter. As a socialist, I am not obligated to believe (as [Vladimir] Lenin[10] sought to persuade us) that [Immanuel] Kant's[11] conceptions of the *Ding-an-sich* [German for "the thing in itself"] and the "world of phenomena"[12] were merely capitalist "tricks" calculated to beguile the innocent in this ingenious fashion: if a worker believes in the absolute reality of phenomena, he perceives that the factory owner eats well—seasoned ham whereas he eats dry bread; consequently, he may become enraged and revolt. Should he become a disciple of Kant, however, he will assume that ham and bread are merely "appearances," and not true "things," so why bother to mount the barricades for unrealities, for fictions? In the socialist movement no one asks me for a declaration of faith or faithlessness. There is room in it for such "heretics" as [Hendrik] de Man,[13] who liquidated his Marxianism and rediscovered for himself what he chose to call "Christianity." There is room in it for a man like [George] Lansbury,[14] whose socialism proceeds logically from his religious conception of the world. Official Communism is the enemy of my freedom of conscience.

You see, I have begun with purely philosophical differences, and you may be inclined to reproach me for ascribing so great an importance to such differences. The issue, you may argue, is not the particular dogmas assumed by Communism, but its achievements. Romain Rolland,[15] I know, has simplified the account in this way: the Communist philosophy, like all materialism, is unfortunate, but the policies of Bolshevism[16] are a blessing for the world.[17] Is this the case?

At this point I shall have to redefine my concept of socialism. What is the goal of socialism? Forgive my further heresies. Under no circumstances can I reduce the goal of socialism to economic equality. I know three institutions where (excluding a small number of officials) economic equality exists: the monastery, the prison, and the army. Can I consider them cells of a socialist society? One can find true "communism," not the variety you have in Russia where you still have the hungry and the sated, or at any rate some hungrier and some more sated, in the far north of the American continent, among the Eskimo tribes where either all eat or all hunger. Nevertheless, we do not propose to learn socialism from monks, soldiers, prisoners, or Eskimos. Nationalization of industry, economic planning—all these fundamental reforms whose sum is economic equality—are means, not goals in themselves. Economic security and equality have significance for us because they can serve another purpose: the creation of a new spiritual status for man, a new mentality. I do not believe that security and equality can bring man happiness or absolute contentment, but they can bring him something no less important—dignity—a sense of social value and individual worth. Human dignity is the sense and goal of socialism, the only sense and the only goal for which all else is an instrument. Every man, no matter how great or small, must be viewed not as a means to an end, but as an end in himself. This is an elementary truth which is not scientifically demonstrable. Science sees no equality among men: it sees the strong and the weak, the more and the less productive, the bright and the dull—all largely biological evaluations. Darwinism may be a completely proven and consistent scientific theory, but one cannot build a social ethic, a new socialist society on the theory of "the survival of the fittest."[18] The conception of economic equality stands on a purely metaphysical, or if you will, a purely religious base. It rests on the belief that in the last analysis, "before someone's eyes," "in the eyes of God, the Father," as the evangelist would say, all men are of equal worth. Without equal worth, there can be no equal rights; without equal rights—no economic equality. (Plato[19] lacked this *a priori* knowledge of the equal worth of man, else he would not have recognized slavery in his "ideal" state.[20]) Whoever lacks this *a priori* knowledge, has no reason to be a socialist and cannot be one.

A generation may create objective means and instruments for a following generation, but there can be no greater profanation than the reduction of man to merely a "means," or primarily a means. There can be no "better" man for whom a man may be sacrificed, and there can be no "better" generation for whom the immediate generation can be surrendered. One of the greatest "sins" of the Old Testament God was his extinguishing the generation of the exodus from Egypt in the desert, so that a better generation might enter the Promised Land. One of the greatest sins of the Communist godlessness is its viewing millions of human beings as "objects" and its transformation of an entire generation merely into a means for a future generation.

Is this a groundless accusation? Then what is the sense of dictatorship—that very dictatorship which is first called the dictatorship of the peasantry and proletariat, then merely of the proletariat, then of the party, then of a wing of the party, till it finally becomes the dictatorship of one man? I know all the arguments. The dictatorship is temporary, the political slavery that you have introduced is a sad necessity. These will disappear in the future, when the final goal of socialism will have been realized. But how can one transform a man into something worthless in order to endow him with worth? How can we introduce slavery for the sake of freedom, an epidemic in the interests of sanitation?

From this distance, it is hard for me to judge your economic achievements. I assume that all that I read in your press—I still read the Soviet publications—

is correct. You have collectivized agriculture, built up industry, and electrified the country. These are great achievements even though many such have been attained in other countries without dictatorship, without terror, without millions of human sacrifices, and without the degradation of an entire people to a state of subjection. When I tell ordinary Americans that you have liquidated illiteracy, they laugh. Capitalists have managed to do that in America, they say, perhaps to promote their own interests. Danes have told me of their huge peasant cooperatives[21] (which resemble your collectives in many respects), introduced without whips. Swedes have told me of their electrification projects[22]—the finest in the world—built without bloodshed. I know, of course, that in Russia all this came about with infinitely more difficulty. I would now congratulate you heartily upon your success, if I did not know how costly it has been, if I did not know what a price millions of men have paid for it. Without human dignity, without elementary freedom, what is all this worth? Of what value are these achievements, if the individual is degraded, if he is surrounded by spies, if he is perpetually terrified? For almost twenty years you have been conducting a system of physical and moral terror for the sake of human happiness; you have been employing the unholy to achieve the holy. Is it so hard to understand that darkness is not the road to light, that dictatorship and paternalism are not the paths to freedom and independence, that terror is no express train to the golden age?

Ends and means in politics are analogous to form and content in art. Form in art is not merely technique; means in politics are not merely instruments. The content must be felt in the form. The means must contain the basic elements of the end. When this minimal harmony between ends and means is lacking, we get the stake at which the holy inquisition burns unbelievers to save their souls.[23] I cannot subscribe to [Sergei] Niechaev's[24] famous slogan: "Full speed ahead, right through the mud."[25]

That is why I began with your philosophy. Your philosophy contains a rationalization of your behavior, your politics, your disbelief in the true worth of the individual, of every individual. You have changed human beings into material for the building of a socialist Pithom and Rameses.[26] But a socialist pharaoh is still a pharaoh, and his injuries cut deeper than those of the ancient Egyptian tyrants.

I know that the collapse of the Soviet regime at present would be a catastrophe, that on the ruins of the Soviet world no free democratic society would arise but a fascism possibly more zoological than Hitlerism. I hope that in time there will be changes for the better in your regime, but I would not repeat in other countries what you have endured for almost two decades, and what I endured during the three bloody years of [Russian] civil war. There is no end for which I would pay such a price. The slaughter of thousands, no matter how politically inactive, in order to terrorize the population; the instincts of hate and enmity kindled in millions of disturbed souls, whose pain and hurt might have been sublimated in a welling up of social and ethical energy; the creation of privileges for some and a status without rights or protection for others; the widespread use of capital punishment for "pedagogic" reasons—I do not care to reach socialism by such a road. When I speak in this fashion to Americans of Communist leanings they do not hesitate to tell me that I exaggerate or that I lie. (What can be expected of a political émigré?) Their ignorance of the history and methods of the Russian Revolution is indescribable. But they are sufficiently naive and sentimental to believe that America or other countries can follow the Moscow way of revolution without going through a period of economic ruin, savagery, and terror. They visualize the social revolution as a kind of dramatic final battle from which the proletariat will emerge victorious, after which it will proceed to celebrate the triumph by offering a choral rendition of [Friedrich von] Schiller's[27] "Ode to [Joy]":[28]

Auszgesoehnt die ganze Welt.
Unsern Erbfeind sei verziehen,
Unser Schuldbuch sei vernichtet,
Auszgesoehnt die ganze Welt.[29]

A year ago, [Leon] Trotsky[30] sought to persuade the American Philistines that, in case of a revolution, America would not have to endure the agony of body and spirit that Russia had experienced. America, he claimed, was economically and technologically better prepared for socialism than Russia of twenty years ago. Here the transition will be easier. But on what can one base such a belief? Is not the opposite true? Would not a revolution in an economically progressive country encounter a better organized resistance? In Russia you had to deal with a decayed aristocracy, with a middle class that never had influence on the political life of the country, with a downtrodden fatalistic peasantry, and with an army disorganized by severe defeats. Such a combination of circumstances does not recur often. I should like to quote Harold Laski,[31] a warm friend of the Soviet Union, who received a hearty reception in Moscow last year. This is what he writes in his *Democracy in Crisis* [1933]: "It is more than likely, I myself believe, that the first consequences of revolution, both in Great Britain and America, would be in fact a dictatorship of the middle class in kind, though not in form, akin to that of the new Italy. Proletarian dictatorship, as in Russia, is helped, rather than retarded, where it can be built upon the ruins of an autocracy. Lenin's victory was immensely aided by the fact that he did not have to cope with a large middle class habituated to domination and privilege, and that masses whose support he won both lacked a clear lead from his opponents and had been schooled by centuries of experience into a temper which made it natural for them to pass from one dictatorship to another. No Western democracy has these circumstances, upon which it may legitimately count."[32]

I believe that social revolutions in the western countries would prove more appalling than anything we have known. Even in the event of success, a victorious revolution is victorious in a military rather than a social sense. [Ralph] Norman Angell[33] wrote a few months ago: "It may be possible to get very simple things done by compulsion: a galley oar pulled, but not a medical operation performed. In the latter case, threats are likely to be less effective than bargain, agreement, persuasion, fees."[34]

I want to stress my conviction that nothing can be achieved by means of force and terror. Revolution must go along the way of evolution, of compromise, opportunism, concession, retreat, and of periods of stagnation. Does not the Soviet experiment itself bear out the truth of my contention?

Do you remember the summer of 1918 when [Yuri] Larin[35] worked out a scheme (accepted by Lenin) according to which Russia would be so socialized that by 1919 it would be possible to dispense with money as a medium of exchange? Instead of one year, eighteen years have passed and I know that your economists are seriously concerned with stabilizing the currency, rather than abolishing money.

In the year that the civil war ended, when imperialist Europe gave up military intervention, when it seemed possible that the building of socialism could begin, Lenin introduced the [New Economic Policy (NEP)][36] partially restoring capitalism. [Nikolai] Bukharin[37] began to hymn the peasant desire "to get rich." Later, [Joseph] Stalin[38] suddenly decided that the restoration of capitalism had gone too far. The NEP was liquidated; a new wave of terror broke over the vast country; several million peasants were allowed to perish; the five-year plan[39] was enforced; the villages were collectivized, socialism was being built—built but still not completed. The first man now to mock economic equality is Stalin. He views it as a petty bourgeois, almost counter-revolutionary, notion of those "sick with leftism"—to use Lenin's phrase.[40] You have introduced a system of premiums in industry, Stakhanovism[41] in the mines, seventeen scales of wages, capitalist bookkeeping in the *kolkhoz*,[42] and partial private ownership in your collectivized agriculture. You still have class distinctions in consumption, some having very much, and some very little indeed. Nor would any of you venture to set a date as to when the economic inequality of Soviet neocapitalism will end. This is no reflection on your capacities. I do not mean that someone else would have done better. I only want you to understand that even a victorious revolution cannot dispense with compromise. The social organism must be healed. But amputation is not necessarily the cure. A slow convalescence is preferable to remedies which in themselves create a new disease. You yourselves, despite your theoretical antagonism to compromise, have been obliged to resort to it for considerations of economic development. Other considerations equally weighty if more imponderable are as imperative for me.

Therefore I still remain the same pacifist that I have always been—a pacifist in international relations, a pacifist in interclass relations. I consider revolution little nobler than war. Revolution is war, a zoological rather than a human method. I still cannot understand why it is a sin for a German soldier to kill a French soldier on the battlefront, but a virtue for a German to kill a German, or a Frenchman another Frenchman, in periods of civil war, terror, or dictatorship. I still believe that the socialist movement can pursue a militant policy of peace and reconstruction, and that such a policy will achieve our end.

If you will answer, as is the fashion, that these are the sentimental considerations of feeble liberals, I will cite your own bible, Karl Marx: "We do not assert that the way to this goal [seizure of political power by the working class] is the same everywhere. We know that the institutions, the manners and the customs of the various countries must be considered, and we do not deny that there are countries like England and America, and, if I understood your arrangements better, I might even add Holland, where the worker may attain his object by peaceful means."[43] These are the words of Marx at the Hague Congress in 1872.[44]

I am certain that Russia could have followed a clearer, and therefore more direct, road to socialism. Even if you are sure that in Russia there could have been no path other than that taken by the Bolshevik revolution, I believe with Marx that in other countries ways flowing more naturally from socialism itself will be found. You must not demand that all of us view Moscow as a kind of socialist Mecca.

I know that I have not expressed my thoughts systematically, and perhaps I have emphasized certain aspects unduly. But you understand the general trend of my thought. When you write to me, please do not answer me with quotations from [Georgi] Dimitrov;[45] do not tell me about your new tactics in connection with the united front. I know that for the present you have changed your tune. The word "revolution" as a slogan has suddenly become taboo. You have suddenly become enthusiastic advocates of democracy, of parliamentary institutions, of reform through constitutional changes and developments. You seem to be more mildly disposed to that entire "social-fascist" baggage against which you directed your sharpest thrusts and because of which you split the labor movement throughout the whole world. You no longer deride all the principles of social democracy which, according to your contention, raised the demon of fascism in Europe.

On my table, I have a book *What Is Communism?* [1936][46] written by Earl Browder, secretary of the American Communist Party.[47] A year ago you would have expelled him from the party because of his bourgeois democratic tone and his Menshevist conceptions.

Please be as upright with me as I have been with you. Either your new direction is merely a tactical move dictated by present urgencies, or else it is a fundamental change in your approach to the problem. If it is merely a tactic dictated by necessity, you will return to the old fashion when the situation changes. If, however, there has been a genuine change of heart, if your viewpoint has undergone a fundamental alteration, then come out into the open with a clear statement. Say that you have erred. Say that you renounce your doctrines about armed uprisings in democratic countries; say that you have lost faith in dictatorship even though that be the dictatorship of the proletariat; state plainly that you will return to free democratic socialism. But should you do this, what will remain of your Communism, of your special dedication, of your difference from the socialist movement?

10

Open Letter to the Third International

(1936)

In the 1920s and 1930s, many Western socialists viewed the Soviet Union and the Third International, the international Marxist association established in 1919 by the Bolshevik leader Vladimir Lenin, as harbingers of a new utopian future for humanity. At the same time, for Jewish socialists the Third International's attitude to Jewish political interests and cultural strivings, which vacillated between indifference and contempt, was highly problematic. Nonetheless, Jewish socialist groups in Europe, Palestine, and the Americas—buffeted by rising European antisemitism, emerging Polish, Italian, and German fascism, and the onset of the Great Depression in the United States, which seemed to herald the end of capitalism—looked to Mother Russia as a beacon of hope. Inspired by the idealistic Marxist vision of creating a new egalitarian society, they thought of themselves as partners in an unfolding worldwide revolution, and they found ways to rationalize their marginalization by the Soviet regime and the Third International. As the gap between Communism and Jewish socialism widened, a vigorous debate ensued in socialist Zionist circles concerning the Labor Zionist movement's relationship to the Third International. In the early 1920s, several Palestine labor leaders, notably Berl Katznelson, broke with the movement's prevailing worshipful attitude to revolutionary Russia and publicly disavowed the Bolshevik agenda and, soon thereafter, the Stalin regime. Outside of the Yishuv, Hayim Greenberg was likewise an outspoken critic—on moral and political grounds—of Bolshevism and the Soviet-dominated Third International. In this essay, written in the wake of Arab rioting in Palestine and the Moscow purge trials (see headnote to the preceding essay), Greenberg addresses the Third International's ideological hostility to Zionism, the issue of Arab rights in Palestine, and the future of Arab-Jewish relations.

I believe that this is the first time that a man of my political persuasion is addressing you directly in an open letter.[1] I know that I have no grounds for optimism in regard to the probable effect of my communication on your views and position. Nevertheless I cannot free myself from the faith which has been mine all my life that no outcry in the universe is wholly lost, that though apparently unheeded it registers somewhere, somehow. And I write to you now in this belief that no protest against injustice is ever senseless.

I shall deal with the grave accusation that thousands, perhaps millions, of Jews have made against you because of your attitude toward the drama, one act of which is now unfolding in Palestine. I have received no mandate from these masses but I am certain that I express a widespread sense of pain and astonishment.

What is the accusation?

No one can accuse you of enmity or indifference toward the national liberation movements of our time. You have never suffered from the superstition of "cosmopolitanism,"[2] and you have more than once stated your conviction that the satisfaction of legitimate national aspirations is the prerequisite of a true internationalism. You oppose the crushing of any national group by stronger one, even though the group in question be without a "history" in the accepted sense, or even the rudiments of a national culture. Tchukches[3] and Mordvins,[4] people whose names are unknown in the Western hemisphere save to students, have been accorded the status of recognized nations by Soviet Russia. I do not believe that [Joseph] Stalin's[5] formula—"socialist in content and national in form"[6] bears logical dissection because form and content are as indissoluble in national culture as they are in painting or music. However, an unsuccessful formula may sometimes enable a successful pursuit of a wise policy.

Speaking more specifically of the Jewish question, no one can accuse you of antisemitism. It would be better perhaps if you did not occasionally betray the bad taste of boasting that under the Soviet regime no pogroms occur and that antisemitism is energetically fought. The fact that an antisemitic government cannot be classed among civilized nations does not mean that a "philo-Semitic" one should claim an order of special merit. Nevertheless, leaving aside fine points of taste, no one can charge you either with that peculiar form of ultra-friendliness which holds that the Jews are fine fellows and should therefore lose their identity in a general amalgam. The Soviet regime has limitations which I do not propose to discuss now, but within the confines of the measure of liberty possible in Russia, Jews have received the maximum opportunities for national existence and national development. You have gone even further. You are giving a symbolic demonstration of the fact that the Jews are a nation and have a right to national existence by your attempted creation of a Jewish republic in Birobidzhan.[7] By this alone you have subscribed to our old Zionist contention that the *national* problems of Jews cannot be solved without a Jewish territory. Obviously you recognize the right of the Jewish people to a territorial center. But you have announced more than once (through President [Mikhail] Kalinin[8] and the declarations of the Komzet[9]) that the colonization of Birobidzhan must not be considered as a "new Zionism" and that the autonomous region in Birobidzhan must not be viewed as a "new Zion" for world Jewry. Through these warnings you have left unsolved the question of a more extensive territorial center, suitable for the six-sevenths of the Jewish people who live outside the Soviet Union. Russia does not propose to fling open her doors to mass immigration. As far as Birobidzhan is concerned, the Russian official press has made it clear that only small numbers of foreign Jews would be permitted to enter, chiefly in cases of a shortage of given categories of qualified workers among Soviet Jews. By this I wish to state that neither you nor the Soviet Government (I hope you will not take amiss my identification of you with the Soviet Government without further diplomatic hocus-pocus) have set up Birobidzhan as a rival to Palestine. You have not declared that a Jewish territorial center should be created not in Palestine, but in Birobidzhan; you have not said that the millions of Jews from various countries who need a national home should go to Birobidzhan rather than Palestine. Up to date you have offered to develop Jewish colonization in Birobidzhan till it can be proclaimed a Jewish republic. I do not recall off-hand how large the population of a region must be before, according to the Soviet constitution, it can receive the status of a republic. I do remember, however, that the Soviet Union contains many republics whose population is negligible: the Abkhazian republic, proclaimed in 1921, had at the time no more than 200,000 inhabitants; the Adjarian republic, proclaimed in the same year, had no more than 131,000; the Nakhichevan republic, established in 1923, had a population of only 104,000.[10] I am pointing out that you can fulfill your promise to create a Jewish republic merely by bringing a trifling number of the sixteen million Jews in the world into Birobidzhan. This of course would still leave the Jewish territorial problem unsolved. Millions of Jews have directly or indirectly shown their Zionist will by their participation in various Palestinian activities. However, instead of welcoming the revival of creative energy in an ancient, martyred people, you are doing all in your power, morally and politically, to discredit and injure the liberation movement of the Jewish people. Far though you be from antisemitism, you actually serve an antisemitic purpose by hindering the reconstruction of our people.

I know how you answer accusations of this kind: the national emancipation of one people must not be achieved at the expense of another people. Zionism, you claim, builds Jewish weal on Arab woe. Were that really so, were Zionism to be achieved through the destruction and exploitation of the Arabs, not only every communist and socialist, but every decent man would be obliged to fight it as an unforgivable form of national egoism. But the time has come for you to revise your conception of Zionism as well as to analyze critically some of the deductions you have drawn from principles correct in themselves.

One people may exploit another economically, culturally, and politically. The most vicious form of exploitation is the economic because both the cultural and political status of a people depend in a large measure on its economic condition. The first question in our controversy therefore is whether the Arabs of Palestine are being exploited economically by the Jewish settlers and the Zionist movement.

I have good reason to be weary of this particular theme. One grows tired of endlessly answering a libel which some spread through malice and others believe through ignorance and intellectual apathy. Possibly you will never free yourselves of your misconception of the economic role of the Jew in Palestine until you send a delegation (consisting not of party politicians but of experts in economics, your experienced *sovnarkhoz*[11] [Russian for "supreme economic council"] men) to study the situation on the spot. I propose this plan in all seriousness, and I should like to take the liberty of making two concrete suggestions; first, acquaint yourselves with the data of the Mandates Commission of the League of Nations[12] in regard to the mythological "displaced Arabs" (if you consider the available information at Geneva insufficient, Russia's representative at the League of Nations will easily be able to secure a new investigation); secondly; send a delegation to Palestine. I have reason to believe that both the government and the Jewish Agency [for Palestine][13] would assist the delegation in its investigation, though I cannot guarantee the attitude of the Arab leaders toward a Bolshevist Commission despite your pro-Arab policies. In the meantime, I think it will be enough for me to mention a few of the grosser fictions in the legend of the Jew's economic exploitation of the Arab.

First of all, let me remind you that the overwhelming majority of the Jewish population of Palestine consists of laboring elements. Zionism liberates the modern Jew from the curse which has pursued him for centuries in the diaspora—the curse of unproductive occupations. You know what difficulties the Soviets encountered because of the peculiar, one-sided economic life of the Russian Jew, a life ill suited to a workers' society. In most European countries with a large Jewish population the Jews have a very limited scope of functions in the economic structure of the country. In Poland, for instance, 65 percent of all the tradesmen are Jews; in Lithuania, 77 percent; in Hungary where Jews are only 5 percent of the population, they form 50 percent of the merchants. This situation is the inevitable result of the restrictions and quotas placed on Jews in practically every form of employment and profession. Outside the Soviet-Russia where, thanks to the revolution, Jew have become economically restratified, Palestine is the only place where, *due to an inner revolution,* Jews are developing without those social-economic anomalies to which history has doomed them. The Jewish population of Palestine is proportionately larger than that of any other country, but only 33 percent of the traders are Jews, whereas the majority of the Jewish population is engaged in agriculture, manual labor, industry, and the professions. Jewish immigration of the last fifteen years consists primarily of workers; it has none of the earmarks characteristics of imperialist invasion of colonial lords. The occupational distribution of the Jewish settlers in itself makes the charge of exploitation absurd. Furthermore, if one compares conditions in Palestine with those in Syria, one realizes what the economic influence of Jewish immigration has been. Thanks to the Histadrut, the eight-hour day has been introduced into numerous enterprises in Palestine, whereas in Syria the twelve-hour day is still in force. If one compares conditions in industries that exist in both neighboring countries, one is startled by the difference in wages. In the Syrian shoe industry the unskilled workers gets 50 to 90 mils[14] and the skilled worker from 100 to 150 mils per day, whereas in Palestine the unskilled worker gets 100 to 150 mils and the skilled worker 300 to 400 mils per day. In the silk industry a Syrian worker gets 60 to 80 mils per day, a Palestinian 400 to 500 mils. In the macaroni factories a Syrian male worker gets 80 to 100 mils a day and a woman as little as 30 to 40 mils, whereas in Palestine men get 300 mils per day and women 200 to 250 mils. These figures, only a small part of similar statistical data which I would furnish for you, speak for themselves; such victories for the working class would be impossible if Jews came to Palestine as exploiters, or if Jewish workers strove to "capture" work from the Arab or to "underlive" him. It is true that the average Jew in Palestine lives better than the average Arab, but is a higher degree of economic well-being always a sign of exploitation? You have now in Soviet Russia some workers barely able to get necessities, while others ride around in their own automobiles. Are you prepared to admit that one group of workers exploits another in the socialist fatherland? Your explanation is that one group is more capable, more energetic, and more productive than the other. It is not our fault that a Jewish hen lays an average of 150 eggs, annually, whereas an Arab one lays no more than 80; nor are we to blame because a Jewish cow gives an average of 4000 liters of milk annually, while an Arab cow produces not more than 700.[15] The Jewish pioneers responsible for these economic "crimes" deserve awards rather than abuse. Jonathan Swift[16] must have had such pioneers in mind when he wrote: "Whoever could make two ears of corn or two blades of grass grow upon a spot where only one grew before, would deserve better of mankind and do more essential service to his country than the whole race of politicians put together."[17]

Since the Jews do not keep their knowledge secret—an esoteric mystery to be shared with none—Arab farmers are gradually learning modern methods. Judging from their present rate of adaptation they may attain a high degree of economic development within our generation.

The growth of a population is a significant index to economic conditions. Before the war there were not more than 600,000 Arabs in Palestine. The number remained static for the fifty years preceding the World War. Today, there are about 900,000 Arabs. This means that the Arab population increased by 50 percent in the very years of intensive Jewish immigration. True, the addition of 300,000 was not due solely to the rate of national increase (excess of births over deaths) but also to Arab immigration from adjacent countries, but the very fact that Arab immigration into Palestine has greatly increased—it would perhaps be truer to say has begun—demonstrates the economic value of Zionist colonization in the country in general and the Arabs in particular. It is no accident that in the very midst of the present tragic occurrences in Palestine[18] the Grand Mufti's party[19] has come out for a mass immigration of Arabs from other Arab countries which are much larger in circumference and much more thinly populated. This approval is being made at a time when the cry is raised that Jewish immigration be stopped, a cry in which your press joins presumably on the grounds that Palestine is "over-populated." It is a little hard to reconcile these circumstances. Apparently "over-population" is a relative term depending on who is to do the populating. In antiquity nearly five million people lived in Palestine on both sides of the Jordan [River].[20] Today there is still room for millions of new immigrants. The demand to stop Jewish immigration and prohibit the sale of land to Jews (a "reform" reminiscent of the policy of the Russian tsars) is motivated not by economic, but by purely political considerations.

I shall be able to pass quickly to the political phase of the question, because, fortunately, no one charges us with cultural exploitation. No one dares to accuse Zionism of degrading the cultural standard of the Arab population. Everyone recognizes that the immigration of elements with a higher cultural level stimulates the original creative energy of the Arab. No Arab will claim that there were better Arab schools, or a more highly developed Arab press before the "Zionist invasion." Our bitterest enemy will not accuse us of attempting to Hebraize the Arabs, or of interfering in any way with their cultural development. On the contrary, if there is any academic institution seriously devoted to the study of Arab history and philology, it is the Hebrew University of Jerusalem, which receives assistance neither from the Arabs, nor from the government, but is open to Arabs, Christians, and foreigners from all lands. I shall dwell no longer on the question of cultural exploitation because in this respect, at least, no one has yet accused us of "poisoning the wells."

The only charge which has some shadow of justification—true, of a purely outward and superficial character—is the political one. Honest Arab leaders are prepared to admit that Zionism constitutes no cultural or economic danger for the Arabs—Communists in Moscow and Catholics in the Vatican talk more about economic exploitation than do the Arabs in Palestine. However, they claim that we represent a serious political menace, because unless Jewish immigration is stopped we will soon become a majority in the country and the land will lose its "Arab" character. One must agree that there is considerable truth in this argument. We are convinced that Palestine, if properly developed through intensive agriculture and industry, has room for many more millions, and that these millions, unless artificially checked, will be Jews. No other people has the devotion or the will for the reconstruction of the country to make mass immigration possible. This means that in the course of time the Jews will become a majority, even though the number of Arabs will not decrease, but will increase much more rapidly than before Zionism. Nationalist Arabs and international communists believe that this means "seizing a country" from its rightful owners, that this is imperialism.

Yet this charge of Zionist imperialism, which you advance so often, is in its essence a discrimination against Jews. You do not realize how antisemitic it is objectively, though not subjectively or consciously. Assuming the status of a national minority to be less than ideal, you are prepared to let the Jews be a minority in every country, but the Arabs not in a single land. Remember that you yourselves do not consider the Palestinian Arabs as a separate national entity; you view them as a part of a larger nation. Therefore your proclamations demand the union of all Arab countries into a larger national federation.[21] You know very well that the Arab nation branches out over a large area. Even if we exclude the Arab-speaking lands of north Africa—Syria, Mesopotamia, and Saudi Arabia still occupy approximately 615,000 square miles (that is somewhat more than France, Germany, Italy, Belgium, Czechoslovakia, Denmark, and Holland put together). Palestine, on the other hand, together with Transjordania,[22] is only 26,000 square miles in area—less than 1/23 of all the land under Arab rule. You know the geographical fact as well as we do, but the deductions that you make resemble Hottentot[23] rather than socialist morality; your conclusion seems to be that 22/23 are not enough for 10 to 12 million Arabs, but 1/23 is too much for 16 million Jews, and, finally, that Arabs must not be a minority anywhere, the Jews everywhere.

I don't know what will happen in the distant future. Possibly the dream of [the] central European reformer [Johann Kaspar] Bluntschli[24] will come true, and the world's population will be so regrouped that there will no longer be national minorities.[25] For the present, national minorities cannot be avoided. Millions of Russians live outside of Russia—they live in the Ukraine, in White Russia, in Turkestan, and outside the Soviet Union as national minorities. Millions of Germans live in Czechoslovakia, in Hungary, in Romania, in Russia, and in the United States. Millions of Italians, Magyars, and other peoples have been incorporated as minorities in larger national organisms. But when the Arabs are involved you consider it an imperialistic crime to place a small number of them in a position of a national minority in a comparatively small area of land—even though this should be done in the interests of the most completely homeless and landless people in the world. Unless my information is wrong, the recently deceased Henri Barbusse[26] put the same question to you in a letter which he sent you in the last months of his illness. His death freed you from the necessity of answering his charge that your attitude toward Zionism was the contrary of communist principles and of true internationalism, that it was motivated by a dubious political opportunism, rather than by socialist ideology. But has not the time come for you to give yourselves a conscientious answer?

And may I ask, whether within the Soviet Union you have always practiced the theory which you wish to apply to Arab-Jewish relations? Because of weighty political considerations which I need not discuss now, I know that in 1924 you founded a Moldavian Republic in south Ukraine with Balta as [its] capital. The Moldavians happen to be a minority in that region, and the Ukrainians a majority. Where was your adherence to the principle of majorities in this case, and why did you give preference to the minority? Was it not because Ukrainian nationalism could find free scope in a comparatively large territory, while Moldavian nationalism had only this small corner of Ukrainia in which to express itself? May I point out still another fact? Several years before the Birobidzhan project hove into view, you planned to transform Crimea into a Soviet Jewish territory.[27] (Our Jewish communists in America[28] once nurtured the same tender patriotism for Crimea that they now do for Birobidzhan.) The Soviet government even negotiated with representatives of the American Jewish bourgeoisie in regard to financing the Crimean project.[29] Was Crimea uninhabited at the time? Did not a non-Jewish majority of several hundred thousand live there? Were not the Tartars[30] the most considerable national group in that region? In other words, did not Crimea have its Arabs? Nevertheless President Kalinin permitted himself the optimistic prophecy that should Jewish colonization develop at a sufficiently rapid tempo, the time would come when the Sea of Azov[31] would be called the "Jewish Sea."[32]

There even appeared Russian historians who unearthed the fact that blooming Jewish communities had existed in Crimea in ancient times. They were delighted to remember that in the early centuries of the Christian Era, Hellenized Jews had come together with Greeks on the shores of the Black Sea and the Sea of Azov, and that as late as the eighth century, the city of Phanagoria on the peninsula of Taman[33] was practically a Jewish city. These excursions into history were to demonstrate the Jewish "historic right" to the region of Crimea.[34] I do not quite understand why the Soviet government gave up the Crimea project so quickly. However, its place was eventually taken by Birobidzhan. Yet Birobidzhan, after a number of years of Jewish colonization, still has its non-Jewish majority. Have you ever inquired whether this majority is willing to become a minority? Do you hold a referendum in regard to the right of the Jews to colonize there? Did the Jews receive an invitation from the non-Jews of Birobidzhan?

I ask these questions because I wish you to consider a geographic fact with which we Jews must reckon and which you cannot possibly ignore. On the whole globe there is no corner which is wholly uninhabited, which has not its "majority," its "Arabs." Wherever Jews may now go to build a national center, no matter how large or uncultivated the land may be, they will always find inhabitants with no enthusiasm for being transformed into a minority. Even Greenland has a population of 16,000 with "historic rights." Should a hundred Jewish immigrants arrive there with the intention of bringing over thousands of others—assuming that the absorptive capacity of the country permitted—the Greenlanders would probably soon raise the cry of "Zionist imperialist invasion." True, there is a difference between the population in Birobidzhan, or Greenland, and the Arabs. Arabs are a *historic* people, whereas the others are not. But I should not care to hear such an answer from you, because that would mean that you give premiums for *historicity* and penalties for *non-historicity,* that you make distinctions between higher races whose rights must be respected and lower races which may be injured. No, such an explanation would be motivated not by ethics, but by convenience. It is not more just, but simply easier to exploit an "unhistoric people." It is the exploiters' line of least resistance.

The situation is such that you can approach the Jewish national problem in only one of two ways. You can tell us—if you have the temerity: "You have come too late. The world has already been parceled out. Every people has its place and every place its people. Do what you will—go under, commit national suicide, jump into the sea—there is no share for you."

If you do not say this, if you dare not say it, if you recognize our right to a national life and the importance of a territorial center for the normalization of our existence, then you must come to another conclusion. You must admit that a people which owns a number of large territories and does not cultivate all of the soil at its disposal is duty-bound to permit Jewish national colonization even though that should mean a Jewish majority. You must realize that the principle of national equality demands that Jews be not hindered in their attempt to reconstruct a national center in a land which represents 1/23 of the total area which Arabs hold, as national territory. I need not point out to you which of these two conclusions is truer to the spirit of socialism and internationalism. Until you change your fundamentally false attitude toward Zionism, I shall charge you with supporting a narrow, greedy Arab nationalism at the expense of the most elementary right of the Jewish people.

I have grave and difficult differences with communism. But no matter how deep the division between us—in regard to your means, not to your goal—I should not want the objective historian of the future to write: "Jews finally rebuilt their national center in Palestine, despite the enmity of Arab chauvinists, despite the propaganda of [Adolf] Hitler[35] and Italian fascism, despite the duplicity of British imperialism and the intrigues of the Vatican, and despite the criminal heedlessness with which the Communist International supported these reactionary forces."

[Karl] Marx[36] has a great utterance familiar to everyone: "From each according to his means, to each according to his need."[37] These words represent the new ethical concept which socialism offers the world. The principle guides your reorganization of economic order, and your view of the relations between individuals. It is no less valid for determining the rights of nations. You, as socialists, should be the last to claim that formal or physical possession whether for use or abuse constitutes a moral title of ownership. You do not recognize the rights of an idle heiress to squander a fortune which she has not earned. Such social outrage seems to you the dark remnant of a barbaric economic order. Similarly, no nation has the right to place "no trespassing" signs around lands which it does not use, around soil which goes to waste. The draining of a marsh by a Jewish pioneer makes more room for Arabs as well as Jews. There is no question of dispossessing the Palestinian Arab. His numbers will continue to grow, as they have grown, thanks to the economic enlargement of the country resulting from Jewish colonization. Nor are his interests in any way injured by the still greater increase of the Jewish population in accordance with the absorptive capacity of the country. Or do you really believe that the perpetuation of barren Arab marsh and desert represents a higher social equity than the transformation of this waste into fields cultivated by Arabs and Jews according to their means, and used according to their needs?

11

An Answer to Gandhi

(1939)

Hayim Greenberg admired the Indian leader and pacifist Mohandas K. Gandhi, and he emphatically supported the Indian national liberation movement known as "Young India." Originally a pacifist, Greenberg was particularly drawn to Gandhi's concepts of satyagraha *(soul force) and* ahimsa *(nonviolence). Like Martin Buber, Judah L. Magnes, and other prominent Jewish leaders, however, Greenberg was also deeply troubled by Gandhi's opposition to Zionism and dismissal of the Jewish claim to autonomy in British-controlled Palestine. In 1921, referring to the Balfour Declaration and the terms of the Versailles Treaty, Gandhi asserted that "no canon . . . of ethics or war can possibly justify the gift by the Allies of Palestine to Jews." Gandhi's opposition to Zionism remained steadfast even after the rise of the Nazi regime and the persecution of the Jews in central Europe. "Why should [the Jews] not, like other peoples of the earth," he argued in 1938, "make that country their home where they are born and where they earn their livelihood? Palestine belongs to the Arabs in the same sense that England belongs to the English or France to the French. It is wrong and inhuman to impose the Jews on the Arabs." When in 1939 Gandhi further argued that "the Jews are not angels" and ought to practice nonviolence in Nazi Germany, Greenberg, unable to abide the Indian leader's readiness to sacrifice human life in the name of pacifist idealism, penned the following essay.*

I

In [Mohandas K. Gandhi's][1] article concerning the Jewish question,[2] a statement for which certain elements in Jewry have long waited with impatience, the spiritual leader of "Young India"[3] directs against us two important accusations. He blames us for not exhibiting the heroism of militant pacifism in those lands where Jews are persecuted, and especially in Germany. On the other hand, he accuses us of following an aggressively nationalist—almost imperialist—policy in Palestine and of a desire to deprive the Arabs of their fatherland.[4]

[Mohandas K.] Gandhi's first accusation is quite natural and is in complete harmony with his entire world outlook. His temperament does not tolerate passivity and his ethical-religious convictions dictate to him the duty of heroic and active resistance according to the Indian principle of *satyagraha* [Gujarati phrase meaning "soul force"].[5]

The motivating idea of *satyagraha* is not, as some claim, a practical strategy which Gandhi "made to order" to meet the concrete demands of the Indian situation. Long ago he advocated it as a universal ideal which could be applied by all the oppressed and injured everywhere and independently of the specific historical situation. Personally, I feel that the individual and the group struggles according to the plan of *satyagraha*—aside from its moral-religious implications—have proved to be practical and effective. The truth of the *satyagraha* teaching—which in another form has been expressed by Jesus and other Jewish teachers many generations ago—is in my eyes as self-evident as a mathematical axiom. But I must admit to myself that in order to apply Gandhi's method of struggle, it is necessary to accept it not only on a purely intellectual plane; it is also imperative that it be assimilated emotionally, that it should be believed in with all the force of one's being. Such faith the Jews of Germany do not possess. Faith in the principle of *satyagraha* is a matter of special predisposition which, for numerous reasons, the German Jews have not developed. The civilization in which German Jews have lived for so many generations, and to the creation of which they have so energetically and ably contributed, has not prepared them for the "pathos" of *satyagraha*. As a result, they are now defenseless. The accepted defense methods of the European-American world cannot be applied by the German Jews. They cannot resort to passive resistance because they lack the heroism, the faith, and the specific imaginative powers which alone can stimulate such heroism. When Gandhi accuses German Jews of lacking that mentality which, in his estimation, is the only truly heroic mentality, I am ready to concur with him, but with one reservation which he also must accept—that this accusation should also be leveled against the millions of non-Jewish Germans who wear the yoke of the Hitler regime with impotent hatred and show no more affinity for *satyagraha* methods than do the Jews; against the millions of Italians who for years have breathed the contaminated air of their own tyranny; against the tens of millions Russians who have exhausted their strength in civil war and do not find their way to the Gandhi method of resisting the Red despotism; against hundreds of millions of Chinese who by their military resistance aid the Japanese aggressors to ravage their country instead of following the path of non-cooperation.

It is true that one may demand—as Gandhi does—that Jews, and particularly the Jews of Germany, should be "pioneers" of new forms of social struggle in the Western world and should be the first to embrace the practice of *satyagraha*. Gandhi wishes that we should set an example to the non-Jewish Germans, that we should point the way to a spiritual crusade against their wicked government. He may have a sound reason for believing that the incomparable suffering and degradation to which German Jews are subjected "compels" them to act more heroically and to be more "adventurous" spiritually than their neighbors. I do not question the idea implicit in Gandhi's demand, that there is a mutual relationship between the intensity of suffering and the intensity of the moral reaction to suffering. But there is no reason to assume that when suffering and insults transgress certain bounds it is quite natural that the reaction should be a feeling of futility and despair instead of that heroism which Gandhi suggests. This is especially true when the group concerned is historically and psychologically not prepared for such a catastrophe and therefore looks upon it as a sudden and unexpected occurrence. The prophet of "Young India" has in this instance exhibited an unusual lack of psychological understanding.

Gandhi should have also understood that it is far less simple to preach *satyagraha* to German Jews than it is to Indian masses, even to the lowest caste of "untouchables."[6] We all know the evils of English rule and administration in India. But one should be wary of drawing comparisons between the situation of the Indian masses today, or even twenty years ago, and the position of the German Jews today. Throughout the years that the Indian National Congress[7] conducted its struggles for emancipation, there existed in India tens of *legal* newspapers and journals which voiced the needs and the political demands of the people. The British government never questioned the right of the oppressed population to live, to work, and to earn their bread; it did not even question their right to hold responsible government positions. The most brutal British administration bore in mind that it had to deal with 350 million people living compactly in one area. Together with Gandhi it understood that, to use his (Gandhi's) own words, "If we Indians could only spit in unison, we would form a puddle big enough to drown 300,000 Englishmen"[8]—the entire number of Englishmen that live in India and govern it. When *satyagraha* is practiced by an organized group that is backed by such an immense population (even if these people wanted to flee the country and had where to go, England is interested that they should remain in the land—the exact opposite of the attitude of the Nazi regime toward the Jews) it is a potential force of which the scattered half million German Jews cannot even dream. And may I add something else? I will use the words of one of Gandhi's disciples and colleagues[9] who, just before he was sent to prison,[10] declared: "We can thank our lucky stars that we are fighting the British and not someone else, for the British have something in them to which we can appeal."[11] The same British judge[12] who sentenced Gandhi to prison found it possible and *unpunishable* to declare, after pronouncing sentence, that it was the law which sends Gandhi to prison but that he personally looks upon him as "a great patriot and a great leader"; that "even those who differed from Gandhi look upon him as a man of high ideals and of noble and even saintly life."[13] At the same time one of the most prominent British missionaries compared Gandhi's trial to the trials of Jesus and Socrates, and the English Bishop of Madras [Henry Whitehead][14] declared to the entire world: "I frankly confess, although it deeply grieves me to say it, that I see in Mr. Gandhi the patient sufferer for the cause of righteousness and mercy, a truer representative of the crucified Savior than the men who have thrown him into prison and yet call themselves by the name of Christ."[15]

Only recently I met an Englishman, an ex-army officer in India (now a member of [British] parliament)[16] who had been noble enough to refuse to carry out the command to arrest Gandhi, with the full knowledge of the punishment prescribed for such insubordination. That punishment was *not* meted out. Even during the days of General [Reginald] Dyer's[17] brutal administration in India there did not rein that bestiality and "moral anesthesia" which characterize the Germany of today. A Jewish Gandhi in Germany, should one arise, could "function" for about five minutes—until the first Gestapo agent would lead him, not to a concentration camp, but directly to the guillotine.

If Gandhi demands heroism from the Indians, he demands of the German Jews a measure of *super-heroism* unexampled in history. Gandhi's comparison between the situation of the Indians and that of the German Jews contains an element of unfairness which crept in against his will and against his intentions.

II

But if Gandhi demands that we practice super-heroism in Germany, he requests that in Palestine we should renounce the most elementary rights which every people may and should claim. When he asks why we do not "like the other peoples of the earth"[18] make our home in the land where we were born and where we earn our livelihood, he indicates that he has not pondered the unusual drama of the paradoxical Jewish history. Jews have been dispersed for many generations and it could not be an accident that after sojourning in so many lands and with so many peoples they have not become so rooted in those countries that these should cease being "stepmother lands." Gandhi should have known of the numerous attempts the Jews have made throughout the ages to transform lands of refuge into true homes, beginning with Babylonia[19] and the Hellenic city of Alexandria in Egypt.[20] The contribution of the Jews to the economic growth and the cultural blossoming of those countries is sufficient proof of this attempt to become rooted which has so frequently ended in failure. Gandhi's question rings like a veiled accusation; it sounds as if we have purposely refused to become rooted in any country but Palestine. If it should be true that we have condemned ourselves to remain eternal strangers, then such an unusual phenomenon in human history should have evoked Gandhi's wonder and he should have asked whether the Jews do not bear within themselves unrealized forces which can only manifest themselves in a Jewish territorial environment where these may come to fruition.

But Gandhi refuses to recognize our right to a distinct territorial settlement, a right which is enjoyed, almost without exception, by all the peoples of the world. Were it not so, he would see the Palestine problem in an altogether different political and moral light. For when he says that "it would be a crime against humanity to reduce the proud Arabs, so that Palestine can be restored to the Jews partly or wholly as their national home"[21] he forgets that if national *honor* is at stake (this is the burden of his statement and he knows full well that one may not repeat the discredited allegations of economic or cultural harm that Jews supposedly caused to Arabs) he should also have thought of Jewish honor. Either it is dishonorable to be a minority in a country or it is merely a question of fictitious prestige for which he can have no sympathy. If only pseudo-honor is involved, why should he be concerned lest the "proud Arabs" be deprived of the enjoyment of an inflated pride? But if real national honor is at stake, why should the Arabs enjoy it throughout the length and breadth of the Arabian peninsula, Iraq, Syria, Lebanon, Trans-Jordan, Egypt (an area almost as large as the European continent) while the Jews should be deprived of this honor even in an area which occupied about one percent of the above mentioned lands, an area to which they have historical claims and the natural right they acquired during two generations of diligent work, initiative, heroism, and suffering?

I do not claim that so-called historical rights possess absolute validity. If it is true, for instance, that Gypsies came to Europe from a certain section of India and that section is not completely settled, no intelligent being would claim that the Gypsies have a right to return to build their national home in that area. They could do so only through the expulsion of the present population. Jewish historical rights to Palestine are of an altogether different nature. The country is underpopulated and inadequately cultivated; it contains room for several times the number of people that now reside in it. For Jews Palestine is the cradle and the "laboratory" of their civilization and their spiritual bond with the country was not broken at any time during their history. For the Arabs Palestine is, in a certain sense, an "accidental" geographical unit for which they do not even have a name. To this day Palestine is only "South Syria" to the Arabs.[22]

Need anything more be added to explain Jewish rights to Palestine? In eastern Europe an anecdote is current (an anecdote the implications of which are altogether too frequently overlooked) concerning a thief whom the judge chided in the following words: "Don't you know that it is forbidden to take anything that belongs to others?" But the thief posed an intellectual dilemma before the judge. "What shall I do," he asked the judge, "since at the time of my birth everything already belonged to other people?" Absolute poverty, in a world filled with riches, confers a natural right upon those whom fate mistreated to demand their share, first of all at the expense of those who possess too much, more than they need or can use. One may not say to Jews: "The world is already divided up; some received more and others less but there is nothing left for you and no one is obliged to share with you; even though he possesses fields which he cannot or does not wish to cultivate, or factories where the machines are left to rust in inaction, simply because at one time he succeeded in obtaining these possessions by force or through trickery." Gandhi does not realize that he has erred in sanctioning the "absolute" nature of private property and its inviolability. Group ownership of territories is also a form of private ownership which should be subjected to control and regulation by a broader human or internationalist principle. Although he is not a socialist in the accepted meaning of the term, Gandhi is aware that the property relationships between individual members of society will have to be modified in some way in order to attain a minimum of justice. Earnest and logical consideration should have led him to the conclusion that the same criterion of justice—the assurance of the necessary minimum to every creature that is stamped with "the image of God"—must also be applied to entire nations, races, and tribes. Another non-socialist and non-internationalist (in the modern sense of the terms), Benjamin Franklin,[23] several generations ago admirably expressed the simple idea in a letter to Robert Morris.[24] He said: "All property except the savage's temporary cabin, his bow, his matchcoat, and other little acquisitions absolutely necessary for his subsistence, seems to me the creature of public convention. Hence, the public has the right of regulating descents, and all other conveyances of property, and even limiting the quantity and the uses of it. All property that is necessary to a man, for the conservation of the individual and the propagation of the species, is his natural right which none may justly deprive him of; but all property superfluous to such purposes is the property of the public, who, by their laws, have created it, and who may therefore, by other laws, dispose of it, whenever the welfare of the public shall demand such disposition. He that does not like civil society on these terms, let him retire and live among the savages. He can have no right to the benefits of society, who will not pay his club toward the support of it."[25]

Had Gandhi taken the trouble to consider this elementary truth in relation to present-day reality, he would also not have written in such a tone of near-disdain about the [British] mandate.[26] From a purely legalistic point of view, it may be possible to agree with him that "the mandates have no sanction but that of the last war."[27] This does not mean, however, that the basic idea of the mandates, and even the mandatory system as it has been practiced during the past twenty years, was born from the war. The idea underlying the mandate which, according to the constitution of the League of Nations,[28] should be applied in territories where the population is not ready for self-government or where local interests must be subordinated to more important considerations of an international character, is potentially of great humanitarian significance. It is a prelude to that "civil society" of which Franklin wrote in the eighteenth century; it is a way to a more rational and just collective-international control of the world's wealth. I am not unaware of the shortcomings with which the League of Nations is weighed down nor of its sad fate during recent years which also brought misfortune to all humanity.[29] But whoever observed closely the activities of the League in the administration of mandated territories—naturally excluding those areas mandated to Japan, a country which cynically mocked League control even when its representatives were still sitting at Geneva—must admit that the mandatory system is a step forward when compared with the uncontrolled colonial regimes of the past and the present. The fact that a mandatory government is responsible to the Permanent Mandates Commission,[30] in which the majority of the members represent governments possessing neither mandates nor colonial possessions, is in itself an advance in the direction of internationalism and the humanization of the world.

It is regrettable that Gandhi approached our problem without that fundamental earnestness and passionate search for truth which are so characteristic of his usual treatment of problems. He therefore missed the deeper implications of the mandates system. He therefore also failed to grasp the unequalled tragedy of Jewish existence. This is the reason why he can justify the phenomenon of five Arab states demanding in London the establishment of a sixth one on the eve of the founding of two other sovereign Arab governments in Syria and Lebanon, while at the same time sanctioning the denial of refuge to Jews in their old home.[31] This also explains his stand that Arabs must nowhere be reduced to the status of a minority while tens of millions of Russians, Poles, Czechs, Germans, Irish, and Italians live in dozens of countries as ethnic minorities and while Jews live as a persecuted minority on the entire globe.

With all my respect for the Mahatma[32] (I doubt if there is another living man who evokes within me such a moral awareness of his loftiness), I cannot help but feeling that in the present instance he has betrayed his inner nature. I cannot avoid the suspicion that so far as the Palestine problem is concerned, Gandhi allowed himself to be influenced by the anti-Zionist propaganda being conducted among fanatic pan-Islamists. His understandable and praiseworthy desire for a united front with the [Muslims][33] apparently misguided and blinded him to significant realities and deprived him of that analytical clarity which is a part of his moral being. Years ago he was, for the same reason, misguided into supporting the agitation for the reestablishment of the [formerly Ottoman] caliphate,[34] an institution that is at such variance with his general views. Gandhi was wrong then; he is also mistaken in the present instance, and the source of these mistakes seems to be the same.

I know that this is a serious accusation—at any rate a serious suspicion. But when it comes from a Jew, such an accusation does not indicate a lack of veneration. Hero worship among Jews is traditionally circumscribed. We venerate Moses, our first prophet and liberator. But we do not forget that also he was sinful—so sinful that God denied him entry into the Promised Land and his earthly remains were interred on the solitary height of Mount Nebo.[35]

12

Leon Trotsky

(1939, 1940)

5. Jewish National Workers' Alliance (JNWA/Farband) Banquet in Honor of Chaim Weizmann (c. 1942), sketched by Saul Raskin for *Der tog* (The Day). Top row, *right to left*: David Pinsky (1872–1959), major Yiddish writer and playwright; Louis Segal (1895–1964), JNWA leader; Chaim Weizmann (center), head of Jewish Agency for Palestine and president of World Zionist Organization; and Hayim Greenberg. Middle row, *right to left*: Samuel Bonchek (1890–1974), JNWA leader; and an unknown person. Bottom row, *right to left*: Samuel Goldenberg (1884–1945), Yiddish and English actor; Isidor Pelarsky; Zalman Shneur (1887–1959), major Hebrew poet; Haim Tchernowitz (1871–1949), also known as Rav Zair (Young Rabbi), Talmud scholar; Nathan Ratnoff (1875–1947), physician and communal leader; Nahum Goldmann, (1895–1982), major Zionist leader; Meir Brown (1889–1965), JNWA leader; and two unknown people.

Hayim Greenberg's oeuvre includes sketches and profiles of a variety of significant non-Jewish cultural, literary, religious, and political figures, including the German leader of the Protestant Reformation Martin Luther, the French writer and dramatist Romain Rolland, the American humorist Mark Twain, the Russian revolutionary leader Vladimir Lenin, and the Japanese Christian pacifist Toyohiko Kagawa. The essay below on exiled Russian revolutionary leader Leon Trotsky synthesizes two pieces by Greenberg originally published in Der yidisher kemfer*: the first part appeared in 1939 shortly after Trotsky and his followers, having been expelled from the Third International (Comintern), created the alternative Fourth International; the second part was published in 1940 following Trotsky's assassination. Written against the backdrop of the anti-Stalinist Communist left's glorification of Trotskyism and the Fourth International, Greenberg examines Trotsky's radical Marxist politics and underscores what he views as the equally destructive, dangerous, and criminal tendencies of Trotsky and the Soviet dictator Joseph Stalin.*

I

It may seem strange (and may the future historian forgive me for the seeming pettiness and vulgarity of the recollection) but one of the associations evoked in me by [Leon] Trotsky's[1] name is . . . gastronomic. I recall how in 1920 I was confronted with a serious problem: for urgent personal reasons I had to go from Kiev to Moscow for a couple of weeks. But it was then almost impossible to obtain a travel permit for private purposes, and even if I had somehow succeeded in obtaining the necessary papers from the dozen or so different offices, how could I have gotten a place in a train—an ordinary seat on a hard bench—for the several days which such a trip then lasted? Luckily, some kind-hearted Communist acquaintances arranged for me an appointment with one of Trotsky's assistants who just then happened to be in Kiev in "his own railroad car." He consented to take me into his car when he was ready to return to Moscow and gave me a document granting me permission to travel, and also containing a paragraph dealing with what was then a very delicate matter—provisions. I had the right, this paragraph stated, to go to a certain government store where I would be issued provisions for the three days I would be en route. When I came to the specified store (where ordinary Soviet mortals could buy nothing because its supplies were reserved for the elite) I was at once issued a ration which made my head swim: white bread, butter, biscuits, pounds of cheese and smoked meat, tea and sugar enough to supply an entire family for weeks, salami, smoked fish—this at a time when nine-tenths of the urban population in the country literally starved. Later I learned that not even the privileged categories in the population could get such supplies, that even among the elite there was a select super-elite of Bolshevik aristocrats who alone could claim such luxuries, and that it was the magic of Trotsky's name that stood me in good stead in this case. Anyone traveling in one of "Trotsky's trains" must have some very special connections, and for such a one even the starved and tattered Russia of that day could be a land of milk and honey.

In the light of cosmic events, this incident is naturally trivial and I should perhaps be ashamed to tell it in polite society. ("Is that all that stuck in your mind from the days of the Russian Revolution?" I may be asked. "Are you looking for spots on the sun's glory?") However, this "trivia" stuck in my memory because at that very same time a doctor warned me of the early death of the person dearest to me because, as the doctor said, he could not treat diseased lungs without the aid of bread and butter.[2] I might still not have thought of it at this time were it not for the fact that I came upon Trotsky's treatise on proletarian ethics (*Their Morals and Ours* [1938][3] in which, in the course of a cynically witty polemic, he accuses the modest and semi-ascetic Norman Thomas[4] of living like a bourgeois despite his socialist speeches and writings.[5]

Trotsky enjoys a deserved reputation as a first-class polemicist. Yet every competent polemicist conceals a sadist. Among Jews it is said of *shokhtim* [pl., ritual slaughterers] that providence had originally destined them to be highwaymen, but because of the merit of their pious forefathers their verdict was changed and the aggression of the highwayman became sublimated into the religiously approved bloodshed of the *shokhet* [ritual slaughterer]. Trotsky's laboratory of polemical instruments is a kind of sublimated *cheka* [Russian for "Soviet state security organization"].[6] Let anyone dare commit the counter-revolutionary sin of disagreeing with him, and he will at once pass sentence and "execute" the personal reputation of his opponent.

What is most deplorable is the fact that in certain liberal circles Trotsky is still considered an innocent sufferer and, what is more important, is looked upon as a temporarily defeated fighter for all those great values which [Joseph] Stalin[7] so brutally tramples with his despotic boots. But in the final analysis, Trotsky is a good Stalinist and Stalin is not such a bad Trotskyist. The ideological differences between them are not nearly as overwhelming as each of them tries to persuade us. Stalin is not [Pontius] Pilate,[8] neither is Trotsky Jesus. The conflict between the two is not a clash between a Cain soul and an Abel soul,[9] but between two Cains for whom the world is too small to be divided equitably. Trotsky has had a sufficiently long time and adequate opportunities to demonstrate in fact how dearly he prized those values and principles which Stalin degraded. He demonstrated that when power over Russia rested to such a large extent in his hands he acted, and permitted others to act, as Stalinists. Under the Lenin-Trotsky rule[10] (the golden and righteous epoch in the history of Bolshevism) no fewer people were shot than in all of Stalin's bloody purges,[11] nor was it ever clear why and to what purposes this was done. In recent years Trotsky tried to excuse himself with the argument that although he had displayed no little cruelty during the time of his rule, he never degraded his victims. This, too, could be considered an accomplishment, had it been true. But Trotsky apparently has his own private concepts, not only of justice but also of what constitutes historical truth. On a number of occasions he described the falsehoods which [Vladimir] Lenin[12] employed in the course of his political career as "mild exaggeration." He permits himself such "mild exaggeration" also when dealing with historical facts in which he was involved. Trotsky does not even deny that thousands of Kronstadt sailors were shot in 1921 with his knowledge and consent.[13] But, he maintains, they were not slandered, they were not framed-up. To this day he maintains that the mutiny of the Kronstadt sailors was counter-revolutionary whereas all one has to do is read the so-called Petropavlovsk Resolution[14] adopted by them to see how thoroughly false and what a frame-up Trotsky's contention is. Among the fifteen points raised by the sincere Communists of Kronstadt, we find some demands which the Lenin-Trotsky government put into effect a few weeks after the "counter-revolutionaries" who proposed them were executed, or protests and exceptions which Trotsky himself has for years past used as a basis for his political program. (Among these are protests against the bureaucratization of the regime, against deadening the democratic spirit in the Soviets, in the party and in the army.) Nor is Kronstadt an isolated instance. It would be well for many to recall the trials of socialists, anarchists, and technical experts at the time when he still exerted a certain control over events in the Soviet Union.

Trotsky is the last person in the world who has a right to protest against Stalin's injustice. In fact, Stalin practices Trotsky's justice. Trotsky always acted in accordance with Lenin's recipe, and Lenin was a true disciple of [Sergei] Nechaev,[15] that ultimate source of revolutionary nihilism, who made himself immortal with his formula: "Everything that helps the triumph of the revolution is ethical; everything that hinders it is unethical and criminal."[16] But who is to say the last word regarding what helps and what hinders the triumph of the revolution? Naturally, the one who succeeds in grasping revolutionary power. Today Stalin has it. Once Trotsky had it to some extent and millions of people remember the beating they got from him and the blows from which other people perished.

Fundamentally, both Stalin and Trotsky are birds of a feather. Today Stalin considers Trotsky to be in his debt—he owes him his head. Trotsky reciprocates with wish-fulfillment dreams: "Should either one of us lose his head or in some other way be gotten rid of, then *I* will return to Moscow." It could have been the other way around: Stalin in hiding somewhere and Trotsky in the Kremlin. The destinies of Russia and of the world in general would not have been altered by such an arrangement. Danger of Bolshevist imperialist expansion into new countries and over more peoples? In the past it was objectively ruled out for Trotsky. Should such chances now arise as a result of the war, Stalin will certainly not miss any opportunities.

Trotsky's suffering in recent years has not chastened him nor evoked within him any repentant thoughts. As in the past, he still has unqualified faith in himself and is enamored with himself. At any rate, he wants to convince us that he has never erred in the past and did no wrong (excepting perhaps a few faulty strategic moves). Should anyone point to his blood-stained hands, he would insolently sneer at such bourgeois hypocritical morality and he would dialectically demonstrate that his hands are really *baptized* in blood and that the *cheka* for which he is intellectually and politically responsible, was in reality a revolutionary tribunal as long as it was in the right hands. His last treatise on revolutionary morality, which is a model of vulgarity and irresponsibility, he dedicated to the memory of his son,[17] "who also abhorred Pharisees."[18] That Trotsky knew nothing about the Pharisees is beside the point. He never took the trouble to find out who they were. But what he lacks is precisely some of the Pharisees' spirit, some of their sensitiveness to the differences between the clean and the unclean, between things that are permitted and things that are taboo under all circumstances, even when ostensibly indulged in for sacred ends.

But if Trotsky did not acquire such a sensitivity in the sixty years of his life, and especially in his late years which brought him so much suffering and persecution, he will not revise his truth in the future. He will not renounce his posture of final revolutionary authority to his dying day. Just as he seems to be incapable of personal friendship (this definition of Trotsky's character was made last summer by Diego Rivera,[19] a man who was of incalculable service to Trotsky[20]), so is he also incapable of experiencing the consoling melancholy of aloneness and of self-confrontation. The world for him is like a well-packed theatre balcony which at the present time is not doing right by him—it does not applaud or shout hysterically, "Hurrah for Trotsky." He looks forward hopefully to millions of disciples; he looks to every corner of the world—will they ever appear? Will they ever appear again? Is a new pedestal being readied for him?

II

Leon Trotsky was "liquidated," without an official trial, without the customary sadistic speech by the Soviet prosecutor and also without the, by now, classical confession. He was "liquidated" on alien soil, thousands of miles from the Kremlin, at the hands of a creature of Stalin who carried out his orders in the guise of a friend and admirer of Trotsky.

It would be naive to speculate why Stalin needed Trotsky's death at the particular time when he was murdered. For many years there was not a moment when Stalin did *not* need Trotsky's death. It is folly to think that one man's desire to remove another man from off the face of the earth must always be motivated by some clear and practical motive. The first mythical murder was never rationally explained. In a "material" sense Cain and Abel were not rivals. The world was big enough for both, and each found fulfillment in a different sphere. Of course, Trotsky was no Abel, and a comparison with Cain might be too complimentary for Stalin. (Stalin never displayed those symptoms of guilt which legend ascribes to Cain.) But for a long time it had become impossible for the two to coexist on the same planet, and even a bigger planet than our earth would not have sufficed for two such extreme egomaniacs.

Granted that for some time before his death Trotsky had become politically a corpse and could not have materially hindered Stalin's plans and ambitions. But for many years Stalin was no longer concerned with the harm which Trotsky could have caused him, only with the existence of the man whose diabolical hatred he so well knew because it was a true copy of the hatred which Stalin felt toward him. The trouble with these two genial haters was that they were not contemplative types but possessed active natures. Not for them the role of the passive hater of the popular anecdote who had but one request to God: that he should become a millionaire so that he could buy a villa in some quiet spot and there, in the midst of idyllic surroundings, he would have nothing to do but sit on a porch surrounded by flowers and indulge in hating his enemy. Both Stalin and Trotsky were not sufficiently introverted for this type of hatred. Like their Petcheneg[21] predecessors on the soil of Russia one thousand years earlier, they needed each other's lopped off heads to display before their followers with outcries of jubilation, and then to drink toasts from their enemy's skull. Therefore, even a politically powerless and helpless Trotsky posed a threat to Stalin. The fact that he existed, breathed, thought, remembered, hated, and reminded others, the fact that he knew too much, and so thoroughly understood Stalin's true nature, the fact that somewhere on earth there existed an acute analyst who understood every dark and murderous corner of Stalin's soul—these became the greatest griefs of Stalin's life, the constant destroyers of his peace, the permanent murderers of his sleep.

Furthermore, Stalin knew all along with the sure knowledge of animal instinct what Trotsky would have done to him were he to have come out on top, were he to have seized Lenin's heritage and the mighty and omnipresent apparatus of power. Thus Stalin could justify his actions with a fair degree of inner conviction: I did to Trotsky what he would have done to me had he the power to do so, what he longed to do to me in his revenge fantasies, what he in fact tried to do a number of times when he sent emissaries from his exile in Constantinople with the mission to get me out of the way.[22]

Nor must we rule out altogether the possibility that Trotsky maintained the "courier service" to Russia (which he operated with so little success from his exile in Turkey) to the day of his death.[23] Stalin had adequate grounds to consider Trotsky an active, agile, and constant conspirator. He might well have thought: It does not matter that the Fourth International[24] has no permanent address and that only a handful of people stand by Trotsky. The original group of Bolsheviks in 1917 was still smaller, yet that group knew how to exploit a favorable moment. The world situation is so charged with dangers and possible surprises that—who can tell?—if the handful of Trotskyites is not to be decapitated in time, it might take advantage of an opportune moment, just as the handful of Bolsheviks did in the summer of 1917. The masses of people whom it is possible to lead into the streets in parades chanting demands of death to Trotsky, may, in other circumstances, in some moment of twilight for a revolutionary idol, hoist the so recently and passionately hated Trotsky to their shoulders and proclaim him as the new idol.

The foregoing might appear to some as a defense of Stalin and a kind of justification for the gruesome murder which the Bolshevist Judas committed in Mexico.[25] It is hardly necessary to point out again how revolting was this act of calculated brutality executed under the cloak of hypocritical friendship. But it was necessary to consider the event for an instant in Stalin's terms which were essentially, though not formally, Trotskyist. Under the impact of the tragic aspects of the murder one is inclined to forget Trotsky's role before his power waned, the sadistic nature of his revolutionism, his initiative in establishing the *cheka* and introducing inquisitorial methods, his approval of mass terror, his theory of revolutionary morality which sanctioned punishment not only of persons who had transgressed against the Soviet government but also of their wives, children, friends, and neighbors (Trotsky's well-known policy of taking hostages), his theory and practice of punitive expeditions against villages and entire districts, the executions he ordered in the army and the mass slaughter in Kronstadt of fellow Bolsheviks who rebelled against the bureaucracy which Trotsky so energetically and capably established and which in later years he sought to destroy because it came into the service of his enemy. The differences between Trotsky and Stalin were primarily intellectual. Trotsky was an intellectual—Stalin a lowbrow; Trotsky was well informed and keenly analytical—Stalin oversimplified matters and was not concerned with socialist doctrine; Trotsky was a man of varied knowledge—Stalin had only the wisdom of primitive instinct.

The scope and value of the differences in principles between the two has long been exaggerated. Trotsky called for world revolution as against socialism in one country primarily because he was in the opposition, and it is a standing rule that for an opposition those in authority are always wrong. But Stalin, too, never renounced the idea of world revolution. Given a favorable situation he would be more than glad to "rescue" and "liberate" one country after another.

The murder of Trotsky must arouse serious thought in the minds of intellectually sound and sensitive persons. If Trotsky and Stalin are typical of revolutionary salvationists, if those who undertake to redeem humanity bear within themselves such volcanoes of hate, brutality, and criminality, and if redemption is not to be obtained from other sources, then social redemption is a curse. Perhaps we should no longer laugh at the Jewish village woman who, when her husband told her that the messiah was about to come in a few days, exclaimed that the God who had saved us from Pharaoh[26] and Haman[27] and others of their kind would have mercy and also save us from the messiah's hands.

In his volume of essays *To the Finland Station* [1940],[28] Edmund Wilson[29] mentions a detail in Trotsky's biography—how Lev Davidovich Bronstein acquired his new name. It was not simply chosen at random, nor was it dreamed up by Trotsky. Nor did it have anything to do with the town of Troki in the Vilna district whence came a number of Trotskys. When Trotsky escaped from his Siberian exile in 1902, some associates at a small railway station gave him some clothing and a blank passport. On his way to Samara[30] he had to fill out the passport. When he came to the choice of a name he did not give the matter much thought and put down the name of the chief supervisor of the Odessa prison where he had been jailed for some months.[31]

Why did he choose the name of a supervisor of a jail? Edmund Wilson pays no attention to this detail. Some thirty or forty years ago such a question would only have evoked a smile. What do you mean, why? It just happened, an accident. Who knows? Perhaps this was the first name that came to his mind, and it came to his mind just like that, "without any reason." But today, though one reject some premises of psychoanalysis and smile condescendingly at some of its extravagances, yet one would no longer maintain that there are accidents in one's psychology. Adopted names are certainly not accidental; very frequently they are closely bound up with the most intimate states of one's soul.

I will not undertake to provide an explanation in this case. I lack both the specialized knowledge and, still more so, familiarity with the techniques of analysis. Nevertheless, I am convinced that in this instance we are dealing with a most unusual case; an extremist revolutionary adopts the name of a prison official and lives with it all his days. Under the name of the tsarist supervisor of prisoners Trotsky founded the Red Army,[32] conducted the [Russian] civil war,[33] wrote books, delivered speeches, went into exile, wandered from country to country, and finally fell under the axe of a traitor. During nearly three decades he had more than one opportunity to change this name (or to reclaim his original name) yet he did not do so. Had he forgotten whose name he had adopted? Did this name never evoke any associations within him? Let us say he had forgotten, but such forgetfulness is far from accidental.

Reading Trotsky's autobiography one is impressed by his remarkable memory.[34] (He never forgot anyone who ever even attempted to step on one of his corns.) But he was also a remarkable "forgetter." Writing his autobiography he clearly remembered who his father was. In Bolshevik terminology Trotsky's father would have been classified as a *kulak* [Russian for "independent farmer"].[35] He succeeded in gaining possession of 650 acres of land from Colonel Yanowsky's estate[36] and he ran his establishment with much gusto. Well-to-do himself, he was not above allowing some poor peasant woman to come to him on foot twice, a distance of seven miles, to get a ruble which he owed her for work done. The peasants whom he employed as wage workers would only get soup and *kasha* [Russian for "cooked buckwheat groats"] for their meals. In order to obtain some meat from time to time they would have to stage protest demonstrations in the course of which they would lie on the ground face downward. Trotsky also well remembered the tears of peasant women whose cattle his father held for ransom when they trespassed on his pasture land. About the only good thing Trotsky could say of his father was that he had been an atheist. He observed neither Sabbath nor holidays and often declared that he believed neither in *haroset* [a Passover dish of chopped nuts and fruit][37] nor in the existence of God. His "education" seems to have consisted in not talking Yiddish at home, for we get the impression from Trotsky's biography that his father was illiterate in both languages. As to his manners and general behavior, we can gauge these from Trotsky's praise for his uncle in Odessa with whom he lived for some time when he went to high school. That uncle taught Trotsky "Russian grammar, how to wash himself, and how to hold a glass."[38]

All of these things Trotsky remembered and it should be said to his credit that he did not choose to pass over them in silence. But in later years he completely seemed to have forgotten one detail of his childhood environment—the fact that from that environment there emerged a Trotsky, and that any man's career, psychology, and destiny are not necessarily determined by the economic class from which he came. When Trotsky had power in Russia he was the greatest enemy of the *kulaks* and he defined a *kulak* as a peasant who did not own even one-twentieth part of what his own father had owned. Following his system of reasoning, he naturally had every right to desire to destroy every peasant who owned his own goat and every shopkeeper whose shelves boasted merchandise worth a few rubles. But what could he have against these people's children? How could he tell how many potential Trotskys were growing up in the huts of his class enemies? But it was precisely under Trotsky's regime that the concept of *declassed* (persons deprived of equal rights as Soviet citizens because of their bourgeois origins) with all its murderous consequences was introduced.

Trotsky conveniently forgot that it was possible for "world redeemers" to emerge from the homes of *kulaks*. Having forgotten this he caused the murder of so many *kulak* children that he could not himself know their exact number.

***

The measure of Trotsky's tolerance when he was still a youngster becomes evident from a letter he then wrote to the public library of Nikolaev.[39] When he was still a high school student, the later dialectician of Marxist kabbalah was a *Narodnik*[40] [Narodnaya Volya member] and proclaimed as unclean anything that smacked of historical materialism. It so happened then that a magazine published by the *Narodniks* slipped out of their control and was taken over by Social Democrats[41] (incidentally, this was the first periodical that legally advocated Marxism in Russia). Trotsky at once petitioned the public library to cancel its subscription to that journal.[42] The enthusiasm for censorship of ideas burned brightly within him even then. When in 1918, together with Lenin, he suppressed the press of the Social Revolutionaries (the spiritual heirs of the *Narodniks)*, petitions of any sort were no longer in fashion in Russia.

***

"A plague on all Marxists and on all those who seek to introduce hardness and dryness into all human relations."[43] It is hard to believe that Trotsky uttered these words, yet this was the New Year toast of the still young but quickly maturing Trotsky in Nikolaev.

The chief protagonist of Marxism in Trotsky's social circle at the time was a young lady, Alexandra Lvovna Sokolovskaya.[44] (The Slavic name need not mislead anyone. This apostle of historical materialism in the provincial town of Nikolaev was a good Jewish girl.) At that time Trotsky considered Marxism a threat to individual freedom and autonomy. There were frequent, sharp and spiteful arguments between him and Alexandra Lvovna, to whom he was far from indifferent. During their frequent meetings Trotsky would tease her: "I can't understand how a young woman so full of life can tolerate such constricted, dry as dust, impractical stuff."[45] She in turn would reply flirtatiously, "And I can't imagine how a man who thinks he is logical can be satisfied with such fuzzy idealistic emotions."[46] For a time these clashes were partly flirtatious, partly ideological encounters. In the end, the Marxist young lady triumphed, both theoretically as well as erotically. Trotsky experienced a Marxist revelation—and surrendered.

For the rest of his life he remained true to the theoretical associations of his first love affair, and ever after the formerly intolerant anti-Marxist waved the sword of Marx over the heads of all unbelievers and skeptics. Long before the

October Revolution[47] he proclaimed Victor Adler[48] a renegade to socialism because the latter had told him that he would undertake to predict political developments on the basis of the apocalypse with more confidence than on the basis of dialectical materialism.[49]

There is something suspect in Trotsky's intellectual stubbornness and his almost inquisitorial dogmatism. He had a keen mind, cutting sarcasm, and much understanding of humor and skepticism. Yet he devoted all his mental energies, resorting to hair-splitting, intellectual acrobatics and casuistry, to a desperate clinging to the confines of Marxist *halakhah*.

It is not for me to draw conclusions, but it might be worthwhile for some trained psychoanalyst to attempt to reveal the erotic factors and the infantilisms in Trotsky's "consistent" Marxism. What was the role of the image of Alexandra Lvovna in the shaping of his personality?

Once, while talking about a man known to both of us, Rabbi [Yaakov] Mazeh[50] of Moscow said to me: "In God's name tell him that he should not go to *tashlikh*[51] on *Rosh Hashanah* [Jewish New Year], for if he were to see his reflection in the water he would not be able to bear it—he might think for a moment that there is another one like him in the world and that he is not unique in the universe."

This malicious jibe came to my mind while reading [R. H.] Bruce Lockhart's[52] diaries.[53] After meeting Trotsky in 1918, he wrote: "He makes the impression of a man who would gladly sacrifice his life in the struggle for Russia—on one condition, that a great crowd should witness his doing so."[54]

It should be added perhaps, "and that he should be *the only one* to do so."

***

At one time Trotsky read only one book each day for months on end—the Bible. When he was imprisoned in Odessa he was treated harshly and was not permitted to receive books.[55] But the tsarist officials could not very well deny him the Holy Scriptures and his sister brought him the Bible in four languages: Russian, German, French, and Italian.

It is remarkable how little Trotsky was impressed by the "Book of Books." His style, his associations, the rhythms of his speech and writing remained completely unaffected by biblical literary influence. He merely *used* the Bible to learn foreign languages. The prophets,[56] the Book of Job,[57] the Song of Songs[58]—these were merely linguistic aids.

Trotsky once told this to the writer [O. L.] D'Or[59] and the latter responded with the Russian peasant maxim that was often quoted by Lenin: "In a good household every piece of trash comes in handy."

***

Naturally, Trotsky did not believe in immortality, but seldom was there a man so obsessed with his own *historical immortality.* (In our time only [Adolf] Hitler[60] with his inflated ego and unabashed melodramatics and the taciturn and secretive Stalin, equal Trotsky in this regard.) A monument to Trotsky in some remote corner of Tibet in the twenty-ninth century would appear logical in the light of his conception of the future. While addressing the first congress of Soviets immediately after the October Revolution, Trotsky shouted to [Julius] Martov[61] and his followers (they were still "legal" and their membership in the Soviet was still recognized): "You are miserable, isolated individuals; you are bankrupt; your role is finished. Go where you belong from this day—*on the trash heap of history*."[62] The seats of honor in history? Valhalla[63] he reserved for all Bolsheviks, and for himself—the speaker's platform.

But in order to be sure of such a place of honor in the historical hereafter, one must first acquire a good share of it in the present, a commanding position in one's own generation. This passion for power burned within Trotsky ever since his boyhood days, and in this connection it is interesting to hear what he says in his autobiography regarding his high school experiences. He relates that he divided his classmates into three categories: those who "betrayed" him, those who "defended" him, and "neutrals." (The center of the high school universe was Trotsky himself, naturally.) With his "betrayers," he informs us, he broke off unconditionally; his "defenders" he cultivated; and the "neutrals" he ignored. A high school boy who was neither for nor against Trotsky simply didn't count.[64]

Trotsky's high school sociology was not unlike that of the waiter in the restaurant where I have my lunch. For him, too, humanity is divisible into three categories: those who finish their meal and leave no tip (to hell with the cheapskates); those who leave only a dime or two (okay, let them live); and customers who leave a generous tip (blessings and long life to them). Without wishing to hurt my waiter's feelings, I'd say that, in another dimension, he was almost Napoleonic. The server of stew and the author of the permanent revolution were both, each in his own way and on his appropriate scale, Napoleonic characters, so far as their classification of their fellow men was concerned.

13
Prayer
(1940)

Hayim Greenberg's world outlook was animated by a deep moral sensibility. He sustained a lifelong fascination with and attachment to humanitarian and communitarian values and principles associated with religious belief—those derived from Judaism in particular, but also ideas and notions stemming from Christianity, Islam, Buddhism, and Hinduism. Greenberg himself, however, was far from a true believer. His philosophical orientation might best be described as a hybrid of agnosticism and atheism. Discussing the purpose of faith, he asserted that "religion is neither able nor called upon to explain the mystery of life." Rather than a God-centered system of divine reward and punishment, he argued that "the role of religion [in human society] is altogether different: it arouses and cultivates an attitude of confidence in the basis of existence." In other words, religion enables cultures, societies, and peoples to thrive—not only in strictly geopolitical and demographic terms, but also in the sense of creating vital frameworks that offer humanity purposeful, meaningful, and desirable road maps for existence. In the following essay, Greenberg draws on a wide range of theological traditions and philosophical understandings of prayer to explore the place of spiritual expression in modern society.

Praying, one often feels, is a forgotten art today even among those who still consider themselves pious, and who may pray regularly, every day. Possibly there never were men who could *really* pray; perhaps we have merely deluded ourselves that in other times the art of devotion was more widespread than it is now. Men with the gift of prayer may always have been emotional, and for ordinary people, praying may always have been more a matter of routine than of immediacy. We find an instructive admonition in the Mishnah: "Do not practice set prayer"[1] [Pirkei Avot 2:18]—as much as to say, avoid making your prayer commonplace and mechanical. Rabbi Oshaya[2] would have exempted from prayer any Jew "who found praying burdensome" [B. Brakhot 29b], who prayed only as a kind of dull duty, a conventional act that one performed to be rid of it. Other rabbis as well as

Rabbi Yosef,[3] as the same mishnah tells us, went so far as to invalidate the prayer of anyone "who could not create some new aspect in it" [B. Brakhot 29b]—probably meaning not new words or sentences, but the capacity of continually bringing to the same ancient, well-known text a fresh comprehension and sensitivity. Thus, even some of our early sages were already shocked by the stiffness and dullness of prayer formulas, and they sought praying men for whom every act of prayer was a new, unique experience.

Yet it *was* easier in olden times to bring oneself to pray. And, if a man today believes not only that there is a God above us, but that he can be moved by the power of prayer to lay aside his "attribute of anger" and turn to his "attribute of mercy;"[4] if a man has not yet lost the sense of the "magical" power of prayer, of its hypnotic effect upon the Lord of the Universe—why should such a man refrain from using that power?

The power of prayer is not, indeed, unlimited, nor is it always possible to strike the very moment when God is "accessible" and allows himself to be swayed. It is related of Rabbi Hanina ben Dosa,[5] for example, that he would often pray for sick persons, and in the very act of praying he would know for whom his prayer would be answered and for whom not: "This one will live, that one will die" [B. Brakhot 34a]. He had his signs: if the prayer came from his lips smoothly, in a flowing stream, he knew it would have effect; if not, it was evident that the sick man was doomed—or as he put it, *metoraf* [Hebrew for "delirious"], a "gone goose," as we would say [B. Brakhot 34a].

I do not know whether Rabbi Hanina anywhere explains why his prayer was sometimes successful and sometimes failed to register. Was it because he himself was not always properly attuned to devotion, or because the almighty sometimes showed himself a poor, insensitive "medium"? Yet it was always worthwhile to knock on the heavenly gates: one could never know with certainty when one would succeed and when one would fail. What is important is that there be someone there to pray to, and that he hearken to prayer and, from time to time, let himself be swayed by it. It is essential that, even if only on rare occasions, one be able to come "in contact" with God and that God have the capacity to give what one asks of him. Then one is always in a position to think that he may strike just such an "hour of grace" as that which Rabbi Ishmael ben Elisha[6] described. Rabbi Ishmael ben Elisha once went into the Holy of Holies[7] to offer up incense, and all at once saw the Lord himself, "Akatriel Yah,[8] Lord of Hosts, sitting on a high and lofty throne" [B. Brakhot 7a]. Not only did he see him, but the apparition even approached him with a request: "Ishmael, My son, bless Me" [B. Brakhot 7a]. Ishmael didn't think twice, and blessed him, that his mercy overcome his wrath, that kindness rule over his attributes, and he treat his children lovingly, passing over what is due to himself [B. Brakhot 7a]. Religious experience is full of paradoxes, and it is pointless to ask how Rabbi Ishmael dared to be so impertinent in the face of heaven. Actually, in his blessing he had appealed to some power other than God, and necessarily higher than God (!), to make God a little more humane. But what is significant is the outcome of this act which, to a strictly Judaic mind, was more in the nature of sacrilege than of prayer—"And He nodded His head to him" [B. Brakhot 7a]. The ineffable, that is, in effect agreed that somewhat more tenderness on his part would be good for the world. But it makes sense to pray even to such a God, though he may need a Rabbi Ishmael to set him on the path of righteousness, for he has the power and capacity to give man what he asks of him, if he only will.

But what shall a modern man do, one for whom such a God no longer exists? What can be the purpose of prayer for a man of our time, deeply imbued with the scientific way of thinking, however great or little may be the sum of his knowledge? The difficulty was well expressed by the Spinozist,[9] [Ivan Sergeyvich] Turgenev,[10] in his *Poems in Prose* [1882],[11] when he said that to pray means asking: "Dear God, do something to make two and two not equal four"[12]—that is, to break the chain of necessary causes of progressing by eternal, iron laws, to break it with some exception, with a miracle, with some act of lawlessness. Alter the immutable cosmic order on my behalf. If God himself is bound by an eternal system of laws, if he is perhaps no more than that very system (if he is the kind of creator—according to an image of certain early Jewish sages, who were of course far from any pantheist philosophy—who "consulted the Torah" and who governs the world by its unalterable precepts), then what is the use of raising one's arms in prayer, calling to him for help? It would be the same as begging a circle to become a square, if only for a moment, to suit our convenience.

But the modern man who is not so atavistic as to believe in the anthropomorphic God of his ancestors, or who is without the courage of the mystic to make him transcend the bounds that scientific method has set down for him, generally knows nothing of [Baruch] Spinoza's[13] God either, or of that "God-Substance" that rests eternally content in his almighty confinement.[14] A man of this kind may have no metaphysical sense at all, and his vacuity was once bewailed by [Haim Nahman] Bialik[15] in these verses:

Behold, about and within me
Is darkness, dear friend, is darkness;
Behold, about and within me
Desolation, dear friend, desolation.[16]

With darkness and desolation all about and within, one cannot pray: "As for me—my heart is dead, and my lips no longer can pray—"[17] But if such a person will nevertheless pray, it is with "lips wilting in prayer."[18]

In Eugene O'Neill's drama *Dynamo* [1929],[19] young Reuben Light, the scion of generations of Protestant clergymen, ceased to believe in the God of his fathers. He became completely fixated upon the world of modern technology, specifically upon electricity: electric power was everything, eternity, the source and secret of existence. However, gradually he brought over into his atheism that organic piety that he could never uproot from his soul, and he became the mystic of physics: he transferred his sense of awe to the electric dynamo, and the hydroelectric plant in his little Connecticut town became his divine temple. In a moment of crisis, when his mother dies, he prostrates himself before the dynamo, and a desperate prayer bursts convulsively from him to the mysterious power that animates the machine. But his prayer is of no avail. In a fit of insanity, he shoots his sweetheart and then puts an end to his own life. O'Neill is no sadist; he would certainly let his hero live, if he could. But Reuben no longer has anything to live for: there is no true God any more. Electricity? Twentieth-century man is terrified to discover that atheism has driven him back into fetishistic idolatry. Reuben Light wants to pray, but has no one to pray to. He tries to pray to *something* instead of *someone,* but the *thing* is deaf and dumb. The praying man, in hysteria, finds himself suddenly alone, at the mercy of un-God, in the jungle, with no way leading from the jungle to civilization—nor would it help if there were such a way, for there is no "civilization" either.

A new profession has sprung up recently in New York, one poignantly characteristic of our time: the profession of listeners—men and women whose job consists in listening. For a fee of three dollars a visit, they are ready to sit quietly, attentively and listen to whatever you may wish to tell about yourself—all your failures, difficulties, doubts, and despairs, all your mental confusions and spiritual agonies. They offer no consolation nor counsel, they do not undertake to "cure" anyone nor foretell the future. They are unusual postal clerks who receive from you unaddressed lyrical letters, which are not to be delivered anywhere, nor ever to be answered.

There exists a perpetual need for soul-outpouring—not to friends, parents, wives, or one's beloved, but to a stranger, an unknown, anonymous "thou," because only to such a being can the most fateful, the ultimate intimacies be entrusted. Those who no longer have any address for the metaphysical anonymous find the address of a "substitute" in some newspaper advertisement.

In every civilization, however advanced or backward it may be, there exist (sometimes simultaneously) both sublime and profane levels of religious awareness, and similarly, various stages of prayer. The Zulu issues ultimata to his idol: "Help me, or I'll see you die of starvation."[20] The prayer and sacrifices he offers to his spirits are no more than a crude commercial transaction. Whoever cares to may console himself with the thought that the Zulu is a pagan, and that all pre-monotheistic religions were morally, aesthetically, and intellectually, on a very low level. But such an explanation would be an unjustified generalization.

Pagan cults had their own expressions of sublimity. When a pagan tribesman in the Indian Himalayas addresses to that god whom he holds the greatest of all gods this brief prayer: "God, we know not what is for our good; you know better than we what is good for us; do, then, that which to your knowledge is the best,"[21] his prayer is on same lofty plane as the noble verse in the Jewish *siddur* [prayer book]:[22] "And put it in my heart to do Thy will, and decree Thy good decree upon me."[23] Confronted with the prayer of the ancient Aztecs (undoubtedly a highly civilized people compared to the Zulus, but still idolaters possessed of entire pyramids of superstitions), "God of mercy, may the suffering you have sent upon us free us of wickedness and of vanities,"[24] one feels impelled to say to all the contemporary Christian (and Jewish) advocates of pure prayer, prayer that is wholly trust and entirely free of petition, that basically they have said nothing new; great, though anonymous, thinkers of old pagan civilizations conceived this very thought before them. When Plato[25] composed his noble prayer: "King Zeus, grant us the good, whether we pray for it or not, and take from us the evil, even if we yearn to have it,"[26] the foundation upon which he built was an existing, if not very prominent, element in the pagan folklore of his people. On the other hand, "monotheistic" Christianity is full of so-called petitionary prayers, and our own Jewish *siddur* cannot boast that it contains no prayer-petitions, in the narrow sense, trying to obtain from God special boons, which he, as it were, is not prepared to grant unless "influence" is brought to bear upon him.

Buddhism is, in some respects, the most notable of world religions. No other religion can compare with the Buddhist doctrine in refinement of thought and metaphysical imagination. Classical Buddhism is freer from anthropomorphic conceptions than any other religion, and its cogency of structure is beyond compare. But there was never a religious system in the entire history of man which could be "guaranteed" against decadence and vulgarization. The Tibetan Buddhists, the so-called "Lamaists," are a shocking example of the decline of a religion.[27] They strongly believe in the efficacy of prayer, and above all of *quantities* of prayer: the more praying, and the more often, the better for the salvation of the human soul. But day has not enough hours nor can lips move rapidly enough to recite the necessary number of prayers. Hence in a country of extreme technical backwardness, they invented a sort of "motorized" praying. Pious Lamaists in Tibet use a prayer-wheel,[28] a mechanical device, which, when wound up, ejects on behalf of whoever has set the machine thousands upon thousands of paper slips, with the pious inscription, "The [jewel in] the lotus, Amen."[29] Whatever number of slips the apparatus produces, so many are the prayers credited to that person on that particular day. Prayer has thus been transformed into a kind of debt settlement, with no relation to the praying man's own experience, or to any psychic process or act whatever.

But Tibet need not feel ashamed even in comparison with so highly civilized a country as the United States. Some time ago there existed a Protestant "Bible Institute" in Pittsburgh[30] with a large staff of professional praying men, ready at any time, upon telephoned or telegraphed orders, to obtain (or try to) by prayer whatever any client desired. Among the recorded orders, there were all kinds of needs and requirements: to pass an examination, win a lawsuit, heal a sore finger, get a good maid, rent a house on good terms, get rid of an undesirable boarder, and so on. A similar Catholic organization for prayer "on order" existed in the United States (perhaps it still does) and, as I read in James Bissett Pratt's instructive study of religious psychology,[31] it received almost five million letters from its "clients" in the month of August 1919, asking to be prayed for. The difference between Tibet and America in this respect is not great. The desecration (and mechanization) of prayer is identical.

[Ralph Waldo] Emerson[32] once chanced to attend a solemn divine service in Boston at which the preacher went all out in an effort to induce God to send rain, abundant rain—the longer and heavier the better. His locality was suffering a dry spell at the time. After the service was over, Emerson approached him and said, "I do not like public scenes, as a rule, but this time I strongly felt like causing a disturbance during the service. You see, I live in Concord now, and if God should really hearken to your prayer and send as much rain as you asked for it may be good for you, but we'll have a flood. What have I done to deserve that?"[33]

I mention this incident, because modern Protestantism has begun to question more and more strongly the right and the meaning of praying for specific benefits. What sense is there, some ask (or have long asked), in praying for a particular benefaction from a just and omniscient God who knows everything every individual creature needs in any case? They also ask, what is God expected to do about the multitude of our individual and collective prayers, so many of which are mutually contradictory? Whose prayer should he prefer? Because of such reflections, liberal Protestantism tends more and more to eliminate the element of "petition" from prayer: prayer is not to have practical results as its aim; it is to be simply "communication," devotion, reuniting oneself with the whole; its aim is to be subjective, not objective—self-purification, consecration, the cleansing and making whole of one's self, the achievement of resignation unmixed with bitterness, of joyous submission to whatever must come, of absolute trust.

I am by no means certain that the theologians of this school are correct in their views. It may be that "petition" has a place of its own in prayer, and will continue to have a place in the future, too. But the times are certainly more favorable to a conception of religion whose prayer books exclude such supplications as are intended to "get something" out of the almighty.

When men recover the gift of prayer (I advisedly say "when," and not "if"), they will no doubt pray only to an anonymous, quite unknown God, a God without attributes and beyond understanding. Any God that submits to definition or description, that allows himself to be compressed within a theological or philosophical formula, will then belong to the dead past, preserved only in a museum, together with the deities of Assyria,[34] Egypt, and Greece. The old ban, "Ye shall make you no idols" [Lev. 26:1], you shall create no image of God, will be given a wider extension.[35] It will then apply not only to painted and sculptured images, but also to the "portraits" of the divinity contained in the various theological systems, no matter how spiritualized and ethically sublime they may be.

It was not simply a meaningless circumstance that, many years before Jewish theologians in the Middle Ages began to grapple with the difficult problem of God's attributes, there was a rabbi (could he have been the only one of his time?) who apparently was shocked by any definition of God. Once, when prayer was offered up at the rostrum in Rabbi Hanina's presence, the prayer leader recited the chain of God's titles: "*Hael hagadol hagibor vehanora haadir veheazuz vehayarui, heazak vehaamitz vehavadai vehanihbad*"[36]—Great God, mighty and awesome, powerful and terrible, etc. (I will not undertake to translate all these glorifications into another language [*sic*].) When he was finished, Rabbi Hanina asked him with irony and resentment: "Are these all the praises you have to offer your Lord in Heaven? Even the three titles of glorification that we regularly use in our prayer (Great, Mighty, and Awesome), ought never to be uttered by our lips if it were not that we find them used by Moses in the Bible and if they had not been established in our order of prayer by the men of the Great Synagogue; yet here you come and add praises of your own. Imagine if a flesh-and-blood monarch possessed a store of a thousand sacks of gold, would one praise him by extolling the sacks of silver in his treasury? Would not this be an insult to him?" [B. Brakhot 34a].

Even then Rabbi Hanina felt that any definition (or "praise") of God was a falsification, a dwarfing and a desecration of [God's] name. There is profound significance in the fact that one of God's titles is simply "the name" [*hashem*]—*the one,* unique name that, fundamentally, is no name at all.

A progressive Christian theologian of our time, trying to prove to a skeptic the effectiveness of prayer, once said: "What makes you think God does not answer man's prayers? He always answers, and His answer, according to circumstances or according to His Will, is one of three: Yes, No, or Wait."[37] This was undoubtedly a clever gambit on the part of the theologian: he set up a kind of lottery in which he could never lose. Were one to assume that God listens to and heeds everything any man asks of him, then whatever happened afterward could be interpreted as an answer to the prayer. Either the request is granted, or God refuses it, knowing that to do so would be to the detriment of the man himself or of his fellowmen, or finally, he postpones granting it for some future time. In any case, the prayer is never ignored.

There is a point of view according to which one can dispense with all three answers and still believe that prayer is effective, and has its pragmatic value. If a man's prayer is genuine and offered in sincerity, it has an effect, first of all, upon himself. He cannot alter the cosmic order by his prayer, he cannot break through the chain of law and necessity that binds natural events and bring about a miracle, but he can integrate, or reintegrate, himself in the general scheme of existence and events, and thus obtain succor for his need. If a man's legs have been amputated he knows quite well that no matter how much he may pray, new legs will not grow on the stumps. But prayer may give him the strength to live in harmony (or in greater harmony) with himself and with the world, even without legs. Through prayer he has the power to "de-egocentrize" himself (if I may use so barbarous an expression), and achieve a state of reconciliation with his fate. Through prayer he may sometimes discover in himself such hidden or dormant sources of delight in and gratitude for his very existence as will greatly compensate him for his loss.

One of the aspects of prayer, undoubtedly, is just this turning to oneself, this navigation of the depths of one's own so largely unexplored soul, this discovery of strata of our own being with which there is hardly any contact in daily, diffuse living. Traditional believers, too, whether they know it or not, pray not only to God but to themselves as well. Prayer to oneself is certainly answered, more often than we may imagine. There are (and have been through the ages) thousands of trustworthy, living witnesses to testify to that. Every one of us, at bottom, is potentially his own witness to it, as Emerson discovered through his personal experience.

Perhaps I am mistaken. It is possible that the future may hold several parallel developments of religion, including one trend based on a God "with a name"—not an anonymous God. The physicist-metaphysician [Gustav Theodore] Fechner[38] has suggested such a conception. Like Auguste Comte,[39] he was a religious man, and both the French philosopher and the Leipzig scientist sought an empirical, naturalistic basis for their piety. But Comte imprisoned himself within the bounds of humanity. For him mankind was (or was presumed to be) the absolute, the same supreme and normative substance that is meant by "God" in theistic religion. His entire religious philosophy could be epitomized in this sentence: "Generation cometh and generation goeth, but Man remaineth forever."[40] Individuals come and depart, generations rise and vanish, but humankind lives eternally. In a transient world, it is the only truly spiritual and eternal reality. Comte transformed humanity from an empirical to a purely metaphysical concept, and declared it to be the possible object of religious worship and religious tension. He replaced God with his concept of "*le Grande Être*"[41] [French for "the great being"], the eternal creativity of the human species, in whose name temples were to be erected and to whom one should also pray. Comte permitted himself to ignore so bold a fact as that the history of the world has vast stretches of time—billions upon billions of years—when his absolute substance simply did not yet exist, and that there may still come other periods in which the creature whom he deifies will no longer exist; that the universe itself, in its present form, may be obliterated. He did not care to think that, from a broader view, the entire human species is a mere episode, and that it would be utterly senseless to address prayer to an episode.

Fechner, however, realized the "human, all-too-human,"[42] the extremely relative aspects of all such constructions as Comte's. He tried to find a new foundation for his religiosity in a pantheistic conception of his own: he sought an Archimedean point to which prayer might be addressed. At one stage in his thought, he found it quite a "simple" matter, after all. Everything in the universe (apart from the universe itself, as the totality of all existence) is both part of something greater and also something whole in and to itself. A cell is part of an organ, but each cell is a living, individual being with consciousness, with pleasure and pain. An organ is part of an organism, but each organ is itself a cosmos with its own fate and destiny. A human individual is part of humankind, but also a being existing entirely in his own right. Humankind as a whole is both an individual entity and a part, or "member," of a greater "body," the organic world. The organic world is, on the one hand, an "individual" with individual consciousness, and on the other hand part of earth, which in turn is, in itself, a living organism, and a "member" of a greater "body," the solar system. There are many, many stellar galaxies, each constituting a part, or "organ," of an encompassing universe: this alone is no longer part of something else, but the first and last thing, the all-embracing being of beings. To this being, conscious, eternally willing and creating, Fechner held, one can and should offer prayer. Does it hear our prayer? Certainly! Fechner even offers an illustration to prove it: When I, Fechner, have a sore finger, it is the pain of the finger as an individual that transmits "telegraphic" signals through the nervous system to "me," the greater individual, reporting its pain. This is the finger's prayer to Fechner, and it is effective prayer, or at least it may be. In its externals, certainly in its terminology, Fechner's religious principle remains naturalistic—a sort of neo-biology raised to the level of metaphysics. But his "cosmism" is far broader, and far less liable to endow the relative with absolute attributes than Comte's "humanism," the religion of humanity and of prayer to the spirit of mortal flesh.

Thus it is not inconceivable that even for the liberal religious belief of the future there may exist not only the absolute anonymous deity, but also a recognition of a sort of cosmic divinity as conceived by Fechner, and that prayer to such a divinity may well have a greater emotional significance than Fechner himself imagined. On the other hand, who can tell? It may turn out that for all the knowledge we now possess and may still acquire, the cosmos may become no less obscure, no less anonymous than he whom Jews call "the name," because it is impossible to suit him with any appropriate name.

When one reads the [Christian Bible], one gets the impression that in his last moments Jesus weakened and yielded to the urge of "petitionary" prayer. He ventured to pray to our "Father in Heaven" to let the destined cup of suffering pass from him. Then, as though he recalled that almighty God foreknew what was to happen anyway, he closed his prayer with contrition: "Thy will be done," whatever it might be and whithersoever it might lead.[43]

I note a similar attitude to prayer in a *zadik* [righteous man] of our own time. In Rabbi Abraham Isaac Hacohen Kook's[44] writings, we find the following conception of prayer: "When one's intention is to request some thing in prayer, one must take care that the intention (*kavanah*) be to remove evil and darkness from the world and increase goodness and light, the fullness of the divine life, so that when it manifests itself, it will not merely fill a particular lack alone but supply all lacks and repair all flaws whatsoever—for as our soul is large, our desire is precisely the final and the absolute perfection."[45] The meaning of Rabbi Kook's formula is that if one prays and has in mind a request he wishes to make of God, his "intention" should be directed not to definite, concrete petitions that may be beneficial to some but harmful to others, good today and bad tomorrow; his "intention" should be to "remove evil and darkness from the world and increase goodness and light, the fullness of the divine life." Rabbi Kook instructs us to pray essentially for the world's perfection, its redemption from conflict, or, in other words, for the realization, as speedily as may be, of God's will. Let "not my will but Thy will" be done. To pray so is at bottom to supplicate without soliciting.

14
Einstein Discusses Religion
(1940)

In the first half of the twentieth century, few Jewish figures garnered the universal recognition and acclaim of the German Jewish scientist Albert Einstein. Hailed as one of the Jewish people's most distinguished representatives, Einstein's statements on a variety of topics including politics, culture, and theology were widely viewed as moral and philosophical imperatives. In the following essay, Hayim Greenberg explores Einstein's views on the nexus between science and religion. The trajectory of Einstein's evolving attitude, Greenberg suggests, bears scrutiny in relation to the multiple traditions of Judaism, classical philosophy, Christianity, European rationalism, and Buddhism. He argues that Einstein's views oscillated between the conception of "truth" as demonstrable "outside the limits of human thought" and his implied belief in "the possible existence of a personal God."

It is related that Victor Hugo[1] once "discredited" himself with a question he asked in the company of professional natural scientists. The French astronomer [François] Arago[2] developed his views on the nature of comets before a group of friends, and when he ended Victor Hugo said: "But tell me, my dear Arago, what is the nature of a comet's soul?" Those present were shocked at such a pointless query. What sense is there in asking a physicist or an astronomer about the soul of any thing when his branch of science has nothing to do with psychic processes or manifestations?

But Albert Einstein[3] need not feel shocked if a similar question is addressed to him. No man must answer questions which have nothing to do with his specialty as long as he confines himself to the boundaries of his scientific sphere. But when a mathematician or natural scientist encroaches on the field of philosophy and expresses opinions or convictions amounting to or indicative of a *Weltanschauung*, it is perfectly legitimate to question him concerning the soul of the universe and whether the universe has a soul.

In his paper submitted to the Conference on Science, Philosophy and Religion,[4] Albert Einstein again raised the old question of the interrelation between science and religion. Those who expected him to discuss this problem in the light of the theory of relativity and of modern physics[5] in general were disappointed. Einstein made no mention of his own theories in mathematics and physics despite the fact that during the last two decades there has grown up a considerable literature on the philosophical implications of his doctrine. In explaining his views on religion and its place in our civilization he applied no special gnoseological method and approached the subject on the basis of conventional logic and what is accepted as common sense. This made it possible for those unable to follow Einstein's mathematical abstractions to understand the pattern of his philosophical thoughts and gave them the right to question his premises.

Einstein does not concede the existence of any inherent conflict between reason and faith. The countless clashes between scientific truths and the religious world outlook occurred, in Einstein's estimation, when either science attempted to transcend its legitimate functions and to become an arbiter of spiritual and moral values, or religion pretended to be the source and the only authority in matters that can best be settled in a scientific manner. It is naturally impossible to reconcile [Charles] Darwin[6] with Bishop [John] Lightfoot[7] who, at the beginning of the seventeenth century, categorically declared that no one must doubt the fact that God or the Holy Trinity created man on a Friday of the year 4004 BCE at nine o'clock in the morning.[8] A conflict must also arise in every case when science, whose function it is to study facts and their interrelationship, attempts to deny spiritual values or to set up its own system of values.

In this respect Einstein, naturally, did not intend to reveal anything new. The boundary lines between science and religion have long been clearly drawn. The scientifically minded man can also be genuinely religious and Einstein has a word of censure for those who seek to prove that science is coextensive with the sum total of human cultural processes. To put it in his own words: "Representatives of science have often attempted to arrive at fundamental judgments with respect to values and ends on the basis of scientific method, and in this way have set themselves in opposition to religion," but "these conflicts have all sprung from fatal errors."[9]

After such an introduction it could have been expected that Einstein would approach the fundamental religious concepts unencumbered with dogmatized patterns of purely scientific understanding for those aspects of spiritual life that are not within the sphere of mathematics or physics. But this time too he clung to the old, and by now classical, opposition to the so-called "theistic" religious concepts. In this respect he redefined, in his own manner, the doubts of many scientific—or predominantly scientific—minds concerning faith in a God who cannot be conceived in the specific terms of mathematics and the natural sciences.

It is the fault of most historical religions, according to Einstein, that they have made the concept of a personal God the foundation stone of their religious structures. But a personal God—he maintains—is but a fiction created by non-scientific, or pre-scientific reasoning. To a large extent it is alleged to be also a sublimation of one time primitive faith in idols. But, Einstein declares, belief in a Godhead is not essential to leading a truly religious life which finds expression in being "preoccupied with thoughts, feelings and aspirations to which one clings because of their super-personal value."[10]

It would take us too far afield to examine why such large sections of the human race abandoned faith in a deity which represented a sum of *impersonal* forces, for a belief in a *personal* God, and especially why this transition occurred during a period of progressive development in the human race. At any rate, such a transition would not have occurred had the pre-theistic religions been capable of gratifying human religious thirst and of providing a satisfactory answer to metaphysical yearnings. Neither does Einstein provide a satisfactory solution to these human yearnings. And the two basic elements of his religious outlook—a strict, orderly, and logical procedure of natural events (instead of a personal God) and man's self-identification with super-personal values—will provide no consolation and will not make the world more "acceptable" to man.

I purposely employ the largely hedonistic term "consolation" for no matter how one may interpret the concept "religion" it would have no significance, in the final analysis, unless it were to provide humanity with the certainty (or probability, as some philosophical minimalists would claim) that the values which the human spirit has produced or manifested are not illusory but belong somehow to ultimate reality, and are rooted in the very essence of the world. In his address Einstein spoke with unconcealed contempt of "fear" and "hope" as the sources of theistic religions and philosophies. But why should fear and hope be considered illegitimate stimuli? And why should the conception of a personal God, who is conceived as the eternal guardian and bearer of values and who is not indifferent to the fate of man, be considered false? Is such a conception of God too pragmatic, too much made-to-order to fit our needs and desires? Is such a conception too good to be true? Is it enough to prove that a certain idea is based on wish-fulfillment in order to discredit it? If this were so, science itself would be discredited. For is not science itself, abstract as well as applied, an answer to man's hedonistic emotions—a product of man's fear of the natural forces and his hopes to control and rule them, a product of man's fear of darkness, the unknown, the lawless, and the chaotic?

There is no doubt that religion, and especially theistic religion, is largely stimulated by fear and the need to overcome this feeling and to establish a harmonious relationship between man and his cosmic environment. If this fear were unfounded and merely a result of superstition and false notions, the religious mentality, as we know it, would not exist. But the feeling of fear which is at the root of most creative religious processes is not aroused only by floods, deluges, or by such imaginary dangers as devils. On the contrary, the source of this fear is primarily a "worrying about" the fate of human values. Fear of death, for instance, is a primary element of those psychic tensions which contributed to the formation of the religious mentality we are most familiar with. But this fear is not baseless. If we do not wish to deceive ourselves, we will realize that this fear will not be eliminated by any theory purporting to prove that death is a natural and orderly phenomenon in the cosmic set-up. A person may accept such a theory rationally, but its implications about the "naturalness" of death will not gain his moral approbation. Einstein is inclined to consider the belief in survival after death as an expression of fear, and he refuses to see the eternal moral protest against destruction of life and the values of life that is expressed in the various manifestations of belief in immortality.

Here we approach what appears to me to be the most essential element in the process of religious creativity.

I will not undertake to add one more general definition of religion to the dozens already advanced. But it would be difficult to find fault with the claim that, from a certain point of view, religion is probably the most daring attempt to conceive the totality of world existence in ethical terms. Fear *plus* Promethean ethical demands on a responsive cosmos—demands which, if met, would put an end to fear—are the foundation of religion. (Were fear the *only* source of theistic religion, there might even be some truth in the old anecdote that [Friedrich] Schleiermacher's dog was more pious than his master.)[11]

But Einstein seems to ignore the thesis that, whatever the relationship between religion and ethics, religion is, from a certain point of view, the product of human inability to acquiesce to an unmoral or amoral world-totality. Einstein concedes the validity of moral values in and for humanity; he even accepts worship of these values as the quintessence of religious life. But at the same time he appears unable to find any basis for considering these values as really anchored in the attributes of the cosmos. But the creative significance of the theistic religious mentality consists precisely in that it projects higher human values into the cosmos and in that it assumes that these values belong to its very essence.

Belief in immortality should therefore be looked upon not merely as wish fulfillment, nor only as a compensation for our fears, but also as a demand of our moral sense and an assumption that within the cosmos there exists an even higher moral awareness which would preclude total annihilation as an epilogue to human fate. It is precisely for this reason that religion gravitates toward some form of theism. Religion finds no sympathy for human values in the impersonal forces of nature. (It finds no antipathy, either, but this does not alter the situation.) But into the concept of a personal God there enters a certain measure of reciprocity in the relations between men and the "supreme power," responsibility for the fate of human values, even though these are on a different plane from the values ascribed to the personal God. Einstein refuses to recognize that if he were to prove the nonexistence of a personal God (something that cannot be demonstrated scientifically, as Einstein himself admitted in his address) he would thereby open broad vistas for a pessimistic world outlook, but not for religion or a cosmodicy. For even those values which Einstein considers to be the main elements in religion—truth, goodness, beauty—are real and can have objective worth under one condition only—if they are accepted as values by somebody or something in addition to humankind. (Not in vain do we find in talmudic literature an expression of the notion that the Torah—law—is obligatory also for God and that he studies it before making decisions [B. Avodah Zarah 3b]. This is a highly anthropomorphic approach. An even more "shocking" example is another popular conception, also to be found in the talmudic literature, according to which God puts on phylacteries [B. Brakhot 6a]. A delicate ear, however, will detect in these conceptions the vibrations of a creative religious force, the striving after ultimate certainty that "law" is not something merely human that does not affect extra-human existence, thus becoming unreal to all intents and purposes.) For the religious-minded it is not enough to accept the thesis propounded by Einstein that there exists an external rhythm of strict order and logical sequence in the universe. Such a thesis will not make one feel "at home" in the universe. Nor is the assumption that there are in nature "personality building activities"—an assumption advanced by the American theologian [Shailer] Mathews[12]—sufficiently meaningful to make the world "acceptable."[13] Religion requires, in addition, that (granted that there is no extra-cosmic or transcendental God) the natural forces or activities should be aware of their existence and of their own nature. Without such an awareness they remain indifferent, irresponsible, and amoral. No reciprocity can be established with unconscious forces even if we assume that these automatically (according to what mechanical laws?) produce the highest known to us values of the spirit and personality. In order to establish such a spiritual and moral bond with these forces, they must contain within themselves something which can only be characterized as "personal."

In this connection it is easy to understand the irony of the greatest master of this art in our era, Anatole France.[14] Discussing the hypothesis that our entire universe is doomed to physical disintegration as well as the destruction of all spiritual values ever created by any being on any planet, France said: "It is unimportant whether the universe will really perish or not, whether this will occur tomorrow or many billion years hence. What is important is whether, when this has happened, there will be a God who will address His courtiers on the ruins of His creation in somewhat the following words: 'This has been a glorious game. Let us begin from the beginning again.'"[15]

The fundamental question in this instance is very simple: whether the appearance of personality in the world is an accident, or a logical consequence of the essence of our cosmos. Bertrand Russell,[16] for instance, holds that consciousness, spirit, will, and personality are essentially something alien and accidental to our universe.[17] We will not pause to ask at this point how such "accidents" could take place in a self-enclosed universe and whether such accidents are not more miraculous, more irrational than a personal God who creates *ex nihilo*, but if we accept Russell's view, it becomes clear that all our values are, in the final analysis, also accidental and therefore unreal. Einstein, however, refuses to consider human values as accidental or illusory. On the contrary, he is inclined to ascribe to them genuine reality. But whence do they derive their reality if they exist only for the human spirit? It is quite possible that Einstein's denial of the element of personality at the basis of the universe is a result of his thinking in terms of physics. This method of thinking, the only legitimate one for its special sphere, seems to have created in Einstein a kind of "inhibition" whenever such non-physical concepts as personality are involved. He thinks in *physicomorphic* terms, if we may be allowed to use such an adjective.

A biologist will naturally suffer much less from such intellectual "inhibitions," and we find that Henri Bergson,[18] whose philosophical orientation is primarily directed toward biology, easily assimilated the concept of personality on a cosmic scale. "It seems to me," he wrote more than two decades ago, "that personality is in the very intention of the evolution of life, and that the human personality is just one mode in which this intention is realized. It is therefore very probable that the spiritual source of life whence our personality springs should be *personal* itself. Of course, personal in a different way, without all those accidental traits which in our mind form part of our personality and which are bound up with the existence of the body, personal in a large sense of the term—a spiritual unity expressing itself in the creative process of evolution."[19] With such a lantern to light his way, it was therefore not difficult for Bergson to manifest intellectual sympathies even for such an element in Judeo-Christian religiosity as the *fatherhood* of a personal God.

In connection with Einstein's address, it may be permissible to quote from a conversation between him and Rabindranath Tagore.[20] I will only cite a few lines from the dialogue between the European scientist and the Asian poet:

> Einstein: Truth or Beauty is not independent of man?
>
> Tagore: No.
>
> Einstein: If there would be no human beings any more, the Apollo of [the] Belvedere[21] would no longer be beautiful?
>
> Tagore: No.
>
> Einstein: I agree with regard to this conception of Beauty, but not with regard to Truth.

Tagore: Why not? Truth is realized through man.

Einstein: I cannot prove that my conception is right, but that is my religion.

[Tagore: Beauty is in the ideal of perfect harmony, which is in the Universal Being; Truth the perfect comprehension of the Universal Mind. We individuals approach it through our own mistakes and blunders, through our accumulated experience, through our illumined consciousness—how, otherwise, can we know Truth?]

Einstein: I cannot prove scientifically that truth must be conceived as something that is valid independent of humanity; but I believe it firmly. I believe, for instance, that the Pythagorean theorem in geometry[22] states something that is approximately true, independently of the existence of man. Anyway, if there is a *reality* independent of man, there is also a truth relative to this reality; and in the same way the negation of the first engenders a negation of the existence of the latter.[23]

If there is no personal God, then Tagore was absolutely right in this conversation. In order that truth and beauty should have extra-human validity, there must be someone outside of man to know truth and appreciate beauty. With his contention that Pythagoras's theorem would remain true even without human beings, Einstein actually implied the possible existence of a personal God. He could have maintained, with equal justice, that the Apollo of [the] Belvedere would remain beautiful even without the existence of human beings. For if there exists a "someone" who is capable of grasping geometric theorems, there is no reason why that "someone" should not also be capable of appreciating esthetic values.

In the above dialogue Einstein showed himself to be much closer to theism than in his recent address. Were he to return today to his one-time conception of truth as demonstrable also outside the limits of human thought, he would find no difficulty in taking a second step—that goodness and beauty are also of cosmic, and not only human, value. Einstein would then, too, not have to accept the existence of an otherworldly supernatural God, the solely transcendental God of our historical religions. For also an immanent God, one who can be interpreted by pantheists as "coextensive" with nature, can be a living, personal, conscious God, "endowed" with will and responsibility for the fate of his creatures—or, if we were to employ biological terminology, responsible for the fate of his *children*.

If Arago—whom we mentioned at the beginning of this essay—were only an astronomer confining himself to the narrow bounds of his science, he would not have had to answer Victor Hugo's question: What is the soul of a comet? More than that, he would even have been under no obligation to understand such a question. But if Arago had also been a philosophical thinker and religious-minded, Hugo's question should have been familiar and easily understandable to him. And although he might not have known *what* is the soul of a comet, he could have, without any loss of prestige as a scientist, accepted the premise that a comet also has a soul, that the universe has a soul, and that that soul is *at least* as potent a force as man's soul. I purposely stress the words *at least,* because of Einstein's sharp opposition to anthropomorphic concepts and images. It is true that certain degrees and forms of anthropomorphism are the stumbling blocks of all theistic religions as well as of many philosophical systems. But even scientific thinking is not entirely blameless in this respect. It will suffice to recall that the concept "law," a concept without which it would be impossible to make any headway in the natural sciences, originated in human, social affairs, and only later was projected into the realm of natural phenomena. As long as we remain the human beings we are, it appears unlikely that we will ever liberate ourselves entirely from anthropomorphic modes of thought. The history of monotheistic religions relates of many struggles against this inner compulsion to think in anthropomorphic terms, against the tendency to underestimate the supreme power when describing it, against the process of "creating God in our own image." As a result of these struggles many religions have evolved a form of negative dogmatism, a definition of what God is not, in order to avoid imagining him in all too human form. So far as positive definitions are concerned, all theistic religions are fatally anthropomorphic, and there seems to be no complete escape from this dilemma. There can therefore exist only the problem of reducing and purifying the elements of anthropomorphism of primitive stuff. Any too rigorous opposition to the anthropomorphist mode of thought must in the end lead merely to hylomorphism,[24] as it did in Einstein's case, to a large extent. (Hylomorphism is a world outlook expressed in terms of what is lower than man, in terms of matter, of things instead of personality.) But in that case it becomes impossible to answer the question of how spirit and personality arose in a world of impersonal matter and forces, how one drop in the ocean can contain elements not to be found in the ocean as a whole. We are thus trapped in a circle from which there is no escape. All forms of existence—present, possible, and conceivable—must be imagined as either sub-personal (minerals and possibly plants), or personal and super-personal. We have no conception of any fourth category. Unless one is inclined to accept the paradox of a universe of which personality is a part but which is itself sub-personal, one is forced to think in terms of either personality or super-personality. In other words, God must be at least "personal." If he is more than that, it does not follow that he is "impersonal" but rather that he *also* contains personality and individuality among his attributes.

I am not so naive as to assume that I have proved my point. I know that no single metaphysical argument can be considered convincing in the accepted sense of the word. There exists no absolute compulsion of logic as a result of which Einstein should feel impelled to accept the thesis that the universe as a whole must contain *at least* that element of personality which manifests itself in mankind. But a hylomorphic world is incapable of releasing our religious tensions. In such a world the values which Einstein would like to see as the basis of a religious life—truth, goodness, and beauty—would have no reality.

15

Psychoanalysis and Moral Pessimism

(1940)

In the decades after World War I, Sigmund Freud's theory of psychoanalysis gained increasing currency in American society. Public intellectuals, scholars, and laypersons alike were profoundly influenced by Freud's conception of the relationship between the human psyche and social behavior. Up to a point, Hayim Greenberg adopted a Freudian lens in his critique of socialism's mechanistic insistence on Marxist utopianism. At the same time, Greenberg, skeptical of Freud's ideas of sublimation and the Freudian school's tendency toward psychological determinism, argued against the reductionist claims of psychoanalysis. In the following essay, Greenberg investigates Freudian theory and argues for reconceptualizing the liberal vision of social transformation along lines that balance Freud's insights with what he considered to be humanity's organic capacity for ethical choice.

I

One of the chief accusations leveled against psychoanalysis is its ethical pessimism.[1] It has been pointed out that according to [Sigmund] Freud's[2] teachings the very nature of man is amoral, if not anti-moral, and that this leaves no hope that man would at some time begin to behave according to the spirit of genuine moral values. Freud himself provided sufficient occasions for such accusations. In a number of works he described our civilization, especially the elements of ethics in it, as entirely or largely a matter of social compulsion applied to the chaotic, savage, and grasping lusts of the individual. But he did not always agree with his critics that his teachings must lead to despair and that the conclusions to be derived from the psychoanalytic school must be radically pessimistic. Thus he complains in his *A General Introduction to Psychoanalysis* [1920][3] that many have misunderstood him.[4] He stressed the evil in human nature, he claims, only because other sentimental thinkers and authors sought to cover it up and thus made human spiritual life more incomprehensible instead of nobler. His critics, he says, did not sufficiently appreciate the censorship process which he discovered in the human psyche. Much evil within us is repressed, censored, and masked, but our very possession of such an inner censoring force, Freud believed, confirmed our possession of a more or less genuine tendency toward "good." In his treatise on war and death[5] he found it necessary to point out that the existence of marked "evil" desires in children is often a precondition for tendencies to be "good" in the adult; unbearably egotistic children often mature into kind and self-sacrificing citizens, and the majority of those obsessed with feelings of compassion and urges to prevent cruelty derived their greatest pleasure during childhood from tormenting living creatures—so Freud believed.[6] That psychoanalysis is not as pessimistic as some imagine, Freud strongly stressed in his intriguing treatise *The Ego and the Id* [1923]:[7]

> Psychoanalysis has been accused on countless occasions of ignoring the higher moral and spiritual side of human nature. This accusation is doubly unjustified, on grounds of history as well as of methodology. The function of repressing certain frequently evil desires we ascribed from the beginning to the *moral and esthetic tendencies of the ego*. Secondly, certain critics refused to understand that psychoanalytic investigation could not come out at once with a completely finished and rounded theory which could be compared to a philosophical system; that it had to find its way step by step, examining the delicate complexities of the human spirit and operating with an analytical scalpel both in physically normal as well as in abnormal manifestations. . . . But now we can answer all those whose moral feelings were outraged and who argued (against us) that there must be a higher nature in man: that is correct, and that higher nature can be seen in the ideals of the ego or in the super-ego.[8]

But we are not obliged to accept Freud's opinions of his own teachings. Whether the theories of psychoanalysis lead to ethical pessimism or not does not depend on polemical declarations which Freud has made at one time or another in response to critics and opponents, but on its basic assumptions. When Freud invokes the ideals of the ego or the super-ego as proof that his teachings detract nothing from man's moral grandeur, we should first of all analyze the character and functions of the super-ego as conceived by Freud, and see whether it really contains sources of genuine morality.

How does Freud understand the term "super-ego?"

I will first briefly sketch Freud's "anatomy of the mental personality."[9] The individual "consists" of three parts: the id, the ego, and the super-ego. The boundaries between one part and another naturally are not as clear and exact as the boundaries between ordinary anatomical organs. In psychic anatomy the parts are not arranged in topographical order, so to speak; their boundaries are often vague and one part may penetrate and influence another. The "id," a term borrowed by Freud from [Friedrich] Nietzsche,[10] is the impersonal element in one's being, the elemental, unorganized, blindly wild, unthinking drive of the instincts and impulses. The id is non-rational, unethical, insatiable and neither knows nor wishes to know of any hindrances in its way; the id cannot conceive of punishment for acts committed and represents unbridled desire in human nature; the id is the glutton, the drunkard, the seeker after power and possessions, the rapist and the murderer in us. Only a tendency toward superficial analogies could have led one to find a similarity between Freud's "id" and [Henri] Bergson's "*élan vital*."[11] Bergson's *élan* is a constructive force bearing within itself "secret wisdom" and the mystery of unending creative evolution, while Freud's id is the eternal unprincipled fool. The id looks upon itself as the only living entity, all others being merely objects to satisfy its lust for possession, pleasure, murder, and destruction. Freud's id is not only absolutely amoral but also scandalously impractical. It never knows, nor ever can know, how dangerous its lust drives are to its own existence. There does not exist for it any relationship between action and its consequences. Were the id the only or the main factor in human life, society could not exist. Humanity would be transformed into a battlefield of blind forces, into a chaos of mutually annihilating and ultimately self-destroying impulses. The relatively few human examples in whom the id gains the upper hand become a danger to society and must be removed through physical destruction (execution) or social destruction (isolation).

An entirely different function is fulfilled in our spiritual life by the ego. As Freud describes it, the ego is also far from being the perfect example of conduct and it would be risky to expect it to be the bearer of genuine moral values. Primarily the ego is the repository of experience within us, and its value consists to a great extent in its ability to accumulate these experiences. The ego is capable of learning from the past and therefore has a certain ability to foresee the inevitable, the likely, and the possible future. It would be no exaggeration to identify the ego with the intellect. The ego knows that the id is chaotic and incapable of reckoning with the surrounding reality; it therefore assumes the role of overseer, guardian, and censor over everything that seethes within the undisciplined id. The ego draws boundaries for the drives of the id in order to avoid sickness or dangerous collisions with the bearers of similar drives or with the objects of the drives themselves (since the id does not know that the object of its desire is often not only an object but also a being endowed with an id of its own, capable of punishing those who attack it). The ego possesses the empirical wisdom of experience. With the power of that wisdom the ego forces the id to make concessions from time to time and to renounce desires which may lead to conflict with the natural and social environment. In certain situations the ego even decrees a measure of asceticism. If we imagine the ego as exerting its influence on the id through convictions, its argumentation would not be ethical but utilitarian and legalistic. The argument would run as follows: "Do not take this object which you desire, for behind it stands somebody whom you, you eternal fool, do not wish to encounter. That somebody will hit you over the head with a club; in addition, he has arranged with others like himself to pool their forces for punishing anyone who takes something that does not belong to him. Repress your desire for that or some other woman because she has on her side an uncle, a brother, a husband, or a lover, in addition to anonymous society." The id often obeys these quasi-moral commandments out of fear more than out of agreement. Only through fear does the ego succeed in bridling the id. In relation to the id the ego is therefore a counselor and, if we may use the expression, a legal advisor. The ego is boss over the id and, paradoxically, also its servant. When the id refuses to heed the advice of the ego or its warning because the intensity of its desire is too great, the ego not infrequently sanctions the act; the ego is then not ashamed to play the role of a shyster lawyer and recommend to the id clever stratagems for gratifying its desire in such a manner that the controlling factors should remain unaware of the act or incapable of meting out punishment. In relation to certain excesses of the id, the ego simultaneously plays the role of the vice-squad and the panderer. If it is true that were all people to be dominated by the id there could be no society, then it is equally true that if the ego were to dominate our entire spiritual life, then after a long period of development we would only attain the status of a "society of egoists for mutual protection." At the foundation of such a society there would be the legal contract, since the control of the ego over the id is primarily legal and not ethical, and the only behavior that the ego is capable of dictating is at best legitimate but not moral. (We take for granted the trite verity that the morality of even a socially useful act is gauged according to whether it is the result of a direct and spontaneous desire to do the right thing.) The ego, too—as it was characterized by Freud—may therefore be eliminated as a possible source of genuine and unequivocal morality. Moral values cannot come from the unconscious id nor from the morally apathetic but society-conscious ego.

We are therefore compelled to seek the springs of genuinely moral motives—if such exist—in the third part of our personality: the ego-ideal or the super-ego. (Freud employs these two terms interchangeably for one and the same concept.) If the id is blind passion and the ego is administering intelligence, then the super-ego is the seat of conscience. The criterion of the super-ego is not the possible or impossible, the socially tolerated or socially punishable, that which is healthful or that which is physiologically harmful and destructive, but that which is allowed and that which is prohibited, the beautiful and the ugly, the worthy and the unworthy. The super-ego is both a certain standard ideal, according to which all actions should be governed, as well as the court which judges one's personality for deviating from the standard and also grieves (and imparts its grief to the other parts of the personality) when an offense or an unworthy act has been committed. Regret, troubled conscience, and repentance are manifestations that would be unthinkable were our personalities to consist merely of the id and the ego. After an amoral act, the ego will remain untroubled if it is sure no one will find out or that for some reason no punishment will be inflicted. But the super-ego knows of no unpunished transgressions; the super-ego represents the inner judge from whom one cannot hide. Moods of depression and gloom, nervous ailments, shame, despair, and, in especially extreme cases, insanity, are the consequences of "sin."

After this characterization of the super-ego, we could complacently conclude that it is the natural and original source of genuine morality. The functions of the super-ego, as described by Freud, could compensate us for the irresponsible nature of the id and for the moral hypocrisy of the ego, and we could then agree with Freud's declaration that his teachings destroy none of the bases of our moral values and there exists therefore no ground for pessimism. But the founder of psychoanalysis gave us not merely a description of the super-ego but also its history. If Freud's genealogy of the super-ego is correct, then it is not a basic bio-psychological factor in humanity, with its own laws of development, but a result of social evolution, a product of civilization rather than a natural ingredient in the makeup of humanity, something forced upon, or into, the human personality. While the id has been there from the very beginning, the super-ego appeared rather late and, in a certain sense, merely reflects education and social compulsion. For that which we are wont to call conscience is, according to Freud, an inner extension of the outer forces of criticism and threat of punishment. The positive and negative commandments imposed upon the individual, first by parents and later by civilized society, exert a hypnotic influence. The detective and punitive functions of the group are transferred into one's inner life, and outward compulsions become transformed into inner compulsions. Many types of mentally afflicted persons suffer from a delusion that other people (or all other people) know their thoughts and actions and constantly observe them. Such mentally deranged people are often informed of the existence of an investigating and prosecuting factor by "voices," and it is characteristic that these "voices" refer to the patients in the third person: "He thinks again of the same thing. He is going to that place again." Freud claims that these "voices" are actually heard by the patient and that they are quite "real."[12] These are the voices of parents, teachers, religious mentors, and society in general which the patient has often heard before and which have become permanently fixed in the patient's ego or super-ego. In his *Origin and Development of Moral Ideas* [1906–8], [Edvard] Westermark[13] relates a conversation between a young member of an Australian tribe and the well-known explorer [Alfred William Howitt].[14] The two discussed the types of food which are forbidden during the period when young tribesmen are being inducted into the adult society of the tribe. [Howitt] then asked: "Imagine that you are very hungry and have an opportunity to kill one of the animals whose meat is forbidden, why shouldn't you eat it if none of the older men sees you?" "That I cannot do," the young tribesman answered; "that would be a bad thing to do."[15] In this instance Freud would have said that the eyes of the older men already look at this Australian from within and that a reflection of their disapproval has already been transferred into his inner self; outer compulsion has begun to exert an influence in the form of inner conscience. In the last analysis, Freud's conscience, or super-ego, thus appears to be masked compulsion and social hypnotism. To the extent that this is the essence of conscience, it is not native or innate but something introjected from the outside. We can therefore find no free and spontaneous morality even in the super-ego, and the individual must always be subject to the desire to break the spiritual bonds with which society bound him, to liberate himself from the *dybbuk* [Yiddish for "demon"][16] which civilization implanted in him. If conscience is not native to the psyche but is a product of other factors, then it can have no determining value according to a strict interpretation of Freud's basic assumptions. A revolt against the "unnatural" conscience is always possible and would be justifiable biologically. Freud's anatomy of the mental personality thus leaves ample room for ethical pessimism, for the conception of ethical values as artificial or society-made; the origin of the id is *cosmic* while the origin of the super-ego is merely *historical*.

II

When we consider Freud's further detailed descriptions of the functions of conscience and its intensity, the suspicion arises that the founder of psychoanalysis did not stop to consider the philosophical implications of his descriptions. Hardly any of the modern psychologists has manifested such an interest in and such a capacity for observing that very important element in conscience—sense of guilt. It was Freud who called our attention to the type of the "[criminal from] a sense of guilt."[17] He gave us the key to the behavior of a certain type of children who suddenly become "bad" with a definite although subconscious intention to provoke punishment because of their badness. Such children are motivated by a sense of guilt for some other act (which they frequently do not remember) or by an unmotivated sense of guilt, and they will not calm down until they are punished. Freud might have found hints of such paradoxical commission of punishable acts in Nietzsche's speeches of Zarathustra,[18] but his own laboratory provided him with adequate material and intriguing illustrations of this phenomenon. Thus he tells of one of his patients who ran away from home while still a young and adventurous girl.[19] In the course of her travels she met an artist who fell in love with her. For a long time the artist's family refused to allow the two young people to marry. When the opposition of the family was finally overcome and the girl could have enjoyed her triumph, she became mentally ill. Her victory was transformed into a calamity, for somewhere in her mind she bore a sense of guilt and considered herself undeserving of happiness. Undeserved happiness is unjustified and in this case justice triumphed through the girl's insanity. In the same treatise we read of a university instructor who for a long time dreamed of gaining the office of an older colleague, an important professor. The professor suddenly died, and the young instructor was appointed to his post. But instead of enjoying his success the instructor was stricken with melancholy and could do no work for many years: something within him had known that in his dreams of advancement he had wished death for the professor.[20]

We mention these facts with a definite intention. They demonstrate a moral function which is too intense and thorough, which fixes the personality on one point too completely to justify Freud's assumption that its power is borrowed from the outside and is not organically a part of the personality. In psychology, as in mechanics, a movement cannot possess a force greater than the one which brought it into being. Were conscience merely a form of inner compulsion, it could not possess such astounding forces as manifest themselves in sick conscience. Education, social compulsion, and inner brakes logically should result in legitimate behavior rather than in masochistic morality. In his last work concerning the origins of morality and religion,[21] Henri Bergson mentioned the type of criminal who cannot control himself and returns to the scene of his crime as if in obedience to a fatal commandment.[22] (He merely failed to mention that he learned of this phenomenon largely from [Fyodor] Dostoyevsky.[23]) The criminal returns so frequently that he is finally apprehended. Freud was also aware of such manifestations and in his estimation too this type of criminal seeks an opportunity to be apprehended, to be punished and thus to calm the consciousness of guilt. How could the elders of the tribe, institutionalized religion, and civilization in general hypnotize one into such behavior if conscience were merely a gramophone playing the records inserted by the outside world, if the super-ego of one's personality did not contain the germ of basic morality? (So far as the principle underlying such behavior is concerned, it is unimportant whether the number thus affected is small or large.)

Similar questions involuntarily arise also in connection with Freud's conception of sublimation. That which he defines as the moral personality arises as a result of two processes. The warnings and threats of the ego curb or suppress some of the instinctive desires, and the super-ego sublimates to a higher plane of social usefulness or esthetic or religious creativeness some of the amoral energies of the id. A boy, for example, who derives pleasure from torturing animals and cutting them up to see what goes on within them may, under the influence of suitable conditions, grow up to be a surgeon and engage in research of anatomy and physiology. In Jewish literature we find an interesting case of sublimation in the works of Sholem Aleichem.[24] For years Moshke the thief steals horses from neighboring peasants, but when a calamity occurs (a Jewish girl is kidnapped to a convent where she is baptized, and her parents look for someone to rescue her out of the convent and take her across the border where she may live without a stigma of shame) Moshke is the one who finds the necessary moral courage to do so.[25] His criminal energy becomes sublimated in this case into religious, or at least socially useful, energy.

Freud attaches great therapeutic value to the process of sublimation. Mere suppression of desires and lusts only disorganizes the personality and leads to nervous and hysterical states of mind, while sublimation rebuilds the personality and revitalizes it with health and productivity.

But whence comes the necessary strength for sublimation? Naturally, sublimation is looked upon as a process of compensation. Through sublimating our feelings, inclinations and energies we compensate ourselves for the losses suffered through obeying the ego or super-ego and depriving ourselves of pleasures for which we yearned. A definite principle of economy operates in this case, according to Freud: "I have renounced a pleasure for the sake of the ego or super-ego, I am therefore entitled to another pleasure in its stead."[26] But here we may ask whether the new gratifications which we obtain through sublimation merely fill the place of others and are, in a sense, *ersatz* pleasures, or they are independent experiences, original pleasures in themselves, deriving their existence from a different plane of our being. Let us assume that a girl who had been raised as a Catholic is forced to renounce such intensive and basic natural functions as sex life and motherhood because of physical unattractiveness or the desertion of the man she loved. Sometime later we hear that this girl became a nun and went to the Molokai island, where she devotes her entire time serving and healing the isolated colony of lepers.[27] We would say in such a case that the girl compensates for her sexual deprivation and gives expression to her unfulfilled motherhood instincts in the tenderness which she lavishes daily on the unfortunate and often incurable patients. It will be said that we deal with a case of compensatory sublimation. But are we justified in declaring that the strange gratification which the nun derives from working among the lepers is merely a substitute for normal sexual life? If the substitute manifests greater psychic energy than the original and the compensating pleasure is more intense than the original pleasure would have been—as in this case—we may be justified in asking whether sublimation is a form of substitute gratification.

From [Arthur] Schopenhauer's[28] biography we know that he was most creative when he was sexually aroused yet suppressed his erotic urges.[29] But would we be justified in concluding on the basis of this fact that his *World as Will and Idea*

[1818][30] was merely a substitute for his loss of sexual gratification? If a blind man develops a more keen sense of hearing and greater capacity for music, it would be absurd on our part to conclude that hearing is a substitute for sight. Similarly, if a deaf person develops a sharp sense for color and line we would be unjustified in concluding that the eye is a natural substitute for the ear. We would be more justified in assuming that, in the first case, the ear was partly atrophied as a result of the claims of the eye to a share of the energy inherent in the personality and when the time came and the eye no longer required its share of energy, the ear was thereby enriched. The same interpretation may be applied to the second case. If the "sublime" were lacking within us as a special sphere of existence, we could never attain it, and if it were not genuine and a value in itself, it could never become as creative and serviceable as it often appears to be in the realms of religion, science, art, and politics. Freud's description of the processes of sublimation[31] and their results should have led him to a revision of his concept of the super-ego and to an earnest consideration of the question whether the "sublime" is merely an end product of certain developments or it is a basic factor and as elemental as the erotic factor itself.

In one of his short but stimulating essays ["Reflections on War and Death," 1915],[32] Freud attempts to place the moral element on the same plane of nativity with the erotic, and even to consider the moral as a part of the erotic factor. In that essay he hints at an entirely different origin and development of moral emotions and ethical commandments. This hint seems to contradict in principle his interpretation of conscience as a form of compulsion transferred inward. He there reminds us that everyone is at one time inclined to consider himself immortal. We know that death exists, but in a certain sphere of our psychic life we do not know that death concerns us personally. It is as if there existed a species of mortals to which we—i.e., each of us separately—did not belong. In Europe a cynical joke is told concerning a man who tells his wife that in case one of them dies, he would go to Paris. (In the Jewish version, Palestine takes the place of Paris.) According to Freud such a joke could not have come into being had it not contained a germ of psychological truth, a hint of our inclination to harbor the idea, in some absurd corner of our psyche, that death exists but not for us, and a partial tendency to wish death upon others, not excluding people who are dear to us.[33] Freud is not surprised at such a phenomenon because it is consonant with his general conception of ambivalence, of opposing emotional tendencies, of parallel love and hate. The same person can be the object of our love and hatred. This is not only a possibility but in a certain sense it is even an organic inevitability. When confronted with the fact of death, primitive man considered every stranger as an actual or potential enemy deserving to die or to be killed by him. Death of others made no impression upon him and did not induce him to ponder metaphysical questions. But when primitive man saw one of "his own" people die, a wife, a child, or a friend whom he loved in the same manner as we love our own "flesh and blood," his grief led him to the realization that he, too, was subject to death, for his dear ones were, to use Freud's expression, "a part of his own beloved ego." Death of dear ones became associated in his mind with his own death. The end of his own life appeared to primitive man more nearly possible and imaginably inevitable. If we correctly understand Freud's meaning, the death of a person to whom man had an erotic attachment in the broadest sense of the word (a child or a friend) introduced him into the community of fate of the human race as such. This awareness of common fate may be the original source of our moral concepts and attitudes. At the bedside of a deceased beloved person there could arise a spontaneous and socially imposed commandment: "Thou shalt not kill" [Exod. 20:13]. On the other hand, the longing for a beloved person removed by death and the memories concerning him evoked the desire for immortality in a world to come and a conception of such a possible world, for had not the dead person continued to live in memory? As a result of the death of a near one, primitive man began to identify himself with other human beings, at first with beloved ones and later also with strangers. Hatred of strangers could not have been an absolute barrier in the way of self-identification, for even the beloved person always contained some aspect of the stranger and his death, too, as revealed in the above-mentioned anecdote, was desired in some corner of the mind. Freud concedes this when he claims that mourning for a beloved person contains the grief of a stricken conscience for its secret desire that the person should die.[34] The object of our love is also hated by us and the one we hate can also be loved.

According to this interpretation, which Freud regrettably merely hinted at and did not expand, the source of our moral concepts and attitudes is the beloved person or persons, love and not compulsion, eros and not social pressure and hypnosis. Viewed in this light, the moral element within us is rather of an erotic nature or origin, and this implies that it is native to the human psyche and possesses its own unborrowed forces. It is remarkable that Freud did not notice the contradiction between his two interpretations of the origin of conscience. His sociological interpretation leaves enough room for pessimism while his hints at a purely erotic interpretation open wide horizons for the existence of an autonomous morality which is rooted in the primeval elements of our nature. In his attempt at an erotic explanation of conscience, Freud actually reached the classic Hindu formula "I am thou,"[35] the ability to become identified with other beings, in which Schopenhauer saw the only possible source of true morality. To the extent that Freud recognized the existence within us of a capacity for erotic devotion and self-identification with others, he must also have recognized that the way to a broad altruistic attitude is not impossible in principle.

Freud's disciples who will continue to develop his methods of investigation are confronted with an intellectual obligation. Above all, they must critically revise their master's "anatomy of the mental personality" and establish a clearer and more organic relationship between the super-ego and those sources of energy which we bear in our eros.

16

Chosen Peoples

(1941)

The concepts of divine and national election have animated disparate societies, groups, and rulers across the globe since the dawn of human history. In the following essay, Hayim Greenberg considers this durable tradition of "superiority and chosenness complexes" as exemplified by a variety of peoples. Written against the backdrop of Nazi Germany's aggressive racist political ideology, which codified the terrifying fantasy of a master Aryan race as state policy, Greenberg surveys the complex competing spiritual, cultural, ethnic, and national claims professed by a broad spectrum of historical groups—beginning with the ancient Egyptians, Persians, and Greeks through the rise in the nineteenth century of modern Italian, German, Polish, Russian, Indian, and Japanese nationalism. Next, Greenberg applies an exacting "yardstick" to the Jewish case and examines the broad spectrum of traditional and modern ideas of Jewish exceptionalism. In the final analysis, he asserts that despite "minor" differences the "advocates" of Jewish chosenness are generally "united in their outlook, but with minor modifications." In this regard, he concludes, Jews are really no different than other peoples and that chosenness, while valuable to the self-awareness of religious, ethnic, and national groups, must be tempered by a sense of collective humility and social responsibility.

Jews are not the only people in the world who are imbued with a conviction, or at least a vague feeling, that they are "the chosen ones" and are endowed with superiority over other peoples. When the ancient Greeks called all other peoples "barbarians" (a term not entirely alien or distasteful even to Plato[1] and Aristotle[2]), they meant to imply that the Greeks were the only ones to create a worthwhile civilization. Egyptians, Persians, and Jews with whom the Greek came in contact were inferior peoples in the estimation of the Greek. The Egyptians, for their part, despised both the Greeks and the Jews and considered themselves to be the bearers of the highest culture. In the Far East the Aryans,[3] as is evident from an ancient document like the *Institutes of Vishnu*,[4] believed that they were the only ones "to be twice born."[5] All others experienced only one material birth and did not attain the second spiritual and higher birth. "A *brahman*,"[6] we are informed by the sacred laws of the Aryans, "must repent if he served a person of the black race."[7] But it would be erroneous to conclude that only members of the black race were held inferior by the Indo-Aryans. Reading the *Avesta*[8] one is struck by its tone of hauteur and hatred for the white Turanians.[9] Similarly, we learn from the Koran that no true spiritual nobility is to be found outside the Arab tribes, this despite the fact that [Islam] strove to become a world religion from its very inception. Considering modern nations, we again find a number of examples of superiority complexes and cases of nations which are imbued with a faith of a special missionary function in life. Nor are the Germans the only ones to suffer from the illusion of superiority and the belief that they are a "master race."[10] The English are too well mannered to formulate such a belief in their superiority, but it stands to reason that they would not have been able to establish the [British] empire without some such faith in their historic mission. British imperial expansion is the empirical expression of this feeling of chosenness. The people of Britain are too "polite" and too hypocritical to rationalize this feeling into a national theory. (The reference to hypocrisy must be understood as a compliment, instead of a condemnation, today.) So far as the French are concerned, their revolution had imbued them with a deep conviction that they were destined to be an example for other nations on the way to political freedom and democracy. The Italians, like the French, a Latin people, were not free from the chosenness complex either. The progressive revolutionary Italians of the nineteenth century particularly believed that destiny had chosen them as the vanguard of humanity pointing the path to moral regeneration. Thus [Giuseppe] Mazzini[11] wrote that "the people that suffered most and preserved its faith in purity would in the course of time be blessed by God with the will and courage to *triumph and die for others*. Such is the fate of a people that rejuvenates the world; it arises to new struggles. It may triumph or fall, but whether from the ashes or from the triumphal altar, the word that is to guide the epoch would rise and redeem the world."[12] Mazzini considered the Italians to be this type of prophetic people. After the Roman Empire, after the Rome of Catholicism and the Popes, there would arise a third Rome whose function it would be to "harmonize heaven and earth, justice and duty."[13] Thus Mazzini wrote in a call to Young Italy.[14] Much more profound, and also more hysterical, was the sense of chosenness which for a time characterized Russia. In [Fyodor] Dostoyevsky's[15] famous novel *The Possessed* [1871–72] we find the following revealing dialogue. When Shatov, one of the heroes of the novel, is asked whether he believes in God, he replies: "I believe in Russia."[16] Whoever believed in Russia automatically believed in God, because the Russian people were the only true bearers of the divine idea. For Dostoyevsky the entire Western world was steeped in diabolical uncleanness and without Russia it could never attain salvation. Western Europe he visualized as a cemetery with costly monuments, but pervaded with the stench of decaying flesh which could not be used even as fertilizer. The French were vain. The Germans, a second-rate and crude people. The English, dull and superficial rationalists. The Jews reeked of pride. Catholicism was the devil's own teaching and an insult to Christ. Protestantism was a rationalist state church and a miserable parody of true faith. All ideas born in western Europe were but wilted flowers. The only true, genuine, and great idea was the Russian. "We Russians conceive everything; you (non-Russians) are narrow-minded and of little spirit." Russia was therefore a collective Christ, the only redeemer of the world. And Dostoyevsky was not the sole representative of this trend in Russian literature and society. Many others cherished similar beliefs and apocalyptic expectations that fed on these beliefs.

Avoiding definite national or racist formulas, [Leo] Tolstoy[17] expressed a similar conception of the idea that Russians were a "god-bearing people."[18] Nor were "reactionaries" the sole protagonists of this idea. Radicals like the *Narodniki*[19] and the Social Revolutionaries,[20] who believed that Russia, of all countries, could skip from a semi-feudal social order into socialism, and avoid a period of capitalism, also believed that the Russian peasants in particular were a people endowed with special gifts. Even the Bolsheviks,[21] stressing the significance of the October Revolution[22] that would lead the world proletariat to triumph and to a socialist "kingdom of heaven,"[23] seemed to stress a certain superiority of the Russian people and its mission in the world—this despite the internationalist ideology and verbiage that was employed. That the feeling of chosenness was not limited to Russian intellectuals is obvious from the popular Russian reference to their country as "Holy Russia."

Chosen people sentiments were not alien in Poland either. While Mazzini and [Vincenzo] Gioberti[24] looked upon the Italian people as the redeemers of the world, believing that the Italians had suffered more than others and had preserved their faith in eternal values, while [François] Guizot[25] believed that France was a "light unto the nations,"[26] and [Johann] Fichte[27] demanded that Germans be recognized as the leading people, [Adam] Mickiewicz[28] and [August] Cieszkowski[29] tried to see in the martyrdom of the Polish nation the pattern of a prophetic and sacrificial people in the mystery of world redemption. In his [*Books of the Polish Nation and of the Polish Pilgrims* (1833)] which Mickiewicz wrote in his Parisian exile, he developed the idea that every historical period has its "Israel"—a nation that takes upon itself the messianic suffering of all humanity. In ancient times this mission was borne by the Jews; in modern days the Poles are the Israel of the world, redeeming humanity through their suffering.[30]

Considering present day Asiatic peoples, it suffices to mention [Mohandas K.] Gandhi's[31] faith that his people are predisposed to realize in life the principles and methods of non-resistance and that through them salvation would issue to the world. Japan is now engaged in imperial expansion based on a native theory that the Japanese are entrusted by destiny with the task of organizing and ruling over Asia.[32]

We have cited sufficient examples and it would serve no purpose to multiply them still further. There exists hardly a people in the world which is entirely free of illusions of superiority and chosenness complexes. There are differences in the degree to which these complexes are rooted, the forms they assume and the intensity with which they are felt. It must also be borne in mind that not all such complexes assume aggressive or nationalistic forms, as in the case of modern [Nazi] Germany. In India, among the revolutionary Italians, and among the romantically mystical Poles, it took the form of humble martyrdom and was characterized by a conception of the nation as a collective servant of a higher destiny instead of an insistence on political privileges and domination of other peoples.

It would also be incorrect to assume that only cultured peoples are subject to such superiority delusions. The French Jesuits who reached Canada in the seventeenth century met with Indians who looked upon the white explorers as inferior to themselves.[33] When [Wilhelm] von Humboldt[34] visited the Caribbean islands at the beginning of the nineteenth century, he heard a native version of the chosen people theory innumerable times. "Only we are a people," the native Indians would say; "all others were created to serve us."[35] And only a few years ago the psychologist C. G. Jung[36] related in his book *Modern Man in Search of a Soul* [1933][37] that an Indian chief of a Latin American *pueblo* boasted in the following words: "We don't understand the white men; always wanting something, always restless, always looking for something. What is it? We don't know. We can't understand them. They have such sharp noses, such thin cruel lips, such lines in their faces. We think *they are all crazy*."[38]

The Indian chief was not educated enough to develop a theory. But within his heart he knew, as did his tribesmen, that they were far superior to the whites. The same was true of the Aztecs who looked upon the whites as beings not belonging altogether to the human race. I have heard of an Eskimo who had to visit western Canada and there met a Jew. When he was informed of the Jewish custom of pronouncing the words "All who are hungry, let them come and eat"[39] at the *seder* feast on Passover,[40] the Eskimo laughed and declared that the Jews must have learned this custom from Eskimos, except that they learned it badly. For every Eskimo calls out an invitation to others to join him in his meal whenever he hunts alone. And he does so not once a year but every day. "There is nothing," he concluded, "that Eskimos need learn from others, but there are many things that white people could learn from us."[41]

We have cited a number of examples of the chosen people complex among cultured as well as among uncultured peoples. The purpose of these illustrations is not to establish any positive conclusions. None of the above cases in itself proves the existence or the nonexistence of superior peoples. But they are sufficient to arouse a good measure of skepticism concerning the entire business of classifying nations as being *higher* or *lower*. Since there are many claimants to the title of a superior nation, one may conclude that these claims are based on subjective or egocentric evaluations. Thoughtful Jews who refuse to surrender the traditional idea of Jewish superiority despite the tendentious nature of this type of claim should therefore be ready to answer some questions. They should, first of all, indicate the yardstick with which the spiritual stature of a people can be measured. Secondly they must prove that an application of this yardstick proves the Jews to be superior to other peoples. They must also demonstrate that this superiority of Jews is not the product of historical accidents, that the so-called "genius" of the Jewish people is not the result of circumstances that would have evoked similar characteristics among any other people. Only one who can give a satisfactory answer to these three questions is entitled to demand agreement with his theories of Jewish superiority.

The only ones who believe in the chosenness of the Jewish people and are not obliged to answer the above questions are those who still cling firmly to fundamentalist, dogmatic religious concepts. One can demand no explanations from pious Orthodox Jews and it would be senseless to debate this matter with them. They accept the chosen nature of the Jewish people as a cosmic fact, an integral element of the laws governing the universe. If God had made a covenant with Abraham and Jews were the only ones to accept the divine law, if this law is eternal and cannot be superseded or modified by any other and only our limited understanding prevents us from grasping the full meaning of the Torah which encompasses all—as pious Jews believe—then there is no reason why such Orthodox believers should doubt the chosenness of the Jews. Such a Jew is entitled to repeat the daily blessing of God that "He did not make me a *goy*" [gentile][42] or when pronouncing the benediction over the Sabbath wine, to declare: "Thou hast chosen us and sanctified us from among all other peoples,"[43] or to recite on Saturday night the prayer glorifying God for "setting apart the sacred from the profane, the light from the darkness, Israel from the other peoples."[44] Such an Orthodox Jew need not hide his faith in his superiority for, strange as it may seem, it contains no dangers for others. This belief does not permit him to exploit or oppress others and, despite its "racism," it also bears a strong mark of universalism. The Orthodox Jew who blesses God who "did not make us like the peoples of the countries nor did he place us like the families of the earth; he did not make our portion like theirs nor our fate like that of their multitudes," also recites a few pages further on in the same prayer book the following: "We therefore hope to see the glory of thy might to remove the abominations from the earth, to destroy the idols and to perfect the world with the kingdom of heaven that all men shall call thy name and all the wicked of the earth shall turn their hearts to thee."[45] The sense of chosenness does not endow the Orthodox Jew with any special rights but imposes upon him great and special burdens. In the coming kingdom of heaven there is room for all redeemed mankind and he would merely demand recognition of his status as first-born among equals. It would be senseless to ask such an Orthodox Jew how it came about that Israel was chosen of all peoples to be the bearer of God's will. He could, of course, recount the old tradition that God had offered the Torah to all the nations, and they had refused it, and that only the Jews consented to stand before Sinai and accept its commandments.[46] But why it was so, why God had not created other peoples with the same will to take up the burden and to obey, there would be no point in discussing with him. The religious mind is full of paradoxes, and the problem of free will in Jewish theological literature has always resembled an attempt to square the circle. On the one hand, no man may move his little finger on earth unless it has been predetermined from above that he do so, and on the other hand, man is personally responsible for all his actions and intentions. [Moses] Maimonides,[47] who did not deny the theory of Jewish chosenness (yet refrained from including it in his thirteen basic tenets of the faith, thus indicating that he did not consider it an indispensable element of Jewish religion) sought for some explanation for it and finally had to settle the matter by declaring that it was one of the mysterious aspects of God's will which man cannot possibly understand through reason. Any Jew who clings to traditional religious concepts can, as a last recourse, point to the inscrutability of God's ways and decisions and refuse to offer any rational explanations.

But when Reform Jews[48] ([Salomon] Munk,[49] Kaufmann Kohler[50]), who do not believe in a law handed down from heaven, refuse to renounce the chosenness of the Jewish people, or a secular nationalist like Ahad Haam[51] includes in a mild form the theory of Jewish superiority in his philosophy, when the prayer books of certain free Jewish congregations, which have purged them of elements of national import, include grateful thanks to God for dispersing Jews throughout the world so that they might best spread among humanity the spiritual influences of Israel, when we find a modern Yiddish poet (Menahem)[52] who struggles to prove the difference between Jews and other nations by comparing the former to ants with their altruistic and strict social organization and the latter to other asocial or even antisocial beings,[53] then we have the right to ask them just what they mean by "chosenness" and superiority and what yardstick they employ to measure the stature of races and nations. They certainly do not depend blindly on the mystery of God's ways. (Although sometimes one gets the impression that they do not believe in God yet believe in God's choosing the Jewish people. This reminds one of Hermann Cohen's[54] famous characterization of an antisemite as a person who denies the historical existence of Christ yet blames the Jews for crucifying him.[55]) They must therefore, in the last analysis, fall back on some racist interpretation—that Jews bear within their blood something which no other people possesses, and that this "something" is of the greatest importance for the spiritual development of mankind. Whoever does not trace things back to providence must try to interpret things in terms of biology, through the "mystery of blood" which is passed on from generation to generation, no matter how distasteful such terminology might sound today. What, then, is this special "something" which Jews had injected into their blood from the primeval genetic origins of humanity?

None of the apologists for the chosen people theory would vulgarize the matter by explaining Jewish superiority in terms of "abilities" which are mostly an outgrowth of habits and customs formed over a long period of time through adaptation to environmental circumstances. One would have to think in very crude terms to try to depict Jewish superiority in terms of success in commerce, industry, or the professions. The "best student" in the class is seldom a higher type of human being. And although Moses and Jesus, Socrates[56] and Plato, Buddha[57] and Confucius[58] would probably show a lower IQ than some high school boy in Chicago or New York (if they were given a modern intelligence test), that would hardly prove that they were inferior to him. The concept of a chosen people has nothing to do with the ability to learn and deals with the creative genius.

What, then, is the special creative genius of the Jews? So far as building civilizations goes—in the technological and scientific meanings of the terms—Jews have little to boast of. They did not establish great or lasting empires and even in ancient times were inferior, in this respect, to the Babylonians, Egyptians, Greeks, Romans, or Assyrians. It is also clear that Jewish genius does not excel in the sphere of the plastic arts. Artists of significance (including musicians) appeared among Jews only in the nineteenth century. The same is true of science, a field of endeavor in which Greeks, Arabs, and Egyptians surpassed the Jews. Modern Jews may boast that "the greatest scientists of the past two generations—[Karl] Marx,[59] [Sigmund] Freud,[60] [Albert] Einstein[61]—were Jews." But this claim can hardly conceal the fact that for thousands of years Jews were not creative in science. In the realm of speculative philosophy, Jews were "barbarians" in ancient times, when compared with the Greeks. Only in the seventeenth century did the Jews produce their first original philosopher—[Baruch] Spinoza.[62] Were philosophical speculation and musical creativeness the criterion for superiority, the Germans would easily win the laurels—unpleasant as this statement may sound to us today.

The specific Jewish genius must therefore be sought elsewhere, and the advocates of this theory have tried to prove that the universal mission of the Jews which set them apart from other peoples lay in the sphere of religion and morals. Neither scientific research nor philosophical speculations nor the esthetic arts—spheres where some other peoples showed greater ability and inventiveness—

could evoke those religious ideas and moral values which the Jews intuitively developed. This intuitive awareness of a pure religious outlook and the yearning for social morality are supposed to be the special gifts of the Jews who thus fulfill among mankind the same role that a prophet fulfills among his own people. To quote Yehuda Halevi,[63] who lived in the twelfth century, the Jews are the heart of the world and their suffering is due to their position; similarly, the heart is the most sensitive part of an organism and consequently suffers more than the other members.[64]

It was this special affinity for the spiritual and moral bases of the world and their subsequent realization in life that were stressed by Nahman Krochmal,[65] when he pointed to the "absolute spirituality" of Judaism.[66] This was also the core of the ideas of Munk who nearly a century ago wrote with absolute self-confidence that "it was the mission of the Romans to glorify human strength which ends in dust; it was the mission of the Greeks to exalt art and external beauty which is but vanity; while the mission of the Jewish people was above this world and the manifestations of nature. It could be summarized in the following words: to know God and to bring others to know him."[67] Moses Hess,[68] the communist and mystical nationalist, declared that "the spirit of the world manifests itself in nations and races according to their natures and characters. The divine spirit which creates higher forms of religious feelings, manifested itself in Israel during three epochs: the epoch of Moses and the prophets, the epoch of Christ and Islam, and toward the end of the Middle Ages (in Spinoza)." On the basis of these epochs, Hess even tried to establish a law of development: "Whenever the times become ripe for the seeds of new social light, the Jewish people serve as the corporeal form through which the new spirit manifests itself."[69] Ahad Haam, despite his elegantly disguised atheism, also saw in Jewish history something of special value and bearing the stamp of a mission. He explained the Jewish national spirit as expressing itself in "disdain for physical strength" and "the elevation of moral values above the material."[70] The basic feature of the Jewish people he saw in their "compelling conscience" and "ability to reach closer than any other people the ideal of moral perfection."[71] Jewish religion and metaphysics were not important to him per se; they gained significance merely as the abode of social and ethical ideals.

It is thus clear that all advocates of the theory of the chosenness of the Jewish people are united in their outlook, with but minor modifications differentiating between their views.

But since there exists no special chemistry by means of which we could analyze the composition and the attributes of a race or a nation, all advocates of the chosen people concept can base their proofs only on historical facts and experiences. There is available rich and varied material that lends itself for the purpose. But in order that the proof should be objectively valid, these advocates will have to establish two facts without which their argumentation loses much of its convincing power. They must show, first, that when comparing the Jews with other peoples, they take into consideration not only nations alongside of whom the Jews lived, but also those peoples which until a brief century or two ago lived apart and were uninfluenced by the Greco-Hebraic culture. If the Chinese or the Hindus, for example, are left out of the comparison, the entire argumentation on behalf of the chosenness of the Jews becomes one-sided. They must also prove a still more important factor—that those manifestations in Jewish history on which they base their conclusions represent something more than mere chronological precedence. In other words, they must demonstrate that Jews were not only the first to grasp high religious ideals and ethical principles but also that if Jews had not existed or had been annihilated at some early stage of their history, no other people could have fulfilled the same role. (If Jews were only the first to express and practice these religious and ethical ideals, all we could then say for them would be that they were "advanced" while other peoples were more backward in this respect, but such historical priority indicates no organic superiority.) The moment one admits that even without Jews the same religious and ethical concepts would have found expression through the medium of some other people at some point in human history—and the element of the time of the appearance of these ideas is of no importance—the basis for the theory of the chosenness of the Jews loses the major part of its convincing power.[72]

17

Socialism Re-examined

(1941)

The rise of Nazi Germany and the onset of World War II compelled advocates of democratic socialism to reconsider their ideological positions and political strategies. As illustrated by three essays that appear earlier in this volume—"Notes on Marxism" (1935), "To a Communist Friend" (1936), and "Open Letter to the Third International" (1936)—Hayim Greenberg consistently espoused the view that socialism was not merely an economic strategy but, more fundamentally, an ethical and moral vision of a future world order. In contrast to other thinkers who subscribed to doctrinaire positions, Greenberg insisted on distinguishing between socialism as a utopian value and a this-worldly enterprise that offered a strategy for relieving human suffering and enhancing social justice on a universal scale. To this end, he categorically opposed the Marxist theory of "transitional generations" and emphasized the Kantian injunction that human beings ought to be treated as ends in themselves and not as means. By the time Greenberg wrote the following essay (on the eve of the bombing of Pearl Harbor and the US entry into the war), he had already abandoned his decades-old pacifist stance. Now, he paused to reflect on socialism's ideational and historical development as well as the wartime crisis faced by the left. He argued that socialists must act "courageously and responsibly," take considered risks and accept compromises when necessary, and work to become a "social-educational force" that introduces "stability into the world." The unprecedented scale of destruction wrought by the war, including the catastrophic tragedy of the Holocaust, would be revealed in the fullness of time.

It is impossible to predict the shape of the world after the war and what part socialism will play in its reconstruction.[1] In the present conflict there operate dynamic forces and inertias, many of which we can hardly fathom. But it would be altogether impossible to make any kind of prognosis without assuming the following two premises: (1) After a period of armed peace, during which the victorious democracies would exercise broad international police functions, there would be established a stable order of relations based on mutual control and economic cooperation that would eliminate the threat of new wars; (2) Within most countries that control the reserves of natural resources in the world and enjoy a high standard of technological civilization, there would continue to exist (or be reestablished) a liberal political regime guaranteeing unhampered expression and development to all sections of the population and all political ideologies.

These two premises sufficiently prove how minimal are my own "war" aims and how little I expect the world to enjoy a period of complete bliss immediately after the trumpets of victory cease their pealing. But bearing in mind the scope of the destruction that we will be confronted with at the end of the war, even if the democracies should emerge triumphant, the above goals are not as modest as they might appear at first sight. It would be folly to expect a rapid realization of broader socialist aims in a world bled white by the most destructive war in history. But there exists an absolute minimum which must be attained as a result of the war, if there is to be any justification and redemption for the blood that is being shed. This minimum consists of the elimination of further dangers of war through the establishment of a natural equilibrium in international relations, and firmly guaranteeing the basic principles that animated the American and French revolutions. Only these two conditions can create the necessary framework for the free development of socialist thought and the growth of a socialist movement.

Even on the basis of these two premises I do not undertake to draw a detailed portrait of the postwar socialist movement. At best I can try to sketch the outlines of socialism in the coming period, and I am not unaware that I am not free of subjective attitudes and expectations.

The deeper causes underlying the present crisis in socialism are not due so much to strategic errors as to certain "organic deficiencies" from which it suffered. In the future socialism should renounce all pretenses to being a religion. Strange as it may appear at first glance, socialism pretended to be just that, despite the fact that in many European countries it was not only irreligious but even anti-religious. The chief characteristics of a religion are its eschatological predictions and promises. For many years socialist propaganda and education were conducted in such a manner that each new convert was imbued with the consciousness that socialism would not only solve certain economic problems, but would also pave the way to a new earth and a new heaven.

"Happiness" and the establishment of the "kingdom of heaven," these were the promises of socialism for many decades. Aware only of "economic man," believing that social class relationships are the only ones that count while ignoring transcendental factors, socialism imbued its followers with the belief that as soon as the "lazy bellies" of the world would cease wasting the products of honest toil, humanity would be rid of all tensions, inner contradictions, and unstilled desires—humanity would be happy. Thus [Charles] Fourier[2] promised that under socialism people would be at least "ten feet tall";[3] Karl Kautsky,[4] ordinarily a man of pedestrian ideas, announced that the average citizen of a socialist society would be a superman;[5] Antonio Labriola[6] tried to convince his Italian followers that in the socialist utopia geniuses would grow in bunches on every street corner and Galileos,[7] Platos,[8] and Giordano Brunos[9] would run around in herds.[10] [Leon] Trotsky[11] described the future socialist millennium as one in which "man would become immeasurably stronger, wiser, freer, his body more harmoniously proportioned, his movements more rhythmic, his voice more musical, and the forms of his existence permeated with dramatic dynamism."[12] Nor was that all: "the average man would reach the level of an Aristotle,[13] a [Johann Wolfgang von] Goethe,[14] a [Karl] Marx."[15] These were all expressions of the naive optimism that characterized socialist movements, of the mystic, redeeming force which was ascribed to the transition from the capitalist curse to the socialist state of bliss. That economic changes for the better possess no such magic powers to transform humanity, that no conceivable social changes can free mankind of conflicts, that suffering is an integral part of man's fate and socialism can at best solve only the problem of "zoological" suffering, these heresies were strictly avoided in socialist education. [George] Bernard Shaw[16] might have been right at that when he compared the world outlook of an average socialist to an Eskimo's idea of paradise—a land of warm waters in which fat fish swim on the surface and do not resist being caught.[17]

That is what I had in mind when I stated that modern socialism sought to wear the mantle of religion to which it had no right. To what extent such a representation of socialism was pure demagogy or a genuine, albeit primitive, conception of world problems, it is hard to determine. But that its consequences were definitely harmful cannot be doubted. A false outlook on life may be absorbed by one's consciousness, but it does not calm the still voice of nagging doubt. Socialism did itself incalculable harm when it starved broad areas of human spiritual life that do not coincide with economic instincts or the sublimation of those instincts.

Now socialism will have to emerge with a new but legitimate program. It must no longer offer "happiness" (Does anyone know definitely what this term means?) nor the elimination of pain and tragedy. Instead, it can lay claim to a more modest program, which is nevertheless considerably broader than the formula of Herbert Morrison,[18] the English socialist leader that "socialism is a good business proposition."[19]

Should one ask the socialist movement today what its goals are, I do not believe that the answer should be nationalization of the means of production, for we have learned from experience that even with a nationalized economy there can exist class divisions and exploitation. Neither should the answer be that the aim is economic equality. Equality, as an end in itself, is not an ideal state of affairs and can assume the form of a general leveling down such as is practiced in a military barrack. Nor is a high living standard the mark of socialism for even fascist movements promise it as an inducement to their own peoples. The only specific good that socialism can offer is the very thing that it had ignored in the past—the striving after *human dignity* and *social worth* for every individual. (I stress social worth because those who seek a basis for human worth on a cosmic scale will have to continue searching for it in religious sources for millennia to come, even as they did for thousands of years past.) Fundamentally, socialism, which is much older than any of our socialist movements and theories, never sought anything more than to establish the worth of the individual in society. "Every man under his vine and his fig tree" [Micah 4:4]—a formula based on absolute private ownership—does not differ basically from the modern socialist program of complete collectivization. Both aim at that complete equality of each individual without which one can have no social importance. The collectivization advocated today is merely a practical application of the principle of equality in an epoch that is marked by technological industrialism. In other words, nationalization (or socialization) of wealth, high living standards and economic equality are *not goals* of socialism but *only means* toward attaining, not complete happiness, but merely that measure of social worth to which every person is entitled, and which is impossible to achieve without resorting to certain economic changes.

If I have over-stressed the importance of the individual in socialism, it is only because we have failed to learn the necessary lesson on this subject from the two revolutions that occurred during the past quarter century.[20] The *elan* of the October Revolution and of the subsequent civil war in Russia derived its inner pathos more from the striving of the forgotten man of our day for social worth than from purely economic interests. The Russian Revolution lowered the standard of living of the population for many years, but for millions of people it provided a new feeling of social (in this case proletarian) worth for which they were ready to pay the price of hunger and need. Belonging to the proletariat, the new ruling aristocracy in Russia, provided many millions with a sufficient compensation for their degradation in the past, especially since the one-time ruling classes were deprived of all rights. Naturally, reversing the social ladder is not equality. But psychologically it represented a historic reckoning and gave the masses of Russia a new, albeit morally distorted, sense of their importance. The same factor of social worth, although in a different form and feeding on widely diverging sources of energy, figured in the Nazi revolution in Germany. Being part of a "superior ruling race" provided millions of Germans with a new sense of importance which lay not in possessing something, but merely in being something—in being German—in the belief that a higher grade "rulers'" blood flowed through their veins. Both the class as well as the race idolatry were only substitutes, *ersatz* [German for "inferior replacement"], for the genuine sense of worth of which every individual is capable irrespective of race or class. The very fact, however, that even substitutes like the above could evoke such passionate enthusiasm and blind the masses to real economic interests proves how jealous modern mass man is of his dignity, how uneconomic his approach frequently is, and how important it is for the future of socialism to embody the expression of this striving for universal aristocracy.

I have dealt at considerable length with this phase of the subject. If the above thesis is correct, it becomes of great political importance for the future program of socialist education. From it we are almost automatically led to other conclusions, that no genuine socialism is conceivable without a certain minimum of *personal freedom*, that establishing economic forms of collectivism on a foundation of political slavery means sanctifying the means while desecrating the ends. Only the false and harmful belief that "the ends justify the means"[21] which modern socialism (even the non-Bolshevist type) always held to some degree could lead to an instance such as that of [Hendrik] de Man[22] who now preaches collaboration with [Adolf] Hitler[23] because Nazism destroys the foundations of classical capitalism and thus, objectively, leads toward a new world order, ergo to socialism. The illusion that it is possible and permissible to achieve human worth for each individual through despotic means that are in crying contradiction to the avowed goal must be uprooted from our minds and hearts before socialism will again be able to start out on a road of healthy development.

It is now no longer necessary to spend much time in proving that political democracy is a higher and more inclusive concept than socialism. For years we had maintained that political democracy was a means toward attaining socialism. This was wrong. The truth is the exact opposite. Democracy is the ultimate goal and socialism is, under modern industrial conditions, the practical means for the attainment of this goal of individual worth and equality. One who believes that democracy is only a means (to be supplanted by other, better, means, should one happen to run across any) must conclude that in a socialist society there would be no room for it. Actually, it should be clear to everyone that precisely in a socialist order conditions of true democracy should be established, for no matter how thoroughly socialist the economic and social principles put into effect, life will always be full of tensions, conflicts, and contradictions which will have to be solved by citizens enjoying equal rights and equal social standing according to some established democratic procedure.

I now wish to touch upon another aspect which, I hope and trust, will take a prominent place in the consciousness of socialists. This is the idea that *there are no transitional generations in history*. No individual may be considered as a means to advance the interests of another, because each one is an end in himself. Similarly we must not look upon any generation as an instrument to advance the welfare of another, as fertilizer on the fields of future history, because in the endlessness of historical development every generation is also an end in itself. Only one who believes in an ultimate kingdom of heaven, or in some final point in time when all contradictions would be finally solved, can decide that he has a right to sacrifice one generation for the sake of all the future ages so that they should enjoy a state of complete blessedness. But in the future socialism will be more modest and too skeptical to believe in some Canaan for the sake of which it is permissible to sacrifice an entire generation.[24] Socialism must make up its mind that the happiness of no future generation is worth the sacrifice of present-day sinners, that we must not show such exalted love for the yet unborn as would justify indifference to current suffering. I realize that this thesis is liable to cause much misunderstanding. Six years ago, I developed this idea before labor audiences in Palestine, and I was later accused of opposition to *haluziut* [pioneering] because of the rigors it imposes on its followers. I would be an opponent of pioneering in Palestine if the hardships entailed in the rebuilding of a long neglected country were imposed on Jewish youth from above and against its will, if the pioneers in Palestine were considered as manure on the fields of the country so that a future generation of Jews might enjoy its roses. But pioneering in Palestine is a voluntary task assumed after free deliberation by those inclined to it and finding personal satisfaction in following its call. The same can be said about the group of nuns of the Order of the Sacred Heart who some years ago went to the Molokai Islands and dedicated their lives to the lepers living there.[25] No one compelled them to do so. Out of their own free will they drew the determination to devote themselves to people hopelessly afflicted. They are not "fertilizer" on another's field, nor a means to advance other people's welfare. They are an end in and for themselves, and anyone who is even slightly acquainted with the religious context of their lives will realize that they saw the highest expression of their personal fate in their action.

It is hardly necessary to add that if socialism renounces the conception of a transitional generation and the idea of a "final struggle" after which history would take a jump into a state of permanent bliss, it must also renounce the idea of a social revolution of a catastrophic type that is based on a momentary configuration of events, such as was popular among socialists for many years. Socialists as well as democrats should visualize only one situation in which it would be justifiable to fan the flames of revolution—when the liberation of society from political despotism, police tyranny and dictatorship are concerned; when revolution can help the establishment, or the reconstitution, of a legal state possessing that minimum of democracy without which no legal state is conceivable. In other words, revolution may be justified if it serves to attain the freedom of the individual to share in his government, but not if it strives after concrete economic changes only. The moment a state is subordinated to the will of the people and the rights of individuals as well as of groups are guaranteed, socialism has no reason to prepare for revolutions and should strengthen the foundations of legality and try to educate the majority of the population toward becoming conscious and responsible participants of the political set-up.

The theses developed above may impress some readers as being primarily negative, in the sense of setting up inhibitions for socialism rather than presenting a positive program. This impression would not be untrue. I did not aim to develop a program for future socialist action, but rather to outline a number of guiding principles without which the socialist movement will always be open to the dangers of political impressionism and the lure of transitory impulses. If these principles are to be taken seriously, socialism may still meet with defeat, but it could never lose its true stature, its moral force, and its chances for influence on the people.

I doubt that I have revealed anything new. Each of the ideas discussed in this article can be found, in one form or another, in earlier writings. Some readers might even associate them with the revisionist trend in socialism.[26] Fundamentally this would be a correct association. But in stressing some particular aspects of the problem I tried to summarize the difficult lessons we have learned on this subject in the last two decades. The main weakness of the socialist revisionists who followed [Eduard] Bernstein's[27] leadership was that their approach lacked the moral pathos without which socialism cannot become a social-educational force.

I would consider it a misfortune if after the present war,[28] in the general atmosphere of tension, bitterness, and moral let-down, the socialist movement were again to embark on the path of a superficial revolutionism based on transitory factors. Civil wars that may follow the present planetary bloodletting can only lead to still greater chaos, to new destructive psychoses and endless fictitious "liberations." Uninspiring and unromantic as the words may sound, it must be said at this time: After this war, socialism must take upon itself the task of introducing a measure of stability into the world. In a period like the one that will confront us in the near future, stabilization will involve certain compromises. But there are compromises which have a beneficial, healing effect, and facilitate normal changes later, if they are undertaken courageously and responsibly, without obliterating the boundaries between compromise and the basic, unchangeable principle.

18

The Myth of Jewish Parasitism

(1942)

It is a commonplace observation that antisemitism is an irrational form of hatred, prejudice, and hostility directed against Jews and Judaism. It is also a particularly tenacious phenomenon which in its various theological, economic, and political manifestations has bedeviled Jewish and global history for centuries. The following essay, written by Hayim Greenberg before the catastrophic magnitude of the Holocaust became fully known outside Nazi-controlled Europe, explores antisemitism's impact on gentile perceptions of the Jews as well as Jewish self-perceptions. What makes Greenberg's investigation particularly intriguing is his probing discussion of the tradition of Jewish apologetics that developed in response to antisemitism over time. "Expressly or by implication," he notes, Jews, ashamed of their historical function in many Western societies as middlemen, have come to accept the proposition of constituting "a useless and an unlovely element in the economic set-up of every country." In the final analysis, he argues, Jews are neither "economically wicked" nor do they bear "collective guilt" for their economic roles in Western society. His observations, which challenged the prevailing wisdom of the Labor Zionist movement, also extend to socialism, Zionism, and American society.

In the antisemitic propaganda which has been flooding every country since 1933 a very prominent place is given to the old charge that Jews are parasites in the world's economic structure. As the economic problems in each country become more accentuated and increase in complexity, the average man has more difficulty in finding his bearings in this maze, and easily accepts the truth of the charge. It even influences people who have until lately been comparatively free of anti-Jewish bias.

Jews also have been considerably influenced by the notion that they constitute an unproductive, or even a destructive force, in the world's economy. We speak of Jews as essentially a people of *luftmenshen*[1] engaged in *luftparnoses,*[2] that is, individuals whose occupations are unsubstantial, who are exploiters, speculators, and traffickers in the labors of others.

Signs of this self-condemnation first appear in the literature of our "enlightenment."[3] Jews who felt spiritually emancipated from the civilization of the ghetto even before they were emancipated from its legal disabilities developed a great admiration for European culture and were in no mean degree affected by its anti-Jewish prejudices. Certainly they shared the European's disdain for the Jew as a trader. During the past hundred years or so wealthy Jews have always been ready to help in the proletarianization of Jewry. But their motives were different from those of the Zionists or the nationalists. The latter see in Jewish economic restratification a means to ensure a more rounded national existence, or a better possibility for surviving crises, while the former view the transition of many Jews from urban to rural life or from trade to manual labor mainly as a way of wiping out a blot on the Jewish name.

The views of many Jewish socialists in regard to the economic role of the Jews have usually been tinged by a certain antisemitic bias. This is especially true of Jewish socialists who are not interested in Jewish survival. Not that every Jewish Marxist has actually read Marx's essay on the Jewish question[4] where Judaism is made synonymous with capitalist exploitation, greed, and usury. But some of the spirit of that shocking accusation is to be found in the attitude of the average Jewish socialist.

Non-Jewish socialists, and not necessarily Marxian socialists, have tended to look down on the Jew in the world's economy. The Russian *Narodnaya Volya* [People's Will Party][5] of the late nineteenth century, which glorified the peasant and which was characterized by more humanism than any socialist or reformist movement of modern times, could be expected to be immune from antisemitism. Nevertheless, the *Narodovolzi*[6] once issued a proclamation to the peasants calling on them "to burn the mansions of the nobility, to rob the estates, and to beat up Jews." This was not, as some believe, a mere demagogic device to rouse the peasants to revolt by appealing to their prejudices. The authors of this proclamation would not have issued it if they did not, at least vaguely, entertain the idea that the Jew was essentially a "bloodsucker." Socialists and other reformers who stressed the agrarian problem and who saw in the peasant the chief potential carrier of their ideal generally tended to see in the Jew the extreme expression of urban life and of the iniquitous exploitation they associate with the city man. This also explains [Leo] Tolstoy's[7] rather unfriendly attitude toward the Jews, an attitude most eloquently expressed by his repeated failure to speak up on behalf of the persecuted Jews. Tolstoy had the peasant's primitive notions of economic life, the peasant's narrow horizon in determining economic values, and the peasant's suspicion of urban sophistication as mere crookedness.

The literary influence of Tolstoy and the influence of some schools of socialist propaganda are largely responsible for the tendency for self-depreciation and self-condemnation so common to many Jewish socialists and Jewish intellectuals.

Nor is Zionism free from its share of responsibility. There was a time when it used to be the fashion for Zionist speakers (including the writer) to declare from the platform that "to be a good Zionist one must first be somewhat of an anti-semite." One can sense this attitude in some of [Leon] Pinsker's[8] writings: there is a great deal of it in [Nahman] Syrkin[9] and in [Dov Ber] Borochov,[10] the two main theoreticians of the Labor Zionist movement; A. D. Gordon,[11] the author of the idea of the "religion of labor" (*dat haavodah*),[12] wrote, in a spirit of extreme contrition, about the national sins of the Jews which must be atoned for by manual labor; [Yosef Haim] Brenner,[13] the nearest to Dostoyevsky in Hebrew literature, indulged in a masochistic self-flagellation. To this day Labor Zionist circles are under the influence of the idea that the "return to Zion" involves a process of purification from our economic uncleanliness. Whosoever does not engage in so-called "productive" manual labor is believed to be a sinner against Israel and against mankind.

When addressing the non-Jewish world we become exceedingly apologetic and talk of extenuating circumstances to explain our supposedly incriminating economic position. We quote the [Hebrew] Bible to prove that as a nation we were born honest toilers of the soil, and that it was the Canaanite[14] and the Phoenician[15] who were the traders of antiquity. We do not dispute the basic fact contained in the accusation against us. We admit, expressly or by implication, that we constitute a useless and an unlovely element in the economic setup of every country. We merely blame it on our tragic history, on the persecutions, and on the disabilities we have suffered.

Our apology is based on ample evidence. There is no doubt that no religious literature (with the possible exception of the ancient Chinese) contains so much glorification of manual labor as do the [Hebrew] Bible and the Talmud. Nor can there be any doubt that our history made us a people of traders in a much larger measure than we would have become under normal circumstances. In contrast to the Greeks who looked down upon manual labor as an occupation for slaves, the Talmud takes the view that manual labor is ennobling. Even Plato and Aristotle adopted the dominant Greek attitude, but the Talmud says that if labor was good enough for God when he created the world, it ought to be good enough for anybody. The number of passages one could cite from the Talmud which express the same view is legion,[16] and we have a right to be proud of that attitude. But that does not mean that a man who works hard for his living as an honest storekeeper has reason to be ashamed of his occupation or to feel constantly apologetic. In medieval feudal Europe, manual labor and particularly agriculture were so intimately bound up with the Church that for a Jew in many countries to take to the plough was tantamount to baptism. There are many other reasons for the change in Jewish occupations during the Middle Ages. The recitation of these reasons fills our apologetic literature.

The present economic structure of the Jews may not be ideal, but there is nothing shameful or unethical about it. In the first place, we have more manual workers than it is commonly believed and their numbers have increased in the past few decades. In the second place, there is nothing evil or parasitic about useful work which is not manual.

Useful or productive labor does not only mean manual labor, or labor engaged in producing things which can be seen and touched and which have physical dimensions. Any work which satisfied human needs or is socially useful is productive work.

Of all great thinkers of modern times, Tolstoy probably went furthest in stressing the virtue of simple manual labor. At one time he was under the influence of a homely moralist by the name of [Timofey M.] Bondarev,[17] who preached the doctrine that only work which helps produce bread is morally good. A peasant who ploughs and seeds corn is a good man, but a farmer who plants oranges or bananas is a *darmoyed* [Russian for "exploiter"][18] who eats the bread of idleness, since he wastes his time on producing unnecessary and evil luxuries. At about the same time, Tolstoy was under the spell of another homegrown philosopher, a Swede, who taught that every man must produce the grain for his own food. This Swede reprimanded Tolstoy for drinking tea. Drinking tea, he said, encourages the Chinese peasant to plant the ungodly weed and neglect the cultivation of life-giving rice, thus bringing about famines in China. One day when Tolstoy offered his Swedish friend a glass of milk, he refused, saying, "My mother has been dead a long time, and the cow you have milked is someone else's mother."[19] Tolstoy was tremendously impressed by the argument. Most of us think it ludicrous. But it serves to illustrate the absurd state which may be reached by the consistent application of the idea that only work immediately resulting in concrete goods is socially and economically useful.

Modern socialism is free from such extravaganzas, since its object is not to limit human needs but to expand them. The doctrine that man may enjoy only that which he himself produces is alien to a system which looks forward to an abundance requiring an increasing complexity and differentiation of labor. But for many years socialist theory has stubbornly clung to a dogma that stresses the worth of the producers and the relative worthlessness of the intermediary between the producer and the consumer. A "logical" deduction from such a view would declare the milk wagon driver a parasite, and the cow the only producer in the milk industry.

[George] Bernard Shaw[20] was justified in ridiculing this primitive notion. His illustrations are the country boy who shoos away the birds from the seeded field and who performs by his unsubstantial noises the same function as the village carpenter who builds a gate to keep the cows away from the same field, or the housemaid who has nothing of physical substance to show for her hard labor except the odd broken dish.

No one is a parasite who engages in work which makes life more agreeable, more comfortable, and more abundant for his fellow men. In our modern society, the distribution of goods is indispensable to their enjoyment by the largest possible number. Anyone engaged in distribution—the exporter, the importer, the sailor, the wholesaler, the retailer—is doing useful work. We may hold the view that nationalized commerce is more socially beneficial than private commerce. Yet in principle, there is no moral difference between a merchant operating his own store and an employee of a workers' cooperative or of a Soviet state store. Both earn their livelihood, provided they do their work honestly and conscientiously, and provided they do not resort to cunning to extract a remuneration which is not commensurate with their service.

Each one of us owes it to society to do some useful work in order to pay for the things he enjoys as the result of the work of others. But among our creditors, so to speak, are not only the farmer, the tailor, and the mason. There are hundreds of people who produce nothing that is tangible, but without whose labor our life would be much harder or would at least lack many of the amenities and the pleasures which we prize. There is the milkman, the grocer, the bus driver, the waiter in the restaurant, the actor, the writer, the radio announcer—even the exterminator of vermin.

Take any typically Jewish occupation which has long been the butt of our moralists and satirists. I, for one, do not approve of the institution of *shadhones* [Yiddish for "matchmaking"], that is, professional matchmaking. But, after all, this is a matter of taste, and no one forces me to pay for the services of a *shadhan* [Yiddish for "matchmaker"] if I do not employ him. There are others who do, and what right have I to impose my attitude upon other people? Or take the Jewish clerics—the rabbi, the *hazan*,[21] the *mohel*,[22] the *shamash*,[23] types whom our "enlightened" literature has presented in a most uncomplimentary way—again it is a matter of the point of view. Millions of Jews require the services of these functionaries and are willing to pay for them. Compared to the numerous clerics, monks, and nuns of other denominations the Jewish religion has been neither overstaffed nor overpaid. In Poland, before the war, we had several hundred "*einikleh*" that is, grandsons of famous Hasidic rabbis, and we have some of them in this country. These people who trade on their pedigrees constitute to my knowledge the only specific class of unproductive Jews. But then, they are no more so than Siamese twins, or the Dionne quintuplets.[24]

The point I am trying to make is that we have no reason to feel morally apologetic about our economic position. I do not mean to say that all Jews are saints. Nor do I deny the need for a thorough restratification of our economic life. But this restratification ought not to be motivated by a sense of collective guilt. We have to reconstruct our economic life because the present one is fraught with dangers to our well-being, and because a fuller national life requires a more balanced economic setup. We are not economically wicked. We have not eaten unearned bread all these centuries. And under the conditions of modern society, we have been fulfilling a useful economic function.

I have no reason to be proud of the Jewish saloonkeeper in this country or of his antecedent in eastern Europe. But I know they have their counterparts among non-Jews. There is nothing edifying about the Jews in the Ukrainian villages under the feudal system who held the keys to the village churches and opened the churches only when the peasants paid the rent. But the keys were placed in the Jews' hands by the greedy and lazy Polish nobility. We are, on the whole, neither better nor worse than others.

The question may well be asked, what of our Labor Zionist ideology? What of our propaganda about ruralization, the dignity of labor, *haluziut*? These principles are still sound. A reshaping of Jewish economic life is a historic necessity, and it cannot be accomplished without the popular enthusiasm that Zionism generally and Labor Zionism particularly have aroused for these aims. There is nothing wicked in being a middleman, but it is not sound for a whole people to consist of middlemen. We are building a new nation in Palestine, and we cannot succeed unless we make its economic life varied and many-sided and thereby relatively complete. It requires no effort and no propaganda on our part to create a Jewish merchant class in Palestine. But the emergence of a Jewish agricultural class cannot be a spontaneous process. At this juncture in our history, the creation of a class of Jewish farmers in Palestine is of paramount importance and justifies the expenditure of moral and mental energies that have gone into the effort. Sometimes the enthusiasm of the Palestinian pioneers appears to us at a distance as being too naive and narrow. But taken in its historic perspective this exaggerated glorification of manual labor and its achievements is necessary.

I am not oblivious of the desirability for a restratification of Jewish economic life outside of Palestine, say, in the United States of America. I know that our top-heavy economy contains some dangerous possibilities. But mere preaching will not accomplish the desired change. I am not an economist, but I question the feasibility of effecting a complete change in Jewish economic life at the present state of capitalist development in this country. How can we produce large numbers of farmers, coal miners, and metalworkers? If present conditions make such a feat impossible, there is nothing to be gained by continuous moralizing. If it is possible, it ought to be done. But let us stop apologizing for ourselves.

19

Go to Nineveh

(1942)

That Hayim Greenberg was steeped in traditional Jewish discourse is evident in his varied writings. Moreover, his deep and genuine appreciation for Judaism's centuries-old theological and philosophical traditions imbued his modern and secular Jewish worldview with a strong ethical and moral foundation. In the following essay, Greenberg explores the biblical story of Jonah, which is traditionally recited as part of the Yom Kippur (Day of Atonement) liturgy. He pays especially close attention to the story's implications for the ideas of a Jewish ethos and the concept of divine justice. In his view, the Jewish understanding of salvation is not a fatalistic end in itself but instead a "road of repentance" open to all; likewise, Jewish prophecy is "by its function and its character conditional rather than categorical." The lasting importance of the story of Jonah, he suggests, is its "limitlessly universal" moral horizon.

The book of Jonah,[1] read in the synagogues every year on Yom Kippur[2] [the Day of Atonement], has a lasting moral quality which overshadows the scholarly discussions as to when and by whom it was written. The kabbalists[3] and early Christians put a mystical interpretation on the book and connected it with their ideas on the immortality of the soul. But anyone approaching the book without preconceived ideas can see that there are no mystical elements in it.

The style is simple, transparent, and not charged with any particular allusions. The story itself is straightforward and its moral is obvious. Once a man is endowed by God with a prophetic spirit, then he remains, willy-nilly, a servant of the Lord for the rest of his life. No rebellion on his part can change this.

Jonah, the son of Amitai, revolted against God. He wished to place his own will, his own prejudices, and his limited concept of justice above God's command. Should he "go to Nineveh,[4] that great city, and proclaim against it," that it should be destroyed by God's wrath [Jonah 1:2]? Why should he? Nineveh was the capital city of Israel's mightiest enemy, a city rotten with sin and crime, for did not God himself say, "Their wickedness is come up before me?" [Jonah 1:2]. Then let the wicked perish without prophecy, without a warning. To be sure,

God did not send him there merely as a bearer of evil tidings, to inform the inhabitants that the final sentence from which there is no appeal had been passed upon them. He suspected God of "weakness" and a desire to act not according to the strict letter of the law, of seeking to avert a punishment which he had already decreed upon the people of Nineveh. "For I knew that Thou art a gracious God, and compassionate, long-suffering, and abundant in mercy, and repentest Thee of evil" [Jonah 4:2]. Jonah was afraid that perhaps the inhabitants of Nineveh might repent on hearing his prophecy and God would alter his decision. To use later terms, he considered himself the bearer of "the attribute of justice" and suspected God of being inclined toward the "attribute of mercy."[5] What he forgot was that mercy and forgiveness were in themselves part of a righteous judgment.

Jonah had another motive for refusing to go Nineveh. Nineveh lay outside the land of Israel, an alien city of pagan, unclean worship. But he was a prophet of Israel and for Israel. He believed that the spirit of prophecy was given to him with the understanding that he pour it out only upon Jewish soil for Jews to hear, that the gentiles had no part in it. True enough, nearly all the prophets had spoken their word about alien lands and alien peoples. Thus Habbakuk's[6] main theme was the Chaldeans,[7] Obadiah's[8] was Edom,[9] and Nahum's[10] Nineveh itself. But these were prophecies made to the Jews, not directly to the gentiles. With the possible exception of Elijah,[11] whom God once sent to idol-worshipping Sidon,[12] Jonah was the only prophet sent abroad with a direct mission to the uncircumcised. And even Elijah was not sent to the community of Sidon. His mission, as related in the First Book of Kings,[13] seems to have been concerned only with one individual among the non-Jews, the sick child of the Sidonese widow whom he had brought back to life. But Jonah was sent not to an individual but to the whole unclean community of Nineveh whom God should have destroyed long before. To bring to them the prophecy of destruction was risky. They might repent their sins: God might hearken to their prayer and Nineveh might be saved.

"Jonah rose up to flee unto Tarshish[14] from the presence of the Lord," rather than carry out his mission [Jonah 1:3]. A later commentary spoke of that flight, saying that Jonah would rather have perished in the sea than bring misfortune upon his own people by effecting the salvation of Nineveh.[15] Another commentator, evidently more prosaic, says that Jonah paid a sum as great as the value of the whole ship, for his trip from Jaffa[16] to Tarshish, so strong was his desire to see God's condemnation of Nineveh fulfilled.[17] At any rate, he did not want to help save Nineveh. (Signs of this Jewish "particularism" or "chauvinism" may be seen much later in the [Christian Bible]: Jesus himself emphasized on several occasions that he was sent only to the "lost sheep of Israel" and commanded his disciples not to go to the gentiles with their tidings of gladness) [Matt. 15:24].

Jonah fled, but can one flee from God's command? A week later, legend tells us, the storm affected only that one ship, and all other ships proceeded on their way peacefully. Moreover, the fish which swallowed Jonah had been prepared for that task from the very first day of creation. "And the Lord *prepared* a great fish to swallow up Jonah" [Jonah 1:17]; the prophet was not to know of any limitations on the message he was to carry. He must carry it also to the lands of the uncircumcised. And if he wanted to narrow his horizon and narrow his heart, God would show him what narrowness was. He was not to reach Tarshish, and soon God was to hear his prayer "out of the fish's belly" [Jonah 2:1].

The rebellious prophet received his punishment by being incarcerated for days and nights in the dark dungeon of the fish's belly. A later commentary says that after the sailors on the ship had seen Jonah spewed out on dry land by the fish, they went to Jerusalem, had themselves circumcised, and devoted themselves and their wives and their children and their belongings to the service of the Lord.[18] This showed that even these uncircumcised, sinful people were not beyond salvation, and what happened to them could also happen to the inhabitants of Nineveh. The God of Abraham, Isaac, and Jacob[19] was also their God and if they did not serve him today they would be ready to serve him tomorrow. "Go to Nineveh," he told Jonah [Jonah 3:2].[20]

But the story of Jonah is more than a protest against narrow nationalism. Its moral deals also with the very essence of Jewish prophecy. The prophet is not merely one who predicts events which will or which must occur in the future. If he were no more than that, there would be no difference between a prophet and a pagan oracle. For the oracle there is no "if." It only knows that thus it will be under all circumstances, no matter how man should act or fail to act. The decree which the pagan oracle knows is categorical and absolute and ultimate. Neither human will nor even the will of the gods can alter it. It is fate, unchangeable and immutable. A decree of this sort is independent of punishment and retribution, of sin and innocence. The catastrophe predicted by the oracle is not a punishment for transgression, and has very little relation to morality or immorality. Not only with primitive peoples but even with such civilized people as the Greeks, fate was outside of morality. This is evident in all of Greek mythology as well as in the highly developed tragedies of Aeschylus,[21] Sophocles,[22] and Euripides.[23] The essence of classic tragedy is in a large measure the problem of the "innocently guilty," of the criminal who is such against his own will and his own intentions, of the helpless individual whom fate itself leads to sin and crime and misfortune against all his efforts to avoid them. The best-known example of this is the legend of King Oedipus.[24] Jewish prophecy, in contrast to pagan prophecy, knows no fatalism. There is no fate within the whole Jewish concept. There is no faith in blind decrees. But there is Providence watching and listening over the world. Providence may be appealed to, may be prayed to, may be moved to do man's desire, if that desire is just and pure. Jewish prophecy, therefore, is by its function and its character conditional rather than categorical. Jonah wanted to see an immutable decree in God's decision to destroy Nineveh. Had he been certain that God interpreted the decision in the same way, he would not have fled to Tarshish. Therein lay his transgression. Instead of being a prophet whose prophecy would bring warning and move the sinful to repent and to purge themselves of their sin, he preferred being an oracle, a *golem*[25] (automaton) through whom spoke the blind, brutal future. By this he lowered the prophetic calling; he destroyed the conditional nature of God's decrees. He confused God's hatred of evil in man with God's hatred of the evil man, as if the evil man was evil in essence and beyond hope, and condemned forever to be wicked and with no road of repentance open to him. By his disbelief in repentance and in God's "duty" to accept it and to "rend the evil of His decrees" [Jonah 3:10] he became a blasphemer, closer to paganism than to the Jewish God. Still greater was his crime in not wanting to see the uncircumcised of Nineveh begin believing in his God and proclaiming a day of fast, clothing themselves in sackcloth, and the king of Nineveh shed his mantle and cover himself with sackcloth and sit in the ashes on the ground. He was unwilling to rejoice with God at the sight of the drama of human repentance and cleansing. It was for this narrow-minded, unprophet-like inability to rejoice with God that he was severely reprimanded. "Thou hast had pity on the gourd, for which thou hast not labored, neither madest it grow, which came up in a night, and perished in a night; and should not I have pity on Nineveh, that great city, wherein are more than six score thousand persons that cannot discern between their right hand and their left hand, and also much cattle" [Jonah 4:10–11].

That is why the book of Jonah fits so well into the Yom Kippur service. The very sense of the Day of Atonement is faith in providence and denial of fate; faith in repentance and in its redeeming power, hatred of evil in man and hope that man will ultimately overcome that evil. The moral horizon of Yom Kippur is wide and distinct, limitlessly universal, in the perspective of which the barrier between one of the covenant [of Abraham, Isaac, and Jacob] and one of the uncircumcised is obliterated. "And all species may fear Thee, and all creatures may they all become one community to do Thy will with a whole heart."[26] And God is praised for his quality of forgiveness on Yom Kippur: "Thou extendest Thy hand to the sinners and Thy right hand is extended to receive those that return to Thee."[27] For on that day prayers are offered also for the wicked. "For Thou wishest the repentance of the wicked and Thou dost not desire their death, for, as it is said, God said, 'As I live,' says the Lord God, 'I do not desire the death of the wicked, but the return of the wicked from his ways [and live].'"[28] On Yom Kippur prayers are offered for Nineveh, for all the Ninevehs of the world.

20

Halakhah and *Agadah*

(1943)

6. Portrait of Hayim Greenberg (c. 1945); courtesy of NA'AMAT USA.

*This essay intentionally calls to mind Haim Nahman Bialik's well-known essay "*Halakhah *and* Agadah *in Jewish History" (1917). A giant of modern Jewish letters, Bialik was arguably the most important Hebrew poet of the pre-state era. Hayim Greenberg and Bialik were lifelong friends. In 1920, Greenberg translated Bialik's essay from Hebrew into Russian. Subsequently, Bialik's essay attracted the attention of the famous Russian author Maxim Gorky, who became an admirer of his work. In 1921 Gorky helped Bialik* *secure an exit visa from the Soviet authorities. Like Bialik, Greenberg was intensely interested in the relationship between the legal and social strictures he called* halakhah *(codified traditional law) and* agadah *(cultural-folk literature), which he understood as the Jewish people's natural expression of its ethnic-national identity—that is, its spiritual moorings, poetry, mythology, and so on. Here Greenberg reminisces about his lifelong friendship with Bialik, unpacks the radical implications of Bialik's assessment of* halakhah *and* agadah*, and discusses the creative tension between these concepts for the future of the Jewish people.*[1]

[Haim Nahman] Bialik's[2] "*Halakhah* and *Agadah*" is an essay with a moral. In it he intended not merely to define the characteristics of these two classical genres in Jewish (and in a certain sense also in world) literature, but also, while describing them, to point to a great cultural danger which he felt was threatening modern Jewry. I recall a private conversation I had with him once, during which he spoke of the threat of disintegration that has been facing us for quite a few generations, ever since the rise of the *Haskalah* movement to the present day. He said:

> The life of any people must have its specific rhythm. Without a minimum of such rhythm, group life becomes impossible. When this rhythm is no longer sensed, there ensues formlessness and an individualism that verges on irresponsibility and chaos. The modern Jew, even if he is a nationalist and a Zionist, becomes ever more atomized and less a part of a community. He lacks the collective rhythm which in part becomes atrophied by natural means and in part is consciously suppressed. Orthodox Jews sense this and therefore so many of them, perhaps the more sensitive among them, hate us. They hate all of us: Hebraists[3] and Yiddishists,[4] Zionists and autonomists,[5] or whatever we call ourselves. They consider us degenerates. We frighten them. If this is the face of "the spirit of the time" [*Zeitgeist*], they no doubt think, then both the time and its spirit can go to the devil. They are capable of understanding that we, modern Jews, can possibly have a *halakhah* [law] of our own which is as remote from theirs as east is from west. Naturally, this would not please them, but it would make sense to them, as in the case of the story which [S.] Ansky[6] once told about a Jewish woman who wakes her apostate son early on Sunday morning that he should not be late to church—let him at least worship another god. What pious Jews can least tolerate in us is not so much our heresy as our spiritual lawlessness. Even when we have our own law, it is not something to be practiced; it is mere theory, principle, ideology, or program. But it has little to do with our actions. And rules that are not practiced are so much

> forged currency and fundamentally not rules at all. . . . Consider, for instance, our own dear Odessa.[7] For many years now we have been waging battles over exalted matters: Zionists, ordinary nationalists, and assimilationists. But what distinguishes the people in one of these groups from those in another? Not in their press and meetings and discussions, but in their everyday life, at home and in the street, their habits and customs, at work and at rest, in their entertainments, in the education of their children? Aside from rare exceptions, there are almost no differences at all. Without some form of "divine service," without a formulated style and defined duties, without concrete commandments, and—this may shock you—without a kind of marching in formation and especially a type of collective breathing, we will not last long, we will be pulverized.

I probably do not repeat Bialik's words exactly. This conversation took place more than a quarter of a century ago while strolling around Malyi Fontan.[8] (To be more precise, Bialik did the talking, indulging in paradoxes, free associations, and whimsical flights of fancy, while I silently followed his gracefully disorganized leaps of thought.) But I believe that I am correctly conveying the sense of his remarks and their general tenor, as I heard them during this conversation as well as in a number of others, which stimulated with their unorganized and often capricious tone. It was during that time—as I learned later—that he was composing his essay "*Halakhah* and Agadah [*in Jewish History*]."[9]

I recall that during one of these meetings I told him about what was going on in the Russian underground and what I heard and saw in Petersburg, in Moscow, and along the Volga in revolutionary circles. I was convinced that the war would end with a revolution on a grand scale and with the overthrow of the monarchy. Bialik listened carefully to what I was saying, then interrupted me explosively:

> Should I tell you the truth? I am afraid of the [Russian] revolution. I am prepared to say every day, "I look forward to it daily, even though it delay its coming," the way pious Jews say about the coming of the messiah, and yet I am afraid of it, just as some Jews are afraid of the coming of the messiah, or of the labor pains that will precede his coming. . . . For centuries Russia has been living with its special rhythm. Under the Romanovs[10] this is a rhythm that—may a fire consume it. All the same, it is a framework, it has its limits, a system of laws and rules regarding their observance, sometimes voluntarily and sometimes against one's will. You say it is a form of idolatry? Of course. And what idolatry! But idolatry too is a form of service. What service the revolution will bring, I do not know. I don't know whether the revolution has already worked out its laws and their applica-

tion, its new code which should begin to create a new rhythm of life. I am afraid that the revolution is all *agadah*—dream, poetry, enchanting lyric, rebellious temperament. Should this be so, then instead of rhythm we will have pandemonium, we will float on a stormy ocean without a compass, there will be anarchy. Our [Alter] Druyanov[11] says that in Russia a revolution will be no more than a pogrom. Russia will stage a pogrom on itself while reciting a pious benediction over it. But you know Druyanov. He likes to be contrary and he would feel insulted if his remarks were to be taken seriously. All the same, I believe there is something in what he said. A good constructive revolution must have its own revolutionary regiments but also its own codes of law. But in Russia I am afraid that instead of disciplined regiments the revolution will bring ill-kempt gangs. . . . Do you see that policeman with the yellow beard in his grease-stained uniform? Those who want to make the revolution must already have decided what they will do with him after their victory; they must already have made a decision whether to kill him or to let him live, whether to exile him, and, if so, where; and what to do about his wife and children, and how to dispose of his alarm clock and what to do with the canary that sits in a green cage which hangs on the wall of his home next to the icon. Tell them, those dreamers, that they must without delay compose a talmudic tractate dealing with all this.

At this point Bialik burst out in his childish, infectious laughter:

One thing leads to another. Some days ago I expressed these thoughts to Grandfather [Mendele Moykher Sforim][12] and he grinned slyly and said in a sing-song: "How come that Bialik, who is no fool, should talk such nonsense? A tractate on revolution he wants, no less. What a notion! Keep your mouth shut, Bialik, or those boys may yet take you up on it. Then they will at once split into two sects, the House of Hillel and the House of Shammai.[13] Each revolutionist will start bashing in the head of his neighbor and shout, The law is as I say it is. And Herod[14] will sit in his palace surrounded by his saintly concubines and laugh till he is in stitches. What other otherworldly ideas have you to suggest?"

It was interesting to see the old man carry on, but he stopped short—"the walls have ears," he said. On the other hand, one must not forget that revolution is war, and a war has to be planned and one must know in advance what is and what is not permissible in war. How does the Good Book say it? Perhaps it does not say it right, or the way we think today the rules of war should be defined. But the [Hebrew] Bible speaks out on the subject; it

> lays down rules and laws [Deut. 20]. Please recall how the sages later elaborated the rules, how they struggled with the problem of Sabbath in connection with war—when and under what circumstances and to what extent it was permissible to profane the Sabbath because of the needs of a war.[15] Without law—and when I say "law" I mean law that is to be practiced—war becomes plain banditry. And the same holds true for revolution. I'll tell you something. Nearly all the revolutionists whom I ever met were wonderful people, honest, sincere, inspired, but it seems to me that they were all people of *agadah* and not of *halakhah*— they are poets, may God preserve us; and may God further forgive me for my words, but *I hate poets*.

I burst out laughing. Bialik too laughed, adding what he used to call "steam" to the merriment.

> This is all nonsense [he went on]. It's easy to say "I hate poets." But it is possible to go on for a couple of generations without new poetry. The Psalms,[16] [Solomon] ibn Gabirol,[17] [Aleksander Sergeyevich] Pushkin[18]—believe me, one can thrive on them. What the world needs now, and we Jews in particular need, is civilized behavior, and this cannot be had without *halakhah,* without discipline. Who will dare say he loves militarism? But, believe me, a company of soldiers marching in step, rhythmically, to the beating of drums, is in some ways a stronger factor for civilized existence than a loose bunch of spirited bohemians on broken chairs in some café. The underworld does not believe in the Ten Commandments, so it is a constant threat to society. But there also exists a kind of "overworld"—poets, kabbalists, evangelists—who also defy the Ten Commandments and the laws which are based on them. Grammar, they believe, is not for them—they speak sensibly and correctly in any case. Obey any of the commandments? That would be a form of degradation—they can be depended upon to do the right and the beautiful without commandments. Discipline, they say, is superfluous. God requires a pure heart only, and of this commodity they have plenty. And here lies the danger. Take [Dostoyevsky's fictional character] Raskolnikov,[19] he no doubt had a great big heart, but he lost touch with the "collective pulse," so he kicked over the social traces and went to murder an old usurer. Then he was left with an empty pocket and a permanent wound in his soul. If one must be a poet, an *agadah*-man, then let it be one like Rabbi Yosef Karo[20]—Kabbalah by the fistful, but also a rigid code of rules. When you awake in the morning you must be "strong as a lion," in the service of the Lord [Prov. 28:1]. A wonderful phrase. But without the regulations that one must at once pour water over one's finger nails and recite "*modeh ani*,"[21] I am afraid that "the lion" would again put

> his head on the pillow and snore away the time when it is necessary to proclaim the unity of God. . . . This is particularly important for Jews. You say that a similar crisis is felt among *goyim* [gentile nations]. You are probably right. But there is a difference. The nations of the world have their countries and governments, and their own economic milieus, and their languages, therefore the individual cannot become quite so atomized there. There exist objective borderlines, an objective *eruv* [a wire or rope strung around an area to enclose it as a unit] which imposes its authority, and whether the individual knows it or not, he toes the line and breathes in unison with the others. But we (excepting perhaps the truly pious Jews) have to relearn how to breathe together, otherwise we will all in time suffer from asthma. . . . In *Erez Israel*, I am told, this will not be needed, at least not to the extent that we need it here and now. I doubt this. But in order to build up *Erez Israel* we must first liberate ourselves of the vague Zionist *agadah* and impose upon ourselves a Zionist *halakhah*, one to be practiced. For how far can one get with "lovers of Zion" or with—pardon the expression—"lovers of Zionism?"[22]

Before we parted that day I said to Bialik: "Now your first act of *halakhah* should be to write an essay on the relationship between *halakhah* and *agadah*, these two genres in modern life."

He replied with a bashful smile: "Part of this manuscript is already in my desk. In order to complete it, I need some fewer headaches and a little assistance from above."

A few weeks later I received from him the completed manuscript together with a request that I translate it into Russian. I postponed my return to Moscow in order to fulfill his request, though I did not quite understand why he needed at that time a translation of his still unpublished manuscript.[23]

***

A year later, shortly before the March revolution, Bialik came for a visit to Moscow, and at the reception arranged for him at the Polytechnic Museum, he read the Russian translation of "*Halakhah* and *Agadah*" instead of delivering an address. (Tsarist officialdom at that time stubbornly refused to permit the use of Yiddish or Hebrew or any other "foreign" language at public meetings.) The outstanding personages of the Russian intelligentsia—artists, scholars, writers—came to that reception and that evening Bialik impressed them profoundly with his personality and his dynamism, though the substance of the essay which he read aroused opposition among some and misunderstanding among others. Some, including Jews, obtained the impression that Bialik was calling back to the synagogue, to Orthodoxy, to old rituals, to formal religion. Others recalled [Leo] Tolstoy's *What Is Art*?[24] and interpreted Bialik's essay as a new attempt to start a crusade against artistic culture. When the reception ended, the artist [Maria] Andreiyeva [Gorky],[25] Maxim Gorky's[26] wife, came up to me and asked to be introduced to Bialik. She came on behalf of her husband who was then in [Saint] Petersburg, to greet in his name "the great man from Odessa." After she had finished her message and had expressed her own enthusiasm for the reading, Bialik jokingly asked her:

"May I be permitted to ask what you got out of my lecture? After all, all my illustrations, which were taken from talmudic literature, must have sounded completely strange to you. The very terms *halakhah, agadah*."

For a moment Madame Andreiyeva appeared confused, like a pupil before his examiner, then, with the forwardness characteristic of a pampered woman, she said somewhat too assuredly:

> All the same, I followed your labyrinth and I believe I emerged from it safely. The *agadah*-man is more or less the same as the *bosiak* [Russian for "tramp"] in Gorky's early work, and you have your grounds to fear the rule of the *bosiak's* lack of discipline. I will write to Gorky about your lecture. In part he will be angry with you, but he will also understand you with deep sympathy. I believe that he is now through with the cult of the *bosiak*. But I fear that he will not so lightly accept your *halakhah*-man. He might identify him with the *muzhik* [Russian for "peasant"] and you know how little liking he has for the *muzhik*. Or he might identify your *halakhah*-man with the petty bourgeois, this dull urban creature lacking all fantasy which shocks Gorky so with his cowardice, submissiveness, greed, lack of temperament, and stale moral codes. I would very much wish that Gorky should read your essay. It appears to me that you are both on the same track. It seems to me that you are looking for a synthesis of *halakhah* and *agadah*. Gorky, too, is looking for a synthesis. Have you read his "Two Souls"[27] about the contradiction in the nature of the Russian people? But he is now trying to convince himself that such a synthesis has already begun to take shape in Russia. He has abandoned the *bosiak*; the *muzhik* and the petty bourgeois revolt him as ever. He now pins his hopes on the industrial worker. In his opinion the industrial worker possesses both artistic imagination and temperament, yet he is not anarchic, he imposes discipline on himself, that which you call *halakhah*. I would very much wish that you should some day have a talk with Gorky on these matters, though his class standpoint might be alien to you.

***

I will not undertake to judge to what extent the development of the Russian Revolution justified Bialik's fears. The roles of *halakhah* and *agadah* in the revolution and their relative proportions are a delicate and complex matter. During the years of the Russian Civil War I had numerous opportunities to recall the dividing line which Bialik had drawn between these two styles, or trends. When the Soviet government began to introduce its own legal system, after it had done away with the preceding legislation, judicial institutions, and procedures, it in many places appointed as judges citizens without legal training or experience. These were mostly *agadah*-men, and the only instructions they received were to apply "revolutionary consciousness of justice."[28] The Soviet state was willing to depend on the conscience and intuition of persons who were imbued, or possessed, by the romanticism of the revolution. Experience proved in time that revolutionary consciousness was often transformed into blind envy or vengefulness, and intuition assumed the form of prejudice and arbitrariness. Little by little the Soviet government had to return to *halakhah* and to elaborate a precise code of laws and legal procedures which could not be freely interpreted or misinterpreted according to the conscience or taste of the individual judge. It proved completely impossible to establish and to maintain a state on *agadah* alone. Organized society, striving toward a condition of organic community, must resort to *halakhah*. It can, and at times should, do away with old outlived laws, but it cannot continue to function efficiently until in time it creates its own Mishnah and Talmud. Anarchism, for instance, despite the force of its ethical and esthetic strivings, has remained to this day a noble vision that has not assumed flesh and blood.

***

In 1920, when the Russian translation of "*Halakhah* and *Agadah*" was published and had aroused interest in certain non-Jewish literary quarters, I had an opportunity to discuss Bialik's ideas with a prominent [Russian] scholar.[29]

"Don't you think," he asked me, "that Bialik's essay is masked propaganda against Christianity?"

It is not important at this point to repeat what I answered then. The way I see it now, Bialik's essay, in one of its aspects, is not masked but direct "propaganda" against a certain kind of Christianity.

If Christianity is that which the world has inherited from the apostle Paul,[30] then Bialik is certainly its sharp opponent. Paul is the typical—more correctly, the most extreme—*agadah*-man. Faith is everything; deeds count for nothing, and if deeds are not important, or do not lead to salvation, then no compelling *halakhah* is needed. That is why the apostle to the nations aroused so much bitterness in his Jewish environment. It is true that Jesus, too, was primarily an exponent of *agadah,* but to the extent that we may form opinions about him on the basis of the vague and contradictory sources we have regarding him, he never proposed to do away with *halakhah*—laws, customs, ceremonies, and commandments. Perhaps he did not stress them sufficiently. (According to Ahad Haam[31] the prophets also stressed these much less than did the priests.) But Jesus did not regard them as superfluous or harmful. His opposition to the Pharisees[32] is considerably exaggerated in the conventional Christian writings. Jesus was himself a Pharisee in no small degree. But criticism of a certain type of Pharisee—more correctly of a degenerate type of Pharisee mentality—did not originate with Jesus. The sages of the Talmud spoke with bitterness regarding the *hasid shoteh* [foolish pietist], the symbol of petrified Pharisee piety, of the type who sees a woman drowning in a river and refuses to rescue her so that he should not have to see her nakedness [B. Sotah 21b];[33] or, according to a version in the Jerusalem Talmud, of one who permits a child to perish and does not rush to rescue it because he had not yet had an opportunity to remove his phylacteries [J. Sotah 3:4]. In such cases *halakhah* completely emancipated itself from *agadah*—love, compassion, responsibility for the lives of others—and through such emancipation it became formal, dull, and mechanical. The protest against a type of *halakhah* which became an end in itself and thus sanctified means at the expense of the end, or even contrary to the nature of the end, continued in later years. When Rabbenu Bahya Hadayan[34] distinguished between commandments that concern our organs and those that concern our hearts,[35] he also opposed a spiritless type of Pharisaism; and when a kabbalist of the Middle Ages described a certain type of petrified *halakhah*-Jew as a kind of ape, at sight of whom one must recite the benediction blessing God for transforming his creatures, this did not imply that he wished to do away with *halakhah* altogether.[36]

Returning to Jesus we must bear in mind that he was not an exception in the Jewish community of his time also when, according to gospel tradition, he attacked the flatterers and hypocrites among the Pharisees [Matt. 22:18]. Rabbi Yehuda Hanasi[37] and the *amora* Rabbi Elazar[38] employed a very strong expression when they referred to the "Pharisee plague"[39] [B. Sotah 22b] having in mind persons who intentionally resort to the law formally in order to defeat its essence; for instance, giving a poor man who possesses 199 *dinars* a donation of one *dinar*, bearing in mind that an owner of 200 *dinars* becomes ineligible to receive assistance from the public charity funds [B. Peah 8:8–9].[40] Rabbi Hanina[41] and Rabbi Yohanan[42] described such Pharisees as "sly wicked men," who use the law for evil or even for sadistic purposes.[43] Had the gospel critics of Pharisaism stayed within these limits, the break between the *agadah*-men of Jesus' type and other Jews would not have been more severe than that between the *Hasidim* and the so-called rabbinic Jewry [i.e., *Mitnagdim*] in the eighteenth century. The Baal

Shem [Tov][44] and other founders of Hasidism overstressed the value of *agadah,* but they did not try to do away with *halakhah*; they only understressed it.

But Paul and the group which crystallized about him presented a threat to Jewry with which it could not compromise. This threat did not consist in Paul's downgrading *halakhah,* nor even in his willingness to do away with some laws and to substitute others in their place. Similar tendencies had appeared among the Pharisees themselves from time to time. Who, after all, were the disciples who came to Rabbi Elazar ben Horkenos[45] to console him on the death of a woman slave and he rejected their condolences on the ground that these were against the law. He reminded them of the rule, "One does not accept condolences for slaves because slaves are like cattle," and when one's animal dies one merely wishes the loser, "May God recompense you for your loss" [J. Brakhot 2:8, 5b].[46] Is it conceivable that Rabbi Elazar had to remind his disciples of this rule? Could they possibly have forgotten it, or not have known about it? Or was their visit of condolence a kind of demonstration? The social consciousness of the disciples apparently rebelled against the animal status of the slave, and they sought a way to establish a new ruling. Indeed, such a new ruling was introduced by Rabbi [Shimon ben] Gamliel[47] of Yavneh—though he apparently lacked the influence to establish it as binding on the community at large. "Rabbi Gamliel showed special affection for his alien slave Tavi, and received condolences when he died, as if he had been one of his relatives" [B. Brakhot 16b]. Rabbi Gamliel had the vision of a new *agadah*—the absolute equality of worth of all human beings, and during his lifetime it began to assume the outlines of a new *halakhah*.

Such "extravagances" among the evangelical Jews would no doubt have been tolerated both by the sages and by the people.

For instance, they tolerated Rabbi Akiba[48] and Rabbi Tarfon[49] who declared, "Had we been members of the Sanhedrin,[50] no one would ever have been executed" [B. Makot 7a].[51] Both Rabbi Akiba and Rabbi Tarfon knew that the law bound the Sanhedrin to pass death sentences for certain crimes. But they were inspired by a new *agadah*: that the life of an individual, of any individual, was so sacred that there did not exist the crime which could merit a death penalty. They may have been inwardly ready not to act against the law, but to introduce a new law in place of the old one.

With Paul the situation was different. He did not distinguish between one *halakhah* and another; he undertook to do away with the element of *halakhah* as a whole. No more laws, no more commandments, no more obligatory customs—there existed only the messiah *agadah*. Good deeds have no effect on the salvation of the world—there exists only faith. No more Torah—there exists only God's grace. No more duties—from that day and to the end of time there was only love. Jews sensed in their entire beings that here was a great danger for their existence as a people, for the rhythm of their social life, for their religious aspirations in which the "redemption of the world" and "the ways of the world" occupied such a central place, not only for themselves but for the world as a whole.

They became aware of the threat of an *agadah* which in principle rejected being incorporated into some kind of *halakhah*. In our generation and in his own terms, Bialik sensed the threat facing our existence as a people and our spiritual and historical destiny. His essay is permeated with the earnestness of that feeling from which it is possible to draw not a few conclusions for a number of specific problems confronting us in the present.

21

Bankrupt!

(1943)

To appreciate Hayim Greenberg's speech at Madison Square Garden (delivered on February 12, 1943),[1] *it is important to note the complexity of the American political landscape in the 1930s and 1940s. First, although Americans trusted the US government and venerated Franklin D. Roosevelt, the Roosevelt administration faced a steady drumbeat of criticism as it experimented with policies that gradually pulled the country out of the Great Depression, implemented the New Deal, and led the country into World War II. Moreover, while FDR reached the height of his popularity with American Jews in the 1940 and 1944 presidential elections, winning roughly 90 percent of the Jewish vote for his third and fourth terms in office, the long shadow of Jim Crow, the internment of over 110,000 Japanese Americans in camps, and the rise of home-grown antisemitism—to name but a few indicators—illustrate how fraught American society remained. In short, FDR's political fortunes depended on preserving the New Deal coalition, but he had little reason to fear alienating America's Jewish voters. Nor was there was any significant political value in elevating the rescue of European Jewry from a basic humanitarian issue to a paramount wartime objective. Finally, in this period Zionism was a minor force that barely registered in American life outside of the Jewish public arena and had yet to emerge as a key factor in plans for postwar reconstruction.*

The Nazi invasion of the Soviet Union on June 22, 1941 (known as Operation Barbarosa), and the Einsatzgruppen's murder of the Jewish populations of the newly conquered Russian territories inaugurated the Nazi regime's systematic campaign to exterminate European Jewry. Word of Hitler's so-called "Final Solution" did not reach American Jewry's preeminent leader Rabbi Stephen S. Wise until August 28, 1942—some eleven months after the Holocaust began. Today, on the basis of declassified historical records, we know the Allies were aware of the mass Nazi killings and deportations of the Jews as early as March 1942. In retrospect, however, the deception of Wise and other Jewish leaders by the Allied governments demonstrates just how low a priority the Allies assigned to European Jewry's desperate plight. If the latter underscores the predicament of Jewish powerlessness in the pre-state period, it serves equally to accentuate the following bitter assessment by Greenberg of the American Jewish condition.

The time has come, perhaps, when the few Jewish communities remaining in the world which are still free to make their voices heard and to pray in public should proclaim a day of fasting and prayer for American Jews. No—this is not a misprint. I mean specifically that a day of prayer and of fasting should be proclaimed for the five million Jews now living in the United States. They live under the protection of a mighty republic governed by democratic laws. They move about freely through the length and breadth of the land. The vast majority of them have enough food to eat, clothes to wear, and roofs over their heads. And if any wrong is committed against them, they are free to protest and to demand their rights. Nevertheless, they deserve to be prayed for. They are not even aware what a misfortune has befallen them, and if they were to look at themselves with seeing eyes they would realize with shock how intolerable this misfortune is. This misfortune consists of the vacuity, the hardness, and the dullness that has come over them; it consists in a kind of epidemic inability to suffer or to feel compassion that has seized upon the vast majority of American Jews and of their institutions; in pathological fear of pain; in terrifying lack of imagination—a horny shell seems to have formed over the soul of American Jewry to protect and defend it against pain and pity. At a time when the American Jewish community is the largest and most influential in the world, at a time when the eyes of millions of Jews in Europe who are daily threatened with the most terrible and degrading forms of physical extermination are primarily turned to American Jewry, this American Jewish community has fallen lower than perhaps any other in recent times, and displays an unbelievable amount of highly suspect clinical "health" and "evenness of temper." If moral bankruptcy deserves pity, and if this pity is sevenfold[2] for one who is not even aware how shocking his bankruptcy is, then no Jewish community in the world today (not even the Jews who are now in the claws of the Nazi devourer) deserves more compassion from heaven than does American Jewry.

I know how much resentment the above statements will arouse. No one—no organization, no public body—has authorized me to make such an indictment and to publish such a characterization of American Jewry. My own colleagues may very well condemn me for my arrogance in issuing such a "diploma" of miserable moral poverty and criminal indifference to the largest Jewish community in the world. But I do not believe that there exists the person who can disprove the basic fact I am pointing to, even though he may question my right to assume the role of diagnostician or of one who reproaches "in the gate" [Amos 5:10].

The basic fact is evident to any Jew who has the courage to look at the situation as it is: American Jewry has not done—and has made no effort to do—its elementary duty toward the millions of Jews who are captive and doomed to die in Europe!

Some weeks ago a certain important Jewish organization in America (or one that would like to be considered important) received a short telegram from *Erez Israel*: "How long have you known what is happening to the Jews in Nazi-dominated Europe?"[3] I do not know how that telegram was answered, but fundamentally that telegram, signed by a Jew who escaped from Poland, did not ask a question. It was a well-merited slap in the face to the entire Jewish community in the United States, with all its organizations, offices, committees, budgets, and leaders. In *Erez Israel* it is well known that as far back as August [1942], we, here, have received authentic information about the murder of millions of our own flesh and blood in Europe.[4] The real question implied in the telegram was: "Why have you wasted so many precious months? And what are you waiting for now, when every day, every hour, every minute counts? Why haven't we heard that you do something, or that you are at least seeking ways to do what may at least *appear* possible to do? Why, from afar, haven't we seen you take those means that are dictated by the present situation, when the knife is at the throat of one half of the Jewish people—means none of which is guaranteed to improve the situation, but which must nevertheless be tried with the energy and speed which the desperateness of the hour calls for?"

We, Jews in America, have proved incapable of acting even as a herd of cattle will sometimes act when faced with danger—huddling together for protection. We did not even display sufficient ability to set up (temporarily, for the duration of the emergency only) some kind of general staff that should meet every day and think and consult and consider ways to engage the help of people who *may, perhaps,* be in a position to help us. Our "assets" are so great that in normal times we do not know how to apportion them among ourselves. So we quarrel and we fight. One clique tries to outmaneuver the other—Zionists and anti-Zionists,[5] Congressists and anti-Congressists,[6] Orthodox[7] and Reform,[8] synagogue Jews against secularists, a fiction of organized labor against an equally mythical organized all-embracing community. But of what value are all our differences of opinion, all our philosophies, worldviews, analyses, prognoses, and orientations, all our tragi-comically inflated prestige considerations, when the axe of the executioner hangs over the neck of nearly every other Jew in the world? It will never be possible to explain why the chief organizations of American Jewry which regard themselves as called upon to engage in political work—the American Jewish Committee,[9] the American Jewish Congress,[10] Bnai Brith,[11] the Jewish Labor Committee,[12] the [National] Council of Jewish Women[13]—could not in this dire hour, unequalled even in Jewish history, unite for the purpose of seeking ways to forestall the misfortune or at least to reduce its scope; to save those who *perhaps* can still be saved. What differences of principle can there exist in such rescue work? What has such rescue work to do with political differences and with the entire ideological claptrap which we have produced during the past couple of generations? Neither the future historians, nor any normally intelligent person today, will ever be able to conceive how it came about:

a) That the American Jewish Committee should send a mere "observer" to a conference of Jewish organizations[14] convened to deal with the massacre of European Jewry—as if the American Jewish Committee were still in doubt whether this subject concerns it closely, or it is a peripheral, sectarian matter which does not concern persons of another sect.
b) That the Jewish Labor Committee should follow in the footsteps of the American Jewish Committee in non-cooperation, non-action, and keeping apart from common attempts to accomplish something.
c) That an important organization of Orthodox Jews[15] should threaten to withhold its cooperation if, for reasons that are not subject to Jewish control, it should prove impossible to include one of their members in a delegation to a certain important personage or office.
d) That so far as matters of "prestige" and "credit" and petty jealousies are concerned, the American Jewish Congress did not fully disregard its own prestige ambitions in the interests of uniting all central Jewish organizations in what I clumsily described above as a united general staff for Jewish defense.[16]

Yes, there was one brief moment when all (or nearly all) united for an instant—when there arose the question of sending a delegation to the president.[17] And I cannot refrain from making a cynical observation. The president of the United States is the busiest man on earth, but should another possibility of a Jewish delegation being received in the White House appear tomorrow, there will again be union for a moment, until the trip back from Washington to New York when everyone will go his own old separate way and indulge in mutual spites.

Quite some months have passed since representatives of Jewish organizations have even met to engage in earnest discussion whether and what can still be done for European Jewry. The president made his statement,[18] and then came the declarations of some governments[19] of the United Nations regarding the punishment to be meted out to the guilty *after the victory,* and most, or is it all, the Jewish organizations were satisfied and appeared to be calmed by it. (It should be noted that the small Jewish community in England was much more effective in obtaining that declaration than the much larger American Jewish community.[20]) Yet everyone should have understood how much more important it is that millions of Jews should be saved *before the victory,* than that a few thousand Nazis should be punished or executed *after the victory.* Everyone knew that this declaration had little effect on the situation. And now we are informed that both Warsaw and Vienna are completely *Judenrein* [German for "cleansed of Jews"].[21] Everyone knows, or should know, that in recent weeks mass massacres of the survivors of Galician Jewry[22] have been resumed. But even this did not move the few American Jewish leaders at least to meet to discuss what to do.

The murder of two million Jews[23] with the most inhuman methods of torture and degradation which sadistic fantasy has ever devised, still has not sufficiently impressed those among us who have donned the *shtreimels* [Yiddish term for fur hats worn by Orthodox Jewish men] of Jewish guardianship, those who have assumed responsibility for Jewish interests so that they could sit down around one table and look into each other's eyes, and together try to do something to rescue at least one percent of the doomed millions. There have even appeared some Zionists in our midst who have become reconciled to the thought that it is impossible to stay the hand of the murderer, and therefore, they say, it is necessary "to utilize this opportunity" to emphasize to the world the tragedy of Jewish homelessness and to strengthen the demand for a Jewish national home in Palestine.[24] (A home for whom? For the millions of dead in their temporary cemeteries in Europe?) And there have arisen *sages* in our midst who have reached the profound conclusion that the sole response to the mass extermination of our people should be the earliest possible opening of a second front.[25] The delegation of the Bund[26] in America has satisfied the demands of its conscience both as Jews and as human beings, by organizing a protest conference of European socialist leaders, and is now boastfully claiming "sole credit" for its own little clique for this great achievement.[27] And only some days ago the Revisionist-controlled[28] Committee for a Jewish Army,[29] succumbing to its own ambitions and hunger for prestige, has put other Jewish organizations in an uncomfortable position by publishing huge ads in the newspapers[30]—ads which also seek "to utilize the opportunity"—calling for the establishment of a Jewish armed force of 200,000, knowing very well that this is a mythical figure concocted for purposes of cheap and irresponsible propaganda; that there do not exist 200,000 stateless Jews of military age and physically qualified for an armed force; knowing also that even if it were possible to establish such an armed force, all the Jews in Europe, to the last one, would be murdered long before such a force could be recruited, organized, and trained for front-line duty; knowing very well that if all the combined allied armies are still not in a condition to start an invasion of the European continent,[31] a Jewish armed force would not do it either, even if it were to consist of 200,000; knowing that if such a Jewish army existed today, it would not be free to operate at will and would be subject to the orders of the American and British general staffs.

Every "committee" cherishes its own committee interests, its sectarian ambitions, its exclusively wise strategy, and its "power position" in the teapot of Jewish communal competition.

Never before in our history have we displayed such shamefully "strong" nerves as we do now in the days of our greatest catastrophe. We have become so dulled that we have even lost the capacity for madness and—may God not punish me for my words—the fact that in recent months Jews have not produced a substantial number of mentally deranged persons is hardly a symptom of health. It is characteristic that when at a session of the Jewish Labor Committee a colleague from Poland permitted himself to express a few sharp words of rebuke on the subject of their indifference and passivity, he was shouted down publicly as a "hysteric"[32]—as if a state of hysteria is today not more normal for Jews than dull even temper and an attitude of "business as usual."

No less characteristic is the fact that such a highly reputable organization as the American Jewish Committee could hold its annual conference one week ago,[33] at the end of which there was issued a declaration[34] dealing with all the baker's dozen areas in which they differ from the Zionists or from other Jews,[35] but not mentioning with even a single word the extermination of the Jews in Europe and what the American Jewish Committee proposes to do now, today, without delay, so that after the victory there should remain someone across the ocean whom the Committee could defend in accordance with its own program and ideology, someone whose rights and human dignity they could protect.

The only Jewish organization which, formally at least, remained on guard and tries to create the impression that it does something is the American Jewish Congress. But it would be criminal negligence to conceal from the public the fact that at a time when the angel of death uses airplanes, the Congress employs an oxcart-express. The Congress, too, does not display that will and that tempo which it should manifest at such a time. The Congress delegated rescue work in Europe to a special committee—the so-called Planning Committee.[36] The idea behind this committee was that people who are not too loaded down with Congress routine work should devote themselves to this task. But also this committee permits itself the luxury of not meeting *for weeks on end.* And when it does meet, and it decides to do something, this is still far from proof that it will carry out its own decisions. So they set up a subcommittee and empowered it to contact American Christian clerics to discuss a one-time large-scale action on the part of religious bodies throughout the world.[37] (Personally, I believe that such an action would be more effective and would make a greater impression in Germany than the threatening declarations of the democratic governments.) And a chairman[38] was appointed for that subcommittee, one who has the necessary qualifications and contacts for that task. So what became of it all? That subcommittee was not convened even once in *more than two months.* This, in itself, would not have been such a calamity—a subcommittee more, a subcommittee less—let those who enjoy committee meetings grieve over this—had the chairman "usurped" all the work and done it himself. But the chairman is a very busy man, preoccupied with many matters (important, very important matters, to be sure) and after he had obtained the promise of a number of prominent clerics to cooperate in the project, he abandoned them. Since this chairman undertook his office, he had time to attend conferences in two remote cities (once again, very important conferences indeed, but having nothing to do with the Jewish emergency), he even had time to tour the country on behalf of a project which could easily have been postponed or assigned to another person who had not undertaken emergency duties. But he lacked the time to utilize his connections, and the new contacts he had recently made, in order that the planned action should materialize.

On the eve of Christmas a number of German Americans were persuaded to issue a manifesto against Hitler's persecution and massacre of the Jews.[39] This was supposed to have been the first step in a campaign to mobilize public opinion among German Americans. It was felt that once it became known in Germany how German Americans condemned the extermination of the Jews in Europe, this would create a powerful impression, and it might even compel some Nazis to consider what they are doing. But this promising activity was limited to a few score Americans who had to be reminded that they were of German extraction for, with a few exceptions, they had consciously and in terms of their social interests lost all touch with specific German issues. In order to produce an impression in Germany, it was necessary to mobilize the sympathy of broad layers of German American society (German fraternal and charitable organizations, culture and art clubs, sports clubs, and German Lutheran churches). But this has not been done to this day. It is no doubt a difficult task, but no one has yet demonstrated that if the required amount of energy had been invested in this effort, it would not have brought results.

The only direct Jewish appeal to the Pope that he should intervene with his moral authority came from *Erez Israel* and was made by the [Ashkenazi] chief rabbi [Isaac Herzog[40]] of that country.[41] But to the best of my knowledge not even the American Jewish Congress took the necessary steps to move the Vatican to greater, more open, and direct condemnation of Nazi cannibalism, despite the fact that millions of Catholics live in the United States, and there are many liberals among the Catholic clergy. Again, no one can prove that the Vatican could be influenced from America to take more drastic measures than it has taken to date. But this does not mean that we have the right *a priori* to renounce attempts to reach an understanding with certain Catholic forces in this country. This has so far not been done, at least not to the extent nor with the intensity that were called for.[42]

There is a shortage of qualified people, and when a suitable person is found he is busy and overwhelmed with a hundred other matters and of course he cannot be everywhere at the same time, even though some of these "other matters," of undoubted importance, could very well wait, should have been made to wait. And when the American Jewish Congress sent an emissary[43] to Washington, to stay there more or less permanently in daily contact with various government offices—perhaps something might still be done to rescue even a handful of European Jews to no matter what place of asylum—this emissary, with all due respect for his abilities and intentions, is a foreigner who cannot always exert the necessary influence in our capital. (For such an assignment, in Washington of all places, no suitable *American Jew* could be found; everyone is busy with more important and more urgent matters, of course.) During the past year the American Jewish Congress twice sent emissaries to South America on organizational and financial missions,[44] but in recent months, when each day brought its burden of tragic news from Europe, no time was found to send a suitable person to Argentina. Argentine Jews must have some influence, so why was no attempt made to utilize the connections which a neutral American country still had with Germany?[45] Perhaps something could have been accomplished through such mediation?

Yes, also the American Jewish Congress, the only Jewish organization which did not remove the subject of the extermination of the Jews of Europe from its agenda, has proven to be criminally slow and lacking in tempo and temperament in its rescue work. It displayed a lack of the courage of despair, of that "aggressiveness of spirit" which characterizes the hour of doom, of the ability to act on its own on a suitable scope or to attract people from other circles and activate them for such a generally self-evident cause as the attempt to rescue those who can still be rescued.

I confess that I am unable to draw concrete, practical conclusions from the above. If it is still objectively possible to do anything, then I do not know who should do it and how it should be done. I only know this, that we are all—all five million of us, with all our organizations and committees and leaders—politically and morally bankrupt. And I refuse to understand how and why all of us here have fallen to such a state of shameful degradation.

22

Concerning Statehood

(1943)

At a time when many observers questioned the need for a Jewish state—whether on religious, philosophical, or ideological grounds—Hayim Greenberg asserted an unapologetic and forthright explanation of Zionism's ethical foundation and moral claims. Free of the doctrinal fetishes that governed the belief systems of many pacifist, socialist, and Zionist contemporaries, he did not seek to counter anti-Zionist arguments from the refuge of a true believer but rather in terms of Realpolitik. "The colossal dimensions of the world tragedy exceeded all predictions," he declaimed in 1942, "and scored the world powers who stood aside a decade ago when Jewry was undermined by Hitler. Now, they pay with the lives of their own sons and daughters."[1] *Though deeply troubled by World War II's unfolding landscape, particularly Nazi Germany's murderous enterprise aimed at the Jewish people, he did not view the history of Jewish suffering or the Holocaust as the primary justification for Jewish nationalism. Nor did he believe that "socialism alone would automatically solve the Jewish problem without the establishment of a free Jewish commonwealth."*[2] *The "instrumentality" of statehood, he argued, notwithstanding the "sublime" and "lofty" universalistic conception of "statelessness," was a minimal requirement for Jewish national integrity and survival in the modern world.*

> According to Aristotle, the "stateless" must be a God or a beast; nowadays he is usually a Jew.
>
> —[Lewis B.] Namier,[3] *Conflicts* [1942][4]

Henrik Ibsen[5] once wrote in a letter to a friend: "Who needs a Jewish state? The world? The Jews themselves? There are certainly enough political nationalisms as it is without anyone wishing still another one. Or is it that sixty-five governments are not enough, because it takes sixty-six to make an even number?"[6]

The Norwegian playwright had heard that some Jews were agitating for a state of their own, and he thought this yearning was very unfortunate, a symptom of degeneration. For two thousand years, he argued, the world had at least one noble people, a group of spiritual patricians—the Jews. All other peoples had their countries, kingdoms, governments, and were engaged in unaesthetic, scoundrelly acts. The only people which did not descend to the level of having its own police, army, prisons, chain gangs, executioners, brutal wars, endless intrigues, and was not contaminated with the corruption that is organically bound up with the job of governing, were the Jews. Now they seemed eager to sell their birthright for the most demoralizing of all vanities—statehood. Political Zionism was to him a degrading phenomenon, a morbid hankering after lowness. To him it appeared as if an artist and Bohemian by tradition should suddenly decide to marry in conformity with all the conventional regulations, buy a house with a fence around it and a bell at the door, and acquire a dog to guard his possessions. He felt that, should Zionism succeed, the only aristocratic people would disappear from the face of the earth.

Many centuries ago one of the talmudic sages declared that God favored Israel by dispersing him among the nations.[7] The Scandinavian iconoclast was disappointed over the fact that some of his Jewish contemporaries rejected the honor bestowed upon their people.

***

In the years of the Russian Revolution I heard a distinguished writer expound a similar conception of the "aristocratic" nature of the Jewish people. [Mikhail] Gershenzon,[8] the deceased historian of Slavophile literature, attacked Zionism for its "let-us-be-like-other-peoples" attitude. A Jew by birth but thoroughly Russified, he declared Zionism to be a form of extreme assimilationism, a betrayal of the inner sense of Jewish destiny. It is true that when the mystically minded Gershenzon attempted to define the providential sense of Jewish existence, the result was nonsense. But one who has been bitten by the peculiar brand of anarchistic mysticism Gershenzon adhered to does not give up so easily. Jews, in his opinion, were from the outset appointed to be the pioneers of an aimless life, of a purposeless and therefore higher plane of existence. The meaning of life is (if I may use a William James[9] expression) an "is-ness" not an "have-ness," and a people burdened with property—a territory, a state, an institutionalized religion, even a crystallized language of its own—is too busy "having" and "would-be-having," and has no time left for the undisturbed task of "be"-ing.[10] Blessed are the poor, and sevenfold blessed is the poorest of the poor, Israel. Providence deprived him of every conceivable burden—of his land, his statehood, his language, and, in recent generations, it is gradually relieving him even of his most burdensome piece of property, dogmatic religion. The transcendental powers do everything to strip the Jews of any possessions they could call their own and so enable them to perform their mission: to serve as a model for other peoples and lead them into the realm of "true" freedom. Gershenzon even believed that the mass desertion of Russian soldiers in 1917, on the eve of and during the Kerensky Revolution,[11] was a manifestation of a great spiritual upheaval. The Russians, it seemed to him, were becoming "Judaized" through Bolshevism; subconsciously they sought to destroy Russia's statehood, her national and political civilization, in order to live "as Jews"—aimless, propertyless, "free." For this reason he was prepared to greet the tide of Bolshevik anarchy: "Judaism" is victorious; the Russians are the first to follow in its path, and if Zionists succeed in their blasphemous rebellion against the "paramount will," then Russia will become Israel. In his argumentation he enlisted, I now recall, the support of John the Baptist:[12] "And think not to say within yourselves, we have Abraham to our father, for I say unto you, that God is able of these stones to raise up children unto Abraham" [Matt. 3:9]. Since we could not deny the Lord's omnipotence, we had to agree that Russians were at least as good material for manufacturing children unto the patriarch as the stones in the wilderness of Judea.

In 1922, after the conclusion of the civil war in Russia, when the Soviets had already become organized into a rigid, all-inclusive and all-regulating state, I met Gershenzon among the émigrés in Berlin. (He was only a visitor, being one of the few nonconformist Russian writers who till the end of their lives were tolerated by the new regime.) I then reminded him that the erstwhile Russian deserters, who were supposed to usher in the new era of "freedom from property" and who had caused him so much joy, were by now disciplined Red soldiers, and that the "Jewish anarchist" outbreak of the first days of the revolution had crystallized into a totalitarian regime, with Marxist hymns soon to be sung from the tops of the new industrial cathedrals. With a deep sigh he admitted that he was disillusioned in the Russians: they have not become "Israel." But this, he concluded, was no indication that Jews should embark on such an unworthy and un-Jewish path as political Zionism.

***

[Mahatma] Gandhi[13] also asked us on two occasions to maintain and cherish our "aristocratic identity." Jews are a spiritual community, he said, and why do they need such terrestrial stuff as a country and a state of their own? Zion is neither a geographical nor a physical concept. It is rather a spiritual entity. Zion can be founded any place where there is even a single Jew faithful to his inherited truth. Why, then, should Jews seek a Zion of square miles? The prophet of Young India advised us to cultivate our celestial Jerusalem, that Kingdom of God which is neither here nor there but everywhere, which is neither of today nor of tomorrow but of eternity. Had Gandhi been better acquainted with European philosophical literature, he would no doubt have quoted [Baruch] Spinoza[14] to the effect that all wars and rivalries are a result of the fact that ignorant human beings cannot satisfactorily divide among themselves the finite things.[15] Were people to interest themselves in the infinite, they would certainly live in peace, since the infinite and the eternal are possessions which each individual can have for himself in their totality, without in the least encroaching on the same totality belonging to others.

Were Gandhi an Indian *sādhu* [Sanskrit for "holy man"], a saint engaged in meditation on things transcendental in the solitude of his retreat, his criticism of Zionism would be morally legitimate. But, despite his genuine religiosity and mysticism, he is also a great political leader, a militant patriot, and reformer. For decades he has been fighting for historical aims and "finite" things, for an earthly India as the basis for a spiritual one. Why, then, does he not understand us?

If Jews have their portable Zion, then Gandhi's countrymen have Hinduism, which gravitates much more toward the "beyond" than Judaism. But what would the Mahatma say if anyone were to advise him not to fight for his people's political liberation, not to demand statehood for his country, but to cultivate the "inner" India instead? What would he say were someone to paraphrase his own words: "India (like Zion) can be found wherever there is a single Hindu who remains true to his tradition, to his fate and faith?"[16]

But Gandhi insists on an independent India and on her territorial integrity. He is not indifferent to "square miles," and Pakistan is to him an invention of the prince of darkness.

***

I am not aware that [Leo] Tolstoy[17] ever expressed any opinion concerning Zionism. But what other man of the twentieth century was as much opposed to the state as he was? Yet he resorted to the state apparatus more than once for his own purposes. In his old age he became concerned with the question of his literary legacy. He had good grounds to fear that after his death his family would seek to gain profit from his works, and his books would thus become inaccessible to poor people. The religious anarchist thought for a long time until he hit on an idea. He secretly arranged to meet in a forest with his secretary and a notary. There the three composed an official will without the knowledge of Tolstoy's shockingly un-Tolstoyan family. This was the famous will, according to which all the works written before this "repentance" were assigned to his heirs, while all his other works were to be published and sold without profit, as "the people's property."

But what was an official will, drawn up and countersigned by an agent of the state before a sworn witness? It was a threat to use governmental authority (violence, coercion!) against the heirs. Should they attempt to gain profits from his late works, the state would intervene, on the basis of the will, with the power of its courts, police, and penalties—the same state which Tolstoy had so courageously refused to recognize. He was unaware (or did he pretend to be unaware?) of the irony of the situation: enlisting the assistance of the prosecuting attorney to make his anti-state propaganda more accessible to the general public.

***

A great Jewish scientist (I am almost tempted to say: "the greatest")[18] came to a Zionist function and uttered some simple and hearty words on behalf of the Jewish community in Palestine. He said he wanted to see it absorb more and more immigrants from abroad and become economically stronger and socially more unified. But the establishment of a Jewish state he also considered as something undignified and . . . un-Jewish. A government of their own, an army, a navy, a police force, prisons, boundaries to be guarded—"*das is kein judisches Geschaeft*" [German for "this is not Jewish business"]. Jews, in his opinion, have already outgrown the stage in which such political idolatry and crass materialism appeal to the feelings and imagination: Why do we need a state when we are in possession of a greater patrimony, the rich tradition of the prophetic culture?

But if statehood is such a nasty business that we Jews must wash our hands of it, why consider only our own purity? Why not undertake the task of ridding the entire world of states? Why does not a humanitarian and internationalist of that scientist's stature feel that what he is advocating is but a new version of the "chosen people" theory? You, Esaus, have not reached spiritual maturity (perhaps you will never reach it) but we, the House of Jacob, graduated long ago and it is not becoming for us to relapse into a second period of primitive civilization. Is this not the unspoken sense of the argument from "prophetism"?

Has anyone a right to advise us not to seek the establishment of a Jewish state? Everyone has this right, but on one condition—that he be ready by the same token to advise [Franklin D.] Roosevelt to do away with American nationhood at the earliest opportunity.

There is no dividing humanity into thoroughbred and plebeian peoples.

***

Let us assume that Jews will renounce their claim to a state of their own in Palestine. What then? Our present and potential settlers in Palestine will live there not in a political vacuum but in a non-Jewish (Arab or British-dominated) state. As a community they will remain true to their lofty tradition of statelessness, but each individual Jew will have dealings with the state in the innumerable details of his everyday life. He will be affected in many respects by the general structure and mechanisms of the state, and he will naturally seek to use its instrumentalities for his own legitimate benefit. There will be no Jewish prisons, no Jewish army or police, but individual Jews will serve in the police force, in the army or militia, in the established courts and the various branches of administration, in the supervision of prisons and in patrolling the borders (non-Jewish borders, it is true). Should they be prevented from sharing in the above positions, they would shout in protest against discrimination, and all those among us who pretend to think that statehood is something incompatible with the sublime destiny of the Jew, would join them in condemning such infringement on the right of Jewish individuals to be employed by the state. Unless we envisage universal anarchy—a vision even most of the anarchist doctrinaires were compelled to renounce—there is no room for a beyond-state status for any people. To the extent that the average person chooses to look down upon the state, this attitude expresses itself in smuggling, bootlegging, bribing, tax-evading, and pork barrel snatching rather than in ethical anarchism. A people without a state is not above statehood but beneath it, and if statehood be despicable (as some of its manifestations certainly are), then statelessness is even worse.

Gypsies may not have learned this yet. We should have learned a long time ago that with all its inherent imperfections Jewish statehood will be a promotion, not a demotion.

23
Notes on the Melting Pot
(1944)

The term "melting pot" was popularized in the early twentieth century by the British Jewish playwright Israel Zangwill in the Broadway production The Melting Pot: The Great American Drama *(1909). Drawing loosely on William Shakespeare's* Romeo and Juliet, *Zangwill's play depicts an interethnic love affair between a Russian Jewish composer and the daughter of an anti-semitic Russian Christian aristocrat. Unlike* Romeo and Juliet, *in* The Melting Pot *ancestral boundaries are transcended, past misdeeds are forgiven, and the young lovers are united. The proposition humanity would elect to choose a harmonious future—by dint of divine and/or this-worldly incentives—is a centuries-old theme for gentiles and Jews. In the American context, the notion of creating a unified and exceptional society dates back to the European colonization of the New World, which according to the seventeenth-century Puritan leader John Winthrop was to be "as a city upon a hill." This remained a familiar refrain throughout American history. Thus, for example, in 1863 President Abraham Lincoln proclaimed the idea of America's universal mission as "the last best hope of earth." That Greenberg imbibed a passion for the United States while squarely facing the problematic of liberalism in the American setting (what scholars today call the "insider/outsider" phenomenon) is evident in much of his writing. Of special importance for Greenberg, as illustrated by the essay below, are the mutual interdependencies and creative tensions, including the delicate balance between cosmopolitanism and particularism, at the core of the American experience.*

Karl Kautsky,[1] the great exponent of Marxism, once took up the cudgels on behalf of the Jews, to answer certain uncomplimentary assertions made by Werner Sombart,[2] in his famous work *Jews and Modern Capitalism* [1913]. In an article entitled "Race and Judaism" published in 1915 in *Die Neue Zeit* [German for "The New Times"],[3] Kautsky, paying us many compliments, assured us that our historic martyrdom was bound to come to an end as soon as mankind progressed toward a better future. That end, as he saw it, was Nirvana. Israel would find its salvation by dissolving like sugar in a cup of tea.

"Once lawlessness and persecution of the Jews have ended," the Marxist prophet comforted our people, "they will then of themselves cease to exist as an entity.... We shall not be able to say that we have passed out of the Middle Ages as long is Judaism exists in our midst. To the extent that Judaism begins to disappear, both the world and the Jews will be better off. The result will be the rise of a higher type of human being. Ahasuerus,[4] the wandering Jew, will at last have found his paradise of rest. He will live on in the memory of humanity as the greatest martyr of history, as one whose reward at the hands of mankind for all the blessings he bestowed upon it had been brutality."[5]

Kautsky was incomparably kinder to the Jews than [Karl] Marx,[6] for whom Judaism was synonymous with social corruption and evil. And yet the only solace that he could offer us was the promise of extinction, and in later generations, encomiums in history books. Banish all your cares about the future, oh, poor, suffering men; rest assured that you shall some day have an elaborate funeral and at least a monument with a poetic epitaph inscribed in gold.

Kautsky's "philosemitic" treatise came to my mind, when I read a review by Pearl Buck[7] of a [three-]volume book on the Jews of China published by the University of Toronto [Press].[8] In the paragraphs she wrote on the work in a monthly magazine, Miss Buck, though disclaiming any special knowledge in that field, does arrive at certain general conclusions about the Jews and sees a lesson in the fact that China today has no Jews and no Jewish problem. The large Jewish community which once lived in China is now almost completely extinct, not because it has been physically exterminated in the European fashion, but because China has been more humane and more tolerant than the Christian nations of the West. The Chinese did not persecute the Jews; so the Jews, of their own free will, became submerged, not only culturally, but also socially and biologically.[9]

Pearl Buck, a great admirer of Chinese civilization, believes that America ought to learn from that experiment with the Jews in the great country of the Mongols. Let Americans desist from discriminating against Jews, and the Jews will of themselves dissolve as an ethnic group, leaving no traces behind them.

The greatest ideal which a certain type of liberalism holds out for us is still one of painless death.

***

These days, there are even some Zionists among my acquaintances who object to the inclusion of America in the *galut*. They are shocked to hear that term, which means exile, applied to American Jewry. To put God's country on the map of Jewish homelessness, they argue, is an insult to America and a misrepresentation of the position of American Jewry. It is true that Polish Jews live (or rather *lived*) in *galut*, and the same is true of Hungarian, Romanian, German, and other Jews; and when no one is around, they will even admit that Soviet Russia lies in the *galut* zone, but not the United States. Latterly they have been using a special term to designate the sociopolitical character of America in relation to the Jews. By the grace of God and George Washington, we, the Jews of America, are said to be living not in *galut*, but in *tefuzah* [diaspora]. This Hebrew term, denoting dispersion, is pronounced in such accents as to carry overtones of meaning like expansion, growth, and prosperity.

The Italian who sells newspapers in my neighborhood is naturally uninformed about this disputation among Jewish intellectuals. He may or may not look upon himself as an exile from Italy, and nostalgia for his Sicilian village may or may not be strong; but he lives in America and knows that his Jewish customers ought to be treated with proper "delicacy." When a man buys an English and a Jewish newspaper from him, the vendor, scrupulously observing the ethics of his profession, quickly wraps the Jewish paper inside the English, making the former invisible, and so inoffensive to the eye.

The other day his thirteen-year-old boy sold me my bundle of papers. But he arranged them so that the [*New York*] *Times* and the *Herald Tribune* were hidden inside the Yiddish *Forward*[10] and the *Morning Journal*.[11] The father quickly noticed the offense and, furiously snatching the papers away from the boy, rearranged them in the proper way for the "convenience" of his customer. At the same time he explained to the lad that such a one as he, the offspring of a female canine, far from being of any benefit to the business, was merely an affliction on one's anatomy. Clearly the Italian who sells newspapers in my neighborhood operates on the theory that American Jews live in *galut*.

Some time ago a well-known United States judge tried to expound to me the theory of *tefuzah*, or Felicitous Dispersion. I did not argue the matter. Congenital inertia prevented me from engaging in polemics on an over-discussed subject. But if one could debate by proxy, I should gladly delegate the newsman in my neighborhood to dispute with the judge. He does not see well when it comes to the printed page (even in his native Italian), but in other respects he is not blind at all. In fact, he is quite perspicacious.

***

The Greek restaurant-owner in Atlantic City sat at my table, watching with hospitable pleasure while I drank the small cup of Turkish coffee and nibbled my *rahat lukum* [Turkish Delight].[12] The bridge between us was a gastronomic one. In America, he said, he seldom meets real connoisseurs. When he heard that I was ready at any time for a dish of Greek *tefteli* [Russian for "meatballs"][13] he beamed even more: he sensed in me a man after his own heart. *Tefteli* was not a small matter. . . . His mother was once a cook for [Eleutherios] Venizelos,[14] who could not find enough words to praise her art in making *tefteli*. If I only should come to visit at his home, he said, he would show me a picture of Venizelos with an inscription, a present his mother had once received from her great master. . . .

I thought of the large placards I saw three years ago, "Get Americanized—Drink Coca-Cola."[15] I asked my host whether he had not in all these years accustomed himself to American foods. No, he said, he could not get used to them at all. "Their" dishes have no taste and "their" drinks make one sick. He added that even his children could not take "their" stuff.

I asked him what he meant when he said his children were "Americanized"; don't they feel any longer that they are Greek? My host thought for a moment, looking far away into invisible distances and heaved a quiet, deep sigh: "My children, dear friend, are *chulemos*." That was farther than my erudition in modern Greek went. I asked him the meaning of the word *chulemos*. It turned out that in the mountainous region of Greece from which he hailed, the peasants use such an expression for ducklings hatched by hens from ducks' eggs. They are your own, it would seem, yet they are strangers to you and sometimes they are downright distasteful.

"What is going to become of them I don't know. Many times I get such a gnawing feeling at my heart, so that I would readily leave everything here and run away with my wife and children back to Greece or to Macedonia. Let them grow up to be shepherds or swineherds and go around in rags, as long as they are merry and there is some fun in their life. All week, things are not so bad. I am busy, they are busy at school, and the time passes. But when Sundays come, they don't know what to do with themselves. Especially the oldest son; he is sixteen years old. The younger ones we take along to church every Sunday morning. We have a place of worship of our own here. It's a small building, but neat and pretty, with a few beautiful icons that were once brought from Constantinople. We beg our eldest boy to come along with us, but it's years now since we have been able to induce him to come. He says he is bored, why should he sit there and yawn? You see, our prayers are all in Greek and the priest insists on preaching in Greek, and my Theodoros has forgotten how to speak his mother tongue, and he can't read the prayer book either. It hurts me. So while we are at church he loafs on the boardwalk all by himself. . . . My mind is not at ease: what's going to happen to him when he grows up? And what's going to become of the younger ones? Without God, without religion, without a *basilica*[16]—you know how many gangsters have grown up in America on account of that? . . . So one day I took heart and said to my Theodoros: 'I'll tell you what, my son. Here, only two or three blocks away from us there is another church, a Presbyterian one. I don't know what that means, but, after all, they too are Christians, they believe in God and pray to Him and read out of the Scriptures. Go over there,' I said, 'everything there is in English, you won't be bored.' Next Sunday he went to the Presbyterians. He came back in high spirits; he even brought home a tune from there—some old English hymn I think it was. So I think to myself—all right, let it be that way, even if it is not our own, as long as he does not grow up without a faith and a church, like a wild nettle in the field. But the Sunday after, he came back home upset and irritated. . . . He would not eat, and lay down to sleep in the middle of the day. No matter how much we kept asking him, it did no good; he was as mute as the wall. Not till evening did we manage to get a few words out of him, which I can't make out to this day: *I don't belong*. . . . The devil knows what that means. No matter how many times we ask him to tell us what happened to him in church, all we get out of him is, 'I don't belong, that's all.'"

The two of us were silent for a few minutes. The restaurant owner, after one of those coughs which help to overcome hesitation, quickly asked me: "And how is it with you, the Jews?"

It is of little importance what I replied. It was commonplace.

On the way to my hotel I thought of only one thing: "What would be the Jewish equivalent of *chulemos*?"

24

The Universalism of the Chosen People

(1945)

Hayim Greenberg was neither a rabbi nor an academic, but his learned, insightful, and masterful analyses of Jewish culture, thought, and history compare favorably with the very best work of Jewish thinkers and scholars of his day. The following essay—a tour de force of exegesis and philosophical probity—represents the fruit of decades of intellectual searching and study of the relationship of the Jews to global history. Written at the close of World War II, Greenberg provocatively opens his essay by unpacking the facile comparison of the Nazi fantasy of Aryan racial superiority to the religiously inspired Jewish doctrine of election. Rather than merely refuting this false dualism, he uses it as a point of departure and casts a broad net to investigate the "chosen people concept" in relation to a variety of religious, ethnic, and national groups. Drawing on a rich spectrum of Jewish and non-Jewish sources from the ancient and classical periods down to the modern era, he systematically traces the origins of the idea of chosenness in human history, its development across time and space, and the implications of election and exceptionalism for various societies. In parallel, as Greenberg's investigation unfolds, he pays close attention to the internal tensions and dynamics informing the Jewish people's desire to be both apart from and a part of the sea of humanity. Ultimately, he arrives at a paradoxical assessment, namely, that centuries-old Jewish concept "Thou hast chosen us" is fundamentally a universalistic idea.

I

In what sense is Judaism racist? Does it in general recognize the holiness of race and, if so, what practical deductions have Jews made from such a theory?

In connection with the Nazi racist propaganda, these questions about Jewry and Judaism have been dealt with extensively in the past few years. Jews regard themselves as a "chosen people," and the Germans of our generation also proclaimed their superiority to the rest of mankind. Does this mean that Jews, or at least tradition-minded Jews, subscribe to the same theory as the Nazis, but only as applied to themselves? [George] Bernard Shaw[1] seems to think so, and when some years ago he was asked for his opinion of the Nazi theories of racial purity and racial contamination, he replied that the fault of the Jew is his enormous arrogance based on his claim to belong to God's chosen race, that the Nordic nonsense is only an attempt to imitate the posterity of Abraham, and that the antisemites do not see how intensely Jewish is the Nazi thesis of race pollution.[2]

H. G. Wells[3] also leveled accusations against the Jews for their willfully remaining a peculiar people in the French- and English-speaking countries, because they are history-ridden and haunted by a persuasion that they are a chosen people with distinctive privileges over their gentile fellow-creatures.[4] Even Wells sees in the Jewish theory of election a similarity to the impulses of racial pride on which Hitlerism was based.

But Shaw and Wells are not the only Englishmen who have pointed out the racist character of Judaism and of the Jews' attitude toward the world. Similar statements have been made on various occasions by prominent spokesmen of the Anglican Church.[5] The Nazis, they said, seek to destroy world Jewry with a racial theory which they have pirated from the Jews themselves; they wish to undermine the Holy Book but they do not realize that their *Kulturkampf*[6] is directed not against the entire Bible, but merely against the New Testament, since the religion of the Old Testament is purely tribal, exalting the same elements as those on which Hitler seeks to erect his false gods—Blood and Soil.[7] Even in Germany itself the few Protestant and Catholic dignitaries who were courageous enough to criticize certain aspects of the Nazi philosophy denounced it as "Teutonic Judaism," a reversion to the ancient Semitic racial particularism from which Christ sought to liberate his people.

Here in America, we have been chided on another score, though the same basic line of argument is followed. The influential coterie of Protestant intellectuals grouped about the Chicago weekly, *The Christian Century*,[8] has never ceased to argue that the ancient teaching of election to which the Jews still adhere is highly detrimental to the development of integral democracy in America. It is not so important, they reason, that Jews refuse to relinquish their own faith and Christianity is thus deprived of new souls—it is naturally the duty and right of every man to cling to his own religion provided that his conscience is organically and intimately bound up with it—but the Jew's offense is that he regards his religion as a racial monopoly, a heritage of great price which he is loath to share with his fellow men. Every good Protestant in America would like to see all his fellow citizens belong to the Protestant Church, just as every true Catholic would like to have all his fellow Americans see the light and embrace the only true faith. But the Jews display no desire to convert either Protestants or Catholics to Judaism, preferring to remain a separate entity within and for themselves; they do not wish to defile themselves through religious union with gentiles; they believe, in other words, that members of other, inferior, races are not worthy of becoming their co-religionists. Where, we are asked, is your Jewish missionary zeal and work? If it is true that we are all groping blindly in the dark, why do you not bring us *your* light? Why do we send our missionaries to the most far-flung and wildest wastes, even to cannibal tribes, while you do not even undertake to convert to your faith your nearest neighbors?

It must be admitted that this argumentation has made an impression on certain Jews. Some Jewish writers have even gone so far as to demand that before we attack Nazi racial theories, we first renounce our own. One author even declared that Hitler pursued the same line followed by Ezra the Scribe:[9] Did not Ezra regard intermarriage as racial pollution, and did he not even harangue his fellow Jews to cast off their non-Jewish wives, ruthlessly break up their homes, and thus purge themselves of gentile contamination?[10]

II

The notion of election as a divine endowment is certainly an important element of Jewish religious and historic consciousness. The concept of "Thou hast chosen us," if not predominant in Jewish dogma—as far as we can assume the existence of a systematic Jewish *Dogmenlehre* [German for "dogma doctrine"]—permeates much of our folklore, Jewish prayers and rites, and our religious poetry. To Jewish national consciousness our past history presents, to a marked degree, the picture of a patrician in the midst of a plebeian world.

True, the idea, or rather the unformulated conviction, of election is not uniquely Jewish. No people, race, or tribe is without ethnocentricity. A certain degree of narcissism is requisite for the survival of an ethnic group, just as every man necessarily possesses a measure of egocentricity. But with the Jews, even in the earliest period of their history, this attitude of spiritual superiority assumed the proportions of a fixation which great sections of our people have still not been able to relinquish. Even early Jewish Christendom was unable to free itself completely from the chosen people concept, and even from chauvinistic extremes, so deeply had that motif become ingrained in the Jew. However earnestly Christian theologians may try to prove that the message of Christ spelled liberation from national or ethnic particularism, and despite the elements of truth to be found in these arguments, it is an undeniable fact that the traces of Jewish particularism can never be eradicated from the pages of the [Christian Bible].

When Jesus sent forth his disciples he admonished them thus: "Go not into the way of the gentiles, and into any city of the Samaritans enter ye not: But go rather to the lost sheep of the house of Israel" (Matt. 10:5–6). And later, when he came to the coasts of Tyre[11] and Sidon[12] and a Canaanite[13] woman cried to him, "Have mercy on me . . . my daughter is grievously vexed with a devil," Jesus answered her, "I am not sent but unto the lost sheep of the house of Israel." And when the woman persisted and bowed before him, pleading for help, he answered her more harshly, "It is not meet to take the children's bread, and to cast it to dogs" (Matt. 15:21–26).

It was certainly not to the advantage of the redactors of the [Christian Bible], which was compiled at a period when the young faith embraced more non-Jews than Jews, to include these and similar passages in their final canon. They were certainly not interested to present this new religion before the Greco-Roman world as a Jewish nationalist lore, their missionary work being based on the precept that in the Kingdom of God there is no distinction between Jew or Greek, and their Church even then aspiring to all-embracing cosmopolitanism. If the various chauvinistic expressions ascribed to Jesus have remained in the text, it indicates that they held significance for his followers, having been transmitted by word of mouth for several generations.

For the clarification of this problem we are not so much interested in the bare fact that Jews were persuaded of their superiority as in the concrete meaning which they attached to the belief in their election and the manner in which this conviction affected their relations with non-Jews.

The belief in their own superiority was not interpreted as entitling Jews to specific rights or privileges of an economic or political nature. It never constituted a theoretical basis for Jewish domination over other, inferior, races or peoples. No matter how the Jews managed to seize Canaan, their claim to the Promised Land was not based on any special rights to land and worldly goods, granted to God's favorite. True, God had pledged to give Canaan to Abraham, his children and their descendants, but there was no element of privilege in his promise. Canaan was the legitimate heritage of the Jews, and such heritages—actually far larger and more fertile—were recognized as the due right of other peoples. We detect a hint of this in Moses' ode *Haazinu:*[14] "When the Most High divided to the nations their inheritance, When He separated the sons of Adam, He set the bounds of the peoples" (Deut. 32:8). All the surrounding countries were, in a certain respect, promised, and only in Palestine could Jewish sovereignty hold sway. Speaking for God, Moses impresses upon his people, that on their way to the Promised Land they would have to "pass through the border of your brethren the children of Esau and that they must be careful not to come into any conflict with these people since not so much as a foot-breadth of this land would be vouchsafed the Jews because I have given Mount Seir[15] unto Esau for a possession" (Deut. 2:3–5). The same injunction is given to the people before they traverse the wilderness of Moab:[16] "Distress not the Moabites, neither contend with them in battle, for I will not give thee of their land for a possession; because I have given Ar[17] unto the children of Lot for a possession" (Deut. 2:9). The children of Esau and Lot have the same rights to the lands allotted them as have the

Jews to their land, and these rights must not be infringed upon. Not only were the Jews forbidden to deprive the owners of their lands and conquer them, but even in passing they were warned to take nothing by force: "Ye shall purchase food of them for money, that ye may eat; and ye shall also buy water of them for money, that ye may drink" [Deut. 2:6]. If ever there was an imperialistic urge, a desire for expansion, among the Jews, it certainly had no religious sanction behind it, nor was it based on any special rights supposedly accorded to the elect.

In comparison with the rest of the ancient world, legislation in Palestine displayed relatively little discrimination against the alien: "One ordinance shall be both for you of the congregation, and also for the stranger that sojourneth with you, an ordinance forever in your generations; as ye are, so shall the stranger be before the Lord. One law and one ordinance shall be both for you, and for the stranger that sojourneth with you" (Num. 15:15–16). This was the Jewish religious principle which strove to regulate the treatment of non-Jews. Love for one's neighbor, which was later, by the Hillel formula,[18] declared to be the quintessence of the Torah, was in biblical times extended to people of alien blood: "And if a stranger sojourn with thee in your land, ye shall not vex him. But the stranger that dwelleth with you shall be unto you as one born among you, and thou shalt love him as thyself; for ye were strangers in the land of Egypt: I am the Lord your God" (Lev. 19:33–34).

Naturally, the alien in the Jewish land could not enjoy full rights, despite the ethical regulations and the command of the "golden rule." The Jewish state was to exist as an organized theocratic society—so that a stranger in its midst, who did not recognize the rule of God as the Jews interpreted it, could not be accorded all the rights granted to Jews as professing members of that society; the limitation of his right was commensurate with the curtailment of his duties. Only a minimum of Jewish religious duties was imposed on the non-Jew: "At the end of every seven years, in the solemnity of the year of release, in the Feast of Tabernacles [Sukkot],[19] when all Israel is come to appear before the Lord thy God in the place which He shall choose, thou shalt read this law before all Israel in their hearing. Gather the people together, men and women, and children, and thy stranger that is within thy gates, that they may hear and that they may learn, and fear the Lord your God, and observe to do all the works of this law" (Deut. 31:10–12).

From these passages it might appear that the sojourn of a stranger in Palestine was conditional upon his acceptance of the Jewish law in its entirety—since he was compelled to be present at the reading of the law before all Israel. The fallacy of such a conclusion is proven not only by the restrictions imposed on the non-Jew but by the special privileges accorded him. In Exodus 12:48 we read: "And when a stranger shall sojourn with thee, and will keep the Passover[20] to the Lord, let all his males be circumcised, and let him come near and keep it and he shall be as one that is born in the land: for no uncircumcised person shall eat thereof." Participation in the Passover ceremony was regarded as an important religious act, and the stranger, far from being forced to take part, was forbidden to do so. This rule expressed no racial discrimination, but was the natural exclusion from participation in an intimate religious ritual of people who did not identify themselves with the Jewish faith. The stranger referred to in the quoted passage is not the same as the *ger* [proselyte] of a later period but merely an alien who found himself in the midst of Jews in the Jewish land and did not accept the Torah of that people. The circumcision which entitled him to share in and eat of the Passover sacrificial flesh was not only important in itself as a physical symbol of spiritual solidarity with other Jews, but was the accepted ritual for the full-fledged convert. By this token, a Jew by race who had never been circumcised—if such there were—would not be admitted to the Passover ceremony. On the other hand, we see that the stranger—in the early biblical sense of the word—enjoyed certain rights and privileges withheld from his Jewish neighbor. In Deuteronomy 14:21 we read: "Ye shall not eat of any thing that dieth of itself: thou shalt give it unto the stranger that is in thy gates, that he may eat it."

The Torah makes no attempt to force on the stranger the dietetic restrictions imposed on Jews, since his code requires no such bans. The stranger's duty to be present, once every seven years, at the reading of the law before all Israel in their hearing may therefore be interpreted not as an effort to coerce the non-Jew into acceptance of the Jewish faith, but rather as a social obligation to acquaint himself with the civilization of the land and the laws under whose protection he lived. It is very possible that there was a design behind this constraint—the thought that periodic inoculations of Jewish lore and introduction into the theocratic structure of the Jewish state would eventually impel the idol worshipper to see the error of his ways; this assumption was, however (at any rate, in principle), never driven to the point of religious pressure. Despite the nebulousness surrounding certain terms applied in the Pentateuch to non-Jews living in the Jewish state—and there are still differences of opinion about such words as *ger* and *toshav* [resident], of which not least interesting are the comments on the subject made by Rav Zair[21] in the first volume of his monumental work *Toldot hahalakhah* [The History of the *Halakhah*][22]—we may conclude that according to the juridico-ethical concept of ancient Jews, strangers fell into one of three categories.

III

In the first category were the "seven nations"—those from whom the Jews had to wrest their land by force.[23] These peoples were, so to speak, outside the law, and the Torah itself decreed severe treatment for them. During the period when the Jews were conquering the land from the Hittites,[24] Girgashites,[25] Amorites,[26]

Canaanites, Perizzites,[27] Hivites[28] and the Jebusites[29]—"seven nations greater and mightier than thou" [Deut. 7:1]—they were enjoined to show them no mercy: "And when the Lord thy God shall deliver them before thee; thou shalt smite them, and utterly destroy them; thou shalt make no covenant with them, nor show mercy unto them. Neither shalt thou make marriages with them; thy daughter thou shalt not give unto his son, nor his daughter shalt thou take unto thy son" (Deut. 7:2–3).

The religiously sanctioned treatment of these natives whom the Jews had undertaken to conquer was a very simple one—physical extermination.[30] Great numbers of them were virtually wiped out (approximating the fate of the American Indians upon the arrival of the white men) and the survivors became slaves or half-slaves. In the First Book of Kings, the following account is given of them with almost epic calm: "And all the people that were left which were not of the children of Israel,[31] their children that were left after them in the land, whom the children of Israel also were not able utterly to destroy, upon those did Solomon[32] levy a tribute of bond service unto this day" (1 Kgs. 9:20–21).

It would be utterly false to see in this treatment of the inhabitants of Canaan the application of any racial principle in the present-day sense of the words. The "seven nations" presented a danger to the Jews since they had claims on the land promised to the children of Israel. We find here a conflict between two political or territorial claims, and the Jews felt that they had moral and religious justification to regard the pretensions of the natives as unwarranted. To have lived at peace with the "seven nations" in their midst, even if they had envisaged the economic and political possibility to do so, would have meant to tolerate the polluting presence of great numbers of pagans. The pagans in foreign, distant lands could scarcely have any demoralizing or corrupting influence upon the religious life of the Jews with their new and still uncrystallized monotheism and the stringent moral code which they were in the process of constructing on the basis of it. Native pagans were regarded as tempters and seducers. The reason for the interdiction against marriage with the indigenous nations is clearly given in Deuteronomy 7:4–5: "For they will turn away thy son from following Me, that they may serve other gods."

Israel was destined to become a holy people, and its Promised Land a holy land, and the impurities of alien peoples had to be eliminated from it. Marriages with pagans of other peoples and lands were, on the other hand, tolerated to a great degree: because of limited opportunities for contact, there could not be many such marriages, and since the foreigners residing in the country were so few in number they could easily be absorbed into Jewish life, whereas the native heathen conducted their own community life and practiced their local pagan cult. Marital bonds with these close neighbors who had not even relinquished their claim to the land would, from the Jewish standpoint, have jeopardized not only

Jewish domination over the country but the very existence of the unique, budding, and essentially antipodal faith of Israel. The rationalization advanced by the Jews for the nationalistic aggressiveness they displayed toward the inhabitants of the land they seized and for their tyrannical policy as occupants was essentially religious in nature, not racist.

The second category embraced aliens in their own native lands. As shown above, the Jews were not especially antagonistic to these people, or, at any rate, not as aggressive as their ethico-religious viewpoint could have dictated or sanctioned. True, the Jews regarded themselves as superior to those foreigners, feeling that they were a chosen people in intimate relations with God (with the one and only God whom the peoples of the earth had not yet learned to recognize). Their position as God's favorites and the fact that a covenant had been concluded between them and the almighty was in no way synonymous in the minds of the Jewish people with a claim to political or economic advantages of any specific sort. Every people is entitled to its land and independence and, despite the intense religious impatience which Jews as a monotheistic people displayed toward the rest of the nations of the world, they nevertheless recognized their right even to idol worship. Their emphasized, or as some choose to regard it, overstressed self-esteem never led to contempt of other peoples: "Thou shalt not despise the Edomite[33] and the Egyptian" [Deut. 23:8].[34] In this connection, Rav Zair is right when he points out in his *Toldot hahalakhah* that the antagonism of the Jews was leveled at paganism, but not at the pagan himself. An exception to this was the Amalekites,[35] whose remembrance under heaven it was considered a virtue to blot out. Jews had freed themselves comparatively soon of their hatred for the Egyptians—even for the Egyptians! But Amalek they could not forgive, as long as he existed. "Remember what Amalek did unto thee by the way, when ye were come forth out of Egypt; how he met thee by the way, and smote the hindmost of thee, even all that were feeble behind thee, when thou wast faint and weary; and he feared not God" (Deut. 25:17–18). If I am not mistaken, Amalek is the only alien people against whom Israel's eternal hate and revenge is invoked in the [Hebrew] Bible.

From the prophets we hear of God's blessing the other peoples of the earth. "Blessed be Egypt my people, and Assyria[36] the work of my hands, and Israel mine inheritance" (Isa. 19:25). In the vision of the prophet, the people which had subjected Israel to generations of slavery and had come to symbolize for the Jew impurity and evil, is elevated to the status of the people of God; Egypt and Assur[37] which for so many years had represented the most mighty factors in the political life of the world known to the Jews will, in the envisioned future, unite with Israel to fight a holy battle for justice and right, in the name of the Lord. Zephaniah[38] expresses this universalistic expectation in even clearer terms: "For then will I turn to the peoples a pure language, that they may all call upon the name of the Lord, to serve him with one consent" (Zeph. 3:9). Zephaniah no longer found it possible to apply his visions to individual peoples; he foresaw a purified and spiritually elevated mankind, united in the service of the one and only God. Jeremiah[39] regarded himself from the very first as the prophet unto the nations, and despite his warning that in the day of God's wrath Egypt, Babylon,[40] Canaan, Elam,[41] and other nations would be severely punished for their sins (almost all the prophets threatened the world, and foremost of all, their own people, with dire retribution), he nevertheless accords them their share in the future salvation: "But it shall come to pass in the latter days, that I will bring again the captivity of Elam, said the Lord" (Jer. 49:39). Jeremiah believed that God would pluck from off their lands all the evil neighbors who had touched the inheritance of the Jews, but the punishment for their evil deeds would not last eternally; God would eventually relent and return each to his possessions and each to his land: "And it shall come to pass, after that I have plucked them out I will return, and have compassion on them, and will bring them again every man to his land" (Jer. 12:15). The prophet had faith in these nations and in their moral future. Even the evil neighbors would eventually mend their ways, and God would heed their penance and restore them each to his place in the world. God entertains no arbitrary prejudices or aversions; his wrath is temporary and his punishments are not unconditional. Jeremiah, and not only he, already believed in those open gates about which we read, many generations later, in the [*Mekhilta*]:[42] "The Lord, blessed be His name, rejects none of His creatures; He accepts them all. The gates are opened hourly that all who wish may enter."[43]

When we pass from the [Hebrew] Bible to the unique and more lyrical sphere of *agadah* and *midrash* we find this universalist tendency of the prophets more defined and articulate. Both are rich in countless expressions of an almost pathological egocentrism and naive self-praise; certain forms of narcissism are often palliative measures against the contempt and persecution of the outside world. At the same time we find the people revolting against narrow separatism and national vainglory which is a denial of universal solidarity and the organic oneness of mankind. The same religious awareness which produced the election concept on the basis of the actual or imagined spiritual and moral distinctions between Israel and the rest of the world refused to accept the idea that the Jews were *organically* different from their neighbors, not merely *historically* more advanced. Religious conscience began, as it were, to seek a form of apologia for the inferiority of the rest of the world, and for Israel's supremacy. Echoes of this subterranean but, according to many signs, very keen moral disturbance can still be detected in certain [talmudic] passages: "Why are the gentiles polluted? Since the Jews were present on Mount Sinai,[44] their pollution has ceased; since the gentiles were not present on Mount Sinai, their pollution has not ceased" [B. Avodah Zarah 22b].

Jews, in other words, were not always as pure as now; there was a time when they were no less polluted than the heathen, but their presence on Mount Sinai purified them. In very cautious, veiled terms, the theory of the spiritual evolution of peoples is set forth: Jews were the *first* to experience revelation, but under the divine plan, revelation will also be vouchsafed to all other peoples; they must merely wait for *their* Mount Sinai. The barrier between Jew and non-Jew is not absolute but conditional, not permanent but temporary, historical. Other peoples still have no Torah—the most precious and important gift to man—but *wisdom* they possess in no less degree than the Jews. Midrash [*Eikhah Rabbah* 2][45] tells us: "If you are told there is wisdom among the gentiles, believe; that the gentiles have Torah, do not believe." The sages of the Talmud even created a blessing to be recited upon meeting a non-Jewish sage: "Upon seeing a sage of Israel one says 'Blessed is the Almighty who has granted of His wisdom to those who fear Him,' and upon meeting sages of other nations, one says, 'Blessed is He who has distributed wisdom to His creatures'" (B. Brakhot 58[a]).[46] The respect in which Jews of the talmudic era held certain spiritual qualities of the gentiles is indicated, for instance, in the interpretation they gave to the passage, "God shall enlarge Japheth,[47] and He shall dwell in the tents of Shem;[48] and Canaan shall be His servant" (Gen. 9:27). This vague sentence is taken to allude to a form of synthesis of cultures. "The magnificence of Japheth shall be in the tents of Shem" (B. Megillah 9[b])[49]—that is, the grandeur and beauty of Japheth (the esthetic values of the gentiles) shall rest in the tents of Shem. Japheth, the gentile, is here indirectly characterized as higher, in a specified spiritual sense, than Shem, the ancestor of the Jews. But esthetics and wisdom do not exhaust the total spiritual strength of the gentile nations. The greatest religious and moral abundance to which man can aspire—the Holy Spirit—is not barred to them. In the *Tanna devei Eliyahu* [Teachings of the School of Elijah][50] we read the following characteristic passage: "I summon the heavens and the earth as witness, and they will confirm that whether gentile or Jew, whether man or woman, whether a serf or an enslaved woman, according to their deeds shall the Holy Spirit rest upon them."[51] The individual, in other words, is not rated by sex, by social degree or by race: in every man lies the ability to rise, to achieve the Holy Spirit.

The Talmud and various *midrashim*, as is well known, contain hundreds of passages of harsh criticism and prejudice against other nations, but only very rarely is an outright prejudice expressed against the entirety of the non-Jewish world. The *agadah* and the *midrashim* are not less, and frequently far more, outspokenly universalist in tendency than the Prophets. According to one *midrash*, the Torah was given to the Jews in the wilderness—a sort of no-man's-land—and not in Palestine, as an indication that in principle the Torah was a gift to all of mankind and not merely to the Jews.[52] Potentially, in the final historical analysis, all peoples are worthy to receive the Torah. According to another legend, the Torah was presented simultaneously in seventy tongues to all the peoples of the earth so that the three score and ten nations might hear it, each in its own language and perhaps, some among them, might accept it [B. Avodah Zarah 2a–2b]. According to another version, the Torah was borne from land to land, from nation to nation: the creator was, as it were, "experimenting" with his creatures, since he was himself "not certain" who among them would be prepared to accept it. The experiment failed since all the nations refused the gift, and even Israel (here we again see that symptomatic apology for possessing a "precious vessel" denied to others) did not accept the Torah willingly, not being mature enough to evaluate it properly, but under compulsion [B. Avodah Zarah 2b]. "The mountain was overturned upon them like a vat" [B. Shabbat 88a]:[53] Either you shoulder the burden of the Torah or the mountain will destroy you. The moral behind this and other *midrashim* is that Jews must be more restrained in their boasts of superiority over other peoples. In the original scheme of the world, the Torah was to belong to all, regardless of land, tongue or origin. For the time being, this plan has failed, but eventually it will be realized ("and the earth shall be ripe with wisdom") [Isa. 11:9; B. Brakhot 55a]; Jews are only the first ones to have made a covenant with God. This attitude toward the gentile bears no similarity to the scientific racial theories of today. Blood, origin, biological heritage shape the individual, but more powerful than all these factors is the spirit of every man, and the *zelem elohim* (the image of God) which leaves its stamp on each human face is, in the final analysis, more determinative than the heritage of flesh and blood.

It would be extremely naive to seek in the [Hebrew] Bible, or even later in the Talmud or *midrashim*, any systematic psycho-biological theories. Jewish classical literature expresses a purely intuitive reasoning: the spirit is not a slave to matter, it is autonomous, and possesses the power to free man from the mastery of flesh and blood; man is beyond biology. Spirit is not simply an attendant phenomenon of the body; man therefore should be regarded as a free agent, morally responsible for his own actions. The relation between spirit and matter is presented once in [the Talmud] in graphic anatomical fashion: "There are three partners in man—God, and his father and mother; his father plants in him the male seed (*loben*), from which spring his bones, veins, nails, brain-matter and the whites of his eyes; his mother implants in him the red fluid (*odom*) whence come his skin, flesh, hair and the pupil of his eye; and God bestows on him spirit, soul, facial features, the ability to see and to hear and to speak and to walk on his feet, understanding, reason and wisdom; and when the time comes for man to depart from this earth, God takes back His share and leaves to the parents *their* share" [B. Niddah 31a].[54] Everything in man which is vital, dynamic and spiritual comes from God, not from the family tree, and, by the same token, not from race. In terms of modern psychology, we realize that our sages meant that the part which parents (and race) play in the development of man can perhaps stimulate or retard the unfolding of his soul; they cannot, however, permanently bind or determine his character and moral destiny. To the Jews, the gentiles appeared as sinful creatures but certainly Judaism never regarded sinful as synonymous with damned. The gates of repentance were open to everyone, and it is significant that during Sukkot seventy oxen were sacrificed in the Temple of Jerusalem[55] to atone for the sins of the "seventy nations" [B. Sukkah 55b]. This rite demonstrates more than anything else, and perhaps even more than the universalist visions of the prophets and the latter anti-particularistic interpretations of many of our sages, that however many faults the Jews might have found in their gentile neighbors and with however many virtues they might have credited themselves—frequently out of sheer naive boastfulness, and at other times in a spirit of refined triumph over their oppressors—when it came to a spiritual summation (which found expression in cult, worship and in the mysteries of sacrifice) they evolved a ritual which solemnly stressed the unity of mankind in sin, repentance, and atonement.

And now we come to the third category of gentiles—not those of distant lands, but individuals or small groups from neighboring countries whom circumstances had brought to the land of Israel. At the beginning of this chapter we have already indicated the social status of this group and will therefore confine ourselves here to a few more brief remarks. Biblical legislation distinguished between the *nokhri*—the foreigner who sojourned only temporarily in the Jewish land in the pursuit of his business, for instance—and the *ger* who, though of foreign origin, had established himself permanently in Palestine. Their rights and duties differed greatly (like the tourist and the bona fide immigrant in the United States, for example). The *nokhri* was bound by the general laws of the land but was not regarded as a resident or member of the community in any economic sense of the word. The restrictions against usury did not apply to him. You may charge the *nokhri* interest but not your brother—here, the *nokhri* is not simply a non-Jew, but a visiting foreigner who did not fit into the permanent social-economic structure of the country, while the term brother applies to all fellow residents of the Jewish state whether ethnically Jewish or not. (We find similar restrictions in other states, both ancient and modern, e.g., a tourist seeks employment or accepts relief only at the risk of deportation in France, Switzerland, and the United States.) The status of the *ger* who is frequently referred to as *ger toshav* [foreign resident] or, simply, *toshav* [resident], to distinguish him from the *nokhri*, is different. We are not always able to grasp the psychological and emotional nuances of certain Hebrew words, but that in the expression *ger toshav* there lay no slightest disparagement is proven by the passage in Leviticus 25:23: "And the land shall not be sold in perpetuity; for the land is mine; for ye are *gerim* [pl., proselytes] and *toshavim* [pl., residents] with me." The idea behind Mosaic agrarian legislation was that no man had absolute proprietary rights over the land since it belongs to God, and men and nations are simply his tenant farmers. The Jews in their own land were also, in a sense, only *gerim* and *toshavim* on God's soil. By the same token, the gentile living in the land of Israel was also one of God's tenants and under his protection. The *ger* must therefore not be wronged or abused: "Thou shalt neither vex a stranger, nor oppress him; for ye were strangers in the land of Egypt" (Exod. 23:21). And in the same breath, comes the injunction: "Ye shall not afflict any widow or fatherless child" (Exod. 22:29). No discrimination must be displayed against the strangers in matters of law and justice: "Ye shall have one manner of law, as well for the stranger, as for the home-born; for I am the Lord your God" (Lev. 24:22).

Biblical law enjoined equal help for the impoverished Jew and non-Jew—the *ger toshav* being placed on an equal footing with fellow-Jews: "And if thy brother be waxen poor, and fallen in decay with thee; then thou shalt relieve him; yea, though he be a stranger, or a sojourner; that he may live with thee" (Lev. 25:35). It is also forbidden to give him money upon usury or lend him victuals for increase. The Mishnah attempted, many generations later, to interpret the word *toshav* differently in order to prove that the prohibition against charging interest applied only to Jews. But this is not the only example of a law which had to be adapted to changing social and economic conditions. *Prosbul*[56] was basically an infraction against a clear biblical law, and the exegetical justification for the emendation is only euphonistic casuistry. *Prosbul* is the classic example of religio-juridical circumvention in which a number of the sages and later Jewish religious authorities specialized—a device by which the word of the law could remain inviolate and, at the same time, not be put into effect. Debts should definitely have been cancelled during the sabbatical year, but when the Jews began to change their patriarchal agricultural life for a more complicated economic system in which trade and commerce played an ever-increasing part, the *shmitah* [sabbatical year] rules were found to impede the development of an extensive credit system. From the Mishnah we learn that when Hillel saw that people were becoming reluctant to extend loans for fear that they would be cancelled on the seventh year, and thus offended against a command of the Torah (the duty to help the needy), he established a new procedure that permitted lenders to grant loans on condition that they could collect them on demand. Similar economic conditions apparently dictated certain revisions in the rules governing the charging of interest on loans to *gerim* and *toshavim*.

One significant social-economic discrimination against the alien deserves mention here. According to biblical law, Jewish bonded servants attained their liberty after six years of service or during a year of jubilee, whereas non-Jewish slaves had no claims to freedom. The formula used in the Torah for the liberation of Jewish bondmen is interesting: "And then shall he depart from thee, both he and his children with him, *and shall return unto his own family, and unto the possession of his fathers shall he return*" (Lev. 28:41). As can be seen from this passage, the jubilee laws were twofold in purpose—restoration of liberty and reestablishment of a certain economic equilibrium in the country. The Jewish slave, upon attaining his freedom, knew what to do with it and did not fall a burden on his neighbors; he returned to the bosom of his family and to the possession of his fathers which was his by right of inheritance. This was not, however, the case with the *ger* or the *toshav*. Under the economic conditions then obtaining, restored freedom could prove disastrous. For the most part, free men lived from the soil, and under the laws of jubilee land could never pass over to those who had not previously owned it. Yehezkel Kaufmann,[57] in the first volume of his *Golah venekhar* [Exile and Alienation], correctly pictures the special economic status of the alien in the Jewish land: "The ancient Israelite tribal system made it practically impossible for strangers to merge with the Jewish people, even after many generations, and thus they remained a separate social entity. The land was apportioned among the tribes and only through membership in a tribe was it generally possible to receive one's share of land and be regarded as a citizen of the country. Land was the 'possession of the fathers,' and the family-tribal alliance jealously guarded its own entity and its own corner of the earth so that no stranger could penetrate. . . . The tribe formed a strong barrier, even among the Jews themselves. In ancient times this division was a strong factor in Jewish social and political life and there was no way for a person to transfer from one tribe to the other."[58] In other words, the tribal structure of Jewish economic life was an automatic barrier to the absorption of the stranger. We find similar features in the unique structure of the Russian *mir*[59] [Russian for "communal village"] which prevailed for many generations, even as late as the beginning of the twentieth century, and in the Swiss canton system[60] with its peculiar economic commune organization which no stranger could enter unless agreed upon by both canton and commune. Had the non-Jewish slave been released he would, apparently, not have known what to do with his freedom and might easily have become a sort of pariah, in a situation worse than that of a slave, whose Jewish owner bore no little responsibility for his needs and well-being.

For these reasons we find in biblical law no economic discrimination against the alien as compared with the attitude toward the needy or declassed section of the Jewish population. "At the end of three years thou shalt bring forth all the tithe of thine increase the same year, and shalt lay it up within the gates; and the Levite (because he hath no part nor inheritance with thee), and the stranger, and the fatherless, and the widow, which are within thy gates, shall come, and shall eat and be satisfied" (Deut. 14:28–29). As we see from this passage, the *ger toshav* is regarded as on the same social level with the Levite, Jewish orphans, and widows, rather than as belonging to a different race. But it is in Ezekiel that we see that religio-ethical consciousness could no longer reconcile itself to this status of the alien and to regulations barring him from fuller integration into the economic structure of Jewish life. "So shall ye divide this land unto you according to the tribes of Israel. And it shall come to pass, that ye shall divide it by lot for an inheritance unto you, *and to the strangers that sojourn among you*; and they shall be unto you as born in the country *among the children of Israel; they shall have inheritance with you among the tribes of Israel.* And it shall come to pass, that in *what tribe the stranger sojourneth, there shall ye give him his inheritance,* saith the Lord God" (Ezek. 47:21–23).

IV

On the basis of its law, social relationships, and religious ritual, we may summarize the attitude of Israel to the three categories of strangers it knew, in the following fashion: The only objects of Jewish chauvinism were the "seven nations" from whom the Jews had recovered their heritage, the land of Israel. (To these seven should be added Amalek which had, as previously mentioned, roused the particular antipathy of the Jews for certain historic-psychological reasons.) The primitive hate displayed by the Jews toward the indigenous population of Canaan had, however, no racial motivation. On the one hand, the antagonism of the Jews stemmed from their determination, once and for all, to occupy the "promised" land and establish incontestably their domination, despite the opposition of the native inhabitants of the country; on the other, it was fed by their passion to wipe out local idol worshipping and purge God's land of the "uncleanness of the heathens" [B. Shabbat 83a].

Far more universalistic, as we have already seen, was the Jewish attitude toward the alien who had come from a foreign land. Discriminations directed against him were the objective results of the economic structure of the country as well as of the great religious differences between the Jew and the uncircumcised alien who was not identified either with the Jewish faith or with the Jewish mode of life. Modern analogies to this situation can sooner be found in the restrictions endured by Protestants in some Catholic countries (or vice-versa, by Catholics in some Protestant lands) than in the prejudices of the white men against the Negro, on the score of racial principles. When aliens were circumcised and assumed a certain number of ritual duties, they could, in the space of a few generations (in later periods, when the ancient tribal structure of the Jewish economy gave way to a freer system of individual property and enterprise), become completely integrated in the Jewish social organism their ethnic origin proving no deterrent whatsoever. In the talmudic era, their equal status was very clearly defined: "The needy stranger and the needy Jew are to be fed equally, and the sick stranger and the sick Jew are to be visited equally, and the alien dead and the Jewish dead are to be given equal burial, for the sake of maintaining peace" (B. Gittin 61[a]).[61] Jewish universalism, as we have shown before and as we shall further demonstrate, was more sharply illustrated by the attitude toward the gentile nations in their own lands, who presented no perils to Jewish existence or independence and could not be regarded as seducers to idolatry.

In this connection, it is interesting to compare the Jewish mentality as reflected in the [Hebrew] Bible and in talmudic literature, with that of the Greek election theories. According to Jewish understanding, all non-Jews were *goyim* or *akum*[62]—heathens who still idol-worshipped, as the Jews had formerly done. But still, they were all eligible to become Jews (in the religious sense). *Goyim* were backward but not damned. To the Greek, the barbarian represented a biologically inferior creature. So profound was the Greek conviction of superiority that it even affected the finer and nobler type of Hellenized Jew. Even Philo[63] regarded the man who spoke no Greek as an ignoramus, a barbarian. But, of course, for the philosopher of Alexandria this could simply have meant that the man who did not know that language could have no access to the sources of science and philosophy, which, at that period, were predominantly Greek. For Aristotle,[64] however, a barbarian meant an uncouth person to whom the only worthwhile civilization was organically alien, who was unable to grasp it by his very nature, not only because of his nurture. He divided mankind into natural slaves and natural masters, into nations whose mission it was to rule and nations eternally fated to be dominated, into those predestined for civilization and those condemned to remain undeveloped.[65] (The modern Nazi concept of the *Herrenrasse* [master race]!) The vision of Isaiah of universal brotherhood in the end of the days, of eternal peace based on solidarity and equality of all races and nations, was entirely foreign to the spirit of Aristotle (nor was he unique in the Greek philosophical world). Despite their intellectual and other faults, the Sophists[66] were the first philosophers in Greece to preach the essential equality of men, regardless of any functional differences among them. But this line of thought left little mark on the social point of view of that period. Much more popular was Aristotelian racism, according to which differences in character and degree of culture among various races were predetermined by God or by nature. Racial conflicts were not interpreted historically or sociologically, but from the natural science standpoint. The reasons behind such conflicts were all part of the eternal plan, and wars will only end when each race will finally recognize and reconcile itself to its own place in the world in other words, when the inferior races will, of their own volition or by submitting to their fate, capitulate to the Greek *Herrenvolk* [German for "master nation"] or to other superior races. In his treatise *Alexander, or on [Behalf of Colonists]*,[67] Aristotle calls the attention of Alexander the Great[68] to the dangers of miscegenation. He criticizes the attempts of the conqueror to establish an equal political status for the various races in his empire, and strives to prove that only the Greeks require constitutional rule while all non-Greeks, as inferior creatures, must submit to a despotic regime.[69] Racial theories of such violence—if we were required to draw a comparison between Judaism and Hellenism—are not to be found in the entire Jewish literature.

Despite any feelings of superiority entertained by Jews, even the most chauvinistic among them were not unaware of the universalistic view expressed by Rabbi Meir:[70] "The dust from which the Almighty molded the first man was taken from all the earth" (B. Sanhedrin 38[a]).[71] It was not by accident that Jews interpreted God's creation of only one man from whom all human beings, until the end of the ages, must descend, as symbolic of the equality and equal worthiness of every single human individual: "Therefore every one is obliged to say the world was created for my sake" (B. Sanhedrin 37[a]). While in Greece Aristotle's racial theories were contested chiefly by the Sophists, a sect considered as intellectually irresponsible,[72] among Jews they were rejected by the highest authorities of the people—that anonymous circle which is known in the Talmud as the *hakhamim* (sages). "The sages taught us: man was originally created alone. Why? Because of the righteous and because of the wicked; so that the righteous might not say, we are descended from a righteous man, and the wicked, we are descended from a wicked man. There is another explanation: because of families, so that they might not quarrel with one another; now then, if, knowing that man was created alone, families still dispute with one another, how much more would they quarrel had God originally created two men" (B. Sanhedrin 38[a]). From its very inception, as evidenced by the first chapters of the Book of Genesis, Judaism was strongly monogenistic. The monogenistic myth is the fountainhead of Jewish universalism and catholicity.

V

There is no object now in indulging in speculations as to the degree to which the Jews were justified in entertaining feelings of religio-moral superiority over other peoples. The Jews of antiquity were scarcely aware of the great civilizations of the Far East (China, India); even had they known them well, who can tell how they would have reacted? Confucius and his doctrine were the product of an older civilization, too saturated with skepticism, intellectual reserve, and over-sophistication to appeal to a comparatively young and temperamental people still in the early stages of self-formation. And if Buddhism had been familiar to them, they could neither have grasped the unrivalled structure of its daring abstractions and the severe circumscription of its metaphysical system, nor could they, as a young nation with a passionate acceptance of *this* world, its joys and its seemingly infinite possibilities, respond sympathetically to such fatalism and all-embracing pessimism. In addition they would, in rather short order, have discovered the disturbing degeneration of Buddhism: its descent from the spiritually lofty heights which it had once attained, to the level of a new and rather coarse form of idolatry adapted to the masses—a level above which most of the countries which embraced Buddhism have, to this day, not been able to rise.

But these are purely hypothetical considerations, since both China and India represented, as it were, distant planets to the Jews of antiquity; the world with which they had contact was little affected by the Far East. The environment in which the Jews existed was primarily Semitic, then Egyptian and Persian, and later Greek and Roman. Were they not justified, when comparing themselves with these neighbors, in feeling preeminent?

Modern Semitologists have bent over backward to find early traces of monotheism in ancient non-Jewish Semitic literature. They may, indeed, have found flashes of pure monotheistic speculation antedating the Jewish adoption of the idea of a one and only God. But the history of civilization is not concerned simply with any individual whose reasoning, imagination, or intuition first revealed to him the idea of a one and only God. The fact that some great human mind did, for a short time, entertain such an idea, which later evanesced or was crushed, can only be of *biographical* moment, but it has little *historical* significance. Even though we assume that the first known monotheist was Akhenaton[73] (this is not the place for a controversy with [Sigmund] Freud[74] with regard to his theories in the field of Mosaic research[75]) and not Moses or Abraham, the monotheism of this Egyptian king was no more than an episode, a felicitous accident in the life of one man, or perhaps of a limited number of followers. Egyptian life and thought were not fired by this spark, nor were the people drawn to it. To the Jews, the concept of the oneness of God was completely original since only among them did the idea take root as a social force and burgeon forth into a new code of ethics and a new mode of life. Abraham, whom Jewish tradition recognizes as the first monotheist, was perhaps ethnically not a member of the Hebrew race (so that the copyright of this idea may belong to an alien race, after all) but it is significant that he gained neophytes for this new faith chiefly among the Hebrews. The question of which individual first "discovered" the monotheistic idea reduces itself, after all, to an *archeological* problem; which group first embraced the idea, is of *historical* significance. In the days of antiquity, only the Jews accepted it, and only for them did it become a spiritual force in the life of the people as a whole. If we subscribe to the theory that even the Jewish god was originally more of a tribal god than the lord of the universe, that in the early stages he was not the one-and-only God, since the gods of the surrounding non-Jewish world were also considered as real entities, each operating within his own ethnic circle—he was nevertheless the supreme, the most powerful, and the holiest of all. He was expected, sooner or later, to destroy all other gods of the surrounding tribes and nations, and his supremacy contained the potential elements of unity, oneness, and universalism.

Jews met the Greeks in a relationship of contact and friction much later than they did their Semitic neighbors, or the Egyptians and the Ethiopians. But even the Greek national religion and mode of life caused them no feeling of inferiority, despite the hypnotic spell certain of its aspects exerted on the upper classes among Jews. Even had the Jews been conversant with the daring metaphysical speculations of the pre-Socratics[76] (and how many among the Greeks themselves knew about or could understand them?), what possible impression could these philosophers make on them? The pre-Socratics were in search of the world's oneness, of its substance-elements, and the principles on which it is based. However, they were more concerned with the monistic *what* (earth, water, fire, air) than the monistic *who*. Monistic atheism could not satisfy the Jewish thirst for monistic theism. One might even question what possible influence the great metaphysical reflections of a Plato[77] could have had on the Jews, provided of course, that they were aware of Plato. (How many people in Greece, in the most golden time of its "golden age," were familiar with Plato's philosophy or could assimilate it? For that matter, how many moderns are able to grasp even the most general outlines of his philosophical structure?) In the context of Greek spiritual life, even Plato was, to a great degree, only an episode; as for the concrete religious concepts of the Greeks as a people, these could only produce an impression of chaos and confusion on the Jews—the very elements from which they sought so passionately to free themselves.

Greek mythology never succeeded in organizing the world, in unifying it or in transforming it into a real cosmos. There were too many gods on Olympus both unwilling and unable to establish accord among themselves; and immorality was much too prevalent among them: "Homer[78] and Hesiod[79] have ascribed to the gods all deeds that are a shame and a disgrace among men: thieving, adultery, fraud" (Xenophanes).[80] In Homer's *Iliad*, for instance (in the final analysis, Homer is more representative of the culture of the Greek people than were Socrates,[81] Plato, or the tragic and unsupported thinkers who preceded Socrates), the chief theme is the wrath of Achilles,[82] and the disaster which his choler brought down upon the nation. The unfair treatment accorded him by King Agamemnon[83] was the cause of his fury. But how does Agamemnon explain his own behavior?

> Oft have our peers of Greece much blamed my forcing of the prize
> Due to Achilles; of which act not I, but destinies
> And Jove[84] himself, and black Erinys[85] . . .
> Are authors. What could I do then?[86]

To the Jews this must have seemed equivalent to having Adam declare that God had implanted in him a wicked desire to eat of the forbidden fruit,[87] or to insistence by Cain that God had implanted in him the lust to kill Abel.[88] Further in the same book, Achilles lends support to Agamemnon's explanation:

O father Jupiter,[89] from thee descends the confluence
Of all man's ill, for now I see the mighty king of men
At no hand forced away my prize, nor first inflamed my spleen
With any set ill in himself, but thou, the King of Gods,
Incensed with Greece, made that the mean to all their periods.[90]

A god who was not the supreme source and sanction of the moral will, the example of perfection for the virtuous, must have repelled the Jews, for whom God was the embodiment of everything they regarded as good and sacred.

In Greek mythological religion the certainty of God's omnipotence is lacking, whereas the Jew had the awareness of his omnipotence as something inseparable from his moral perfection: without the one, he could not possess the other. In Greek mythology there was, to be sure, one god who was king over all his colleagues and underlings. Some scholars choose to regard the Jove concept as a version of monotheism. But even Jove was powerless to exercise fully his own will unless it coincided with that of a still higher, more absolute and inflexible power—fate, destiny, or, as the Greeks termed it, *Moerae* [Greek for "the fates"].[91] When Jove's favorite son, Sarpedon,[92] fought against Patroclus,[93] Jove—the mightiest of all the gods—knew that his son would be overpowered and killed because it had so been decreed by fate. He was torn between his paternal love and the bitter decree of destiny, and Hera[94] reminded him of his duty to bow before it. We read in *The Iliad* that he, the father of the gods, carefully listened to her and caused bloody rain drops to fall upon the earth, thus doing honor to his beloved son about to be slain by Patroclus.[95] Jove's limited omnipotence is only effective when there is no conflict between his will and the categoric foreordainments of fate. To the Jewish religious mind, this was equivalent to virtual impotence. If there exists in the world a being or power more mighty than a god, then not he is god but that being or power which operates through the medium of Jove's "powerless will."[96] If God is subordinate to fate, then the true ruler of the world is fate. And what is fate? A power far less explicable than God and, moreover, a power to which no moral attributes can be assigned and no moral appeal can be made. During the talmudic era, in their religious folklore, Jews subscribed to a certain anthropomorphic theory, according to which God rules the world by consulting the Torah. Such a concept could not be interpreted to mean that God was a lesser power than the Torah, since he himself had given it to the Jews, to the world and to himself as well; and if he consults it, it is not because he subordinates his will to the directives of the Torah—if we can conceive of the two as being contradictory—but because he seeks to avoid any hasty judgments or caprices of the moment, and, by referring to the Torah which is the essence of his will, he refreshes his memory, as it were, regarding his *real* will and saves himself from acceding to any momentary desires. In this peculiar folklore interpretation, the principle of moral lawfulness in the world triumphs; it is, so to speak, a guarantee that caprice, temper, chance, amoral volitions, blind destiny, have, in the final analysis, no power. Jews did not believe that the heavenly bodies determine events and the span of man's life; they also refused to believe in the invisible and morally undiscriminating fate which looms in the background of the Greek religious worldview. The unity of the world and the unity of God had a meaning for the Jews only insofar as they indicated a watchful eye, guarding the world and bearing moral responsibility for it. *Providence* rather than *fate*.

There must have been far more fascination for the Jews of antiquity in the Persian religion, in the great vision of Zoroaster[97] with its peculiar mystical nationalism and still profounder faith in the moral destination of the world. Even modern man finds himself stirred by the teachings of Zoroaster, if only because of his tragic search for an explanation of the world's disunity, of the simultaneous existence of good and evil. Ormazd[98] is the source of truth, purity, lawfulness, friendship and goodness; whereas in Ahriman[99] is concentrated everything evil—two separate divine spirits, each seeking complete domination over the world. These two gods are twins, in constant conflict with one another. The two separate and antagonistic (and yet in some mysterious fashion, fraternal) spirits are both creative forces and the history of their struggle is the history of the world and all that occurs in it. The great ethical principle underlying this concept is that human beings are not only witnesses of the struggle but are themselves the protagonists. Man is the center of this conflict, his soul is, to a great degree, the battleground for mastery over which both spirits fight. By his very life and being, his faith and emotions, sympathies, action or inaction, and by his dreams and wishes, man allies himself with either Ormazd or Ahriman. His good deeds lend strength to Ormazd, and his sins, to Ahriman. Although the outcome of the conflict is a foregone conclusion (eventually Ormazd must completely overpower his rival and gain sole mastery over the world) it can never be attained without man's cooperation. No other religion has invested man with a nobler role. But despite the fascination it certainly had for the more inquisitive minds, Zoroastrianism met with a stubborn spiritual resistance from the Jews.

The Jews had already become too sensitive to any form of limitation of God's omnipotence, and they saw in the Persian religion a god whose true power was still post-existent. According to Zoroaster, Ahriman—the god of darkness—not only exerts a great influence upon the world but is partly its maker as well. A number of the heavenly bodies—Behram (Mars), Kevan (Saturn), and others—were created by him and peopled with devils and evil spirits. This strange, though only temporary, dualism could not but repel the Jewish mind, although the high moral plane of Zoroastrianism and the laws regarding purity and defilement, set forth in the *Avesta*[100] and in other Persian scriptures, must have touched a responsive chord and evoked its admiration. The typical reaction of Jewish monotheism to the Persian concept of a dual divinity is expressed by the anonymous diaspora prophet commonly referred to as the Second Isaiah. He bore Persia no ill will; on the contrary, he predicted that its gracious king would yet bring deliverance to the Jews. He regarded Cyrus[101] as one of the "anointed," as "God's shepherd" who served the true God although he was himself not aware of doing so [Isa. 44:28, 45:1]. The prophet clearly discerns, however, a line of demarcation between Jewish monotheism and Persian dualism: "I am the Lord and there is none else, there is no God beside me. . . . That they may know from the rising of the sun, and from the west, that there is none beside me. I am the Lord and there is none else. I form the light and create darkness; I make peace and create evil; I, the Lord, do all these things" [Isa. 45:5–7]. The prophet failed to, or perhaps could not, explain *why* and *for what purpose* darkness and evil must exist; but he did know that they could not have been created by anyone other than the one-and-only God whose very oneness is a guarantee of ultimate goodness and light. If, as we read in the *Avesta*, Ahriman possesses sufficient power to people the earth with dragons, poisonous snakes, sickness and pestilence, and even cruel rulers, then, although temporarily, he outshines Ormazd and places in question the fundamentality of goodness and light in the world. Ormazd even resorts to the same strategies employed by a human ruler: realizing his weakness, he offers Ahriman an armistice to last nine thousand years, in the belief that after the lapse of that time his enemy would have become so weakened as to be easily overcome and destroyed. But the essential concept of a god who must for a long period tolerate and recognize the partial dominion of a negative god, must have grated on the Jewish metaphysical sense. In addition, Ormazd and Ahriman were not the *source* of everything which exists: both were *born*. The *Avesta* tells of other eternals which do not emanate from either of them: limitless *space* and limitless *time*. Ormazd created his world from light, with the sanction of Zarvan[102] who, accordingly, surpasses him and has the power either to withhold or to grant his approval. According to later versions, Ormazd and Ahriman proceed from Zarvan, who is still not the highest power: he renders sacrifices (to whom?); he is the victim of doubts and hesitations and does not know what he himself will bring forth. It must not be forgotten that, according to popular conception, Ormazd brings creatures to life through a form of propagation of himself. His wife is also his daughter, [Spenta] Armaiti,[103] who bore him sons and daughters. (One can well imagine the revulsion this evoked in Jews, with their stern antipathy toward incest.) Ather[104] (fire) is his son and Mithra[105] (the sun) is his daughter. When his son Gayumart[106] lay dying, he impregnated his own mother, and the issue of this union were the first two humans. It was not Ormazd who determined the fate of Gayumart but Zarvan or, according to another version, the stars. Even when Ormazd takes sick, he is powerless to help himself but must appeal to other gods.

Of all the religions with which the Jews of antiquity came in contact, the Persian most closely approximated monotheism, and its ethical principles and ritual found greatest favor with them. But they found even Zoroastrianism to contain too many idolatrous elements and to present too many spiritual and moral pitfalls, although they undoubtedly discerned in the Persian conception a subterranean struggle which was bound eventually to discover the "oneness of the Creator."[107]

The names which Jews at various periods assigned to God are indicative of the tendency or line of development which motivated their religious conscience from the very beginning: *ribono shel olam*—lord of the universe, the absolute ruler who shares his dominion with no one, even for a moment; *manhigo shel olam*—leader of the world; *atiko shel olam*—the pristine elder of the world whom nothing and no one could precede since he is the one "who spoke and the world came into being" [Ps. 33:9]; *hagvurah*—the power, the one and only, without which all else is powerless; *hadibur* or *memra*—the word, which is the basis of all existence and all happenings; the "only one" who is, according to Maimonides,[108] *mekhuyav hameziyut* [the necessary existent]—whose existence is logically obligatory since all other existence is dependent upon him; the name of *Shadai*[109] which, in the interpretation of Maimonides, is the same as *Asher dai*[110]—one who is sufficient unto himself, lives only within and for himself, and seeks no support elsewhere for his existence (the Spinozan concept of "substance");[111] or, simply, *hu*—"he," the only genuine "he" in the universe. This tendency, from the moment of revelation among the Jews, became the dominating directive and overtone in their religious development; and since the world is so full of contradictions and the mind of man is not capable of understanding God's plan in ruling the world, the Jews added another to his names, in a spirit of intellectual resignation and agnostic reverence: *sitro shel olam*—mystery of the world, into which we cannot delve—*Deus absconditus* [Latin for "hidden god"].

With such absolute monotheism as a driving force and directive for development, and with a superior standard of national morals which was so natural an aspect of this monotheistic tendency (by national morals we mean that set of ethical values which shape a mode of life and exert an influence on the average member of a democratically minded people—although there were periods when other peoples produced individuals of an ethical cast far superior to any then found among the Jews), the Jews had more than a mere subjective or egocentric cause to feel superior to all the other nations with whom they came in contact. This feeling of superiority naturally expressed itself in the belief that they had been *elected*: the "Thou-hast-chosen-us" concept. The fact that so many of their neighbors later embraced either Christianity or Islam in no wise served to dim this belief. Whatever criticism the Jews may have directed against the two new faiths, they were both the children of Judaism. Both Christianity and [Islam] accepted the [Hebrew] Bible as their Holy Book, thereby alone recognizing the superiority of the Jews. In other words, a great part of the surrounding world implicitly confirmed the election of Israel.

VI

The belief in *election* did not, however, in any way stifle the Jews' sense of moral responsibility toward the non-Jewish world, nor did it blind them to the actual or potential *worth* of their neighbors. The gentile world is sinful far more so than the Jewish but, despite its iniquity, it must and can be redeemed, and it is the task of the Jews to help in this redemption. The prophet Jonah[112] was severely punished for his chauvinism, and was forced, against his will, to go to Nineveh[113] and present there his prophecies before the gentiles, stirring their hearts to repentance and thus saving their city from destruction.

Perhaps the story of Jonah is not the best illustration of Israel's religious propensity to recognize the essentially equal worth of Jew and non-Jew: he was a Jew addressing gentiles. True, it was the Jew who saved the non-Jewish city of Nineveh, but he held himself aloof throughout—the Jew was here an active agent, and the non-Jew merely the receptive spirit. To a far greater degree the universalist trend of Jewish religion manifests itself in the Book of Ruth.[114] Not only does the woman of Moab embrace the faith of Israel, but she becomes completely absorbed in Jewish life: from this daughter of the gentiles no less a figure than King David[115] issued; and, whenever he arrives and whoever he may be, the messiah will have to remember that his great-great-ancestress was once a gentile of Moab.[116]

A still more radical universalist view is manifest in that most profoundly devotional book of the entire biblical canon: Job.[117] It is immaterial who the author was, or what the period of this magnificent opus, or whether Job actually existed or is merely the figment of some poet's imagination. ("Job never was, never existed; the story is merely a parable" [B. Bava Batra 15a]—a saying prevalent among some of the *amoraim*). What is significant is that the word "Jew" is not once mentioned in the entire book. The dramatic duel between man and God, man's pious resignation, his penitence all take place on a cosmic plane.

The reverence in which the Book of Job is held by Jews can be seen from the fact that they ascribed it to the same hand which had written the Torah: "Moses wrote his own book and the Book of Job" (B. Bava Batra [15a]).[118] However, neither in its prologue, epilogue, nor in any other portion of the book is there any indication of the relationship between Jews and non-Jews—it *completely ignores* the existence of nations and peoples. The only realities are God, world, and man—man in general, without regard for any ethnical, historical, or local aspects. The locale of the book is given as Uz.[119] This would seem to indicate that Job was a non-Jew, but the author does not attach any significance to this, and Job's three companions are aliens bearing non-Jewish names.[120] These purely external references have no connection with the content of the book itself. They may be compared with the stage directions in *Hamlet*[121] which identify the hero as a Danish prince and set the action in Denmark. This does not mean that Shakespeare intended his play as a *Danish* tragedy or that it could not equally well have taken place in England or Siam.[122] The very fact that an actual or imaginary non-Jew could be portrayed as an example for all men to follow in their religious lives is the clearest proof of the strong universalist tendency of Judaism. No number of dissertations on Jewish narrow particularism can possibly refute this.

But the decisive moment in this entire problem is to be found in another field. The degree to which Jews considered themselves a consecrated ethnic group or race can be seen more clearly in their attitude toward non-Jews in the specific question of mixed marriages. Had the conviction of their superiority formed an integral and determining part of the conscience, and more particularly of the sensibilities of the Jews, and had it been interpreted in terms of modern racism, or according to the theories of an Aristotle (in the sense of the sharp, native distinction between "higher" and "lower" peoples),[123] they would first and foremost have adopted hard and fast measures against any biological contact with other peoples. If the Jewish race is holy and all other races impure, then the Jews should not risk pollution through mixed marriages. If man's spirit is bound to his body, to his biological heritage, then no gentile flesh or blood should be permitted to intrude upon the Jewish organism, and a union between Jews and non-Jews would thus become not only racial but spiritual pollution as well.

But the [Hebrew] Bible speaks openly of the Negro wife of Moses, the "woman of Cush."[124] Aaron[125] and Miriam[126] are the racial chauvinists who reproach their brother, but God himself sides with Moses and summons them before him in the "tent of meeting" to voice his displeasure [Num. 12:4–9]. Rav Zair refers, in the same connection,[127] to the manner in which Samson's[128] parents berated him for having taken a Philistine woman to wife: "Is there never a woman among the daughters of thy brethren, or among all my people, that thou goest to take a wife of the uncircumcised Philistine?" (Judg. 14:3). The meaning here being, that such action is unseemly but not necessarily forbidden or censurable. The writer of Judges[129] himself adds the comment: "But his father and mother knew not that it was of the Lord" (Judg. 14:4), that this was, as the later Jews expressed it, a "marriage made in Heaven."[130]

The laws of the [Hebrew] Bible sanctioned marriage with any "comely woman" taken prisoner in war [Deut. 21:11]; but it was found necessary to impose certain procedures so that the woman might be spared as much grief as possible at the separation from her home, her parents, and the burial grounds of her ancestors. The only ban on intermarriage referred to in the [Hebrew] Bible is in the previously mentioned case of the "seven nations" in Palestine itself; this was due to certain political and religious motivations which we have already discussed. On the whole, however, the [Hebrew] Bible made no attempt to insist on preservation by the Jews of their ethnic purity.

An exception to the general Jewish attitude toward mixed marriages are the well-known strictures laid down by Ezra and Nehemiah.[131] The ban[132] they declared was stern and aimed at the radical biological segregation of non-Jews from Jews, both in Palestine and abroad. Their interdiction was unconditional, uncompromising, without regard for any possible extenuating circumstances, and was intended for eternity.

The drastic regulations for biological segregation, introduced by Ezra and Nehemiah and so determinedly implemented by them in Jewish life, have a special interest for us.[133] Their decrees should be accorded their proper place in history. The "for eternity" formula of Ezra and Nehemiah was not upheld and, with time, their uncompromising interdictions were abolished. There is cause to believe that the obdurate insistence on endogamy by Ezra and Nehemiah was due to the special conditions prevailing during the return from captivity, and, as [R. Travers] Herford[134] points out, very possibly, if not for their bans, Judaism would in time have perished and there might not have remained even that nucleus from which Christianity later sprang. A relatively short time after this enforced biological segregation from the gentile world, the Jews became exogamous, making marriage conditional only upon the conversion to Judaism of the gentile spouse.

Discrimination against marriages with members of alien races was almost unknown during the talmudic era. The ban only referred to "gentiles in spirit"—those who worshipped pagan gods and were unwilling to embrace Judaism, or to *minim*, Jews seduced to the Christian heresy.[135] The consecrated *nation* was thus in a certain measure transformed into a consecrated *congregation*, to which people of all origins were welcome, provided they assumed its religious beliefs and duties. In other words, a Jew is not only one who was born of Jewish parents, but anyone who has undergone the process of Jewish "religious naturalization."[136] In the soul of the people there gradually emerged the sentiment that all traces of division between the native Jew and the naturalized Jew must be eradicated. "If a man repents, say not to him: 'Remember thy former deeds.' If a man derives from the gentiles, say not to him: 'Remember the deeds of thy forebears'" [B. Bava Mezia 58b]. The *ger* who embraces Judaism in good faith is the same as Israel [B. Bava Mezia 59b], or, as we read further in the same passage, "The Almighty saith that the name of the *gerim* is more beloved than the libations of wine poured to me" (*Bamidbar Rabbah* 88).[137] The words "towards the righteous and the pious . . . toward the *proselyte of righteousness* . . . may Thy tender mercies be stirred" still form part of the *Shmoneh Esreh* [Eighteen Benedictions] prayer.[138]

As time passed it was realized that religious discrimination against certain peoples—practiced for historico-political reasons rather than out of contempt for any particular "race"—had lost its meaning. In [the Talmud][139] we read that "Judah, a convert from the tribe of Ammon,"[140] asked the famous heads of the Yavneh Academy:[141] "What is my status in Israel?" Am I a member of the congregation, an equal among equals, or does the ban of the Torah—"Neither Moabite nor Ammonite may enter the congregation of God" [Deut. 23:4]—still apply to me? Rabbi Gamliel's[142] decision was that since he was a convert, he could not "enter the congregation." But Rabbi Joshua[143] insisted that the ban was no longer in effect, giving as his reason: "Sennacherib,[144] King of the Assyrians, came up and confused all the nations." We know from the Talmud that the decision of Rabbi Joshua triumphed and the Ammonite was "admitted to the congregation" [B. Brakhot 28a]. The argument advanced by him was almost that of a modern anthropologist: using the Sennacherib formula, he proved that there were no longer any pure races, nor was it possible any more to determine the origins of peoples, and it was therefore futile to submit the genealogical background of individuals to a minute inspection. Rabbi Gamliel's judgment, on the other hand, was based on the convert's own admission to being an Ammonite, and he turned to the written law for support of his contention that one may not be "admitted to the congregation" even though there were only a suspicion that he was a son of Ammon [B. Brakhot 28a]. Behind Rabbi Joshua's decision was the tacit conviction that what we have termed "religious naturalization" makes a "natural" Jew of the *ger*, regardless of his origin, that conversion is equivalent to rebirth (a notion which later played an important role in Christianity), and that "he who makes welcome the *ger* is as though he had created him" (Bereshit Rabbah [84:4]).[145] The religious transformation of a non-Jew, his moral determination to become a Jew and enter into the Jewish covenant with God, cancels, to a great degree, his entire past and he now begins to live anew: "A convert is comparable to a newborn child" (B. Yevamot [22a, 62a]).[146] Resh Lakish[147] went even further, insisting that a *ger* was not to be regarded as the equal of but as superior to a "native" Jew, because Jews had accepted the Torah at Mount Sinai under duress or under the impression of various miracles, whereas the convert embraced his new faith voluntarily and out of an unshakable conviction.[148] (This is reminiscent of the contention of naturalized Americans: "I, the immigrant, am a better American than you; you could not help yourself; you were born here; but I had a choice and I selected America as my homeland.") The glorification of the convert rose to such a pitch that [Resh Lakish asserted] an insult to a *ger* was declared tantamount to insulting God (B. Hagigah 5[a]).[149] Such an attitude inevitably led to extremes, even to a belligerent insistence that Torah is everything, and blood and heritage, nothing. Rabbi Meir—apparently in the course of a polemic attack on the Jewish racists of his day—declared that even the idol worshipper who applies himself to Torah is as the high priest himself (B. Bava Kama 38[a]).[150] This was, of course, intentional exaggeration on the part of Rabbi Meir, who knew that he could not so summarily dismiss the categorical law which states that not only an idolator, but even a convert of the first generation could not attain the high priesthood.[151] Rabbi Meir certainly had no hope that his aphorism would be accepted and embodied in normative law. We cite his defiant opinion merely as an illustration of the processes and conflicts then prevailing in Jewish religious thought. It was in character with the polemical methods employed by the universalists against the particularists.

It is a significant commentary on that period that many of the *tannaim* were casually referred to as *gerim* or descendants of *gerim*. It would be a fruitless task to attempt to trace the genealogical tree of the various *tannaim* and *amoraim*. It is possible that the classification of some of them as racial non-Jews was only based on rumor, but it is characteristic that such rumors could find their way into the records of Jewish tradition; nor did the redactors of the Talmud feel that they in any way lowered the status or social station of the *hakhamim* [sages] in question. The compilers and redactors of the [Christian Bible] found no difficulty in establishing a genealogical line which proved that Jesus was a direct descendant of King David ("a shoot out of the stock of Jesse" [Isa. 11:1]); it would have been equally simple for the compilers of the Talmud to represent Rabbi Akiba as a descendant of, let us say, Ezra or Nehemiah. They could easily have concealed his true lineage, but apparently they were not the least disconcerted to learn that not only was he descended from *gerim* but that one of his ancestors was none other than *Sisera*![152] We must not forget the profound reverence in which Rabbi Akiba was held by the Jews, not only as a great man of *halakhah* but also as one of the most prominent Jewish political nationalists and martyrs for the faith. Jews nevertheless readily adjusted themselves to the "fact" that the man who was worthy of receiving the law—about whom Moses said to God: "My Lord, having such a man as this, why didst Thou give Thy Torah through me?" (B. Menahot 29[b])[153]—was not only a non-Jew by race but was, into the bargain, descended from Sisera. The talmudic sages were not forced to disclose that [Rabbi] Shemayah[154] and [Rabbi] Avtalyon[155] were also the offspring of *gerim*; nevertheless they did so. Nor was it essential for them to record that Rabbi Meir, who lives in the memory of Jews as the miracle worker, came of non-Jews (B. Gittin 56[a]), and that his real name was Measha but the name of Meir (one who enlightens) was given to him because "he enlightened the wise in the law" [B. Eruvin 13b].

There was indeed much opposition to those efforts at broadening the universalistic base of Judaism. Within the people itself, and among some of its highest circles, the antagonistic forces of narrow nationalism and racism were at work, and the struggle against these forces was very bitter. This can be seen from more than one passage in the Talmud. We have, for instance, the story of the high priest who issued from the Temple, followed by the multitude of worshippers. Shemayah and Avtalyon (as told above, descended from *gerim*) passed by, and the congregation deserted the high priest for the two scholars. When both men approached the high priest to pay their respects, he addressed them slightingly, thus: "Enter in peace, sons of *gerim*," to which they replied: "Yea, let those *gerim* enter in peace who act in the manner of Aaron the Priest, but let not those enter who descend from Aaron (the high priest himself) and act not in the manner of Aaron" (i.e., act as disturbers of the peace and insult the people) [B. Yoma 71b].[156] In this talmudic parable, racial background is scathingly held up to ridicule and emphasis is laid on personal character, deeds, and merit.

Whatever the stages through which it passed, one fact is clear: that, from the time the Jews freed themselves from the prohibitions imposed by Ezra and Nehemiah, the ban on mixed marriages began to lose its quondam racial motivation and finally assumed an outspokenly religious character. The marriage laws and practices of later Judaism—dating from the period of the Pharisees—can in no way be compared to the racial laws of modern Germany or to laws still prevailing in certain sections of this country where marriage to a Negro (or, as the formula goes, with anyone in whose veins there flows more than one-sixteenth of Negro blood)[157] is a breach of the law, even though both parties are members of the same church. Jews discriminate, in the matter of mixed marriages, against non-Jews in the same sense that "universalist Christianity" or Islam discriminates against adherents of other faiths. From the very inception of the Christian Church as a consolidated institution, marriage with non-Christians has been frowned upon. On the basis of certain pronouncements ascribed to Tertullian[158] and St. Cyprian,[159] the Synod of Elvira[160] (300–306 CE) forbade Christian girls to marry "the unfaithful, Jews, heretics, and pagan priests."[161] In 339 CE Emperor Constantine[162] forbade mixed marriages between Christians and Jews. Later, in 388 CE, by the decree of Valentinian,[163] Theodosius,[164] and Arcadius,[165] such unions were denounced as "whoring and adultery" and their issue as "bastards."[166] The Roman and Greek Catholic Churches have never lifted this ban (although there have been some occasions when popes granted special dispensations in cases of mixed marriage). Furthermore, after the Reformation, the Catholic Church extended this interdiction to include errant Christians. Marriage out of the Catholic Church was most harshly condemned by the Popes Urban VIII,[167] Clement XI,[168] Benedict XIV,[169] Pius XI,[170] and Leo XIII.[171] We find in the "Westminster Confession of Faith"[172] of the comparatively young Church of England, the statement that members of the true reformed church are enjoined from marriage with the unfaithful, papists [Catholics], and other heathens. Jews were not mentioned in this document for the simple reason that there were none in England at that time.[173] According to an Irish law of 1697, a Protestant woman who possessed more than five hundred pounds forfeited her property upon marriage with a "papist" (there we have, of course, also an economic consideration hiding behind a religious rationalization),[174] and, according to a later law of 1745 (also in Ireland), Catholic priests performing marriage ceremonies between Protestants and Catholics were condemned to death.[175] Islam is far more tolerant in this respect. A Muslim may not marry a woman who is a non-believer but the Koran permits exceptions in the case of a so-called *Kitubaya*—a woman who recognizes the *Ktav*, the holy scriptures (thus a Jew or a Christian, but not a pagan). Such unions are regarded by [Muslims] as lawful but are looked upon askance, especially when they take place in non-Muslim countries where the influence of other religions presents a greater danger than in lands where Islam is dominant.

All these examples fortify our contention that the Jewish ban on mixed marriages is purely religious in nature and has nothing whatsoever to do with motives of race preservation. It is noteworthy that in the eighteenth century, some rabbinical authorities forbade marriages between Jews and certain other Jews. We have in mind, specifically, the ban imposed by heads of the *Mitnagdim*[176] and their warnings to pious Jews not to countenance any unions with the *Hasidim*[177] since it is their daughters who were meant in the passage "Cursed be he that lieth with any manner of beast" (Deut. 28:21). Certainly there could have been no racial motives involved here, but the clash between the *Mitnagdim* and the *Hasidim* rose to such a fever pitch during the time of the Gaon of Vilna that the stigma of being likened to "beasts" could be flung at the racially pure daughter of one's opponent.[178] Fortunately, such a situation could not long endure; but it is characteristic of the attitude of so-called Pharisaic Judaism[179] toward the question of marriage, which was regarded not only as a civil act but, primarily, as a spiritual union demanding a certain measure of religious conformity and spiritual harmony.

The conclusion to be reached from our discussion thus far is clear: the concept of election did not in any way resolve itself into a sanctification of the Jewish race. By opening wide its doors to *gerim* and by removing all obstacles to marriages between them and Jews by birth, Judaism has presented to the world pragmatic proof that what we designate in modern jargon as "race" is not regarded by the Jew as holy, nor does he make a fetish of it.

VII

Jewish attitudes toward the gentile world were naturally colored by contemporary political conditions. Consider, for example, the ban on the sale of cattle to non-Jews, which was enforced for a time [B. Avodah Zarah 16a–16b]. At first glance, this would seem to be an economic discrimination against the members of an alien race. Yet the motivation of this ban seems to be purely religious. According to Rabbi Ashi,[180] it was a form of assuring that cattle bred and raised by Jews would not be used for work on the Sabbath. Rabbi Ashi himself opposed this ban, arguing that the cattle might very well be purchased for slaughter only (B. Avodah Zarah 15[b]).[181] His opinion does not necessarily mark him as a universalist and the authors of the law as particularists. Very likely, he was more sensitive (or more submissive) to the economic exigencies of his day—compare Hillel's institution of "Prosbul"—and more inclined to broad construction than his colleagues. It would be misleading to assume that every pronouncement of the sages of the Talmud, or even every law on which they were unanimously agreed, resulted from a clearly defined and immutable *Weltanschauung*. Local and temporary conditions, individual mentalities, the pressure of worldly affairs left their mark in many cases.

At one time, for example, Jews were forbidden to sell arms to gentiles [B. Avodah Zarah 15b]. The same Rabbi Ashi excluded the Persians from this interdiction, his motive being purely historico-political and not in any way indicative of racial preference. The Persians, he argued, were on good terms with the Jews and protected them. In the case of other hostile nations, there was always the chance that they might turn against the Jews the very arms purchased from them [B. Avodah Zarah 16b].

Similar factors undoubtedly molded the attitude toward proselytes. Rabbi Helbo[182] declared that the convert was "a burden to the Jew, like leprosy" [B. Yevamot 47b]. He probably was an extreme racial chauvinist, but many later scholars see in his harsh words no more than a protest against the behavior of certain proselytes and charge him only with being too extravagant in his generalizations. The dynasty of Herod,[183] who was himself of Idumean[184] origin, a nation which [Yohanan Horekenos][185] had forced to embrace Judaism, was thoroughly detested by the Jewish people, and there is every reason to believe that Herod's actions inspired revulsion against converts in general. The failure of certain *gerim* to abide by the Jewish code, which they had vowed to uphold, caused at times great bitterness and gave rise to the belief that "by their misdeeds they delay the coming of the messiah" (B. Niddah 13[b]). It even provoked such a condemnation of Jewish missionaries as, "Evil befall the receivers of proselytes" (*mekabelei gerim*) ([B.] Yevamot 109[b]). These are all, of course, purely emotional reactions and should not be taken to represent the general feeling, or to be regarded as enduring in character. Rabbi Eliezer ben Horkenos's[186] comparison of "breaking bread with the Cutheans,[187] or Samaritans,"[188] with "eating of the flesh of the pig" was not meant to be accepted literally or as a rule [B. Hullin 13a]. Rabbi [Shimon] ben Gamliel[189] voiced an entirely different opinion: "The Samaritans are the peers of the Jews, in every sense" ([B.] Kidushin 76[b]).[190] Each of these statements is the reflection of individual reactions and idiosyncrasies.

Of much greater importance is the general trend as reflected in accepted laws, in rituals, and ceremonial procedure—and the general trend was to welcome the proselyte with open arms, although the sages of the day had good cause to warn against light-minded *gerim* and those who embraced Judaism for ulterior motives. In dwelling on this question, we believe it wrong to impute to Hillel and Shammai[191] two completely divergent viewpoints regarding proselytism—characterizing Hillel as the universalist who was eager to welcome as many new members to Judaism as possible, and Shammai as the particularist or racist who resented the intrusion of other strains into the Jewish bloodstream. A close examination of what is told in the Talmud of the methods Hillel and Shammai applied in their examination of applicants for conversion reveals an entirely different distinction between their viewpoints. The challenge of the prospective proselyte, who asked Shammai to convert him on condition that he be taught the wisdom of the Torah as he stood on one foot, was neither an attempt to embarrass the Jewish scholar nor to scoff at him, nor was it necessarily a proof of laziness on the part of the *ger*. Actually, he earnestly desired to know the fundamental or normative principles of the Jewish faith. He wanted a condensed formula for the philosophy of Judaism. But Shammai, the rigorous ritualist and nomist, angrily dismissed the questioner. He refused to tolerate what he construed as a frivolous approach to Judaism because he was shocked by the request to have its quintessence formulated. He feared that the convert might be content with the essence of Judaism and thereafter neglect the prescribed specific commandments. (During the Middle Ages, similar conflicts arose among Jews, not over the question of conversion, but over that of the *ikarim* [fundamental dogmas] of the Jewish religion; many Jewish theologians were shocked by Maimonides' reduction of the number of *ikarim* to thirteen and were still more confounded by those who held that the number was even smaller. They emphatically rejected any condensation of the codified six hundred and thirteen commandments.) Hillel, on the other hand, accepted the *ger's* challenge and, as the convert stood on one leg, summarized the entire Torah: "What is hateful to thee, do not unto thy fellowman; this is the whole Law, the rest is mere commentary" [B. Shabbat 31a].[192]

It certainly was not Hillel's intention to exempt the convert from the code of *mizvot* [religious commandments], from studying and then applying what he called the "commentary." He was aware, as well as Shammai, that the mere avoidance of moral evil did not in itself make a man a Jew. The "seven laws given to the sons of Noah"[193]—which all mankind must observe—was a known formula, a kind of natural theology in the days of Hillel; but certainly no recognized sage could have advocated that the observance of these *mizvot* alone (which were actually an elaboration of Hillel's "golden rule") entitled one to membership in the Jewish congregation.[194] Jews realized that there were God-fearing men of other faiths, whose belief in God approximated the Jewish concept of divinity. Those *yerei elohim* [ones who fear God][195] led pure and moral lives, without any desire to become converts. Jews also knew that there were gentiles who had earned a place in the next world, and were not Jews for all of that. Hillel's formula is therefore far more complex than would appear at first glance. It is inconceivable that he would have regarded a man as a genuine convert solely on the strength of an acceptance of his humanistic formula. Without a supporting belief in God, in the *one* God, this formula could only be considered a noble principle of human relations, but it was still not a faith. Man's duty to God played no small part in Hillel's religious philosophy, and however highly he regarded man's responsibility for his fellow man, he knew that this alone fell far short of satisfying God's requirements of his followers. It is also inconceivable that Hillel would accept a non-circumcised convert—although no mention of this ritual requirement is made in the story. The story, we believe, is not to be taken literally but interpreted as an illustration of the essential conflict between Hillel and Shammai—not on the score of universalism or particularism, but on that of *emphasis*: which is more important? The observance of prescribed *mizvot*, or moral intention and a general habit of good deeds? Shammai was more of the fanatic type, more insistent on the observance of ritual, and the problem of what was of primary or of secondary importance could not have had the same significance for him as it did for Hillel. This does not mean that Hillel was an anti-ritualist. This charge cannot even be brought against Jesus, who for the most part observed the code, indulging only in minor infringements. *Mizvot* were precious to Hillel as the religious lore of his people, but he did not ascribe to them any absolute value. He was distressed by the mechanistic or ostentatious observance of the code by some of his co-religionists just as, generations later, were the Baal Shem [Tov],[196] Rabbi Nahman Breslover,[197] and the Rabbi of Kotzk.[198]

It would be highly improbable to suggest that Hillel's attitude toward ritual paralleled that of the Nazarene; but it cannot be denied that even before the advent of Christianity there was a tendency, though not so boldly formulated, to relegate the code of *mizvot* to a position of secondary importance—or at least not to accord it paramount importance—and it is this tendency which is illustrated in the dialogue between Hillel and the gentile. Though he spoke to the gentile, Hillel by implication directed his remarks to his colleagues. Shammai's attitude, on the other hand, must not be taken as a general policy to discourage proselytes on racial grounds but as a protest against the tendency to accord only secondary importance to ritual commandments. The conflict between Hillel and Shammai must be interpreted in the terms of orthodoxy versus liberalism rather than of universalism versus particularism.

Notwithstanding the adverse criticism or derogatory comments directed against *gerim* to be found in talmudic literature (and there are many), they are in no way to be regarded as typical of the main trend of Judaism, which was definitely universalistic. Within the framework of the *agadah*, the sages of the Talmud and the *baalei hamidrash* [expounders of *midrash*] permitted themselves certain artistic flights and liberties, airing their prejudices and idiosyncrasies; but when it came to *halakhah*—the interpretation of the law—they exerted more self-restraint and were guided in their decisions by religious considerations, sternly avoiding any possible thought-habits or impressions attributable to momentary mundane concerns. The *halakhah* distinctly states that if a gentile's desire to become a Jew is earnest and pure, he must be accepted. Even Rabbi Helbo, who compared the convert to a leper, could not have refused to accept a proselyte who declared his faith in the God of Israel and agreed to undergo circumcision and assume all the prescribed *mizvot*. The *halakhah*, the custom of the day, and age-old precedent would all have militated in favor of the convert. Rabbi Helbo could probably brush aside any personal aversion he might have entertained by referring to the *agadah* which relates that in some mysterious fashion, the gentiles were present at Mount Sinai (B. Shabbat 145[a]). "'What of the gentiles? The Jews were purified by being present at Sinai, but since no gentiles were there, does that mean that they remain impure?' To which Rabbi Ashi replied, 'Though they were not actually there, their destiny was present.'" They were, so to speak, spiritually represented at Mount Sinai, through their fate or their "[guiding] stars" [B. Shabbat 146a]. Their physical absence was therefore not of decisive importance.

For a thorough understanding of talmudic Jewry, Rabbi Helbo is not so characteristic as is Eleazar ben Pedat,[199] who regarded the dispersion of Jews throughout alien lands as a divine plan to gain proselytes for Judaism (B. Pesakhim 87[b]).[200] The attitude of Eleazar ben Pedat found its expression in normative law, in *halakhah*, while Rabbi Helbo's aphorism has remained a private opinion, or rather a *lapsus linguae* [Latin for "slip of the tongue"] in the heat of argument.

The talmudic controversies about *gerim* did not rest on the question of their acceptance or rejection—since all the sages of the Talmud were more or less in accord on that subject—but on the procedure or conditions under which a gentile might become a Jew. A discussion on this problem is known to have taken place among some of the first *tannaim*. Rabbi Joshua ben Hanania maintained that when a gentile undergoes *tvilah* [ritual ablution] he attains the status of a *ger* even though he has not been circumcised; while Rabbi Eliezer ben Horkenos contended that "a gentile who has been circumcised is a *ger* even without *tvilah*" [B. Yevamot 46a]. Other sages insisted that both ceremonies were required.[201] Even here we find, not a conflict between particularism and universalism but, rather, between orthodoxy and liberalism. *Tvilah* is less trying than circumcision; Rabbi Joshua ben Hanania was apparently willing to replace the surgical operation with the easier ceremony, accepting it as a symbol of renunciation of the alien, and assumption of the Jewish faith. Like Hillel—though he probably never formulated it to himself so concretely—he was reluctant to ascribe absolute value to the code of *mizvot* as did his fellow sages who opposed any such reforms in Judaism, claiming that to exempt the *ger* from circumcision might eventually lead to total abrogation of this requirement for the racial Jews as well. History is vague about the identity of Ananias, the merchant of Judea,[202] who, Josephus[203] tells, was a close friend of Izates, king of Adiabene.[204] When the king's mother and wife embraced Judaism, he decided to follow suit and it was the Jew Ananias who attempted to dissuade him from submitting to circumcision, assuring him that "one may serve God without it; observance of the traditions of the Jewish patriarchs is more essential than the ceremony of circumcision"[205] (reminiscent, in a sense, of Hillel's formula). The merchant of Judea voiced an opinion which was apparently then current in certain circles; it is otherwise inconceivable that, having no specific claim to scholarship, he should have taken it upon himself to offer such advice.

The question of procedure in proselytizing was later taken over by the young Christian community and apparently assumed the same importance as it had for the *hakhamim*. Those apostles who opposed the admission to Christianity of gentiles who balked at circumcision while agreeing to baptism (the sacrament of immersion), were no less universalistic than Paul,[206] who demanded the complete abolition of circumcision as a requisite for conversion to the new faith. They did not object to the missionary work of Paul and his followers among gentiles in Syria, Greece, and the Mediterranean islands, but merely refused to renounce their own Orthodox standards for conversion.[207]

At various periods, it must be admitted, Jews showed an increasingly skeptical attitude toward the *ger*. Many began to question the sincerity of the convert and the degree to which he might be trusted in practicing his new faith. There were those who expressed doubt as to the *ger's* probable behavior in times of distress and persecution: Was he prepared to "sanctify the name" by sacrificing his life?[208] The *Tanna devei Eliyahu*, for instance, differentiates between "the *ger* who is in all respects still an alien, the *ger* who is likened to Hamor,[209] and the *ger* who is likened to the patriarch Abraham."[210] The first, he stated, was a man "in whose place there was filth and unclean foods, snails and crawling creatures; and so he said unto himself: 'Let me embrace Judaism and live among the Jews, for their food is pure, they have holidays and the Sabbath, and all impurities will thus be cleansed from my house.'"[211] This man cannot be regarded as a full-fledged Jew, since he became one only because a certain aspect of Jewish life appealed to him; nevertheless, he must not only be tolerated, but accepted as well. The second type is compared to Hamor, father of Shekhem,[212] who was driven to Judaism by the love of a woman. Of him, God said to Israel, "My children, he seeks peace in your midst, therefore molest him not."[213] In other words, though he has not earned any love or warm welcome, since his conversion was due to ulterior motives, he must nevertheless be tolerated and left in peace. Abraham represents the nobler type of *ger*, who changed his faith because he sought refuge "under the wings of the *shekhinah*" [divine presence] [B. Sanhedrin 96b].[214] This was an act of pure conversion, and the *agadah* tells that God sent Abraham from land to land to urge others to accept the true faith.

Various other types of *gerim* were portrayed in the popular terminology of the day. There was the "proselyte" [B. Yevamot 24b],[215] so called after the Cutheans and Samaritans whom the king of Assyria placed in Samaria and who finally accepted "the manner of the God of the land" [2 Kgs. 17:26] only after they had been preyed upon by the lions of the country. Latter-day Jewry had only contempt for conversion under duress. Another type of opportunist convert were the "*gerei Mordekhai ve-Esther*,"[216] meaning those who had embraced Judaism only after the downfall of Haman, and hoped thus to be saved from Jewish vengeance. Others were the "dream converts," driven to the new faith by "night visions," motivated by fear and superstition [B. Yevamot 24b]. Rabbi Nehemiah[217] said of all these groups that unless they were willing to repeat the conversion ceremony, they should forfeit the right to be regarded as *gerim*. Then there were the "*gerei shulkhan melakhim*" [converts of the royal table]—the social climbers who could not attain the position they aspired to in their own milieu, and so assumed Judaism in the hope of "sitting at a kingly table" [B. Yevamot 24b] (like the legendary gentile who asked Shammai to convert him provided he would then become high priest) [B. Shabbat 31a]. There are countless instances in the Talmud where *gerim* are rebuked for their ignorance of the *mizvot* and for still retaining "the ways of their forefathers" [B. Bava Mezia 58b]. Rabbi Eliezer [ben Horkenos] estimated that there were thirty-six warnings in the Torah directed against the *ger*, "for his ways are evil" and it is not easy for him to renounce "the ways of his ancestors"[218] (B. Bava Mezia 59[b]).[219] In B. Yevamot [47a–47b], the fear is expressed that the *ger* might regret his action and recant after having taken unto himself a daughter of Israel. Rabbi Yossi[220] jeered at the *ger's* weakness of character and lack of valor: "When the messiah comes, they will be so terrified by the anguish of battle between Gog and Magog[221] that they will refuse to fulfill the required *mizvot*" [B. Avodah Zarah 3b].

The practical outcome of all these doubts, complaints, and suspicions was not the summary repudiation of the *ger* or the denial of his right to be admitted to the Jewish congregation. Careful judgment and observation dictated only greater caution in the acceptance of the proselyte, the establishment of a more or less rigorous procedure. In B. Yevamot [47a] we read of a strict examination to which a candidate for conversion was subjected. He was asked: "Why do you seek conversion? Do you not know that in these days Jews are in distress, oppressed, rejected, and subjected to endless suffering?" If the answer was, "'I know, and am unworthy of becoming a Jew,' the applicant was received into Jewry, for his reply shows that he *is* worthy, and he is to be taught the simpler *mizvot* and only a few of the more complex." Latter-day Jewry insisted on sincerity of motive in the *ger*, on his willingness to assume the role of martyr, accept suffering with exaltation, and be closely bound to the Jewish faith and the community which it represented. There was the constant fear, which past events had justified, that the *ger* might treat his new faith and its accompanying obligations too lightly or that he would possess too little courage to withstand temptations in his path. Then there was always the possibility of his reversion to idolatry. Various *baalei agadah* [expounders of *agadah*] have interpreted the description of Hagar's[222] leaving Abraham—"and she departed and strayed in the wilderness" [Gen. 21:14]—to mean that, despite her sojourn in the household of Abraham and her learning to believe in the one and only God, as soon as she left his influence she strayed back to the worship and faith of her forefathers.

It is this reversion or recantation which had to be avoided in the acceptance of proselytes. At the risk of repetition, we must make it clear that this fear was of a religious nature and in no way connected with racial principles. It must not be forgotten that the very *agadah* which so often warned against and scorned the convert, also knew how to evaluate the high-minded and pure *ger*. Just as the penitent was held higher than the saint with a sinless past, so the *ger* was regarded not only as the peer of the Jew, but frequently as his superior.

In *Yalkut Shimoni*[223] we read the following allegory: "Moses asked the Lord, 'Is this *ger* as worthy as the Levite?' To which God replied, 'In my eyes, more so, for in my name he became a convert.' It is told that a deer which was raised in the wilderness voluntarily joined a herd of sheep. The shepherd gave it food and water and favored it above all his other charges, explaining to those who questioned him, 'How much effort I have expended over my sheep, leading them out to pasture in the morning and taking them back at eventide, watching over them until they were full-grown. But here is a deer, raised in the wilderness, which joined my fold of its own accord. Why should I not love it more?' Such also was God's reply to Moses, 'How I labored over Israel, bringing them up out of Egypt, lighting the way before them, dropping *manna* to them, and protecting them in a cloud of majesty, until they accepted my Torah; but here is the *ger* who comes to me of his own free will therefore he is as dear to me as a Levite and as an Israelite'" [*Yalkut Shimoni, Bo*, 213].[224]

While we can find in this and similar *agadot* a latent protest against those allegories which sought to discredit certain types of *gerim*, the *halakhah* openly favored an attitude of respect toward the *ger*, and supported the theory that racial origin cannot deter the proselyte from entering into an eternal covenant with God, nor need it prevent him from attaining full membership in the Jewish congregation. Saadia Gaon,[225] leaning heavily on the *agadah*, but even more strongly on *halakhah*, stated that though we are the "chosen people," this does not signify that any one creature is God's favorite. "All men are equal in His eyes."[226]

Maimonides, the greatest codifier of *halakhah*, did not deny the concept of election (though he conspicuously omitted it from his "thirteen essentials") but extended it to embrace even the proselyte. In contrast to Yehuda Halevi,[227] with his Jewish ethnocentrism, Maimonides vouchsafed to all peoples of the world the gift of prophecy. He insisted that the Torah was meant both for the Jew and the *ger* (and thus, by extension of the term, for all of mankind). Thus, when a convert asked Maimonides whether he might include in his daily prayers the words of the traditional invocation "Our God and the God of our forefathers," he was assured that he might recite all the prayers "like every other citizen in Israel," for he had accepted the Jewish faith, "for all generations to come," thereby becoming a disciple of Abraham and a member of his household.[228] The *ger* may even thank the Lord for having led *him* out of Egypt, for after he had cast himself upon the grace of God "there is no longer any difference between you and us, and all miracles performed on our behalf are as though performed *for you as well*, and *God has chosen you from among all peoples* and given his Torah to *you*."[229] The spiritual and moral background of the gentile who accepts Judaism, according to Maimonides, becomes merged with that of Jewry, and the *ger* shares in the collective spiritual biography of his new co-religionists. The Jewish people and its religious congregation thus become, to borrow a term employed by Henri Bergson,[230] an *open* rather than a *closed* society, a community which is, in principle, prepared to become all-embracing and to welcome all men, regardless of their racial origin.

The conclusions to be drawn from the development of Jewish religious attitudes are apparent. God is one, the world is one, and humankind is also a unity. Mankind is still divided into Jews and non-Jews, but eventually this hiatus will be bridged, and men will become one—in the religio-moral, if not in the ethnical sense. This will be accomplished not by the acceptance by Jews of the faiths about them but by the gentiles' acceptance of the Jewish Torah. Otherwise, there can be no possibility of *eschatos*,[231] and God cannot triumph. "Thou hast chosen us"[232] must not be taken to signify a superior race but a superior faith, destined to become the faith of the entire world. Jewish religious awareness at its deepest knows of no higher and lower races or peoples; the Jew, through his faith, is merely advanced, while the rest of the world is retarded. The eyes of the Jew have been opened while those of the gentile world are still closed. Both are equally equipped with eyes—to see the divine light.

Jacob and Esau are different, but not organically. Esau represents a different state of mind, not a different and immutable mind-substance. Each Jacob is a former Esau, and each Esau a potential Jacob. Jacob's spiritual awakening, his "rebirth" preceded that of Esau—therefore he is the elder of the two: maturer, but not superior. His special relationship to God is based on primogeniture rather than on superiority.

25

Current Alternatives in Palestine

(1947)

In the months following World War II, several factors complicated and brought enormous pressure to bear on the Zionist movement's campaign for Jewish statehood in Palestine: the plight of thousands of homeless European Jewish refugees; the British blockade and deportation of so-called "illegal" Jewish immigrants whose numbers exceeded the prevailing mandatory quota; growing political restlessness among the Yishuv's population, including the amplified demand for Jewish autonomy; categorical Arab opposition to changing Palestine's status quo in ways that would assist the country's Jewish community; and the new postwar geopolitical reality in which the United States, Britain, and the Soviet Union vied for influence and control in the Middle East. Against this backdrop, in May 1947 the UN established a Special Committee on Palestine (UNSCOP). Charged with formulating a new proposal to resolve Palestine's political future, UNSCOP embarked on a ninety-day process of investigation and deliberation as it sought to move beyond the failed mandatory, federalization, cantonization, and trusteeship plans of the past. During this interval, Jewish Agency chairman David Ben-Gurion, who officially adhered to the position of the Twenty-second World Zionist Congress (1946) and affirmed the Jewish claim to all of Palestine, sidestepped maximalist demands when he publicly announced the Zionist movement's readiness to "consider a viable Jewish state in an adequate area of Palestine" as an acceptable "basis for discussion." A lively internal debate ensued in which the Zionist ranks split over competing ideas of partition and self-rule, whether to embrace a transitional period of British and/or American administration and work toward achieving a Jewish majority in Palestine, or to pursue the prospect of bi-nationalism and the establishment of an Arab-Jewish state. To this complex discussion, Hayim Greenberg contributed the following analysis—adding his own farsighted view of the Jewish state-in-the-making, including the unprecedented challenge of absorbing masses of Jewish refugees and Displaced Persons destined to increase by half again the size of the Yishuv's Jewish population.

The time is approaching when the Jewish Agency [for Palestine][1]—as well as those sections of organized Jewry which are prepared to support the essential aims of the Zionist movement—will have to state in clear terms its aspirations and demands. It will not be enough to state our principles and our needs. The UN Special Committee,[2] the coming session of the General Assembly, those individual governments whose sympathies we shall endeavor to enlist, will all expect us to go beyond generalities. In our contacts with the United Nations and its varied constituency, we will have to offer during the coming few months a concrete, if not a detailed, program, and outline a definite political framework within which the realization of our aims should appear both justified and feasible. Do we want a Jewish state, and, if so, what should be its constitutional basis? Do we want this state to be established immediately, or only after the fulfillment of certain conditions, during a transitional period of some international management? Should the establishment of Jewish statehood be postponed for a definite number of years, what kind of regime do we wish instituted in Palestine for the interim period? Do we want the British to continue for any length of time, and subject to what provisions, as the mandatory power? Is the Palestine mandate still "workable," and, if so, how do we visualize its further (or rather renewed) implementation under the supervision of the United Nations? Is there, in our opinion, any feasible way of breaking British calculated resistance to the continued development of the [Jewish] National Home,[3] of making the thoroughly discredited mandatory government adhere to the letter and spirit of its international obligations? And if the mandate should prove unworkable or obsolete, are we prepared to advocate the placing of Palestine under a United Nations trusteeship? What is our attitude toward the so-called bi-national state, and would such an entity, if created, satisfy our vital needs?[4] Would we be prepared to renounce our political claim to a certain part of Palestine, if that should give us immediate sovereignty in another definite area of the country?

Such are some of the specific questions we probably will be asked to answer, and it is in our own interest at this time not to limit ourselves to statements of a general or ideological nature. There is also more than one reason to assume that from the viewpoint of strategy it is not desirable that we should occupy for any length of time a position of passive waiting, no matter how watchful, and let others try to decipher our aims or to translate them into definite political terms.

What, then, should be our concrete demands to be addressed to the United Nations, or for that matter to any government in its capacity as a member of the international organization?

The Mandate

We would certainly commit a grave mistake were we to ask the United Nations for the implementation of our claims on the basis of the old mandate, with the

British continuing in the administration of Palestine. It is absolutely useless and irrelevant to discuss whether the mandate is still workable or not. As an instrument the mandate has, for all practical purposes, become unworkable since the British government has openly demonstrated its unwillingness (or its inability) to operate it in the spirit in which it was created. This must not be construed in the sense that we are no longer to attach any importance to the mandate as a piece of international legislation. We have every right to insist that the essential content of the mandate—the rights and opportunities which it guaranteed to us—is as binding upon England, and the concert of nations as a whole, today as it was in the past. But it would be folly to demand that our rights, which we believe to be embodied in the mandate, should be gradually realized in the future within the framework of the existing, degenerated, mandatory regime.

Mandates granted or endorsed by the League of Nations[5] have no legal validity for the UN. It is true that the UN is heir to the defunct League of Nations, but the heritage of the League does not automatically pass to the UN without any modifications. The UN reckons with mandates as facts which it has no power to vote out of existence, but it does not recognize them as legal instruments within the scope of its own jurisdiction under the charter.[6] The UN cannot deprive England of the mandate over Palestine—the charter contains no such provision—nor can it impose changes in the mandate or new administrative methods that would be more in the original spirit of the mandate. Were the UN to make such decisions it would find itself in the awkward position of claiming authority on matters which, in principle, are outside its jurisdiction, and of assuming responsibility for situations over which it has no control. The UN can exert no control over a mandatory administration for the simple reason that its charter fails to recognize, in the realm of its duties or functions, the very term of mandates. It should also be borne in mind that some countries belonging to the UN were not members of the League of Nations, which laid the legal foundation for the mandates system. Among the great powers, the United States is a case in point;[7] of the smaller countries, Syria and Lebanon. On the other hand, a number of countries which belonged to the League of Nations and were technically responsible for the system of mandates are not members of the UN: Japan, Germany, Austria, Hungary, Italy, Spain, Ireland, Portugal, Romania, Bulgaria, Finland.[8] The UN recognizes in principle only two types of non-self-governing territories: colonies and trusteeship regions. Mandated territories are merely leftovers of a past era. If they are not transformed into independent states or made organic parts of other states, as was the case with South-West Africa,[9] they may in time be put under a trusteeship and thus come under control of the UN. If they attain neither status—of all the mandated territories Palestine is today the sole country in this situation—they remain suspended in a legal void. The UN, at least, wouldn't know what to do with them.

The Biltmore Program

The Biltmore Program[10] still has a great appeal within the Zionist movement. One might claim that the political resolutions adopted by the recent Zionist Congress are fundamentally a reaffirmation of the program adopted in New York in 1942, and subsequently approved in Palestine and in a number of other countries. In essence the Biltmore Program is very simple: Palestine—all of Palestine—should be established as a "Jewish Commonwealth."[11] We will not, at this time, attempt to define the expression "all of Palestine," whether only western Palestine, the present mandated area, is implied, or whether Transjordan is to be included. We may assume that the majority of Zionists are at present prepared to reckon with the fact that Transjordan now enjoys the status of an independent state.[12] No matter how grave the injustice committed by Great Britain in detaching the eastern and larger part of Palestine, it would be a fantastic delusion to assume that the UN might for our sake abrogate the independence which they officially sanctioned during last year's session of the General Assembly. But the moment we demand a Jewish state in all of western Palestine—"undivided and undiminished" as it is phrased in some quarters for greater clarity—we will undoubtedly be asked a number of questions. We might be told the following:

> "Yours is a logical demand and you have good grounds for making it, but kindly clarify the matter. Should a Jewish state in all of western Palestine be established *at once*, or at some later date? In the latter case, when should that date be and what conditions should determine it? If you believe that a Jewish state should be established forthwith, does that imply that you are in favor of Jewish sovereignty in Palestine before Jews have become a majority of the population? Are we to conclude that, for some years at least, this state will not be a democratic one because it will be run by and based on a minority, every Jewish resident being granted the status of a full-fledged citizen and the Arabs being only subjects? Will Jews coming to Palestine from Germany or Austria be granted immediate political rights while the non-Jewish inhabitants of the country will have to wait many years before they can be *naturalized* in their native land?"

I have intentionally phrased these questions in a sharp and politically embarrassing form. It is quite possible that we will be asked these questions in an even sharper manner. As we go before the United Nations we must be prepared for dialogues and not merely for our soliloquies, and we must have ready answers for probable queries and objections. A mere formulation of the question indicates the type of answer we will be compelled to give. There is no point in recalling the mood and the atmosphere of the days when the Biltmore Program was adopted and in reiterating what we meant at that time. None of us will *today* offer such a program to the UN or any of its subsidiary bodies for immediate implementation. It would be a waste of time to discuss whether the carrying out of such program would be politically moral or immoral. Impossibilities are beyond good and evil. What is important is that among all the governments with whom we will have to deal in the UN there is not a single one that would openly recognize the right of Jews—even temporarily—to govern a country where the non-Jewish population is twice as large as the Jewish. Even the government of South Africa, where a white minority rules a colored majority at least four times as large, would not support such an arrangement for Palestine, on the ground that one cannot compare the Arabs, who have been a civilized people for many centuries and gave the world one of its three monotheistic religions, to the Bantus of South Africa.[13] Those who would demand a Jewish state in all of Palestine—and none among us questions the historical, political, and moral legitimacy of such a demand in its essence—must therefore add that *for the present* such a state cannot be established, and that for some years Palestine would have to be governed by an international authority whose aim it should be to extend effective aid to Jewish expansion until Jews become a majority. This aim has been foreshadowed in the mandate.

The Biltmore Program, translated from a declaration of principles into the language of political realities, implies a transition period of some duration, in the course of which Palestine would not be independent but subject to international administration. Such an administration, in terms of the UN and its jurisdiction, can be organized primarily in the form of a trusteeship. Whether we like it or not, we are thus compelled to recognize that in the year 1947 the Biltmore Program is to a great extent identifiable with, or calls for, some sort of trusteeship.

Trusteeship

Conceptually there hardly exists any difference between a mandate and a trusteeship. However, we are not dealing with abstract logical concepts but with political realities and qualified mechanisms.

A trusteeship for Palestine might, under certain circumstances, be of great positive significance for us. By means of a trusteeship the unity of Palestine—at least of that part of Palestine which has so far remained politically and administratively whole—might be preserved. Palestine is in many respects an economic unity. Any partition of the country into independent states would immediately raise complex economic problems which could only be solved with great effort. Some technological projects have been outlined without whose implementation there is little opportunity for the maximal economic development of the country. It is sufficient to mention the problem of irrigation as an adequate illustration of this point. The projects we referred to can be put into effect either in a unified Palestine, or in a process of very close cooperation between the two states that would come into being as an outcome of partition. Administrative unity is naturally much preferable, as a basis for economic development, to geographical and administrative division. A favorable trusteeship sincerely striving for the maximal economic development of the country, and cooperating honestly and effectively with the authorized Jewish bodies to the end of absorbing as many new Jewish settlers as the economy of the country permits, would no doubt be the most rational solution—for a number of years—of Palestine's political problem as well as of the acute problem of Jewish rehabilitation.

Were such a trusteeship possible we could all wisely refrain for some years from demanding the establishment of a Jewish state. Under such a trusteeship a Jewish majority would gradually be created in all of Palestine, and at the end of this period a Jewish state could come into being without any great difficulty, as a natural outgrowth of organic development.

(And may we venture another "heresy"? It is quite possible that under such circumstances there would be no need to cling to the term "Jewish state." The resulting state might bear any name at all; it would in fact be a Jewish state, because it would be based on the equal rights of a mixed population within which the Jews would form a majority.)

However, the questions confronting us in connection with a future international administration of Palestine appear to be quite complex and the prospect must be considered none too encouraging. Granted that a certain kind of trusteeship could well serve Jewish needs and aspirations in Palestine, what are the chances of its establishment?

It is not too difficult to prove that a trusteeship favorable to Jewish interests and developments is not in the realm of the impossible. According to the charter of the UN, trusteeships must not all follow one pattern. Separate, individual agreements have to be made regarding each territory to be placed under the control of the Trusteeship Council. These agreements must outline the special conditions for the administration of each territory. There exists, therefore, no legal barrier to the inclusion of an adequate guarantee for Jewish immigration and colonization in an agreement to cover a trusteeship for Palestine.

However, a great distance separates the legal and formal possibilities based on a penetrating interpretation of the UN charter from the political probability that such a trusteeship would indeed be adopted and implemented. The following doubts and considerations must be taken into account:

(1) Nearly all territories (excepting Palestine) which were governed by mandatory administrations after World War I, and have not in the meantime attained independence, have been transformed into [territorial] trustee-

ships under control of the UN.[14] Only the mandate for South-West Africa was abrogated in a different way. The government of General [Jan Christiaan] Smuts[15] has refused to place this territory under a trusteeship and has decided to incorporate it as an organic part of the Union of South Africa.[16] For all other mandated territories, special agreements have been drawn up. Not one of these agreements can serve even as a partial model for a trusteeship over Palestine. None of those territories has an immigration problem, whereas the chief problem of Palestine, from the Jewish standpoint, is the question of absorbing large numbers of additional Jewish immigrants.[17] The idea underlying those articles of the charter which deal with trusteeships cannot easily be stretched to cover problems of such a specific and dynamic nature as the problems of Zionism. Article 73 of the charter speaks with some accentuation of recognizing the principle that in non-self-governing territories "the interests of the *inhabitants* of these regions are paramount" and considers "as a sacred trust the obligation to promote to the utmost the well-being of the *inhabitants* of these territories."[18] Article 76 also deals with the duty "to promote the political, economic, social, and educational advancement of the *inhabitants*," and refers further to the "freely expressed wishes of the people concerned."[19] In the paragraphs dealing with non-independent territories there is not even the faintest reference to "immigration," because they are motivated by but one concern and chief obligation: the obligation toward the indigenous population of the trust territories. The trusteeship system, on the whole, was designed for more or less static situations, not for the development envisaged by Zionism.

(2) Let us assume that this general attitude toward trusteeship territories does not exclude the possibility of a special approach to the unique situation prevailing in Palestine.

On the basis of the accepted procedure, however, the terms of each trusteeship are to be formulated by the power which had previously administered the territory under a mandate. In our case Great Britain would be the power to outline the terms of the trusteeship for Palestine. A second stage, preceding a vote on the trusteeship by the General Assembly of the UN, involves consent of "the states directly concerned" to the terms of the agreement.[20]

It would be vain to ask what principle governs the selection of "states directly concerned" with the new trusteeship. No one can give a clear answer to this question. This item in the charter of UN was intentionally couched in nebulous language. The founders of the new international organization and the authors of its charter could not come to a clear agreement, and the interpretation of this clause was postponed to a future occasion. This is the reason why the Soviet Union is not, to this day, an actual member of the Trusteeship Council, although a permanent seat on the council is reserved for it.[21] No matter with what measure of justification, the Soviet Union considered itself to be a "state directly concerned" in all the trusteeship agreements already approved by the UN. But Great Britain, Belgium, France, New Zealand, and Australia submitted their trusteeship agreements without consultation with the Soviet Union. More recently a practice of questionable moral validity has been established, according to which the power drawing up the proposed trusteeship agreement (England, in our case) is the one to determine which are the "states directly concerned" whose consent must be obtained before the draft is submitted to the General Assembly. It is to be anticipated that Great Britain will recognize the Arab states as directly concerned in the trusteeship over Palestine. Indeed, England may no longer have too much choice in the matter. Since the summer of 1936 she has consistently invited the rulers and representatives of the Arab states whenever official or semiofficial conferences were held concerning the solution of the Palestine problem.[22] By its behavior in the course of the past eleven years, England has endowed the Arab states with a claim to the status of "directly concerned" parties in the Palestine dispute. It is not difficult to visualize the terms of a trusteeship for Palestine drawn up by the present government of England and endorsed by the five Arab states—assuming that England will agree to a trusteeship over Palestine altogether.

(3) Iraq is now a member of the Trusteeship Council. It is true that the veto right cannot be exercised here as it can in the Security Council. However, a full-fledged member of the council has many opportunities to exert his influence. In the present instance the influence will be directed against our interests. Iraq's membership is for a limited time, but it is not far-fetched to assume that at the expiration of its term another Arab state or a pro-Arab Muslim power will replace Iraq.

(4) According to the charter of the UN a trusteeship territory may be administered by a single power, by a group of powers, or by the United Nations as a collective entity. It is hard to prognosticate which of these administrative forms would be better—or worse. If a single power is to be entrusted with the administration of Palestine, there is hardly any doubt that it will be, again, the old [British] mandatory functioning under a new tide. Should the trusteeship be delegated to a group of powers, the question arises whether these states will be able and willing to cooperate with one another. The same holds true for the eventuality that Palestine is administered by the UN as a whole. Should that be the case there would apparently be formed a special board to which the UN would delegate its au-

thority. The previous question again reappears: Which states would be represented on that board, and would they be capable of cooperating? In the case of the erstwhile Italian colonies in Africa,[23] the United States recommended some time ago the formation of a board to administer them in the name of the UN. The board was to consist of the following governments: England, France, Italy, the US, and the Arab countries. Few delegates to the UN believed that such a board could function more or less effectively and not to the detriment of the populace. The entire subject remained undecided.

(5) Should a part of Palestine be declared as a "strategic area," that area would be placed under the jurisdiction of the Security Council, in accordance with the terms of the charter. Such an arrangement is liable to complicate the administration of the country still further. Two separate administrations would then have to cooperate, and the one operating under the authority of the Security Council would be constantly subject to a veto of its decisions.

(6) Were we to ask at this time that Palestine be placed under a trusteeship, we would have to weigh seriously the effect of such a step on the Soviet Union. If the so-called "Gromyko Declaration"[24] is to be taken as a genuine expression of policy, then we cannot afford to ignore the question, under what conditions the Soviet Union may be willing to support Zionist demands. An examination of the attitude of the Soviet delegation at the special session of the UN reveals that in regard to Palestine the Soviet Union has ample grounds to support a radical solution of the Palestine problem, a solution that would make the further existence of a British mandate over Palestine impossible, and would also rule out an international trusteeship under which British hegemony over Palestine might continue. The Soviet Union's program for Palestine can be expressed in three words: "Independence without delay." The change from Russia's former anti-Zionist policy to its present more pro-Zionist orientation is a change in means rather than in aims. If not independence in the form of an Arab state with certain safeguards for Jewish rights and interests—a solution acceptable to the Soviet Union until very recently—then independence in the form of a bi-national, Jewish-Arab state with a status of equality for both people. Should this plan prove impracticable, then let the independence of Palestine emerge through partition of the country and the formation of two separate states. In any case, the present interests of the Soviet Union are not along the line of a Palestine trusteeship.

It should not be inferred that the Soviet Union will have the decisive voice in the solution of the Palestine problem. Nor should anyone ascribe to us a readiness to follow the Russian lead irrespective of its nature, merely to obtain Soviet support and friendship. The orientation of the Soviet Union must, however, be evaluated, at least, as one of the paramount factors in the present lineup of forces, and conditions may easily arise in which it would be a fatal mistake to ignore her attitude.

Recently some Zionists have discussed another possible solution of the Palestine problem. We are referring to the "synthetic" plan according to which those parts of Palestine where Jews are already in the majority, or "on the eve" of becoming a majority, should at once be established as a Jewish state, the remaining area to be a trusteeship.[25]

All the factors outlined above in our discussion of trusteeship must be seriously considered also in connection with a trusteeship over a part of the country. To the extent that we ought to reckon with the attitude of the Soviet Union, we should expect Soviet opposition to a formula of "half state and half trusteeship" no less than to any other formula which does not recognize the principle of immediate independence and allows of continued English rule, even if that rule is to be in "cooperation" with other powers. There is also the danger that should such a plan be accepted, the area designated for the further development of the Jewish state would be very small. It might be argued that opportunities for further development would exist in the trusteeship zone and the narrow confines of the Jewish state should thus not be considered a serious limitation. On the other hand, restrictions on Jewish immigration and colonization in the trusteeship zone might then be justified by the argument that within the boundaries of their own state Jews have complete freedom of immigration, which should compensate them for restrictions imposed in the rest of the country.

Special Status

Is there no other framework for an international administration of Palestine? Cannot a special arrangement be made, neither on the basis of the old [British] mandate nor under a trusteeship scheme? According to Article 22 of the Charter, "the General Assembly may establish such subsidiary organs as it deems necessary for the performance of its functions."[26] The formula employed for this authorization is so vague that it is not easy to draw any final conclusion whether on this basis the UN can establish a special form of administration for a country which for one reason or another cannot be granted immediate independence. However, let us conditionally assume that such is the case and that the foregoing article can be thus interpreted. What type of regime can then be established in Palestine under the supervision of a special subsidiary organ?

Any attempt to answer this question leads one down the slippery path of speculations. We have so far only one concrete example from which we may draw some conclusions. Within the small territory of Trieste[27] there has been established a regime unlike that of a mandated territory but also outside the scope of the

Trusteeship Council. The district of Trieste has a mixed population of Italians and Yugoslavs. Both Italy and Yugoslavia have historic claims to that region. In the resulting compromise Trieste was set up as an area belonging to neither of the two states. By the terms of the peace treaty Trieste is almost a self-governing country so far as domestic matters are concerned. It will have its own democratic parliament, independent courts, etc. Only paramount power will be vested in the UN, and the governor of Trieste, who will enjoy broad administrative rights, including the right to appoint the chief of police, will derive his authority from the Security Council. To be sure, the case of Trieste lacks those specific elements which complicate the Palestine problem. Neither Italians nor Yugoslavs turn to the small area of Trieste as a goal of immigration. Complex as the Trieste situation may be it still cannot compare with the political labyrinth which history has created in Palestine.

Despite this advantage there exists little reason for envying the Triestinos. The agreement drawn up by the victorious Allies specifies who may *not* be governor of Trieste. He may be neither Italian nor Yugoslav nor, ironically enough, a citizen of Trieste itself. By origin or nationality he must be "neutral, nonpartisan, and objective." Months have passed since the agreement on Trieste was signed, yet no governor has been appointed. It is apparently difficult to find a neutral person whom all would trust. Candidates suggested by the Western powers are rejected by the Soviet Union, and candidates recommended by Russia are frowned upon by the West. In view of this less than idyllic situation within the Security Council there is no telling how long it will be necessary to wait before a candidate for governor is accepted by all and can begin his experiment of initiating a more or less normal course of life in that unhappy area.

An ad hoc international regime in Palestine must not be an exact replica of the sad state of affairs now prevailing in Trieste. It may prove to be better—or worse. But to the extent that one considers Trieste—this latter-day Danzig[28]—a characteristic precedent, the possibility of a similar regime in Palestine can only arouse many doubts and serious misgivings.

Bi-National State

Some Jews employ the term "bi-national state" as if this were a clearly defined concept whose implications are universally understood. In his "pro-Zionist" declaration, the Soviet representative, [Andrei] Gromyko,[29] also used this term and even stressed that such a dual state would provide the best solution to the Palestine problem, although he did not expound even in a few brief words what such a state would be like.

There exists no general definition of a bi-national state, nor any code of constitutional law from which we could learn the shape of such an entity. States governed by more than one nationality are not "inventions" but products of long, and more or less organic development. Switzerland is not, as it appears to the uninformed, a tri-national state, created as a kind of compromise by the three main ethnic groups of the population. Switzerland is a confederation, not of three peoples (German, French, and Italian) but of twenty-two territorial and administrative units, some of which use the German language and others French and Italian.[30] (In a part of one canton a Latin dialect spoken only by 100,000 people has attained in recent years the status of an official language.) Constitutionally, Switzerland is a confederation not of the German, Italian, and French national groups, but of the autonomous cantons which merely happen to be coterminous with linguistic areas.

Are there in existence other models more closely approximating the problems that must be solved in Palestine? There is our neighbor to the north, for instance. Canada may in a certain sense be considered a bi-national state. But Canada represents not only a political union of the English and the French. Primarily it is a union of two territories, a French area in Quebec and the rest of the country where Anglo-Saxon elements predominate. The same holds true of still another bi-national state, Czechoslovakia, which is not merely a political union of organized Czechs and organized Slovaks but a political merger of two states, or two national territories.

Should this principle be applied to Palestine, it would result in a form of partition which would delineate the borders of a Jewish province and of an Arab province, or provinces, in Palestine. Granted a large measure of self-government in each of the two provinces, the Arab part of the country, which is now the larger one, could utilize its local legislative and administrative authority to block Jewish settlement outside the borders of the Jewish province. Nor would this be all. Were a bi-national state to be established in Palestine now, based on Gromyko's formula of "equal rights for Jews and Arabs" and on the territorial model of Canada or Czechoslovakia, the Arabs would have a majority in the parliament and could easily dominate the legislative processes of the country. It would be folly to assume that such legislation would manifest a liberal attitude toward further Jewish immigration. How then can we be satisfied with the formula of "equal rights for Jews and Arabs" which a bi-national state can offer us? Arabs can even afford to use their numerical strength for prohibiting all immigration into Palestine, Arab as well as Jewish, for the simple reason that Arabs nowhere suffer from an emigration problem, whereas for Jews immigration into Palestine is a crucial need. On a strictly legal basis such a prohibition would not be discriminatory toward Jews. On the surface it would even appear to be in harmony with the principle of equal rights—or equal lack of rights—for both Jews and Arabs. But such equality would in fact be a death sentence to all our hopes and aspirations.

Others speak of a different type of bi-national state unlike either Canada or Czechoslovakia, a new creation at present unparalleled anywhere in the world. It is suggested that the principle of *parity* be introduced as the constitutional basis of the new state: Jews should not dominate Arabs nor Arabs dominate Jews; the minority should have no less power than the majority, and vice versa. In parliament Jews and Arabs would have an equal number of representatives, irrespective of their ratio within the population of the country. Some extreme advocates of this plan hold that the administrative apparatus of the government should likewise be composed on a fifty-fifty basis.[31] Whether Gromyko had in mind such an arrangement when he spoke of equal rights for Jews and Arabs is not certain, since he did not define his formula. At any rate the parity principle of the proposed bi-national state is not reconcilable with our needs, mainly for two reasons:

(1) The inhabitants of Palestine would have to be separated into two separate electoral colleges of Jews and Arabs. The fifty percent Arab representatives in parliament would represent Arabs only; the Jewish representatives, Jews only. In elections Arabs could vote only for Arabs; Jews only for Jews. Social and political cooperation between the two national groups would be extremely difficult. For a long time, until the Arabs become more politically alert and socially differentiated, their representatives would mainly vote as a bloc. This would compel Jewish representatives to vote similarly. Those who believe that a bi-national state of such a structure would be less nationalistic than a state of another type are therefore guilty of a grievous error. Chaining the individual voter to an electoral college of his ethnic group will make him more nationalistic, rather than less. The Arab bloc, which will apparently remain politically retarded and socially conservative for some time to come, would be in a position to block progressive social legislation through the use of their fifty percent representation.

(2) Were control of immigration to be denied to the new state, it could not then be considered sovereign and independent. This again poses the question, who should be responsible for the regulation of immigration? Under present conditions, only the UN could create a special body to deal with immigration and colonization in Palestine. (Both are closely interrelated and even inseparable.) But such an arrangement would in fact be a form of *trusteeship*. All the objections to an outright trusteeship enumerated above are equally valid in the case of such limited international supervision.

Partition

This is not a new plan. During the past decade, since the issuance of the well-known Peel [Commission] Report,[32] there has arisen a considerable, largely polemical, literature on this subject. No purpose would be served in repeating at this moment all the arguments *pro* and *contra* such a surgical solution of the Palestine problem.[33] The objections to the partitioning of Palestine into two separate states are not alien even to those who have become reconciled to the idea of a Jewish state in a part of Palestine. Little could be added to the arguments in favor of partition. Some adherents of the partition plan are now putting greater stress on the urgency of Jewish statehood than ever before. It is pointed out that it is becoming increasingly difficult, psychologically, for Jews in Palestine to live under foreign rule.

We have no reason, of course, to underestimate our achievements in Palestine even under the mandatory regime. In spite of the numerous obstacles put in our way by the semi-colonial administration of Palestine, we managed to rehabilitate, in the country, hundreds of thousands of Jews, to expand our agriculture, and lay the foundation for a promising Jewish industry. However, there is a growing awareness among us, and particularly in Palestine itself, of the increasing difficulties our further development faces because of a policy clearly tending toward the crystallization of the Yishuv. If we are really to absorb large numbers of new Jewish settlers in agriculture and industry, we ought to be given more freedom and independence in releasing the pent-up economic forces in Palestine. Without actual control of the government machinery, without the right of eminent domain to carry out a number of long overdue technological projects, it will hardly be possible to create the necessary conditions for mass employment. What the country needs—particularly for *our* purposes—is a social and economic *élan*, which is not to be expected under a more or less disinterested and un-dynamic foreign administration. The thesis that Jewish mass immigration and large-scale colonization should precede the establishment of a Jewish state may be logically correct and even appealing. Political realities, however, have their own inherent "logic," and many among us are becoming convinced that in our case, and at present, some measure of Jewish sovereignty is a prerequisite of Jewish immigration and resettlement.[34] All other solutions appear to be bound up with so many complications and delays, with so many opportunities for hostile forces to sabotage our plans and efforts, that a part of Palestine under an independent Jewish government should be considered in effect "larger" as a basis for immigration and colonization than a continued mandate or some kind of trusteeship-tutelage.

In this case, too, difficult questions arise which must not be ignored. We have pointed out before that any substantial part of Palestine set aside as a Jewish state would depend on areas outside its boundaries for its economic development and for the execution of a number of important irrigation and electrification projects. The cooperation of the Arab state to be set up in the other parts of Palestine—or of the Arab state in which the other parts of Palestine might become incorporated—would thus be essential. Partition, too, is dependent on a number of factors without which the potential development of a Jewish state becomes problematical. Still another danger must not be overlooked. Assuming that the Special Committee of the UN adopts a project of partition, and the session of UN in the autumn approves its recommendation, it is still possible that the area assigned for the Jewish state should be so small that its potentialities for immigration and colonization would be negligible. Much depends on the criterion employed—on how many Jews will be taken into consideration as prospective citizens of the planned state. If only the interest of those Jews already in Palestine are considered, then the boundaries of the Jewish state would be narrow and unacceptable to us. The situation would not be altered noticeably even if the needs of a relatively small number of refugees—200,000 to 250,000—are taken into account. But should a decision concerning a Jewish state be adopted with a view to accommodating the hundreds of thousands of Jews who, though technically not homeless still have sound reason for refusing to remain in their present lands of domicile, then the partition scheme might assume an entirely different character.

The United Nations and the individual governments interested in the solution of the Palestine problem ought to know in advance that we are not interested in mere "symbolism," and that even the most ardent advocates of partition will never reconcile themselves to a token state. Any discussion of a Jewish state in a partitioned Palestine may become senseless, unless assisted by a map, unless the vital interests of a minimum of two million Jews are seriously taken into account.

26

Patriotism and Plural Loyalties

(1948)

A groundswell of American Jewish support in the years following World War II played a consequential role in the Zionist campaign for Jewish statehood. Many American Jews now embraced the formula articulated by Louis D. Brandeis, the venerable American Jewish leader and US Supreme Court justice, who proffered a synergy between Zionism and Americanism. "Let no American imagine that Zionism is inconsistent with patriotism," Brandeis had famously declared in 1915. "Multiple loyalties are objectionable only if they are inconsistent. . . . Every American Jew who aids in advancing the Jewish settlement in Palestine, though he feels that neither he nor his descendants will ever live there . . . [will be] a better American for doing so." Nonetheless, a sizable albeit steadily diminishing segment of American Jewry adhered to the American Jewish Committee's view that Palestine was not "the only haven to which Jews want or should have a right to immigrate" and that the "Jewish Agency [did] not speak for non-Zionists." Though it would take another decade for tensions between American Jewry's pro-Zionist and non-Zionist camps to be resolved, the creation of the State of Israel in 1948 ushered in a sea change in the relationship of American Jewry to the new Jewish state, the United States, and the Jewish people as a whole. In the following philosophical exposition, Greenberg builds upon and extends Brandeis's defense of "plural loyalties" in Jewish life and America in the post-state era. He explores the competing demands of overlapping social, cultural, ethnic, and national attachments and makes the case for the meaningful symbiosis of cultures and identities in democratic societies. Such ideas and themes would become central to late twentieth- and early twenty-first-century philosophical discourse on multiculturalism and anticipated the views of Charles Taylor (b. 1931), Michael Walzer (b. 1935), Kwame Anthony Appiah (b. 1954), and other prominent contemporary public intellectuals.

One may well imagine a future, and not necessarily in a messianic era, when the national sovereignties and local patriotism of our time will be universally regarded as archaic features of a defunct civilization. It is entirely possible that the relations of the individual to his local group, his people, nation, or religio-ethnic community may, some generations hence, lose much of the emotionally tinged quality of modern nationalism, or patriotism. Particular patriotisms, which in our time easily engender hostility and even bloodshed, may then be no more than local nuances of a single "world patriotism," whose fatherland will be the globe.

The idea of a world-fatherland is, of course, not new. It was not unknown to the prophets, and it finds expression in later Jewish messianic and eschatological literature also. In the Hellenic world, Diogenes[1] was not the only one to hold that no state had the right to exist except a world state. Meleager,[2] the father of the *Greek Anthology*, went even farther than he. For him, all humans dwell in the bosom of one and the same *motherland* (this substitution for *fatherland* was intentional)—and the cosmos.[3] Aristotle,[4] with his empirical approach to social and political phenomena, would naturally have rejected such cosmological mysticism in an analysis of "patriotism": the borders of a state, in his view, should be confined within "earshot" distance—literally, to an area over all of which a human voice can be heard.[5] (Such "parochialism" may seem less bizarre to us in the case of Aristotle, who lived after all in a world of little city-states, if we recall the following observation in *The Federalist Papers*,[6] about the optimal extent of a state: "The natural limit [of a republic] is that distance from the center which barely allow the representatives to meet as often as may be necessary."[7]) An Aristotle of the twentieth century would certainly have a different opinion from the Stagyrite[8] sage: the distance between Tokyo and Washington today is "smaller" than the distance between Athens and Sparta in his time; in a world with radio communication, to talk of "earshot" distance no longer makes sense. The ancient utopias of a political universalism are becoming more and more capable of realization.

But however practicable the idea of a global state, based upon a federal principal with local national autonomy, may already seem, we shall undoubtedly have to deal for a considerable period to come, with a multiplicity of political sovereignties, as well as with greedy and suspicious nationalisms. The emergence of Israel as a sovereign state thus confronts certain Jewish groups with a new problem, whether their active interest in the upbuilding and political defense of the Jewish state may not in some sense be opposed to their patriotic obligations as citizens of the countries where they live. Both in Britain and America, certain organizations and bodies (not always anti-Zionist) have already issued special declarations concerning the indivisibility of their patriotism and loyalties, which are not to be affected by the fact that a Jewish state has arisen in Palestine.

It is hard to judge how convincing such declarations will be to elements in the non-Jewish world who feel that they have a reason to suspect pro-Zionist Jews of a lack of patriotism or of dual loyalties. A pathologically jealous woman will not believe any man faithful; to a man who considers the state as the object of absolute loyalty, to which all other loyalties must be subordinate at all times and under any circumstances (or to one who pretends to hold this opinion), all his co-citizens are under constant suspicion of actual or potential treason. For idolators of the state—of *one's own* state—every dissenter from this view is a traitor, in mind if not in deed. What, for example, was the attitude of such an idolator as André Gide[9] in his ultra-nationalistic period? In a letter written to a friend concerning the Dreyfus Affair[10] in 1898, he said: "If saving an innocent Dreyfus involves any injury to the French state, everything should be done to make Dreyfus guilty, so that France may remain unstained."[11] Gide subordinated all other values and loyalties to the "supreme" loyalty which he at that time recognized—loyalty to "*la patrie*" [French for "the nation"], even if the latter fails in loyalty to its own deepest meaning.

The nineteenth-century "patriots" who called Anatole France[12] a traitor and avenged themselves upon Émile Zola[13] by excluding him from the *Légion d'Honneur*[14] for the crime of defending Dreyfus "against France," never charged, even at the height of the affair, that their opponents lacked feeling for, or even devotion to their country. As a matter of fact, the charge made against Dreyfusards by the French nationalists of the time was one of "dual loyalties," and of giving precedence to a subordinate loyalty—to truth, to justice, to the cause of the republic's moral physiognomy—over their patriotic duties to France. Had these men been Englishmen in the days of [Oliver] Cromwell,[15] they would undoubtedly have made the same accusation of "dual loyalty" against [John] Milton.[16] To English loyalists of that period, the king has the same significance as the army had to the French nationalists in the time of the Dreyfus Affair—he was the symbol of one's country and the supreme object of loyalty. Milton, who boldly preached the right to execute a king, if he is a tyrant, and who accused some of the Puritans[17] of having "seditious pity" for the crowned head, did not deny that "the crown" as an institution could have its place as an element in, or symbol of, English patriotism. The problem he confronted was, which was the higher loyalty in the given historical situation? To this question he answered clearly and simply: "I only preferred Queen Truth to King Charles"[18] (*Eikonoclastes*).[19] In saying this, he was convinced that to serve Queen Truth was, not only in the specific situation of England at that time, but at all times and under all circumstances, much more patriotic, in the final historic analysis, than to spare King Charles.

It is worth noting that the attitudes which some are inclined to condemn as "dual loyalties" may be found not only among citizens whose ethnic descent gives them cultural and emotional bonds with the inhabitants of some other sovereign country, or who have established such bonds though their personal experiences. It also occurs among citizens of a more average type, whose ethnic relationships, whether inherited or personally established, are exclusively with the majority, or the native stock of their country, and who have no sentimental ties with any other land. The Doukhobors[20] in Russia, the Hutterites[21] and Mennonites[22] in Germany, and the Quakers[23] in England and America entertained (and, to a certain extent, still entertain) parallel loyalties, even though they were otherwise indistinguishable from the rest of their co-nationals. The conflict between them and the patriotic fetishists of the state did not arise from a clash of two *national loyalties*, such as might have been the case, let us say with an Irishman living in England twenty-odd years ago. It was in a certain sense, a far deeper and more basic conflict: a conflict between imposed duties of a political and "anti-religious" character, on the one hand, and immediately presented ethical and religious, or, so to speak, "transcendental" duties, on the other.

It was in essence the same clash between loyalties of relative value and relative validity and loyalties of absolute value and of a more metaphysical character which two millennia and a half ago already concerned not only Socrates[24] and Plato,[25] but also the Greek tragedians, especially Sophocles.[26] Antigone[27] knew that her brother Polynices,[28] who fell in battle, had betrayed his county, and that the king had a right, under the laws of the state, to exact from his slain foe the penalty prescribed for such cases: "Leave him unwept, unburied, for the birds to watch and feed on at their own sweet will."[29] But she also knew of another kingdom where gods rule, and not flesh and blood. She was, in parallel allegiance, a citizen of that other kingdom of immortals, and under its laws, as she knew them to be, no crime is great enough to leave a body unburied and unwept: a dead man not brought to his grave is forever cut off from the "other" world, from the eternal. For this reason, she herself rebelled against sovereignty, through bringing Polynices to his grave with due rites. She committed, as she herself says, a "holy crime"[30]—a crime by the lights of the state, but a holy act, according to the demands of the gods.

Antigone's way, subordinating political loyalty to religious loyalty, giving the "law of heaven" precedence over the "law of the realm,"[31] was meant to be the way of Christianity. But this tendency found expression historically in Christian heresies, not in its major current. The [Christian Bible] maxim to "render unto Caesar what is Caesar's and unto God what is God's"[32] sounds very idyllic, but also very illusory. Caesar often demands what belongs to the almighty, and God often quite categorically demands what Caesar claims for himself. Whatever grave faults we may ascribe to the Roman Church as a social or political factor in Western history, Catholicism was not only right, but true to its source, when it so vigorously opposed the famous principle of the Protestant Reformation (particularly in Germany): *Cuius regio, eius religio* [Latin for "Whose rule, his religion"];[33] a principle which empowers sovereigns to impose their own religion, whatever it might be, upon the whole population of their country. Catholicism rightly saw in this principle a secularization of matters of the spirit, an attempt to place loyalty to a prince, the contemporary form of patriotism, above all other duties and loyalties.

Without attempting to trace the whole history of this conflict between church and state on the point, it suffices to say that what some call "dual loyalties" is far from new. The modern democratic state has had to accommodate itself to the existence, among its citizens, of minorities—indistinguishable in stock and speech and culture from the majority—whose "patriotism," in the conventional sense of the word, is not absolute and who make it quite clear that in *principle*—as well as in practice—they cannot be expected to place loyalty and obedience to the state above other (from their point of view) more important loyalties. Nor are the members of such minorities universally regarded as low-grade citizens, even though there may be critical situations, in wartime for instance, when they refuse to perform their prescribed patriotic duties. It suffices to recall the high esteem and social position enjoyed by the Quakers in both England and America. Thorstein Veblen[34] was far from wrong in the distinction he drew between the good citizen and the patriot, even though he expressed his view in a provocatively paradoxical form: "There is, indeed, nothing to hinder a bad citizen from being a good patriot; nor does it follow that a good citizen, in other respects, may not be a very indifferent patriot."[35]

As Jews, our present social interest in the problem is not mainly in the general issue of multiple loyalties, and the hierarchical order of such loyalties among non-ethnic minorities. The concrete question which concerns us is how far Zionism, or even pro-Zionism, may be regarded as in conflict with the local political loyalties of diaspora Jews. Is the loyalty of an American Jew open to question if he cultivates his bonds with the Jewish people and sees in the State of Israel the embodiment of one of his personal ideals? Is he, and may he expect to be regarded as, a *whole* American (or Englishman, or Frenchman), or is he only part-American, an "American with reservations"? Does such a person belong to two nationalities at once, and, if so, can his loyalty to America be wholly relied on? Does such a Jew regard America as merely a "boarding house"[36] (to use an expression of Theodore Roosevelt's[37] which Charles Beard[38] thought it necessary to employ on the eve of the last World War, when he charged non-Anglo-Saxon immigrant groups with a lack of patriotism[39]), or as his country?

As a preliminary, it may be useful to define anew the concept of patriotism, as it is currently understood. In the Middle Ages, as we have already remarked, the dynastic ruler, the prince or king, was the sole object of political loyalty. Then, there was no place for loyalty to the state *per se,* for basically it had no true existence of its own apart from the person of the monarch, or the dynasty. "*L'état, c'est moi*" [French for "I am the state"][40] was no mere boast of a vainglorious emperor, but a more or less accurate description of most states. In so far as the loyalty of subjects (not, let it be noted, of *citizens*) to the ruler or ruling family could be called patriotism, it necessarily had to be an exclusive patriotism. One could not be simultaneously loyal to two monarchs, both, in principle, exercising unlimited authority.

Except for such outlandish anachronisms as the kingdoms of Saudi Arabia and Yemen, there is no room in our present world for this kind of loyalty.[41] It would be quite mistaken to describe modern patriotism as involving loyalty to the *government* of one's country. A constitutional government in a democratic country, by the very fact that under the constitution it exercises *delegated* authority granted by the sovereign people, and is always of uncertain duration and dependent on popular approval, can make no claim to the absolute, almost mystical loyalty which was considered the due of "divine monarchs." A democratic government is entitled to demand that its citizenry obey its regulations—unless they are unconstitutional—but it cannot demand love or devotion, or immunity from criticism, nor can it expect the citizens to refrain from trying by every legal means to depose it and replace it with a new government. When the United States Congress passed the Sedition Act of 1798,[42] providing fines and imprisonment "for anyone who should publish false, malicious, or scandalous statements about the members of the national government with the intent to bring them into disrepute,"[43] the legislatures of Virginia and Kentucky immediately replied with resolutions holding that such an act was unconstitutional.[44] To bring a government or its members into disrepute is a citizen's right, so long as this is done without resorting to false reports. Except in totalitarian countries, no one would dream, in our time, of making a government, or its members, the object of patriotic loyalties. It is the state, not the government, upon which patriotism centers.

But what, empirically speaking, is the state? Anyone who does not assume that the state is a substantial entity existing independently of the individuals of whom it is constituted, anyone who does not succumb to a state mystique, knows that the state is, primarily, an organized social framework for coordinating the behavior of its constituent individuals and groups. Hence, in the final analysis, loyalty to the state is loyalty to one's fellow citizens, to the society existing on the state territory, to the *people*. A patriot is one who experiences a more or less intimate relationship to the entire group of his fellow citizens and sympathetically considers, in governing his actions, the interests, well-being, moral character, and reputation of his people in relation to other peoples.

At this point we may ask: Does loyalty (as well as a certain intimacy of relationship) to one people preclude similar, parallel loyalty to another ethnic group, living in a different country under a different state organization? Is it possible to maintain what some would call "dual nationality," and, if so, is this a legitimate and more or less normal phenomenon? Are people, nation, and state such hermetically closed bodies that their members are normally prevented from maintaining similar relationships to groups in other compartments? In other words, is there any room for pluralistic social relationships, attachments, sentiments, and loyalties?

The answer is presented to us in concrete reality. Let us take as an example an Italian-speaking Swiss citizen. He may hardly know himself how many different loyalties, in various degrees, he harbors. He is a Swiss, and nobody can question his Swiss patriotism, his loyalty to the [Swiss] Confederation.[45] He is, at the same time, a patriot of his canton. Ticino[46] is the part of his *patria* [homeland] which claims his most intimate attachments. No matter what his "race" may be, he feels a bond of cultural and linguistic sentiment allying him with millions of Italians across the border. Religiously, in most cases, he is a Catholic, and as such he is intimately connected with a vast number of Catholics all over the globe, and, furthermore, for certain purposes and in certain situations, he respects the "sovereignty" of a unique authority called the Vatican. If tomorrow he should become a UN official, he would take a new oath of allegiance and acquire a new loyalty—to the "world" as a whole.

If he were to be interviewed and made to give an accounting of his "allegiance," which he probably never before had occasion to do, he would undoubtedly say that there are no contradictions between the many parallel loyalties we have enumerated. If we were to tell him he is a less normal psychological or social type than other citizens with fewer loyalties, he would probably deny it; or he might say that, first of all, there are some phenomena for which there is no objective measure of normality, and secondly, "That's how I am"—and there is no authority that can, or ought to set up rules of "normality" for him. And if someone should plainly demonstrate a contradiction or disharmony in his condition and relationships, he would quote you a verse from a Swiss poet:[47]

Ich bin kein ausgekluegelt Buch,
Ich bin ein Mensch mit allem seinen Widerspruch.[48]

The Swiss is only one illustration; he is by no means exceptional. A Scot is, first of all, a patriot of Scotland (objectively speaking, it would be abnormal if he were not); secondly, a loyal citizen of Great Britain; third, he has a certain sentimental political relationship to the British dominions; fourth, if he is devout, he still entertains a definite and far from superficial relationship to the High Church,[49] which unites him with co-religionists overseas and separates him from quite a number of his British compatriots. In addition, he may, perhaps, be a loyal adherent of international socialism. Similar plural loyalties are found among Englishmen and, even more, among Frenchmen in Canada, or Boers and Englishmen in South Africa.

One of the most important foundations of true democracy is the right to be different: not only the right to hold different opinions and beliefs than the majority, but to *be* different, including the right to maintain a living, fraternal relationship with an ethnic group living outside one's own state, and as a separate organized state. An Italian American who does not wish to forget his Italian, who bears Italy in the innermost recesses of his memory or in his imagination, who suffers and rejoices with Italy, who puts something aside from his earnings to help the needy in Italy, too, who uses his influence as an American to urge his government to help Italy in her need, and who may occasionally be so homesick for Italy that he must take a trip to the Old Country, or even settle there—such a person is basically not a worse American than one who has no specific attachment to any ethnic group outside the United States. When such things chance to happen to a "hundred percent American" (as, for example, to the Virginia-born Lady Astor,[50] who acquired naturalization in England and even became a member of [the British] parliament), no one dreams of accusing him or her of "treason" or "disloyalty." America is not interested—no country is interested—in having citizens with defective memories and shrunken horizons, citizens afflicted with aphasia and amnesia.

Ernest Renan[51] once said that the very existence of a nation is "*un plébiscite de tous les jours*" [French for "a plebiscite every day"].[52] The statement, of course, is considerably exaggerated. But it is true that the scope of social, cultural, and political loyalties is not constantly the same, and historic events and developments can contract or expand their extent. A Norwegian today, in independent Norway, has a narrower focus for his political nationalism than his father or elder brother had, when Norway was still a part of the State of Denmark.[53] The object of Muslim patriotism in Pakistan is "smaller" than the object of all-Indian nationalism ten or fifteen years ago. Not every Englishman is now well described by the popular song:

> In spite of all the temptations
> To belong to other nations,
> He remains an Englishman.[54]

The Englishman in Australia, New Zealand, and South Africa (not to speak of the Englishman who has settled in the United States) is no longer the same Englishman as in the United Kingdom. In a sense, he belongs to "other nations," to nations which he and his like themselves created, and which made more extensive and more varied the sphere of his loyalties.

In summer 1940, Winston Churchill[55] proposed to the French government, in the name of Great Britain, to continue the war against Germany in spite of the tragic difficulties of those days, and at the same time to lay groundwork for a joint Franco-British state.[56] What if France had accepted? Frenchmen and Englishmen would today be citizens of a common state; a Frenchman in time would become an English patriot, and an Englishman, a French patriot. Over the period of a generation, a sort of federal patriotism might have crystallized, something not unlike Swiss nationalism. Both Frenchmen and Englishmen (together with their Scotch and Welsh compatriots) would slowly discover that, although the human capacity for loyalties and intimate relationships is not unlimited, it is nonetheless significantly greater, more dynamic, and more elastic than many of them had imagined.

Human loyalties involve the deepest and most intimate relations of personal integrity. They cannot be mechanically regulated under any monistic principle of social control.

***

The American Jew is not faced with any fundamental conflict between his duties to America and his bond with the Jewish community in Israel. Not even in time of war could there arise any earnest clash of loyalties. There are some, however, who feel that American Jews are confronted with a moral and political dilemma when they are asked to contribute to Israel not only funds but also human resources, volunteers who should go to Israel "for good" and merge their personal destinies with those of the Land of Israel. You would not ask non-Jews to emigrate to Israel—thus runs the argument—nor would you appeal to non-Jewish Americans to return to the countries from which they and their forbears came. There are millions of such Americans, yet you would not proclaim a general slogan that all those Americans who are not of Anglo-Saxon extraction or of "pure" American descent should go back to their erstwhile fatherlands. It is therefore obvious that you believe that American Jews as a group possess specific traits and interests not shared by any other group in the country. Doesn't this imply an assumption that American Jews are not truly American, that they are hyphenated Americans, citizens with mental reservations of which other ethnic groups in the country are free? Don't you think that stressing this exceptionalism of the American Jew might place him in an unenviable and equivocal position?

Though I doubt that I can provide a formula that will satisfy everybody in answer to the above arguments, I would like to offer my personal approach to these matters.

I do not believe that Jews living in America are not genuine Americans. Instead of hyphenated Americanism we should rather speak of uniqueness. *We are unique.*

Everyone, Jew or non-Jew, is different, and possesses a certain degree of distinctiveness if only he or she represents something specific and is not totally lacking in individuality. A true democracy rests on the differences between its citizens, as individuals or as groups. The day these differences disappear will also mark the end of the still imperfect democracy which we now enjoy.

It is not the function of democracy to obliterate or suppress these differences which, whether one likes them or not, stem from historic and cultural developments and are also based to some extent on factors which may be classified for lack of a better term as biological. It is democracy's task to harmonize them. Education must strive neither to destroy nor to ignore these differences but to sublimate them, to find the fruitful elements within them and to raise them to a higher level so that they may make their unique contribution to the general civilization of the country.

In America we are blessed (and I say "blessed" advisedly) with a number of group differences which do not generally stem from ethnic descent. Quakers are not distinguishable in any respect from the basic American racial stock (assuming that "basic American racial stock" is a fact and not a myth). They are a native Anglo-American phenomenon, yet one cannot say of them that they are "as American as baked beans." They stand out by reason of some essential differences, yet it will not occur to anyone to question their Americanism.

Or, let us consider another ethnic group, less "respectable" than the Quakers and lacking the spiritually aristocratic background which characterizes the Quakers in England as well as in America. I am referring to the sect known as Jehovah's Witnesses.[57] The nonconformist character of this group has in recent years gained them a certain notoriety. They do not, for instance, recognize the sanctity of the flag and their children have refused to salute the national colors on certain festive observances in the public schools. Were it up to me, I would advise the parents of these children not to bring them up in a spirit of such rabid dogmatism. But Jehovah's Witnesses consider saluting the American flag—any national flag—as a form of idol worship, an infringement on the prerogatives of God's kingdom on earth, a fetishist rite. It may be true that their extremist avoidance of homage for symbols of American solidarity, such as the national flag, is in itself a form of taboo of which they should rid themselves. I realize my inability to dissuade them from their extremism, nevertheless I would not question their Americanism, especially when I recall that they are a native growth of the American soil, not transplanted from any foreign land. They do occasionally cause some inconvenience, but with all the rigidity of their concepts of what is right and what is wrong they are more valuable for America than millions of others who ask no questions and indiscriminately take for granted all the elements of the status quo.

I know the objections that will be raised against these analogies. Both Quakers and Jehovah's Witnesses, it will be said, are religious sects, and toleration of religious difference is an organic part of our American heritage. But I have noticed that the concept of religious tolerance as understood by the average American is based on an incorrect appraisal of what constitutes religious differences. The commonly accepted idea on the subject is that differences between religions are of a purely metaphysical character and express themselves in varied rituals. It is therefore easy to maintain that it is nobody's business what holy days are privately practiced by citizens in their houses of worship. The state, organized society in general, has no interest in such "private" affairs of the citizenry, and these have no relations to the citizen's duties and responsibilities.

While maintaining such a point of view, we overlook that there exist religious minorities whose difference from the rest of the community is not merely of a metaphysical nature, but manifests itself in definite attitudes toward political, economic, and social problems. Thus the political differences that divide Quakers from the rest of the American community are far more earnest than those between Lutherans and Episcopalians or even the differences between Jews and Christians.

The United States does not impose any civic obligations on its citizens which both Jews and Christians cannot meet equally without violating their religious conscience, but there are civic duties which, though acceptable to Jews and Christian denominations, are not acceptable to Quakers and Jehovah's Witnesses (e.g., military service, specific oaths of loyalty, etc.). Here we are confronted with a category of differences affecting social and political attitudes and not only variations in the mode of worship. A democracy that wishes to remain true to itself makes allowances for such differences. It may even value them highly, despite the inconvenience which they cause from time to time.

So far as American Jews are concerned, we too are characterized by certain differences with whose existence American democracy must reckon and for which allowances must be made. Our differences are not the same as those of other nonconformist groups. But it is in the nature of differences that they *differ* from each other, that they are dissimilar.

The unique mentality of the Jewish people (also of Jews in America) contains a potentiality of emigration, especially emigration to the Land of Israel. This is a potentiality and not an inevitability.

In this respect Jews may not be so unique after all. Judging from my observations, such a mental tendency toward repatriation exists also among Italian Americans, although object conditions do not permit its fruition. Italy cannot accept any appreciable numbers of its sons and daughters from abroad. Because of its economic situation, Italy today is a land of emigration, not of immigration. The same is also true more or less of the Irish. Subjectively, a considerable number of Irish in America were in a mood to return to Ireland, especially after that country achieved independence.[58] This is so despite the fact that the Irish have no reason to feel uncomfortable in America. In this instance, too, objective conditions in Ireland preclude such a return. The economy of Ireland, even after its liberation, is not of a sort that can attract immigrants or repatriates. To this day, thousands of young people in Ireland dream of lands overseas, especially in America. Gaelic, the Irish national tongue, has made little progress despite its official status in Ireland and the efforts on its behalf by the government and the public schools. One of the causes for this failure is the fact that a large part of the youth in Ireland still thinks in terms of emigration and therefore feels that the English language would be of greater benefit to them than the Gaelic, which no one abroad understands and whose position in the [Irish] Free State is still conspicuously weak.

It is true that for American Jews migration to Israel would not be a repatriation in the strict, etymological sense of the word. Such a migration would rather be in the nature of the fulfillment of an old traditional sentiment, a longing which in a certain social climate can easily lose its impetus but which can also, under definite conditions, be rearoused and gain new strength.

This potential revitalization of an old dream is part of the Jew's being "different." It is part of the heritage which Jews brought with themselves to America from other lands and which they possessed, consciously or subconsciously, even when some of them felt compelled to deny its existence for ideological and other reasons.

Jews need not feel apologetic for this element in their heritage. It never interfered with the conscientious fulfillment of their duties as citizens of the United States or with their love for the country and its civilization, nor did it hinder the growth of bonds of intimacy between them and the land of their adoption. This unrealized longing, often subconscious, did not lessen their contribution to American life, well-being, and civilization.

In any case, that is how Jews are. Whether this is a perfectly normal phenomenon, I do not know. I have long since given up trying to apply exact measurements to normalcy, and though I realize that the following analogy is far from being a perfect one, I would nevertheless like to point out that while a horse with a hump on its back is definitely a monstrosity, the same deformity on a camel's back is quite normal and may even be esthetically pleasing.

Will American Jews go to Israel in coming years? And in what numbers? I have already stated that there exists a subjective potentiality for such migration. How, when, and under what conditions this potentiality may be realized I cannot say.

I rule out altogether the elements of catastrophe. I do not care to presuppose a migration of Jews from America on the basis of prophecies of social cataclysms which will force the Jews to flee. Despite our tragic experiences in the Old World, I believe that "It can't happen here!" And were I not to believe so, I would have no reason to look to Israel as a haven of refuge. Should the sun be blotted out in America, I could not then see any light anywhere on this planet. A fascist America would mean a fascist world; a viciously antisemitic America would mean a viciously antisemitic world. Should America betray herself, it would mean a moral eclipse on a global scale from which there could be no escape—not even in Israel.

I do not share the defiance of that Jewish woman in the anecdote who went to the synagogue on [Yom Kippur][59] and presented an ultimatum to the almighty: "Either you grant me a prosperous year, or I will go to live with my aunt in the country." The aunt in the country is also subject to the jurisdiction of the lord from whose wrath one cannot escape. The State of Israel can exist and endure only if a certain measure of justice and fair play prevails in the world. Should the world descend below that standard (and we all know how low that standard is at present), Israel could not exist for even a day.

When I think of migration of American Jews to Israel, I think in terms of *aliyah* [ascent] not of flight, in terms of Jews departing from America with a blessing on their lips, with love and gratitude in their hearts, and even with homesickness for America at the very moment when they wish it farewell. For we must not assume that all situations call for a choice between love and hatred. Sometimes it is a choice between two loves, one of which transcends the other.

I have already remarked that I cannot prophesy when, how, and in what numbers American Jews might migrate to Israel. I recognize the right of being different in some respects not only as between Jew and non-Jew but also between Jews and themselves. I am not inclined to stereotype the Jewish community in any country, and especially not the one in the United States.

I can easily visualize a more or less organic differentiation of American Jewry in our era into three probably unequal groups. One of these groups may in time entirely dissolve in the American melting pot. Though assimilation is no longer preached as an ideology and social doctrine, we must not conclude that objective as well as subjective factors working toward group dissolution have ceased to operate. Not all Jews are equally gifted with a will to persevere as Jews, and I am willing to concede that some elements in the American Jewish community would welcome some form of "kiss of death." I would not like to see those Jews lost to the body of the Jewish community, but if they yearn after complete assimilation and the non-Jewish environment does not hinder them, my preferences in the matter will not avail.

I also visualize another segment of the Jewish community, possessing more vitality and a stronger will to continued existence. These elements will seek to survive as American Jews and will draw the strength to endure as a distinct group from the wellsprings of Jewish tradition as well as from the emergent Jewish civilization in Israel. I do not know what the shape and the essence of such continuity of Jewish life in America will be. However, we must not rule out possibilities of creative energy to be displayed in the future, even though symptoms of such creativeness are still invisible to the naked eye.

I also foresee a third element, with still greater Jewish vitality that will orient itself toward a full, dynamic Jewish life in Israel. It was this element I had in mind when I spoke above concerning two loves, one of which transcends the other.

Assuming that my prognosis is correct, we should not delude ourselves into believing that it is already possible to classify individual American Jews into these three categories. In this respect we should be prepared for many paradoxes, surprises, and disappointments. Pilgrims and pioneers for Israel may come from elements which are today non-Zionist or indifferent. Similarly, it is possible that some Zionists of today and their children will seek and find their place in the other two categories. Today, we can only point out those Jews who are ideologically pro-Israel, but it is not at all easy to discover who among them has "a talent for Israel"; talents so often smolder in the depths.

The size of migration from America to Israel will depend on many factors, some of which cannot even be listed today. The economic situation and the development of Israel on one hand, and socioeconomic changes in America on the other hand, will contribute their share. Whether a significant economic restratification will take place in the United States will also be a factor, since persons who have to change their occupations or status are more prone to migration than those whose economic routine remains unbroken. The cultural and moral shape of Israel will also determine its power of attraction. The degree of Jewish isolation or integration in America, as well as the type of education young Jews receive in America in coming years, will likewise exert their influence.

It is impossible today to weigh these factors, nor was it my intention to do so. I only wished to point out that the migration of certain elements of the American Jewish community to Israel must be considered by Jews and non-Jews alike as a legitimate process.

It may not be irrelevant to stress one other point. American law and American political thought has long recognized the possibilities of the type of repatriation which I consider as a justifiable. As early as 1779, Thomas Jefferson sponsored a resolution in the legislature of Virginia defining the rights and duties of a citizen. One of the most significant paragraphs in that resolution outlines "the natural right which all men have of relinquishing the country in which birth or other accident may have thrown them and seeking subsistence and happiness wheresoever they may be able, or may hope to find them."[60]

Professor [Hersch] Lauterpacht[61] (in his *An International Bill of the Rights of Man*)[62] recalls that the same principle was again formulated in 1868 in a joint resolution of both Houses of Congress which recognized "the right of expatriation as a natural and inherent right of all people, indispensable to the enjoyment of the right of life, liberty, and the pursuit of happiness."[63]

In our own day the spokesman of the American delegation to the Hague Conference on Codification of International Law [1930][64] made the following declaration: "For a century past it has been the policy of my country that the right to expatriation is an inherent and natural right of all persons. True it is that allegiance is a duty, but it is not a chain that holds one in bondage. . . . This principle is not a little thing. It is not a question of language, or of formulas, or of phrases. It is a principle of the rights of man and of the liberty of the human race."[65]

27
Concerning an Israel Constitution
(1949)

7. Photo of Hayim Greenberg in Palestine (c. 1947); courtesy of Ameinu.

Israel's Declaration of Independence called for the completion of a constitution by October 1, 1949. The War of Independence and the lack of consensus about the composition of the state's constitution made this target unrealizable. In 1950 the Knesset adopted a proposal by the lawyer and politician Yizhar Harari (1908–78) (known as the "Harari Decision") to create a series of legal chapters (called "Basic Laws") that would incrementally outline the fledgling state's political structure, resolve constitutional legal issues, and ultimately yield an overarching constitutional matrix. Owing to significant religious and political controversies that had long bedeviled the Zionist movement, the constitution did not materialize—nor was the matter resolved in subsequent decades. In the absence of a unitary constitutional document, the state continues to rely on the Basic Laws as an uncodified constitutional framework. To date, the state has created twelve Basic Laws on the following themes: legislative structure of the Knesset (1958); nationalization of Israeli lands (1960); function and powers of the president (1964); authority of the government (1968, 1992, 2001); regulation of the domestic economy (1975); role and administration of the military (the Israel Defense Forces) (1976); the Jerusalem Law establishing the unified city of Jerusalem as capital of Israel (1980); authority and powers of the civil judiciary (1984); authority and powers of the state comptroller (1988); human dignity and liberty (1992); freedom to engage in any occupation, profession, or trade (1992, 1994); and protocol for and regulation of governmental referendums (2014). Additionally, the Law of Return (1950) ("Every Jew has the right to immigrate to Israel"), though technically not a Basic Law, is regarded as integral to the latter framework. In the following essay, Hayim Greenberg explores the spectrum of clashing ideas and opinions that impeded efforts to develop a state constitution. His analysis places the stormy public debate of 1949 in cultural, historical, and political context.

I

In what sense and to what extent should the constitution of the Jewish state bear a specifically Jewish character? The question is not of universal interest. There are many Jews, both in and outside Israel, who are persuaded that no special measures are necessary to give the Jewish state a characteristically Jewish aspect. A free republic of and for Jews, with the bulk of its population already Jewish, and destined for the future to be Jewish, would naturally have specifically Jewish qualities, without requiring constitutional guarantees of its Jewishness. Jews settled and created an independent political framework of their own, not in order to discard their Jewishness, but quite the opposite, in order to enrich it, make it more spontaneous, creative, and true in its expression. From this point of view, an Israel constitution ought to be "good," just, humane, and realistically adapted to the complex conditions and requirements of our time; it will be "Jewish" automatically, in so far as it expresses the judgment and conscience of contemporary Jews, who consciously or unconsciously bear within them the higher impulses and aspirations of past Jewish ages.

However, we may expect a severe and unavoidable *Kulturkampf*[1] when the Israeli parliament begins its discussion of the various paragraphs of the draft constitution.[2] The Orthodox group in Israel (not only the combined Orthodox bloc of Mizrahi and Agudat Israel, but also religious Jews not attached to any religious political party) intends to demand certain constitutional guarantees of the "Jewish" character of the state, according to their own definition—or definitions—of "Jewishness." Even before the state was founded, they used to tell us that Israel ought to be governed "in the spirit of the Torah." Some were not satisfied with so abstract a formula. The *spirit* of the Torah, they pointed out with justified concern, can be variously interpreted by different interpreters, especially by unqualified amateurs. They prefer, accordingly, a "safer" formula, and demand that the state be governed according to the *laws* of the Torah, in which case the spirit of the Torah would necessarily prevail in Jewish life.

The draft constitution, which will serve as the basis of a severe and inevitably lengthy debate in the parliament (and, of course, also in the other forums of public opinion), takes account in no small measure of the easily understood and certainly quite natural attraction of traditional piety among Jews all over the world and especially in Israel. The author, or chief author, of the draft, Dr. Leo Kohn,[3] is himself by education and personal feelings close to an Orthodox religious approach to the principles of a Jewish political philosophy. Nevertheless he was forced to include provisions concerning the basic structure and fundamental laws of the state which find no support in a strictly fundamentalist conception of Jewish religion.

Let us take, for example, Article 4, paragraph 2 of the draft constitution, which guarantees equal civil and political rights to all Israeli citizens, without discrimination on grounds of race, religion, language, or sex. The citizens of Israel include not only Jews but non-Jews as well—Muslims, Christians, and small numbers of other religions. According to the above Article 4, and also according to Article 49 which grants every citizen, without regard to religion, the right to be elected president of Israel, the highest office in the land may be occupied by an Arab or a Druze,[4] a Muslim, a Christian, or even, theoretically, an idolater. It does not matter that neither a Christian nor a Muslim in actuality has any chance to be elected president of Israel by its parliament, the Knesset. A resident of ancient Israel with the status of a *mamzer* (an illegitimate child) or of Amalekite[5] descent undoubtedly had less than the proverbial "Chinaman's chance" to be chosen high priest. But still it was thought necessary to frame a specific prohibition on this point as a *matter of principle*. It needs no deep research to discover that in principle such political equality is not countenanced by Jewish religious tradition. Even a proselyte, declares so late an authority as Maimonides,[6] may not become king among Jews "unless his mother is of Israel"; that is, only converts of *Jewish maternal descent* were qualified for the highest office in the Jewish state.[7] Lest anyone contend that the traditional law of kings does not apply to the presidency, highest office in a republic, we may quote what Maimonides has to say further in the same connection: "Not for kingship alone but for any office in Israel"—a non-Jew is not only disqualified from becoming king, but from holding any position of authority in Israel.[8]

The above-mentioned paragraphs in the draft constitution are opposed to Jewish traditional law in another respect also—in granting absolute equality to women. One may orate forever about Judaism's not being discriminatory against women in spirit and invoke the memory of such great figures as Miriam,[9] Deborah,[10] Bruriah,[11] et al. But whatever may be its spirit, Jewish *law* (and we are dealing here with rules for practice, not principles for preaching) is clearly and sharply discriminatory in regard to women. Together with slaves, minors, and deaf-mutes, women are inadmissible as witnesses under the law. As for woman's political rights, let us see what the great codifier Maimonides has to say on this point, expressing, of course, not a personal view but the position of the Torah: "Women are not placed in kingship . . . and similarly regarding all offices in Israel, only men are appointed to them."[12]

Jewish law is by no means uniquely backward in these matters. How long ago was it that civilized Christian states began to allow non-Christians to exercise the rights of citizenship and serve as public officials (although the phraseology of Christianity is, of course, outstandingly cosmopolitan)?[13] Anything in Jewish tradition is more than matched by those Catholic Church conclaves where lengthy debates were conducted, with an ingenuity which might well have been spared for better purposes, on the peculiar question of whether women, too, have souls.[14] And may an American or an Englishman forget that woman suffrage was introduced in their countries only in our own days?[15] Or may not western Europe, the cradle of modern civilization, be reminded that countries like France and Belgium have not to this very day been fully reconciled to the idea of political equality for women, or even of equality in such purely economic spheres as property and inheritance rights?[16] But none of this alters the fact that traditional Jewish law recognizes equal rights neither for non-Jews nor for women.

If Jewish orthodoxy wished (or were bold enough) to be entirely consistent with its abstract professions, it would have to object strenuously to certain glaring violations of Jewish law already accepted in Israel, even before a constitution has been adopted. The Knesset has some [members] who are non-Jews and an even larger number of women.[17] Members of the fair sex have already distinguished themselves as officers in the Israel army;[18] and a woman [Golda Meir][19] already sits in the Israel cabinet, holding a portfolio of major importance, alongside fellow ministers and rabbis of the Mizrahi and Agudat Israel parties. The Orthodox have not yet been heard to protest very seriously against these departures from traditional Jewish law. On the contrary, from certain recent indications it appears that they may cooperate in ratifying them. In the Knesset debate after Premier [David] Ben-Gurion[20] presented his cabinet list (comprising three ministers from the United Religious bloc[21]) he said: "In the very near future a law will be promulgated in Israel making every man and woman equal in matters of inheritance, maintenance, and juridical rights, whether before a rabbinic, Muslim, or Christian court."[22] The rabbis in the Ben-Gurion cabinet, as well as the parties they represent, are undoubtedly bound by this statement.

The same sort of comment must be made on the very significant subject of capital punishment. Article 12 of the draft constitution recognizes the absolute sanctity of human life and expressly prohibits capital punishment in any form. This provision has, to be sure, been criticized by a number of (Jewish) jurists, sociologists, and political leaders. There are still any number of "civilized" states which have not yet abolished the death penalty. It is still sanctioned by United States federal law (and by many states of the union), as well as in France and the United Kingdom. In Switzerland, capital punishment was abolished by a constitutional enactment in 1874, but only five years later this "humanitarian calamity," as some called it, was rescinded, because a number of particularly shocking crimes evoked a popular trend to return to the "good old days." Capital punishment then became permissive under the law of the Swiss Confederation, with each of its twenty-two cantons entitled to include or abolish it in its own penal code. Today Catholic theologians in Switzerland assiduously argue out of Thomas Aquinas that "judges who pronounce death sentences act as the agents of God"—and the almighty, of course, may take anyone's life as he pleases—or that "judges are society's surgeons, who amputate diseased members of the social organism."[23] It is one of the ironies of our time that capital punishment has been abolished precisely in totalitarian countries—Russia, Romania, Spain. In states where the idea of a writ of *habeas corpus* is not recognized, and the police may hold a prisoner *incommunicado,* the government needs no law to authorize executions: it can remove its opponents by a far simpler procedure. The author of the draft constitution for Israel evidently felt that, first, capital punishment is so important a question in the relation between the individual and organized society, that it must be dealt with constitutionally, and not left to statutory enactment; second, that even though the death penalty exists in many "progressive" states, and it was even reintroduced in certain countries where it had been previously abolished, on the plea that it was premature or "impractical" to deny the state so powerful a weapon in fighting crime, such a penal system was nevertheless intolerable for the new State of Israel.

This is not the place to discuss whether a state has or has not the right to take the life of even the most dangerous criminal, or whether, speaking in strictly practical terms, capital punishment is an effective "deterrent" to crime. This writer agrees fully with Dr. Leo Kohn, author of the draft constitution for Israel, that the conception of the "sanctity of human life," a basic assumption in the structure of his entire draft, necessarily implies an absolute prohibition of the death penalty. But it is impossible to agree with one of Dr. Kohn's arguments on this point, namely, that the death penalty is contrary to the spirit of Jewish religious tradition.[24]

Of course, many a citation can be quoted from the Talmud expressing strong opposition to judicial executions. The statement, for example, that a Sanhedrin issuing one death sentence in seven years deserves to be called a "destructive Sanhedrin" or a "murderous Sanhedrin" is certainly very impressive [B. Makot 7a]. Eleazar ben Azariah[25] applied the same derogatory terms to a Sanhedrin that issued a death sentence once in seventy years, and Rabbi Tarfon[26] and Rabbi Akiba[27] went even further: "If we were members of the Sanhedrin, death sentences would never be imposed" [B. Makot 7a]. But all this is the realm of ethical literature, not law. These are personal views of individuals whose own religious conscience could not accept the idea of punishment by death. If the same Rabbi Tarfon and Rabbi Akiba had been asked what was the *law,* and according to what rule a Sanhedrin was obliged to proceed in practice, they would probably have had no choice but to conclude, however painful it might have been for them, that under the law certain crimes might, or rather, had to, be punished by death. How essentially private were these views of theirs—or strictly speaking, their humanitarian sentiments, rather than views—may be seen from the criticism their statements evoked. No less an authority than Rabban Shimon ben Gamliel[28] expressed himself very sharply about such "sentimentalism": "Such an attitude would increase the murderers in Israel" [B. Makot 7a]. The right of the state, or of organized society generally, to impose the death penalty is recognized in Jewish religious tradition both by scriptural and rabbinic legislation. Not only murder—under the maxim of "a life for a life"—but many other crimes call for capital punishment, as for example participation in pagan cult rituals, incitement to crime, magical practices, desecration of the Sabbath, and cursing one's father and mother. Death through strangling is the penalty decreed for a false prophet who prophesies in the names of idols. On cardinal questions, the authority of Maimonides as codifier is unquestioned to this day, and he lists thirty-six crimes for which the law imposes the death penalty.[29]

It is true that in capital cases, Jewish law demands an extraordinarily cautious judicial procedure that is without parallel in the jurisprudence of other civilizations, whether in antiquity or in modern times. There are categories of citizens who are disqualified from judging such cases, in order to guarantee the greatest possible justice and impartiality for the accused. "Neither the senile nor the emasculated may be appointed to the Sanhedrin, because there is cruelty in them; nor may a childless man; for he must be merciful."[30] Modern jurisprudence, even in the most advanced states, could learn a good deal from Jewish law concerning the qualifications of judges and procedure in capital cases. But the law itself is not altered in principle by such procedural provisions, and though Maimonides is not under the slightest suspicion of sadistic tendencies, he yet declared (because his conception of the law obliged him to hold this view) that not only may a pregnant woman be condemned to death, but in such an event, "one does not wait until the child is born, but one beats her against the womb until the child in her is dead" and then she herself is executed.[31] According to Maimonides, judges who issue a death sentence must fast the whole day of the execution.[32] To take a human life, even of a man who forfeited his right to life, is not a trivial matter, and one may not pass directly and heedlessly from such a responsibility to one's ordinary, everyday affairs. But, again, from legal prescriptions like these, which express a view of judicial execution as a dread and *tragic duty,* one can hardly leap as lightly as does so excellent a scholar as Rav Zair[33] to the conclusion that the laws of Sanhedrin and of capital cases may never have been practiced at all, but were merely studied as purely theoretical, academic exercises, without any connection with reality.[34] Maimonides, for example, regards all these laws as practically applicable, and he states expressly that, if all the precautions in procedure, and particularly in the manner of questioning witnesses, have been scrupulously observed, no court is required to refrain from frequent executions, if they should be necessary. "If it happens that they must execute daily, they do so."[35] The court must refrain only from condemning to death two people on the same day. In his important work *Penalties in the Period after the Redaction of the Talmud* [1922],[36] Prof. [Simha] Assaf[37] stated that death sentences were issued by Jewish courts for a considerable period after the destruction of the Temple.

It should also be noted that a "Torah constitution," to use a phrase currently in fashion in some Orthodox circles (in the sense of strict adherence to the law, not merely to a conception so inexact and tenuous as "the spirit of Judaism"), can also contain no categorical prohibition of corporal punishment, which is also categorically banned in the Israeli draft constitution. Flogging is used (or is legally permitted) as a penalty for certain crimes to this very day in many "progressive" states. There are a number of states in the United States where this scandalous practice has not yet been wiped out: Alabama, Louisiana, South Carolina, Mississippi, Texas, and even [Thomas] Jefferson's home state, Virginia. Nor has England yet been persuaded that flogging is not the best means to teach certain citizens better habits and instill discipline. The classical punishment by cat-o-nine-tails for robbery attended by a certain degree of violence has not yet been eliminated from the British common law system. In English schools, too, it is not officially forbidden to punish by hand or rod in cases of unruly students. The author of the Israeli draft constitution, however, believed that every man's body is his absolute property, and that even criminals may not be beaten. But he would be defending a very shaky position were he to argue that whippings are opposed to the spirit of Jewish tradition, not to speak of Jewish law. Floggings are an entirely legitimate method of punishment in Jewish law.[38]

In this regard, there is no essential difference between the scriptural and rabbinic categories of law. One must merely be careful that the caning be done "with restraint" or "according to capacity," so that the person whipped may not die or be badly hurt—a special procedure for the "operation" was worked out to ensure this—but Maimonides has a long list of crimes and offenses for which flogging is the legitimate and, so to speak, natural penalty. Among over two hundred offenses listed there are, of course, a number of anti-social, perverted, and unnatural acts.[39] But whippings were also prescribed for those who violate purely ritual laws or permit themselves a kind of behavior which shocks society as a breach of convention or etiquette: eating or working on Yom Kippur [Day of Atonement],[40] eating from a loaf without ritually sacrificing a first portion of the dough, following the ways of the gentiles, eating ritually unclean animals, fowl, or prohibited sea foods, reptiles, insects or the worms in fruits, walking farther than the permitted distance on Sabbath, working on festive days, tattooing oneself, wearing clothes of *shatnez*—mixed wool and flax—a man dressing like a woman or a woman dressing like a man.[41]

It is well known that floggings were in practice among Jews at almost all times, and though non-Jews did not need us to teach it to them, they did take over from Jews, at certain times, the method of regulating (and, in a sense, humanizing) this penalty. The forty stripes less one of the Puritans in Massachusetts were a direct carryover from Jewish practice.[42] Thus whippings acquired a sort of religious sanction among the Massachusetts Protestants. The same was true in Connecticut and New Jersey, where judges were under general instructions to punish "in accordance with God's law."[43]

The purpose of this over-long digression was to show that a number of fundamental provisions of the Israeli draft constitution—though undoubtedly desirable in themselves and in harmony with our legal conscience today—are not in accord with Jewish traditional law. Yet Jewish orthodoxy raised no protest against these proposals. More than that, in a brochure concerning the problems of the Israeli constitution, which contains comments by prominent Orthodox leaders, both of Mizrahi and of Agudat Israel, they declared themselves in opposition to the death penalty, though not to corporal punishment.[44] It would be useless to ask on what grounds in Torah they would seek to abolish capital punishment. We may assume that such a penalty is simply abhorrent to their ethical and spontaneous religious sense.

If they were pressed with questions from the basis of Jewish dogma, or as Americans say, from the standpoint of their own "fundamentalism," they might perhaps take refuge in the argument that full redemption has not yet come with the establishment of the Jewish state and there are certain laws which still cannot be revived. This writer has heard it argued that death penalties cannot be imposed by ordinary courts, but only by the Sanhedrin; that the Sanhedrin must sit in Jerusalem as the recognized capital of the kingdom of the House of David;

that it is still a moot and very difficult question how a member of the Sanhedrin can be ordained in our day, that perhaps the Sanhedrin cannot be reestablished at all until the Temple is rebuilt, and all this may be ritually as well as eschatologically possible only after the advent of the messiah. The irony in such an argument is blatant: Jews in Israel will have to manage as best they can under humanitarian laws so long as full redemption has not yet come; but when, with God's help, the messiah arrives we will be able to reestablish a number of brutal laws, to which, in the final analysis, the sensitive conscience of a pious Jew in our time cannot reconcile itself. If this is a paradox, it is not the first in the history of institutional religion . . .

II

One of the great achievements in the field of political and spiritual liberty is undoubtedly freedom of religious conscience. But the concept of religious freedom includes not only the right of every citizen to belong to any religion he chooses; it also implies his right to be absolutely indifferent to all religion, or even hostile to the very idea of religious belief and practice; or, on the other hand, if he is able to do so, to live his own, purely individual religious life, without ties to any organization or institution, and to be held to account by no one as to its content. Other citizens (they may be the majority) have the right to consider anyone utterly indifferent to religion as mentally and spiritually defective, they may be convinced that anyone hostile to religion is either a pathological case or a villain, and they may freely consider as an idle boaster and phrase-monger anyone who pretends that he is religiously self-sufficient and needs no one's counsel. All this has nothing to do with the democratic state itself and the social contract upon which it must be established: the state is tolerant of every religion as well as of irreligion, except where these are opposed to the criminal code or basically violate accepted standards of public order and decorum. Such a state extends its patronage to no single religion, nor does it discriminate against any religion; it forces no citizen to carry out any religious duty or participate in any ceremony against his wish.

The draft constitution for Israel is, in general, based on the principles of tolerance and equality. It establishes no special privileges for the Jewish religion and contains no explicit discrimination against any other religion. Its shortcomings are of quite a different kind. It does not provide for a strict separation of church and state; in fact, it instructs the state to extend its protection to the three major religions of the country. In a sense one may say that instead of establishing any one religion as dominant, the constitution would provide for Jewish, Muslim, and Christian established churches on a plane of equality. Certain legal procedures which are generally regarded as organic functions of the modern state as a whole have been delegated to the "religious communities," to be administered by them under the budget of the whole state.

This is clearly seen in chapter V of the draft constitution (Articles 70–74). This chapter provides for the establishment of five kinds of courts in Israel. We cannot here describe the hierarchical order of the proposed system of courts, their rights and duties. This writer, incidentally, is in full sympathy with the principle of *appointment* of judges (by the president of the republic, upon the recommendation of certain recognized bodies) underlying the proposed judicial system. The authors of the draft constitution preferred to follow the example of England and the dominions rather than that of the United States, where a large proportion of the judiciary is directly elected by the voters. Experience has shown that the system of appointment offers greater guarantees of justice and impartial judgment, and provides more favorable conditions for an independent judiciary than does the elective system, which puts judges at the mercy of party bosses, if they wish to be certain of re-election at the end of their terms. In the present connection, we are interested in those provisions of the draft constitution which delegate certain powers to the religious communities. Questions of "personal status" (i.e., marriage, divorce, registration of births, burials, identification of parents, separation of [husband] and wife, certain aspects of inheritance, etc.) are assigned by the draft constitution to special "religious courts" of the Jewish, Muslim, and Christian communities. The judges in these courts, too, are to be appointed by the president of the republic in consultation with the minister of religious affairs, whose proposals in turn shall take into account the recommendations of the supreme religious council of the community concerned.

Upon examination of Articles 70–72, it is clear that the state is obligated under them to consider every citizen as belonging to one of the three (or more) religious communities of the country. A citizen of the State of Israel, whether he likes it or not, is automatically considered a member of one of the recognized churches or religious organizations. In certain important matters affecting him personally and the vital interests of his family, he must be either a Jew, a Christian, or a Muslim. If one is not a "Jew" (that is, he does not consider himself a member of the Jewish religious community, or is unwilling to submit to the authority of the chief rabbinate), nor a Christian by faith and belief (though his parents may have been Christians, and he may have been baptized as an infant), nor yet a Muslim, he has no official agency, according to the existing draft, to appeal to in the most vital questions of personal status. If he refuses to apply to the recognized religious courts, he has no way of legalizing or even simply registering his marriage or the birth of a child; he has no one to grant him a divorce, and it is not clear who will be responsible for probating his will, and dividing his inheritance among his heirs if he dies intestate. The draft constitution does not provide for a secular non-religious court with jurisdiction in these matters.

The State of Israel would make no provision for the personal status of atheists, agnostics, or adherents of a private religion. It is easy to see that we have here a plain violation of the principle of equal rights and personal freedom: the state assumes the character of a tripartite theocracy.

Although the draft constitution does not say so, the simple division into three religious communities, to which it repeatedly refers, could hardly be carried out in practice. The [British] mandate[45] government recognized a good many more, as the State of Israel will also undoubtedly do, but even then difficulties arose in fitting all the differences into the official framework.

This writer does not pretend to know very clearly whether the Muslims in Israel are all of the same school. But everyone knows there is no such thing in Palestine as a "Christian community." The Christian population of Israel is quite variegated. Nowhere do a Protestant, a Roman Catholic, and a Greek Orthodox Christian belong to the same religious community, nor do they in Israel. The relations between them are far from idyllic, and though they are all Christians, they lay most stress on the theological, liturgical, and other differences that divide them. Consequently, there is not, nor can there be, a supreme religious council of the "Christian community." Nobody would recognize the authority of such a council. Precisely in questions of personal status, the Christian denominations differ sharply. Most Protestant churches, for example, do not recognize the ban on marriage of first cousins; it is still maintained by the two "classical" churches, the Roman Catholic and Greek Orthodox. Roman Catholicism does not recognize divorce at all, except in rare, exceptional cases ("what God hath joined, let no man put asunder" [Mark 10:9]); the Greek Orthodox Church recognizes divorce, but requires a very painful, one might almost say pornographic procedure, proving beyond any doubt that one of the parties was guilty of sexual transgression.[46] It would certainly be impossible to bring all these variegated groups under the roof of a single "religious community," and the Israel government will undoubtedly have to recognize several Christian communities, as did the mandate government.

But, beyond this problem, why should the state force a citizen who is classified as a Catholic to accept a personal status which involves all the severe restrictions of the Roman church, if he himself does not care to observe them? Why shouldn't there be a general civil jurisdiction for anyone seeking to marry or be divorced on conditions a particular church fails to recognize? And why must anyone born a Muslim submit to the anachronistic Islamic laws about inheritance and the relations between man and wife or parents and children, if he wishes to be free of the compulsion of such laws?[47] Let the church treat such cases as it likes, or as its canon prescribes—excommunicate them, deny them salvation, or take other punitive measures. That has nothing to do with the state, which must grant its citizens the liberty to ignore such sanctions, if they choose.

There are also a number of religious groups in Israel which do not fall under the draft constitution's classification of Jews, Muslims, and Christians. The Bahai[48] group in Haifa cannot be satisfactorily assigned to the jurisdiction of any of the three major religious communities. The Druze are not Christians, even though they regard Jesus of Nazareth as one of the incarnations in which God revealed himself on earth. Nor are they Muslims, although they regard Mecca as a holy place. They are not pagans, for although their ritual contains certain elements reminiscent of ancient idolatry (What monotheistic religion is entirely free of them?), the unity of the creator is a fundamental and profoundly conceived belief among them. They have their own laws and customs concerning marriage and the family, and women occupy a far higher position socially as well as in religious functions among them than in the system of Islam. To what court should they appeal in matters of religious status, under a draft constitution which refers only to the Jewish, Muslim, and Christian "religious communities"?

The Jewish community itself in the State of Israel is not entirely homogeneous. There are [Sephardic] Jewish communities in Israel which have never adopted the ban on polygamy.[49] Should the Jewish court forbid them to marry more than one wife, or should it recognize distinct and opposed laws for different parts of the same religious community as the mandate courts did? What will be the status in Israel of Conservative synagogues and rabbis?[50] Will marriages and divorces authorized by such rabbis be considered valid by the Jewish religious courts, which will probably consist entirely of Orthodox judges? Will the children of such marriages be recognized by the courts as legitimate, or will their official documents bear the stamp of illegitimacy? What would be the status before the publicly recognized "Jewish community" in Israel of, let us say, a congregation similar to the New York Society for the Advancement of Judaism,[51] which denies that the tenet of Israel as the "chosen people" is binding upon a modern Jew, and which has deleted *Kol Nidrei*[52] from its [Yom Kippur] liturgy? Shall we say that such religious "eccentrics" are permissible among Jews in exile, in America, but cannot be allowed to exist in the State of Israel, where every Jew, whether he likes it or not, must be subject to orthodoxy? And what will be the status in Israel of Reform or Liberal Judaism,[53] some of whose rabbis, incidentally, occupy leading positions in the World Zionist Organization? Will they and their doctrines have a legitimate status before the Jewish court, or will they merely be "subjects" of the Orthodox jurisdiction? May the state delegate authority to them also in questions of personal status?

We raise these questions because the formulation in the draft constitution, instead of simplifying all these problems, makes them much more complex and involved. Even in England, where the [Anglican] church still enjoys a definitely official status, there are certain liberties which the authors of the Israel draft constitution have not sought to secure for the citizen. The king of England is still head of the church (to be sure, by some mysterious device, he manages to be an Episcopalian in England and a Presbyterian in Scotland) and only parliament may authorize changes in the prayer book (hence, comical though it may sound to our ears, it is still technically true that Jewish members of Parliament, as well as Catholics and the handful of Communists in the House of Commons, are entitled to vote on the kind of prayers which may be recited in the Anglican church). Yet the concept of civil marriage and divorce is not foreign to British jurisprudence and legal practice. In these questions, the citizen is not chained to any given ecclesiastical organization.

Many other questions arise which even further complicate the situation. The religious courts are to be maintained out of the government budget. By what right, one may ask, is a Jew by belief to be forced to pay taxes in order to maintain, let us say, a Roman Catholic religious court? Or were the authors of the draft thinking of an arrangement by which each community would pay special taxes to maintain its own courts, and the state machinery would simply enforce and collect the taxation? One may also anticipate conflict with the canon law of some of the religions. This writer is not certain whether it is acceptable to Roman Catholic or Greek Orthodox law that judges in their religious courts should be appointed—even though only nominally—by someone not among their own ordained authorities, but by a secular authority, by the president of the republic, who, incidentally, is hardly likely to be anything but a Jew.

A thoroughgoing separation of church (or churches, in this case) and state would not only be a just solution, but would also be much simpler in practice. The state can set up its civil courts and civil procedures dealing with personal status in general for all its citizens. This would not preclude the functioning of religious courts for those citizens who might wish to live under their jurisdiction. Such courts could be partly private, partly public institutions, maintained by those citizens who want them and are willing to support them. A marriage recognized by such a court could also be recognized by the state; a divorce granted by such a court would be valid in the eyes of the state, and if heirs agree to allow a religious court to divide their inheritance among them, after taxes are deducted, there is no reason for the state to interfere—just as no state would prevent its citizens from settling certain disputes by voluntary arbitration, rather than in the civil courts. Thus we do not wish to question *toleration* by Israel of religious courts, for those who want to have recourse to them. The state may even delegate, under clearly defined conditions, certain essentially governmental functions to such religious courts. What is to be criticized is the *obligatory* character of their jurisdiction over citizens—no matter how large or small their number may be—who have their own reasons, true or false, for refusing to accept it. Civil courts must be available with jurisdiction in all questions of personal status also.

One final question calls for comment. In Article 77 of the draft constitution it is stated, "Future legislation in Israel shall be guided by the basic principles of Jewish law," and "Wherever the existing law does not provide adequate guidance, the courts of law shall have recourse to these basic principles." If this Article is to be considered as something more than a mere rhetorical statement—and, of course, *every* constitution contains certain purely declamatory elements—it sets future legislative and judicial proceedings on a very obscure and dangerous road. If the criterion set up were defined as the existing Jewish normative religious law, it would, at least, constitute fairly clear instructions: in uncertain cases, one would simply consult the well-known relevant texts and, if one were sufficiently expert in this vast domain, *find* the law. But the draft constitution speaks not of *laws,* but of *basic principles* of Jewish religious jurisprudence. Such "instructions" leave open a broad field to speculative and quite subjective interpretation. The affirmation of a basic principle—or even of a major tendency—in Jewish law would depend on individual judgment and highly theoretical generalizations, which in each judge would depend on his personal background and education, his preferences and ethical valuations. This is about the same as invoking the "spirit of Judaism." How many different aspects has this "spirit of Judaism" put on in modern times, according to the individual leanings of its various portraitists!

We might learn a great deal about how dangerous such abstract instructions may be from the Soviet judicial system, as it functioned in the years following the October Revolution. At that time there was not yet in existence a codified Soviet law, and judges were instructed to decide cases according to their revolutionary legal conscience.[54] The "revolutionary conscience" showed itself in far too many cases to be extremely subjective and elastic. When judges in colonial times in Massachusetts were instructed to punish the guilty "according to the law of God," the meaning was far more concrete than that of the corresponding article in the draft constitution for Israel: for certain purposes, the Puritans regarded the Mosaic law as their chief source book. To be sure, they interpreted certain biblical laws all too literally, and thus they actually observed the commandment "thou shalt not let a witch live" [Exod. 22:18]. (In later years, Washington Irving[55] made this the occasion for his sarcastic comment that the New Englanders had to govern themselves by the laws of God until they found time to make better ones. . . .[56]) Naturally, it is not easy—especially for a layman—to propose how the courts in the young State of Israel should guide themselves in cases for which no clear legislative rule has yet been adopted and where old laws are not in accord with the constitution. It will probably take some time until Israel will work out its own system of civil and criminal normative law, and the courts in the meantime will require some temporary guidance. But more realistic methods must be sought for this purpose, since the method proposed by the authors of the draft constitution is, at best, an abstraction.

The above comments may impress some readers as reflecting an anti-religious bias. It is far from our wish to destroy religion generally and Judaism in particular. Nor do we imagine that the life being sown and nurtured and taking shape in Israel can fail to be enriched and fructified in certain ways by Jewish tradition. It is quite possible that Jewish religious life may now experience a new efflorescence in the stimulating atmosphere of its own land and in a social milieu of its own. A religious view is surely entitled to hope that the return to Zion will be accompanied by a Jewish religious renascence. But such a rebirth, if it is destined to come, must come spontaneously, not by way of a "protectionist" policy on the part of the state. The state must only secure to all believers the opportunity of a full and undisturbed life in the spirit of their faith and in harmony with their tradition. The Jewish republic can have no other obligations to the religious. It cannot force upon other citizens any religion, traditional way of life, or obedience to religious authorities. These things cannot, in any true sense, be achieved by coercion. Only in freedom can those who have wandered from the straight road (in the religious sense) be brought to repentance, and not by regimentation. Organized religion may and should seek to act through persuasion, not through authority; by its own, inner spiritual power—not by the power of the judge and the policeman.

28

Jewish Culture and Education in the Diaspora

(1951)

Hayim Greenberg delivered the following address on August 18, 1951, at the Twenty-third World Zionist Congress, the first Zionist congress to be held in the newly established State of Israel—and against the backdrop of an ongoing controversy occasioned in 1950 by Israel prime minister David Ben-Gurion's urging that young American Jews ought to immigrate to the Jewish state. Ben-Gurion's remarks led to a public dispute with Jacob Blaustein, president of the American Jewish Committee, and eventuated in a rapprochement known as the "Blaustein-Ben-Gurion Agreement" that stated the option of aliyah *"rests with the free discretion of each American Jew himself; it is entirely a matter of his own volition." In this piece, Greenberg, well known for his profound appreciation of the diaspora and undogmatic Zionist views, publicly challenged the Zionist movement* and *American Jews to rethink the nature of the Israel-America relationship as well as the place of the Jewish state in modern Jewish life. To drive home his point—and in an ironic twist given his role as head of the Jewish Agency's Department of Education and Culture—he deliberately addressed the Zionist Congress in Yiddish.*

My subject today is the problem of Jewish culture and education in the diaspora. The [Culture and Education] department [of the World Zionist Organization and the Jewish Agency for Israel] I have conducted for the past two years does not include the State of Israel in the scope of its activities. Our area of operation lies in the *galut* [exile] countries, and accordingly I must begin with a few remarks about the conception *galut* [Jewish life in exile].

In a sense, *galut* is an algebraic expression. Concretely, over the two thousand years of our dispersion, we have had varying types of exile. Our sense of living in exile was not one and the same in all periods and in all countries. The acuteness and intensity of that feeling depended upon the particular environments and civilizations in which we lived. Jews everywhere might believe the old midrashic saying: "Exile is hard, for it is equal to the weight of all the curses set forth in the anathema"[1] [B. Sanhedrin 37b], but in their concrete historical perspective, Jews differentiated between one exile and another. There were exiles that were worse, and others that were better, so to speak; exiles in which Jews sensed their foreignness, helplessness, and state of outlawry with every fiber of their being, and other exiles in which they felt themselves partially rooted, or at least enjoyed the illusion of relative integration or adjustment.

Any country outside the dreamed-of Land of Israel was exile for the Jew, yet over a period of generations Jews came to regard some of the lands of their dispersion with a sort of "at-homeness" in an alien environment. If it is a paradox, it is not one I have invented. History and social fact create their own paradoxes and ambivalences. Portugal and the Netherlands, Spain and Turkey in the fifteenth and sixteenth centuries were all, in principle, exiles. Yet it was not mere accident that refugees fled from the Iberian peninsula to the Low Countries or to the Ottoman Empire. One exile offered the Inquisition and *autos-da-fé* [Portuguese for "act of faith"][2] the other, tolerance and relative hospitality. In one exile were Marranos [crypto-Jews],[3] in the other exile a process of "de-Marranization" took place, if such an expression may be permitted. In our time, too, every country of the diaspora—every one without exception!—is *galut*. Even Israel itself was for many, many centuries, in essence, *galut*. Wherever Jews live as a minority, where they are not politically or socially independent, where they rely on the good graces of the non-Jewish majority and are subject to the everyday pressures of its civilization and mode of life, such a place is *galut*. In this respect, the United States today and, let us say, Iraq, are both "exiles," in the broad psycho-historical sense. But the concrete difference between the two is unspeakably great. Jews are compelled to flee from Iraq; no one drives them out of any part of America. If, in a general sense, exile may be conceived of symbolically as night, then there are some exiles of pitch-black night, and some where the night is moonlit.

In rough generalities, the exile complex of our day may be divided into three main areas.

The first zone of *galut* is that to which we have no access whatever and from which no one can emerge. Expulsion is a calamity in the life of a people; but in some situations it is still greater torture to be incarcerated without any visible prospect of ever being freed. It would be a bitter jest if I were to pretend to outline any principles or methods for cultural activities among the Jews in the vastness of the hermetically sealed Soviet prison.[4]

The second zone includes countries of a feudal and Islamic social structure and way of life. Jews are among the oldest inhabitants of those countries, but in none of them does any Jew today have a sense of security, and the roots they have struck there may be torn out by brutal hands at any moment. The Jews of those countries must depart as soon as possible from their step-motherlands and settle in Israel. Indeed, they are doing it before our very eyes, and we may hope that in a relatively short time they will break free from the intolerable situation to which they are doomed in that part of the world.[5]

The United States and England are typical countries of the third zone of the *galut*. A very substantial part of our people today resides in Western countries with traditions of liberty, with a high order of civilization and technological development, with progressive economies creating sound opportunities for achieving in time modern standards of social justice. Those countries do not constitute for Jews the best of all possible worlds. But it would be wrong to say that Jews have not struck roots there, that they are totally unintegrated, or that they are faced with immediate threats to their existence. Jews have already attained there a degree of relative well-being economically, and though they are socially segregated to no small extent, still they are not regarded by the majority as aliens in the sense they are so branded in backward countries or countries experiencing the convulsions of a perverse nationalism.

As I have already remarked, I have no remedy for the Jewish communities in Russia and the Soviet satellite countries. They can neither appeal to us, nor can we bring them consolation and encouragement. The way is barred, and who knows when or how it will be reopened.

In the second zone—the Arabic speaking countries and the Muslim area generally—our cultural tasks are not easy, but they are not too complex either. Our educational aims in that zone must be concentrated upon preparation for resettlement in Israel—[Hebrew] language training, ideological, and also technical and professional readjustment. In that zone there are hardly any differences of opinion among Jews as to their situation and prospects. The State of Israel is their only aspiration.

However, we cannot apply the same simple approach to the third zone—the Jewish communities in the democratic West, and particularly the five million Jews of the United States. Mass emigration is not currently on the agenda of American Jewry. You may adopt here as many resolutions as you please concerning the "ingathering of the exiles," asserting that it also applies to the Western communities, including American Jewry—[World Zionist] Congress resolutions are not effective in creating either pressure or active will toward migration.[6] American Jewry especially is far from a panic situation. There are diaspora communities in a state of "self-liquidation," without benefit of congress resolutions, "Jerusalem Programs,"[7] or other exhortations. The Jewish community in the American *galut* is not today prepared to "liquidate" itself through migration to Israel. This does not mean that American Jews will never settle in Israel at all. It should not be interpreted as an assertion that a time can never come when a massive number of American Jews will become full participants in the drama of redemption which is unfolding in Israel. But it is not something to be achieved simply by adding a new paragraph to the Zionist *vade mecum* [Latin for "go with me"].[8]

I have heard this argument in the past few days: "You, American Jews, are an alien body in the organism of the American people; you are cherishing vain illusions; you forget that other Jews had the same illusions in other countries, and you know what happened to them." May I say here that such prognostications make no great impression on the average American Jew. He has no reason to consider his position as ideal, but he has become conditioned to believe that "it can't happen here." Not without justification, he regards the American Revolution as the most successful revolution in world history. He is prepared "to boast" that even though political shifts occur in American affairs and occasionally threatening omens of reaction appear on the horizon, there never was an American counterrevolution, nor does any prospect of one appear in the future, at least as indicated in present realities. He persuades himself that America shows a rational patriotism, but none of that nationalistic mythology that led Germany astray, making it drunk and toxic with political idolatry.

Such a typical American Jew may be wrong, unrealistic, and you may say that in his blindness he fails to note the handwriting on the wall. Others may be convinced that their prognosis is the correct one, that Western Jewry generally, and American Jewry in particular, face more or less the same dangers that befell so large a part of European Jewry, but no one can make him feel these threats as actual. May I add one thing more? It is difficult to refute the argument that if America is doomed in time to become a land of fascist antisemitism, a Gehenna [Greek for "purgatory"][9] for its millions of Jews, then there may be no safety even in timely flight to the Jewish state. If we should ever see a bestialized America, how long could the State of Israel exist in a world capable of producing such a monster, even should Israel's population be increased by several million Jews? There is no room for redemption in a monstrous world, amidst universal wickedness. If the time ever comes, as I believe it will, when considerable numbers of American Jews will go to live in Israel, they will do so not because America will have ejected them, but out of Israel's attraction and inspiration, not in fear, but in love. At the present time, I can see no such trend in American Jewish life. Zionism has not become a matter of direct personal bearing for the bulk of American Jewry, nor will it become such a matter unless the younger generation receives a deeper and more organic Jewish education in coming years. The same may be said, with certain modifications, concerning the Jews in a number of other countries of the democratic West, where a flow of *aliyah* may be hoped for, but where propaganda for mass *flight* would be utterly meaningless.

Whoever enjoys futile gestures may adopt a tone of simple, very simple, Zionist "consistency" and address American Jews in such terms as these: "Have no fond illusions that you are Americans; the genuine Americans regard you as *strangers*; you are not an organic part of the American scene, and your citizenship, in the final analysis, hardly amounts to anything; better make up your minds to leave America as soon as possible, and if you cannot arrange your transport to Israel at once, seriously consider yourselves in the meantime as potential Israelis, and educate your children toward the objective of migration." This would be an appeal for the mental "denaturalization" of American Jews. If anyone feels entitled to demand this of American Jews, or even only of American Zionists, then let him take consistency a step further and say: "Be honest with yourselves and with your non-Jewish neighbors, and do not keep a double set of accounts. You are not, and can never hope to be, an accepted part of America, and therefore you ought to act already as 'temporary sojourners' in the country. Accept no nominations to [the US] Congress or the state legislatures. Occupy no governorships, supreme court seats, or other magistracies. Accept no professorships in American colleges and universities. Recall from their posts the thousands of Jewish men and women teaching in municipal [public] schools and sharing, whether for good or ill, in molding the character of American youth. Do no service on the police force, accept no commissions in the American army, refrain from participating in American journalism and literature, in art, theatre and music. Take no stand on political questions. In short, 'denaturalize' yourselves, if not technically, then at least morally, socially, and intellectually." This, at least, would be complete doctrinal consistency, but I have yet to see a delegate at this [Zionist] Congress with "courage" enough to make such a demand on American Jewry, and we can all learn something from this lack of courage. . . .

It is an easy transition for me to pass to another proposition which should not arouse controversy among us, if we do not adhere to fruitless dogmatism. The American Jew (and wherever I use the word "American" my remarks might equally well be applied to a number of other Western countries) is bound by objective circumstances to live in a certain cultural dualism which must naturally be reflected in his educational processes. Culturally, he is at one and the same time both an American and a Jew. Whoever wishes may argue that such a dualism is unhealthy, "abnormal." Cultural monism may be regarded as a much more normal condition than a person's living in the spheres of two cultures. But none of us has the power to create monistic wholeness by decree. A certain degree of cultural integration with the milieu is inevitable for Jews wherever they live as a minority in a country of high civilization, and criteria of "normality" and "abnormality" are irrelevant when applied to situations of objective inevitability. Of course, the degree of cultural integration I have referred to involves considerable danger of assimilation, but in a *galut* situation there is always such danger, and we already agreed to classify the West (including America) as *galut*, though of a different sort than the one of Morocco or Iran. Now, in order to avoid harmful complexes as well as conflicts with their environment, Jews in the West must clearly and boldly declare their cultural dualism and uphold its legitimacy. If some see in this a "double set of accounts," we need not argue over terms and expressions. I am prepared to accept this description. What causes friction and trouble is not so much "double" or parallel accounts, as the keeping of *secret* accounts. The American Jew has the right to identify himself as a Jew, to live a Jewish cultural life (if he possesses the necessary vitality and content), to preserve and, if he can, revitalize his own cultural values, but on one condition: if he does it openly, if he makes no secret of it, if he tells his non-Jewish fellow-citizens about it in all honesty. I would deplore the spiritual and moral fate of any country that imposed among the duties of citizenship an obligation of amnesia, of becoming oblivious of oneself, of erasing one's memories, one's past, one's intimate group relationships. I know that no man of sense in America demands from American Jews such a spiritual suicide, such a self-abduction from the Jewish folk from which they stem.

In the West we face no problem of combating assimilation as a dictum imposed from above or from "around," nor even as a formal ideology among Jews. The chief danger is that of plain indifference to the whole matter of being a Jew. Zionism as such, or rather merely platonic Zionism—which is no less platonic even when it takes the form of helping Israel from a distance—is not enough to stimulate the will in Jews outside Israel to live as Jews, to have a taste for Jewish life and sense a meaning in it. If one is not to be indifferent to Jewish survival and to one's own belonging to Jewry, one must be imbued with the content and values of Jewish culture and Jewish spirit. This cannot be achieved by propaganda. It demands a more fundamental and organic Jewish education than is given to a great portion of Western Jewry in our time. From the standpoint of Jewish survival in the West, consequently, education to "Jewishness" is far more vital than what we call specifically "Zionist education." One can never be a "Zionist by will" (in contrast to a merely sentimental Zionist) if one is not a "Jew by will," if one lacks the awareness of participating in the long, dramatic history of being a Jew.

The living Israel is, naturally, a far more effective stimulus for diaspora Jews in strengthening the will to maintain and cultivate their Jewish identity than is Zionism as a doctrine or a *Weltanschauung*. But the influence of present-day Israel can be a fertilizing factor for Jewish cultural life in the diaspora only on one condition: if the civilization of Israel should lean on certain, so to speak, extra-geographical elements in traditional Jewish culture, elements that have demonstrated their capacity to survive without the support and nourishment of a national soil.

I find it hard to express this point clearly, and I should like as far as possible to avoid using abstract or philosophical terms. In a sense one may say that the Jews have for many centuries—throughout the so-called *galut* period—lived more in the sphere of *time* than in the sphere of *space*, or perhaps more in the sphere of "music" than in the sphere of the "plastic." Plastic art is quite inconceivable apart from space. A painting, a sculptural or architectural work, must occupy room or ground; a melody is spaceless. Basically, it has no way of grasping what space is; it exists, moves, and makes its way in the dimension of time. In a symbolic sense, Jewish culture was more of the historical and musical type than of the geographic and plastic type, and from this point of view, until a few generations ago, the *galut* was perhaps the only example in history (at any rate, the most prominent example) of an ex-territorial civilization. Undoubtedly, a civilization without a soil of its own, without territorial bounds, is from many angles an abnormal phenomenon. But Jews were successful in sublimating this abnormality. They brought something with them into exile which I might seek to compare, if I were a poet, to Father Jacob's visionary (yet still real) ladder, which requires no more space than a ladder needs for its support in order to reach to heaven ("a ladder set up on the earth and the top of it reached to heaven") [Gen. 28:12–13]. And, looking backward, who can say today that the almost fantastic history of the Jew was without significance, or dull, or fruitless? Upon vast expanses of time and apparently out of nothing more than memories, strivings, and aspirations, our people created such grand structures as the Babylonian Talmud, the palaces of Kabbalah and Hasidism, the gardens of medieval philosophy and poetry, the self-discipline and inspirational ritualism of the *Shulkhan Arukh* [Prepared Table][10] the color and aroma of Sabbaths and holidays. All these to a great extent are creations of the *galut*, ex-territorial conquests, and however onerous was our isolation from the world we lived in, still it gave us a sense of aristocratic exclusiveness, of lineage, of superiority. We were without territory—yet possessed of clear and fixed boundaries that Jews devotedly guarded; without armies—and yet so much heroism; without a Temple—and yet so much sanctity; without a priesthood—and yet each Jew, in effect, a priest; without kingship—and yet with such unexcelled spiritual "sovereignty." Should we be ashamed of the exile? I am proud of it, and if *galut* was a calamity (Who can pretend it was not?), I am proud of what we were able to perform in that calamity. Let others be ashamed of what they did to us in exile. We have every reason to consider our exilic past with heads proudly lifted. None of us would idealize a prison; but let those be ashamed who torment in prisons the better representatives of mankind, not those captives who in the darkness of their prison cell were inspired to compose paeans to freedom and truth.

True, the *galut* in which Jews live today is no longer that in which they lived so many generations in the past. The Jewish capacity for living creatively as a people in the sphere of time alone has been sadly depleted. This is neither the place nor the time to analyze the historical causes that deprived us of that rather unique capacity. But we know—and this is one of the most important elements of the Zionist idea—that not only our political and socioeconomic position in many countries of the diaspora, but also our spiritual and cultural situation everywhere demand that we resume national life in the sphere of space, of territorial rootedness, and of political independence. It is needless to explain to a Zionist Congress that without such a return to the soil, without building anew a Jewish landscape, we face a general withering of our spiritual life. The spiritual *Judennot* [German for "Jewish plight"] was by no means the least among the factors that gave force and momentum to the Zionist movement and to the actual building of Zion.

I would be less than honest with you if I failed to note in a few words a new spiritual danger which may arise from the accentuation—or rather, the hyperemphasis—of our new orientation toward space. In some circles one no longer talks of *Jewish culture* but of *Israeli culture*. This term is used (perhaps only in restricted circles) with clear reference to the state, as though in the three and a half years of its existence there has already arisen a characteristic or original culture of the State of Israel. I do not intend now to discuss the general relations between state and culture. A state can stir and quicken a people's spirit and establish a sound environment for its cultural development; but sometimes a state can also throttle, degrade, and stultify a people's spiritual life. It depends on what sort of state it is, what it does with its citizens, or, more properly perhaps, what its citizens do with it. But the best of states, even the ideal one, has no power to produce an original or characteristic culture of its own in a few years' time. Least of all does it possess this power if it regards itself as an end in itself, if it apotheosizes itself and cuts itself off from the spiritual history of its people, from its past, and from the values created in the past. When I hear so frequently the verse "For from Zion shall go forth Torah" [Isa. 2:3] reverently quoted with reference to the Zion of our day, the present state in Zion, I too believe, as others do, that new and lofty cultural values will in time be created here—values of universal scope and significance. But for the present I should rather rephrase it to say "For from Zion *went forth* the Torah"; a Torah once came forth from this land, and in virtue of that Torah, later, generation upon generation, in one exile after another, Jews created spiritual values which bear the stamp of creative effort and achievement. Those values and the psychic energies embodied in them must continue to be cultivated on the soil of the State of Israel, no doubt in new forms, with new stresses, and by different methods; they must be the foundation of that new civilization that is beginning—with much more severe birth pangs than many of us preferred to imagine—to emerge in the State of Israel. There will be no culture of tomorrow without a culture of yesterday and of the remoter past, unless we want to reconcile ourselves to a shallow pseudo-cultural style attuned to the local ethnography and narrow horizons of a small irritably nationalistic state.

But our cultural history of the recent and remote past is stocked with elements bearing the stamp "Made in *galut*." Should we refuse to recognize them because of this stamp? I pose this question not because I attach great weight to such a pathological phenomenon as the small group of "Canaanites"[11] with their penchant for a "blood and soil" nationalism,[12] for a futurism that pretends to find support in ancient Semitic paganism. A trace of this lunatic "Canaanitism" is to be found among other, far broader, and by no means clinical groups, and its presence is enough to indicate certain perils. It is from these quarters that there arises a contempt for the recent Jewish past in the *galut*, for the so-called "ghetto Jew," his style, his values, his way of life; that contempt to which not long ago an Israeli Hebrew writer devoted a pamphlet of such signal brilliance. I refer to [Avraham] Kariv[13] and to his book *Adaberah veyirvah li* ["Let me speak, then, and get relief" (1950)].[14] At bottom, it is an appeal for a renewed Hebrew humanism, lacking which the civilization of the State of Israel may be led into false and sterile paths and prove incapable of exercising any significant cultural influence on Jewish life abroad.

During these few days of the [Zionist] Congress we have heard several times the slogan of "Hebraizing the *galut*." I need hardly declare here that such a slogan is far from alien to me and my like. I accept it with all my heart, but what is its substantial content and aim? Simply to diffuse knowledge of the Hebrew language in diaspora countries, primarily because it is today the official language of a Jewish state? This, too, is certainly a worthy aim toward which we must all strive. But Hebrew has credentials that antedate the reborn Jewish state, and, as we all know, it is neither an accident nor the result of an individual's perseverance that Hebrew has won the position it enjoys, and today still displays such vigor and élan, such dynamic force and elasticity.

In our time, almost simultaneously with the Jewish state, one of the oldest and noblest nations in the world, India, also experienced its national rebirth.[15] I am revealing nothing everyone here does not already know when I note that the official language of the Indian Union is still English, the language of the former occupying power, the invader, from whose yoke that great country has just been freed. India still lacks a common national language that could bind together all its provinces and ethnic components, even though the Indians—let us not forget—lived continuously in their own land for the whole extent of their long history. Take a second example: Ireland. Nominally, independent Eire has its own official language, Gaelic. But in fact, how many of the Irish speak Gaelic? How large and how widely distributed is their Gaelic literature? In what language are their newspapers and journals published? What language is chiefly used in their parliament? The Irish have had no great success in their attempts to revive Gaelic even in the period of full political independence, and English, the language of the historic "foe," is still actually the language of Ireland. The Irish, like the Jews, have their own diaspora, and by no means a small one, but the several million Irishmen who live in their homeland have always lived there, have never emigrated, have been continuously rooted in their own soil and milieu. Why then were they unable to do for Gaelic what we did for Hebrew? We succeeded not because we are more skilled than they, but because Hebrew in all generations was our sacred tongue, while Gaelic was never for the Irish more than a folk tongue, part of a local ethnographic culture. For many centuries, even since the days of St. Patrick,[16] Ireland's sacred tongue was the same as in all Roman Catholic countries, the universal denationalized Latin language, not their own tongue. Hebrew was able to exist for two thousand years, without state or territory, and not as a museum exhibit but as a functional organ, because the language itself was a kind of a "territory," a spiritual "home," and because the *pathos* of Jewish life and creativity, of inner Jewish struggles and victories, was chiefly expressed in the Hebrew language. Hebrew in our own time had the power of becoming a secular vernacular not in spite of but because of the fact that for so many generations it was our sacred tongue. If Hebrew (together with its sister language, Aramaic,[17] in certain periods) had not been the organ of sublimation in Jewish life, it would long have become a dead language. If one takes the modern Hebrew of Israel, of which we are so justly proud, it is not simply a fresh new growth sprouted from the soil in a few decades. Modern Hebrew would have been impossible if it had not sprung from the stock of "*galut* Hebrew"—the prose of Mendele Moykher Sforim,[18] the essay style of Ahad Haam,[19] the poetry of [Haim Nahman] Bialik,[20] and the recreation of Sholem Aleichem[21] by [Yitzhak Dov] Berkovitch.[22] But this "*galut* Hebrew" itself drew its sustenance from the depths of traditional Hebrew, from the *lingua sancta* [Latin for "sanctified tongues"] from a spiritual stream which contained much more than nationalism, from the Jewish reservoir of great collective and individual spiritual endeavors. Without that background—without the background of Judaism in the broad historical sense—Hebrew in Israel today, if it existed at all, would be a kind of Esperanto for immigrants bringing a Babel of tongues,[23] perhaps no more than a pidgin Hebrew. But, of course, without that background Zionism itself would probably not exist.

If my observations are generally correct, then they apply both to Israel and the diaspora, and with particular force to the latter. The fundamental objective of Jewish education in the diaspora is thus, in my view, not Zionism, in the specific or programmatic sense of the word, but *Jewishness*. Zionism should be the natural product of an organic education to Jewishness, the culmination, not the point of departure. Without such education, Zionism may be a doctrine, a convincing theory, a program, a plan, an undertaking of desperate urgency, an appeal to sentiment, a noble humanitarian enterprise, but not a profound creative experience. Hebrew is naturally a very, very important element in this sort of education, but I should prefer to use the term "Hebraism" rather than "Hebrew." I use the word Hebraism here not in that polemical sense which in our time signifies an extreme language preference, a purely linguistic shibboleth, but in the same way that I should use such a term, for example, as Hellenism. Hellenism is more than the Greek language, more than ancient Greek mythology or religion, more than the art of Greek antiquity. It is a current in the infinite ocean of mankind's searching, of humanity's passionate will to find security within itself, an anchorage in the cosmos in the striving toward truth, beauty, and harmony. Judaism, too, is such a mighty current. All civilizations, even the greatest and most sumptuous, are more experiment than consummation. But a viable civilization, one that has not reached exhaustion in its experimenting with itself and still contains potentialities of self-renewal, rejuvenation, and new modulations, should rather be compared to a melody than to a sculpture. Ancient Egyptian civilization, for instance, has long been no more than statuary which can produce no new life. It has more archaeological than historical significance. We have every reason to regard Judaism not in terms of a completed plastic "petrification" but in terms of melody, and melody—precisely because the "area" of its existence is time—has in principle an unending continuity. There is always room for possible variations, even for creative mutations, deviations, and complementary contrasts for new experiments upon itself, but such experiments as do not lose their link (their "memory") with the past, and with those forces that created the past.

That brings us, willingly or not, to the question of religion. But religion is not something sealed away somewhere in private seclusion, without relation to a people's, or to humanity's, culture. Religion is itself culture, and I am inclined to believe that, potentially, it is indeed the peak of all possible cultural achievement. I should not wish to speak at length on the subject, but it has so transpired that Judaism, Jewish culture, was chiefly religious in its most significant manifestations. In other words, the archetypal motivation of the Jewish people, its struggles with itself, with the despotism of nature, and the pressure of the peoples of the world, sought religious channels, religious implements, and religious forms for their expression. The chief tensions of the Jewish collective psyche were religious; its energies spoke to themselves and to the world of their ethical-religious drama, in a sacred tongue. Abstract from the skein of our fate the strand of religious drama, especially in our long, martyred exile, and any attempt to interpret Jewish history becomes senseless. Jewish life over the past two thousand years was either a mystery (and a mystery has meaning and destination) or a misunderstanding. I assume that it was a mystery, and I would be sorry for Zionism, for the whole ideal of Jewish renaissance, if it could be regarded as the product of something incongruous, of a historical *faux pas*. I have compared Judaism to a melody. If I should be held to this analogy, then Genesis is the prelude to the melody, the messianic era (in the striving toward it, not in achieved historical reality) its epilogue, while "Let there be!"[24] is its recurrent refrain. Thus it is quite unnecessary to be religious in a dogmatic or institutional sense of the word, to be orthodox—if I were to use American parlance, I should say it is unnecessary to be a fundamentalist—in order to recognize the inseparable significance in our embodiments of the Jewish religious genius.

I am far from being unappreciative of the importance of diffusing in the diaspora, let alone Israel itself, the knowledge of Hebrew—modern, spoken, so to say practical Hebrew. I see in this, first of all, a sort of social medium of contact between Jews abroad, as well as between Israeli Jews themselves, speaking as they do such a multitude of languages brought over from their old homes. But may I be permitted to say that a Jew who can name all the plants in Israel in Hebrew, or call all the parts of a tractor or some other complicated machine by their correct designations (in new Hebrew coinages), possesses one qualification for useful service in the State of Israel. And who among us could fail to see in this not merely a technical or utilitarian but a cultural value as well? But if he does not know to their deepest sounding and in their context of spiritual tensions such Hebrew expressions as *mizvah* [divine commandment], *averah* [transgression], *geulah* [redemption], *tikkun* [repair], *tumah* [impurity], *taharah* [ritual purity], *yirah* [fear], *ahavah* [love], *zedakah* [righteousness], *hesed* [lovingkindness], *mesirut nefesh* [self-abnegation], *kidush hashem* [sanctification of the name], *dvekut* [cleaving (to God)], *teshuvah* [repentance], he cannot carry a part in that choir that gives voice, consciously or not, to what I have called "the Jewish melody." Even so-called secular Jewish education in Israel and in the *galut* as well, if it is not to be drained of those powers that build a Jewish personality, must therefore be nourished from sources which are regarded, at least formally, as religious.

I do not propose a detailed practical program nor a curriculum for Jewish schools. It is much to be doubted whether I am the man for such a task. I have simply tried today, perhaps too abstractly, to sketch the lines along which our thought should be directed. The Hebrew language must naturally occupy a central place in our whole folk pedagogy; there can be no Hebraism without a sound background in Hebrew. This does not mean, however, that in my opinion we should use in our educational processes Hebrew exclusively, or that we must wait until the bulk of the people will wish, and be able, to learn Hebrew in such a measure that the language becomes a source of enjoyment, without which genuine spiritual experience is impossible. In conveying the values of what I call "Hebraism" at various stages and to various strata of our people in *galut*, we shall have to use other languages, too. Regardless of what fate may hold in store for it in the future, we shall have to use Yiddish, too, for those Jews to whom the language still has an organic, intimate relation, making them receptive to cultural influences. We shall also have to use non-Jewish languages, foreign to Jews as a collectivity but native to or fully acquired by millions of individual Jews who live and grow spiritually through them.

Such earnest, deep-plowing, cultural work permeated with Jewish individuality will in time, I am certain, bring forth a profounder Zionism, an appreciation of our historic drama, and an active will to play a role in it. It will lead even to *haluzism* [Zionist pioneering] which will draw its strength from the depths of Jewish being. Only such an organic and wide-ranging educational program can create in the *galut* the inner resolution to identify oneself in full, in deed, with the grand process of Jewish revival.

Such a program is not easy. It cannot be accomplished or even adequately prepared overnight. No one in this hall, perhaps, knows better than I how great are the difficulties of carrying out such a task in the diaspora. More than once in the course of the work one feels as if pouring wine into a broken cask. But I believe that without this work Zionism is doomed, especially in the advanced and free lands of the West, to become ever drabber, duller, more anemic and withered.

In the final historical analysis, the State of Israel should be interested in the spiritual growth of diaspora Jewry no less than the Jews of the *galut* themselves. All Jewish roads—sooner or later, directly or indirectly, with landmarks or without them—lead to the same destination: to *Erez Israel*.

29
The Future of American Jewry
(1951)

Hayim Greenberg delivered the following address on April 10, 1951, to a conference of the New York Board of Rabbis. Originally established in 1881 as a transdenominational association, the board grew to include rabbis affiliated with Reform, Conservative, and Orthodox Judaism and, somewhat later, rabbis from other walks of American Jewish life. It is likely that Mordecai M. Kaplan (1881–1983), the founder of Reconstructionist Judaism, Israel Goldstein (1896–1986), rabbi of Congregation Bnai Jeshurun, or Dr. Louis Finkelstein (1895–1991), chancellor of the Jewish Theological Seminary of America—leading communal figures with whom Greenberg was friendly and shared an expansive view of the American Jewish diaspora, Jewish moral and spiritual values, and Israel in modern Jewish life—arranged for Greenberg's appearance before the New York gathering. (For an interesting parallel, see also Greenberg's address to the Conservative movement's rabbinical conference four years earlier: "Present Prospects for a Jewish Palestine," reprinted in Proceedings of the Rabbinical Assembly of America *11 [1947]: 161–169.)*

I stand before you and I wonder: How did it come about that you invited me to address your conference? I was never ordained a rabbi. I am probably the only one here who never attended a *yeshivah*, nor a modern substitute for a *yeshivah*. I also cannot boast of religious scholarship. I even suspect that those who invited me did not check to which of the three types of religious institutions[1] which are united in your organization for specific purposes I belong, or even whether I belong to any congregation. Was this invitation a misunderstanding, or an expression of undeserved confidence in me? Be that as it may, the fact that I gladly accepted your invitation—which I regard as a great compliment to me—does not testify to much modesty on my part.

I will no doubt digress from the limits which you assigned for my talk: "Jewish Life in the Second Half of the Twentieth Century." None of us is a prophet, and to the extent that we permit ourselves to make prognoses, we must not confine them to specific dates or sharply defined periods. In any case, I will make my assignment both easier and more convenient. Instead of offering solutions to problems, I will limit myself to analyzing the existing condition. I realize that defining a problem is only half the job, but [neither, according to Rabbi Tarfon, is it] . . . "incumbent upon (me) to complete it" [Pirkei Avot 2:21].

Not long ago, while traveling from France to Israel on a Jewish ship, I was present at a discussion between some rabbis of the eastern European type. One of them asked: "Since, thank God, there now exists a Jewish state, may we not say that redemption has become a reality, and since our two-thousand-year old hope has been realized, is it not time to do away with *Tisha Beav* [the Ninth of Av]?"[2] An older rabbi pondered the question and decided: In a general sense, it is permissible to do away with this fast day. But, he added, he was inclined to wait till the other half of Jerusalem, where the Temple once stood and where the Wailing Wall[3] is now, as well as other Jewish holy places are, pass from Arab possession to Israel.[4] It was the youngest of the rabbis who vehemently protested:

"Nothing has happened to justify doing away with *Tisha Beav*," he said. The State of Israel? He did not deny that its existence was a very important event which should inspire the heart of every pious Jew. But its existence had nothing to do with redemption, for the time being. What was it we mourned during so many generations at our midnight vigils? And why did we fast and weep each year on the ninth day of [the Hebrew month of] Av? Was it because the Jewish state had been destroyed? But *Erez Israel* had not been an independent Jewish land for a good many years before the destruction of the Second Temple. *Erez Israel* had been a Roman province, a kind of protectorate of the Roman Empire.[5] Large numbers of Jews already lived in dispersion before the flames consumed the Temple. Does it mean, then, that we mourned the Temple itself, and not the state? But what does it signify to mourn for the Temple? Because we lost a valuable building? Who can say with assurance that there had been no political opportunities during the years to rebuild the Temple? Nobody can prove that even under Roman rule there had not been liberal periods when we could have rebuilt the Temple without interference, had we given guarantees that the rebuilt Temple would not become the focus of a movement of liberation from Roman political rule. . . . On *Tisha Beav*, he continued, we have been mourning for generations because of something else . . . because of the dominion of Edom[6] in the world. More than the walls of Jerusalem had been destroyed. The spirit of Edom triumphed over the spirit of Jerusalem. At that time Edom was known as Rome. But Rome had no monopoly on the Edom spirit. Every generation, or every few generations, Edom rises under a new name and rules the world. The names change, but the evil and the uncleanness remain the same. Now, I ask, he continued, has Edom been overcome? Does the spirit of Jerusalem rule in the world? Are we, Jews, entirely free of the Edom spirit? And now that a Jewish state exists, does its spirit prevail in the world? And, let us be honest with ourselves, is the Jewish state itself a kingdom of heaven? Can it be such today, with us as we are, ridden with evil desires, consumed with envies and hatreds? Is redemption something that comes from outside and has nothing to do with the inner being? No. *Tisha Beav* must still be preserved whether half or all of Jerusalem is in Jewish hands, and midnight mourning must go on. . . .

It is not necessary that I identify myself with that young rabbi in order to understand him. I quoted him because he expressed a specific, and historically very important, aspect of the Jewish attitude toward the world and themselves. From a broad historical perspective he regarded the emergence of the Jewish state as a kind of equalization with the nations of the world. Other nations have independent states; now we too have one. For two thousand years we had been politically castrated. Today we are no longer so, both in our own estimation and also in the eyes of the world. It is a great event, this young rabbi agrees, but it is not redemption. He regards redemption as a moral, spiritual, and religious concept, and not as a political or economic idea. He does not regard the desire to be "like other nations" [1 Sam. 8:4–20] as an ideal. He regards the existence of the Jewish people as a divine drama on a universal scale, and no local epilogue in the form of a small or large Jewish state constitutes, in his estimation, the conclusion of that unique drama.

But neither the State of Israel and the Jews who live in it, nor even the ones who will in time settle there, are the subject of our present discussion. I will not undertake this evening to project an image of Israel one generation or two or three hence. But whatever the spiritual face of Israel may be in the future, the Jews who live there will remain Jews. Their existence as a people is assured and their unique and specific Jewish image will not be blurred. It is the Jews who live in *galut* [exile], those Jews who will remain in the diaspora for many generations, or perhaps forever, that are our problem. From the standpoint of their spiritual destiny and continuity, it is the Jews in America who are our problem.

We have been living here for three centuries altogether. We began our life here as a minute, unwanted, barely tolerated, and unambitious group. One of the very first documents pertaining to Jewish life in America always saddens me. This was a petition which the Jews of New Amsterdam[7] addressed to Peter Stuyvesant[8] requesting that he permit them to purchase a plot of land for a cemetery.[9] Jewish communal possession in America thus began, if I do not err, with a small cemetery in Chatham Square in New York[10] which they bought in 1655—not with a house of prayer or a school or a *yeshivah* or a club, but with a cemetery—a piece of land to assure Jewishness after death and not for the continuation of life as Jews. In time, other Jews came in greater numbers and the external as well as the internal situation of the Jewish community changed. American Jews never displayed any conscious, programmatic assimilatory tendencies such as prevailed among western European Jews commencing with the last generation of the eighteenth century. As a general rule the Jews tried to strike roots in America and at the same time to preserve their traditional and specific image.

There may be differences of opinion regarding the degree to which Jews have become rooted in America (and how strong and secure these roots are), but it is a fact that our right to live here as Americans and as Jews is not questioned. It is true also that, without any intent on the part of the law or of the authorities to erase Jewish identity, pressures producing this effect are consciously or unconsciously exerted by the environment to which we are subject. Rabbi Isaac Mayer Wise,[11] basically a traditional Jew whose destiny it was to lay a strong foundation for the Reform movement[12] in America, once stated (naturally employing the terms and images of his time): "There [were] Episcopalian Jews in New York, Quaker Jews in Philadelphia, Huguenot Jews in Charleston, [and so on], everywhere [according to the prevailing] sect."[13] His statement was no doubt exaggerated, but no one will deny that, no matter how Jewish we feel and how hard we try to preserve our Jewishness, the surrounding environment imposes its stamp upon us. It were not normal were it otherwise. The question is how great is this American influence today and how much greater is it likely to become in time, and whether there does not exist a grave danger that the specific Jewishness of which we are still the bearers may not in time become totally atrophied.

It would be pointless to harbor illusions, or to resort to patent medicines to guarantee our continued vital existence. Cultural Zionists of a certain type tried to console themselves, as well as us, with the idea of a "spiritual center" in Israel which would in time replenish Jews all over the world. The light of a new, independent Jewish life in a Jewish land will no doubt reach far out and will warm and nourish and illuminate our lives. No one here will deny that diaspora Jews who possess a vitality of their own will become still more vital and creative under the influence of the inspiration emanating from a Jewish center which is completely autonomous. But whence will we replenish a more or less permanent vitality of our own when it threatens to become ever weaker, paler, more desiccated under the pressure of the forceful non-Jewish environment within which we are a minority? From diaspora culturists[14] we have heard their own remedy: Cultivate the Yiddish language and you will have vitality. Yiddish saves from death. Others proclaimed: Cultivate Hebrew and you will have genuine vital continuity. I cannot oppose the cultivation of Yiddish, and still less so can I be opposed to cultivating Hebrew. But I know that there was a time when Jews survived without either Yiddish or Hebrew; and in another epoch they cultivated these languages (though they did not employ this term and did not do so programmatically) not in order to draw vitality from them, but precisely because they already possessed vitality, because they had the will to live and the energies to nourish that will.

What was the secret of our ability to remain firm in our Jewishness during so many generations despite the fact that we were everywhere a minority, and a severely persecuted one at that? I realize that it is very seldom that anyone has something new to offer in a discussion of this question. The explanation is, if you care, an oft-repeated one, and yet it is necessary to repeat it again and again, especially in the light of our new experience with ourselves.

Until recent times we were, fundamentally, not a minority. We were a minority statistically only, but not psychologically. A soloist in a large philharmonic orchestra is not a minority of one among scores of other musicians. The early Christians who were persecuted in pagan Rome were not a minority in the sense in which we should understand this term. The Quakers in England three hundred years ago were spiritually not a minority, though numerically they were insignificant. In the area of spiritual influences and cultural pressures we are justified in using the terms "majority" and "minority" only when we deal with two groups which are basically more akin than they are different; when the less numerous, statistical minority differs from its environment in matters which it does not regard as sanctities. Jews survived as a numerical and persecuted minority in an alien world not because they were a separate *tribe*, a distinct *people* (in the modern, nationalist sense), or a different *race*. Tribes, peoples, racial groups disappeared many times when they mingled with others more numerous and stronger than they. The world cemetery is filled with the graves of such dead entities. We were also a distinct people with specific characteristics of a people; perhaps we were also a separate racial group. But it is not these that gave us vitality and continuity. While we were all these things, we were at the same time also something else: an exclusive group of believers, the Congregation of Israel. This is much more than a group sharing common memories (time and environment frequently eradicate group memories and eliminate them as influencing factors); it is more than blood kinship. In other words, we survived not simply because we were a people—how many peoples did not Jews see go under in the course of their long history, so that not a trace was left of them—but because we were a "chosen people" with a special place in the history of the world, and a central position in the destiny of the cosmos as such.

It is not important how any of us understands the chosenness element in the Jewish religion. Personally, I am inclined to believe that it is possible to be a Jew without faith in this chosenness. It was not by accident that Maimonides[15] failed to include belief in Jewish chosenness among his thirteen dogmas.[16] But however one evaluates the concept of chosenness from an objective historical or from a psychological standpoint, the fact remains that this concept was accepted as a great subjective truth in the consciousness of the people during many generations, and a subjective truth is always historically more dynamic than an objective truth which has failed to penetrate the consciousness of the people. During many centuries Jews were aware that, in addition to being a people like any other, a collective physical entity, they were also (and this is very important) a group of "conspirators" against the forces of darkness and uncleanness in the world, and that this "conspiracy" was part of providence's plan leading to the "end of days," which would come about sooner or later—time was not a factor and it was not desirable to hasten the end. Perhaps we should paraphrase this belief in chosenness and instead of saying "Thou hast chosen us," we should say "I have chosen You." According to the *Agadah* God offered the Torah to all the peoples, to each in its own language, and the only people which finally accepted it were the Jews [Sifré to Deut. 33:2]. The Jews chose the one God and the only true Torah. How then can one apply to a people with such an aristocratic self-awareness (even if this be no more than a notion of a group of stubborn snobs) the same yardstick that we apply to ordinary ethnic groups? A group of "conspirators," even if they are few in number, but who have God on their side, are infinitely more numerous than the greatest majority. Finding himself in Sodom or Gomorrah,[17] Abraham would be alone and physically defenseless, but spiritually he would not be a minority there.[18]

We now come to the question: To what extent are contemporary Jews still aware that their life as Jews constitutes an "open conspiracy" (to use a term coined by H. G. Wells)[19] in which God is a partner? In a survey of Jewish cultural history in America[20] by Dr. Moshe Davis,[21] I recently came across the story of an incident that impressed me strongly. In 1817 Joseph Jonas,[22] the first Jew to settle in that region, came to Cincinnati. Many Christians there who had never seen a Jew before came to look at him as at a wonder. An elderly Quaker lady specially made a long trip to look at him. "Are you a Jew," she asked him, "one of God's chosen people? Let me take a good look at you." After she examined him from all sides, she remarked, in apparent disappointment: "You are not different from other people."[23] I know nothing about Joseph Jonas, but now, some generations after that incident, I doubt that we impress our neighbors differently. We often feel that we no longer impress the non-Jews in any particular way, the way our forebears did, either as an inspiration or as a vague threat. [Friedrich] Nietzsche[24] once sarcastically remarked regarding Christians: "Christianity, I have been told all my life, is the religion of salvation. But I know my Christians well and they don't look saved." I could paraphrase this to read: "Jews, I have been told all my life, are a chosen people. But knowing my contemporary Jews, they somehow don't look chosen." Yet it may not be so very important how Jews appear in the eyes of non-Jews; but it is important how they appear to themselves. Our chosenness has become a tradition rather than a living, nourishing faith.

What I wish to emphasize is that we are in grave danger of becoming merely an ethnic group in the conventional sense of the term—no more a sacred congregation, no more the Congregation of Israel, but only a group with a long and heroic history, with memories which, when cultivated, can arouse much justified pride (thus still not quite a mere banal minority) but without the consciousness of a specific spiritual drama and tension in its life. In the perspective of history this also means to be without a future. We have few grounds for assuming that in a progressive—or progressing—technological society with a high degree of general civilization, ordinary ethnic minorities will be able to survive as such, without in time mingling with the majority culturally, socially, and perhaps also biologically. The French in Louisiana, for instance, have no reason to feel inferior when they recall their descent and cultural traditions, but little by little they are losing their identity and the distinct elements of their cultural life, and, I hope they will forgive me for saying so, their French distinctiveness is becoming primarily gastronomical. Were some chemical to be discovered that could overnight change the color of the millions of American Negroes from black to white, they would, I believe, assimilate and disappear in the ethnically anonymous American environment within a few generations. Insofar as we Jews become a mere ethnic minority we, too, cannot escape such a fate.

This need not be interpreted to mean that extinction is around the corner. Such processes are slow and do not always follow a straight line. They are marked by zigzags, by ups and downs. Even when tradition becomes mere inertia it remains a force capable of sustaining a social group for many years. But in the end the force of inertia must exhaust itself, and unless tradition acquires new vitality and style, it must in time become desiccated and lose its color. More power to everyone among us who does something positive to strengthen Jewish spiritual life, to restrain, or even simply to delay the process of disintegration. This is in itself a great good deed. But I cannot imagine the continued existence of a Jewish community in America in a distant future (and I must stress again that I am not limiting myself to the calendric bounds set for my talk—the second half of the twentieth century) without a religious basis and without a stimulating religious content.

I do not now wish to step on anyone's corns. It is not desirable today to discuss the differences between Orthodox,[25] Conservative,[26] and Reform Jews, and their respective merits or shortcomings. But there is one danger which they must all eschew: the danger of tedium. Tedium is, fundamentally, the greatest sin which can be committed in religious life. When Satan wishes to undermine religious life, he afflicts it—if he is successful—with a yawn, and then no efforts to exorcise the tedium with extra-religious means are of any avail. When congregations try to attract their audiences by means of dances, fine concerts, or lectures on interesting secular themes, they do not thereby eliminate the boredom afflicting the specific religious life of the congregations if such boredom already exists. The attachment of the public to the congregation is then not for its own sake, but becomes technical, and, so to say, topographic. I need hardly stress that I am not opposed to dances or concerts or lectures on general themes. I am convinced that they can also fulfill a specific religious function, as long as religion remains central and all projects glow with its light. But is religion central today? By its very nature religion cannot be a peripheral matter. Either it stands at the core of things, and all other cultural activities intentionally or unintentionally serve as its periphery—or it ceases to be religion. Either religion inspires the entire man, the totality of his being, or it ekes out a miserable existence on the sidelines, and then it knows that, in time, it will probably not be tolerated at all and will be driven out also from its corner.

Should we now be honest with ourselves, we would be compelled to conclude that today there are in America hundreds of thousands of Jews who are, in the religious sense, not Jews. They are Jews only insofar as they are not Christians. They are Jews—and this is the bitter irony of it—because they don't believe anything but also lack the courage to call themselves agnostics. My friend, the Israeli author Rabbi Binyamin,[27] has been calling in recent years for the creation of a "Jewish mission." Judaism, he maintains, is universal, the Torah was intended not for Jews alone and it would be well were we to send missionaries to other peoples for the purpose of proselyting them. I too think that a people which believes that its religion is an expression of eternal truth is duty-bound to proselytize: it must not monopolize the truth for itself but should spread it also among others. In certain eras Judaism has in fact displayed marked missionary tendencies and has also achieved substantial conquests, and it was only the extreme intolerance of militant medieval Christianity, and the fanaticism of Islam—the two chief areas where Jews moved—which for a long time precluded Jewish missionary activity. But on more than one occasion I felt impelled to say to Rabbi Binyamin: "Before you send missionaries to the Chinese or the Japanese, to the Hottentots[28] or the Zulus,[29] it were better that you send Jewish missionaries to the Jews." Very many of them must first be converted, if possible. Recently we have been hearing much about an *anti-shmad* campaign.[30] I do not know who (and for what purpose) raised this alarm. At times I am inclined to say that, regrettably, we are not threatened by *shmad* (conversion to Christianity), especially not in America. Many Jews are so indifferent to religion altogether that conversion to Christianity does not enter their thoughts, except on rare occasions as a degenerate act of convenience for careerist purposes. The attitude of very many thousands among us toward religion (even among persons belonging to congregations) is well characterized by a certain American author who once described it as follows, using the answer of a Sunday School pupil to the question of what is religion: "Religion is something to profess which you know ain't true."[31]

Some eight centuries ago we produced a man who was a great authority on law and a great philosophic thinker. Responding to the need of his time, he wrote *The Guide for the Perplexed*.[32] Were we to have a Maimonides today, he would have to write another kind of book, a "Guide of the Non-Perplexed." For the trouble with the modern Jew—and I am not referring here to the surviving spiritual remnant of authentically pious, rooted Jews who live only calendrically in modern times, but have little relationship to it—is that he is shockingly untroubled and finds himself, at least consciously, in no spiritual dilemma. I do not know whether this type of Jew of whom I now speak is an atheist: most likely he never took the time or trouble to analyze this question and to formulate an answer for himself. I need hardly say that I am not hankering after atheists, though I am inclined to believe that a tragic or melancholy atheist, one with "an ache in his heart"[33]—and not the type of cheerful vulgar atheist who is perfectly content to believe that there is no God, for it is more convenient this way—is essentially and potentially closer to genuine religious life than most inert "believers." I am therefore not overwhelmed when I read that, statistically, synagogue attendance has increased here or there, or that new congregations are established.[34] Among Jews, as also among some American Christians where Protestant family traditions persist, belonging to a congregation is conventionally approved as a sign of social solidity and respectability. Among Jews there operates the added incentive to express in some way one's belonging to the community, a measure of nostalgia and pious respect for parents and a dim fear of making the total break. But in most cases the specific religious impulse is both weak and unsure.

Can such elements (which have a visible tendency to increase) be converted, or reconverted to religious Judaism? Should this be possible it would present a very serious pedagogical problem. And, pedagogically speaking, it would be very difficult—if at all possible—to transform one into a religious Jew if he is not a religious human being.

I would not wish to be misunderstood. Anti-religiousness, or what is much more common, religious indifference, naturally is not a specific Jewish trait. It is the result of a number of developments and mental changes which have taken place (and are still taking place) during recent generations. Let me point out some of them.

A) Religion has been discredited in certain segments of modern society because it tried to provide answers to some questions that are not in its province. To the extent that religion pretends to be a kind of science that solves problems which can only be studied experimentally, it must fail. Though science in itself is not and cannot be anti-religious, scientists of a certain type have become enemies of religion. Religion aroused their distaste with pretensions to which it was not entitled. A formulated or unformulated conviction thus became prevalent among many that religion as such is the enemy of clear and dependable knowledge, instead of the more logical conclusion that certain claims of some religions, developed in specific eras of religious evolution, are anti-scientific. But true religion is agnostic when it is true to its own nature. I use the term "agnostic" in its strict etymological sense. Religion is "uninformed" in all those areas where research by means of the application of strict logical rules and experimental techniques are called for. Even in questions which would appear to be the natural province of religion, such as the existence of God, free will, immortality, etc., religion cannot provide rational answers. The role of religion is altogether different: it arouses and cultivates a specific ethic-poetic orientation toward the world, life and destiny, and it cultivates an attitude of confidence in the basis of existence and its intentions. Religion is neither able nor called upon to explain the mystery of life. But it stresses, by means of its specific and largely artistic means, the existence of mystery, veneration of it as well as confidence in it. God, as the prophet Isaiah expressed it, is an *el mistater*, a God who seeks concealment (Isa. 8:17).[35]

B) Religion has lost its one-time influence and prominence among many people because it (or rather the institutions which represented it publicly) was too long and too frequently anti-religious: because religion allowed itself to be dominated by powerful social classes for their own anti-social, and consequently anti-religious purposes.

C) Technological progress of recent generations and the great utilitarian benefits which resulted from scientific achievements and discoveries have created a widespread illusion that man is fundamentally not dependent on powers outside himself or above himself, that science is capable of solving all problems and contradictions of human existence without exception, and that therefore religion is no longer necessary, that it is useless. The conception that man is something created, that all he possesses or is potentially capable of acquiring is borrowed or received as a gift, that he is essentially poor and helpless and destined to remain so, this conception has been weakened and watered down by the above-mentioned illusion. This is particularly apparent among the masses of the West and in "awakening Asia,"[36] but also many genuine and even prominent scientists belong, in this regard, to the type of mass man.

D) A new climate of "scientism" has engulfed millions who have no direct relation or access to science. In this climate, people are carried away by materialist conceptions because matter in all its forms is the chief theme with which science can and should deal. This enthusiasm contributed in no small degree to the dulling and weakening of intuitive faculties without which it is impossible to consider the world metaphysically or religiously. It is impossible for one person to arouse esthetic elation in another with his beauty, if he is to be regarded too long or permanently only from an anatomic-physiological standpoint.

An anatomist or physiologist in love is a psychological impossibility, to the extent that he is exclusively a physiologist or an anatomist and is no longer capable of considering another person from a synthetically intuitive standpoint. This obsession with matter leads many to doubt or to despair about the reality of psychic existence. Among the more sensitive this reaches a mood which a European author once characteristically described with the text of a skeptic's prayer: "Oh, God—if there is a God; save my soul—if there is a soul; if I am I; and if I has an existence."[37]

E) The life of great masses in a metropolitan, industrial civilization with its tempo and extreme concentration on economic interests deprived modern man of his capacity (and opportunities) for altruistic contemplation, for that type of contemplation of the world and of the self which leads man to wonder and amazement. For a man who lacks this contemplation, the world and all that happens in it becomes trivial, and triviality is the opposite and the enemy of religion, just as it is the enemy of art which sees sense and the eternally solemn in everything. In the rushing tempo of his life, modern man lacks the time (psychological as well as chronological time), or does not set aside the time for disinterested contemplation.

I have touched only on a few circumstances in the condition of modern man which deprive him of the capacity for religion. I am not sure that I described them exactly, or that these are the most important ones. But they should provide a general description of the condition of modern man and of his spiritual image. And I do not believe that in this area there exists any basic difference between modern man in general and the modern Jew. If this condition is indeed as I see it, then it is a morbid condition and this morbidity applies also to Jews. And this is what I meant when I said above that one cannot be a religious Jew if one is not fundamentally a religious man.

For this reason I can ignore theological, ceremonial, or other differences which today distinguish the three types of institutional Jewish religion in America.[38] The essence of the matter is elsewhere. All three trends suffer the same lack which afflicts the entire contemporary world: genuine and direct religious experience. This lack cannot be concealed with the chilly "dignity" of the Reform Temple, nor with the respectful but distant attitude to tradition of Conservative Judaism, nor also with the petrified loyalty of Orthodox Jewry to inherited religious forms which no longer contain the profound and rooted content of such a short time ago. The intrusion of nationalism and Zionism into what we define as religious life is no doubt a positive social fact which should not be underestimated, but it cannot lead to religious resurgence in Jewry. The evolution taking place in the State of Israel is, for the time being at least, a factor leading to secularization rather than to a revival of Jewish religiosity, despite the fact that Orthodoxy wields dictatorial influence in certain institutional areas of life in Israel.

It would be erroneous to conclude from what I said thus far that I am calling for some new kind of "reform" in Jewry in the accepted sense of the term. Jews have gained little from the Reform movement in Germany and later in America. Criticize the Protestant Reform movement as we may—and indeed it bore within itself a religious sanction for capitalism, the germs of extreme nationalism, and an idolatrous attitude toward the state and its authority and also a sanction for race hatred—it aimed not to dilute but to intensify the religious life of the individual. Protestantism did not come to make the life of the individual more comfortable or morally easier and less responsible. On the contrary, it introduced greater strictness than Catholicism did in many areas of life. Its demands were more stringent. The Jewish Reform movement relieved its followers of the heavy "ballast" of commandments, but it did not demand more profound and personalized religious experience. It did not lead to increased spiritual tension. It is no accident that Reform Jews, in contrast to Protestant reformers, did not produce even one more or less prominent mystic. What I have in mind here are not reforms in the sense of the so-called "Liberal Jewry," nor the decent but tragically earth-bound modifications "in the spirit of the time" of Conservative Jewry, but something similar to that which Hasidism once upon a time introduced into our life.

Hasidism did not reform Judaism—it reformed the Jews. Hasidism did not repudiate a single one of the 613 commandments,[39] it did not do away with even one of the strictures of the *Shulkhan Arukh* [Prepared Table].[40] It did not undertake to introduce any changes into Jewish theology (insofar as Judaism has a systematic theology) or ritual. It added nothing and detracted nothing. But it introduced new spirit into that which existed and was traditionally hallowed. It introduced *kavanah* (intention) and *dvekut* (cleaving [to God]) into the mechanics of religious life. Hasidism's reform consisted in providing or returning to its followers the capacity for experiencing and beholding the miracle in the everyday, in the normal lawful order of things, the capacity for marveling and being entranced. Hasidism did not revise the prayer book, but to the act of praying it imparted new dimensions and a lyricism which is perhaps the sole convincing justification for praying.

Religious life throughout the world now requires a revitalization through a new kind of Hasidism (I employ this term because I have no other), and this is perhaps especially true of Jewish religious life. Without such a revitalization religion is becoming ever more flat and horizontal, whereas its true mission is to be vertical.

I would not undertake to prove that such a reform is possible in our time. Such a basic reform of religious man, of modern man in general and of the modern Jew, is essentially a process of sanctification, a reawakening of intuitive forces, of the visionary and artistic capacities in man. And this requires that man should be less organized, more of a spiritual vagabond, and that within the framework of society there should be room also for community. More time is also needed. I am convinced that without a removal of the obstacles which stand in the way of what I called contemplation, without a curing of that specific blindness that affects so many people as a result of their fixation on the material and on those problems of the material which can be experimentally solved, there is no room for authentic religious life, and naturally also not for authentic Jewish religious life.

30

Church and State: Seven Theses

(1952)

Hayim Greenberg believed profoundly in the values of political liberty and freedom of religious conscience. Rather than mere abstractions, he regarded them as fundamental to the equilibrium and flourishing of democratic societies and modern civilization. In the following statement, composed against the backdrop of nascent Israel's vigorous public debate over the development of a state constitution (see chapter 27), Greenberg provides a systematic intellectual and moral framework that elucidates his symbiotic outlook. On the one hand, he believed religion to be "potentially, if not actually, the peak of all possible human achievements." On the other, he subscribed to the Jeffersonian notion of church-state separation. "The Jewish republic," he asserted, "should not force upon unwilling citizens any religious conformity, any obedience to ecclesiastical authorities."

The individual is not a part of a mechanism, neither is he only a cell in the social organism. Within his own dimensions the individual is an entity, or as our sages of old visualized it, a universe in and for himself, a little world.[1] The individual's allegiance to specific groups or social bodies, irrespective of their number or the profundity of his involvement with them, does not constitute the total sum of his being or of his spiritual and emotional life. The individual can abandon his community or his religious organization; he can renounce citizenship in his country or his voluntary adherence to his people; he can become naturalized in another country and pledge allegiance to another state; he may even abandon his clan to which he is more deeply attached than to other social formations if another clan consents to adopt him—he can do all of these things and he still remains an individual, a better or a worse one, more or less normal, elevated by these renunciations or crippled by them, but still conscious of his uniqueness and individual identity. The act of uprooting himself from an organization or some other collective organism need not lead to the individual's extinction or total depersonalization. Such radical changes in his allegiances may make him more free, or less so, but they do not alter his existence as a little world in himself. They do not deprive him of his memory of the past nor of his anticipation for the future nor of his vague but very real awareness of his own unique destiny.

The individual, by definition, is indivisible, whereas society, in principle and frequently as a matter of historical reality, is often divided. A people, a clan, a religious alliance, even a tribe can, under certain circumstances, break apart, be atomized, or even disappear as an entity possessing a specific character and will. From this standpoint, biography is a more real factor than history, and the individual bears within himself more essential reality, more substance than any community of human beings, and consequently also more than the community's legal and administrative embodiments. The state, which is the largest and most potent collective organism, cannot create a single new individual, whereas a number of individuals can, and under certain circumstances must, create a society.

1. The essence of the state is of a temporal and secular nature, even when it decks itself out in religious or metaphysical garb for specific purposes, consciously or unconsciously. The essence of the individual, on the other hand, is transcendental in nature and reaches out beyond time. The consciousness of eternity (or the illusion of eternity, as some might call it), the yearning for immortality and the faith in extra-corporal existence—irrespective of whether it embodies a truth or a fiction—stem primarily, if not exclusively, from individualist roots. The believer is therefore inclined to assume that in the eternity of the hereafter there exist only individuals and not collectives, or, in the terminology of the [Christian Bible], entities which are neither Greeks nor Jews.
2. This leads to the second thesis that the state, be it ever so perfect and harmonious in its construction, cannot, by its very nature, comprise the totality of the individual existences of which it is composed. The state is not the sum of the individuals within it, but only of certain aspects of their lives, interests, relationships, and wills. The more profound and less rational aspects of the individual lives do not enter into the state's collective being. These remain potentially free or autonomous, even when the state temporarily succeeds in dominating and regimenting them superficially. From this standpoint, anarchism, the most utopian extension of liberalism, may be regarded as the most religious of all social systems. Single anarchists, even very many of them, may claim to be atheists or philosophical materialists; but anarchism as an idea, is essentially an idealistic and even a religious teaching, if it is pursued to its origins. It would not be difficult to demonstrate that genuine anarchism is a logical abstraction which may perhaps never find true embodiment in historical reality. But the positive element of anarchism is its accentuation of the incomparable value of the individual

as such, of his cosmic reality, and of the relative value of all possible forms of state and social organization.

3. The authority or power of the state is largely delegated. Directly or indirectly, the state derives its ability to organize the individuals of which it is composed, to impose upon them specific actions, to bend or even to break their wills, to fuse their will into collective decisions, to permit and to prohibit, to discipline the disobedient, to punish and to reward, from the individual citizens themselves. In principle as well as in its origins, the state is an outgrowth of a social contract, or of a mandate which it receives from its individual citizens. Its strength, and its very existence, stem from vaguely formulated or unformulated attitudes of individuals and the groups to which they belong, in a certain historical period. The basis on which the state rests is the will of its citizens or subjects. On the part of some, this may be a conscious will, or even an enthusiastic devotion to the idea and the image of the particular state; others may grant their consent half-heartedly, saying their "yea" for lack of alternative (which, though in a weaker form, is also consent), an acknowledged or concealed kind of capitulation; still others give their consent out of apathy which, paradoxical as this may sound, is also an aspect (perhaps a negative aspect) of will and of partial consent.
4. On the basis of the foregoing it is possible to formulate briefly a fourth thesis. In the hierarchy of values, the believer must place religion far above the state. Religion exists and reveals itself in the realm of the absolute; the state comes into being, exists, and disappears in the realm of the relative.
5. The fifth thesis is a logical result of the fourth. When laws or ordinances of the state conflict with the fundamental principles or commandments of religion, the believing citizen must naturally remain loyal to the requirements of his faith (to the absolute but transcendental) and disobey the state. When the citizen decides to be loyal to the state and disobedient to his faith, he relegates religion to the category of relative values (and thus falsifies its character) and at the same time he ascribes to the state an absolute value transforming it into a fetish, an object of idolatry. The relative obligations to God and to Caesar cannot always be reconciled as lightly and almost idyllically as Jesus did when he said, "Render unto Caesar what is Caesar's and unto God what is God's" [Matt. 22:21]. Such solutions would be possible were God and Caesar peacefully to divide between themselves the rule over man, with God ruling over one strictly limited area of man's life and Caesar over another equally defined area. But Caesar frequently demands for himself what, by its very nature, belongs to God. The conflict between state and religion is much more forcefully described in Greek drama than in the [Christian Bible]. Sophocles'[2] Antigone[3] realized that she had com-

mitted a "sacred crime" when she buried her brother according to accepted ritual though he had committed treason against the state and contrary to the order of the ruler that the traitor's dead body should be abandoned in the open field. A "sacred crime" is not a crime. By using this paradoxical expression, Sophocles' heroine emphasized that what she did was a crime only from the limited and basically false standpoint of Caesar, of the state, but that this act, for which she was preparing to pay with her life, was regarded by God as the fulfillment of his sacred will. God wills it that even the most sinful among sinners should be brought to his eternal rest with the required dignity and ritual. The authority of temporal law thus covers only a limited range of duties, and its application must be subjected to rigid limitations. Purely semantically it is no accident that in Hebrew God is so often described as "king of the kings of kings,"[4] implying that there exists no royal authority that can challenge the authority of God. (Or, as John Milton[5] said, "When I am confronted with a conflict between the demands of Queen Truth and those of King Charles, I have to obey Queen Truth."[6])

6. The state thus has no right to impose upon its citizens any laws or regulations which are contrary to their religious conscience. It is true that one of the most characteristic and self-evident traits of the state is its power and right to compel. It would be impossible to imagine the existence of a state without the right to exert compulsion. But if, as was stated in preceding theses, the essence and the value of the state are relative, and the area in which it operates is secular-empirical, then its authority to exercise compulsion should be limited to those areas in life where it does not conflict with religious conscience. (In a general way those areas can be defined as covering police protection, the administration of justice in civil or criminal cases, public health, social security, education and, insofar as these do not imply the imposition of religious or anti-religious attitudes, the preparation of youth for productive participation in economic life, etc.)

   The modern democratic state tends, to some extent, to avoid action which could seriously infringe upon the religious sensibilities of certain groups of citizens. In England as well as in the United States, Quakers[7] are generally exempt from military service since the use of arms is contrary to their religious convictions. The state naturally reserves the right to mobilize also Quakers for specific tasks, but it is worth noting that, in the Anglo-Saxon countries at least, ever greater care is taken not to mobilize conscientious objectors for labor in the arms industries, and the tendency is to assign them to types of labor that would be required and important also in a world without wars.

7. Should religion, on the other hand—in this case, organized religion—remain true to its essence and specific tasks, it must not use, or seek to use,

the state and its instruments for its aims. Just as the outstanding characteristic of the state is its power and capacity to use power for purposes of compulsion, it should be the characteristic trait of religion to base itself on the freedom of the individual. It is impossible to demand a specific conviction from any individual if his reason (and be his reasoning logical or distorted) rebels against such a conviction. One may not demand of an individual to hold a specific faith, if the totality of his personality rejects it. The forced performance of a religious ceremony that is lacking in intent and in experiencing the symbolism expressed in the particular ceremony is valueless from a religious standpoint and is basically anti-religious. That which we describe in our political jargon as a "theocratic state" is in the final reckoning an anti-religious and Godless state. When the army and police are called upon to aid God's rule, they limit his rule instead of extending it. Their "help" is an insult to the concept of God's dominion over the destiny of man and the world. The power which religion claims must go hand-in-hand with political powerlessness. The separation of church, of all organized religion, from the state, is thus fundamentally a religious idea.

31

Religious Tolerance

(n.d.)

In the wake of the Hitler regime's murderous assault on European Jewry, Hayim Greenberg penned an essay titled "In Dust and Ashes" (1940). "What is God doing now?" he lamented, "Where is he, if he exists anywhere at all?" The question was, of course, rhetorical. Though Greenberg's writings on politics, art, history, culture, philosophy, and literature are frequently punctuated with references to God, religion, and traditional Jewish sources, he himself was not religious. Nor did he believe religion could "explain the mystery of life." The purpose and value of religion, he argued, is to "arouse" and "cultivate" a "specific ethic-poetic orientation toward the world, life, and destiny." By cultivating such an "attitude of confidence," he explained, societies and peoples become equipped with the tools necessary to survive and thrive. He further asserted it to be the responsibility of modern democratic polities to both respect humanity's "religious self-searching" and uphold civic structures that ensure the rights of believers and nonbelievers of all varieties. This dualism, he asserted, is fundamentally in harmony with authentic religious belief: "True religion is agnostic when it is true to its own nature." In the following piece, apparently delivered as a public talk in the late 1930s or early 1940s, Greenberg explores the communal and historical relationship of American Jews to the concept of freedom of religious conscience.

I believe that we Jews, particularly American Jews, should redefine the concept of tolerance, especially religious tolerance.

It appears to me that in no other country are people half as preoccupied with the business of tolerance and nowhere does this concept seem to be so vague and even purposely veiled as it is in the United States. There are large cities in this country where two-thirds of the time and energy of the rabbis is consumed in manufacturing religious tolerance. Who knows how many "good will" committees have been organized in recent years? But just try and ask one of the large army of "good will" rabbis, what is tolerance, and he will most likely avoid giving a direct and clear answer. Deep within his heart he may even realize that he speaks of tolerance but actually means indifference. Such a person conceives of tolerance as a sort of inter-religious armistice—let us make an agreement that you, a Christian minister, will not speak against my religion, while I, a rabbi, will refrain from uttering even a word against your religion. Were I inclined to speak in Marxist terms I would explain this situation as a reflection of certain "fair practices" employed by the large commercial firms in the country—to limit competition and under no circumstances to claim, publicly or otherwise, that the products of one firm are superior in quality or cheaper than the products of another firm. In other words, tolerance amounts to an agreement to refrain from criticism.

If this is the nature of tolerance, then it amounts to no more than indifference and one may legitimately ask the question whether a truly religious person can be tolerant. A nonbeliever, an atheist, can be tolerant in this fashion, for he considers all religions to be nonsense of the same variety. The princess described by [Heinrich] Heine[1] was tolerant. For hours she listened to a theological dispute between a rabbi and a priest, and when she was later asked who of the two was correct, in her opinion, she promptly answered that according to her royal way of thinking both didn't know what they were talking about.[2] But what is the meaning of tolerance when rabbis and Christian ministers speak of it? Does it mean that a member of one religion should be told not to criticize any other religion? Why should not a religious man believe that his own religion is more true, more noble and inspired, in fact the only genuinely inspired faith? Is it not the duty of such a person to combat beliefs and notions which he considers to be false?

My neighbor is a Catholic. He believes that God handed "the keys" to the popes in Rome; he is convinced that priests are authorized to grant remission of sins; he is sure that I will burn in hell if I die unsaved. If we are friends, he will pity me on account of the fate that awaits my unsaved self in the world to come and I will pity him for his beliefs, which to me appear strange, to say the least. Should I be "tolerant" toward his religious beliefs? Is it not my duty to exert my efforts in order that he may see the light? Was there no justification for intellectual and moral pressure against the Mormons because of their adoption of polygamy as a religious institution?[3] And if the Reverend [Wilbur Glenn] Voliva[4] preaches a theory according to which the earth is flat and anyone who disputes this view is doomed to perdition, must I restrain myself and never tell his followers that their leader is a crackpot?

In Russia there was a sect which believed that man was by nature physically immortal and that only those die who do not believe in this immortality.[5] As proof of their contention they would trot out their leader who, they claimed, was none other than John the Baptist,[6] born before Jesus, and over whom death has no control. Should one exhibit tolerance even toward such a belief? There was still another Russian sect that practiced castration for the sake of God.[7] They believed that it was God's will that all males should emasculate themselves in order to bring this sinful world of humanity to an end. Should one tolerate such a sect and avoid pointing out the psychopathic nature of its followers? And why not criticize a religion, such as the one in India, which condemns tens of millions of people to the status of untouchables and kindly advises widows to allow themselves to be burned on a pyre in order to follow their husbands and lords into the hereafter?[8]

It is true that it is mostly Jews that conceive of tolerance as a form of indifference, a prohibition of debate, an attitude of "do not bother me and I will not bother you." Catholics frequently deviate from this rule. Protestants may tell their followers to recognize the inhuman wrong done to Jews by Christians but, on the other hand, they call upon Jews to gather beneath the redeeming wings of the Christian Church in joint congregations or in separate Hebrew-Christian communities. The rabbis do not call upon Christians to be converted. They merely ask that Christians bear with the Jews if the latter insist on remaining such. In order to add some strength to this petition, they often cite [Gotthold Ephraim] Lessing's[9] *Nathan the Wise* [1754][10] and the well-known story of the three rings.[11]

For several generations "liberal" Jews have been retelling this story which has by now become quite threadbare. The great German humanist Lessing has manifested an unforgivable shallowness in the field of theological reasoning. For whoever seriously accepts his parable of the three rings (which symbolize Judaism, Christianity, and [Islam]) must come to the following conclusion: all three religions are equally true and equally inspired and one must therefore remain unconcerned if one of the rings is substituted for another and a person shifts his religious allegiance from one of the three religions to another. No one should sigh in disappointment if one beautiful day all Jews and Christians adopt [Islam]. The rabbi adopting such an attitude would have to manifest a peculiar sort or tolerance. He would have to remain coolly indifferent were he to awake one day to find that his entire congregation has overnight deserted him for another faith. For, what would have happened in such a case? The members of his congregation would merely have changed one gold ring for another; in the worst possible case, they would have broken with a habit and even if it is an old historical habit, there could still be no justification for loudly bewailing the fact.

True tolerance—as against the kind espoused by "good will" rabbis—is the antithesis of ignoring differences and is diametrically opposed to indifference toward another's convictions. Tolerance is fundamentally no more than a method of behavior toward people holding varying beliefs, but it has nothing to do with the beliefs themselves. It implies retention of the self-assurance that one's own faith is the correct one and the desire to convince others of the justness of one's views. But it implies that, as long as persuasion has proved futile, it is one's duty to tolerate the views of his unconverted neighbor, to look upon him as an equal, morally, and to consider him to be a person earnestly seeking after truth who had been misled in the course of this search. Tolerance implies the readiness to renounce any intention of chastising an ideological opponent or of relegating him to an inferior position socially, economically, or politically. Such tolerance does not rule out the right to attack convictions which one holds to be untrue and the hope of persuading the non-conformers to the beliefs which one holds to be the only correct ones; it does not rule out the missionary spirit. On the contrary, in a certain sense it even presupposes such a spirit. To tolerate means to respect deeply one's fellow man, to believe that in his search for truth and in his natural ability to grasp the truth he is fundamentally capable of attaining the same high conclusions that are cherished by oneself. In this sense every genuinely religious faith—as well as every deeply felt political conviction—is of necessity aggressive, militant, and missionary in spirit.

At this point we reach the tragic aspect of Jewish religiosity. Modern Jews do not want to act in a missionary spirit. Jews claim, not entirely without foundation, that they were the first in the history of humanity to grasp and to formulate the idea of monotheism, of a universal God. But Jews in their diaspora did not seek to convert other people to their faith. They always strove, and they still strive to keep their religion for themselves as a sort of family heritage in which no outsider can share. On the one hand, we see a belief in one God who is the lord of the entire universe—an unlimited cosmic conception of the subject. On the other hand, we are confronted with the cry "Hear, O Israel"[12]—only Israel, instead of "Hear, O humanity." Instinctively, even though not ideologically, Jews have manifested a historical inclination to consider their religious values as a national monopoly, the exclusive property of the Jewish tribe. In this connection it is interesting to cite the Jewish legend that the land of Palestine trembled six hundred by six hundred miles when the [Hebrew] Bible was translated into Greek.[13] One might have expected the Jews of that time to celebrate the occasion—the universalist conception of God was beginning to penetrate the heathen world. Instead, they were in mourning; their monopoly over monotheism was being threatened and the danger arose that some Greeks might embrace Judaism.

Naturally there are historical causes for this phenomenon, important, tragic, and paradoxical causes. But they do not change the basic fact that ever since we can remember Jews [have been] suffering from a prodigy complex. Jews admit that they are not God's only child and that he has plenty of others, but they look upon themselves as the Joseph of the family,[14] the eternal darling whom God loves even more than the angels, or, to quote [Rabbi Shimon],[15] "God overlooked His own honor and revealed Himself in a place of idolatry and impurity in order to redeem the Jews."[16] It has been the Jewish attitude that if gentiles wish to be redeemed they should not be driven away, but that it was not necessary to assume the mission of redeeming them. [It has been said:] "Proselytes are difficult for Jews like a malignant growth"[17] and "gentiles need only fulfill the seven commandments given to Noah"[18]—the much larger number of [613] commandments listed in the [Hebrew] Bible were specially reserved for Jews.[19] These and similar talmudic statements amply illustrate the attitude [noted above] and many Jews have [consequently] felt it was unnecessary to indulge in internationalist hospitality in the way of welcoming proselytes.

Jews were instinctively opposed to missionary endeavors and the universality of their conception of God did not interfere—and does not to this day—with their pampered, monopolistic possessiveness when they referred to "Him" as "the God of Israel" or "the God of Zion." The few ecstatic kabbalists in medieval times who went, or dreamed of going, to Rome to convert the popes to Judaism were merely deviators from the general line of Jewish spiritual history.[20]

Was Jesus personally free of this monopolistic tribal psychology? Even he could not lightly liberate himself from this specific Jewish nationalist bond. The apostles relate (although it might have been wiser on their part to pass over these matters in silence) that when a Canaanite woman appeared to Jesus to expel an evil spirit that had possessed her daughter, he forthwith replied that he had been sent only to the lost sheep of Israel.[21] The apostles he enjoined to avoid going to the gentiles and to refrain from entering the city of Samaria[22] and only to preach to the children of Israel.[23] Who knows what path Christianity might have followed—if, indeed, it would have developed into considerable proportions at all—were it not for the later appearance of Paul's internationalist religious teachings in the Greco-Roman world.[24]

But so long as Judaism as a religion remains non-missionary and even anti-missionary, so long as it strives to remain a tribal religion and a family monopoly, there will exist grave misunderstandings between Jews and religious non-Jews. There will always remain the following difficult question: "We, Christians, would like to see all Jews converted to our faith because we look upon them as people of equal worth. But you, Jews, would not wish to see us all converted to Judaism. Does not that imply disdain on your part? Is it not proof that you consider us inferior and incapable, or unworthy, of seeing the light which you hold to be the only true one?" These are definitely uncomfortable questions and one need not be an antisemite to ask them.

What is the conclusion? I am not affiliated with any religious institution or institutionalized religion. I therefore am not obliged, and possibly I also have no right, to draw conclusions. But every contemporary Jew who considers himself religious in the traditional sense of the word must seriously ponder the historical anachronism of Jewish religiosity and the difficult problems which it creates for us under present conditions in the sphere of the cultural relationship between us and our non-Jewish neighbors.

Notes

Foreword

1. See Alan Wolfe, "The Calling of the Public Intellectual," in *Public Intellectuals: An Endangered Species?*, ed. Amitai Etzioni and Alyssa Bowitch (Oxford: Rowman and Littlefield, 2006), 91–94.

2. Marie Syrkin, ed., *Hayim Greenberg Anthology* (Detroit: Wayne State University Press, 1968), 17.

3. See chapter 5, "Our Stand," in this volume, 87.

4. Martina Urban, *Theodicy of Culture and the Jewish Ethos: David Koigen's Contribution to the Sociology of Religion* (Berlin: Walter de Gruyter, 2012), 38f.

5. Before the outbreak of World War I Greenberg edited a Russian weekly on Jewish affairs, *Razswiet* (Dawn).

6. See "Introduction," in Syrkin, *Hayim Greenberg Anthology*, 9.

7. Greenberg surely would have agreed with the late Jean Bethke Elshtain, who held that "intellectuals and others who speak in a public moral voice do not carry a card that says 'Have Ideology, Will Talk.' Instead, they embrace Hannah Arendt's description of the task of the political theorist as one who helps think about what we are doing. In a culture that is always doing, the responsibility to think is too often evaded. . . . The role for public intellectuals . . . is to bestir the quiet voice of ethically engaged reason." Jean Bethke Elshtain, "Why Public Intellectuals?," in Etzioni and Bowitch, *Public Intellectuals*, 89.

Acknowledgments

Epigraph taken from the transcript of Hayim Greenberg's remarks ("Our Cultural Objectives") in *Excerpts of Freedom Convention of Pioneer Women Held at the Benjamin Franklin Hotel, Philadelphia, PA, June 11–15, 1949*, 235, NA'AMAT USA Archives, Canoga Park, CA.

Introduction

Note: This essay is a revised and expanded version of Mark A. Raider, "Toward a Reexamination of American Zionist Leadership: The Case of Hayim Greenberg," *Journal of Israeli History* 15:2 (Summer 1994): 133–160. It also includes elements from Mark

A. Raider, "Culture and Education in the Diaspora: Hayim Greenberg," *Jewish Review of Books* 4:2 (Summer 2013): 44–45. I am grateful to Allan Arkush, Matthew A. Cahn, Aryeh Goren, Miriam B. Raider-Roth, and Robert M. Seltzer for their valuable criticisms and suggestions.

1. Irving Howe, *World of Our Fathers: The Journey of the East European Jews to America and the Life They Found and Made* (New York: Simon and Schuster, 1976), 503.

2. Resolution of the American Zionist Emergency Council, February 13, 1945, Stephen S. Wise Papers, P-134, Box 99: American Zionist Emergency Council, American Jewish Historical Society, New York, New York; Walter Laqueur, *A History of Zionism*, rev. ed. (New York: Schocken Books, 1989), 567; Israel Goldstein, *My World As a Jew: The Memoirs of Israel Goldstein*, vol. 2 (New York: Herzl Press and London: Cornwall Books, 1984), 333.

3. Eliahu Elath, *Zionism at the UN: A Diary of the First Days* (Philadelphia: Jewish Publication Society of America, 1976), 313.

4. "Hayim Greenberg, Zionist, Dies at 63: Head of Education, Culture Unit of World Organization Was Israeli Leaders' Adviser," *New York Times* (March 15, 1953), 93.

5. See the following from *JTA Daily News Bulletin* 20:51 (March 16, 1953), http://pdfs.jta.org/1953/1953-03-16_051.pdf: "Dr. Hayim Greenberg, Jewish Agency Leader, Dead; Funeral Today," 2; "Israel President, Jewish Agency Mourn Death of Dr. Greenberg," 3.

6. See "Thousands Attend Dr. Greenberg's Funeral: Israel Ministers Present," *JTA Daily News Bulletin* 20:52 (March 16, 1953), 1; http://pdfs.jta.org/1953/1953-03-17_052.pdf; "W.Z.O. Publication Issues Special Hayim Greenberg Memorial Edition," *JTA Daily News Bulletin* 21:101 (May 26, 1954), 5; http://www.jta.org/1954/05/26/archive/w-z-o-publication-issues-special-hayim-greenberg-memorial-edition.

7. See, e.g., Laura G. Sharon, "Lives of Our Times: Hayim Greenberg," *Wisconsin Jewish Chronicle* (1948), Central Zionist Archives, Jerusalem, Israel (hereafter CZA); Israel Goldstein, "Memorial Tribute to Hayim Greenberg," Israel Goldstein Papers, A364/86c, CZA; Rose L. Halprin, "Address at the Hayim Greenberg Memorial Meeting at the Jewish Theological Seminary, February 1954," reprinted as "Dedicatory Preface to Hayim Greenberg," in *Israel: Its Role in Civilization*, ed. Moshe Davis (New York: Harper and Brothers, 1954), xv–xvii; Arthur Hertzberg, "Hayim Greenberg: Zionist *Rebbe*," March 1963, photocopy of published ms., Hayim Greenberg Collection, American Jewish Archives, Cincinnati, Ohio (hereafter AJA); Samuel M. Blumenfeld, "Hayim Greenberg: Zionist Educator," *Jewish Frontier* 30:2 (March 1963): 11–12; Jacob J. Weinstein, "Hayim Greenberg: The Religious Roots of Zionism," *Jewish Frontier* 30:2 (March 1963): 8–10; Morris Adler, "Hayim Greenberg: The Whole Man," *Jewish Frontier* 30:4 (May 1963): 20–23; Shlomo Grodzensky, "*Hayim Greenberg in di fareinikte shtaten,*" in *Geklibene shriftn* (Tel Aviv: I. L. Peretz Publishing House, 1973), 343–347.

8. See Ben Hecht, *A Child of the Century* (New York: Simon and Schuster, 1954), 548–550.

9. "Truman Named to Receive 1952 Stephen Wise Award," *JTA Daily News Bulletin* 20:52 (March 17, 1953), 4, http://pdfs.jta.org/1953/1953-03-17_052.pdf.

10. Rose L. Halprin, "Address at the Hayim Greenberg Memorial Meeting," xv. It

has been observed that in contrast to Greenberg and "other critical figures," only Louis D. Brandeis and Henrietta Szold "achieved special 'canonical status' among American Zionist leaders." See Jonathan D. Sarna, "America's Most Memorable Zionist Leaders," in *The Individual in History: Essays in Honor of Jehuda Reinharz*, ed. ChaeRan Y. Freeze, Sylvia Fuks Fried, and Eugene R. Sheppard (Waltham, MA: Brandeis University Press, 2015), 129.

11. Stephen J. Whitfield, "A Tale of Two Critics," *American Jewish History* 86:1 (March 1998), 1.

12. Ezra Mendelsohn, *On Modern Jewish Politics* (New York: Oxford University Press, 1993), 141–145.

13. Samuel M. Blumenfeld, president of Chicago's College of Jewish Studies, recalled that Greenberg "maintained a certain distance between himself and his associates, no matter how close and warm the contact with co-workers and disciples." Blumenfeld, "Hayim Greenberg," 11.

14. Howe, *World of Our Fathers*, 511.

15. The felicitous phrase "free associations" stems from the title of an essay (originally published in Yiddish in 1938) in which Greenberg stitches together vignettes and musings on the themes of listening, solitude, silence, and independence for writers, thinkers, and philosophers. See Hayim Greenberg, *Bletlekh fun a tog-bukh* (New York: Yidisher Kemfer, 1954), 73–79; Greenberg, *The Inner Eye: Selected Essays*, vol. 2, ed. Shlomo Katz (New York: Jewish Frontier Association, 1964), 2:298–303.

16. Lloyd P. Gartner, "Jewish Gold and Prussian Iron," *Jewish Journal of Sociology* 19:2 (December 1977): 197.

17. For a corrective concerning Greenberg and other figures, see Carole S. Kessner, ed., *The Other New York Jewish Intellectuals* (Albany: SUNY Press, 1994).

18. The notable exception in this regard is, arguably, Greenberg's "The Universalism of the Chosen People," included in the present volume (chapter 24).

19. Dan Ben-Amos, "Jewish Folk Literature," *Oral Tradition* 14:1 (1999): 230.

20. See Carole S. Kessner, *Marie Syrkin: Values Beyond the Self* (Waltham, MA: Brandeis University Press, 2008), 249–251.

21. Marie Syrkin, ed., *Hayim Greenberg Anthology* (Detroit: Wayne State University Press, 1968), 18–19.

22. For Greenberg's Yiddish essays, see *Yid un velt* (New York: Yidisher Kemfer, 1953); *Mentshn un vertn* (New York: Yidisher Kemfer, 1953); *Bletlekh fun a tog-bukh* (New York: Yidisher Kemfer, 1954). Many of Greenberg's essays were translated into English and can be found in Greenberg, *The Inner Eye*, 2 vols. (vol. 1, New York: Jewish Frontier Association, 1953, 2nd ed., 1958; vol. 2, New York: Jewish Frontier Association, 1964), and Syrkin, *Hayim Greenberg Anthology*. A selection of Greenberg's Hebrew essays appears in *Ayin roi: Sefer masot vehegyonot* (Jerusalem: Mosad Bialik, 1958).

23. Dwight F. Reynolds, "Folklore," in *The Cambridge Companion to Modern Arab Culture*, ed. Dwight F. Reynolds (Cambridge: Cambridge University Press, 2015), 249.

24. Rose L. Halprin, "Dedicatory Preface to Hayim Greenberg," xv–xvii.

25. See chapter 26, "Patriotism and Plural Loyalties," in this volume, 287.

26. Marc Lee Raphael, *Abba Hillel Silver: A Profile in American Judaism* (New York:

Holmes and Meier, 1989), 201–205; Ofer Shiff, *The Downfall of Abba Hillel Silver and the Foundation of Israel* (Syracuse: Syracuse University Press, 2014), chap. 7.

27. Confirmed in oral histories conducted and recorded by the author with David Breslau (1993), Abe Cohen (1993), Saadia Gelb (1990), Jacob Katzman (1990), and Nahum Guttman (1993), in the author's possession. See also letter from David Breslau to Mark A. Raider, December 19, 1994, in the author's possession.

28. Even some colleagues with whom Greenberg shared a lifetime of Zionist organizational and political engagement defaulted to a doctrinaire position. The Hebrew literary critic Zvi Woyslawski asserted Greenberg "played a part in public affairs all his life as a scintillating writer and brilliant orator . . . but [he] was no [A. D.] Gordon, no [Ber] Borochov, nor [Nahman] Syrkin." The implication here is that Greenberg's importance, unlike that of his Labor Zionist predecessors Gordon (who lived in Palestine) or Borochov and Syrkin (both of whom died before settling in Palestine), was diminished by his choice to live outside of the Land of Israel; Zvi Woyslawski, "On Hayim Greenberg," *Forum for the Problems of Zionism, World Jewry and the State of Israel* 1 (December 1953), 189. Likewise, Zalman Shazar depicted Greenberg in melancholic terms as "the servant of *Erez Israel* and of the labor movement. . . . But like the legendary page, he carried the train of his beloved all his life without approaching her . . . and his comrades lowered his body into remote soil." Zalman Shazar, "The Man Apart," *Jewish Frontier* 20:5 (May 1953): 11.

29. See chapter 28, "Jewish Culture and Education in the Diaspora," in this volume, 317.

30. Robert E. Park, "Human Migration and the Marginal Man," *American Journal of Sociology* 33:6 (1928): 892.

31. See Kessner, *The Other New York Jewish Intellectuals*.

32. The absence of Hayim Greenberg's personal and professional papers presents myriad challenges for the researcher. Apparently, Greenberg's widow and son, Leah and Emanuel, disposed of most of his papers after his death. The *Yidisher kemfer*'s and *Jewish Frontier*'s records were lost in the 1940s and 1950s when the journals' New York City offices changed locations. Confirmed in oral histories conducted and recorded by the author with David Breslau (1993), Abe Cohen (1993), Saadia Gelb (1990), Jacob Katzman (1990), and Nahum Guttman (1993), in the author's possession. The CZA has a small collection of Greenberg papers, and the AJA's holdings include several boxes of American Labor Zionist movement records. Other Greenberg papers from the 1920s to the 1950s are scattered among the records of major Jewish, Zionist, and Israeli leaders and organizations. A few boxes of Greenberg's papers are in the private possession of a woman in Hackensack, New Jersey, who claims to have been friendly with Leah Greenberg. She is willing to sell the papers, but has not otherwise permitted access to them. Some personal data included in this essay concerning Hayim, Leah, and Emanuel Greenberg was culled from the following items on Ancestry.com: (a) *Petitions for Naturalization from the US District Court for the Southern District of New York, 1897–1944* (Washington, DC: National Archives and Records Administration, n.d.), series M1972, roll 1453; (b) *US Social Security Applications and Claims Index, 1936–2007* [database on-line]; *Fifteenth Census of*

the United States, 1930 (Washington, DC: National Archives and Records Administration, 1930), roll 1483, page 3B; enumeration district 0520; image 470.0; FHL microfilm 2341218.

33. A portion of Greenberg's writings in Yiddish and English were previously published in the following anthologies: Greenberg, *Yid un velt*; Greenberg, *Mentshn un verten*; Greenberg, *Bletlekh fun a tog-bukh*; Greenberg, *The Inner Eye*.

34. Syrkin, *Hayim Greenberg Anthology*, 7.

35. David Biale, *Not in the Heavens: The Tradition of Secular Jewish Thought* (Princeton, NJ: Princeton University Press, 2011), 11–12. See also Anita Shapira, "The Religious Motifs of the Labor Movement," in *Zionism and Religion*, ed. Shmuel Almog, Jehuda Reinharz, and Anita Shapira (Hanover, NH: Brandeis University Press, 1998), 251–272.

36. See *Enziklopedyah shel galuyot* (1971), 11:295–296.

37. See Ben Halpern, *A Clash of Heroes: Brandeis, Weizmann, and American Zionism* (New York: Oxford University Press, 1987), 39–40; Kalman Weiser, *Jewish People, Yiddish Nation: Noah Prylucki and the Folkists in Poland* (Toronto: University of Toronto Press, 2011), 154.

38. Elath, *Zionism at the UN*, 121.

39. Edward K. Kaplan and Samuel H. Dresner, *Abraham Joshua Heschel: Prophetic Witness* (New Haven, CT: Yale University Press, 1998), 127.

40. See "With Romain Rolland," in Greenberg, *The Inner Eye*, 2:271–278.

41. *Enziklopedyah shel galuyot* (1971), 11:589–590.

42. Quoted in Laqueur, *A History of Zionism*, 432. See also Vladimir Lenin, "Critical Remarks on the National Question," in *The Jew in the Modern World: A Documentary History*, ed. Paul Mendes-Flohr and Jehuda Reinharz, 3rd ed. (New York: Oxford University Press, 2011), 407–409.

43. Michael Brenner, *The Renaissance of Jewish Culture in Weimar Germany* (New Haven, CT: Yale University Press, 1996), chap. 7.

44. See chapter 28, "Jewish Culture and Education in the Diaspora," in this volume, 317.

45. See Robert M. Seltzer, "Hayim Greenberg, Jewish Intellectual," in *The "Other" New York Jewish Intellectuals*, ed. Carole S. Kessner (New York: New York University Press, 1994), 33.

46. Arnold M. Eisen, *The Chosen People in America: A Study in Jewish Religious Ideology (Bloomington: Indiana University Press, 1983)*, 121–122.

47. See Hayim Greenberg, "*Mediniyut vaavodah*," *Haolam*, February 7, 1923, 70–71. The complete English translation of this essay appears in this volume as "Policy and Labor" (chapter 2).

48. Jehuda Reinharz, *Fatherland or Promised Land? The Dilemma of the German Jew, 1893–1914* (Ann Arbor: University of Michigan Press, 1975), 158.

49. Ibid., 154–158.

50. Yosef Sprinzak, "Hayim Greenberg," *Shnaton Davar* (Tel Aviv: Davar, 1953), 495; see also Chaim Arlosoroff's letters to Hayim Greenberg dated February 1, 1930, and April 21, 1930, Chaim Arlosoroff Papers, A44/5-I, CZA.

51. Shlomo Avineri, *The Making of Modern Zionism: The Intellectual Origins of the Jewish State* (New York: Basic Books, 1981), 158; Shlomo Avineri, *Arlosoroff* (New York: Grove Weidenfeld, 1989), 8–9, 28–29.

52. A. D. Gordon, "People and Labor," in *The Zionist Idea: A Historical Analysis and Reader*, ed. Arthur Hertzberg (New York: Atheneum, 1981), 372.

53. See "*Hasozialism haamami shel hayehudim,*" in *Kitvei Chaim Arlosoroff*, ed. Yaakov Steinberg, vol. 3 (Palestine: A. J. Stybel Publishing House, 1934), 86–88. On the impact of Arlosoroff's approach, to which other Zionist officials also subscribed, see Anita Shapira, *Land and Power: The Zionist Resort to Force, 1881–1948* (New York: Oxford University Press, 1992), 206–209.

54. Jehuda Reinharz, *Writing the Biography of Chaim Weizmann* (Rehovot: Yad Chaim Weizmann, 1992), 16.

55. See chapter 2, "Policy and Labor," in this volume, 65.

56. Mendelsohn, *On Modern Jewish Politics,* 132–139.

57. Abraham Goldberg, "Zionism in America: A Chronicle of Its Development," in *Theodor Herzl: A Memorial*, ed. Meyer W. Weisgal (New York: New Palestine, 1929), 220–222; Evyatar Friesel, "Brandeis' Role in American Zionism Historically Reconsidered," *American Jewish History* 89:1 (September 1979): 47.

58. Ben Halpern, "The Americanization of Zionism, 1880–1930," *American Jewish History* 89:1 (September 1979): 15–33; Deborah E. Lipstadt, "Louis Lipsky and the Emergence of Opposition to Brandeis, 1917–1920," in *Herzl Year Book*, ed. Melvin I. Urofsky, vol. 8 (New York: Herzl Press, 1978), 37–60.

59. Jonathan Frankel, *Prophecy and Politics: Socialism, Nationalism, and the Russian Jews, 1862–1917* (Cambridge: Cambridge University Press, 1981), chap. 9.

60. Chaim Arlosoroff, *Surveying American Zionism* (New York: Zionist Labor Party "Hitachduth" [*sic*] of America, 1929), 23–24; emphasis in the original.

61. Louis D. Brandeis, "Zionism Is Consistent with American Patriotism," in Mendes-Flohr and Reinharz, *The Jew in the Modern World*, 555.

62. Whitfield, "A Tale of Two Critics," 22.

63. K. Weitmann, "*Parzufim,*" in *Sefer hayovel shel Hadoar*, ed. Menahem Ribalov (New York: Hozaat Hahistadrut Haivrit Beamerikah, 1927), 143–145.

64. Letter from Mitchell Cohen to Mark A. Raider, November 8, 1994, in the author's possession.

65. From an interview conducted and recorded by the author with Jacob Katzman (1990), in the author's possession.

66. Ben Halpern, "Hayim Greenberg in America," in *In Memoriam: Hayim Greenberg* (Jerusalem: Information Department and Department for Education and Culture in the Diaspora, 1953), 56.

67. Matityahu Mintz, *Zmanim hadashim, zmirot hadashot: Ber Borochov, 1914–1917* (Tel Aviv: Hozaat Am Oved, 1986), 98–125.

68. Marie Syrkin, *Nachman Syrkin, Socialist Zionist: A Biographical Memoir and Selected Essays* (New York: Herzl Press, 1961), 162–163.

69. Frankel, *Prophecy and Politics*, 258, 442, 486.

70. Shapira, "The Religious Motifs of the Labor Movement," 251–272.

71. Jacob Katzman, *Commitment: The Labor Zionist Life-style in America* (New York: Labor Zionist Letters, 1975), 200.

72. Anita Shapira, *Berl: The Biography of a Socialist Zionist, 1887–1944* (Cambridge: Cambridge University Press, 1984), 343; Ben Halpern, "Greenberg in His Generation," *Jewish Frontier* 30:2 (March 1963): 5–7.

73. Daniel Katz, *All Together Different: Yiddish Socialist, Garment Workers, and the Labor Roots of Multiculturalism* (New York: New York University Press, 2011), 192–197; Ron Chernow, *The Warburgs* (New York: Random House, 1993), 162–164; Shiff, *The Downfall of Abba Hillel Silver*, 8–10, 21–22, 157–166.

74. Golda Meyerson, "He Who Sees and Knows," in *In Memoriam: Hayim Greenberg* (Jerusalem: Information Department and Department for Education and Culture in the Diaspora, 1953), 36–37.

75. Jonathan D. Sarna, "The Spectrum of Jewish Leadership in Ante-Bellum America," *Journal of American Ethnic History* 1:2 (Spring 1982): 61–62.

76. Ben Halpern and Jehuda Reinharz, *Zionism and the Creation of a New Society* (1998; reprint, Hanover, NH: Brandeis University Press, 2000), 261–267, 301–302.

77. See chapter 5, "Our Stand," in this volume, 87.

78. From an address to the 15th Zionist Congress (September 1927) reprinted in Arthur Ruppin, *Three Decades of Palestine: Speeches and Papers on the Upbuilding of the Jewish National Home* (Jerusalem: Schocken, 1936), 153.

79. Ibid., 159–160.

80. Henry L. Feingold, *A Time for Searching: Entering the Mainstream, 1920–1945* (Baltimore: Johns Hopkins University Press, 1992), chap. 7.

81. Theodore Peterson, *Magazines in the Twentieth Century* (Urbana: University of Illinois Press, 1956), 40–45, 50–53, 66–70, 94–98, 209–210; Arthur A. Goren, "The Jewish Press," in *The Ethnic Press in the United States: A Historical Analysis and Handbook*, ed. Sally M. Miller (New York: Greenwood Press, 1987), 220; Lou Siegel and Jeff Stansbury, "Beyond English: The Labor Press in a Multicultural Environment," in *The New Labor Press: Journalism for a Changing Union Movement*, ed. Sam Pizzigati and Fred J. Solowey (Ithaca, NY: ILR Press, Cornell University, 1992), 86; "Labor Press," *Encyclopedia of American Journalism*, ed. Stephen L. Vaughn (New York: Routledge, 2008), 250–251; Christopher Daly, *Covering America: A Narrative History of a Nation's Journalism* (Amherst: University of Massachusetts Press, 2012), chaps. 7–8.

82. Goren, "The Jewish Press," 219.

83. Berman, *Nazism, the Jews and American Zionism*, 17.

84. Marie Syrkin, "Looking Back—and Forward," *Jewish Frontier* 28:3 (March 1961): 7.

85. See chapter 5, "Our Stand," in this volume, 87.

86. Ber Borochov, *Nationalism and the Class Struggle* (New York: Young Poale Zion Alliance, 1937), 196.

87. Ahad Haam, "The Negation of the Diaspora" in *The Zionist Idea: A Historical Analysis and Reader, ed. Arthur Hertzberg (New York: Atheneum, 1981)*, 276.

88. See chapter 5, "Our Stand," 87.

89. See Shapira, "The Religious Motifs of the Labor Movement," 251–272.

90. See chapter 9, "To a Communist Friend," in this volume, 109.

91. See chapter 17, "Socialism Re-examined," in this volume, 187.

92. Greenberg's assessment echoes A. D. Gordon's view of Zionist pioneering. For example, consider the following statement by Gordon: "The most important of the fundamentals is human life in all its breadth and depth. The individual and the community participate equally in its creation. What we seek here is a perfect harmony which cannot be attained by minimizing the personality of the individual and by obliterating it. On the contrary, the power of the individual must be increased and the lofty understanding and freedom of his personality must be recognized." A. D. Gordon, *Selected Essays*, ed. Frances Burnce (New York: League for Labor Palestine, 1938), 263–264. On the historical development of Labor Zionism, see Gideon Shimoni, *The Zionist Ideology* (Waltham, MA: Brandeis University Press, 1995), chap. 5.

93. See Frankel, *Prophecy and Politics*, 303–305.

94. See chapter 6, "Jew and Arab," in this volume, 92.

95. Ibid.

96. See also Hayim Greenberg, "Is Zionism Imperialistic?," in *Jews and Arabs in Palestine: Studies in a National and Colonial Problem*, ed. Enzo Sereni and R. E. Ashery (New York: Hechalutz Press, 1936), 247–257.

97. Klara Moricz, *Jewish Identities: Nationalism, Racism, and Utopianism in Twentieth-Century Music* (Berkeley: University of California Press, 2008), 69.

98. Hillel Halkin, *Jabotinsky: A Life* (New Haven, CT: Yale University Press, 2014), 140–141, 159–161; Chanoch (Howard) Rosenblum, "The New Zionist Organization's American Campaign, 1936–1939," *Studies in Zionism* 12:2 (Autumn 1991): 169–185; Joseph B. Schechtman, *Rebel and Statesman: The Vladimir Jabotinsky Story, The Early Years* (New York: Thomas Yoseloff, 1958), 388–394; Elias Ginsburg, "Is Revision-Zionism [*sic*] Fascist?" *Menorah Journal* 22:2 (October-December 1934): 190–206.

99. Chapter 7, "Revisionism," in this volume, 95. Other examples are Hayim Greenberg, "Jabotinsky's Army Marches," *Jewish Frontier* 2:3 (January 1935): 6; Greenberg, "Revisionism: A Self-Portrait," *Jewish Frontier* 2:3 (January 1935): 15–16; Greenberg, "The Irresponsible Revisionists," *Jewish Frontier* 10:11 (November 1943): 7–8. See also Marie Syrkin, "The Essence of Revisionism: An Analysis of a Fascist Tendency in Jewry," *Jewish Frontier* 7:4 (April 1940): 6–10.

100. The trial was followed intensely in the Jewish press. See, e.g., the following *JTA Daily News Bulletin* items: "Arlosoroff Murder Trial Starts in Jerusalem; Police Guard Court as Hundreds Seek Entrance" (April 24, 1934), 1, 8, http://pdfs.jta.org/1934/1934-04-24_2827.pdf; "Hanging for Stavsky, Rosenblatt Is Freed; Death Verdict Comes as Shock after Lengthy Arlosoroff Trial," June 10, 1934, 1, 12, http://pdfs.jta.org/1934/1934-06-10_2867.pdf; "Stavsky Free on Appeal; Appeals Court Reverses Death Verdict, Jabotinsky Hails Freeing of Revisionist," July 22, 1934, 1, 12, http://pdfs.jta.org/1934/1934-07-22_2903.pdf.

101. Hayim Greenberg, "The Threat of Revisionist Irresponsibility," *Jewish Frontier* 5:8 (August 1938): 7–9.

102. Chapter 7, "Revisionism," in this volume, 95.

103. Mitchell Cohen, *Zion and State: Nation, Class, and the Shaping of Israel* (1987; reprint, New York: Columbia University Press, 1992), 184–192.

104. Chapter 7, "Revisionism," in this volume, 95.

105. Michael Brown, *The Israeli-American Connection: Its Roots in the Yishuv* (Detroit: Wayne State University Press, 1996), 37–42.

106. Stephen S. Wise, "Why Zionists Cannot Support Jabotinsky and Revisionism: Excerpts of Address Delivered before the Free Synagogue at Carnegie Hall," March 10, 1935, 3, 4, and 7, AJA.

107. Chapter 9, "To a Communist Friend," in this volume, 109.

108. Chapter 8, "Notes on Marxism," in this volume, 102.

109. Burnce, *A. D. Gordon*, 9.

110. Chapter 9, "To a Communist Friend," in this volume, 109.

111. See Hayim Greenberg's statement in "Report of Eastern Conference [of PZ-ZZ]," *Jewish Frontier* 6:7 (July 1939): 30–31.

112. Hayim Greenberg, "To Young India . . . An Open Letter to Gandhi," *Jewish Frontier* 4:4 (April 1937): 7; Maurice S. Friedman, *Martin Buber: The Life of Dialogue* (New York: Harper and Row, 1960), 205–207. For Buber's open letters to Gandhi, see "The Land and Its Possessors," in Martin Buber, *Israel and the World: Essays in a Time of Crisis* (New York: Schocken Books, 1963), 227–233; "A Letter to Gandhi," in Martin Buber, *Pointing the Way*, trans. and ed. Maurice S. Friedman (New York: Harper Torchbooks, 1957), 139–147.

113. Mahatma Gandhi, "Death Has No Terror," *Jewish Frontier* 6:5 (March 1939): 9.

114. Hayim Greenberg, "We Are Treated as Subhumans—We Are Asked to Be Superhuman," *Jewish Frontier* 6:5 (March 1939): 13. The complete essay is reprinted in this volume under the title "An Answer to Gandhi" (chapter 11).

115. George P. Fletcher and Jens P. Ohlin, *Defending Humanity: When Force Is Justified and Why* (New York: Oxford University Press, 2008), 217. On American pacifism during World War II, see W. Edward Orser, "World War II and the Pacifist Controversy in the Major Protestant Churches," *American Studies* 14:2 (Fall 1973): 5–24.

116. Scott H. Bennet, *Radical Pacifism: The War Resisters League and Gandhian Nonviolence in America, 1915–1963* (Syracuse: Syracuse University Press, 2003), chap. 2; Naomi W. Cohen, "An Overview of American Jewish Defense," in *Jews and the American Public Square: Debating Religion and Republic*, ed. Alan Mittlemen, Robert Licht, and Jonathan D. Sarna (Lanham, MD: Rowman and Littlefield, 2002), 23–24, 31–35, 43.

117. Deborah E. Lipstadt, *Beyond Belief: The American Press and the Coming of the Holocaust, 1933–1945* (New York: Free Press, 1986), 155–156.

118. Hayim Greenberg, "Palestine Administration Indicted," *Jewish Frontier* 8:2 (February 1941): 7–9.

119. Ibid.

120. Chaim Weizmann to Christopher Eastwood, March 10, 1941, *The Letters and Papers of Chaim Weizmann, July 1940–January 1943*, ed., Meyer W. Weisgal et al., English ed., ser. A, vol. 20 (New Brunswick, NJ: Transaction Books, 1979), 124; Chaim Weizmann, *Trial and Error* (New York: Harper and Brothers, 1949), 425.

121. Yosef Gorny, *The Jewish Press and the Holocaust, 1939–1945: Palestine, Britain, the United States, and the Soviet Union* (Cambridge: Cambridge University Press, 2012), 91–92; Kessner, *Marie Syrkin*, 340–343; Lipstadt, *Beyond Belief*, 165–166.

122. In his memoir, Hecht notes that he learned about the details of the Nazi genocide in a private meeting with Greenberg and that his article "Remember Us," which appeared in *Reader's Digest* in February 1943, was also "based on Dr. Greenberg's data." Ben Hecht, *A Child of the Century*, 548–550.

123. Hayim Greenberg, "Under the Axis," *Jewish Frontier* 9:10 (November 1942): 3.

124. Berman, *Nazism, the Jews, and American Zionism*, 96–100.

125. Hecht's memoir includes an intriguing but suspect account of his encounter with Greenberg. See "The Goodness of a Jew," in Hecht, *A Child of the Century*, 548–550:

> "Dr. Hayim Greenberg, editor of *Jewish Frontier*, a New York weekly [*sic*] written in English, removed a heap of papers from his brief case.
>
> "'I think these contain the facts you wish to know,' he said. 'Some are from eyewitnesses and some from underground sources. They come to us through Switzerland.'
>
> "We were lunching in a crowded kosher restaurant. I had been told that Dr. Greenberg was one of the best-informed people in New York on the massacre of the Jews.
>
> "I read the documents he had taken from his brief case. I read of the execution of the Jewish population in Munich, of the extermination camp in Tremblinka [*sic*]. A survivor reported the dark cloud of smoke that hung over the crematorium in which thousands of Jews were being burned alive daily.
>
> "I read of the freight cars. . . . [Here follows a page of detailed observations of instances of the killing and murder of Jews by the Nazis.]
>
> "Dr. Greenberg had sat silent as I read the dispatches. He asked me now,
>
> "'What sort of an article are you going to write, Mr. Hecht?'
>
> "'I'm going to write something about the Germans,' I said.
>
> "'From what point of view do you intend to write of the Germans?' Dr. Greenberg asked.
>
> "'From the point of view that the Germans are a nation of murderers,' I said.
>
> "'I don't think it is wise to accuse all the Germans of being murderers,' Dr. Greenberg said. 'I would like to ask you to consider carefully before denouncing the German people. To denounce a people is to do what the Germans are doing to the Jews.'
>
> "'They are not denouncing Jews,' I said. 'They're killing them.'
>
> "'I know,' said Dr. Greenberg. His eyes looked painfully at the documents heaped on the table. 'But, please, may I point out to you that it will be bad for the Jews if you make the Jews seem as cruel and unthinking as those whom you are trying to attack. More than ever before in our history, the Jew today must have a philosophical view. He must keep his mind undarkened by hate and look with clear eyes on the world. He must rise above his bitterness and not fight back only out of his pain. The evil ones should be punished. But, please, let us not become like them. It is not ethical to attack a whole race—even the race of Germans.'
>
> "I thanked this man whose kindness I understood. But his way was not my way. I was unable to answer his philosophical words. My head was full of faraway screams."

126. Ben Hecht, "The Extermination of the Jews," *American Mercury* 56 (February 1943): 194–199; Ben Hecht, "Remember Us," *Reader's Digest* (February 1943): 107–110.

127. Bret Werb, "We Will Never Die: A Pageant to Save the Jews of Europe," note iv; http://orelfoundation.org/index.php/journal/journalArticle/we_will_never_die_a_pageant_to_save_the_jews_of_europe/#fniv.

128. Quoted in Hecht, *A Child of the Century*, 550. For reprints of full-page newspaper ads the Bergson group placed in the *New York Times* in February-December 1943, see the plates between pp. 78–79 in David S. Wyman and Rafael Medoff, *A Race against Death: Peter Bergson, America, and the Holocaust* (New York: New Press, 2002). See also Mark A. Raider, "'Irresponsible, Undisciplined Opposition': Ben Halpern on the Bergson Group and Jewish Terrorism in Pre-State Palestine," *American Jewish History* 92:3 (September 2004): 313–360.

129. Chapter 21, "Bankrupt!," in this volume, 215.

130. Haskel Lookstein, "Rabbi Joseph Soloveitchik and American Jewry's Response to the Holocaust," *Journal of Ecumenical Studies* 40:4 (Fall 2003): 457–460.

131. Charles F. Howlett, "A. J. Muste: Portrait of a Twentieth-Century Pacifist," in *The Human Tradition in America between the Wars, 1920–1945*, ed. Donald W. Whisenhunt (Wilmington, DE: Scholarly Resources, 2002), 1–19; Joseph Kip Kosek, *Acts of Conscience: Christian Nonviolence and Modern American Democracy* (New York: Columbia University Press, 2009), 152–155; Michael W. Casey, "The Ethics of War: Pacifism and Militarism in the American Restoration Movement," *Leaven* 7:4, Article 7; http://digitalcommons.pepperdine.edu/leaven/vol7/iss4/7.

132. Harvard Sitkoff, *Toward Freedom Land: The Long Struggle for Racial Equality in America* (Lexington: University Press of Kentucky, 2010), 150–151.

133. A full discussion of Jewish and Zionist leaders, American society, and the Holocaust goes beyond the scope of this study. For useful scholarly analyses, see Anita Shapira, "Did the Zionist Leadership Foresee the Holocaust," in *Living with Antisemitism: Modern Jewish Responses*, ed. Jehuda Reinharz (Hanover, NH: University Press of New England, 1987), 397–412; Verne W. Newton, ed., *FDR and the Holocaust* (New York: St. Martin's Press, 1996); Richard Breitman and Allan J. Lichtman, *FDR and the Jews* (Cambridge, MA: Harvard University Press, 2013).

134. Alexander M. Dushkin, "The Role of American Jews in Postwar Reconstruction," *Journal of Educational Sociology* 18:5 (January 1945): 261.

135. For example, see Reinhold Niebuhr's open letter to Hayim Greenberg in *Jewish Frontier* 3:6 (June 1936): 26; Hayim Greenberg, "Israel and Assur Meet in Manhattan," *Jewish Frontier* 10:12 (December 1943): 17–19; Pearl S. Buck's open letter to Hayim Greenberg in *Jewish Frontier* 11:6 (June 1944): 25; Jacques Maritain's open letter to Hayim Greenberg: "A Catholic View of the Crucifixion," *Jewish Frontier* 11:8 (August 1944): 14–15; "With Romain Rolland," in Greenberg, *The Inner Eye*, 2:271–278.

136. Israel Goldstein, *Israel at Home and Abroad, 1962–1972* (Jerusalem: Rubin Mass, 1973), 392; Rose L. Halprin, "Dedicatory Preface to Hayim Greenberg," xv–xvii.

137. Halpern and Reinharz, *Zionism and the Creation of a New Society*, chap. 11.

138. Brown, *The Israeli-American Connection*, 242–246.

139. Peter Y. Medding, *The Founding of Israeli Democracy, 1948–1967* (New York: Oxford University Press, 1990), 8–16, 30–42.

140. Michael Ottolenghi, "Harry Truman's Recognition of Israel," *Historical Journal* 47:4 (2004): 978, 982–984; Yosef Gorny, *The State of Israel in Jewish Public Thought: The Quest for Collective Identity* (New York: New York University Press, 1994), chap. 2.

141. Zvi Ganin, *An Uneasy Relationship: American Jewish Leadership and Israel, 1948–1967* (Syracuse: Syracuse University Press, 2005), 123–124.

142. See "The President's Day," Wednesday, November 15, 1950, Harry S. Truman Library and Museum, http://www.trumanlibrary.org/calendar/main.php?currYear=1950&currMonth=11&currDay=15.

143. Alfred Werner, "*Jewish Frontier Anthology, 1934–1944*," *Jewish Social Studies* 8:3 (July 1946): 215.

144. See Rufus Learsi (Israel Goldberg), *Fulfillment: The Epic Story of Zionism* (Cleveland: World Publishing Company, 1951), 306; Stanley F. Chyet, "American Jewish Literary Productivity: A Selected Bicentennial Bibliography," *Studies in Bibliography and Booklore* 11:1/2 (Winter 1975/76): 5. Neither *N. W. Ayer & Son's Directory* nor *Ulrich's Periodicals Directory*, the standard reference works on US periodicals, include *Jewish Frontier's* circulation figures for the early 1950s. It is likely *Jewish Frontier* chose not to report this data. (It was not until the 1970s that state and federal law required publication of such information.) Some American Jewish periodicals did disclose such data, e.g., *Jewish Daily Forward* (over 112,000), *Jewish Forum* (16,500), *Jewish Journal* (over 39,000); *N. W. Ayer & Son's Directory: Newspapers and Periodicals 1952*, ed. J. Percy H. Johnson (Philadelphia: N. W. Ayer & Son, 1952), 684. Meanwhile, after World War II, it has been observed, groups such as Bnai Brith and Hadassah produced "mass-circulation" magazines, the cost of which was included in members' dues, "giving the *Hadassah Magazine* an impressive circulation of 400,000 and Bnai Brith's *Jewish Monthly* close to 200,000." Such marketing potential no doubt "attracted advertisers and helped to underwrite production costs." Goren, "The Jewish Press," 220. In the absence of precise data concerning *Jewish Frontier*, the estimates presented here reflect a synthesis of the aforementioned context (see also note 81 above) and the following sources: (a) *Report of Farband-Labor Zionist Order* (1951), 2, NA'AMAT USA Archives, Canoga Park, CA (hereafter NUA); (b) Samuel Halperin, *The Political World of American Zionism* (Detroit: Wayne State University Press, 1961), 327; (c) Theodore Peterson, *Magazines in the Twentieth Century*, chap. 13; (d) Sam Pizzigati and Fred J. Solowey, *The New Labor Press*, xii–xiii.

145. Peterson, *Magazines in the Twentieth Century*, 363.

146. Pizzigati and Solowey, *The New Labor Press*, xiii.

147. Israel Knox, "Frontier or Frontiers," *Commentary* 1:3 (January 1, 1946): 92–93.

148. Hebrew Union College–Jewish Institute of Religion Records, MS-20, Box A3–6, AJA.

149. In 1943 Greenberg challenged a conference of American Habonim youth leaders to be wary of the Zionist movement's doctrinaire tendencies: "West is West and East is East. When you go to the West, you come to the East. When you go to the East, you come to the West." Quoted in a letter from Aryeh Goren to Mark A. Raider, August 4, 2014, in the author's possession.

150. For example, consider the similarities between Hayim Greenberg, "Patriotism and Plural Loyalties" (reprinted in this volume, chapter 26), and Simon Rawidowicz,

Bavel veyerushalayim, vol. 2 (Waltham, MA: Ararat, 1957), 369–371; Rawidowicz, *Israel: The Ever-Dying People and Other Essays*, ed. Benjamin C.I. Ravid (London: Associated University Presses, 1986), 194–204. See also David N. Myers, *Between Jew and Arab: The Lost Voice of Simon Rawidowicz* (Waltham, MA: Brandeis University Press, 2008), 121.

151. Transcript of Hayim Greenberg's remarks ("Our Cultural Objectives") in *Excerpts of Freedom Convention of Pioneer Women held at the Benjamin Franklin Hotel, Philadelphia, PA, June 11–15, 1949*, 268–272, NUA.

152. Mordecai M. Kaplan, *The Meaning of God in Modern Jewish Religion* (1937; reprint, Detroit: Wayne State University Press, 1994), 182.

153. See "The Future of American Jewry," in Greenberg, *The Inner Eye*, 2:66. The complete essay is reprinted in this volume, chapter 29. At another point in this address, Greenberg underscored his inability to accept the concept of divine redemption. Paraphrasing Nietzsche, he cast a sidelong glance at the tradition of desacralization in modern Jewish life: "Nietzsche once sarcastically remarked regarding Christians, 'Christianity, I have been told all my life, is the religion of salvation. But I know my Christians well and they don't look saved.' I could paraphrase this to read: 'Jews, I have been told all my life, are a chosen people. But knowing my contemporary Jews, they somehow don't look chosen.' Yet it may not be so very important how Jews appear in the eyes of non-Jews; but it is important how they appear to themselves." Greenberg, *The Inner Eye*, 2:67. See also "New York Board of Rabbis Completes Three-Day Celebration of its 70th Anniversary," *JTA Daily News Bulletin* 28:71 (April 11, 1951), 4, http://pdfs.jta.org/1951/1951-04-11_071.pdf.

154. "US Members of Jewish Agency Oppose Recruitment of American Jewish Youth for Israel," *JTA Daily News Bulletin* (August 7, 1951), 1, http://pdfs.jta.org/1951/1951-08-07_153.pdf.

155. Quoted in *American Jewish Year Book* 53 (1952): 564. See also Charles S. Liebman, "Diaspora Influence on Israel: The Ben-Gurion-Blaustein 'Exchange' and Its Aftermath," *Jewish Social Studies* 36:3–4 (July-October 1974): 271–280.

156. Gorny, *The State of Israel in Jewish Public Thought*, 33–34.

157. "Jewish Agency Functions in US Divided among Executive Members," *JTA Daily News Bulletin* 28:198 (October 15, 1951), 4, http://pdfs.jta.org/1951/1951-10-15_198.pdf. In a related vein, Greenberg was instrumental in helping to create a chair in Yiddish literature at the Hebrew University in 1951. See Rachel Rojanski, "The Status of Yiddish in Israel, 1948–1951: An Overview (1)," *Mendele Review: Yiddish Literature and Language* 9:2 (February 2005); http://yiddish.haifa.ac.il/tmr/tmr09/tmr09002.htm.

158. See chapter 28, "Jewish Culture and Education in the Diaspora," in this volume, 317.

159. Ibid.

160. Lawrence H. Fuchs, *The American Kaleidoscope: Race, Ethnicity and the Civic Culture* (Hanover, NH: University Press of New England, 1990), 1–6, 65–69, 73–74.

161. See chapter 28, "Jewish Culture and Education in the Diaspora," in this volume, 317.

162. Quoted in Simon N. Herman, *Jewish Identity: A Social-Psychological Perspective*, 2nd ed. (1978; reprint, New Brunswick, NJ: Transaction Publishers, 1989), 130–131.

Chapter 1

Source: Hayim Greenberg, "The Meaning of Zionism," in *The Inner Eye: Selected Essays*, vol. 2, ed. Shlomo Katz (New York: Jewish Frontier Association, 1964), 25–59.

1. Diogenes (c. 412–323 BCE), a Greek Cynic philosopher, asserted that virtue is revealed in action. He publicly disdained Plato (see note 19 in chapter 9, "To a Communist Friend," in this volume) and Socrates (see note 56 in chapter 16, "Chosen Peoples," in this volume), and he is reported to have demonstrated his quest for an honest man by carrying a lantern with him.

2. The Hellenistic school of Greek philosophy known as "Cynicism" centered on living one's life in accord with nature, relying on only bare necessities for sustenance, and rejecting the conventions of wealth, power, and social status. An exemplar of Greek Cynicism, Diogenes opted for a life of abject poverty.

3. Stoicism, a school of Greek philosophy founded by Zeno of Citium in c. 200 BCE, held that a universal divine force pervades the world and all reality is material. Stoics sought to live consistently with nature and set aside unjust passions and actions in order to achieve true freedom through civic duty. The philosophers Seneca (c. 4 BCE–65 CE) and Epictetus (c. 55–135 CE) and the Roman emperor Marcus Aurelius (c. 121–180 CE) were notable adherents of Stoicism.

4. The Russian writer and religious philosopher Leo Tolstoy's (1828–1910) most famous works are *War and Peace* (1869), a prose epic of the Napoleonic wars, and *Anna Karenina* (1875–77), a tragedy about Russian life in St. Petersburg society at the time of Tsar Alexander II.

5. Tolstoy's negative view of the tsarist regime, especially imperial Russia's intense militarism, patriotism, and nationalism, is amplified in the novel *War and Peace* (1869). In later life, Tolstoy became a devout Christian pacifist and advocated a doctrine of political non-resistance.

6. Jules Ferry (1832–93), a French statesman who rose through the Third Republic's ranks, was instrumental in establishing France's universal system of free compulsory secular education. As prime minister, he was a key architect of the French colonial system.

7. Engelbert Pernerstorfer (1850–1918), an Austrian journalist and Social Democratic Party leader, advocated anti-Habsburg nationalism. His sympathetic attitude to the Jewish predicament in central European society made him exceptional in a time of rising Austrian antisemitism.

8. Jean Jaurès (1859–1914), a French social democratic leader and antimilitarist, played a key role in the Dreyfus Affair as a public champion of Alfred Dreyfus's innocence (see notes 10 and 13 in chapter 26, "Patriotism and Plural Loyalities," in this volume). He was assassinated in 1914 by a French nationalist.

9. See Jean Jaurès, *Studies in Socialism*, trans. Mildred Minturn (New York: G. P. Putnam's Sons, 1906), 9.

10. German philosopher Georg Wilhelm Friedrich Hegel (1770–1831) changed the course of European philosophy with *The Phenomenology of Spirit* (1807), which posits an enveloping absolute in a state of perpetual self-creation. The worldwide *Geist* (German for "spirit" or "mind") is to be discerned through a search for meaning and purpose

to history. Known as the "Hegelian dialectic," the contemplation of dialectical knowledge begins with a concept (thesis), which evokes its opposite (antithesis), and the two interact to form a new concept (synthesis), which in turn becomes a new thesis. Hegel asserted that nations possess unique national spirits, which are part of an unfolding universal historical experience, and he viewed Christianity as the successor to paganism and Judaism. His ideas had a profound impact on socialist theory and Marxist dialectical materialism.

11. In his *Philosophical Letters* (1836), the Russian philosopher Pyotr Yakovlevich Chaadaev (1794–1856) posited Russia to be an isolated and primitive society in desperate need of catching up with the West. Rejecting Chaadaev's call, a loose pan-Slavic coalition of liberal and conservative elements led by the Russian poet Aleksey Stepanovich Khmyakov (1804–60) and the Russian literary critic Ivan Vasilyevich Kireyevsky (1806–56) founded the Slavophile movement. They valorized Russia's non-Western national heritage, cultural traditions, and the religious dogmas of the Russian Orthodox Church. The writer Fyodor Dostoyevsky (see note 14 in chapter 8, "Notes on Marxism," in this volume) later became a key representative of the Russian Slavophile sensibility.

12. Ahad Haam (Hebrew for "one of the people") was the pen name of Asher Zvi Ginsberg (1856–1927), the Hebrew essayist and cultural Zionist philosopher. He argued that Zionism could not solve the "problem of the Jews" (i.e., their social, economic, and political plight) but rather the "problem of Judaism" (i.e., the trend of Jewish assimilation into European society). In his view, cultural and spiritual renewal was a necessary precondition to creating a new Jewish society. He urged the use of Hebrew as a secular language and the Hebrew Bible as the basis for morality and culture rather than religiosity.

13. For example, Ahad Haam described as "dangerous" those who seek "salvation in a future not connected with our past, and [believe] that after a history extending over thousands of years a people can begin again, like a newborn child, and create for itself a new national land, a new national life and aims. . . . [They forget] that it is the nation—that is, the national ego in the form given to it by history—that desires to live: not some other nation, but just this one, with all its essentials, and all its memories, and all its hopes. . . . They err who think it is possible to lead [the national ego of the Jewish people] along the path of their own choice." Ahad Haam, *Selected Essays*, trans. Leon Simon (Philadelphia: Jewish Publication Society of America, 1912), 89–90.

14. The phrase "uninterrupted process of becoming" is derived from Friedrich Engels, "Ludwig Feuerbach and the End of Classical German Philosophy" (1886). See Karl Marx and Friedrich Engels, *Selected Works* (New York: International Publishers, 1972), 627.

15. Christianity is the dominant religious faith of Great Britain. In addition to the Church of England (the Anglican Church), British Christianity historically included and produced a broad spectrum of denominational subgroups, splinter groups, and dissenters (e.g., Presbyterianism, Roman Catholicism, Methodism, Quakers, Baptists, Anabaptists, Mennonites, Charismatics, and Pentecostals).

16. The Ukrainian Hebrew novelist and essayist Micah Yosef Berdichevsky (1865–1921) was deeply influenced by the Haskalah and secular European culture, particularly the German philosopher Friedrich Nietzsche (1844–1900), who asserted the necessity

of establishing a new basis for social values. In opposition to the ideas of Ahad Haam and Theodor Herzl, Berdichevsky declaimed a Nietzschean demand for the "transvaluation" of Judaism and Jewish history.

17. The Jewish philosopher Martin Buber (1878–1965) is best known for his work *I and Thou* (1923), which posits a direct personal dialogue between God and the individual. Born in Vienna, Buber was deeply influenced by the Zionist philosophers Ahad Haam and A. D. Gordon. As a young man, he assumed an active role in Zionist affairs as a champion of Jewish educational, cultural, and spiritual concerns, calling himself a spokesman for "Hebrew humanism." From 1924 to 1933 Buber taught philosophy and religion at the University of Frankfurt-am-Main. In this period, he was a founder of Brit Shalom, a group of liberal Jewish intellectuals that advocated the creation of a binational Jewish-Arab state within the framework of the British mandate. The rise of Nazism prompted Buber to leave Germany and in 1938 he immigrated to Palestine and became a professor of social philosophy at the Hebrew University of Jerusalem, a position he held until his retirement in 1951. Buber was a vigorous advocate of Arab-Jewish reconciliation and consistently strove to infuse political Zionism with ethical and spiritual values.

18. Greenberg is apparently referring to themes Berdichevsky developed in a series of essays republished in 1922 in a collection titled *Baderekh* (On the Way). In the latter, Berdichevsky, who viewed ancient Jerusalem as a fulcrum of Jewish history, rejected Ahad Haam's proposition that Judaism esteems spiritual superiority over physical strength. He elevated the memory of the zealots and Masada, traditionally scorned in the Talmud, and proposed an innovative scheme of Jewish history divided into two eras: he described the first (the "age of Shammai") as a period of vitality and strength, and the second (the "age of Hillel") as a period of repressive and stultifying rabbinic authority. In Berdichevsky's Nietzschean view, the latter marked the start of the Jews' estrangement from nature and history. See Gideon Shimoni, *The Zionist Ideology* (Hanover, NH: University Press of New England, 1995), 288–292.

19. Berdichevsky was not an entirely consistent thinker and his writings contain many contradictions. In various instances, he views the Jewish past as "wholly dispensable," while in others he actually concurs with Ahad Haam's argument about "building upon the heritage of the [Jewish] past." Gideon Shimoni, *The Zionist Ideology* (Hanover, NH: Brandeis University Press, 1995), 290–291.

20. The Russian Jewish historian Simon Dubnow (1860–1941) articulated the theory of autonomism. He described the Jewish people as a "spiritual community" united by religious, cultural, and historical bonds, and believed the Jews had entered a higher stage of post-territorial history that anticipated the future of all nations. In the meanwhile, however, he believed Jews should enjoy cultural autonomy and even a measure of Jewish self-government in their respective host societies. See also note 30 in chapter 4, "Sabbatai Zevi," in this volume.

21. Gabriel de Tarde (1843–1904), a French sociologist and criminologist, was known for his general social theory distinguishing between inventive and imitative persons. His major works include *The Laws of Imitation* (1890) and *Social Laws: An Outline of Sociology* (1899).

22. Gaul is the ancient designation for the land south and west of the Rhine, west of

the Alps, and north of the Pyrenees. The name comes from the Celts, who were called Gauls by the Romans.

23. This is the common designation for the Norsemen (Northmen), who conquered Normandy in the tenth century CE and adopted Christianity and the customs and language of France. In 1066 they conquered England and displaced the local Anglo-Saxon nobility.

24. In the ninth century CE, the Varangians, Scandinavian merchant warriors who raided the eastern shores of the Baltic, penetrated into Europe. Their chieftain, Rurik (c. 830–879), established himself in Novgorod in 862 and laid the foundations for Kievan Rus.

25. Tartar (also Tatar) refers to a member of any of the Turkic or Mongolian peoples of central Asia. These groups originally invaded western Asia and eastern Europe in the medieval period.

26. This may refer to the work of Marcel Mauss (1872–1950), the pioneering French anthropologist and author of *The Gift* (1925), whose studies included observations of the gait of men and women in the West. See Marcel Fournier, *Marcell Mauss: A Biography*, trans. Jane Marie Todd (Princeton, NJ: Princeton University Press, 2006), 247, 261, 277, 290, 397n.15.

27. Gustav Le Bon (1841–1931), a French sociologist and social psychologist, was a pioneer of the study of psychosocial bases of criminal behavior. His works include the pseudo-scientific eugenics study *Applications of Psychology to the Classification of Races* (1886), *The Crowd: A Study of the Popular Mind* (1895), and *The Psychology of Peoples* (1898).

28. Heinrich Heine (1797–1856), one of the greatest German lyric poets, was a significant figure in the revolutionary literary movement "Young Germany." Despite converting to Christianity, Jewish themes featured prominently in many of his best-known works.

29. Ludwig Boerne (1786–1837), a German Jewish writer and the first great journalist-critic in German history, edited the journal *Die Waage* (The Scales) during the brief window of liberalism before the Prussian reaction closed it down in 1821. He was later blamed by the nationalist Henrich von Treitschke (1834–96) for corrupting the Germans with "dilettante politics" and was driven into exile in Paris.

30. Mark Antokolsky (1843–1902), born in Vilna, Lithuania, was a prominent Russian Jewish sculptor whose work conveyed a spiritual and social message. After the pogroms of 1882 he emigrated to Paris.

31. The German social philosopher Karl Marx (1818–83) was descended from a family of central European rabbis. However, Marx's parents converted to Christianity before he was born and he was baptized at age six. In 1842 he earned a doctorate from the University of Jena. The following year, while in Paris, he began his lifelong collaboration with Friedrich Engels (1820–95). Together they published *The Communist Manifesto* (1848), a seminal work in the development of Marxism. In 1850 Marx relocated to London, where in 1864 he founded the International Workingmen's Association (also known as the First International). During this period he wrote his monumental treatise *Das Kapital* in which he adapted Hegelian thought to produce the theory of dialectical materialism. Marx published the first volume of *Das Kapital* in 1867; Engels published the sec-

ond and third volumes after Marx's death in 1885 and 1894. Marx's theory of dynamic social change proved to be hugely influential worldwide and spawned the modern forms of socialism and communism. Though Marx advocated Jewish emancipation in Europe, his essay "On the Jewish Problem" (1844), written as a critique of the German Protestant philosopher Bruno Bauer's (1809–82) tract "The Jewish Problem" (1843), relies on explicitly negative Jewish stereotypes and is considered a key text in the history of antisemitism. The Bauer-Marx exchange is reprinted in *The Jew in the Modern World: A Documentary History*, 3rd ed., ed. Paul Mendes-Flohr and Jehuda Reinharz (New York: Oxford University Press, 2011), 297–302.

32. Ferdinand Lassalle (1825–64), a German Jewish socialist leader and theoretician, was a major figure in the development of German workers movement. In contrast to Karl Marx, who did not regard him as ideologically pure, Lassalle favored the notion of collaborating with the state to create a system of labor cooperatives. In 1863 he founded the first German labor party. After Lassalle was killed in a duel, it was discovered he had secretly corresponded and met with Chancellor Otto von Bismarck (1815–98) in an attempt to make common cause with the Prussian government.

33. The term *Weltschmerz* (German for "world grief") is associated with the German poets of the Romantic era and refers to a mood of pessimism and melancholy arising from the refusal or inability to adjust to realities seen as destructive to the rights of personal freedom.

34. Isaac Ilyich Levitan (1860–1900), a celebrated Russian Jewish painter, produced over a thousand artistic works, mostly in the decade from 1887 to 1897. His works are characterized by a thorough knowledge of Russian scenery and life.

35. Ivan Sergeyvich Turgenev (1818–83) was a Russian novelist, dramatist, and short story writer. Considered one of Russia's foremost authors, Turgenev dealt with complex social and political issues in his work. His best-known novel, *Fathers and Sons* (1862), is considered a masterpiece of modern Russian fiction.

36. Maxim Gorky (1868–1936), a Russian Marxist writer whose social realism emphasized descriptions of the outcasts of society as the hope of the future, is considered the father of Soviet literature. Exiled from tsarist Russia in 1905, he mostly lived abroad until 1928 when he returned to Soviet Russia as a celebrated figure. Among his important works are the novels *Three of Them* (1900), *The Mother* (1906), and *The Life of Matvey Kozhemyakin* (1910). His plays include *The Lower Depths* (1902), *The Zykovs* (1913), and *Yegor Bulychov and Others* (1932).

37. The Russian author and dramatist Anton Pavlovich Chekhov (1860–1904) is known for his sensitive portrayal of characters whose struggles with the loneliness, frustration, and stagnation of tsarist Russian society raise issues of universal concern. His significant dramas include *The Sea Gull* (1898), *Uncle Vanya* (1899), *The Three Sisters* (1901), and *The Cherry Orchard* (1904).

38. In 1933, the writer and poet Ivan Alekseyvich Bunin (1870–1953) became the first Russian to win the Nobel Prize in Literature. He is best known for the novellas *The Village* (1910) and *Dry Valley* (1912), the autobiographical novel *The Life of Arseniev* (1933), and the book of short stories *Dark Avenues* (1946).

39. It is unclear to whom Greenberg is referring here.

40. In William Shakespeare's *The Merchant of Venice* (c. 1596), the Jewish money-

lender Shylock, a proud and tragic figure abused by medieval Christian society, is paradoxically both a victim and a potential villain.

41. In *The Merchant of Venice*, Shylock's only daughter, Jessica, elopes with Lorenzo, her Christian suitor.

42. Shakespeare, *The Merchant of Venice*, 2.5.34–36.

43. Greenberg is referring to the opening stanzas of Heinrich Heine's "Princess Sabbath" (1851): "Yet the magic time expires, / And once more and of a sudden / We behold his royal highness / Changed into a shaggy monster. / Of a prince of such-like fortune / Sings my song. His name is Israel, / And a witch's art has changed him / To the figure of a dog. / As a dog, with doggish notions, / All the week his time he muddles / Through life's filthiness and sweepings, / To the scavengers' derision. / But upon each Friday evening, / Just at twilight, the enchantment / Ceases suddenly,—the dog / Once more is a human being." *The Poems of Heine*, trans. Edgar Alfred Bowring (London: George Bell and Sons, 1891), 466.

44. Haim Nahman Bialik (1873–1934), considered the poet laureate of modern Hebrew, was raised in a traditional Jewish household in the Pale of Settlement. He broke with Orthodox Judaism at the age of eighteen and thereafter devoted himself to secular Jewish culture. He became a Hebrew teacher and a Zionist, and he was particularly drawn to the socialist Zionist pioneers of Palestine. His poetry and prose deals with a broad range of subjects. Among his most famous poems is "The City of Slaughter," composed in the aftermath of the Kishinev pogrom of 1903, which became a symbol of the Zionist revolt against Jewish vulnerability in the diaspora. In 1924, he immigrated to Palestine.

45. Quoted from "*Megilat haesh*" (The Scroll of Fire) (1905). For an English translation, see *Complete Poetic Works of Hayyim Nahman Bialik*, ed. Israel Efros (New York: Histadruth Ivrith of America, 1948), 164. For the original Hebrew, see *Haim Nahman Bialik: Shirim, 1899–1934*, ed. Dan Miron, vol. 2 (Tel Aviv: Dvir, 1990), 224.

46. The biblical Hebrew term *avadon* (Abaddon) refers to both a destroying angel and the realm of the dead. In Christianity it signifies the antichrist and Satan, the angel-prince of hell. In Western literature it connotes a vast evil wilderness and the source of the River Styx.

47. See *Complete Poetic Works of Hayyim Nahman Bialik*, 197; *Haim Nahman Bialik: Shirim*, 233.

48. Greenberg is referring to the Turkish mystic Sabbatai Zevi (see note 53, below) and the Polish merchant Jacob Frank (1726–91), both false self-proclaimed Jewish messiahs, as well as their followers and other lesser known figures.

49. Greenberg is referring to the sojourns of Sabbatai Zevi, Jacob Frank, and their followers across Europe and northern Africa. Meanwhile, he is suggesting the Sabbateans, Frankists, and other premodern Jewish messianic groups underwent a key psychological shift insofar as they believed it possible to escape the oppressive reality of medieval Christian Europe.

50. The Dutch Jewish philosopher Baruch (Benedict) Spinoza (1632–77) was excommunicated in 1656 by the Sephardic Jewish community of Amsterdam for his allegedly heretical views. Spinoza, who never expressed remorse about his separation from Jewish life, substantially influenced modern Jewish thought and was a precursor of modern secular Jewish identity. Spinoza's philosophical work laid the groundwork of modern bib-

lical criticism and helped to usher in the European Enlightenment. He favored democratic government and argued humanity should adjust to and accept the infinite order of the universe, seeing all events as an aspect of eternity. His major works are *The Theological-Political Treatise* (1670), a critical analysis of the composition and transmission of the Hebrew Bible and its impact on society, and *Ethics, Demonstrated in Geometrical Order* (1677), in which he deploys Euclidean thought to analyze God and nature.

51. In 1617 Uriel Acosta (c. 1590–1647), a Portuguese Sephardic Jew whose family were *conversos* (New Christians), decided to flee to Amsterdam and return to Judaism. In 1624 he published *An Examination of the Traditions of the Pharisees*, which openly questioned the doctrine of the immortality of the soul and challenged the authority of rabbinic Judaism. Acosta's views generated considerable controversy and he was excommunicated by the Amsterdam Jewish community. After a brief stay in Hamburg, he returned to Amsterdam, recanted, and was permitted to rejoin the Jewish community. When in 1633 he was discovered espousing heretical views, he was excommunicated for a second time. He lived in virtual isolation for seven years until he again recanted, acceded to lashings and public humiliation, and was permitted to rejoin the Jewish community. Broken and demoralized, he wrote a memoir titled *Exemplar Vitae* (1640) and afterward took his own life.

52. The Venetian rabbi Leon de Modena (1571–1648) was a scholar, poet, translator, and publicist. His personal life was troubled by considerable misfortune, including the deaths of three of his children and his wife's mental illness. His resources were depleted by a gambling addiction and he suffered from perpetual anxiety in this regard. Nonetheless, he proved to be a prolific author, engaged in biblical criticism, and compiled a Hebrew-Italian dictionary. His major work, *Ari nohem* (The Lion Roars, 1840), is a defense of traditional Judaism and an attack on the authority of the *Zohar* (Book of Splendor), a thirteenth-century Jewish mystical text redacted by the Castilian kabbalist Moses de Léon (c. 1250–1305).

53. In 1648 Sabbatai Zevi (1626–76), a Sephardic rabbi and kabbalist born in Izmir (Smyrna), Turkey, proclaimed he heard a "heavenly voice" and declared himself to be the messiah. In 1654 he was excommunicated by the rabbis of Izmir and left for Salonica, where he attracted a large following. He next traveled to Rhodes, Tripoli, and Egypt before arriving in Gaza in 1665, where Nathan Benjamin ben Elisha Halevy (Nathan of Gaza) (1643–80) proclaimed him the messiah. Against the backdrop of rising messianic expectations, Zevi embarked on a grand tour via Jerusalem and Aleppo to Istanbul, where he was seized and imprisoned by the Turkish vizier. In 1666 he was taken to Adrianople, where the sultan forced him to choose between conversion to Islam or death. Following his conversion, Zevi assumed a new name and was granted a title and a government pension. Though he continued to practice Judaism secretly, Zevi's conversion undermined the Sabbatean movement and it quickly collapsed.

54. The central European Jewish philosopher Moses Mendelssohn (1729–86) is considered the founding figure of the Haskalah. He sought to synthesize Judaism with the rationalism of the Enlightenment, and his general writings, which anticipated the aesthetics of the central European philosopher Immanuel Kant (1724–1804) and the German poet Friedrich Schiller (1759–1805), include *Philosophical Speeches* (1755) and *Phaedo, or On the*

Immortality of the Soul (1767). His seminal theological-philosophical work, *Jerusalem, or On Religious Power and Judaism* (1783), argues religious truths can be discovered through reason and declaims Judaism's uniqueness as a divinely revealed code of ritual, moral, and legal obligations. He translated the Hebrew Bible into German, strove to develop positive relations between Jews and Christians, and defended the legitimacy of the world's multiple faiths. The composers Felix Mendelssohn (1809–47) and Fanny Mendelssohn Hensel (1805–47) were his grandchildren. See also note 9 in chapter 31, "Religious Tolerance," in this volume.

55. Greenberg may be alluding to "The Way Out" (1919), a short story by the Hebrew writer Yosef Haim Brenner (see note 13 in chapter 18, "The Myth of Jewish Parasitism," in this volume) set during the Turkish and British wartime struggles over Palestine.

56. [Greenberg's note:] We include in this Jewry the eastern European Jews as well, despite their not having been emancipated until very recently [by the Paris Peace Conference of 1919], for thanks to the influences coming from the West the Russian Jews underwent approximately the same evolution as their western European brothers before their own emancipation.

57. The French Jewish philosopher Henri-Louis Bergson (1859–1941) originally trained as a mathematician before gravitating to philosophy. In 1900 he was appointed to a faculty position at the Collège de France. With the publication of *Creative Evolution* (1907), he rapidly garnered worldwide acclaim. What came to be known as Bergsonism—the theory that the world is perpetually evolving, time is the central fact of experience, and the *élan vital* which governs all organic processes can only be apprehended intuitively—influenced William James's (1842–1910) formulation of American pragmatism, the prose of Willa Cather (1873–1947), Wallace Stevens (1879–1955), and other Modernist writers, and the painting of Jean Metzinger (1883–1956), Albert Gleizes (1881–1953), and other Cubist artists associated with the *avant garde* Puteaux group. In 1914 Bergson became the first Jew elected to the Académie Française. His major works include *Matter and Memory* (1896), *Laughter: An Essay on the Meaning of the Comic* (1900), *Mind Energy* (1919), *The Two Sources of Morality and Religion* (1932), and *The Creative Mind* (1934). He won the 1927 Nobel Prize in Literature.

58. In literary and popular legend, Ahasuerus, a Jew who supposedly mocked or mistreated Jesus while he was en route to be crucified, was condemned to a life of wandering on earth until Judgment Day. The story, common in the folklore of premodern and early modern western Europe, was accentuated by regional variations.

59. In Greek mythology, Prometheus stole fire and arts from the gods and gave them to man. The supreme god Zeus punished him by tying him to a mountain where a vulture devoured his liver until Hercules freed him. In Western literature, Prometheus is a symbol of deliverance and redemption.

Chapter 2

Source: Hayim Greenberg, "*Mediniyut veavodah*," *Haolam*, February 7, 1923, 70–71. Translated from Hebrew by Yaron Peleg and Mark A. Raider.

1. Greenberg is referring to the traditional Jewish prayer known as "*Asher yazar*"

(Who has formed [humankind]) that is recited after using the bathroom and as part of the daily morning benedictions. The prayer concludes with the phrase, "Blessed are you, God, who heals all flesh and acts wondrously."

2. During World War I, the British and Turkish forces fought for control of the Mediterranean theatre, including the southwestern region of the Ottoman Empire. The British government's determination to gain control of Palestine gave added impetus to London's military strategy, which began in 1917 with the capture of the Beer Sheva and Gaza districts. The new conquests added to the British-controlled areas stretching from Hebron to Tiberias and Safed as provided for in the Sykes-Picot Agreement of 1916. On November 2, 1917, the British government issued the Balfour Declaration expressing "sympathy with Jewish Zionist aspirations" in Palestine. The declaration, which marked a pivotal shift in the Zionism's political fortunes, catapulted Chaim Weizmann (1874–1952) into the international limelight as the movement's premiere leader. (In this period, Weizmann, who from 1892 to 1901 had trained in Germany and Switzerland as a scientist and emigrated in 1904 to England to assume a post at the University of Manchester, devised a synthetic method for producing acetone used in munitions that helped to boost Britain's war effort. After the war, he assumed the leadership of the Jewish Agency and World Zionist Organization, serving as president of the latter in 1920–31 and 1935–46. In 1948 he became Israel's first president.) At the end of December 1917 British forces entered Jerusalem under General Edmund H.H. Allenby (1861–1936), ending four hundred years of Ottoman rule over the Holy Land. After the war, the Zionist position was further advanced when the League of Nations assigned the mandate for Palestine to Great Britain and the Yishuv's political future became an international concern.

3. Theodor Herzl (1860–1904), father of modern political Zionism and founder of the World Zionist Organization, was originally a highly acculturated Jew with few attachments to Judaism and Jewish life. In many ways, Herzl's trajectory exemplified the experience of modern European Jewry. Caught between the twin promise of liberalism and emancipation on the one hand and the rise of antisemitism and anti-Jewish violence on the other, Herzl was shocked to the core by the Dreyfus Affair in 1894 (see notes 10 and 13 in chapter 26, "Patriotism and Plural Loyalties," in this volume). Herzl, who covered the affair as the Paris correspondent of the *Neue Freie Presse* (New Free Press) of Vienna, concluded the only solution to the "Jewish problem" was a mass exodus of Jews from their host societies and resettlement in a land of their own. He spelled out this idea in a treatise titled *The Jews' State: An Attempt at a Modern Solution of the Jewish Question* (1896). Herzl was responsible for convening the first World Zionist Congress in 1897 and the establishment of the movement's main instruments, the World Zionist Organization, the Jewish Colonial Trust, and *Die Welt* (The World), a Zionist weekly. In 1902 he published *Altneuland* (Old-New Land), a utopian depiction of the Jewish society he envisioned. Although he failed to reach lasting agreements with European leaders or convince wealthy Jewish benefactors to fund his plans, Herzl's tireless leadership paved the way for subsequent Zionist political activity.

4. Herzl sought to procure a charter from a world imperial power in order to sanction the Zionist movement's aims and establish international legitimacy. To this end, he assiduously laid the groundwork for an eventual encounter in 1898 with Kaiser Wilhelm II (1859–1941) that, although unproductive, helped boost Zionism's visibility. In

1900 he publicly asserted the need for a charter at the Fourth Zionist Congress in London. In 1901 Herzl met with Ottoman Sultan Abdulhamid II (1842–1918) and unsuccessfully sought to persuade him to allow large-scale Jewish colonial settlement in Palestine in exchange for help consolidating the Turkish empire's debts. Herzl also used his contact with members of the British government, particularly secretary of state for the colonies Joseph Chamberlain (1836–1914), to broker a charter that would permit Jewish settlement in the British-occupied Sinai peninsula. While Herzl's charter idea did not bear fruit in his lifetime, his efforts elevated Zionism's standing in the global arena and laid the groundwork for the Jewish claim to sovereignty in Palestine.

5. Cyrus the Great (c. 600–529 BCE) founded the vast Achaemenid empire (c. 550–330 BCE). Centered in Persia, Cyrus's empire stretched from the Aegean Sea in the west to the Indus River in the east. In the course of expanding and consolidating his empire, Cyrus freed the Jews from Babylonian captivity and facilitated the restoration of Jewish political power in ancient Palestine. The Greek historian Herodotus (c. 484–425 BCE) and the writer Xenophanes (see note 80 in chapter 24, "The Universalism of the Chosen People," in this volume) are chiefly responsible for chronicling Cyrus's legacy as a military strategist and imperial leader.

6. On Haim Nahman Bialik, see note 44 in chapter 1, "The Meaning of Zionism," in this volume, 371.

7. On Bialik's conceptualization of *agadah*, see chapter 20, "*Halakhah* and *Agadah*," in this volume, 204.

Chapter 3

Source: Hayim Greenberg, "East and West," in *The Inner Eye: Selected Essays*, vol. 2, ed. Shlomo Katz (New York: Jewish Frontier Publishing Association, 1964), 77–83.

1. Magyars, the principal ethnic group of Hungary, also live in Romania, Ukraine, Slovakia, and Yugoslavia.

2. On the Tartars, see note 25 in chapter 1, "The Meaning of Zionism," in this volume.

3. The reference is to natives of Kalmykia, a region of southwest Russia on the Caspian Sea, who are mostly Buddhist Mongols. Kalmykia came under Russian control in the mid-seventeenth century.

4. The reference is to natives of a region in west-central Asia bordering on northwest China. Kirghiz was probably inhabited before the thirteenth century by a Turkish-speaking people and was annexed by Russia in 1864. After the Bolshevik revolution, it became a semi-autonomous region. In 1926, one year after Greenberg wrote this essay, Kirghiz was reorganized by the Soviets and in 1936 it officially became a constituent republic of the Soviet Union.

5. The German term for a comprehensive philosophy of the world and human society.

6. Born in Odessa, Russia, Yizhak Epstein (1862–1943) was a writer and linguist. In 1886 he immigrated to Palestine and found work as a laborer in Zikhron Yaakov and Rosh Pinah. In 1891 he became principal of a new public school in Safed and later taught in Metulah and Rosh Pinah. Between 1902 and 1908 he completed his studies in education at the University of Lausanne and subsequently directed a school of the Alliance

Israélite Universelle in Salonika. After World War I he returned to Palestine, where he settled in Jerusalem and became the supervisor of schools administered by the Zionist movement. An advocate of Arab-Jewish reconciliation, he was a founding member of Brit Shalom (see note 10 in chapter 7, "Revisionism," in this volume) but later resigned from the organization because of ideological conflicts with other members of the group.

7. Menahem Mendel Ussishkin (1863–1941) was born in the Russian town of Dubrovno to a Hasidic family. In 1884 he was among the founders of the Bnei Zion society, and in 1887 he was sent as the society's delegate to the Hovevei Zion conference in Durzkeniki, where he attracted attention as an articulate and forceful young leader. In 1889 he joined Ahad Haam's (see note 12 in chapter 1, "The Meaning of Zionsim," in this volume) Bnei Moshe society, and in 1891 he visited Palestine for the first time. Settling in Yekaterinoslav, he became a prominent leader of Russian Zionism. In 1903 Ussishkin traveled to Palestine on behalf of the Russian Zionist Geulah company in order to purchase land for would-be settlers. During his stay, he organized a three-day conference at Zikhron Yaakov. He used the occasion to urge the organization of Palestine's Jewish community and to establish the Hebrew Teachers' Association. In 1904 he published *Our Program*, a treatise calling for a synthesis of political and pragmatic Zionism. The following year he helped to spearhead the Zionei Zion group that successfully defeated the Uganda scheme at the Seventh Zionist Congress, thereby affirming the Palestinocentric orientation of the Zionist movement as a whole. In 1919 Ussishkin settled in Palestine, where he continued to play an active role as head of the local Zionist commission. His major contribution to the practical development of Palestine took place between 1923 and 1941, when he served as chairman of the Jewish National Fund.

8. In 1885 the Russian Zionist activist Yehiel Mikhael Halpern (1860–1919), son of a prominent Hebrew Bible scholar, immigrated to Palestine. In 1887 he helped organize Agudat Poalim (Workers Association), the first Jewish workers union in the country. He subsequently returned to Russia to organize would-be Zionist pioneers and socialist Zionist workers groups; he was also one of the initiators of the Marxist Zionist Poalei Zion Party. In 1905 he helped found Hashomer (The Watchguard), Palestine's first Jewish self-defense organization.

9. On Martin Buber, see note 17 in chapter 1, "The Meaning of Zionism," in this volume.

10. This refers to World War I.

11. Greenberg is referring to the modernizing impact of the West and the fledgling Indian nationalist movement comprising a spectrum of moderate constitutionalist and revolutionary groups. In this period, Mohandas K. Gandhi (1869–1948) emerged as the dominant figure in Indian nationalism. Gandhi fully supported the British during World War I and was initially inclined to accept British plans for the gradual implementation of increased Indian autonomy after the war. In 1920, however, he changed his position and started a nonviolent campaign of non-cooperation with the government. His distinctive achievement was his capacity to promote unity among the disparate Indian nationalist groups and stamp the movement as a whole with a self-awareness that emphasized the needs of the masses, appeals for non-violent action, and the renunciation of modes of Western living.

12. At the time Greenberg wrote this essay, China was undergoing a dramatic transformation. Following World War I, the country was beset by social, economic, and political upheaval that provided the scope and inducement for the emergence of dissident Western strains of anarchism, liberalism, materialism, socialism, and communism. The new ideas and attitudes invigorated vast segments of Chinese society and brought to the fore the Kuomintang nationalist party, which placed a premium on anti-imperialism and the nationalization of major industries. In 1923 Soviet Russia threw its support behind the ascendant Kuomintang, which in 1924 reorganized itself along the lines of Bolshevik "democratic centralism" and extended its influence and reach countrywide. The years 1926 to 1928 witnessed the unification of China under the Nationalist leader Chang Kai-shek (1887–1975), who would later split with the Communists, setting the stage for a decisive conflict with Mao Zedong (1893–1976) and the Chinese Communist Party.

13. The reference is to the belief and practice of the Russian Bolshevik regime in the immediate post-revolutionary years. In this period, the Bolshevik leaders attempted to spread Marxist Communism to Asia and Africa, arguing that the peoples of these disenfranchised and exploited regions possessed a natural disinclination toward Western capitalism and non-Communist societies.

14. A German historian and philosopher, Oswald Spengler (1880–1936) is best known for *The Decline of the West* (1918–22), in which he argued that civilizations and cultures are subject to the same cycle of growth and decay as human beings. Spengler upheld the ideal of obedience to the state and supported German hegemony in Europe. His refusal to support Nazi theories of racial superiority led to his ostracism after the Nazis came to power in 1933.

15. The Druze Arabs are natives of present-day Lebanon, Syria, Jordan, and Israel. The Druze monotheistic faith, which is generally cloaked in secrecy, stems from Shia Islam and centers on the divinity of the eleventh-century Fatimid caliph Abu Ali Mansur Tariqu al-Hakim (c. 985–1021), who, it is believed, will return and usher in a messianic age.

16. St. Francis of Assisi (c. 1181–1226) was an Italian Roman Catholic monk who founded the Franciscan order in 1209. He was canonized in 1228.

17. Rabindranath Tagore (1861–1941), a Bengali writer born in Calcutta, was involved in the Indian nationalist movement. His myriad writings—dramas, books of verse, novels, shorter works of fiction, and numerous philosophical works—combine natural descriptions with religious and philosophical speculation. His best-known collection of poetry, *Gitanjali* (1912), is derived from traditional Hindu themes. He denounced nationalism and violence and was severely critical of the Indian caste system. He was awarded the Nobel Prize in Literature in 1913.

18. Count Maurice Maeterlinck (1862–1949) was a Belgian writer whose literary corpus, particularly the play *Pelléas et Mélisande* (1892), epitomized the spirit of a generation of French intellectuals before World War I. His poetry, essays, and symbolic dramas reflected his mysticism and strong anti-materialism. An avid supporter of European socialism, in 1911 he was awarded the Nobel Prize in Literature.

19. On Ludwig Boerne, see note 29 in chapter 1, "The Meaning of Zionism," in this volume.

20. On Heinrich Heine, see note 28 in chapter 1, "The Meaning of Zionism," in this volume.

21. Berthold Auerbach (1812–82), a celebrated German Jewish novelist and poet, originated the genre of rural peasant-story realism in German literature.

22. Arthur Schnitzler (1862–1931), an Austrian Jewish dramatist and novelist, was the son of a prominent Viennese physician. Though Schnitzler trained to be a medical doctor, he gravitated to literature and attracted critical notice with his drama *Anatol* (1893), a cycle of one-act plays concerning a philanderer.

23. August von Wasserman (1866–1925), a German Jewish scientist, was a pioneer in the field of immunology and is best known for the Wassermann test for syphilis.

24. Otto Weininger (1880–1903), an Austrian-born Jewish philosopher, converted to Protestantism and published a study on bisexuality entitled *Sex and Character* (1903), which expounded misogynist and antisemitic beliefs. He committed suicide a few months after its publication.

25. On Henri Bergson, see note 57 in chapter 1, "The Meaning of Zionism," in this volume.

26. Georg Morris Cohen Brandes (1842–1927) was a Danish Jewish literary critic and philosopher whose work was influenced by Hippolyte Adolphe Taine (1828–1923). In 1870 Brandes was refused a chair in aesthetics at the University of Copenhagen because he was a Jew, an atheist, and a radical. He was awarded the same chair thirty-two years later.

27. Born to a Sephardic Jewish family in London, Benjamin Disraeli (1804–81), later the first Earl of Beaconsfield, was baptized at the age of thirteen. He rose to prominence as a British author and statesman and eventually served as prime minister during the reign of Queen Victoria. He is regarded as the founder of the modern Conservative Party in Britain.

28. Léon Gambetta (1838–82), a French Jewish political leader, gained worldwide recognition for his organization of a government of national defense and his vigorous opposition to the Prussian empire. He was influential in shaping France's constitution of 1875 and as a leader of the country's republican forces.

29. Walter Rathenau (1867–1922), a German Jewish industrialist, social theorist, and statesman, directed the distribution of raw materials during World War I. He became minister of reconstruction in 1921 and foreign minister in 1922. He represented Germany at the Cannes and Genoa reparations conferences and negotiated the Treaty of Rapallo with Russia. He was assassinated by German fanatics belonging to a secret ultranationalist political group.

30. Leon Trotsky (1879–1940) was a prominent Russian revolutionary theoretician and one of the principal leaders of the Bolshevik Party. Born Lev Davidovich Bronstein, Trotsky broke away from Judaism in his youth and later played a central role in the Russian Revolution of 1917. In 1927 he was expelled from the Communist Party and in 1929 he was banished for his opposition to the authoritarianism of Joseph Stalin (see note 38 in chapter 9, "To a Communist Friend," in this volume). His writings include *Literature and Revolution* (1925) and *My Life* (1930). Trotsky was murdered while in exile in Mexico.

31. The reference here is to the collaboration between Karl Marx, the eminent political thinker and philosopher (see note 31 in chapter 1, "The Meaning of Zionism," in

this volume), and Moses Hess (1812–75), a Russian Jewish socialist thinker considered a precursor of socialist Zionism. In the 1840s, as editor of the *Rheinische Zeitung*, Hess developed a close working relationship with Marx. Indeed, Hess is credited with having influenced key elements of *The Communist Manifesto* (1848), the seminal treatise by Marx and Friedrich Engels (1820–95). Hess later developed his own theory of socialist Zionism in *Rome and Jerusalem* (1862).

32. On Mark Antokolsky, see note 30 in chapter 1, "The Meaning of Zionism," in this volume.

33. On Isaac Ilyich Levitan, see note 34 in chapter 1, "The Meaning of Zionism," in this volume.

34. Joseph Israels (Jozef Israëls) (1824–1911) was a Dutch Jewish painter known for his depictions of rural life and fishermen. The recipient of many significant awards and honors, Israels's paintings were displayed throughout Europe in art exhibits.

35. Max Liebermann (1847–1935), a German Jewish impressionist painter and printmaker, was especially well known for his etching and lithography. In 1920, he became president of the Berlin Academy of Art. When the Nazis came to power in 1933, he was dismissed from this position.

36. Felix Mendelssohn (Jakob Ludwig Felix Mendelssohn Bartholdy) (1809–47) was one of the early nineteenth century's outstanding Romantic composers, conductors, and musicians. Among his most famous compositions are *A Midsummer Night's Dream* (1826, 1842), the *Scottish* (1829), *Reformation* (1830), and *Italian* (1831) Symphonies, and two oratorios, *St. Paul* (1836) and *Elijah* (1846). Mendelssohn was baptized a Christian by his parents, who converted from Judaism to become members of the Calvinist Reformed Church. Despite the era's rising current of antisemitism, Mendelssohn remained proud of his Jewish ancestry and in particular of his paternal grandfather, the philosopher Moses Mendelssohn (see note 54 in chapter 1, "The Meaning of Zionism").

37. Arthur Rubenstein (1887–1982), Polish-born American Jewish musician and conductor. By the time of his immigration to the United States in 1937, Rubenstein was regarded as one of the world's finest concert pianists. He was closely associated with the Hebrew University of Jerusalem, where a chair of musicology is named for him.

38. The *numerous clausus* (Latin for "closed number") was used by religious and temporal authorities to curtail and restrict Jewish participation in Western society. It was variously applied in Europe and the Americas beginning in the early modern era and lasting into the mid-twentieth century.

39. Greenberg is referring to the emergent nationalist movement in India, which was inspired by intellectuals like Gandhi and Tagore (see notes 11 and 17, above).

Chapter 4

Source: Hayim Greenberg, "Sabbatai Zevi: The Messiah as Apostate," in *The Inner Eye: Selected Essays*, vol. 2, ed. Shlomo Katz (New York: Jewish Frontier Association, 1964), 84–98.

1. On Sabbatai Zevi, see note 53 in chapter 1, "The Meaning of Zionism," in this volume.

2. A *mufti* is an Islamic religious and legal scholar.

3. For a detailed analysis of contemporaneous Jewish responses to Sabbatai Zevi's conversion to Islam, see Gershom Scholem, *Sabbatai Sevi: The Mystical Messiah, 1626–1676* (Princeton, NJ: Princeton University Press, 1973), 693–705.

4. "Applied kabbalah" (*kabbalah iyunit*) refers to the pursuit of Jewish mysticism in the temporal arena through theological study and meditative practices.

5. Isaac Luria (1534–72) of Safed, a founder of Jewish mysticism, was known as "*Haari Hakadosh*" (the holy lion). Following Luria's death, his teachings (referred to collectively as "Lurianic kabbalah") were studied by kabbalists through hagiographic compilations of letters written from Safed by Shlomo Shlumil of Dresnitz, Poland in the early seventeenth century. Published as *Shivhei haari* (Praises of the Ari) and *Toldot haari* (History of the Ari), the volumes convey detailed information about Luria and relate miraculous stories that have become part of kabbalistic lore.

6. Hayim ben Yosef Vital (1543–1620), a Safed rabbi and Isaac Luria's chief protégé, compiled and annotated Luria's quotations and teachings in a volume titled *Ez hayim* (Tree of Life). The latter did not achieve widespread circulation until after Vital's death.

7. Nathan of Gaza (1643–80), also referred to as "Nathan Gazati" and "Nathan Benyamin Ashkenazi," encountered Sabbatai Zevi during the latter's return journey from Cairo. Thereafter Nathan of Gaza proclaimed himself a prophet, professed revelations concerning Sabbatai Zevi's messiahship, and became Sabbatai Zevi's chief tribune and disciple.

8. The Zohar (Radiance), the main corpus of Jewish mystical literature, is a collection of exegetical and kabbalistic texts that interpret the Hebrew Bible and discuss God's influence on the world. Compiled in the late thirteenth century, the work is largely attributed to the Spanish rabbi and kabbalist Moses de León (c. 1250–1305).

9. The term "Ishmaelite" derives from Ishmael, the eldest son of the biblical patriarch Abraham who is considered to be the father of the Arab peoples (Gen. 16:11–16). It is used here to refer to a follower of Islam.

10. On Esther, Ahasuerus, and the Purim fable, see note 216 in chapter 24, "The Universalism of the Chosen People," in this volume.

11. See Scholem, *Sabbatai Sevi*, 872.

12. The reference is to Laban's daughters, Rachel and Leah (Gen. 29:1–30).

13. The reference is to the story of Moses' escape from Pharaoh after having killed an Egyptian taskmaster and his subsequent flight to Midian. There Moses came to the aid of the daughters of Jethro (also called Reuel), including Zipporah, whom he subsequently married and who bore him two sons, Gershom and Eliezer (Exod. 2:11–22, 18:3–4).

14. The notion of the "suffering God" has been the subject of Christian theological debate for centuries. Though fundamental to Christian doctrine, theologians have historically offered varied and competing interpretations of the story of Jesus' suffering recounted in the gospels. A unifying theme in this regard is the idea that God's suffering mitigates evil and opens the door to humanity's redemption.

15. See Matthew 27:20–37; Mark 14:55–15:32; Luke 22:63–23:39; John 19:1–19.

16. See Matthew 27:29; Mark 15:17; John 19:2, 5.

17. The Christian "passion of the Lord" refers to final period of Jesus' life, starting with his visit to Jerusalem and ending with his crucifixion.

18. The notion of messianic redemption in Judaism is complex. The Hebrew Bible does not explicitly speak of a messiah; however, it does use the term *mashakh* (to anoint) in reference to kings and priests. Cyrus is singled out as God's anointed servant and permits the Israelites to return to Palestine from their Babylonian exile (Isa. 45:1–25). Rabbinic literature has long debated the concept of a messiah, but there is no uniform discourse or theology in this regard. In general, most religious Jewish commentators assert *hevlei mashiakh* (birth pangs of the messiah) will precede the messianic era. Next, the exile of the Jews will end, the Jews will return to the Land of Israel, the Davidic monarchy will be restored, and the one true God of the Hebrew Bible will be acknowledged by all of humanity.

19. Following Sabbatai Zevi's death, Abraham Miguel Cardozo (1627–1707) emerged as a leading disciple and theologian of Sabbateanism. Born into a Castilian Marrano family, Cardozo grew up in Madrid, where he received a Jewish education from his older brother Isaac Cardozo (1604–80). He later studied medicine and Catholic theology. In 1648 he relocated to Livorno, where he returned to Judaism. He subsequently traveled throughout the Mediterranean basin and acquired a reputation as an accomplished student of Kabbalah and Midrash. In 1663 he settled in Tripoli and was employed as a physician to the pasha Osman Saqili (1649–1762). He professed having visions and revelations concerning the forthcoming messianic era and humanity's redemption.

20. In 1668 Abraham Miguel Cardozo wrote a letter in which he explained that two years earlier—at the zenith of the Sabbatean movement—he foresaw "that King Messiah would don the garb of a forced convert . . . that on account of that garb the Jews would not recognize him; that he would become, in short, a Marrano like me." Quoted in *Abraham Miguel Cardozo: Selected Writings*, trans. David J. Halperin (Mahwah, NJ: Paulist Press, 2001), 55.

21. It is interesting to note that Vladimir Lenin used the phrase "swindler-scoundrelly elements" to describe anti-Bolshevik opponents in 1919. See George S. N. Luckyj, *Literary Politics in the Soviet Ukraine, 1917–1934*, rev. ed. (Durham, NC: Duke University Press, 1990), 18.

22. Maimonides (1135–1204), known in rabbinic literature as Rambam (from the Hebrew acronym for Rabbi Moses ben Maimon), was the premier rabbinic authority and Jewish philosopher of the Iberian peninsula in the medieval period. His two most famous writings are *Mishneh Torah* (1170–80), a fourteen-volume codified collection of rabbinic law, and *The Guide for the Perplexed* (1204), a synthesis of Judaism and neoplatonic Aristotelian philosophy that seeks to resolve the conflict between religious knowledge and the secular arena. The latter sparked the two-hundred-year "Maimonidean controversy," which pitted Jewish traditionalists against rational philosophers. Maimonides also conceived the thirteen fundamental principles of Jewish faith (see note 16 in chapter 29, "The Future of American Jewry," in this volume). His enduring impact on Jewish thought is profound. He also influenced philosophers of other faiths, notably the Italian theologian Thomas Aquinas (1225–74).

23. Written in 1172, Maimonides' letter (or epistle) was a response to Yemen's Jewish community leaders who requested his advice about a regional manifestation of Sabbateanism and the forced conversion of the Jews by Islamic authorities. In reply, Mai-

monides discouraged Jewish messianic activity and asserted the messianic era would be heralded not by social upheaval but rather the restoration of order. In the meanwhile, he counseled Yemen's Jews to remain steadfast in their commitment to Judaism and pragmatic in their daily affairs. See Joel L. Kraemmer, trans., "Maimonides' Epistle to Yemen (1172)," in *Maimonides' Empire of Light: Popular Enlightenment in an Age of Belief*, ed. Ralph Lerner (Chicago: University of Chicago Press, 2000), 99–132.

24. Jacob Israel Emden (1697–1776), a central European Orthodox rabbinic scholar, theologian, and leading opponent of the Sabbatean movement, presided over a synagogue and operated a printing press in Altona, a Danish-ruled western borough of Hamburg. In the late 1740s, Emden began actively campaigning to unmask his contemporary Rabbi Jonathan Eibeschütz (1690–1764) of Prague as a Sabbatean—a charge the latter vigorously denied. When in 1751 Eibeschütz became chief rabbi of the Altona, Hamburg, and Wandsbek Jewish communities, Emden publicly called for his excommunication for heresy. Due to the ensuing vitriolic Emden-Eibeschütz controversy, Emden was forced to seek safety and refuge in Amsterdam. In 1752 the court of Frederick V (1723–56) of Denmark intervened on Emden's behalf, fined and censured the three Jewish communities for mistreating him, and provided for his return to his synagogue and printing establishment. Notwithstanding Eibeschütz's denial, his attitude to Sabbateanism was never conclusively resolved. Upon his death, his son openly declared himself to be a Sabbatean. See *Megilat Sefer: The Autobiography of Rabbi Jacob Emden*, trans. S. B. Leperer and M. H. Wise (Baltimore: PublishYourSefer.com, 2011).

25. Originally published in 1752, Jacob Emden's *Torat hakenaot* (The Doctrine of Zealotry) is a polemical study of Sabbatai Zevi that includes criticisms of Jonathan Eibeschütz, Nehemiah Hayon (c. 1655–1730), and other kabbalists.

26. The historian Heinrich Graetz (see note 27, below) notes that Hakim Bashi, also known as Guidon, was the sultan's physician and a "Jewish renegade." See Heinrich Graetz, *History of the Jews*, vol. 5 (Philadelphia: Jewish Publication Society of America, 1895), 153.

27. Heinrich Graetz (1817–91), a German Jewish historian and biblical scholar, is best known for his eleven-volume work *History of the Jews* (1853–75). Notwithstanding its biases and inconsistencies, *History of the Jews* is regarded as a seminal text, and the author's ambitious effort to write a comprehensive rational history of the Jewish people helped lay the groundwork for the field of Jewish history. Translated into English, Yiddish, Hebrew, and French, the study also played a significant role in the emergence of modern Jewish self-understanding and consciousness.

28. These phrases appear to have been translated into English by Greenberg from Heinrich Graetz's original German work (*Geschichte der Juden von den ältesten Zeiten bis auf die Gegenwart*, 11 vols., 1853–75). For the English equivalent, see Graetz, *History of the Jews*, 5:153–154.

29. Like Heinrich Graetz (see note 27, above), the Russian Jewish historian Simon Dubnow (1860–1941) produced an influential ten-volume *World History of the Jewish People* (1925–29). Much more than Graetz, however, Dubnow focused on social and political factors in Jewish history and on eastern European Jewry. In addition to Dubnow's pioneering research, he was deeply involved in the creation of the Jewish political move-

ment known as autonomism, which distinguished itself from Zionism by emphasizing the national identity of the Jews in the diaspora (see note 20 in chapter 1, "The Meaning of Zionism," in this volume).

30. These phrases appear to have been translated into English by Greenberg from the German edition of Simon Dubnow's work (*Weltgeschichte des Jüdischen Volkes*, 10 vols., 1925–29). For the English equivalent, see Simon Dubnow, *History of the Jews: From Cromwell's Commonwealth to the Napoleonic Era*, vol. 4, trans. Moshe Spiegel (South Brunswick, NJ: Thomas Yoseloff, 1971), 73.

31. Among others, Greenberg is likely referring to the work of Heinrich Graetz (see note 28, above). For a related discussion of "historical and sociological explanations of the Sabbatean movement and their deficiencies," see Scholem, *Sabbatai Sevi*, 1–7. In particular, Scholem references the limitations of Graetz's *History of the Jews*, David (Kohn) Kahana's (1838–1915) *Toldot hamekubalim, hashabtaim vehahasidim al pi mekorot yeshanim vehadashim* (1915), and Solomon Abraham Rosanes's (1862–1938) *Korot hayehudim beturkyah vearzot hakedem* (1930–45); *Sabbatai Sevi*, xi–xii.

32. According to the Christian Bible, Judas Iscariot, one of the twelve original apostles of Jesus, betrayed Jesus, identifying him for capture by kissing him, and delivering him into the hands of the Sanhedrin in exchange for a payment of thirty silver coins. Judas subsequently hanged himself. See Matthew 26:20–25, 47–49; 27:3–10.

33. The nature of Nehemiah Kohen's relationship to Sabbatai Zevi remains an open question. In 1666, during Sabbatai Zevi's imprisonment in Abydos by Turkish authorities, he learned Nehemiah Kohen of Lvov had prophesied the advent of the messiah. Whether he sent for Kohen or not is unclear, but when the two men later met they clashed. Next, Kohen briefly converted to Islam and publicly denounced Sabbatai Zevi to the Turkish court. The chain of events resulted in Sabbatai Zevi's appearance before the sultan's vizier, and he was forced to choose between death and conversion to Islam. Thereafter, Kohen recanted and fled to Poland, where he was apparently reviled as a traitor. See Scholem, *Sabbatai Sevi*, 658–688.

34. Sabbatai Zevi traveled to Gaza in April 1665. With great fanfare, he was anointed messiah the following month in the local synagogue. The news was conveyed in letters to various diaspora Jewish communities and triggered widespread jubilation.

35. On Baruch Spinoza, see note 50 in chapter 1, "The Meaning of Zionism," in this volume.

36. On Uriel Acosta, see note 51 in chapter 1, "The Meaning of Zionism," in this volume.

37. For a useful discussion of Cardozo's views, see Scholem, *Sabbatai Sevi*, 814–820.

38. "Practical kabbalah" (*kabbalah maasit*) is a term used to describe the substream of Jewish mystical tradition identified with magical incantations, amulets, healing, and cursing.

39. Shortly after Sabbatai Zevi's meeting in Abydos with Nehemiah Kohen, the Turkish authorities moved him to the city of Adrianople.

40. Greenberg is referring to the kabbalistic fable in which the historical figure Rabbi Joseph della Reyna seeks the counsel of Elijah the prophet in order to vanquish Satan. According to the legend, Elijah "enumerated what measures and tactics he would have

to observe in his combat with the fallen angel. . . . The rabbi followed out Elijah's directions carefully, and succeeded in summoning Sandalphon to his assistance. If he had continued to obey instructions implicitly, and had carried out all Sandalphon advised, the rabbi would have triumphed over Satan and hastened the redemption of the world. Unfortunately, at one point the rabbi committed an indiscretion, and he lost the great advantages he had gained over Satan, who used his restored power to bring ruin upon him and his disciples." Quoted in Louis Ginzberg, *The Legends of the Jews*, vol. 4 (Philadelphia: Jewish Publication Society of America, 1913), 231.

Chapter 5

Source: Hayim Greenberg, "Our Stand," *Jewish Frontier* 2:2 (December 1934): 3–5.

1. The October Revolution, a violent military coup executed in November 1917 (or October according to the Julian calendar then in use in Russia), was led by Vladimir Lenin (see note 9 in chapter 6, "Jew and Arab," in this volume) and Leon Trotsky (see note 30 in chapter 3, "East and West," in this volume). In the event, Lenin and Trotsky seized power, arrested the authorities of Alexander Kerensky's (see note 16 in chapter 9, "To a Communist Friend," and note 11 in chapter 22, "Concerning Statehood," in this volume) moderate provisional government, and established a new Bolshevik-dominated Soviet regime. The revolution resulted in countrywide social and political instability, coupled with economic chaos. The new regime benefited enormously from signing the Treaty of Brest-Litovsk in March 1918 and ending the war with the Central Powers on the eastern front. This enabled the Lenin-Trotsky regime to focus attention on consolidating its authority and suppressing anti-Bolshevik resistance in the ensuing Russian Civil War. The revolution's global impact was mixed. Though hailed by radical socialists in many parts of the globe, it particularly frightened democratic governments and societies in the West, including the United States, which became gripped by a Red Scare that lasted decades.

2. This reference applies to Jewish colonization in the Birobidzhan territory. In 1928 the Soviet regime, having recognized the Jews as a nationality and Yiddish as an official language, authorized the creation of Birobidzhan, a special *oblast* (Russian for "administrative division") for Jewish colonization located on the Manchuria border in the far east of the USSR. Viewed as the Communist alternative to Zionism, the new territory was in many respects the outcome of decades of public debate about how to Russify the Jews, turn them into productive members of society, and advance the Soviet agenda vis-à-vis its constituent ethnic minorities. The territory (14,000 square miles) was originally conceived as a society of Jewish farmers organized in *kolkhozes* (collective farms); however, the population generally gravitated away from agriculture and toward industry. In 1934, Birobidzhan was declared an "autonomous Jewish region"—with the intention of eventually becoming a "Jewish national republic." Though it initially seemed to be a promising foothold for the secular-national Jewish culture in eastern Europe, the project ultimately failed due to longstanding Soviet ambivalence to Jewish Communist aspirations, coupled with Stalin's purges of the mid-1930s and the resurgence of Russian antisemitism. Waning Jewish interest in the project also limited its success.

3. For useful analyses of Soviet sponsorship of Jewish communal institutions in the 1920s and 1930s, see Salo W. Baron, *The Russian Jew under Tsars and Soviets* (New York:

Macmillan, 1976), 223–226, 278–287; Benjamin Pinkus, *The Jews of the Soviet Union* (Cambridge: Cambridge University Press, 1988), 106–126; David Shneer, *Yiddish and the Creation of Soviet Jewish Culture, 1918–1930* (Cambridge: Cambridge University Press, 2004), chap. 4.

4. Greenberg is referring to the process by which the Bolshevik government hastened the integration of ethnic minorities into the Soviet state. No less than other groups, many Russian Jews were enthusiastic about this prospect. See Baron, *The Russian Jew under Tsars and Soviets*, chap. 13; Pinkus, *The Jews of the Soviet Union*, 136–137; Benjamin Pinkus, *The Soviet Government and the Jews, 1948–1967* (Cambridge: Cambridge University Press, 1984), 12–13, 545n.37.

5. See note 3 above.

6. Founded in 1934 by Hayim Greenberg, *Jewish Frontier*, the monthly English-language journal of the American Labor Zionist movement, was published continuously until 2005.

7. The waves of Jewish immigration to Palestine rose dramatically in the early 1930s. Net annual Jewish immigration climbed from 9,553 in 1932 to 30,327 in 1933, to 42,359 in 1934, and to 61,458 in 1935. The total Jewish population in Palestine in 1934 reached approximately 175,000. It climbed to 348,078 in 1936, then to 543,000 in 1946, and 716,700 in 1948 at the time of Israel's War of Independence. Data compiled from L. Hersch, "Jewish Migrations during the Last Hundred Years," in *The Jewish People, Past and Present*, vol. 1 (New York: Central Yiddish Culture Organization, 1946), 417; *American Jewish Year Book* 37 (1935): 362, 380–385; *American Jewish Year Book* 38 (1936): 562, 580–585; *Israel in the Middle East: Documents and Readings on Society, Politics, and Foreign Relations, Pre-1948 to the Present*, ed. Itamar Rabinovich and Jehuda Reinharz, 2nd. ed. (Waltham, MA: Brandeis University Press, 2008), "Appendix 5. Jewish and Non-Jewish Population of Palestine-Israel, 1517–2004," 571.

8. In the early 1930s, the Belgian Congo (see also note 27 in chapter 7, "Revisionism," in this volume) and Liberia were dominated by non-native minority groups. Several hundred Belgian-born administrators maintained firm control over the Congo, a region eighty times the size of Belgium, and severely restricted the territory's opportunities for self-governance and autonomy. Likewise, Liberia was dominated by a class of Americo-Liberians, never more than five percent of the country's population, whose Eurocentric worldview manifest itself in a rigid racial hierarchy imposed on the indigenous peoples. The Belgian and Americo-Liberian overlords exploited, respectively, the natural resources of the Congo and Liberia, subjected the native peoples to impoverished and subsistence-level conditions, and used modern technology, commercial success, and political clout to maintain their dominant status.

Chapter 6

Source: Hayim Greenberg, "Jew and Arab," *Jewish Frontier* 2:2 (December 1934): 23–24.

1. Greenberg frequently returned to this question. See, e.g., Hayim Greenberg, "Is Zionism Imperialistic?" in *Jews and Arabs in Palestine: Studies in a National and Colonial Problem*, ed. Enzo Sereni and R. E. Ashery (New York: Hechalutz Press, 1936), 247–257.

2. In the Hebrew Bible, Adam and Eve give birth to two sons, Cain and Abel. The

first-born Cain is described as a "tiller of the soil" and Abel as a shepherd (Gen. 4:1–2). Sibling rivalry results in Cain's murder of Abel. In the story, God inquires of Cain, "Where is your brother Abel?" Cain answers, "I do not know. Am I my brother's keeper?" (Gen. 4:9). Next God punishes Cain but also promises to protect him (Gen. 4:11–16). The story raises fundamental questions about the ethic of responsibility for one's kinsman and neighbor. It proved to be a generative source of centuries-old theological and philosophical debate.

3. The Austrian Jewish poet and dramatist Richard Beer-Hofmann (1866–1945) initially earned a doctorate in law at the University of Vienna. In the 1890s he emerged as a prominent member of the *fin de siècle* Young Vienna movement, a group of literati who challenged prevailing central European artistic and aesthetic forms; they experimented with sexuality, impressionism, and symbolism in their work. He was also a friend of Theodor Herzl (see note 3 in chapter 2, "Policy and Labor," in this volume) and active in German Zionist circles. In the 1920s, he worked closely with the Austrian Jewish theatre and film director Max Reinhardt (1873–1943). With the rise of Nazi Germany, Beer-Hofmann's writings were burned and his plays banned. In 1938 he fled to the United States and settled in New York City.

4. Richard Beer-Hofmann's *Jacob's Dream* (1915) is a biblical drama that explores the concept of the divine election of the Jewish people. First performed in Vienna in 1919, the play emphasizes the themes of suffering, self-doubt, and heroism in the context of the patriarch Jacob's struggle and covenant with God. In addition to retelling the biblical story, its raises existential questions about the place of the artist in society and the fate of the Jewish people in history. See Richard Beer-Hofmann, *Jacob's Dream*, trans. Ida Bension Wynn (Philadelphia: Jewish Publication Society of America, 1946).

5. In the play, Esau "repeatedly challenges Jacob to a fight, but Jacob, by standing unmoved and unafraid, eventually obliges [Esau] to kneel before him and plead for reconciliation. Jacob offers him the ceremony of blood-brotherhood, but refuses to expiate his deceit by being sacrificed. . . . In rejecting sacrifice, Jacob is affirming complete nonviolence. His election separates him from the cycle of violence and sacrifice in which Edom—and, by extension, the gentile world—is caught." Quoted from *The German-Jewish Dialogue: An Anthology of Literary Texts, 1749–1993*, ed. Ritchie Robertson (New York: Oxford University Press, 1999), 202.

6. Greenberg appears to be paraphrasing the original German text. For the English version of this interaction, see Beer-Hofmann, *Jacob's Dream*, 123–125.

7. The German philosopher Friedrich Wilhelm Nietzsche (1844–1900) was appointed professor of philology at the University of Basle in 1869. Ill health caused him to resign his position in 1879. He suffered a complete mental breakdown a decade later and went insane. In *Thus Spake Zarathustra* (1883–85) Nietzsche, who spoke of the "death of God," decries traditional Christian morality as the code of the herd (the slavish masses) and stresses the superior morality of the masters (the natural aristocrats) from which arises the will to power. According to Nietzsche the will of man invariably yields the *Übermensch* (German for "superman") destined to transcend good and evil and by his own power destroy hypocritical liberal society and refashion it. Among Nietzsche's other influential works are *The Birth of Tragedy* (1872), *The Gay Science* (1882), and *Beyond Good*

and Evil (1886). Though Nietzsche displayed an ambivalent attitude to Judaism, he was a vocal critic of contemporary antisemitism as boorish and superficial. See Yirmiyahu Yovel, *Dark Riddle: Hegel, Nietzsche, and the Jews* (Cambridge: Polity Press, 1988), 103–185.

8. The Austrian Jewish physician and psychotherapist Alfred Adler (1870–1937), whose understanding of power dynamics in society was strongly influenced by the philosophical work of Friedrich Nietzsche, founded the school of individual psychology. In contrast to Sigmund Freud (see note 42 in chapter 8, "Notes on Marxism," in this volume), Adler's approach underscores a holistic study of the individual's character. He also emphasized the significance of the inferiority complex in personality development. With the rise of Nazi Germany, Adler fled to the United States. The Adlerian school of psychology profoundly impacted the twentieth-century arena of counseling and psychotherapy. A prolific writer, Adler's major publications include *Understanding Human Nature* (1927), *The Practice and Theory of Individual Psychology* (1927), and *What Life Could Mean to You* (1931).

9. The Russian revolutionary leader Vladimir (Ulyanov) Lenin (1870–1924) originally studied law in St. Petersburg but gave up his university training to pursue Marxism and radical political activity. Twice exiled to Siberia by tsarist authorities, he left Russia in 1900. While in London he fomented the split in 1903 of the Russian Social Democratic Party into Bolshevik and Menshevik factions (see note 16 in chapter 9, "To a Communist Friend," in this volume). In 1905–7 he was responsible for the participation of the Bolsheviks in the imperial duma. He spent much of World War I in Switzerland where he denounced imperialism as the last stage of capitalism and called for a worldwide proletarian struggle against the imperialist war of society's capitalist rulers. After the outbreak of the February Revolution of 1917, the German government helped Lenin to return to Russia. In November 1917 Lenin engineered the overthrow of the Kerensky government (see note 16 in chapter 9, "To a Communist Friend," and note 11 in chapter 22, "Concerning Statehood," in this volume) and became chairman of the Council of the People's Commissars. He saw the Bolshevik revolution through to victory in the Russian Civil War of 1918–20 and the subsequent creation of the Union of Soviet Socialist Republics. The death of Lenin, who ruled Soviet Russia as a virtual dictator, opened up a struggle for succession among key Bolshevik leaders from which Joseph Stalin (see note 38 in chapter 9, "To a Communist Friend," in this volume) emerged victorious. Lenin's elaboration of Marxist theory, known as Leninism, emphasizes what he viewed as imperialism's insidiousness, the need for a highly disciplined Communist Party to lead the proletarian revolution, uncompromising ideological maximalism, and atheism. Though Lenin opposed antisemitism on moral and political grounds, declaring it reactionary and counterrevolutionary, he believed assimilation to be the only solution to the Jewish problem.

10. The Austrian-born German politician Adolf Hitler (1889–1945) was dictator of Nazi Germany from 1934 to 1945.

Chapter 7

Source: Hayim Greenberg, "Revisionism," in *Revisionists and Mizrachi: A Symposium Held in New York on Saturday Evening, February 3, 1934, at Which the Speakers Were*

Hayim Greenberg and Joseph Sprinzak, trans. Maximillian Hurwitz (Milwaukee, WI: Poale Zion–Zeire Zion of America, 1934), 2–10, Mizrachi Organization of America Files, American Jewish Historical Society, New York.

1. Almost from the outset, tensions arose in the Zionist movement over the nature and purpose of Jewish colonization in Palestine. In the decade prior to World War I, advocates of an activist settlement policy argued the Second and Third Aliyah pioneers would enhance and strengthen the achievements of the First Aliyah colonies. Adopting Theodor Herzl's (see note 3 in chapter 2, "Policy and Labor," in this volume) vision of a Zionist "vanguard," they believed the *haluzim* would lay the foundation for the Yishuv's future. In contrast, proponents of large-scale colonization asserted the Yishuv's development required major economic investment and international support for Jewish immigration on a mass scale.

2. The Turkish regime, which ruled Palestine from the early sixteenth century until 1917, was generally antipathetic to the Zionist movement. In addition to Ottoman sultan Abdulhamid II's (1842–1918) absolutist and anti-liberal disposition, the Porte regarded the nationalist-inspired Jewish colonies with suspicion. Although the Zionist movement managed to operate within the narrow constraints permitted by the fraying Ottoman Empire (e.g., negotiating land purchases, constructing buildings, paving roads), the Turks severely limited Jewish colonization in Palestine.

3. Hibat Zion (Love of Zion), a proto-Zionist movement, emerged in the early 1880s in Russia and Romania. A loose coalition of Jewish nationalist groups and intellectual circles that cut across religious and ideological lines, the movement was initially led by Eliezer Ben-Yehuda (1858–1922), who championed the revival of Hebrew as a modern language, the scholar Moshe Leib Lilienblum (see note 5 below), and the Hebrew novelist Peretz Smolenskin (1842–85). In reaction to pogroms in the Ukraine, the physician and Zionist theoretician Leon Pinsker (1821–91) joined Hibat Zion and asserted that antisemitism was inherent to diaspora Jewish life and the Jewish future could be ensured only through "auto-emancipation" and settlement in the Land of Israel. Hibat Zion succeeded in establishing a handful of colonies in Palestine. In time, it merged into Theodor Herzl's World Zionist Organization.

4. *Hovevei Zion* (pl., lovers of Zion) refers to members of the Hibat Zion movement.

5. Moshe Leib Lilienblum (1843–1910), a Hebrew author and Jewish scholar, hailed from a traditional eastern European background. Influenced by the Haskalah, he became a religious moderate and a founder of the Hibat Zion movement. When Theodor Herzl burst on the scene in 1896 and thereafter established the World Zionist Organization, Lilienblum became one of his ardent champions in Russia.

6. Greenberg appears to be citing the Anglo-Jewish novelist Israel Zangwill's (1864–1926) characterization of Theodor Herzl's diplomatic strategy which, he argued, emphasized "the object of Zionism is to create, not things, but conditions." Quoted in Martin Sicker, *Reshaping Palestine: From Muhammad Ali to the British Mandate, 1831–1922* (Westport, CT: Praeger Publishers, 1999), 90.

7. Greenberg is referring to a debate that arose in the World Zionist Organization concerning the movement's political and settlement activity. Many of Theodor Herzl's

followers, including a faction known as "maximalists," insisted on the primacy of diplomatic and political work aimed at garnering international recognition of Jewish rights in Palestine. Like Herzl, they opposed expending the movement's scarce resources on generating Zionist settlement activity absent an internationally recognized charter that secured Jewish rights in Palestine. Meanwhile, the so-called "practical Zionists," led by Russian Zionist leader Menahem Mendel Ussishkin (see note 7 in chapter 3, "East and West," in this volume) believed investing in the Yishuv's fledgling infrastructure, particularly its emerging Jewish towns, villages, and labor communes, and new Zionist settlement activity to be critically important to the future of an independent Jewish national home.

8. This refers to the Arab Riots of 1929 which resulted in the massacre of Jews in Hebron and other places, and dramatically altered the Yishuv's internal debate over the issues of Jewish sovereignty and security.

9. Transjordania (also Transjordan) was the name given to the area east of the Jordan River, spanning from Mt. Hermon to the Dead Sea, but excluding the Golan Heights and the Bashan Valley.

10. In 1925 the Zionist technocrat Arthur Ruppin (1876–1943) convened a small group of Jewish intellectuals in Palestine to establish Brit Shalom (Covenant of Peace). The group, which advocated the creation of a bi-national Jewish-Arab state within the framework of the British mandate, derived its name from Ezekiel 34:25. A mix of secular and religious Jews, Hebrew writers and scholars, and liberal and left-wing political activists, the group viewed itself as an intellectual forum and did not seek to become a political party.

11. Close contact between Revisionist leader Vladimir Jabotinsky (see note 16 below) and the Labor Zionist movement was established during World War I when, together with labor leaders Yosef Trumpeldor (1880–1920), Pinhas Rutenberg (1879–1942), and David Ben-Gurion (see note 20 in chapter 27, "Concerning an Israel Constitution," in this volume), and Yitzhak Ben-Zvi (1884–1963), Jabotinsky created the Jewish Legion, a Jewish military battalion organized under the auspices of the British army that included a sizable Labor Zionist faction. Thereafter, notwithstanding Jabotinsky's anti-socialist views, he was favorably impressed by the determination and achievements of the *haluzim* and maintained cordial relations with several key left-wing Zionist leaders. In the mid-1920s, however, Jabotinsky adopted an aggressive anti-labor stance against the backdrop of the Fourth Aliyah and the Yishuv's postwar economic crisis. At the Fourteenth and Fifteenth Zionist Congresses, held respectively in Vienna in 1925 and Basel in 1927, he forcefully opposed the Palestine labor movement and championed the interests of the lower- and middle-class Polish Jewish immigrants attracted to the country's developing urban centers. For a summary of Jabotinsky's attitude to labor in this period, see the 1925 articles "*Hasmol*" and "*Bastah*" reprinted in Zeev Jabotinsky, *Basaar* (Jerusalem: Eri Jabotinsky, 1952), 13–29.

12. In the 1930s, Revisionism stood "unconditionally on the side of private ownership and private enterprise," while the Mapai party "operated on a reformist and pragmatic basis of cooperation with private entrepreneurs and capitalists." Yaacov Shavit, *Jabotinsky and the Revisionist Movement, 1925–1948* (London: Frank Cass, 1988), 73.

13. Greenberg's use of the term "Nazirite" (Num. 6) alludes to the tradition of self-sacrifice and devotion to God exemplified by Samson. As a form of self-offering in the biblical and postbiblical periods, Nazirites vowed not to cut their hair, come into contact with corpses, or become intoxicated.

14. Greenberg is alluding to the escalating antagonism between the Labor Zionists and Revisionists following the assassination in June 1933 of Labor Zionist leader Chaim Arlosoroff (1899–1933) and the subsequent Eighteenth Zionist Congress, held in Prague in August-September 1933, at which Labor Zionism emerged as the movement's dominant political faction. Palestine labor's growing strength in the Yishuv and Zionism generally resulted in a decisive shift in the balance of power in the World Zionist Organization at the Nineteenth World Zionist Congress, held in Lucerne, Switzerland, in August-September 1935. In the event, Mapai swept the congress elections, winning 44 percent of the world vote (including 71 percent of the Palestine vote), and attained virtual hegemony in Zionist affairs. David Ben-Gurion subsequently became chairman of the Jewish Agency for Palestine.

15. The relationship between Revisionism and fascism is complex. Though influenced by European models of liberalism and fascism, Revisionism's major leader Vladimir Jabotinsky consistently advocated democracy as a paramount value and a fundamental tenet of Jewish and Zionist politics. Many of Jabotinsky's extreme and maximalist followers, however, including the activist Abba Ahimeir (1897–1962), Hebrew poet Uri Zvi Greenberg (1896–1981), and journalist Yehoshua Yevin (1891–1970), who cofounded the clandestine Brit Habiryonim (Alliance of Roughnecks) in 1930, believed in the supremacy of the nation over all other interests, and advocated centralized political authority and the use of military force to achieve political ends.

16. Vladimir (Zeev) Jabotinsky (1880–1940) became a Zionist after the 1903 Odessa pogrom, during which he helped to organize self-defense. A charismatic Zionist leader as well as a brilliant orator, writer, and translator, Jabotinsky was a central figure in the Jewish public arena in the decades leading up to the establishment of the State of Israel. He led the campaign for the creation of the Jewish Legion during World War I. In 1920, predicting imminent Arab riots in Jerusalem, he formed clandestine Jewish self-defense units and led them into action without the permission of the British authorities. For this offense, he was sentenced to fifteen years' hard labor, but he was granted amnesty within a year, in part due to the international outcry following his imprisonment. He served on the Zionist executive, founded the right-wing Betar youth movement in 1923, and was head of the World Union of Revisionist Zionists. Jabotinsky later supported "illegal" immigration and was commander of the Irgun Zvai Leumi (National Military Organization). He vigorously opposed the Labor Zionist movement throughout his career, believing that socialism was secondary to Jewish nationalist concerns, and argued against the partition of Palestine.

17. Vladimir Jabotinsky originally stated: "So very wise was the philosopher who proclaimed '*Homo homini lupus*'... He who trusts integrity and justice is a fool in that integrity exists only for the powerful and the stubborn..."; Vladimir Jabotinsky, "*Homo homini lupus*," *Odesskie Novostoi* [Odessa News] (July 18, 1910), 3, http://en.jabotinsky.org/media/9742/homo-homini-lupus.pdf.

18. In the pre-state era, the major Hebrew newspapers associated with the Revisionist movement were *Doar hayom* (Daily Mail) (1928–31), *Haam* (The People) (1931), *Hamashkif* (The Observer) (1939–49), *Hayarden* (The Jordan) (1934–36), and *Hazafon* (The North) (1926–27). Other significant right-wing periodicals in this period were *Hayishuv* (The Community) (1924–27), *Hazit haam* (The Popular Front) (1932–35), and *Betar* (1933–34).

19. The Austrian Social Democratic Party stemmed from the revolutionary Marxist fervor of the fin-de-siecle but over time adopted a pragmatic strategy known as a "third way to socialism." Led by Victor Adler (1852–1918), Karl Renner (1870–1950), and Otto Bauer (1881–1938)—the latter served as Austria's chancellor and foreign minister in a post-World War I coalition government—the Social Democrats championed women's rights and introduced significant protections for workers. In February 1934, the Social Democrats mounted a failed political uprising against the dictatorship of Christian Social Party leader Engelbert Dollfuss (1892–1934). Dollfuss suppressed the revolt and outlawed the socialist movement. Hundreds of civilians were killed in the clash and Austrian authorities arrested thousands of dissidents. Bauer was forced into exile and continued his resistance activity from Brno (Brünn) and Paris.

20. Greenberg is probably quoting a source from Palestine's Revisionist press (see note 17 above). It is unlikely Vladimir Jabotinsky himself would have uttered such a statement.

21. On this idealistic notion in Revisionism, see Shavit, *Jabotinsky and the Revisionist Movement, 1925–1948*, 139–142.

22. In this period, the Revisionist movement engaged in a variety of educational and propaganda activities in Poland and Palestine. Like the Labor Zionist groups, they recognized the value of maintaining their own *hakhsharot* (pioneer training camps) and fostering camaraderie among Betar members. The camps provided Hebrew classes and paramilitary instruction for Polish Jewish youth preparing to live in Palestine. They also served as vehicles for distributing immigration certificates. In Palestine, the Revisionists created their own work brigades, paramilitary groups, and other channels to absorb newcomers who shared their ideological worldview.

23. Following Chaim Arlosoroff's assassination in June 1933, the ideological clash between the Labor Zionist and Revisionist movements became vitriolic. Left-wing activists compared Jabotinsky to Hitler, while right-wing activists equated the Mapai party with the Russian Bolsheviks.

24. In 1934 a faction of right-wing workers withdrew from the Histadrut to form the National Labor Federation. Of the new organization's 4,000 members, roughly half belonged to the Betar youth movement and the Revisionist party.

25. In the early decades of the twentieth century, many private American businesses created and ran internal labor groups called "company unions." In general, the latter were inordinately dependent on the companies that created them and they fought bitterly with independent trade unions seeking to improve workers' rights. In 1935 the National Labor Relations Act outlawed company unions in the United States.

26. "Contract labor" (also "yellow-dog contracts") refers to the late nineteenth- and early twentieth-century American business practice whereby employees, as a condition of employment, were barred from joining independent unions. This practice, which under-

mined the rights of workers to freely associate and organize professionally, was outlawed by the Norris-LaGuardia Act (1932).

27. At the turn of the nineteenth and twentieth centuries, eastern European Jewish immigrants to the United States generally worked in the ready-made clothing industry, alongside large numbers of Italian, German, and Irish workers. In New York City the garment industry included the notorious sweatshops where employees often worked for ten or more hours a day. The regulation of the sweatshops coincided with the countrywide expansion of American trade unionism generally and the successful organization of Jewish labor. At its peak between World Wars I and II, approximately 40 percent of all Jewish laborers could be found in the American garment industry, including a sizable quotient of women, the majority of whom belonged to the Amalgamated Clothing Workers of America and the International Ladies' Garment Workers' Union.

28. In 1878 King Leopold II of Belgium (1835–1909) commissioned the British explorer Henry Morton Stanley (1841–1904) to survey the African Congo and conclude treaties with its native rulers. As a result, the Congo Free State, a corporate state privately controlled by Leopold II, was established in 1885. In ensuing decades, the Congo Free State, whose raw products included copper, diamonds, gold, and tin, proved to be an abundant source of revenue for the Belgian crown. Meanwhile, the region's native populace was cruelly oppressed and violently exploited. In 1908, following an international public outcry, Leopold was forced to relinquish control over the region to the Kingdom of Belgium and it was renamed the Belgian Congo. Though the natives' situation improved marginally, they did not achieve independence until 1960.

29. From 1894 to 1962, Great Britain ruled the colonial British Protectorate of Uganda, an entity comprising several regions and native ethnic groups. The British Indian Army officer John Hanning Speke (1827–64) and the explorer Henry Morton Stanley (see note 28 above) were among the first Europeans to survey the region. In 1890, following a struggle against British imperial forces, the central Bugandan kingdom came under the control of the British East Africa Company. In 1894 the British government established a protectorate over Buganda and it thereafter acquired several adjacent regions. The British renamed the country Uganda and instituted a system of limited self-government. With its abundant natural resources, Uganda became a leading exporter of cotton, coffee, and sugar.

30. The island of Java was a Dutch colony from the late sixteenth century until it gained independence in 1945. Over the course of this 400-year period, the Netherlands lay claim to most of the Indonesian archipelago with brief interludes of British and French conquest. By the early nineteenth century, however, Dutch imperial and commercial control of the region was secure. Java's main exports were quinine, rubber, sugar, and teak.

31. In the fall 1934, Vladimir Jabotinsky and David Ben-Gurion conducted secret talks in London, the purpose of which was to reach a political compromise and prevent the Revisionist movement from leaving the World Zionist Organization. In the encounter, both men agreed to unprecedented concessions and displayed remarkable warmth and goodwill. Their accord, described by the right-wing maximalist Abba Ahimeir as a "stab in the back," was ultimately rejected in March 1935 by a Histadrut plebiscite. See Shabtai Teveth, *Ben-Gurion: The Burning Ground, 1886–1948* (Boston: Houghton Mifflin, 1987), 481–493.

Chapter 8

Source: Hayim Greenberg, "Notes on Marxism," *Jewish Frontier* 2:7 (May 1935): 19–22.

1. On Karl Marx, see note 31 in chapter 1, "The Meaning of Zionism," in this volume.

2. The Greek philosopher Heraclitus (c. 535–475 BCE) asserted that permanence is an illusion and change is the only reality. All things and states, he argued, contain their opposites, thus transition is the only genuine state of being. He identified life and reason with fire and believed that no man had a soul of his own but that each shared in a universal soul.

3. On Georg Wilhelm Friedrich Hegel, see note 10 in chapter 1, "The Meaning of Zionism," in this volume.

4. See Songsuk Susan Hahn, *Contradiction in Motion: Hegel's Organic Concept of Life and Value* (Ithaca, NY: Cornell University Press, 2007), 28–30.

5. Ibid., 26–27.

6. The demon Mephistopheles utters this well-known German phrase ("for everything that is created is worth destroying") in part 1, scene III of Johann Wolfgang von Goethe's *Faust* (1808): "I am the Spirit that Denies! / And justly so: for all things from the Void / Called forth, deserve to be destroyed." Johann Wolfgang von Goethe, *Faust: A Tragedy*, trans. Bayard Taylor (London: Ward, Lock and Company, 1889), 38.

7. Appalled by the poverty of imperial Russia's serfs and the brutality of the class of nobles to which he belonged, the Russian writer and socialist political thinker Alexander Herzen (1812–70) became a leading revolutionary activist. He eventually left Russia, set up the first free Russian press abroad, published the radical journal *Kolokol* (Russian for "the bell"), and wrote several influential books, including his memoir *My Past and Thoughts* (1852).

8. In fact, this phrase was penned by Friedrich Engels. See Paresh Chattopadhyay, "Karl Marx and Friedrich Engels on Communism," in *The Oxford Handbook of the History of Communism*, ed. Stephen A. Smith (New York: Oxford University Press, 2014), 49.

9. George Bernard Shaw (1856–1950), the eminent Irish playwright and literary critic, won the Nobel Prize in Literature in 1925. His major plays include *Caesar and Cleopatra* (1899), *Man and Superman* (1903), *Major Barbara* (1905), *Pygmalion* (1912), and *Saint Joan* (1924). He also wrote for and edited a variety of socialist publications.

10. The reference here is to line 107 in "Maxims for Revolutionists." See George Bernard Shaw, *Man and Superman: A Comedy and Philosophy* (Cambridge: Cambridge University Press, 1903), 237.

11. According to a midrash in *Vayikra Rabbah* 13, the *shor habor* (wild bull) is destined to battle the Leviathan, only to be vanquished and slaughtered by the latter.

12. According to Canaanite mythology, the Leviathan was a sea monster defeated by the storm god Baal. In the Hebrew Bible, the Leviathan is mentioned six times, including a detailed description in Job 40:15–32. For a useful analysis, see *The Jewish Study Bible*, ed. Adele Berlin and Marc Zvi Brettler (New York: Oxford University Press, 2004), 1559–1560.

13. According to talmudic tradition, a special wine known as *yayin hamishumar* (watched wine), supposedly preserved from "the six days of creation," will be served to the righteous at a feast in a future world (B. Brakhot 34b).

14. The works of Fyodor Dostoyevsky (1821–81), an outstanding figure in modern Russian literature, are characterized by deep psychological insight, fascination with guilt and crime, and faith in the possibility of redemption. His famous novels are *The House of the Dead* (1862), *Notes from the Underground* (1864), *The Idiot* (1869), *The Possessed* (1872), and *The Brothers Karamazov* (1879–80). Greenberg greatly admired Dostoyevsky's literary accomplishments despite the latter's antisemitism.

15. Eduard von Hartmann (1842–1906), a German philosopher, attempted to synthesize the philosophies of Georg Wilhelm Friedrich Hegel (1770–1831), Wilhelm Leibniz (1646–1716), Gottfried Friedrich Joseph von Schelling (1775–1854), and Arthur Schopenhauer (see note 19 below). He is best known for *The Philosophy of the Unconscious* (1869).

16. On Friedrich Nietzsche, see note 7 in chapter 6, "Jew and Arab," in this volume.

17. Greenberg is referring to *Shemot Rabbah* 31:12. This midrash cites key moments in Job (Job 1:9–10, 23:3, 36:21) in its explication of the biblical phrases "do not act toward him as a creditor" and "to the poor person who is with you" (Exod. 22:24). The midrashic commentary reads: "The Holy One, blessed be He, said to him [Job]: 'What dost thou wish, poverty or suffering?' Job replied: 'Lord of the Universe! I am ready to accept all the troubles in the world, but not poverty; for if I go to the market without a *prutah* [coin of small value] for buying, what shall I eat?'" *Midrash Rabbah: Exodus*, trans. S. M. Lehrman, 3rd ed. (London: Soncino, 1983), 391.

18. Greenberg is referring to the biblical story of the tower of Babel. According to Genesis 11:1–9, after the great flood (Gen. 6–9) "everyone on earth had the same language" and gathered in the land of Shinar (a reference to Babylonia) to erect "a tower with its top in the sky." Fearing nothing humanity "may propose to do will be out of their reach," God decided to "confound their speech" and "scattered them from there over the face of the whole earth." See Berlin and Brettler, *The Jewish Study Bible*, 29.

19. The German thinker Arthur Schopenhauer (1788–1860), who developed a philosophy of pessimism, asserted that reality is an impelling force expressed in the individual's will. The mutual resistance of various wills causes strife and pain, which can be temporarily alleviated through science and art, but only resolved by negation of the will. His major works include *The World as Will and Idea* (1818) and *Will in Nature* (1836).

20. Schopenhauer argued the "vulgar opinion" of Western philosophy stemmed from Judaism and that Jewish tradition in turn spawned the doctrine of metempsychosis. The essence of the latter, he asserted, which "spread over the whole human race and commends itself alike to the wise and to the vulgar, is Judaism, together with the two religions which have sprung from it, because they teach the creation of man out of nothing." See Arthur Schopenhauer, *The World as Will and Idea*, trans. R. B. Haldane and J. Kemp, vol. 2 (London: Kegan Paul, Trench, Trübner, 1909), 8; and vol 3, 305.

21. Ibid., vol. 3, 397.

22. The Irish-born American writer John Boyle O'Reilly (1844–90) penned these lines in a poem titled "In Bohemia" (1866), which, according to Robert H. Bremner, "contrasted the kindness and generosity of a community of artists, writers, and scholars with the coldness and caution of a society devoted to thrift and trade." Robert H. Bremner, *Giving: Charity and Philanthropy in History* (1996; reprint, New Brunswick, NJ: Transaction Books, 2000), 160.

23. Greenberg is referring to a statement by the nineteenth-century English social theorist John Ruskin (see note 24 below): "The only wealth is life; all else is not wealth but 'ill-th.'" See *Unto This Last* (1862), which originally appeared in 1860 as series of articles in *Cornhill Magazine*, in *The Works of John Ruskin*, vol. 17, ed. E. T. Cook and Alexander Weddeburn (London: George Allen, 1903–1912), 105.

24. The English social theorist and art critic John Ruskin (1819–1900) wrote several books on art history and architecture in which he developed the idea of art as a reflection of a nation's integrity and morality. A prolific writer and speaker, he attacked the problematic of socioeconomic inequality in the West and proposed reforms in the philosophic works *Munera Pulveris* (1863), *The Crown of the Wild Olive* (1866), and *Time and Tide* (1867).

25. The Greek Sophists, a class of itinerant intellectuals who flourished in the late fifth century BCE, were paid teachers of the nobility who advanced moral skepticism in philosophical discourse and denied the possibility of arriving at objective truth. They specialized in teaching philosophy, rhetoric, mathematics, and the arts.

26. *De Tribus Impostoribus*, an anti-religious polemical tract commonly known in English as *The Treatise of the Three Impostors*, dates back to the early medieval period and evolved over the course of several centuries. Variously attributed to different authors, it refutes the beliefs and teachings of Judaism, Christianity, and Islam. For a useful analysis, see George Mionois, *The Atheist's Bible: The Most Dangerous Book That Never Existed*, trans. Lys Ann Weiss (Chicago: University of Chicago Press, 2012).

27. Greenberg is paraphrasing the famous egalitarian assertion of the medieval English priest John Ball (c. 1338–81): "When Adam dalf, and Eve span, who was thanne a gentilman? From the beginning all men were created equal by nature, and that servitude had been introduced by the unjust and evil oppression of men, against the will of God, who, if it had pleased Him to create serfs, surely in the beginning of the world would have appointed who should be a serf and who a lord." Quoted in Richard B. Dobson, *The Peasants Revolt of 1381* (London: Macmillan, 1970), 374–375.

28. On Moses Hess, see note 31 in chapter 3, "East and West," in this volume.

29. On Ferdinand Lassalle, see note 32 in chapter 1, "The Meaning of Zionism," in this volume.

30. Issued in 1891 by Pope Leo XIII (see note 171 in chapter 24, "The Universalism of the Chosen People," in this volume), the papal encyclical *Rerum Novarum* ("Rights and Duties of Capital and Labor") was an arraignment of capitalism that also attacked Marxist socialism.

31. Greenberg is referencing Marx's famous comment: "Religious suffering is at one and the same time the expression of real suffering and a protest against real suffering. Religion is the sigh of the oppressed creature, the heart of a heartless world and the soul of soulless conditions. It is the opium of the people." Quoted in "A Contribution to the Critique of Hegel's Philosophy of Right" (1843–44) in Karl Marx, *Early Writings*, trans. Rodney Livingstone and Gregor Benton (London: Penguin Books, 1992) 244.

32. On Baruch Spinoza, see note 50 in chapter 1, "The Meaning of Zionism," in this volume.

33. Auguste Comte (1798–1857), a French philosopher who conceived of the "religion of humanity" as a substitute for traditional belief and an answer to France's post-

revolutionary social crisis, believed in the possibility of reforming society through empirical investigation, critical analysis, and social planning. Comte's major works are *The Course of Positivist Philosophy* (1853) and *A General View of Positivism* (1848). The latter is considered a founding document of the discipline of sociology. Comte's theories were critical to the development of secular humanism in the nineteenth century.

34. Over the course of his career, the German philosopher and anthropologist Ludwig Feuerbach (1804–72) abandoned Hegelian idealism for naturalistic materialism. His critical analysis of religion and society in *The Essence of Christianity* (1841) prefigured Karl Marx's theory of dialectical materialism.

35. On Feuerbach's notion, see Jeffrey J. Kripal, *The Serpent's Gift: Gnostic Reflections on the Study of Religion* (Chicago: University of Chicago Press, 2007), 73–75.

36. Though unrecognized in his lifetime, the artist and poet William Blake (1757–1827) came to be regarded as a seminal figure in English Romanticism. His major works include *Songs of Innocence* (1789) and *Songs of Experience* (1794).

37. This couplet is from lines 146–147 of William Blake's "The Everlasting Gospel" (1818). See also *The Visionary Company: A Reading of English Romantic Poetry*, ed. Harold Bloom (Ithaca, NY: Cornell University Press, 1971), 5–6.

38. Quoted from Karl Marx's "Theses on Feuerbach" (1845). See *Karl Marx: Selected Writings*, ed. David McLellan, 2nd ed. (New York: Oxford University Press, 2000), 173.

39. Anatoly Lunacharsky (1875–1933), a Russian revolutionary leader, dramatist, and poet, served as the Soviet Union's first commissar of education (1917–29). Influential in the development of Soviet Russian theatre, he wrote a memoir titled *Revolutionary Silhouettes* (1923).

40. Both Georg Wilhelm Friedrich Hegel and Friedrich Nietzsche asserted this idea in their respective works. As Greenberg notes here, however, Nietzsche applied it most famously in a parable which first appeared in *The Gay Science* (1882). See Walter Kaufmann, *Nietzsche: Philosopher, Psychologist, Antichrist*, 4th ed. (Princeton, NJ: Princeton University Press, 1974), 96–97.

41. The American philosopher and psychologist William James (1842–1910) taught at Harvard University. He considered consciousness as active and purposeful. In his "radical empiricism" he rejected all transcendent principles and argued that knowledge derives from direct experience. His works include *The Principles of Psychology* (1890), *The Will to Believe* (1897), *The Varieties of Religious Experience* (1902), and *Pragmatism* (1907).

42. Sigmund Freud (1856–1939), the Austrian psychiatrist and founder of psychoanalysis, was raised in Vienna in an acculturated Jewish household. He initially collaborated with his mentor, the Austrian Jewish physician Josef Breuer (1842–1925), leading to their joint publication of *Studies on Hysteria* (1895). In time, the two separated over disagreements about the role of sexuality in psychoanalysis. Freud subsequently substituted hypnosis with the process of free association. In 1902 Freud founded the Wednesday Psychological Society (which later became the Vienna Psychoanalytic Society), and in 1906 he entered into close working relationships with Paul Eugen Bleuler (1857–1939), Carl Jung (1875–1961), and Alfred W. Adler (1870–1937). Between 1911 and 1913 Jung and Adler broke away from Freud and formed their own schools of psychoanalysis. In 1938, after the Nazi occupation of Austria, Freud escaped to London. His major works

include *The Interpretation of Dreams* (1900), *The Psychopathology of Everyday Life* (1904), *Three Essays on the Theory of Sexuality* (1905), *Totem and Taboo* (1913); *Beyond the Pleasure Principle* (1920), *The Ego and the Id* (1923), *Civilization and Its Discontents* (1930), and *Moses and Monotheism* (1937). Freud's work continues to exert considerable influence in the modern fields of medicine, cultural studies, anthropology, education, literature, and art. For a full discussion by Greenberg of Freud, see chapter 15, "Psychoanalysis and Moral Pessimism," in this volume.

43. Quoted from the "Fourth and Last Part" of Friedrich Nietzsche, *Thus Spake Zarathustra*, trans. Thomas Common (New York: Macmillan, 1911), 335.

44. Zarathustra is the central character in *Thus Spake Zarathustra* (1883–85), a philosophical epic by Friedrich Nietzsche. Zarathustra's namesake is the founder of the Persian religion Zoroastrianism (see note 8 in chapter 16, "Chosen Peoples," and note 97 in chapter 24, "The Universalism of the Chosen People," in this volume).

45. Mount Vesuvius, the only active volcano on the European mainland, is located in southern Italy. It is famous for erupting in 79 CE and destroying the Roman cities of Pompeii and Herculaneum.

46. Quoted from Friedrich Nietzsche, *The Gay Science; with a Prelude of Rhymes and an Appendix of Songs*, trans. Walter Kaufmann (New York: Random House, 1974), 283.

Chapter 9

Source: Hayim Greenberg, "To a Communist Friend," *Jewish Frontier* 3:5 (May 1936): 15–20.

1. The Russian Civil War (1918–21), a countrywide rebellion following the October Revolution of 1917 (see note 1 in chapter 5, "Our Stand," in this volume), was spurred by the White Army, a loose coalition of counter-revolutionary and anti-Bolshevik factions as well as military forces formerly loyal to the tsarist regime. The civil war era witnessed widespread political turmoil, widespread anarchy, food shortages, and regional fighting. In contrast to the White forces, which lacked unity and strategic coherence, Leon Trotsky (see note 30 in chapter 3, "East and West," in this volume), in his capacity as war commissar, pursued a sustained strategy that maximized the Red Army's superior artillery and munitions. In late 1919, the White Army started to collapse and in time the Red Army succeeded in stamping out all resistance to the Bolshevik regime.

2. Yemelyan Mikhailovich Yaroslavsky (1878–1943), a Russian revolutionary and Bolshevik leader of Jewish ancestry, served as the Communist Party's official historian. An outspoken atheist, he edited the satirical journal *Bezbozhnik* (Russian for "The Godless") and was head of the League of Militant Atheists.

3. The Italian religious reformer Girolamo Savonarola (1452–98), a popular Dominican preacher, was sent to Florence by the Vatican. When the Medici family was exiled in 1494, he became the virtual ruler of Florence and imposed rigidly puritanical order. He opposed the corruption of Pope Alexander VI (Rodrigo de Borgia, 1431–1503) and allied himself with King Charles VIII (1470–98) of France, who invaded Italy. In 1497, Savonarola was excommunicated and he denounced the pope. When tensions in Florence turned to violence, he was arrested, tortured, and hanged.

4. François-Marie Arouet de Voltaire (1694–1778), a preeminent philosopher, historian, and writer of the French Enlightenment, was a rationalist and deist known for his wit and satirical style. He asserted that "if God did not exist, he would have to be invented." He vigorously opposed religious fanaticism, declaring, "*Écrasez l'infame*!" (French for "crush the infamous one"). His social and political views were generally conservative. Among his major works are the novel *Candide* (1759) and the *Philosophical Dictionary* (1764).

5. On Leo Tolstoy, see note 4 in chapter 1, "The Meaning of Zionism," in this volume.

6. Waldo Frank (1889–1967), a prolific secular Jewish novelist and political activist born in New Jersey, helped to strengthen cultural ties between the United States and Latin America. He authored fourteen novels, eighteen volumes of social history, and over a hundred articles on literary and political subjects.

7. On Karl Marx, see note 31 in chapter 1, "The Meaning of Zionism," in this volume.

8. The reference is to Baruch Spinoza's postulate that all existence is embraced in one "unique substance," namely, God or nature. Spinoza asserted that "no substance or attributes exist in God's infinite [power] which do not formally exist in nature. . . . Everything is equally in God's infinite intellect." See Spinoza's "Short Treatise on God, Man, and His Well-Being," in Edwin M. Curley, *The Collected Works of Spinoza*, vol. 1 (Princeton, NJ: Princeton University Press, 1985), 68–69.

9. Spanish for "swine," the term *marranos* was used in Spain and Portugal to refer to the descendants of baptized Jews suspected of secret adherence to Judaism.

10. On Vladimir Lenin, see note 9 in chapter 6, "Jew and Arab," in this volume.

11. The central European thinker Immanuel Kant (1724–1804), a seminal figure in Western philosophy, resided in Königsberg, where he was professor of logic and metaphysics. Among his major works are *Critique of Pure Reason* (1781), *Foundations of the Metaphysics of Ethics* (1785), *Critique of Practical Reason* (1788), *Critique of Judgment* (1790), and *Religion within the Boundaries of Pure Reason* (1794).

12. Kant distinguished between things of worldly experience (phenomena), which can be categorized according to causality and substantiality, and *Dinge-an-sich* (German for "things in themselves") (noumena), which the intellect cannot comprehend. To illustrate the latter, he pointed to the logical contradictions of principles which cannot be resolved (antinomies). In this way, he sought to demonstrate that time and space are both finite and infinite and likewise God exists and does not exist.

13. Hendrik (Henri) de Man (1885–1953), an antisemitic socialist theoretician and Belgian Labor Party politician, gravitated to fascism in the late 1930s. Following Hitler's occupation of Belgium in 1940, he served as de facto prime minister of the Belgian government and collaborated with the Nazi regime. He soon fell from favor, however, and went into self-imposed exile in France. In 1945, he fled to Switzerland in advance of the Allies' defeat of the Axis powers. After the war, he was convicted of treason in absentia and remained in Switzerland for the remainder of his life.

14. Influenced by Christian socialism, the British writer and politician George Lansbury (1859–1940) founded the *Daily Herald* in 1912 and served as the paper's long-time editor. He eventually entered politics as a member of the British Labour Party. From 1931 to 1935 he led the parliamentary opposition to Ramsay MacDonald's (1866–1937)

Conservative-dominated national government. A staunch pacifist, he favored Great Britain's unilateral disarmament. In 1937 he tried to avoid war with the Axis powers by visiting the fascist dictators Benito Mussolini (1883–1945) of Italy and Adolf Hitler (1889–1945) of Germany.

15. The French novelist, biographer, and playwright Romain Rolland (1866–1944) wrote biographies of Ludwig van Beethoven (1903), Michelangelo (1905), Leo Tolstoy (1911), and Mahatma Gandhi (1924). He won the Nobel Prize in Literature in 1915 and is best known for the play *The Wolves* (1898) and his ten-volume novel *Jean-Christophe* (1904–12). As a result of his pacifism, he spent several years of self-imposed exile in Switzerland.

16. The two main camps of Marxist socialism in Russia between 1903 and 1918 were Bolshevism and Menshevism. In 1903 the Russian Social Democratic Party (founded in 1898) split into the Bolsheviki (majority members), led by Vladimir Lenin, and the Mensheviki (minority members), led by Georgi Valentinovich Plekhanov (1857–1918). Lenin advocated immediate revolution and the establishment of "the dictatorship of the proletariat." By contrast, Plekhanov asserted that before achieving socialism Russian society needed to pass through the intermediate stage of a democratic bourgeois regime like other countries in the West. The Bolsheviks believed in the leadership of a small disciplined party, while the Mensheviks sought to appeal to the masses and find common cause with non-Marxist democratic political parties. Although the Social Democratic Party ostensibly remained united, the Bolsheviks soon lost their majority status and the Mensheviks gained the upper hand. In the Russian Revolution the Mensheviks worked closely with the Kerensky regime (see note 16 in chapter 9, "To a Communist Friend," and note 11 in chapter 22, "Concerning Statehood," in this volume), which the Bolsheviks overthrew in November 1917. In 1918, the fledgling Communist Party dismantled the Menshevik faction and purged its ranks of dissenters.

17. Greenberg wrote this essay on the eve of Soviet Russia's Moscow Trials that lasted from 1936 to 1938. The Stalin regime used these "show trials" as a pretext for purging the Communist ranks and Russian intellectual arena of all dissenting and moderate voices. Here Greenberg refers specifically to the disappointing response of Romain Rolland who, "after making a career of conscientious protests . . . neither endorsed nor criticized the most glaring Communist excess of the era." David James Fisher, *Romain Rolland and the Politics of Intellectual Engagement*, 2nd ed. (New Brunswick, NJ: Transaction Publishers, 2004), 286.

18. Darwinism, the concept of evolution formulated by the naturalist Charles Darwin (1809–82), is predicated on the notion of natural selection. In the fifth edition of Darwin's *On the Origin of Species* (1859), which was published in 1869, Darwin employed the phrase "survival of the fittest." In fact, the English philosopher Herbert Spencer (1820–1903) coined the latter phrase shortly after Darwin's work first appeared.

19. The ancient Greek philosopher Plato (c. 429–347 BCE), among the most significant and profound Western thinkers and writers, was a disciple of Socrates (see note 56 in chapter 16, "Chosen Peoples," in this volume). His studies, including the highly influential Socratic work, *The Republic* (c. 380 BCE), emphasize questions of justice and virtue, the formation of man's character, and the relationship between the individual and so-

ciety. In 387 BCE, he founded the Academy, an Athenian school of learning that spawned Western society's tradition of institutions of higher education. Plato's most famous pupil was Aristotle (see note 2 in chapter 16, "Chosen Peoples," in this volume).

20. Plato viewed disorder as evil and immoral. He envisioned a world of order attained when reason governs human conduct. The ideal state, according to Plato's *Republic* (c. 380 BCE), was to be divided among four classes: the "philosopher kings" who would rule, soldiers, a trade and merchant class, and slaves. In this way, each individual would occupy an assigned place in a fixed sociopolitical environment that benefits the whole.

21. At the turn of the nineteenth and twentieth centuries, the movement to establish Danish peasant cooperatives grew swiftly and achieved remarkable success. The latter proved to be a model for other European efforts. By the eve of World War I, "most Danish, Swedish, Finnish, and Romanian and more than one in three Russian and Irish peasant households belonged to marketing and/or credit cooperatives." Robert Bideleux and Ian Jeffries, *A History of Eastern Europe: Crisis and Change* (London: Routledge, 1998), 450.

22. Before the mid-1930s, most western European countries, including Sweden, outpaced the United States in rural electrification. Electro-Invest, a Swedish holding company established in 1929, held major concessions in Latvia, Poland, Romania, and Yugoslavia. See Paul Wolman, "The New Deal for Electricity in the United States, 1930–1950," in *The Challenge of Rural Electrification: Strategies for Developing Countries*, ed. Douglas F. Barnes (Washington, DC: Resources for the Future, 2007), 261; William J. Hausman, *Global Electrification: Multinational Enterprise and International Finance in the History of Light and Power, 1878–2007* (Cambridge: Cambridge University Press, 2008), 193.

23. The reference is to "*autos-da-fé*" (pl., Portuguese), literally "acts of faith" (also "*autos-de-fe*" in medieval Spanish), the term used by the Spanish and Portuguese Inquisitions to describe the penance required of heretics, apostates, and crypto-Jews. In time, the term came to be identified with the Inquisition's practice of executing its victims by burning them at the stake. Together with Catholic Church authorities, the Spanish and Portuguese regimes wielded *autos-da-fé* as instruments of terror and punishment in their dominions from the late fifteenth to early nineteenth centuries.

24. Sergei Nechaev (1847–82), a Russian Nihilist and revolutionary activist, advocated the use of violence to destroy the tsarist regime and create a new political order. He was closely associated with the Russian political thinkers Mikhail Bakunin (1814–76), Alexander Herzen (see note 7 in chapter 8, "Notes on Marxism," in this volume), and Nikolai Ogarev (1813–77). He was imprisoned for life after being convicted of the murder of Ivan Ivanovich Ivanov (d. 1869), a student and one of Nechaev's former followers. He is best known for the political statement *The Revolutionary Cathechism* (1869) (see note 16 in chapter 12, "Leon Trotsky," in this volume). The Russian author Fyodor Dostoyevsky (see note 14 in chapter 8, "Notes on Marxism," in this volume) drew on Nechaev as a model for the character Pyotr Stepanovich Verkhovensky in his novel *Demons* (1872). See Paul Avrich, *Anarchist Portraits* (Princeton, NJ: Princeton University Press, 1988), chap. 3.

25. It is unclear if Nechaev uttered this statement. However, Maxim Gorky attributed the phrase to Nechaev (see note 36 in chapter 1, "The Meaning of Zionism," in this volume) in his fierce criticisms of the Bolsheviks in 1917, many of which appeared in the

Russian newspaper *Novaya Zhizn* (New Life) published by the Menshevik Party. For example, in December 1917 Gorky characterized "Nechaev's method" as "full steam ahead through the swamp." Maxim Gorky, *Untimely Thoughts: Essays on Revolution, Culture and the Bolsheviks, 1917–1918*, ed. Mark D. Steinberg, trans. Herman Ermolaev, rev. ed. (New Haven, CT: Yale University Press, 1995), 87.

26. According to the Hebrew Bible, the Egyptian pharaoh used Israelite slave labor to erect the garrison cities of Pithom and Rameses (Exod. 1:11). The cities guarded, respectively, the northern and northeastern entry points of Egypt.

27. Friedrich von Schiller (1759–1805), a central European poet, dramatist, historian, and philosopher, was a leading figure of the proto-Romantic *Sturm und Drang* (German for "storm and stress") movement. Deeply influenced by Immanuel Kant, idealism and hatred of autocracy were central to his artistic sensibility. His works include "Ode to Joy" (1785), a hymn Ludwig van Beethoven (1770–1827) incorporated into his Ninth Symphony (1824), the drama *Don Carlos* (1787), *A History of the Thirty Years War* (1793), and *On the Aesthetic Education of Man in a Series of Letters* (1794). Together with the German writer and politician Johann Wolfgang von Goethe (1749–1832), he helped to usher in the period of central European creativity known as "Weimar Classicism."

28. Schiller's "Ode to Joy" (1785) stands out as an iconic example of the German Romantic period. The poem's central theme is humanity's potentiality and this-worldly happiness. In time, owing in large measure to Beethoven's musical rendition of the text, it became an anthem of universal brotherhood.

29. Translated from German, the text reads: "Reconciled the entire world. / Let our arch-enemy be forgiven, / Our debt ledger be destroyed, / Reconciled the whole world." Greenberg appears to be offering a satirical twist on lines 66, 69, and 70 of Schiller's original poem: "*Unserm Todfeind sei verziehen . . . / Unser Schuldbuch sei vernichtet*! / *Ausgesehnt die ganze Welt*!" ("Our deadly enemy be forgiven . . . / The account of our misdeeds be destroyed! / Reconciled the entire world!").

30. On Leon Trotsky, see note 30 in chapter 3, "East and West," in this volume.

31. The British Jewish intellectual and politician Harold J. Laski (1893–1950), a socialist and political theorist, was educated at Oxford and taught at Harvard, where he developed close ties with the American jurist and US Supreme Court justice Oliver Wendell Holmes (1841–1935). He was subsequently appointed to the faculty of the London School of Economics. An articulate and compelling speaker, he emerged as a key figure in the British Fabian Society. In the mid-1930s he played an active role in the British Labour Party and in 1945 he became its chairman. Following Labour's rise to power in 1945, he was shut out of the new government by Prime Minister Clement Atlee (1883–1967) and the party leadership who feared his Marxist views and pro-Soviet inclinations. Though generally inactive in Jewish public life, starting in the mid-1930s he developed a keen interest in British policy vis-à-vis Zionism and Palestine. After World War II, he clashed publicly with British foreign minister Ernest Bevin (1881–1951), questioned the British mandatory regime's postwar policies, and declared his support for the creation of a Jewish commonwealth.

32. Harold J. Laski, *Democracy in Crisis* (Chapel Hill: University of North Carolina Press, 1933), 256–257.

33. The British public intellectual Ralph Norman Angell (1872–1967), a social demo-

cratic activist and internationalist, was a journalist, author, British Labour Party politician, and member of the British parliament. He spent considerable time in the United States in the late nineteenth century, before relocating to Paris, where he covered the Dreyfus Affair (see notes 10 and 13 in chapter 26, "Patriotism and Plural Loyalties," in this volume), and then returning to England. In the 1920s, he became active in the British Labour Party and served as a member of Parliament. An outspoken and prolific advocate for world peace, he was knighted in 1931 and awarded the Nobel Peace Prize in 1933. He first developed his ideas in *Patriotism under Three Flags: A Plea for Rationalism in Politics* (1903). In *The Great Illusion* (1910), which became an international bestseller, he argued the shared economic interests of European nations made militarism and wars futile. Among his other major works are *The Money Game* (1928), *The Unseen Assassins* (1932), *The Steep Places* (1947), and a memoir titled *After All* (1951).

34. Greenberg is quoting a phrase Ralph Norman Angell first used in *Must Britain Travel the Moscow Road?* (1926). Angell subsequently repeated variants of this argument in order to make clear his intellectual disagreement with Marxism, such as in *Can Governments Cure Unemployment?* (1931), with Harold White; *Preface to Peace* (1935); *Does Capitalism Cause War?* (1935), with Henry Brinton and Leonard Woolf; *Raw Materials, Population Pressure and War* (1935), based on a series of lectures he delivered in the United States in the fall of 1935; and *The Money Mystery: An Explanation for Beginners* (1936). On Angell's view of economic incentives and political organization, see Martin Ceadel, *Living the Great Illusion: Sir Norman Angell, 1872–1967* (New York: Oxford University Press, 2009), 285–286, 301, 324–325.

35. Yuri Aleksandrovich Larin (1882–1932), a Russian economist, publicist, and political activist of Jewish ancestry, joined the Russian Social Democratic Party in 1900 and shortly thereafter emerged as a Menshevik leader. He was active in a variety of insurgent activities, spent time in prison and Siberia, and traveled extensively. After the Russian Revolution of 1917, he joined the Bolshevik Party and Vladimir Lenin tapped him as an economic advisor. In 1917–18, he served in the Soviet delegation to the Brest-Litovsk negotiations. His daughter married the Bolshevik activist Nikolai Bukharin (see note 37 below). As Greenberg notes here, Larin's views on labor affairs and the role of capital in the emerging national economy were widely embraced by Soviet leaders in the mid-1920s.

36. The New Economic Policy was a relatively moderate economic policy that the Bolsheviks initiated after they won the Civil War. Under this policy the state would control banking and large industries but allow peasants to sell their goods on capitalist markets and allow for some private trade and property.

37. Nikolai Bukharin (1888–1938) was a Russian socialist and member of the Bolshevik Party during the Russian Revolution. While he was at first a member of the party's left-wing faction, he altered his views and after Lenin's death came to be regarded as the leader of the party's right-wing faction. He supported the gradual building of socialism in the Soviet Union and opposed Joseph Stalin's five-year plans (see note 39 below). In 1929, he was stripped of his party positions, although he remained editor of a party newspaper. In 1938, he was charged with treason and executed.

38. Joseph Vissarionovich (Dzhugashvili) Stalin (1879–1953), the Soviet Russian dictator from the mid-1920s until his death, succeeded the Bolshevik leader Vladimir Lenin.

In 1928 he ended Lenin's New Economic Policy and inaugurated the first Five-Year Plan, an authoritarian national policy whose twin objectives of rapid collectivization and industrialization brushed aside basic civil liberties and caused a staggering countrywide loss of human life. In contrast to Leon Trotsky (see note 30 in chapter 3, "East and West," in this volume), whose exile from Russia he secured in 1927, Stalin asserted the need to achieve "Socialism in One Country" rather than promote Marxist revolution worldwide. In the 1930s, he ruthlessly consolidated his absolutist rule by eliminating all dissent in the Communist Party, imprisoning, terrorizing, forcibly resettling, exiling, and executing his political opponents, and authorizing mass killings. In the early 1940s, he unilaterally reorganized all of the Soviet Union's executive and military leadership functions in the office of "marshal." During World War II, he was a shrewd strategist and ally of the United States and Britain. With the rise of the Cold War era, he became an adept adversary of the West.

39. The Five-Year Plans were economic schemes through which the Soviet Union's leadership sought to rapidly modernize and industrialize the country. The first Five-Year Plan was launched by Stalin in 1928 and had as its goal substantial increases in the output of the Soviet Union's heavy industries and the nationwide collectivization of agriculture. Subsequent plans were routinely implemented as a centerpiece of Soviet domestic planning until 1991 when the USSR dissolved.

40. See Vladimir Lenin, *The Infantile Sickness of "Leftism" in Communism* (Moscow: Executive Committee of the Communist International, 1920), in which he argues that for Marxist Communism to succeed it must vanquish and stamp out all forms of left-wing socialism including Menshevism.

41. Stakhanovism, a movement named after Aleksey Stakhanov (1906–77), a Soviet coal miner who became a Communist celebrity and hero when his team increased its daily output sevenfold, encouraged workers to ramp up their productivity through the utilization of new and more efficient labor techniques. The movement disappeared after World War II.

42. The *kolkhoz* (Russian for "collective Soviet farm") was an agricultural village made up of peasant families, each of which was allocated a plot of land and paid a share of the farm's overall yield.

43. Quoted from Karl Marx, "On the Hague Congress" (Report of Speech Delivered on September 8, 1872) reprinted in Karl Marx and Friedrich Engels, *Collected Works: Marx and Engels, 1871–1874*, trans. Richard Dixon et al., vol. 23 (London: Lawrence and Wishart, 1975), 255.

44. The Hague Congress of 1872, a meeting of the International Workingmen's Association (IWA), also called the First International—a coalition of anarchist, communist, and socialist groups—took place in the aftermath of the failed Paris Commune (March–May 1871), a revolutionary socialist government that briefly ruled Paris and proclaimed its right to govern France. Ideological dissent and strife plagued the congress, while Karl Marx and the radical leader Mikahil Bakunin (1814–76) clashed over the IWA's political agenda. The congress expelled the revolutionary anarchists Bakunin and James Guillaume (1844–1916), which in turn prompted the dissolution of the IWA. Thereafter, the Marxist and anarchist camps established rival internationals.

45. In 1919, Georgi Dimitrov (1882–1949), a socialist revolutionary and opposition leader in the Bulgarian parliament, helped found the Bulgarian Communist Party. Following a failed worker's revolt in 1923, he fled to Yugoslavia and then the Soviet Union. In 1929, he relocated to Germany where he became leader of the region's Marxist Comintern (also known as the Third International). In 1933, he was arrested and tried by the Nazi regime for alleged involvement in the burning of the Reichstag. Upon his release, he returned to the Soviet Union and became a party functionary in Stalin's regime. After World War II, he was installed as the Soviet-backed premier of a Bulgarian puppet state.

46. Earl Browder, *What Is Communism?* (New York: Vanguard Press, 1936).

47. Earl Browder (1891–1973), a key leader of the American Communist Party during the Great Depression and World War II, was a follower of Soviet dictator Joseph Stalin. From the start of his involvement in radical politics, he worked assiduously to bring the Communist Party into the mainstream of American life, and he was imprisoned by the US government on different occasions for charges of espionage, conspiracy, and passport fraud. After the outbreak of World War II, he moderated his views and worked selectively with other American labor, trade union, and socialist groups in opposing Nazi Germany and backing some of the Roosevelt administration's New Deal policies, particularly employment initiatives like the Works Progress Administration. Browder's popular front activity met with modest success and he established relationships with a loose coalition of left and center-left figures and groups. His outlook (known as "Browderism"), which aroused the ire of orthodox Marxists, caused him to be expelled from the Communist Party in 1946.

Chapter 10

Source: Hayim Greenberg, "Open Letter to the Third International," *Jewish Frontier* 3:8 (August 1936): 15–20.

1. In 1919 the Bolshevik leader Vladimir Lenin (see note 9 in chapter 6, "Jew and Arab," in this volume) established the Third International (also called the Comintern), a Soviet-dominated international organization of Marxist-oriented socialist and Communist parties and groups, many of which were directly affiliated with the Soviet Union. Its chief aim was the spread of Marxist revolutionary ideology and activity to the rest of the world. In 1943, the Soviet dictator Joseph Stalin (see note 38 in chapter 9, "To a Communist Friend," in this volume) dissolved the Third International, ostensibly as a gesture of goodwill to his non-Communist allies during World War II.

2. Greenberg is referring to the debates that roiled the left in the 1920s and 1930s concerning the integrity and durability of distinctive ethnic and national groups vis-à-vis the aims of socialism and communism.

3. The Tchukches (also Chukchi) (Russian for "rich in reindeer"), an indigenous tribe inhabiting the Chuckchi peninsula in the Bering Strait, became part of the Soviet Russian federation during World War I.

4. In 1928, the Soviet Union granted the Mordvinians formal status as an "autonomous republic" within the Russian federation. The resulting republic of Mordovia in the Volga River region is home to approximately one-third of Russia's Mordvinic-speaking people.

5. On Joseph Stalin, see note 38 in chapter 9, "To a Communist Friend," in this volume.

6. Quoted from "Political Report of the Central Committee to the Sixteenth Congress of the C.P.S.U.(B.), June 27, 1930," reprinted in J. V. Stalin, *Works, April 1929–June 1930*, vol. 12 (Moscow: Foreign Languages Publishing House, 1954), 378–379. Stalin's explanation includes disparaging comments about the Bundists and other "deviators . . . follow[ing] in their footsteps" allegedly preoccupied by "juggling with the flag of internationalism and slander against Lenin."

7. On Birobidzhan see note 2 in chapter 5, "Our Stand," in this volume.

8. The Bolshevik revolutionary Mikhail Ivanovich Kalinin (1875–1946), a close ally of Joseph Stalin, served as chairman of the Soviet presidium's supreme council from 1922 to 1946. An outspoken advocate of the Birobidzhan project, he made the following argument (known as the "Kalinin Declaration") at an Ozet conference in 1926: "The Jewish people faces a great task—to preserve its nationality—and for this end a large part of the Jewish population, hundreds of thousands at least, must be turned into agricultural peasants settled in a continuous area. Only in these conditions can the Jewish masses hope to preserve the continued existence of Jewish nationality." Quoted in Benjamin Pinkus, *The Jews of the Soviet Union: The History of a National Minority* (Cambridge: Cambridge University Press, 1988), 72.

9. In 1925 the Soviet regime established the Komzet (Russian acronym for the "Committee for the Settlement of Toiling Jews on the Land") in order to promote and assist Russian Jewry's transition from semi-skilled professions to agricultural labor. While the Komzet played a direct role in allocating lands and organizing Jews in *kolkhozes* (collective farms), the Ozet, a complementary public society, channeled funds and provided expertise required for relocation, training, and building public infrastructure, including educational and medical services. The Ozet also interfaced with international Jewish aid and philanthropic agencies, chief among them the American Jewish Joint Distribution Committee, which created the Agro-Joint and contributed $25 million to support Birobidzhan. The latter efforts were discontinued after 1937 when Stalin's purges, which targeted a broad array of intellectuals and internal dissenters as counter-revolutionaries, victimized the Komzet and Ozet leadership.

10. The Abkhazian, Adjarian, and Nakhichevan republics, located in the borderlands separating the former Russian and Turkish empires, were established by the Soviet Union after the conclusion of World War I in accordance with the Treaty of Kars (1921).

11. The *sovnarkhozy* (Russian for "supreme economic councils") were regional branches of a centralized governmental authority that assumed broad responsibility at the provincial level for the nationalization of Soviet economic life including the channeling of government funds, organizing labor exchanges, managing food supplies, distributing raw materials, and so on.

12. The Permanent Mandates Commission was established in 1919 following World War I by the League of Nations (see note 5 in chapter 25, "Current Alternatives in Palestine," in this volume) to oversee the assignation of mandates, a form of colonial administration imposed on former Turkish territories and German colonies by the victorious Allied Powers. Though France and Great Britain, the chief beneficiaries of the new postwar system, were theoretically accountable to the commission, the League lacked any

real political power. In 1946 the UN Trusteeship Council replaced the Mandates Commission. See also notes 1, 14, and 21 in chapter 25, "Current Alternatives in Palestine," in this volume.

13. In 1920 the San Remo conference, representing the victorious "Principal Allied Powers" (with the notable exception of the United States), continued the postwar work of the Paris Peace Conference of 1919 and assigned "mandates" for the ongoing administration of the former Turkish territories and German colonies. The French took control of Syria and Lebanon, while the British assumed authority for Palestine, Transjordan, and Iraq. In 1922, the newly established League of Nations formally approved the British mandate for Palestine. The latter reiterated the provisions of the Balfour Declaration of 1917 (see note 3 in chapter 25, "Current Alternatives in Palestine," in this volume) and stipulated that "an appropriate Jewish agency shall be recognized as a public body for the purpose of advising and cooperating with the Administration of Palestine in such economic, social, and other matters as may affect the establishment of the Jewish national home and the interests of the Jewish population in Palestine. . . . The Zionist organization, so long as its organization and constitution are in the opinion of the mandatory appropriate, shall be recognized as such agency." See Article 4 in League of Nations, *Mandate for Palestine* (London: His Majesty's Stationery Office, 1922), 39–40. Consequently, the Zionist movement's Palestine executive became the new Jewish Agency for Palestine, with Chaim Weizmann (see note 2 in chapter 2, "Policy and Labor," in this volume), president of the World Zionist Organization, as its chairman. The Jewish Agency was thereafter regarded as the official representative body of the Zionist movement in the international arena.

14. From 1927 to 1946 the British Mandatory regime granted the Palestine Currency Board authority to issue the Palestine pound (which bore trilingual legends in English, Arabic, and Hebrew) for regional circulation. Each pound was divided into 1,000 mils and coins were assigned values of 50 and 100 mils. The unit value of a mil was equivalent to 1/1,000 of the British pound sterling.

15. The foregoing data are apparently drawn from "The Palestinian Arabs," *Palestine* 11:3 (March 4, 1936): 4.

16. The Anglo-Irish cleric and author Jonathan Swift (1667–1745) was one of the greatest satirists of the English language. His significant works include *A Tale of a Tub* (1706), *An Argument against Abolishing Christianity* (1708), *Gulliver's Travels* (1726), and *A Modest Proposal* (1729).

17. Quoted from Jonathan Swift's *Gulliver's Travels* (1726). See, e.g., *The Prose Works of Jonathan Swift*, ed. G. Ravenscroft Dennis, vol. 3 (London: George Bell and Sons, 1909), 140.

18. Arab rioting began in Jaffa in mid-April 1936 and soon spread to other towns with mixed Jewish and Arab populations. In the ensuing months, the riots developed into a full-scale Arab rebellion that lasted until 1939. For a useful analysis, see Anita Shapira, *Land and Power: The Zionist Resort to Force, 1881–1948* (New York: Oxford University Press, 1992), chap. 6.

19. The reference is to Haj Effendi Muhammad Amin al-Husayni (1897–1974), who assumed the position Grand Mufti of Jerusalem in 1921 following the death of his brother

Kamil al-Husayni (1867–1921). The al-Husaynis, one of Jerusalem's elite families, opposed Zionism and were among the leaders of the Arab nationalist movement. During the Arab rebellion of 1936–39, al-Husayni escaped arrest by the British and fled to Lebanon, Iraq, Italy, and Germany. During World War II, he collaborated with the Nazi regime. After the war, al-Husayni's influence swiftly declined and in 1948, following Jordan's conquest of eastern Jerusalem, King Abdullah I (see note 6 in chapter 28, "Jewish Culture and Education in the Diaspora," in this volume) deposed and banned him. He spent his remaining decades in Lebanon marginalized and discredited.

20. Speculation about the size and composition of ancient Palestine's population can be traced to Josephus's (see note 203 in chapter 24, "The Universalism of the Chosen People," in this volume) account which included the fanciful estimate of 10–12 million persons. In this instance, Greenberg appears to be drawing on the work of French Jewish historian and lawyer Jean Juster (1886–1916), whose study *Les juifs dans l'empire romain* (1914) includes the estimate of five million inhabitants. For an overview of historians' prevailing assumptions in the 1920s, 1930s, and 1940s concerning ancient Palestine's population, see C. C. McCown, "The Density of Population in Ancient Palestine," *Journal of Biblical Literature* 66:4 (December 1947): 425–436. Contemporary scholars generally believe "the population of Palestine in antiquity did not exceed a million persons." See Magen Broshi, "The Population of Western Palestine in the Roman-Byzantine Period," *Bulletin of the American Schools of Oriental Research* 236 (1979): 7; Yigal Shiloh, "The Population of Iron Age Palestine in the Light of a Sample Analysis of Urban Plans, Areas, and Population Density," *Bulletin of the American Schools of Oriental Research* 239 (1980): 33.

21. Throughout the 1920s and 1930s the Comintern called for an Arab Communist Federation "to include the parties of Syria, Palestine, and Egypt" as well as for "the national unification of all Arab countries." See, e.g., "Extracts from a Resolution of the ECCI [Executive Committee of the Communist International] Political Secretariat on the Insurrection Movement in Arabistan (October 16, 1929)," in *The Communist International: Documents, 1919–1943*, ed. Jane Degras, vol. 3 (London: Royal Institute of International Affairs, 1964), 78, 81.

22. On Transjordan (Transjordania), see note 10 in chapter 7, "Revisionism," and note 12 in chapter 25, "Current Alternatives in Palestine," in this volume.

23. The Khoikhoi (formerly called "Hottentots") are a native southwestern African tribe of farmers and cattle herders. Starting in the sixteenth century, successive European colonial powers, particularly the Dutch East India Company in the seventeenth and eighteenth centuries, exploited and brutalized the Khoikhoi. Except for the Namas, a small remnant in central Namibia, they have mostly disappeared.

24. The Swiss jurist and politician Johann Kaspar Bluntschli (1808–81), a leading student of political science, was among the founders in 1873 of the Institute of International Law in Ghent, Belgium. He is best known for his three-volume work *Lessons of the Modern State* (*Lehre vom modernen Stat*) (1875–76).

25. Bluntschli asserted that when "different nationalities are intermixed with one, there is no danger to the unity of the State, but the weaker will probably be suppressed and destroyed by the stronger; the higher nationality becomes dominant and assimi-

lates by degrees the isolated elements of the rest. Thus it was that the Germans were finally Romanized in what were once Roman provinces. . . . Thus the Irish, German, and French in the United States, after two generations, are assimilated by the Anglo-Saxon population." Johann Kaspar Bluntschli, *The Theory of the State* (first English trans., 1895; reprint, Kitchener, ON: Batoche Books, 2000), 92.

26. The French writer and Communist activist Henri Barbusse (1873–1935) first gained international recognition with the novel *Le Feu* (Under Fire) (1916) about his experiences in World War I. In 1918 he left France for the Soviet Union, where he became intimately involved with the Bolshevik revolution and the Communist Party. In the ensuing decades, Barbusse strove to create a new proletarian literature. He is author of an admiring biography entitled *Stalin: A New World Seen through One Man* (1935).

27. In the years following World War I, the Bolshevik regime, concerned about the persistent anti-Communist leanings of Tartar, Ukrainian, and German communities in the Crimean peninsula, responded favorably to a proposal by Joseph A. Rosen (1877–1949), an agronomist and officer of the American Jewish Joint Distribution Committee (JDC), to resettle persecuted Jews in the region. Meanwhile, as a result of continuing political strife, many Crimean Jews emigrated to Turkey and the United States. In 1923 the Soviet government briefly considered (and then rescinded) a plan to establish a Jewish autonomous region in the Crimea. From 1924 to 1938 the JDC's Russian operation (known as the Agro-Joint) helped to establish numerous collective Jewish farms in the Crimea, many of which became vibrant Yiddish-speaking communities and helped strengthen the regional economy. In 1939, against this backdrop, Soviet foreign minister Vyacheslav Molotov (1890–1986) publicly entertained the possibility of creating a Jewish homeland in the Crimea. With the Nazi invasion of the Soviet Union in 1941, however, all such hopes were dashed and the majority of Jewish colonists in the Crimea fled eastward. After World War II, notwithstanding JDC-sponsored efforts to return Jewish farmers to the region, the Stalin regime's growing hostility to ethnic-national Jewish aspirations hastened the Crimean experiment's dissolution.

28. Greenberg is referring to the broad canvas of American Jewish sympathy for communism and the Soviet Union in the 1920s and 1930s, which rapidly imploded starting in the mid-1930s with the Stalin regime's violent purge of dissent among Communist ranks. For the most part, American Jewish communist activity before World War II was grouped around the Jewish Socialist Federation (the Jewish section of the American Socialist Party) and the Arbeiter Ring (Yiddish for "Workmen's Circle"), a fraternal order that operated a countrywide network of educational, political, and recreational activities including Yiddish supplementary schools.

29. The reference is to Julius Rosenwald (1862–1932), Louis Marshall (1856–1929), Felix Warburg (1871–1937), and other elite American Jews of central European ancestry who together contributed millions of dollars to the Crimean project via the American Jewish Joint Distribution Committee. Several non-Jewish American philanthropists, including John D. Rockefeller (1839–1937), also participated in the project.

30. On the Tartars, see note 25 in chapter 1, "The Meaning of Zionism," in this volume.

31. The Sea of Azov, the northern arm of the Black Sea, with which it is connected by the Kerch Strait, is located at the southern edge of eastern Europe. Fed by the Don and Kuban rivers, the sea and its environs are rich in vegetation, fish, and birds.

32. As noted above, the Soviet leader Mikhael Kalinin publicly endorsed the settlement of Jews in the Crimea. See, e.g., "Road to Jewish Republic in Russia Open, Soviet President Kalinin Tells Land Settling Conference in Moscow," *Jewish Daily Bulletin* 3:623 (November 19, 1926): 1, 3; http://pdfs.jta.org/1926/1926-11-19_623.pdf.

33. The ancient Greek colony of Phanagoria, located on the Taman peninsula between the Sea of Azov and the Black Sea, was settled in the sixth century BCE. Phanagoria flourished as a city-state under the Bosporan kingdom from the fifth to the second centuries BCE and it became an independent state in the first century BCE. Conquered and decimated by nomadic Huns in the fourth century CE, the city thereafter entered a long period of steady decline until its demise in the eleventh century CE.

34. The history of Crimean Jewry can be traced to antiquity when the region's small Jewish community split into two distinct groups: the Krymchaks, who followed mainstream rabbinical Judaism, and the Karaites, a Jewish movement that rejected postbiblical interpretation as spurious and adhered only to the Hebrew Bible. Following the Russian conquest of the Crimean peninsula in the Russo-Turkish War (1787–92), the regime of Catherine the Great (1729–96) opened this part of "New Russia" to increased Jewish settlement. In time, as Crimea became intimately bound up with Russia's Jewish history, the legacy of Crimean Jewry gave rise to a historical mythology including the notion that Jews had dwelled in the Crimea longer than Russian gentiles. The Russian Jewish historian Avram Samuilovich Firkovich (1787–1875) is known to have fabricated colophons, tombstone inscriptions, and a historical narrative to substantiate his claim that Karaite Jews inhabited the Crimea before the era of Jesus Christ.

35. On Adolf Hitler, see note 10 in chapter 6, "Jew and Arab," in this volume.

36. On Karl Marx, see note 31 in chapter 1, "The Meaning of Zionism," in this volume.

37. Quoted from Karl Marx's "Critique of the Gotha Program" (1875). See *Karl Marx: Selected Writings*, ed. David McLellan, rev. ed. (New York: Oxford University Press, 2000), 615.

Chapter 11

Source: Hayim Greenberg, "We Are Treated as Subhumans—We Are Asked to Be Superhuman," *Jewish Frontier* 6:3 (March 1939): 11–15. The essay is the second part of a symposium ("Jews in a World of Violence") that includes essays by Mohandas K. Gandhi ("Death Has No Terror") and Norman Angell ("A Liberal Interprets Zionism") in the same issue of *Jewish Frontier*, 9–17.

1. The Indian leader Mohandas K. Gandhi (1869–1948) was educated in India and Britain. In 1889 he completed his legal training in London and was admitted to the bar. In 1893 he relocated to South Africa where he fought for the rights of Indians in that country. In 1915 he returned to India and took up the struggle for home rule. At this juncture, he gave up Western ways and began to lead a life of abstinence in accordance with Hindu ethics. Asserting humanity's unity under one God, he professed belief in the Hindu, Christian, and Muslim scriptures. In 1921 he became the leader of the Indian National Congress and thereafter vigorously advocated the abolition of untouchability (see note 6 below), eradicating poverty, advancing women's rights, religious and ethnic reconciliation, and national self-determination. In opposition to British rule of India,

he espoused *satyagraha* (see note 5 below), an ethical form of non-violence. In 1930, he was imprisoned for publicly violating the British-imposed state salt monopoly. He was released in 1931 in order to attend a special London conference on India's future. Popularly referred to as the "Mahatma" (Sanskrit for "great souled"), Gandhi's national and global stature skyrocketed in the 1930s. He was capable of exacting political concessions by protesting with "fasts unto death." In the 1940s Gandhi's emphasis on national unity and religious pluralism was challenged by the rise of Muslim nationalists who called for a future Muslim homeland to be established in part of India. With the outbreak of World War II, Gandhi called for the British to "Quit India" in a famous speech which became the rallying cry of Indian nationalism. As a consequence, in 1942 Gandhi and other Indian National Congress activists were imprisoned; he was released in 1944 owing to his failing health. In 1947 Britain partitioned India into two dominions, a Hindu-majority India and Muslim-majority Pakistan. Civil war erupted as displaced Muslims, Hindus, and Sikhs sought refuge in the new territories. Gandhi worked assiduously to quell the violence and promote social and political order. He was assassinated on January 30, 1948, by Nathuram Godse (1910–49), a Hindu extremist.

2. Gandhi's statement was published in the weekly *Harijan* (Hindustani for "Child of God") on November 26, 1938. He flatly asserted that Palestine "belongs to the Arabs" and recommended the Jews remain in Germany to practice non-violent resistance to the Nazi regime. Like Greenberg, the German Jewish philosopher Martin Buber (see note 17 in chapter 1, "The Meaning of Zionism," in this volume) responded publicly to Gandhi. The complete texts of both essays are reprinted in *Martin Buber on Jews and Arabs*, ed. Paul Mendes-Flohr (New York: Oxford University Press, 1983), 107–111, 113–126. See also Gideon Shimoni, *Gandhi, Satyagraha, and the Jews: A Formative Factor in India's Policy toward Israel* (Jerusalem: Hebrew University of Jerusalem, 1977).

3. Greenberg is using the term "Young India" to refer to the Indian national liberation movement. *Young India* was also the name of the English-language weekly published by Gandhi from 1919 to 1932, which served as a forum and vehicle for public opposition to British mandatory rule in India.

4. Greenberg wrote this essay against the backdrop of Nazi Germany's escalating terrorization of central European Jewry, the promulgation of the British White Paper of May 1939, which imposed severe restrictions on Jewish immigration to mandatory Palestine, and the outbreak of World War II in September 1939 following Hitler's invasion of Poland.

5. [Greenberg's footnote:] Gandhi's own translation and interpretation of this term is "holding on to truth," "soul force," "love force." [Gandhi employed the term *satyagraha* to express his religious-ethical conception of nonviolent resistance as a means of pressing for political reform.]

6. In India there exist four chief castes, with many subdivisions: *Brahmans* (priests), *Kshatriyas* (the military), *Vaisyas* (farmers and merchants), and *Sudras* (laborers). The lowest social group—known as the "untouchables"—are outside the caste system and considered pariahs. The latter are excluded from and considered ritually unclean and defiling by the four Hindu castes.

7. Established in 1885, the original purpose of the Indian National Congress was

to make India a British dominion by constitutional means. In 1917 Gandhi and other home-rule advocates forced the resignation of the accommodationist faction and began to call for *Swaraj* (Hindi for "self-rule"). In 1919 the party initiated a countrywide campaign of nonviolent disobedience. During World War II the party's refusal to cooperate with the British mandatory regime led to the arrest of its leadership, and it was outlawed from 1942 to 1945. In conferences leading up to India's independence in 1947, the party was forced to bow to the demand of the Muslim League for a separate state of Pakistan.

8. Though Gandhi's quote appears in numerous sources, its precise origin is unclear. See, e.g., Upton Close (Josef Washington Hall), *The Revolt of Asia: The End of the White Man's World Dominance* (New York: G. P. Putnam's Sons, 1927), 47.

9. This likely refers to the Indian home-rule activist Shankarlal Banker (b. 1889–after 1922), who played a key role in Ahmedabad's labor unrest, edited *Young India*, and was sentenced to imprisonment together with Gandhi in 1920 (see note 10 below).

10. Against the backdrop of India's rising political unrest, Gandhi's call in August 1920 for civil disobedience and a countrywide boycott of the British mandatory regime was electrifying. Together with his disciple Shankarlal Banker, Gandhi was charged with sedition under section 124a of the Indian Penal Code. The immediate impetus in this regard was the publication in *Young India* of a series of articles critical of the governing authority. The trial instantly became a global *cause célèbre*. Gandhi's eloquent testimony ennobled the Indian nationalist cause and elevated the concept of non-violence to a universal ideal: "I hold it to be a virtue to be disaffected towards a government which in its totality has done more harm to India than any previous system. . . . Non-violence is the first article of my faith. It is also the last article of my creed. But I had to make a choice. I had either to submit to a system which I consider has done an irreparable harm to my country or incur the risk of the mad fury of my people bursting forth when they understood the truth from my lips. . . . The only course open to you, the judge, is . . . either to resign your post or to inflict on me the severest penalty, if you believe that the system and law you are assisting to administer are good for the people." Quoted in E. Stanley Jones, *Mahatma Gandhi: An Interpretation* (New York: Abingdon-Cokesbury Press, 1948), 91, 94. Judge C. N. Broomfield, citing the 1908 precedent of the sedition trial of Indian nationalist leader Bal Gangadahr Tilak (1856–1920), sentenced Gandhi and Banker to six years' imprisonment.

11. The provenance of this quote is unknown.

12. The reference is to Judge C. N. Broomfield, who presided over Gandhi's sedition trial. On Broomfield's attitude to Gandhi, see Rajmohan Gandhi, *Gandhi: The Man, His People, and the Empire*, rev. ed. (Berkeley: University of California Press, 2008), 252–254.

13. See "Gandhi Thanked Court for Sentence," *New York Times* (March 20, 1922), 4; Donn Byrne, *Mahtma Gandhi: The Man and His Message* (Hyderabad: Orient Longman, 1984), 77–78.

14. From 1899 to 1922, the Anglican clergyman Henry Whitehead (1863–1947) served as the fifth Bishop of the Diocese of Madras of the Church of South India.

15. Quoted in Jones, *Mahatma Gandhi*, 106.

16. The identity of this figure is uncertain.

17. British career officer Brigadier-General Reginald Dyer (1864–1927) served in a

variety of posts in Britain's Asian colonies. In April 1919, against the backdrop of countrywide martial law and widespread political unrest in India, Dyer employed British infantry to conduct reprisals against Indian civilian protesters in Amristar, resulting in more than a thousand casualties and 379 deaths. Though many conservative Britons applauded Dyer's actions, the massacre generally prompted outrage in India and Britain. British war secretary Winston Churchill (see note 55 in chapter 26, "Patriotism and Plural Loyalties," in this volume) and former prime minister Herbert Henry Asquith (1852–1928) publicly denounced Dyer. Meanwhile, the Asian Nobel laureate Rabindranath Tagore (see note 17 in chapter 3, "East and West," in this volume) renounced his knighthood in protest. Dyer was relieved of his command in the wake of the massacre.

18. Quoted in *The Gandhi Reader: A Sourcebook of His Life and Writings*, ed. Homer A. Jack, rev. ed. (Bloomington: Indiana University Press, 1956), 318.

19. During the period of the Babylonian captivity (587–538 BCE), the Jewish exiles were granted limited autonomy and survived as craftsmen, farmers, and traders. They paid special taxes and fulfilled various communal obligations to the Babylonian regime. While the impact of Babylonian culture on the Jews was profound, the organized community generally retained its monotheistic beliefs and religious traditions. See also note 39 in chapter 24, "The Universalism of the Chosen People," in this volume.

20. Alexandria, the capital of the Ptolemaic empire, emerged as one of the most populous Jewish communities in the ancient world between the third century BCE and the end of the first century CE. The city's several hundred thousand Jewish inhabitants included elite wealthy merchants, shippers, and bankers, as well as a sizable cohort of artisans and shopkeepers.

21. Quoted in Jack, *The Gandhi Reader*, 318.

22. Greenberg is employing terminology characteristic of the Arab leaders of the day. In this period, there existed only isolated pockets of Arab nationalism and few, if any, Arab leaders regarded the area known as Palestine as a separate entity, possessed of its own national significance. Indeed, the term "Palestinian" was used in the West to describe Jews living in Palestine.

23. Benjamin Franklin (1706–90), the American printer, scientist, writer, and statesman, gained recognition as the author of *Poor Richard's Almanac* (1732–57). The success of the publication launched Franklin's political career and he subsequently played a central role in the American Revolution. He negotiated French support for the colonists, signed the Treaty of Paris (1783), and helped draft the US Constitution (1787–89).

24. Robert Morris (1734–1806), an American banker, was called the "financier of the American Revolution." Morris was a signatory of the Declaration of Independence. He later served as the federal government's superintendent of finance and helped create the national bank.

25. Quoted from a letter written by Benjamin Franklin to Robert Morris (December 25, 1783); reprinted in *The Founders' Constitution: Major Themes*, ed. Philip Kurland and Ralph Lerner, vol. 1 (Chicago: University of Chicago Press, 2000), 589.

26. The mandate system, a form of colonial administration and trusteeship established in 1919 by Article 22 of the Covenant of the League of Nations (see note 28 below), divided the former Turkish territories and German colonies into three categories: Turk-

ish territories, with provisional independence; African territories formerly under German control, with significant commercial potential; and other former German colonies deemed to be primitive socially and economically. The mandate system was administered by an eleven-member Permanent Mandates Commission. The main beneficiaries of the system were Great Britain and France, which took control of most of the Middle East, the former Ottoman empire, and much of the African continent.

27. Quoted in Jack, *The Gandhi Reader*, 318.

28. US president Woodrow Wilson (1856–1924) envisioned the League of Nations in his Fourteen Points program of 1918 as a congress of republics dedicated to global peace and security. Established at the Paris Peace Conference of 1919 following World War I, the original League resulted in a fragile association of the European Allied powers (except the Soviet Union), while the defeated Central Powers were excluded. Despite Wilson's herculean efforts, the League failed to win American support and was ultimately rejected by the US Congress. In general, it persisted as a largely ineffective international forum until the outbreak of World War II.

29. Almost from the outset, the League of Nations proved incapable of reining in Europe's aggressive powers. Throughout the 1920s, its weakness and ineffectuality was repeatedly demonstrated as various international commitments forged at the Versailles Peace Conference (1919) were undermined and rapidly dismantled. The political rise of fascism and communism in the 1920s and 1930s, Germany's rearmament in violation of the Versailles treaty and withdrawal from the League in October 1933, and the Nazi and Soviet territorial conquests of the latter decade amplified the League's impotence and irrelevance.

30. See note 26 above.

31. This refers to the meeting in February-March 1939 of the Arab-Jewish Round Table Conference in London (also called the St. James Palace Conference). Chaim Weizmann (see note 2 in chapter 2, "Policy and Labor," in this volume) led the Jewish Agency delegation, which included an advisory committee of Zionist and non-Zionist representatives. The Arab delegation included followers of the mufti of Jerusalem, Hadsh Amin al Husseini (see note 7 in chapter 25, "Current Alternatives in Palestine," in this volume) and rival Arab nationalists. Representatives of the governments of Egypt, Iraq, Saudi Arabia, Yemen, and Transjordan also attended. The British hosts included colonial secretary Malcolm J. MacDonald (1901–81) and foreign secretary E. F. L. Wood (1881–1959). Because the Arab representatives refused to meet directly with the Jewish Agency delegation, the British conducted separate discussions with the Arab and Jewish delegates. There were also informal contacts and off-the-record Arab-Jewish discussions behind the scenes. The Arabs steadfastly opposed continued Jewish immigration to Palestine and insisted on the creation of an independent Arab state, while the Zionists refused to consider new restrictions on Jewish immigration in exchange for deferring decisions about the territory's future status. On March 15 the British presented a proposal to limit Jewish immigration, allow the Arabs to determine future Jewish immigration, and postpone decisions about the country's ultimate status. Both the Arabs and the Zionists rejected the British proposal and the conference concluded without any agreement. Subsequently, the British issued the White Paper of May 1939 (also known as the MacDonald White Paper)

which limited Jewish immigration to a maximum of 75,000 over the next five years, curtailed future Jewish land acquisition, and proposed the creation of a bi-national Arab-Jewish state after a ten-year transition period. The new official British government policy remained in effect until the end of the mandate in 1948.

32. See note 1 above.

33. Shortly after his return to India in 1915, Gandhi undertook efforts to ease Hindu-Muslim tensions and embarked on a campaign to achieve countrywide unity. After March 1940, however, when the Muslim League adopted the Lahore Resolution calling for the creation of an independent Muslim-majority state to be carved out of India, Gandhi's elusive dream imploded.

34. Following World War I, Gandhi and other Indian National Congress activists emerged as supporters of the Caliphate movement (1919–24), an orthodox pan-Islamic protest movement against British rule in India that sought to restore the authority of the former Ottoman caliphs. In February 1922 the alliance between Gandhi and the Caliphate movement collapsed following Muslim violence in Gorakhpur. Though some Muslim activists were later integrated into the wider Indian independence movement, others reacted negatively to Gandhi and blamed him for the Caliphate movement's failure.

35. Mount Nebo is located east of the Jordan River, opposite of Jericho. According to the Hebrew Bible, the Israelites encamped there during the last stage of their journey to the Land of Israel (Num. 33:47). It also relates that Moses, whom God did not permit to enter the Promised Land, was allowed to view it from the top of Mount Nebo before dying (Deut. 32:48–52, 34:4–5).

Chapter 12

Source: Hayim Greenberg, "Leon Trotsky," in *The Inner Eye: Selected Essays*, vol. 2, ed. Shlomo Katz (New York: Jewish Frontier Association, 1964), 229–243. This English translation is a synthesized version of two Yiddish essays originally published in *Der yidisher kemfer* and reprinted in Hayim Greenberg, *Bletlekh fun a tog-bukh* (New York: Yidisher Kemfer, 1954), 173–194. Part 1 was published in 1939 and part 2 appeared in 1940 in the wake of Trotsky's assassination.

1. On Leon Trotsky, see note 30 in chapter 3, "East and West," in this volume.

2. It is unclear to whom Greenberg is referring in this instance.

3. See Leon Trotsky, *Their Morals and Ours: The Class Foundations of Moral Practice* (1938; reprint, New York: Pathfinder Press, 1973).

4. Trained as a Presbyterian minister, Norman M. Thomas (1884–1968), a Christian socialist and pacifist activist, was shaped by the social gospel movement and later emerged as a significant American political figure. On the eve of America's entry into World War I he campaigned for Morris Hillquit (1869–1933), the prominent Jewish labor lawyer and American Socialist Party founder who in 1917 ran for mayor of New York. In ensuing decades, Thomas himself was the American Socialist Party's standard bearer for New York City's mayoralty as well as statewide offices. Following the death of Eugene V. Debs (1855–1926), Thomas emerged as the American Socialist Party's leading spokesperson and was nominated six times as its presidential candidate. Thomas was a formidable

orator and his articulation of democratic socialism, including the differences between the American Socialist Party's agenda and Soviet Marxism, won him wide acclaim. He initially opposed America's entry into World War II but later conceded the necessity of waging battle against the Nazi regime. A lifelong progressive idealist, Thomas embraced a variety of social and political positions that put him at odds with mainstream America, the US government, and the Catholic Church, including anti-militarism and disarmament, the wartime internment of Japanese Americans under the Roosevelt administration, desegregation, and birth control.

5. Trotsky accused Norman Thomas and other non-Marxist leftists of being "social-democratic careerists." In one instance, he noted: "Norman Thomas speaks about 'that strange communist amorality in which nothing matters but the party and its power' (*Socialist Call*, March 12, 1938, p. 5). Moreover, Thomas throws into one heap the present Comintern, that is, the conspiracy of the Kremlin bureaucracy against the working class, with the Bolshevik Party which represented a conspiracy of the advanced workers against the bourgeoisie. This thoroughly dishonest juxtaposition has already been sufficiently exposed. . . . The drawing-room socialist, Thomas, is surprised by and rejects a similar relationship between a revolutionist and revolution because he himself is only a bourgeois with a socialist 'ideal.' In the eyes of Thomas and his kind the party is only a secondary instrument for electoral combinations and other similar uses, not more. His personal life, interests, moral criteria exist outside the party. With hostile astonishment he looks down upon the Bolshevik to whom the party is a weapon for the revolutionary reconstruction of society, including also its morality. To a revolutionary Marxist there can be no contradiction between personal morality and the interests of the party, since the party embodies in his consciousness the very highest tasks and aims of mankind. It is naïve to imagine that Thomas has a higher understanding of morality than the Marxists. He merely has a base conception of the party." See Trotsky, *Their Morals and Ours*, 29, 44–45.

6. *Cheka* (Russian acronym for the "All-Russian Extraordinary Commission for the Suppression of Counterrevolution and Sabotage") was the Soviet Union's secret police agency. In 1922 it was reorganized as the GPU (the Soviet political directorate).

7. On Joseph Stalin, see note 38 in chapter 9, "To a Communist Friend," in this volume.

8. Pontius Pilate (d. c. 36 CE) was the Roman governor of Judea (c. 26–36 CE) under the emperor Tiberius (c. 42 BCE–37 CE). Known for being ruthless and violent, he is featured in the Christian Bible as the Roman official responsible who permitted the crucifixion of Jesus Christ due to pressure from Jewish political and religious leaders.

9. On the biblical story of Cain and Abel, see note 2 in chapter 6, "Jew and Arab," in this volume.

10. Greenberg is referring to the period starting with the October Revolution of 1917 until Vladimir Lenin's death in January 1924 (see notes 12 and 47 below). With outbreak of the October Revolution, Trotsky, previously associated with the Mensheviks, joined the Bolshevik Party and played a key role in toppling the moderate regime of Alexander Kerensky (see note 16 in chapter 9, "To a Communist Friend," and note 11 in chapter 22, "Concerning Statehood," in this volume). Under the new Soviet regime, with Lenin at

its head, Trotsky became foreign commissar and helped to negotiate the terms of Germany's surrender. Next, he was appointed war commissar, engineered the build-up of the Bolshevik-sponsored Red Army, and suppressed the anti-Communist White Army forces. Despite Trotsky's central position in the Communist regime, he failed to consolidate his political authority and engendered enmity among many party adversaries, some of which no doubt stemmed from anti-Jewish hostility. Following Lenin's death in 1924, rivalry among Lenin's political heirs, including Joseph Stalin, resulted in Trotsky being outmaneuvered, thrown out of the party in 1927, banished to Siberia in 1928, and exiled from Russia in 1929.

11. In the decades since Greenberg penned this essay, scholars have established that the Soviet regime executed over 500,000 people and condemned millions more to forced labor and gulag colonies as part of Stalin's purges (1936–39). In all, some 20 million Russians were murdered under Stalin's rule. See, e.g., *The Black Book of Communism: Crimes, Terror, Repression*, ed. Stéphane Courtois et al. (Cambridge, MA: Harvard University Press, 1999), 4.

12. On Vladimir Lenin, see note 9 in chapter 6, "Jew and Arab," in this volume.

13. In the waning months of the Russian Civil War (1918–21) (see note 33 below), the Kronstadt naval base, located in the Gulf of Finland, was the site of an anti-Bolshevik rebellion led by the revolutionary anarchist Stepan Maximovich Petrichenko (1892–1947). By the winter of 1921, widespread Russian economic deprivation had fostered considerable peasant unrest and the Kronstadt sailors, previously important allies of the Bolsheviks, were angered by the regime's authoritarian policies and their poor material conditions. Under Petrichenko, they formed a revolutionary committee to investigate Bolshevik abuses in Petrograd and sent a delegation to meet with the Kronstadt Soviet council. Fueled by Bolshevik allegations of counter-revolutionary activity, the confrontation between the representatives of the Soviet regime and the Kronstadt sailors resulted in arrests and physical violence and prompted a regional rebellion. In late March, Trotsky deployed Soviet troops who violently suppressed the revolt. Many of the rebels were killed or escaped to Finland, while hundreds of Soviet troops were killed and thousands injured.

14. The Petropavlovsk Resolution (March 1, 1921), presented by a delegation of Kronstadt communists to representatives of the Bolshevik regime, asserted "the present soviets do not express the will of the workers and peasants" and called for the liberation of "all political prisoners of socialist parties, as well as all workers, peasants, soldiers, and sailors imprisoned in connection with the labor and peasant movements." Translated in Anton Ciliga, *The Kronstadt Revolt* (London: Freedom Press, 1942), 2.

15. On Sergei Nechaev, see note 25 in chapter 9, "To a Communist Friend," in this volume.

16. See item 4 of "The Duties of the Revolutionary toward Himself," in Sergei Nechaev, *The Revolutionary Cathechism* (1869; reprint, n.p.: Anarchist Library, 2009), 3; http://archive.org/details/al_Sergey_Nechayev_The_Revolutionary_Catechism_a4.

17. Lev Lvovich (Leon) Sedov (1906–38), Trotsky's son from his second marriage to Natalia Sedova (1882–1962), emerged in the 1930s as his father's key European interlocutor and a leader of the Fourth International, the pro-Trotsky international Commu-

nist organization opposed to the Comintern (Third International). Sedov organized anti-Stalinist activity in the West and exposed the criminality of the Soviet regime's purges in *The Red Book on the Moscow Trials* (1936). To this day, it remains an open question whether he died from complications following an appendectomy or if he was murdered by NKVD (Soviet secret) agents.

18. Quoted from Trotsky, *Their Morals and Ours*, 52. Trotsky believed his adversaries to be self-righteous and invidious hypocrites, and he used the term "Pharisees" pejoratively to tar his socialist and communist detractors with the same brush. For a brief historical explanation of the Pharisees, see note 32 in chapter 20, "*Halakhah* and *Agadah,*" in this volume.

19. The Mexican artist and Communist activist Diego Rivera (1886–1957) lived and worked in Europe in 1907–9 and 1912–21. Closely associated with the leading European impressionists of the day, including Chaim Soutine (1893–1943), Amedeo Modigliani (1884–1920), and Pablo Picasso (1881–1973), he also established friendships with many Russian exiles and believed public art should be used to express a vision of new socialist world order. Many of his Mexican murals depict the history and dignity of peasants, farmers, and workers. He visited Moscow in 1927–28 and in 1933 painted a mural for Rockefeller Center in New York that was destroyed by the sponsors because it featured a portrait of Vladimir Lenin. In 1936, after the Stalin regime condemned Trotsky to death, Rivera interceded with the Mexican government to permit Trotsky to enter the country.

20. The friendship between the Leon Trotsky and Diego Rivera dated to the latter's sojourns in Europe. In 1936, Trotsky and his second wife, Natalia Sedova, fled Europe for Mexico, where they lived with Rivera and his wife, the artist Frida Kahlo (1907–54), in Coyoacán for two years. Shortly thereafter, Trotsky and Kahlo had an extramarital affair which, in combination with ideological disagreements between Trotsky and Rivera, sundered the couples' friendship.

21. In c. 880 CE, the Petchenegs (also "Patzinaks"), a semi-nomadic people who originated in central Asia, advanced from the Ural region into the lower Danube area. They controlled parts of Russia in the eighth and ninth centuries CE.

22. After being exiled from the Soviet Union in 1929, Trotsky lived in Turkey for four years. He initially resided in Istanbul's Moda neighborhood before moving to Büyükada, the largest of the Princes' Islands off Istanbul's coast. In 1933 he left Turkey for France and then relocated to Mexico where he was murdered in 1940 (see note 25 below). Historians have yet to confirm whether Trotsky attempted to assassinate Stalin; however, this was indeed the claim put forward by the Soviet press. According to historian Robert Service, Stalin edited an article in *Pravda* published after Trotsky's murder describing Trotsky as "'an international spy' . . . [he] had been a Menshevik and a counter-revolutionary. He had fought for the interests of tsar, landlords, and capitalists. Having infiltrated the Bolshevik Party, he had plotted to assassinate Lenin, Stalin, and [Yakov Mikhailovich] Sverdlov. He had betrayed and sabotaged the Red Army. He had worked as an agent of foreign intelligence agencies since 1921." See Robert Service, *Trotsky: A Biography* (New York: Macmillan, 2009), 493.

23. Following his exile from the Soviet Union in 1929, Trotsky and his followers created a sizable but loosely organized web of anti-Stalinist activity. The Trotskyite network,

which included several highly placed informants, relied on "confidential communications with occasional uses of couriers, safe accommodation addresses, and code names for correspondents. . . . But contrary to [the Stalin regime's assertion] which depicted the movement as a vast international espionage system . . . neither Trotsky nor any of his leading followers maintained any intelligence establishment." Rita T. Kronenbitter, "Leon Trotsky, Dupe of the NKVD," *Studies in Intelligence* 16:1 (1972): 18–19.

24. On the Fourth International, see note 17 above.

25. The reference is to Ramón Mercader (1913–78), a Spanish Communist and Stalinist agent, who fatally wounded Trotsky in 1940 with an ice pick. He subsequently served twenty years in a Mexican prison for Trotsky's murder. When Mexican authorities released Mercader in 1960, he relocated to Cuba and then in 1961 settled in the Soviet Union, where he was welcomed as a national hero.

26. The reference is to Pharaoh in the biblical story of the Israelites' exodus from Egypt. Scholars have yet to precisely determine which pharaoh(s) reigned during the period when this migration presumably occurred.

27. On the Purim holiday story, including the Persian king Ahasuerus's wicked vizier Haman, see note 216 in chapter 24, "The Universalism of the Chosen People," in this volume.

28. Edmund Wilson's *To the Finland Station: A Study in the Writing and Acting of History* (1940) examines the history of radical and revolutionary thought starting with the era of the French Revolution through the rise of Lenin and the Bolshevik Party in 1917. The book's title derives from the story of Lenin's return from exile in Switzerland on the eve of the Russian Revolution. When his train arrived at Finlyandsky Rail Terminal in St. Petersburg on April 16, 1917, he was greeted by a crowd of revolutionaries singing the "Worker's Marseillaise."

29. The literary critic and author Edmund Wilson (1895–1972) was managing editor of *Vanity Fair* and wrote for the *New Republic*, the *New Yorker*, and the *New York Review of Books*. A significant figure in American letters, he played a central role in promoting the work of many key American and European writers.

30. Samara (renamed Kuibyshev from 1935 to 1991 by the Soviet regime) is a city in southeastern Russia situated at the confluence of the Samara and Volga Rivers.

31. See Edmund Wilson, *To the Finland Station: A Study in the Writing and Acting of History* (1940; reprint, New York: Farrar, Straus and Giroux, 1972), 483.

32. The Red Army originated as strike forces marshalled by the provisional government under Alexander Kerensky in the summer of 1917. After the Treaty of Brest-Litovsk, which ended World War I, Trotsky reorganized the Red Army as the permanent military force of the newly established Soviet Union. Red Army forces campaigned throughout the former empire during the ensuing Russian Civil War (1918–21), suppressing remaining imperial White forces and bolstering Bolshevik uprisings in neighboring regions including Poland, Finland, and the Baltic states. Under Trotsky's leadership as war commissar, the Red Army successfully vanquished the remaining White Army forces and brought an end to the Russian Civil War.

33. On the Russian Civil War, see note 2 in chapter 9, "To a Communist Friend," in this volume.

34. See Leon Trotsky, *My Life: An Attempt at Autobiography* (1930; reprint, New York: Pathfinder Press, 1970).

35. The term *kulak* (Russian for "independent farmer") originally referred to a prosperous farmer in tsarist Russia. After the Bolshevik revolution, it took on negative connotations and was used to describe private landowners believed to exploit rural laborers. Kulaks were among the chief targets of the Soviet nationalization and collectivization strategy as well as of Stalin's secret police. In time, the term was also applied to peasants who owned their own livestock or were simply better off than those around them.

36. See Trotsky, *My Life*, 6–10.

37. *Haroset*, a mixture of chopped nuts and fruit, is a symbolic food traditionally eaten as part of the Passover meal. It represents the mortar used by the ancient Israelites as enslaved laborers in Egypt. The ritual derives from the biblical verse: "They made their lives bitter with hard labor in brick and mortar" (Exod. 1:14).

38. Greenberg is apparently quoting from memory. In fact, Trotsky's memoir refers to his mother's nephew Moissey (Monya) Filippovich Schpentzer, with whom he lived in Odessa for four years. Trotsky notes the following in his memoir: "From Monya I learned many things I did not know: how to hold a glass, how to wash, how to pronounce certain words." See Trotsky, *My Life*, 41–42.

39. Nikolaev (the Russian name for Mikolaev) is a city in southern Ukraine.

40. The Narodnaya Volya (Russian for "People's Will"), a revolutionary terrorist party made up of Russian populists and socialists, was active from the mid- to late nineteenth century. The group was responsible for the assassination of Tsar Alexander II (1818–81). It organized small political cells in dozens of Russian cities and promoted a social-economic philosophy of self-governing economic units similar to the traditional *mir* (Russian village commune) (see note 59 in chapter 24, "The Universalism of the Chosen People," in this volume).

41. The reference is to the Russian Social Democratic Party. See note 17 in chapter 9, "To a Communist Friend," in this volume.

42. See Wilson, *To the Finland Station*, 410.

43. Quoted in ibid., 410.

44. Alexandra Lvovna Sokolovskaya (c. 1872–1938), a Russian Marxist revolutionary and Trotsky's first wife, was arrested in 1935 during the Stalinist purges and is believed to have been killed. Trotsky's marriage to Sokolovskaya broke apart in 1902 after he met Natalia Sedova, whom he later married.

45. Quoted in Wilson, *To the Finland Station*, 410. The text actually reads: "I can't imagine how a young girl so full of life can stand that narrow dry impractical stuff!"

46. Quoted in ibid., 410. The text actually reads: "I can't imagine . . . how a person who thinks he is so logical can be satisfied with a headful of vague idealistic emotions."

47. On Russia's October Revolution of 1917, see note 1 in chapter 5, "Our Stand," in this volume.

48. Victor Adler (1852–1918), an Austrian politician, socialist, and journalist of central European Jewish ancestry, was a founder and leader of the Austrian Social Democratic Party (see note 19 in chapter 7, "Revisionism," in this volume). In the 1880s, he published two German-language Marxist journals, *Gleichheit* (Equality) and the *Arbeiter*

Zeitung (Workers' Newspaper). His radical socialist activity, including collaboration with the Marxist thinkers August Bebel (1840–1913), Friedrich Engels (1820–95), and Karl Liebknecht (1871–1919), resulted in his nine-month imprisonment. Rising through the ranks of the Austrian labor movement, he emerged as a leading moderate social democratic voice of the European left and the Second International.

49. Greenberg is referring to a disparaging comment by Trotsky about Victor Adler. See Trotsky, *My Life*, 208.

50. Yaakov Mazeh (1859–1924), Moscow's chief rabbi from 1893 until 1924, was a Hebraist and pro-Zionist communal leader. He contributed frequently to the Russian Hebrew newspaper *Hameliz* (The Advocate). In 1913, he served as an expert witness at the notorious blood libel trial of Menahem Mendel Beilis (1874–1934).

51. *Tashlikh* (Hebrew for "casting off"), a traditional custom observed on the first day of the Jewish New Year, is derived from Micah 7:18–20. The ritual is performed standing beside a body of flowing water such as a stream, river, lake, or sea. According to some traditions, one throws morsels of bread into the water, symbolically casting off the previous year's sins, while reciting prayers and biblical verses, including "Cast away from yourselves all your transgressions, and create within yourselves a new heart and a new spirit" (Ezek. 18:31). See, e.g., *The New Mahzor for Rosh Hashanah and Yom Kippur*, ed. Sidney Greenberg and Jonathan D. Levine, rev. ed. (Bridgeport, CT: Prayer Book Press, 1998), 356–363.

52. Robert Hamilton Bruce Lockhart (1887–1970), a British diplomat, secret agent, and author, was stationed with the British consulate in Moscow in 1912. He served as acting consul general during the February Revolution of 1917 (see note 9 in chapter 6, "Jew and Arab," in this volume) and returned to England shortly before the Bolshevik revolution in October. In 1918, he returned to Soviet Russia as a British special envoy charged with the task of dissuading the Bolshevik regime from signing a separate peace treaty with Germany. He soon became engaged in espionage and was falsely accused of plotting to assassinate the Bolshevik leaders Lenin and Trotsky. Imprisoned in the Kremlin, he was eventually released as part of a hostage exchange between Russia and Britain involving Soviet diplomat Maxim M. Litinov (1876–1951), who had been arrested by the British government.

53. R. H. Bruce Lockhart's *Memoirs of a British Agent* (1932) was an international bestseller. In the book, Lockhardt offers a detailed account of the twilight of the tsarist regime, the impact of World War I on Russian society, and the ensuing Russian Revolution. He also describes his personal encounters with Vladimir Lenin, Leon Trotsky, Joseph Stalin, and other Soviet officials.

54. Greenberg is paraphrasing the following statement: "He strikes me as a man who would willingly die fighting for Russia provided there was a big enough audience to see him do it." R. H. Bruce Lockhart, *British Agent* (New York: G. P. Putnam's Sons, 1933), 224.

55. In 1898 tsarist authorities arrested Trotsky for radical revolutionary activity. He spent two years imprisoned in Nikolaev, Kherson, Odessa, and Moscow. In 1900, during his imprisonment in Moscow, he met and married his first wife, Alexandra Sokolovskaya (1872–1938). Soon afterward, the newly married couple was exiled to Siberia, where they

had two children. In 1902, with Sokolovskaya's support, Trotsky escaped from Siberia to London, where he first met Vladimir Lenin.

56. Greenberg is referring to the figures featured in *Neviim* (Prophets), the second canonical division of the Hebrew Bible. *Neviim* consists of eight discreet books: Joshua, Judges, First and Second Samuel, First and Second Kings, Isaiah, Jeremiah, Ezekiel, and the Twelve Minor Prophets (Hosea, Joel, Amos, Obadiah, Jonah, Micah, Nahum, Habakkuk, Zephaniah, Hagai, Zechariah, and Malachi). The latter are referred to as "minor prophets" owing to the brevity of the texts in each instance.

57. Scholars believe the Book of Job was composed between the sixth and fourth centuries BCE. It appears in *Ketuvim* (Writings), the third division of the Hebrew Bible. Many Sephardic Jewish communities recite Job on *Tisha Beav* (Ninth of Av), the traditional day of mourning commemorating the destruction of the First and Second Temples and other tragedies in Jewish history. The Book of Job centers on a dramatic dialogue between Job and his friends and subsequently between Job and God concerning the problem of good and evil in the world. In the prologue, God and an accusing angel form a plan in heaven to test Job, a truly upright man. Next, Job's property, family, and health are taken from him. Friends who seek to comfort Job accuse him of sin. Though Job protests his innocence, he learns God's judgment is beyond human understanding. In the epilogue Job's losses are restored and he is contented; however, the narrative's core ethical problematic is not explicitly resolved.

58. The Song of Songs appears in the Hebrew Bible in *Ketuvim* (Writings) as one of the *hamesh megilot* (five scrolls). It was likely composed and/or redacted in the fourth and third century CE. Though the text explicitly attributes its authorship to King Solomon (see note 31 in chapter 24, "The Universalism of the Chosen People," in this volume), scholars do not believe this to be historically accurate. The text is structured as a discourse between two lovers in which other voices are frequently interposed. It achieves a richly textured multivalence by employing a variety of linguistic, poetic, and metaphorical strategies. The text emphasizes the relationship of God and Israel but is also suggestive of human erotic love.

59. This is apparently a reference to Yosef (Osip) Lvovich Orsher (1879–1942), the Russian Jewish writer, journalist, and literary critic. Orsher, who used the pseudonym O. L. D'Or, gained fame for his short stories, feuilletons, and parodies. In 1918 he edited the satirical Soviet journal *Guillotine*. During the Russian Civil War he served as the Petrograd (St. Petersburg) correspondent for the state-controlled Russian Telegraph Agency (ROSTA). His publications include the novel *Yakov Markovich Melamedov* (1906) about the world of the eastern European Jewish *shtetl* and a memoir entitled *The Literary Path of a Pre-Revolutionary Journalist* (1930). He died in the siege of Leningrad during World War II.

60. On Adolf Hitler, see note 10 in chapter 6, "Jew and Arab," in this volume.

61. The Russian revolutionary activist Julius Martov (1873–1923), a leader of the Menshevik faction, was the son of a middle-class Turkish Jewish family. Martov, a close associate of Lenin, was a founder of the Russian Social Democratic Party and swiftly emerged as a leader of its moderate wing. He opposed Russia's entry into World War I, which he viewed as an imperialist conflict, and strongly criticized the Bolshevik faction's grow-

ing authoritarianism. After the October Revolution he was marginalized politically. In 1920, he went into exile in Germany where he continued to lead a dwindling Menshevik network.

62. Quoted in Wilson, *To the Finland Station*, 430.

63. The metaphor Valhalla (Norse for "hall of the slain") derives from Norse mythology. Valhalla is the god Odin's eternal home for slain heroes. The heroes are delivered to Valhalla by Valkyries ("choosers of the slain"), Odin's attendants who visit the battlefield, select those who are to die, and bring them back.

64. Quoted from Trotsky, *My Life*, 72.

Chapter 13

Source: Hayim Greenberg, "Prayer," *Jewish Frontier* 21:9 (September 1954): 19–24. The original Yiddish version of this essay, published in 1940 under the title "*Tefilah*," is reprinted in *Mentshn un vertn* (New York: Yidisher Kemfer, 1953), 101–113.

1. "And when you pray, make not your prayer a fixed form, but [a plea for] mercy and supplication." See *Pirkei Avot—Ethics of the Fathers*, trans. Hyman E. Goldin (New York: Hebrew Publishing Company, 1962), 32–34.

2. Rabbi Oshaya (c. 200 CE), a Palestinian *amora* sage, compiled *baraitot* (Aramaic for "teachings") associated with the Jewish oral tradition that existed outside the framework of the Mishnah.

3. Rabbi Yosef ben Hiyya (c. 300 CE), a Babylonian *amora* sage, was head of the Pumbedita academy.

4. According to the Hebrew Bible, when God spoke to Moses on Mount Sinai, he proclaimed himself "slow to anger" and "compassionate and gracious"; see Exodus 34:4. The latter text is the subject of considerable interest in rabbinic discourse; see, e.g., B. Rosh Hashanah 17b.

5. Rabbi Hanina ben Dosa, a *tanna* in ancient Palestine during the first century CE, was noted for his scholarship, piety, and supposed mystical powers. He lived in poverty and his prayers for the sick were believed to be efficacious.

6. Rabbi Ishmael ben Elisha (90–135 CE), a *tanna* from southern Palestine, was noted for his thirteen rules of exegetical interpretation of the Pentateuch. According to some sources, in 135 CE he was martyred in the fall of Betar, the last Jewish fortress to be vanquished by the imperial Roman campaign that suppressed the Bar Kokhba revolt.

7. The inner sanctuary of the ancient Temple in Jerusalem, presumably containing the Ark of the Covenant, was accessible only to the Israelites' high priest on Yom Kippur. The ark reportedly contained the Decalogue given by God to Moses at Mount Sinai. The precise location of the sanctuary is unknown; however, tradition holds that it is located beneath the Dome of the Rock, a seventh-century edifice built atop the Temple mount by the Umayyad Caliph Abd al-Malik ibn Marwan (646–705 CE).

8. In this instance, God is identified by the name "Akatriel," a Hebrew compound of *keter* (throne) and *el* (the name of God). "*Yah*" is a numinous appellation for God, as in "Yahweh."

9. The adjectival modifier "Spinozist" refers, of course, to the Dutch philosopher

Baruch Spinoza, who believed that nature itself was God in its fullness, and that God was not the creator of nature separate and beyond himself.

10. On Ivan Turgenev, see note 35 in chapter 1, "The Meaning of Zionism," in this volume.

11. A collection of anecdotes and meditations, *Poems in Prose* (1882) was Turgenev's last published work.

12. The precise quote is "Whatever a person may pray for, that person prays for a miracle. Every prayer comes down to this: 'Almighty God, grant that two times two not equal four.'" See "Prayer," in *The Essential Turgenev: Ivan Sergeevich Turgenev*, ed. Elizabeth Cheresh Allen (Evanston, IL: Northwestern University Press, 1994), 882.

13. On Spinoza, see note 50 in chapter 1, "The Meaning of Zionism," in this volume.

14. On Spinoza's conception of God, see note 9 in chapter 9, "To a Communist Friend," in this volume.

15. On Haim Nahman Bialik, see note 44 in chapter 1, "The Meaning of Zionism," in this volume.

16. In this instance, Greenberg fuses two separate elements from the first and second stanzas of a poem titled "*Kokhavim mezizim vekhavim*" (Stars Twinkle and Go Out), written in 1901 by Haim Nahman Bialik. It is unclear why Greenberg made this editorial change. See the Yiddish original of this essay, which includes the conjoined elements in Hebrew, in Hayim Greenberg, *Mentshn un verten* (New York: Yidisher Kemfer, 1953), 103. For the unexpurgated Hebrew version of Bialik's poem, see *Haim Nahman Bialik: Shirim, 1899–1934*, ed. Dan Miron (Tel Aviv: Dvir, 1990), 75, especially lines 3–4 and 7–8. For an English translation of the poem, see *Songs from Bialik: Selected Poems of Hayim Nahman Bialik*, ed. and trans. Atar Hadari (Syracuse: Syracuse University Press, 2000), 66.

17. See line 5 in the first stanza of "*Al hashkhitah*" (Upon the Slaughter), which was written by Bialik in 1903 following the Kishinev pogrom. For the original Hebrew text, see Miron, *Haim Nahman Bialik*, 156. For the English translation, see Hadari, *Songs from Bialik*, 11.

18. This line is from "*Kokhavim mezizim vekhavim*"; see note 15 above. See also Miron, *Haim Nahman Bialik*, 75, especially line 10.

19. Eugene O'Neill (1888–1953) was an American playwright who was awarded four Pulitzer Prizes and one Nobel Prize, though *Dynamo*, written in 1929, was not among those which earned him these honors. O'Neill had planned to make it the first in a trilogy, but its failure caused him to drop this plan and to retire from writing plays until 1931.

20. The source of this quotation is unknown. Whether the statement is actually a Zulu prayer or perhaps a denigrative invention found in an essay or memoir by a Christian missionary or traveler is unclear. In the late nineteenth and early twentieth centuries, evangelical American Christian missionaries of various denominations active in Africa, Asia, and Latin America generally dismissed pantheistic and non-Abrahamic religious traditions as ungodly and primitive. Given Greenberg's appreciative comments about the "sublimity" of pre-monotheistic and pagan religions, he appears to be throwing light on such unjustified Western preconceptions.

21. The source of this quotation is unknown.

22. *Siddur* (Hebrew for "order") is the term used by Ashkenazi Jews for the daily prayer book.

23. Greenberg is referring to a phrase from the prayer known as "*Brikh shemeih*" (Aramaic for "Blessed be thy name"), which is traditionally recited in Ashkenazi and Sephardi synagogues prior to removing the Torah scroll from the ark for a public reading. See *Sabbath and Festival Prayer Book*, ed. Robert Gordis et al. (New York: Rabbinical Assembly of America, 1946), 117–118.

24. The provenance of this quote is uncertain. As such terminology does not appear in extant sixteenth-century transcriptions of pre-conquest Aztec (Nahua) writings, the words "mercy," "suffering," "wickedness," and "vanities" appear to be European concepts. Greenberg may be drawing upon on the ethnographic work of the Franciscan missionary Bernardino de Sahagún (1499–1590), whose *Florentine Codex* (c. 1545–1590) and recorded sermons date to the late 1500s and include discussions of Aztec culture and beliefs.

25. On Plato, see note 19 in chapter 9, "To a Communist Friend," in this volume.

26. Quoted from *Alcibiades II*, a Socratic work dubiously attributed to Plato and generally believed to have been composed in the second or third century BCE. In the dialogue, Socrates raises doubts about the efficacy of prayer and seeks to dissuade the Athenian statesman and warrior Alcibiades from indiscriminately praying to the gods.

27. Greenberg's use of the term "Lamaism" (standard nomenclature for his time) refers to Tibetan Buddhism. Though Tibetan monks continue to be called "lamas," in the late twentieth century the designation "Lamaism" evolved into a pejorative term. In this passage, Greenberg is comparing Tibetan Buddhism to what is now known as "Protestant Buddhism," a perceived tradition that arose following the British colonization in the nineteenth century of south Asia. Starting in the 1890s, English-speaking civil servants working in Sri Lanka and Burma (present-day Myanmar), mostly graduates of elite British universities, led a drive to edit and translate the tradition of Buddhist scriptures known as *Theravada,* which they believed to be a rational and superior form of Buddhism. Thus, irrespective of the variety of Buddhist practices, Western observers came to understand the *Theravada*, which is highly logical and includes criticism of Buddhist rituals, to be a religious philosophy devoid of superstition.

28. A prayer wheel is a metal cylinder mounted on a stick that either has a piece of scripture inside it or a *mantra* carved on the outside. It is spun by lay people seeking to invoke Buddhist teachings and to produce a small amount of religious merit. In Buddhist tradition, religious merit is akin to karmic goodwill that can be accumulated (over many lifetimes) and rewarded freely to other individuals. Greenberg apparently read a derisive account of this particular custom.

29. "The jewel in the lotus" (*om mani padme hum*) is a Sanskrit mantra. Each syllable in the mantra represents one of the six virtues enjoined upon all Mahayana Buddhists: generosity, morality, patience, energy or diligence, meditation, and wisdom. The lotus is a favorite Buddhist symbol because it produces a beautiful spotless flower. The jewel represents the quality of mind required to cut through one's egotistical self-perception.

30. Founded by the evangelical faith healer Charles H. Pridgeon (1863–1932), formerly a Presbyterian minister, the Pittsburgh Bible Institute (Pittsburgh, PA) was a transdenominational church that emphasized missionary work.

31. This may be a reference to James Bissett Pratt's (1875–1944) *Why Religions Die* (1940). Pratt studied philosophy at the University of Berlin and Harvard University, where he earned his doctorate under the American philosopher William James (see note 41 in chapter 8, "Notes on Marxism," in this volume). He later taught philosophy at Williams College. His significant works include *The Psychology of Religious Belief* (1907), *What Is Pragmatism* (1909), *India and Its Faiths* (1915), *Religious Consciousness* (1920), *Matter and Spirit* (1922), and *Can We Keep the Faith*? (1941).

32. Ralph Waldo Emerson (1803–82) was a major nineteenth-century American philosopher, essayist, and poet. As a result of *Nature* (1836), he garnered attention as a leading exponent of Transcendentalism. A Harvard lecture published under the title *The American Scholar* (1837) cemented his reputation as a spokesman for intellectual freedom. He posited the idea that the individual can find redemption only in his own soul, a concept he developed fully in a series of lectures and essays published in 1841, including "The Over-Soul," "Compensation," and "Self-Reliance."

33. Most likely, this is not a direct quotation but rather a comment attributed to Emerson.

34. Assyria was an ancient state in West Asia that controlled a large empire starting in c. 2000 BCE. The Assyrian Empire grew stronger as the Hittite and Egyptian empires declined, and it eventually controlled parts of modern-day Iraq, Iran, Syria, Palestine, and Egypt. Its history involves numerous conflicts with the Israelites. Greenberg mentions Assyria here as an example of nation hostile to Israel. The Israelite kings Jehoash and Jeroboam II were leaders of anti-Assyrian alliances around 800 BCE.

35. The full text reads: "You shall not make idols for yourselves, or set up for yourselves carved images or pillars, or place figured stones in your land to worship upon, for I the Lord am your God." See Leviticus 26:1 in *The Jewish Study Bible*, ed. Adele Berlin and Marc Zvi Brettler (New York: Oxford University Press, 2004), 273.

36. This language derives from Deuteronomy 10:17: "For the Lord your God is God supreme and Lord supreme, the great, the mighty, and the awesome God"; Berlin and Brettler, *The Jewish Study Bible*, 388–389. The latter text is included in the *Tefilat haamidah* (Standing Prayer), also known simply as the *Amidah* or *Shmoneh Esreh* (Eighteen Benedictions), a central prayer of traditional Jewish worship recited in morning, afternoon, and evening services.

37. This phrase is a popular saying from Christian folk theology. In all likelihood, Greenberg's quip is not a direct quote.

38. Gustav Theodore Fechner (1801–87) was a German philosopher and physicist and the founder of psychophysics. In *Elemente der Psychophysik* (1860) Fechner demonstrated the relationship between subjective sensation and stimulus intensity, a concept that became known as "Fechner's law" and influenced a broad array of twentieth-century philosophers and scientists.

39. On Auguste Comte, see note 33 in chapter 8, "Notes on Marxism," in this volume.

40. Greenberg's phrase is a play on Ecclesiastes 1:4: "One generation goes, another comes, but the earth remains forever." See Berlin and Brettler, *The Jewish Study Bible*, 1606.

41. Comte's notion of "*le Grande Être*" (French for "the great being"), also referred to as the "*Nouveau Grand-Être Suprême*" ("new supreme great being"), is central to his "re-

ligion of humanity," which has been described as "a complete system of belief and ritual, with liturgy and sacraments, priesthood and pontiff, all organized around the public veneration of Humanity." See Tony Davies, *Humanism* (London: Routledge, 1997), 28–29.

42. Greenberg may have borrowed this phrase from the title of a book by Friedrich Nietzsche (see note 7 in chapter 6, "Jew and Arab," in this volume), *Human, All Too Human*. The latter was written after Nietzsche's break with the German composer Richard Wagner (1813–83) and reflects changes in his thinking since his earlier work, as well as his disillusionment with Wagner's ideas about art and music.

43. See, for example, Matthew 26:39, Luke 22:41–42, and Mark 14:36.

44. Abraham Isaac Hacohen Kook (1865–1935) was a major eastern European rabbinic thinker and religious Zionist leader. After serving as a rabbi in Lithuania, he immigrated in 1904 to Ottoman Palestine to become the rabbi of Jaffa. He spent most of World War I in England and thereafter returned to British mandatory Palestine to become the Ashkenazi rabbi of Jerusalem. From 1921 to 1935, he served as the first Ashkenazi chief rabbi of Palestine. In 1924 he established Merkaz Harav in Jerusalem, a religious academy that became a hub for religious Zionist youth, especially the group Bnei Akiva (Sons of Akiba). A prolific Torah scholar distinguished by his openness to Jewish nationalism and the modern world, Kook's writings and teachings influenced a broad spectrum of religious and nonreligious Jews.

45. Quoted and translated from Abraham Isaac Hacohen Kook's *Olat reiyah* (1939), a collection of liturgical commentaries composed in Palestine between 1917 and 1935, subsequently edited and published posthumously by his son, Zvi Yehuda Kook (1891–1982). The phrase *olat reiyah*, literally "sight offering" (the sacrifice mandated by biblical law on seeing the Holy Temple during a pilgrimage, e.g., Exod. 23:15), also means the "offering of Reiyah" (the Hebrew acronym for Rabbi Avraham Yitzhak Hacohen). For the original Hebrew commentary Greenberg cites here, see http://www.daat.ac.il/daat/vl/olat/olat01.pdf, 6, section 4.

Chapter 14

Source: Hayim Greenberg, "Albert Einstein Discusses Religion," *Jewish Frontier* 7:11 (November 1940): 12–16.

1. The French poet, dramatist, and novelist Victor Hugo (1802–85) is best known for his novels *The Hunchback of Notre Dame* (1831), *Les Misérables* (1862), and *Toilers of the Sea* (1866). A pioneer of French literary romanticism, he transformed from a royalist to a staunch advocate of republicanism and social reform. He opposed Napoleon III (Louis-Napoleon Bonaparte, 1808–73) and fled France in 1851. Over the next fifteen years, he lived in Brussels, Jersey, and Guernsey before returning in triumph to Paris after Napoleon III's fall in 1870.

2. François Jean Dominique Arago (1786–1853), a French physicist, astronomer, and mathematician, is noted for his discoveries in optics and magnetism as well as being the inventor of polariscope and polarimeter. He was a passionate advocate of republicanism and publicly opposed Napoleon III's autocratic regime.

3. In 1905, the German Jewish scientist Albert Einstein (1879–1955) posited the

general theory of relativity on electrodynamics of moving bodies and the equivalence of mass and mechanical energy, subsequently distilled into the famous equation $E = mc^2$. Thereafter, Einstein's rise as one of the world's leading scientists was meteoric. In 1921 he was awarded the Nobel Prize in Physics. Notwithstanding his non-observant upbringing and background, Einstein maintained strong attachments to Jewish culture throughout his life. In 1922, as part of a trip to Asia, he visited Palestine where he was treated to a hero's welcome and witnessed first-hand the Jewish colonies of the Yishuv. This period also marked the start of his association with the Zionist movement. In February 1933, during a visit to the United States, he decided not to return to Germany owing to the rise of Adolf Hitler and the Nazi Party. Thereafter, he spent time in Belgium and England before settling permanently in the United States in October 1933 and assuming a faculty position at the Institute of Advanced Study in Princeton, New Jersey. Though a pacifist, he understood the risk of Nazi Germany developing an atomic bomb before the Allies. Together with other American and émigré scientists, he urged the Roosevelt administration to pursue uranium research which ultimately led to the Manhattan Project. In 1952, following the death of Israel's first president, Chaim Weizmann (see note 2 in chapter 2, "Policy and Labor," in this volume), he was offered the presidency of the Jewish state, a largely ceremonial post, which he declined.

4. [Greenberg's footnote:] This conference was held on September 10–11, 1940, at the Jewish Theological Seminary, New York, N.Y.

5. For Einstein's reflections on the theory of relativity and physics, see Albert Einstein, *Out of My Later Years* (New York: Philosophical Library, 1950), 41–110.

6. On Charles Darwin, see note 18 in chapter 9, "To a Communist Friend," in this volume.

7. Greenberg appears to be confusing John Lightfoot (1602–75), an English clergyman, Old Testament scholar, and master of St. Catherine's College, with James Ussher (1581–1656), the Anglican archbishop of the Church of Ireland (see note 8 below). In his published works, Lightfoot employed a literal reading of the biblical narrative and ascertained that God created the world at the time of the autumnal equinox in 3929 BCE.

8. This year was deduced by James Ussher, the Archbishop of Armagh (Church of Ireland), on the basis of a theologically inspired close reading of the biblical text. Known as the "Ussher chronology," it is often erroneously referred to as the "Ussher-Lightfoot chronology."

9. Quoted from *Science, Philosophy and Religion: A Symposium* (New York: Conference on Science, Philosophy, and Religion in Their Relation to the Democratic Way of Life, 1941); reprinted in Einstein, *Out of My Later Years*, 25–26.

10. Quoted in Einstein, *Out of My Later Years*, 25.

11. The Prussian biblical scholar and theologian Friedrich Schleiermacher (1768–1834), often called "the father of liberal theology," sought to reconcile Protestant Christianity with the principles of the European Enlightenment. He believed religious awareness derived from experience and not revealed doctrine. Greenberg is quoting the anti-ecclesiastical riposte of rationalist philosopher Georg Wilhelm Friedrich Hegel (see note 10 in chapter 1, "The Meaning of Zionism," in this volume) aimed at Schleiermacher's assertion that the essence of authentic religious experience is "the feeling of absolute dependence" (i.e.,

the religious state of mind). See George Behrens, "Feeling of Absolute Dependence or Absolute Feeling of Dependence? (What Schleiermacher Really Said and Why It Matters)," *Religious Studies* 34:4 (December 1998): 471–481.

12. The liberal American Christian theologian Shailer Mathews (1863–1941) served as dean of the Divinity School at the University of Chicago from 1908 to 1933. A prolific author, Mathews espoused a synthesis of religion and science as well as an anthropocentric emphasis on the "distinctiveness" and "personality" of human beings amidst the non-human natural world. Religious experience, he believed, is the process by which humanity adjusts to the natural and social environment and perpetuates its future development. He incorporated evolutionary theory into his sociohistorical approach to religion and argued that "nature reveals a kingdom of ends as well as of histories." Shailer Mathews, *Contributions of Science to Religion* (New York: D. Appleton, 1927), 396.

13. Greenberg is referring to the views of Shailer Mathews (see previous note): "If life has grown more personal while organisms have grown more complicated this must be due in part to the influence of an environment. . . . There must be that in the environment which the *personality-producing* organism can appropriate and with which it can act harmoniously. . . . But be the value of metaphysical speculation of this sort what it may . . . one has come in sight of God." Ibid., 399–401.

14. The French poet, novelist, and journalist Anatole France (1844–1924) authored several widely popular works including *The Crime of Sylvestre Bonnard* (1881), *My Friend's Book* (1885), *Thaïs* (1890), *At the Sign of the Reine Pédauque* (1893), and *The Red Lily* (1894). Following the Dreyfus Affair, in which he publicly supported Émile Zola (see notes 10 and 13 in chapter 26, "Patriotism and Plural Loyalties," in this volume), he turned to political satire with *Penguin Island* (1908) and *The Revolt of the Angels* (1914). In 1921 he was awarded the Nobel Prize in Literature.

15. It appears Greenberg may be paraphrasing ideas and themes in Anatole France's *The Revolt of the Angels* (1914), a satirical novel that draws on John Milton's *Paradise Lost* (1667). In the former, the guardian angel Arcade is converted to free thought by the Roman philosopher Lucretius's didactic poem *De rerum natura* (On the Nature of Things) (c. 50 BCE). He relates: "I am about to reveal to you a secret on which hangs the fate of the universe. . . . Do you not know that the sons of God have already revolted and that a great battle took place in the heavens? . . . It was before the creation of the world. But nothing has changed since then in the heavens. The nature of the angels is no different now from what it was originally. What they did then they could do again now." See Anatole France, *The Revolt of the Angels*, trans. Mrs. Wilfrid Jackson (1929; reprint, New York: Limited Editions Club, 1953), 84.

16. Bertrand Russell (1872–1970), scion of an aristocratic British family, was a philosopher, social reformer, and mathematician. A prolific author, he collaborated with Alfred North Whitehead (1861–1947) on *Principia Mathematica* (1910–13), a pioneer work in symbolic logic. As a realist, Russell sought to infuse philosophy with a scientific basis. As a social thinker, he advocated anti-militarism, anti-imperialism, socialism, pacifism, and nuclear disarmament. In 1950, he won the Nobel Prize in Literature in recognition of his efforts to champion "humanitarian ideals and freedom of thought."

17. This argument is developed in Bertrand Russell, "Our Sexual Ethics," *American Mercury* 38:149 (May 1936): 36–40.

18. On Henri Bergson, see note 57 in chapter 1, "The Meaning of Zionism," in this volume.

19. Quoted in Louis Levine, "Bergson Sees Great Future for American Philosophy," *New York Times* (February 22, 1914), section magazine, 4.

20. On Rabindranath Tagore, see note 17 in chapter 3, "East and West," in this volume.

21. This refers to a second-century CE statue of the Greek god Apollo located in the Belvedere courtyard of the Vatican palace in Rome. It is considered a sublime representation of classical Greek sculpture.

22. Developed by the Greek philosopher Pythagoras (c. 582–507 BCE), the Pythagorean theorem ($a^2 + b^2 = c^2$) posits that the square of the length of the hypotenuse of a right triangle is equal to the sum of the squares of the lengths of the remaining sides.

23. Quoted from "Note on the Nature of Reality (A conversation between Rabindranath Tagore and Professor Albert Einstein in the afternoon of July 14, 1930 at the professor's residence in Kaputh)" in Rabindranath Tagore, *The Religion of Man, Being the Hibbert Lectures for 1930* (New York: Macmillan, 1931), 222–223.

24. The metaphysical notion of hylomorphism (a compound word derived from the Greek terms for "matter" and "shape") is the central doctrine of Aristotle's (see note 2 in chapter 16, "Chosen Peoples," in this volume) philosophy of nature, namely, that every natural body consists of primary matter and substantive form.

Chapter 15

Source: Hayim Greenberg, "Psychoanalysis and Moral Pessimism," *Jewish Frontier* 7:3 (March 1940): 10–15.

1. In this essay, Greenberg uses the terms "ethical pessimism" and "moral pessimism" interchangeably. In doing so, he calls to mind the philosophical school of pessimism identified with Friedrich Schopenhauer (see note 19 in chapter 8, "Notes on Marxism," in this volume). The latter challenged religiously inspired forms of optimism and the notion of progress, instead viewing social and historical change as devoid of intrinsic meaning or value as well as limited in its capacity to elevate or improve the condition of humanity.

2. On Sigmund Freud, see note 42 in chapter 8, "Notes on Marxism," in this volume.

3. Sigmund Freud's *General Introduction to Psychoanalysis* (1920), first published in German as *Vorlesungen zur Einführung in die Psychoanalyse*, outlines the framework of Freud's revolutionary assessment of the unconscious, human sexuality, and the complexity of the mind. The culmination of Freud's pioneering psychoanalytic work at the turn of the nineteenth and twentieth centuries, the book derives from a series of lectures he gave during World War I.

4. The following observation underscores Greenberg's point: "There was great hostility to Freud's science. The combat with psychoanalysis' doubters and critics required much of [Freud's] energy and deeply colored his presentations of psychoanalysis. In *A General Introduction*, for example, the theme of hostility, which Freud psychoanalytically regarded as defensive resistance, is literally present from the first page to the last. On the other hand, Freud portrayed psychoanalysis' practitioners as brave heroes, misunderstood, attacked, and lonely." Michael Oppenheim, *Jewish Philosophy and Psychoanalysis: Narrating the Interhuman* (Lanham, MD: Lexington Books, 2006), 61. See Sigmund Freud, *A*

General Introduction to Psychoanalysis, trans. G. Stanley Hall (New York: Boni and Liveright, 1920).

5. In *Reflections on War and Death* (1915), first published in German as *Zeitgemäßes über Krieg und Tod*, Freud examines Austro-Hungarian society's collective mental profile following the onset of World War I. The state, he asserts, having abdicated responsibility for the treaties and agreements which formerly preserved peace in Europe, now unabashedly resorts to lies, deception, injustice, and violence in its relations with other countries and, in the process, it abuses, exploits, and dishonors its own citizens. "Caught in the whirlwind of these war times," he states, "it is small wonder that we ourselves become confused as to the meaning of impressions which crowd in upon us. . . . It would seem as though no event had ever destroyed so much of the precious heritage of mankind, confused so many of the clearest intellects, or so thoroughly debased what is highest." Sigmund Freud, *Reflections on War and Death*, trans. A. A. Brill and Alfred B. Kuttner (New York: Moffat, Yard and Company, 1918), 1–2. He posits that the public response to the war—the mass casualties, the mechanized means of slaughter, and the military's stunning losses—is a mix of shock, anguish, and disillusionment. Meanwhile, the shifting nature of modern politics and the state's wartime amorality undermines the public's faith in civil society, provokes widespread anxiety, and impacts people's attitudes toward death. Thus, he concludes: "War strips off the later deposits of civilization and allows the primitive man in us to reappear. It forces us again to be heroes who cannot believe in their own death, its stamps all strangers as enemies whose death we ought to cause or wish; it counsels us to rise above the death of those whom we love. . . . Shall we not admit that in our civilized attitude towards death we have again lived psychologically beyond our means?" Freud, *Reflections on War and Death*, 70–71.

6. Greenberg is referring to Freud's assertion that "the earlier infantile existence of intense 'bad' impulses is often the necessary condition of being 'good' in later life. The most pronounced childish egotists may become the most helpful and self-sacrificing citizens; the majority of idealists, humanitarians, and protectors of animals have developed from little sadists and animal tormentors." Ibid., 21.

7. Freud's *The Ego and the Id* (1923), first published in German as *Das Ich und das Es*, outlines his theories of the psychodynamics of the id, ego, and super-ego. He identifies the instinct for life, love, and sexuality (Eros) and contrasts it with the drive toward repulsion, aggression, and death (Thanatos). The former leads to reproduction of the species, the latter to its self-destruction.

8. See Sigmund Freud, *The Ego and the Id*, trans. Joan Riviere, ed. James Strachey, rev. ed. (New York: W. W. Norton, 1960), 25–26.

9. Greenberg is referring to Freud's pathfinding work in which he distinguished the conscious, the pre-conscious, and the unconscious and developed his theory of the id, the ego, and the super-ego. "The Anatomy of the Mental Personality" (1932) is the title of the third chapter of Sigmund Freud, *New Introductory Lectures on Psychoanalysis*, trans. J. H. Sprott (New York: W. W. Norton, 1933).

10. On Friedrich Nietzsche, see note 7 in chapter 6, "Jew and Arab," in this volume.

11. On Henri Bergson, see note 57 in chapter 1, "The Meaning of Zionism," in this volume. Bergson coined the phrase "*élan vital*" (French for "vital impulse") to signify the

original stimulus common to all living species which, in his own words, he explained as "elements that coincided in the vital impulsion common to plants and animals." Henri Bergson, *Creative Evolution*, trans. Arthur Mitchell (London: Macmillan, 1922), 142.

12. Sigmund Freud, *The Psychopathology of Everyday Life* (1901), originally published in German as *Zur Psychopathologie des Alltagslebens*, in *The Standard Edition of the Complete Works of Sigmund Freud*, ed. and trans. James Strachey, vol. 6 (London: Hogarth Press, 1958), 261.

13. Edvard Westermarck (1862–1939), a Finnish philosopher and sociologist, is best known for *The History of Human Marriage* (1891), in which he originated a theory explaining the incest taboo in many cultures (later known known as the "Westermarck effect"), and *The Origin and Development of Moral Ideas*, 2 vols. (1906–8), in which he argues that morality is based on social approval and disapproval. The latter volume includes considerable discussion of Jewish customs and practices.

14. The Australian naturalist Alfred William Howitt (1830–1908) was an anthropologist and explorer. An expert on Australia's indigenous tribes, he authored numerous scientific studies including *The Native Tribes of South-East Australia* (1904), a pioneering investigation of central Australian aborigine culture.

15. Greenberg appears to be paraphrasing a passage in Westermarck's study that draws, in part, on Alfred William Howitt's *The Native Tribes of South-East Australia* (1904). See Edvard Westermarck, *The Origin and Development of Moral Ideas*, vol. 2, 2nd ed. (London: Macmillan, 1924), 319–320.

16. *Dybbuk*, a Yiddish noun derived from the Hebrew root "to cling," connotes a demonic or malicious spirit believed to be the dislocated soul of a dead person. The notion of the dybbuk can be traced to medieval Jewish writings and was later popularized in nineteenth-century folk tales. *The Dybbuk* (1914), a play by the Yiddish writer S. Ansky (see note 6 in chapter 20, "*Halakhah* and *Agadah*," in this volume), relates the story of a young bride possessed by the spirit of her prematurely deceased bridegroom.

17. Greenberg is referring to Freud's observation: "Paradoxical as it may sound, I must maintain that the sense of guilt was present before the misdeed, that it did not arise from it, but conversely—the misdeed arose from the sense of guilt. These people might justly be described as criminals from a sense of guilt." Sigmund Freud, *Some Character Types Met with in Psychoanalytic Work* (1916), in *The Standard Edition of the Complete Psychological Works of Sigmund Freud*, ed. and trans. James Strachey, vol. 14: "On the History of the Psycho-Analytic Movement, Papers on Metapsychology and Other Works (1914–1916)" (London: Hogarth Press, 1957), 332.

18. On Friedrich Nietzsche's *Thus Spoke Zarathustra*, see notes 43 and 44 in chapter 8, "Notes on Marxism," in this volume.

19. See Sigmund Freud, *Those Wrecked by Success* (1916), in *The Standard Edition of the Complete Psychological Works of Sigmund Freud*, ed. and trans. James Strachey, vol. 14: "On the History of the Psycho-Analytic Movement, Papers on Metapsychology and Other Works (1914–1916)" (London: Hogarth Press, 1957), 316.

20. Ibid., 317.

21. Greenberg is referring to Henri Bergson, *The Two Sources of Morality and Religion*, trans. R. Ashley Audra and Cloudesley Brereton (London: Macmillan, 1935).

22. See ibid., 8–9.

23. Greenberg is alluding to the Russian writer Fyodor Dostoyevsky's novel *Crime and Punishment* (1866). On Dostoyevsky, see note 14 in chapter 8, "Notes on Marxism," in this volume.

24. Sholem Aleichem (the pen name of Solomon Naumovich Rabinovich, adopted from the Hebrew/Yiddish greeting and blessing "peace be with you"; 1859–1916), a multilingual eastern European Jewish author, humorist, and playwright, was a central figure in Yiddish letters. He generally favored Jewish socialism and Zionism but never affiliated with any political party or organization. In the wake of Russian pogroms in 1905, he temporarily resettled his family in Geneva, Switzerland, while he immigrated to New York City with the hope his family would immigrate thereafter. To support his family, he wrote plays and lectured widely in the United States and Europe. His funeral, among the largest in New York City's history until then, attracted over 100,000 mourners. Among his most famous works is *Tevye der milkhiker* (Tevye the Dairyman) (1894), a collection of short stories later adapted for stage and film in the American Broadway musical *Fiddler on the Roof* (1964).

25. See Sholem Aleichem, *Moshkele ganev* (Moshkele the Thief) (Warsaw: Familien Bibliotek, 1913).

26. In describing Freud's theory of the "pleasure principle," Greenberg calls attention to the concept's transactional dimensions, namely, the idea that people exchange immediate gratification for long-term certainty. On this economic aspect see also, e.g., Sigmund Freud, *Civilization and Its Discontents: The Standard Edition* (1953–74; reprint, New York: W. W. Norton, 1990), e.g., 35, 48; first published in German as *Das Unbehagen in der Kultur* (1930).

27. The reference is to a group of American Catholic nuns (the Sisters of Saint Francis) who engaged in missionary work on the Hawaiian island of Molokai, site of an isolated leper colony. Inspired by the Belgian priest Joseph de Veuster (1840–89), known as Father Damien, whose pioneer efforts attracted international attention, the nuns devoted themselves to caring for the Molokai colony. Led by Marianne Cope (1838–1918), who was beatified in 2005 by Pope Benedict XVI (Joseph Ratzinger, b. 1927), the nuns augmented and eventually assumed Father Damien's workload, ran a local hospital, and opened a home for women and girls.

28. On Arthur Schopenhauer, see note 19 in chapter 8, "Notes on Marxism," in this volume.

29. Greenberg may be referring to a discussion of Schopenhauer's sexuality in Vivian J. McGill, *Schopenhauer: Pessimist and Pagan* (New York: Brentano's Publishers, 1931), 86–87.

30. Schopenhauer's philosophical pessimism is developed in *The World as Will and Idea* (1818) and *Will in Nature* (1836), which argue reality is a blind impelling force that appears in humanity as will. The constant tension of competing wills causes strife and consequently individuals live in pain because they cannot be truly satisfied. Although temporary refuge can be found in science and art, the only true escape, Schopenhauer concluded, is negation of the will. He also argued ethics rests on one's sympathy for others' pain.

31. In psychology, the process of sublimation refers to one's capacity to transform socially unacceptable impulses into socially acceptable behavior. Freud asserted sublimation to be a key element of civil society because it enables people to function collectively. He emphasized the idea that the transformation of base sexual instincts into culturally acceptable behaviors makes it possible for "higher physical activities, scientific, artistic, or ideological, to play such an important part in civilized life." See Sigmund Freud, *Civilization and Its Discontents* (1930), first published in German as *Das Unbehagen in der Kultur*, in *The Standard Edition of the Complete Psychological Works of Sigmund Freud*, ed. and trans. James Strachey, vol. 21 (London: Hogarth Press, 1961), 79–80.

32. See note 5 above.

33. See Freud's discussion of "cynical jokes" in *Complete Psychological Works*, 66–67. Elsewhere, Freud describes *Galgenhumor* (German for "gallows humor") as "the crudest case of humor"; Sigmund Freud, *Jokes and Their Relation to the Unconscious*, ed. and trans. James Strachey (New York: W. W. Norton and Company, 1960), 284. The latter was originally published in German as *Der Witz und seine Beziehung zum Unbewußten* (1905).

34. Freud discusses the individual's "fear of death" being displaced "upon another beloved person" in his *Totem and Taboo: Resemblances between the Psychic Lives and Savages and Neurotics*, trans. A. A. Brill (New York: Moffat, Yard and Company, 1918), 120–121, 158–159. The work was originally published in German as *Totem und Tabu: Einige Übereinstimmungen im Seelenleben der Wilden und der Neurotiker* (1913).

35. The Hindu formula for spirituality ("I am Thou") underscores the idea that all living beings are both the creation and manifestation of God. This doctrine derives from the *Vedas* (Sanskrit for "knowledge"), the canonical scriptures of Hinduism which originated in ancient India. See also notes 4–7 in chapter 16, "Chosen Peoples," in this volume.

Chapter 16

Source: Hayim Greenberg, "Chosen Peoples," *Jewish Frontier* 10:9 (September 1941): 8–12.

1. On Plato, see note 19 in chapter 9, "To a Communist Friend," in this volume.

2. Aristotle (384–322 BCE), a major Greek philosopher, who studied under Plato and later tutored Alexander the Great (343–336 BCE). Known for emphasizing the close observation and accurate classification of nature, he asserted logic to be the necessary tool of any inquiry. Aristotelianism profoundly influenced medieval Jewish and Islamic philosophical and theological discourse. His extant works, written in the mid-fourth century BCE and published posthumously, are *Organon*, *Metaphysics*, *The Physics*, *On the Heavens*, *History of Animals*, *On the Soul*, *Politics*, *Nicomachean Ethics*, *Rhetoric*, and *Poetics*.

3. The name "Aryan" (Sanskrit for "noble") refers to a group of tribes who spoke an early version of the Indo-European language Sanskrit and settled in the northern Indian subcontinent around 1500 BCE. Later generations of the Aryan people migrated southward to Persia (Iran) and westward to Europe.

4. The *Institutes of Vishnu* (known in Sanskrit as *Vishnu Smiriti*) is the main collection of ancient aphorisms about the sacred Hindu laws of India. Greenberg was likely fa-

miliar with the classic English translation of the Hindu text: *The Institutes of Vishnu Together with Extracts from the Sanskrit Commentary of Nanda Pandita Called Vaijayanti*, ed. Julius Jolly (Calcutta: Asiatic Society, 1881). Vishnu himself is an Indian deity who was originally considered a minor god and whose cults began to grow steadily from the first millennium BCE, absorbing various other local traditions as they did so. In time, Vishnu the Preserver, together with Brahma the Creator and Shiva the Destroyer, came to be regarded as a supreme Hindu deity, of whom all other gods are secondary manifestations.

5. See *The Vishnu Purana, A System of Hindu Mythology and Tradition*, trans. H. H. Wilson (London: John Murray, 1840), 628–629; Arvind Sharma, *Classical Hindu Thought: An Introduction* (New York: Oxford University Press, 2000), 156–157.

6. The term "brahman" refers to the highest of the four castes of India, that which is responsible for officiating at religious rites and teaching the *Vedas* (Sanskrit for "knowledge"), the oldest scriptures of Hinduism. Traditional Hindu culture regards brahmans as a priestly group possessed of greater ritual purity than other castes.

7. The source of this quote is unknown. For a comparable assertion, see Edward A. Blunt, *The Caste System of Northern India* (London: Oxford University Press, 1931), 299–302.

8. Scholars believe the *Avesta*, the sacred book of Zoroastrianism, was originally transmitted orally and evolved over several hundred years. Composed in the Avestan language, it was probably redacted at some point in the third or fourth century CE. According to Avestan legend, a definitive version of the text was lost in 331 BCE when Alexander the Great destroyed Persepolis (near present-day Shiraz in southwest Iran), the capital of the Achaemenid empire (c. 550–330 BCE). The core of the *Avesta* are hymns (called *Gathas*) attributed to Zoroaster; it also contains stories about the creation of humankind, religious and ritual laws, and liturgical elements.

9. Originally the ancient Persian designation for nomadic tribes in central Asia (Turan is Persian for "the land of Tur"), the Turanians are an Iranian people who over time became associated with the Turks. In the modern era, the terms "Turanian" and "Turk" came to be used interchangeably in the West. In the *Avesta* the Turanians are generally identified as the enemies of Zoroastrianism.

10. Greenberg is referring to the German term "*das Herrenvolk*" (master race), a Nazi ideological concept that asserted the supposed Nordic ancestry and purity of the so-called Aryan race. See also note 7 in chapter 24, "The Universalism of the Chosen People," in this volume.

11. The Italian patriot Giuseppe Mazzini (1805–72) was a key revolutionary leader of the Risorgimento. Exiled from Italy in 1831, he spent much of his life in London writing books, editing periodicals, and advocating for the unification of the Italian states in the framework of a democratic republic. He returned to Italy during the 1848 revolution and participated in the short-lived Roman republic (1849). His writings on a variety of topics, including politics, literature, and philosophy, are known for their idealism and compelling stylistic qualities. Many early Zionist activists were inspired by Mazzini's writings.

12. Greenberg is quoting from Giuseppe Mazzini's essay "On the Revolutionary Initiative" (1834). See, e.g., *Life and Writings of Joseph Mazzini*, vol. 3 (London: Smith, Elder and Co., 1891), 60–61.

13. See Giuseppe Mazzini, "General Instructions for the Members of Young Italy" (1831) in *Selected Writings of Giuseppe Mazzini*, ed. Nagendranath Gangulee (London: L. Drummond, 1945), 130.

14. Young Italy, a political movement founded in 1831 by the Italian revolutionary leader Giuseppe Mazzini, sought to foment a popular insurrection among the Italian people and bring about a unified democratic Italian republic. The group's leadership included Giuseppe Garibaldi (1807–82), another central figure of the Italian Risorgimento.

15. On Fyodor Dostoyevsky, see note 14 in chapter 8, "Notes on Marxism," in this volume.

16. Quoted in Fyodor Dostoyevsky, *The Devils (The Possessed)*, trans. David Magarshack (1956; reprint, New York: Penguin Books, 1986), 259.

17. On Leo Tolstoy, see notes 4 and 5 in chapter 1, "The Meaning of Zionism," in this volume.

18. Reference to the Russian people as a "god-bearing people" can be found in Dostoyevsky, *The Devils*, 258. In the novel, the character Shatov introduces the latter concept while revealing "the twofold nature of the messianic consciousness, a twofoldness which existed already among the Hebrew people." As well, Shatov's name is "derived from *shatkij*, which means wavering." See Carnegie Samuel Calian, *The Significance of Eschatology in the Thoughts of Nicolas Berdyaev* (Leiden: E. J. Brill, 1965), 24n.1.

19. On the *Narodniki* (Russian for Narodnaya Volya members), see note 40 in chapter 12, "Leon Trotsky," in this volume.

20. Greenberg is referring to the moderate wing of the Russian Social Democratic Party known as the Menshevik faction, which was led by Georgi Valentinovich Plekhanov (1857–1918). See note 17 in chapter 9, "To a Communist Friend," in this volume.

21. On the Bolshevik faction, see note 17 in chapter 9, "To a Communist Friend," in this volume.

22. On the October Revolution see note 1 in chapter 5, "Our Stand," in this volume.

23. Karl Marx and Friedrich Engels ridiculed the notion of establishing a kingdom of heaven on earth, with roots in Christian biblical sources, as "in every sense a sedative." See, e.g., "'Doctor Georg Kuhlmann of Holstein' or The Prophecies of True Socialism," which carries the subtitle "The New World, or the Kingdom of the Spirit upon the Earth. Annunciation," in Karl Marx and Friedrich Engels, *Collected Works, 1845–47*, vol. 5: "Theses on Feuerbach, The German Ideology and Related Manuscripts," trans. Richard Dixon et al. (New York: International Publishers, 1975), 531–539. Meanwhile, contemporary exponents, detractors, and observers of Marxist socialism used the term liberally. For example, the American author Charles Edward Russell (1860–1941), who visited the fledgling Soviet Union in 1917 with the Root Commission appointed by President Woodrow Wilson, reported "the most active supporters of Bolshevism in principle and in practice" believed "Bolshevik rule was the beginning of the kingdom of heaven on earth, and that [the Russians] would show the rest of the world the way to happiness." Charles Edward Russell, *Bolshevism and the United States* (Indianapolis: Bobbs-Merrill, 1919), 275.

24. Vincenzo Gioberti (1801–52), a liberal Italian priest, philosopher, and statesman, served as premier of Sardinia (1848–49). He originally favored a federation of Italian states under papal authority, but later modified his views and advocated the creation of a unified Italy under a constitutional monarchy.

25. The French historian and politician François Guizot (1787–1874) was a leading intellectual advocate of Louis Phillipe's (1773–1850) bourgeois monarchy (1830–48). He served briefly as the premier of France in 1847–48 and his reactionary policies helped to prompt the February Revolution of 1848. His scholarly studies include *Collection of the Memoirs Relating to the History of France from the Foundation of the French Monarchy to the Thirteenth Century* (1823–26) and *Discourse on the History of the English Revolution* (1849–50).

26. François Guizot believed France to be "the center from which European civilization has emanated" (May 1840). "Guizot's Progress of European Civilization," *Fraser's Magazine for Town and Country* 21:121 (January–June 1840), 582.

27. The German philosopher and political leader Johann Gottlieb Fichte (1762–1814) conceived a form of ethical idealism derived from Kantianism. His important works include *Attempt at a Critique of All Revelation* (1792–93), *Foundations of the Entire Science of Knowledge* (1794–95), *Foundations of Natural Right* (1796–97), *The System of Ethical Theory Based on the Wissenschaftslehre* (Doctrine of Science) (1798), and *The Characteristics of the Present Age and The Way Towards the Blessed Life* (1806). Fichte's *Addresses to the German Nation* (1808) was central to the rise of liberal nationalism in the West.

28. The Polish romantic poet, playwright, and political activist Adam Mickiewicz (1798–1855) was a central figure in eastern European revolutionary politics and *belles lettres*. After he was arrested in 1823 for participating in secret pan-Polish political societies, he was exiled to Russia. In 1829 he fled Russia and thereafter lived in different parts of Europe. He eventually settled in Paris where he taught literature. He died in Istanbul while he was organizing a legion of Polish and Jewish revolutionaries to fight Russia in the Crimean War (1853–56). His literary works, which often utilized Polish folk themes, include the dramatic poem *Forefather's Eve* (1823) and the epic poems *Konrad Wallenrod* (1825–28) and *Pan Tadeusz* (1834).

29. The Polish philosopher August Cieszkowski (1814–94) was a key eastern European exponent of Hegelian thought. He adapted the latter so as to emphasize a threefold division of human history: (a) antiquity, during which humanity existed in its primal state; (b) the Christian era, when humanity developed its self-reflective capacity and confronted the duality of God and temporal existence; and (c) the post-Hegelian era in which the tensions of the Christian era would be overcome. His philosophical worldview was subsequently reformulated in Trinitarian and religious terms. Active in radical political affairs, he helped to found the Polish League and served in the Prussian national assembly (1848–55). His major works include *Prolegomena to a Historiosophy* (1838), *God and Palingenesis* (1842), and *Our Father* (1848). The proto-Zionist German Jewish philosopher Moses Hess (see note 31 in chapter 3, "East and West," in this volume) introduced Karl Marx to Cieszkowski's philosophical writings and ideas.

30. See Adam Mickiewicz, *Poems*, ed. George Raphall Noyer (New York: Polish Institute of Arts and Sciences, 1944): "The Books of the Polish Nation: From the Beginning of the World to the Martyrdom of the Polish Nation," 371–380; "The Pilgrim's Litany," 414–415.

31. On Mohandas K. Gandhi, see note 11 in chapter 3, "East and West," in this volume.

32. Greenberg may be referring to a marginal school of Japanese thought called

Nohonjin-ron (Japanese for "theory of the Japanese people"), which postulates Japanese exceptionalism and racial superiority owing to physical and genetic differences. Historically, a powerful militarist vision animated Japan's conquest of territories in Asia and its presumed destiny for cultural and political dominance of the region. Thus, in the early twentieth century Japan annexed Taiwan (1895), Korea (1910), and Manchuria (1931). In 1938, on the eve of World War II, Japanese prime minister Fumimaro Konoe (1891–1945) proclaimed a New East Asian Order purporting to be an equal partnership between Japan and China. In 1940, poised to expand into Indochina, the Japanese government called for the creation of a Greater East Asia Co-prosperity Sphere inclusive of southeast Asia. Japan rhetorically preached Asian unity (under its leadership) in hopes of mustering Asian support for the war effort. However, the government lacked a systematic strategy for building and administering the latter entity, and varying forms of Japanese-controlled military and civilian rule were instituted in Burma, Thailand, the Philippines, and other territories. In 1942 the Japanese government also created the Greater East Asian Ministry. In general, Japan's efforts to dominate Asia met with little success as the tide of World War II quickly turned against the imperial government. Indeed, between 1942 and 1944 Japan lost most of the territory it had conquered in southeast Asia and China. In July 1944, American planes began flying bombing missions over the Japanese home islands. The ramping up of Allied bombing in early 1945 brought devastation to the Japanese people, and the dropping of the atomic bomb on Hiroshima and Nagasaki in August signaled both the end of the war and the destruction of Japan's imperial social and political order.

33. In the mid-seventeenth century, groups of French Jesuits, a male Catholic evangelizing order, established a foothold along the St. Lawrence River in sparsely populated New France. Unlike Catholic missionaries in the colonial territories of Latin America, the French Jesuits lacked the coercive power of a conquering regime and their efforts to convert the native American Huron tribe proved futile. Over time, the French Jesuits developed friendly relations with the Huron and played an intermediary role in preserving economic, political, and military ties between the latter and New France.

34. The liberal reformer Wilhelm von Humboldt (1767–1835) was a German statesman and philologist. His argument that society's progress is dependent on the free interaction of its members and the limited role of the state strongly influenced the British philosopher and political economist John Stuart Mill (1806–73). In his capacity as Prussian minister of education he was responsible for reforming the country's school system and establishing the Humanistic Gymnasium, which became a normative educational framework throughout Germany. He also helped to found the University of Berlin.

35. The provenance of this quote is unknown.

36. Carl Gustav Jung (1875–1961), founder of the school of analytical psychology, was a colleague, protégé, and rival of Sigmund Freud. As first president of the International Psychoanalytic Association, Jung worked closely with Freud and Alfred Adler (see note 8 in chapter 6, "Jew and Arab," in this volume); they are considered the founding figures of modern psychology. In 1913, Jung and Freud split over conceptual and analytic differences. In contrast to Freud, Jung conceived of libido as primal nonsexual energy and postulated two systems in the unconscious: the personal (repressed events in personal life)

and the collective unconscious (archetypes of inherited tendencies). He is also credited with introducing the psychoanalytic concepts of archetypes, introversion and extraversion, the complex, and synchronicity. Among Jung's important works are *The Psychology of the Unconscious* (1912), *Psychological Types* (1921), and *Modern Man in Search of a Soul* (1933).

37. Reacting against what C. G. Jung considered Sigmund Freud's rigid conceptualization of psychotherapy, he wrote *Modern Man in Search of a Soul* (1933), in which Jung emphasizes the spiritual significance of the unconscious and examines eleven different topics including dream analysis, the problems and aims of psychotherapy, his theory of types, developmental stages, the differences between his and Freud's approaches to analytical psychology, and "the spiritual problem of modern man."

38. Quoted in C. G. Jung, *Modern Man in Search of a Soul* (London: K. Paul, Trench, Trubner and Company, 1933), 213.

39. This phrase is recited at the outset of the traditional Passover service. It is intended as a reminder that "care must be taken to provide for the poor . . . and they—as all other Jews—should be able to celebrate [the holiday] free of worry." Philip Goodman, *The Passover Anthology* (Philadelphia: Jewish Publication Society of America, 1973), 432.

40. The Jewish festival of Passover derives from the Hebrew Bible (Lev. 23:5) and is intended to commemorate the liberation of the ancient Israelites from Egyptian slavery as recounted in Exodus. Observed annually, the holiday starts on the fifteenth day of the Hebrew month of Nisan and lasts for seven days (in the Land of Israel) or eight days (in the diaspora). The holiday includes unique ritual customs and dietary restrictions including the consumption of unleavened flatbread known as *mazah* (pl. *mazot*) (Exod. 12:8).

41. This appears to be an anecdote.

42. The Hebrew phrase is "*Barukh atah adonai eloheinu melekh haolam shelo asani goy*" (Praised are you, eternal our God, ruler of the universe, who has not made me a gentile). The scholar Ruth Langer explains that "*Tosefta Berakhot* 6:18 teaches in the name of Rabbi Yehuda ben Ilai (mid-second century CE) that every (Jewish) man is obligated to recite three blessings daily. These express gratitude for one's station in life through the negative statements: thank God that I am not a gentile, a woman, or a slave (or in earlier formulations, a boor). This language echoes Greek prayers preserved first by Plato. Especially because this text also appears as a legal dictum in the Babylonian Talmud [B. Menahot 43b], these blessings, which modern scholars call the 'blessings of identity,' gradually became part of the preliminary prayers to the daily morning service. They are found in the earliest preserved Jewish prayer books, from the end of the first millennium." Ruth Langer, "Liturgy: Daily Prayers: 'Who has not made me a gentile,'" in *Jewish Understandings of the Other: An Annotated Sourcebook*, ed. Eugene Korn, Shira Lander, and Ruth Langer (Boston: Boston College Center for Christian-Jewish Learning, 2010); http://www.bc.edu/dam/files/research_sites/cjl/texts/cjrelations/resources/sourcebook/shelo_asani_goy.htm.

43. The Hebrew phrase is "*Atah bahartanu mikol haamim*" (You have chosen us from among all the nations). The traditional Jewish liturgy "portrays its community, Israel, as distinctive among human communities" and "calls for daily, explicit acknowledgment of this fact." Ruth Langer, "Theologies of Self and Other in American Jewish Liturgies," *CCAR Journal: A Reform Jewish Quarterly* (Winter 2005): 12.

44. Greenberg is referring to the liturgy of the Jewish *havdalah* (separation) service, a ritual ceremony that concludes the Sabbath and Jewish holidays and symbolizes the start of a new week. The service includes blessings for kindling a braided candle, drinking a cup of wine, and smelling spices. It has been observed that "insofar as *havdalah* is viewed primarily as a ritual to demarcate the conclusion of the Sabbath, it is the categorization of holy/profane, not light/dark, that constitutes the primary binary distinction of Judaism." Lawrence A. Hoffman, *Beyond the Text: A Holistic Approach to Liturgy* (Bloomington: Indiana University Press, 1987), 41.

45. Greenberg is referring to language found in the traditional Jewish prayer known as "*Aleinu*" (it is our duty). This liturgical poem is recited at the conclusion of each of the three daily Jewish worship services, after the monthly blessing for the new moon, and following a ritual circumcision. The first stanza of *Aleinu* is "less a comment on the other nations, per se, than a paean to God for having made Israel distinctive," while the second stanza "presents an eschatological vision of a future in which God will be triumphant over all false gods, and all non-Jews will come to accept God as their sovereign." It is noteworthy that "no other text of the statutory prayers makes an explicit statement about the active participation of non-Jews in the messianic scenario." Ruth Langer, "Liturgy: Daily Prayers: *Aleinu*," in Korn, Lander, and Langer, *Jewish Understandings of the Other*; http://www.bc.edu/content/dam/files/research_sites/cjl/texts/cjrelations/resources/sourcebook/Aleynu.htm.

46. According to the Hebrew Bible, Moses received the Decalogue from God at Mount Sinai (Exod. 19). The precise location of Mount Sinai is unknown, although scholars generally believe the biblical narrative refers to a mountain in the central and northern areas of the Sinai peninsula.

47. On Maimonides, see note 22 in chapter 4, "Sabbatai Zevi," in this volume.

48. The reference here is to the stream of classical liberal Judaism that originated in central Europe. In the early nineteenth century, German-speaking Jewish immigrants to the United States brought this religious sensibility with them and laid the foundation for American Reform Judaism (see note 13 in chapter 29, "The Future of American Jewry," in this volume).

49. Salomon Munk (1803–67), a Prussian-born French Jewish scholar of medieval Arabic and Hebrew literature, is known for the three-volume Arabic translation of Maimonides' *Morei nevukhim* (The Guide for the Perplexed) (1856, 1861, 1866) and his discovery that the medieval Andalusian Jewish philosopher and poet Solomon ibn Gabirol (c. 1021–58) was the author of *Fons Vitae* (Source of Life) (c. 1050) and not, as previously believed, a Christian or Muslim theologian. He also traveled to Egypt with the French Jewish lawyer Adolphe Crémieux (1796–1880) and the British financier Moses Haim Montefiore (1784–1885) to help defend the Jewish community of Damascus when it was falsely accused of ritual murder in the Damascus Affair (1840).

50. Kaufman Kohler (1843–1926), an American Reform rabbi, theologian, and scholar of central European ancestry, immigrated to the United States in 1869. He served as a congregational rabbi in Detroit, Chicago, and New York before becoming chair of Jewish theology and president of Hebrew Union College (1903–21). Known as a chief exponent of classical Reform Judaism, he authored *Jewish Theology, Systematically and Historically Considered* (1918).

51. On Ahad Haam, see notes 12–13 in chapter 1, "The Meaning of Zionism," in this volume.

52. Greenberg is referring to the Yiddish poet and essayist Menahem (Goldberg) Boraisha (1888–1949), known simply as "Menahem." Boraisha drew on traditional Jewish sources as inspiration for his work. Many of his early poems, composed in the form of prayers, were "rhapsodic odes filled with longing for God and holiness." In his later work, he asserted that "revelation was as legitimate a gate to the realm of the absolute as were calculations of reason." Sol Liptzin, *The Maturing of Yiddish Literature* (New York: Jonathan David, 1970), 20.

53. See "*Yidishe noyt un 'Ato bekhartonu*,'" in Menahem Boraisha, *Eseyen* (Buenos Aires: Yidbukh, 1956), 203–204.

54. The German Jewish public intellectual and philosopher Hermann Cohen (1842–1918) was raised in a traditional central European Jewish home and originally pursued rabbinic studies at the Breslau Jewish Theological Seminary. He abandoned his rabbinical training, however, and instead went on to complete a doctorate in philosophy at the University of Halle. From 1873 to 1912 he taught at the University of Marburg. His antipsychologistic interpretation of Immanuel Kant gave rise to the Marburg school of neo-Kantianism that dominated German philosophy in the late nineteenth and early twentieth centuries. After his retirement, he left Marburg for Berlin where he taught Jewish philosophy at the Institute for the Science of Judaism, which occasioned his articulation of a philosophy of religion based on an interpretation of the foundational sources of Judaism. Published posthumously, this work—*Religion of Reason: Out of the Sources of Judaism* (1919)—ascribed in contrast to Kant a crucial role to liturgical prayer in the context of monotheistic faith in the nurturing of ethical reason and commitment to universal justice. With the rise of anti-Jewish hostility in Imperial Germany, Cohen became one of central European Jewry's leading critics of antisemitism. His imprint and widespread influence on twentieth-century Jewish theological and philosophical thought are evident in the work of Martin Buber (see note 17 in chapter 1, "The Meaning of Zionism," in this volume), Franz Rosenzweig (1886–1929), and other leading Jewish thinkers. His important works include *The Logic of Pure Intelligence* (1902), *The Ethics of Pure Will* (1904), *The Aesthetics of Pure Feeling* (1912), and the aforementioned *Religion of Reason: Out of the Sources of Judaism.*

55. The source of this statement attributed to Hermann Cohen is unknown.

56. Socrates (c. 469–399 BCE), a classical Greek philosopher and founder of Western philosophy, is known through the second-hand accounts of the playwright Aristophanes (c. 446–386 BC) and his students Plato and Xenophon (c. 430–354 BCE). Aristotle credits Socrates as the originator of the scientific method, stemming from the "Socratic method," a form of dialectical inquiry that emphasizes the process of observing phenomena, generating questions, stimulating debate, and arriving at hypotheses that withstand rational scrutiny.

57. Buddha (Sanskrit for "enlightened one"), the title given to Siddhartha Gautama (c. 563–483 BCE), was an Indian religious leader and founder of Buddhism. He is the central figure in Buddhism and the account of his life, teachings, and monastic rules are foundational to Buddhist belief and practice.

58. The life of the Chinese philosopher Confucius (551–479 BCE) is surrounded by legend. It is known he lived in the feudal state of Lu, became a public official, and advocated social reform. He urged a system of morality and statecraft to bring about peace, justice, and universal order. His teaching became the basis of Confucianism, an ethical and philosophical system that emphasizes mutuality, the maintenance of respectful relationships, and avoidance of extremes.

59. On Karl Marx, see note 31 in chapter 1, "The Meaning of Zionism," in this volume.

60. On Sigmund Freud, see note 42 in chapter 8, "Notes on Marxism," in this volume.

61. On Albert Einstein, see note 3 in chapter 14, "Einstein Discusses Religion," in this volume.

62. On Baruch Spinoza, see note 50 in chapter 1, "The Meaning of Zionism," in this volume.

63. Born under Muslim rule in Tudela, a town in northeastern Spain, the Sephardic Jewish philosopher and physician Yehuda ben Shmuel Halevi (c. 1075–1141 CE) is a major figure in medieval Hebrew poetry. Rooted in Hebrew and Arabic classical sources, he studied theology, philosophy, science, and medicine. His poetry on religious and secular themes blossomed under the mentorship and patronage of the Spanish poet and philosopher Rabbi Moses ibn Ezra (c. 1055–1138 CE), who brought Halevi to Granada. When Granada fell in 1090 during the Almoravid invasion of the Iberian peninsula, Halevi relocated to Toledo under the patronage of the Castilian official Solomon ibn Ferruziel (c. 1050–1108). When the latter was assassinated in 1108, Halevi traveled throughout North Africa and Egypt. His significant religio-philosophical work the *Kitab al Khazari* (Arabic for "Book of the Khazars") (c. 1140 CE), commonly called the *Kuzari*, is an extended dialectical treatise in the form of dialogue between the pagan king of the Khazars and representatives of different faiths including Judaism. In 1140 Halevi departed Egypt for Palestine, but it is not certain he arrived before his death.

64. Quoted from Yehuda Halevi, *Sefer hakuzari*, second essay, article 36. See Yehuda Halevi, *The Kuzari: In Defense of the Despised Faith*, trans. N. Daniel Korobkin (Nanuet, NY: Feldheim, 2009), 202.

65. Nahman Krochmal (1785–1840), also known by the acronym Ranak (Rav Nahman Krochmal), was a Galician Jewish theologian, philosopher, and historian. Raised in a traditional Ashkenazi environment, he married at age fourteen and moved to the home of his in-laws outside the Ukrainian city of Lviv, where he continued his rabbinic studies and educated himself in ancient and modern languages and European philosophy. He became personally acquainted with many of the leading figures of the Galician Haskalah. Despite his initial trajectory as the son and son-in-law of successful merchants, Krochmal was largely unsuccessful in business and eventually became impoverished. Though he published only a few items during his lifetime, he continued his intellectual labors privately and garnered a reputation as a significant thinker. His innovative theosophical approach emphasizes a synthesis of metaphysics and the philosophy of history to explain Judaism's historical development. For Krochmal, one scholar observes, "the Jewish idea of God was philosophically rational and the inner development of Judaism was a gradual clarification of the idea implicit in the biblical depiction of God" and the "meaning of Jewish existence" became visible though the history of "the people and its spirit,

together forming an indissoluble unity revelatory of the Absolute." Robert M. Seltzer, *Jewish People, Jewish Thought: The Jewish Experience in History* (New York: Macmillan, 1980), 578. Following his death, the German Reform rabbi Leopold Zunz (1794–1886), a key exponent of *Wissenschaft des Judentums* (Science of Judaism), published Krochmal's work posthumously in 1851 under the title *Morei nevukhei hazman* (Guide for the Perplexed of the Time).

66. Krochmal's *Morei nevukhei hazman*, whose title signaled a refutation of Maimonides' famous *Morei nevukhim* (Guide for the Perplexed), argued against the traditional Jewish view of Jewish history as separate from general history as well as the prevailing Enlightenment belief in humanity's infinite progress. Nonetheless, he believed the Jews achieved full awareness of the "absolute spirit" in the postbiblical era: "It was as imprinted on our hearts; throughout the generations we never strayed from it, and we were its teachers to many nations, and with it we remain to this very day, and through it we shall survive and enjoy eternal redemption." Quoted in Jay M. Harris, *Nachman Krochmal: Guiding the Perplexed of the Modern Age* (New York: New York University Press, 1991), 139.

67. The source of this quotation attributed to Salomon Munk is unknown.

68. On Moses Hess, see note 31 in chapter 3, "East and West," in this volume.

69. In this instance, Greenberg appears to be paraphrasing from memory the diffuse and sometimes nebulous arguments in Moses Hess's *Die heilige Geschichte der Menschheit* (The Holy History of Mankind) (1837) and *Rom und Jerusalem, die Letzte Nationalitätsfrage* (Rome and Jerusalem: The Last Nationality Question) (1862). The summative statements here correctly and succinctly convey the essence of Hess's philosophical views, but it seems unlikely they are direct quotations. For passages that approximate Greenberg's references, see *Moses Hess: The Holy History of Mankind and Other Writings*, trans. and ed. Shlomo Avineri (Cambridge: Cambridge University Press, 2004), 17, 21, 44–45, 91–93, and 136–139; Moses Hess, "Rome and Jerusalem," in *The Zionist Idea: A Historical Analysis and Reader*, ed. Arthur Hertzberg (1959; reprint, New York: Atheneum, 1981), 125–126, 129, 131.

70. See "The Transvaluation of Values," in Ahad Haam, *Selected Essays*, trans. Leon Simon (Philadelphia: Jewish Publication Society of America, 1912), 14, 117, 152.

71. Ibid., 49–50, 234.

72. When this article was originally published in 1941, it concluded with the following note: "Whether the proponents of Jewish superiority satisfy the above two requirements, and to what extent they do so, will be discussed in another essay." It does not appear Greenberg composed a follow-up essay. A few years later, however, he continued his discussion of themes introduced here in "The Universalism of the Chosen People" (1945), which is reprinted as chapter 24 in this volume.

Chapter 17

Source: Hayim Greenberg, "Socialism Re-examined," *Jewish Frontier* 8:11 (November 1941): 9–12. This essay was reprinted in the *International Socialist Forum* (June 1942).

1. World War II ended in Europe in early May 1945 with the Allied invasion of Berlin

and the unconditional surrender of the Nazi regime. Next, following the US bombing in August 1945 of Hiroshima and Nagasaki, Japan surrendered to the Allied forces.

2. The French philosopher Charles Fourier (1772–1837) developed a theory of utopian socialism in which the basic social-economic unit, known as the "phalanx," consisted of 1,620 people. The doctrine of Fourierism was popularized and transplanted to the United States by Albert Brisbane (1809–90) and Fourier's protégé Victor Prosper Considerant (1808–93), who in 1855 founded the short-lived Fourierist colony Le Réunion in Texas. Horace Greeley (1811–72), the well-known American reformer and newspaper editor, helped to publicize Fourier's ideas in the United States. In all, Fourierism prompted the establishment of over two dozen American socialist colonies, the most successful of which was located in Red Bank, New Jersey.

3. This is a slight misquote by Greenberg. Charles Fourier claimed that following sixteen generations of harmony people would be on the average seven feet tall owing to "*l'emploi continuel des trois passions distributives*" (French for "the continual use of the three distributive passions"). The original text can be found in *Oeuvres Complètes de Charles Fourier*, 12 vols. (Paris: Anthropos, 1966–68), vol. 12, 64. For a useful analysis, see Jonathan Beecher, *Charles Fourier: The Visionary and His World* (Berkeley: University of California Press, 1986), 332–352.

4. German-Austrian socialist Karl Kautsky (1854–1938) was a leading figure in the effort to spread Marxist doctrine in Germany. His activity set the German Social Democratic Party on an orthodox Marxist path and established him as a dominant figure in the Second International. He opposed the Social Democratic Party's support of the German effort in World War I and helped form the Independent Social Democratic Party. Soon after the Bolshevik revolution in Russia, he condemned it as undemocratic and non-Marxist.

5. In contrast to Friedrich Nietzsche (see note 7 in chapter 6, "Jew and Arab," in this volume), Karl Kautsky described the "superman" from the socialist viewpoint "not as an exception, but as a rule, a superman as compared with his predecessors, but not as opposed to his comrades, a noble man who seeks his satisfaction not by being great among crippled dwarfs, but great among the great, happy among the happy—who does not draw the feeling of his strength from the fact that he raises himself upon the bodies of the downtrodden, but because a union with his fellows gives him courage to dare the attainment of the highest tasks." Quoted in Henry C. Vedder, *Socialism and the Ethics of Jesus* (New York: Macmillan, 1912), 279.

6. The philosopher and socialist theoretician Antonio Labriola (1843–1904), known as the father of Italian Marxism, significantly influenced the political worldview of Antonio Gramsci (1891–1937), Palmiro Togliatti (1893–1964), and other Italian Communist leaders.

7. Galileo Galilei (1564–1642), an Italian mathematician, astronomer, and physicist, laid the foundations of modern experimental science through his investigations of natural law. His observations prefigured Isaac Newton's (1642–1727) laws of motion. In 1609 he constructed the first telescope and his astronomical discoveries confirmed the Copernican theory of the solar system. He was later forced by the Inquisition to recant his view that the earth orbited the sun.

8. On Plato, see note 19 in chapter 9, "To a Communist Friend," in this volume.

9. Giordano Bruno (1548–1600), a free-thinking Italian Dominican friar, was a philosopher, astronomer, mathematician, and poet. He posited the universe to be infinite and asserted the solar system to be made up of planets orbiting stars. Tried by the Inquisition for his pantheistic beliefs, he was found guilty of heresy and burned at the stake in 1600.

10. Greenberg is paraphrasing the following: "In the society of the future . . . there will grow out of all proportion, until they are legion, the number of men who will be able to discourse with that divine joy in research and that heroic courage of truth which we admire in a Plato, a Bruno, a Galilei." Quoted in Antonio Labriola, *Socialism and Philosophy*, trans. Ernest Untermann (Chicago: C. H. Kerr and Company, 1907), 7.

11. On Leon Trotsky, see note 30 in chapter 3, "East and West," in this volume.

12. Leon Trotsky, *Literature and Revolution* (1924; reprint, New York: Russell and Russell, 1957), 256.

13. On Aristotle, see note 2 in chapter 16, "Chosen Peoples," in this volume.

14. The poet, writer, statesman, and scientist Johann Wolfgang von Goethe (1749–1832) was the central German literary figure of the Romantic movement. His philosophical worldview, strongly influenced by Baruch Spinoza (see note 50 in chapter 1, "The Meaning of Zionism," in this volume), was a mystic pantheism. His close friendship with Friedrich von Schiller (see note 27 in chapter 9, "To a Communist Friend," in this volume) informed his view of aesthetics. Among Goethe's major literary works are *Goetz of Berlichingen of the Iron Hand* (1773), *The Sorrows of Young Werther* (1774), and *Faust* (1808, 1832). He also produced numerous poems, ballads, and lyrics as well as several scientific essays on morphology and botany. His discovery in 1784 of the intermaxillary bone proved important to the theory of human evolution. Goethe sustained close personal and professional relationships with many Jews, and he was keenly interested in the Hebrew language and themes drawn from the Hebrew Bible. Even so, he opposed legislation intended to improve the situation of the Jews in central Europe.

15. Trotsky, *Literature and Revolution*, 256.

16. On George Bernard Shaw, see note 9 in chapter 8, "Notes on Marxism," in this volume.

17. Greenberg seems to be mistaken about the attribution in this instance. He may have been thinking of the following statement by Hendrik de Man (see note 22 below): "The earthly paradise of the utopists (the Marxists not excepted), who picture the general happiness on 'the day after the revolution' as a general wellbeing, belong to the same order of guiding fictions as the 'happy hunting grounds' of the Red Indians, who, since their worst misfortune is a lack of game, naturally regard heaven as a place which is teeming with deer and buffalo. The Eskimos, in like manner, dream of heaven as a sea where fish abound." See Hendrik de Man, *The Psychology of Marxian Socialism* (1928; reprint, New Brunswick, NJ: Transaction Books, 1985), 484.

18. Herbert Morrison (1888–1965), a British socialist and Labour Party leader, served as foreign secretary and deputy prime minister in Clement Atlee's (1883–1967) Labour government (1945–51). A key figure in British politics, Morrison is credited with the political strategy that brought Labour to power following World War II. In 1946, together with US ambassador Henry F. Grady (1882–1957), he devised a stillborn proposal (known as the Morrison-Grady Plan) to place Palestine under a British trusteeship.

19. Greenberg is referring to Herbert Morrison's assertion that "the high moral purpose of socialism does not and must not prevent the socialist in public affairs from carrying a sound business head on his shoulders, nor must he feel it in any way a treachery to his ideals if he must elaborate in a realistic spirit the organization and management of socialized industries. . . . It is essential that socialism should be sound public business." Herbert Morrison, *Socialisation and Transport* (London: Constable, 1933), 281. For a useful analysis, see W. H. Greenleaf, *The British Political Tradition: A Much Governed Nation*, vol. 3 (1987; reprint, New York: Routledge, 2003), 382–386.

20. Greenberg is referring to the Russian Revolutions of February 1917 (see note 9 in chapter 6, "Jew and Arab," in this volume) and October 1917 (see note 1 in chapter 5, "Our Stand," in this volume).

21. This expression derives from the Italian political philosopher Niccoló Machiavelli (1469–1527): "In the actions of men, and especially of princes, from which there is no appeal, the end justifies the means. Let a prince therefore aim at conquering and maintaining the state, and the means will always be judged honorable and praised by everyone." Niccoló Machiavelli, *The Prince* (Chicago: Great Books Foundation, 1955), 60.

22. On Hendrik de Man, see note 13 in chapter 9, "To a Communist Friend," in this volume.

23. On Adolf Hitler, see note 10 in chapter 6, "Jew and Arab," in this volume.

24. On the origins of the concept of Canaan as fundamental to a providential or inevitable plan for humanity, see notes 13 and 29 in chapter 24, "The Universalism of the Chosen People," in this volume.

25. On the group of American Catholic nuns (the Sisters of Saint Francis) who engaged in missionary work on the Hawaiian island of Molokai, site of an isolated leper colony, see note 27 in chapter 15, "Psychoanalysis and Moral Pessimism," in this volume.

26. Greenberg is alluding to the longstanding debate on the left concerning the means and ends of socialism. The notion of a "revisionist trend" in socialism can be traced to Vladimir Lenin (see note 9 in chapter 6, "Jew and Arab," in this volume), who asserted that non-Marxist socialists, social democrats, and other left-wing moderates—in contrast to orthodox Marxists—lacked steadfast principles, grasped at opportunism, and generally undermined the socialist cause. Lenin argued: "In the sphere of politics, revisionism did really try to revise the foundation of Marxism, namely, the doctrine of the class struggle. Political freedom, democracy and universal suffrage remove the ground for the class struggle—we were told—and render untrue the old proposition of the *Communist Manifesto* [by Karl Marx and Friedrich Engels (1848)] that the working men have no country. . . . The liberals have always said that bourgeois parliamentarism destroys classes and class divisions. . . . The inevitability of revisionism is determined by its class roots in modern society. Revisionism is an international phenomenon. No thinking socialist who is in the least informed can have the slightest doubt that the relation between the orthodox [Marxists and non-Marxist moderates] is everywhere essentially similar, notwithstanding the immense variety of national conditions and historical factors [worldwide]. . . . The ideological struggle waged by revolutionary Marxism against revisionism at the end of the nineteenth century is but the prelude to the great revolutionary battles of the proletariat, which is marching forward to the complete victory of its cause despite all the waverings and weaknesses of the petty bourgeoisie." See "Marxism and Revision-

ism" (1908) in Vladimir I. Lenin, *Collected Works*, vol. 15, March 1908–August 1909 (Moscow: Progress Publishers, 1977), 36–39.

27. Eduard Bernstein (1850–1932), a German socialist and political theorist of central European Jewish ancestry, was a founder of the German Social Democratic Party. In contrast to Karl Marx and Friedrich Engels, Bernstein emphasized utopian socialist principles and rejected Hegelian dialectics and materialist theories of history. He believed socialism's realization to be possible through peaceful means and legislative reform. He also asserted the state could be mobilized as a useful and positive mechanism to uplift workers and elevate society generally. Vladimir Lenin singled out Bernstein for attack in "Marxism and Revisionism" (1908) (see previous note).

28. The reference is to World War II.

Chapter 18

Source: Hayim Greenberg, "The Myth of Jewish Parasitism," *Jewish Frontier* 9:3 (March 1942): 19–22.

1. A derogatory Yiddish term for an impractical rootless person lacking a viable occupation, literally "one who lives on air."

2. A Yiddish epithet signaling profit derived unfairly from the efforts and at the expense of others, literally an "income from nothing but air."

3. Greenberg is referring to the Haskalah (Jewish Enlightenment).

4. On Karl Marx, see note 31 in chapter 1, "The Meaning of Zionism," in this volume. Marx's essay "On the Jewish Question" (1844) is a critique of "The Jewish Problem" (1843) by Bruno Bauer (1809–82), a German Protestant philosopher and historian. Marx's essay was a crucial step in his formulation of the concepts of dialectical materialism and scientific socialism. Though he called for Jewish emancipation, Marx's negative and vulgar characterizations of the Jews provided substantial fuel for antisemitism on the left. The essay is also commonly regarded as a prime example of Jewish self-loathing. For excerpts of Bruno's and Marx's essays, see *The Jew in the Modern World: A Documentary History*, ed. Paul Mendes-Flohr and Jehuda Reinharz, 3rd ed. (New York: Oxford University Press, 2011), 297–302.

5. The Narodnaya Volya (Russian for "People's Will") was a radical Russian revolutionary party founded in 1879. The group focused on using political violence to overthrow imperial Russia's tsarist regime. After three bomb-throwing Narodnaya Volya members succeeded in killing Tsar Alexander II (1818–81), the group largely disbanded in the face of mass arrests and widespread popular anti-terrorist sentiment.

6. Russian term for members of the Narodnaya Volya Party.

7. On Leo Tolstoy, see note 4 in chapter 1, "The Meaning of Zionism," in this volume.

8. On Leon Pinsker, see note 3 in chapter 7, "Revisionism," in this volume.

9. The socialist Zionist theoretician Nahman Syrkin (1868–1924), a founder of the Labor Zionist movement, received both a traditional Jewish and secular education as a youth. He joined Hibat Zion early on and also gravitated to clandestine Russian revolutionary activity. In 1888 he left Russia for Berlin, where he earned a doctorate in philosophy. In this period, he became active in Zionist and Hebraist circles and began writ-

ing theoretical essays about socialism and its application to the Jewish question. He also developed friendships with Chaim Weizmann (see note 2 in chapter 2, "Policy and Labor," in this volume), Shmaryahu Levin (1867–1935), Leo Motzkin (1867–1933), and other figures in Berlin who later became significant Zionist leaders. In 1897 Syrkin participated in the First Zionist Congress (Basle, Switzerland) as a representative of the fledgling socialist Zionist movement. In 1898 he published his famous treatise "The Jewish Question and the Jewish Socialist State," outlining a voluntaristic brand of Jewish socialism to be realized in Palestine that inspired many early Zionist pioneers. Though Syrkin was a fierce critic of the diplomatic efforts of Theodor Herzl (see notes 3 and 4 in chapter 2, "Policy and Labor," in this volume) and Europe's bourgeois centrist Zionist groups, he remained an ardent champion of the World Zionist Organization and the Jewish National Fund. A superlative orator, he became a familiar figure at Jewish socialist meetings and the World Zionist Congress. He supported himself by lecturing, writing, and translating; he also founded and edited several short-lived Yiddish and Hebrew journals. In the early 1900s Syrkin spent time in Germany, Austria, Switzerland, and Russia before immigrating to the United States in 1907. Thereafter, he became a leader of the American Poalei Zion Party and a regular contributor to the local Yiddish press. He broke ranks with the party in 1916, when he supported America's entry into World War I. Next, he championed convening the American Jewish Congress in 1918 and was elected to the American Jewish delegation that accompanied Woodrow Wilson to the Versailles Peace Conference in 1919. That year, he also toured Palestine with a socialist Zionist study group that produced a plan for the Yishuv's future development along cooperative lines. He died suddenly in 1924 from a heart attack just as he was planning to immigrate to Palestine with his family.

10. Dov Ber Borochov (1881–1917), the leading Marxist Zionist theoretician of his generation, was a brilliant student of Jewish history, culture, and language as well as economics. Born and raised in Ukraine, he attended a Russian-language gymnasium but like other Russian Jews was denied admittance to university. An autodidact by nature, he pursued a vigorous program of self-education and became fluent in Russian, Yiddish, German, and Hebrew. He initially joined the Russian Social Democratic Party, but his desire to synthesize his Jewish and socialist commitments prompted him in 1901 to establish the Zionist Socialist Workers Union and eventually to join the Poalei Zion Party. In his theoretical formulations, Borochov argued the Jews would be integrated into the class struggle through the revolutionary process and that the formation of a Jewish proletariat in Palestine was the precondition for Jewish national liberation. In the Uganda controversy of 1903, when Theodor Herzl raised the possibility of Jewish colonial settlement in eastern Africa, Borochov aligned himself with the Palestine-oriented faction of "Zion Zionists" in the World Zionist Organization, led by Russian Zionist leader Menahem Mendel Usisshkin (see note 7 in chapter 3, "East and West," in this volume). At this juncture, Borochov became a leading voice of the World Union of Poalei Zion and began to travel and speak extensively across Europe. Meanwhile, he supported himself by lecturing as well as writing, editing, and translating philosophical, political, and historical works. In 1914 he relocated to the United States to conduct party work among American Jewry. He immediately assumed a leading position in the American branch of

Poalei Zion and was a key figure in the mobilization of the American Jewish Congress. In 1917, on the eve of the Russian Revolution, he returned to eastern Europe for a speaking tour but contracted pneumonia and died suddenly in Kiev. His major treatises include "On the Question of Zion and Territory" (1905), "The National Question and the Class Struggle" (1905), and (on behalf of the Poalei Zion Party) "Our Platform" (1906).

11. The socialist Zionist ideologue Aaron David Gordon (1856–1922) was a key figure in the development of the Palestine labor movement. Gordon emigrated in 1904 from Russia to the Yishuv at the age of forty-seven. He eventually settled in the Lower Galilee, where he became the spiritual father of the Second Aliyah pioneers clustered around the Kinneret and Dagania communes. Though he cofounded the Hapoel Hazair Party in 1905 and attended the World Zionist Congress in 1911, Gordon generally eschewed politics. His philosophical writings about the relationship of Jews to the Land of Israel, the challenges of building a modern Jewish socialist society in Palestine, man's quest for spiritual fulfillment, and other topics profoundly influenced the Zionist pioneering movement.

12. A. D. Gordon coined the Hebrew phrase "*dat haavodah*." Literally, the "religion of labor," *avodah* refers to both the traditional Jewish concept of "worship" and the modern Zionist idea of "building" and "labor." The duality inherent in the Hebrew term illustrates the quasi-religious impulse of the Palestine labor movement.

13. Yosef Haim Brenner (1881–1921), a prominent Hebrew writer of the Second Aliyah, fled Russia in 1904 to escape forced conscription during the Russo-Japanese War. In London, he became active in the Poalei Zion Party and published the Hebrew periodical *Hameorer* (The Awakener), which influenced many Second Aliyah pioneers. In 1909 he immigrated to Palestine, where he first worked as a laborer in various Zionist colonies. He continued writing fiction, literary criticism, and social commentary and became a leading intellectual influence of the Palestine labor movement. Brenner's writings are generally concerned with the problematic of modern Jewish identity, the tension between secular and traditional Jewish life, and the hardships of life in Palestine. Among his most famous works is the novel *Shekhol vekishalon* (Breakdown and Bereavement) (1920). In 1921 he was killed by Arab rioters in Jaffa.

14. According to the Hebrew Bible, the Canaanites were one of "seven nations" driven out of the Land of Israel by God and the Israelites (Deut. 7:1; Num. 33:51–54; Josh. 22:9). The biblical narrative identifies the Canaanites as a rival Semitic people, associated with the Phoenicians (Isa. 23:11–12), who lived in the northwest region of ancient Palestine.

15. The Phoenicians (a term meaning "red people," derived from the Greek *phoinikes* in reference to reddish-purple cloth exported by merchants of Sidon and Tyre) inhabited present-day Lebanon, Syria, and Israel starting in the third millennium BCE. From the ninth to sixth centuries BCE the Phoenician empire dominated the Mediterranean region and stretched from Cyprus in the east to northern Africa and the Iberian peninsula in the west. After the empire collapsed, the Phoenicians' major cities and towns were destroyed and the evidence and records of the once-flourishing culture disappeared. See also note 15 in chapter 19, "Go to Nineveh," and note 11 in chapter 24, "The Universalism of the Chosen People," in this volume.

16. See, e.g., B. Nedarim 49b; B. Hullin 54b; T. Avot De-Rabbi Natan 11:1.

17. Timofey M. Bondarev (1820–98), a peasant member of the Russian Christian

sect known as Sabbatarians, conducted a famous correspondence with Leo Tolstoy. Tolstoy credited Bondarev with originating the idea of "bread-labor," which called for the simplification of life, a return to working the soil, and the equality of all members of society. Drawing on scripture (Gen. 3:19) and applying this proposition generally to Russian society, Bondarev asserted "the prime duty of man consisted in reducing his consumption to a minimum and in earning his bread . . . by the labor of his own hands." M. J. de K. Holman, "The Purleigh Colony: Tolstoyan Togetherness in the late 1890s," in *New Essays on Tolstoy*, ed. Malcolm Jones (Cambridge: Cambridge University Press, 1978), 200.

18. A Russian epithet used by Communist revolutionaries, *darmoyed* (literally, "eating my gifts of labor") refers to one who exploits the work and toil of others.

19. The origins of this statement are uncertain. It may possibly be traced to a letter Leo Tolstoy wrote to his wife, Sofiia Andreyevna, dated May 1, 1892, in which he notes he recently met a Swede who visited Yasnaya Polyana. Among other things, Tolstoy writes the man was "a vegetarian who refrained from milk and eggs" and "preferred uncooked food" (*predochitaia vse syroe*). See L. N. Tolstoy, *Polnoe sobranie sochinenii* [Russian for "Complete Collected Works"], vol. 84 (Moscow: Gosudarstvennoe izdatel'svo "Khudozhestvennaia literatura," 1949), 145–146.

20. On George Bernard Shaw, see note 9 in chapter 8, "Notes on Marxism," in this volume.

21. Hebrew for "cantor," the term *hazan* originally was used to describe a functionary in the Temple in ancient Jerusalem, though in modern times it refers to the synagogue's precentor.

22. The *mohel* is the person who performs the rite of circumcision on newborn boys according to traditional Jewish custom.

23. The *shamash* is the synagogue beadle.

24. The "Dionne quintuplets"—Annette, Cecile, Emilie, Marie, and Yvonne—born in Ontario, Canada, on May 28, 1934 to Elzire and Oliva Dionne, were the first identical quintuplets in the West known to have survived infancy. In the wake of an international media frenzy, Ontario's provincial government assumed forced custody of the girls and exploited them as public curiosities for monetary gain. In 1943, the children were returned to their parents after a protracted legal battle. However, as a result of their ordeal, exacerbated subsequently by life with their abusive father, they went on to live shattered and dysfunctional lives. In 1998, after decades of public pressure, the Canadian government awarded a $4 million settlement to three surviving Dionne sisters.

Chapter 19

Source: Hayim Greenberg, "Go to Nineveh," *Jewish Frontier* 9:9 (September 1942): 6–8. The Yiddish version of this essay is dated 1941 and appears in Hayim Greenberg, *Yid un velt* (New York: Yidisher Kemfer, 1953), 19–25.

1. Jonah, one of the twelve minor prophets of the Hebrew Bible, is the central character of the Book of Jonah, which scholars believe was written in the late fifth to early fourth century BCE. The text emphasizes Jonah's career as a reluctant prophet called by

God to undertake a divine mission and preach repentance to the people of the city of Nineveh. Owing to its themes of sinfulness, repentance, and forgiveness, the Book of Jonah is typically recited on Yom Kippur (see note 2 below) as the *haftarah*, a selection from the prophetic books that follow the Torah reading in Sabbath and Jewish holiday worship services.

2. The Jewish holiday Yom Kippur (Day of Atonement), a solemn day of repentance and fasting lasting twenty-four hours, occurs on the tenth day of the month of Tishrei in the Hebrew calendar. It is a day of abstention from all manner of food, drink, work, and sexual relations. The regulations for observing Yom Kippur derive from Leviticus 16: 1–34 (where it is called the "Sabbath of Sabbaths") and 23:26–32 as well as Numbers 29:7–11. According to rabbinic tradition, Yom Kippur marks the day Moses descended from Mount Sinai with the Decalogue and announced the divine pardon of the Israelites for the sin of worshipping the golden calf.

3. Kabbalists are those who practice Kabbalah, the mystical religious stream of traditional Judaism.

4. Nineveh was the ancient capital city of the Assyrian empire. Standing on the eastern bank of the Tigris River (opposite present-day Mosul in Iraq), Nineveh was a major commercial juncture between the Mediterranean Sea and the Indian Ocean. Following a period of internal strife, the city was destroyed in 612 CE by warring subject groups. A few years later, the Assyrian empire as a whole collapsed.

5. The Hebrew terms *midat harakhamim* (measure of goodness) and *midat hadin* (measure of punishment) derive from early rabbinic sources. *Bereshit Rabbah* 12:15, for example, a homiletic text that dates to 400–600 CE, asserts: "The Holy One, blessed be He, said, 'If I create the world with attribute of Mercy, its sins would get the upper hand; if with the attribute of Justice, how could the world exist? Therefore I will create it with both the attribute of Justice and the attribute of Mercy.'" Quoted in Reinhard Neudecker, *The Voice of God on Mount Sinai: Rabbinic Commentaries on Exodus 20:1 in the Light of Sufi and Zen-Buddhist Texts* (Rome: Gregorian and Biblical Press, 2012), 44.

6. Bible scholars suggest that Habakkuk was a Hebrew prophet who lived in c. 612 BCE. He may have prophesied at the time of the siege of Nineveh and is unique among the prophets in that he openly questioned God's wisdom (Hab. 1:3 and 1:13). Except for brief references to him in Habakkuk 1:1 and 3:1 there is no record of Habakkuk's life or activity. In time, rabbinic and Christian commentators generated many tales about Habakkuk.

7. The Chaldeans were a Semitic tribe that migrated to south Babylonia and adopted ancient Babylonian culture. From the tenth to the seventh centuries BCE, the Chaldeans were ruled by the Assyrian empire. Following the death of the Assyrian king Ashurbanipal (668–627 BCE) in 626 BCE the empire was weakened by civil strife and began to implode. Meanwhile, a coalition of Assyria's rivals, including the Chaldeans, attacked the empire. Around 625 BCE the Chaldean leader Nabopolassar (658–605 BCE) established himself as the king of Babylonia. In 612 BCE the Chaldeans and Medes destroyed the city of Nineveh. In 605 BCE, Nabopolassar's son Nebuchadnezzar (634–562 BCE) assumed his father's throne. In Nebuchadnezzar's wars of conquest, he laid siege to ancient Jerusalem and destroyed the First Temple in 587 BCE.

8. Obadiah was a minor prophet that scholars generally believe lived at the turn of the sixth and seventh centuries BCE. The text attributed to Obadiah is the shortest book in the Hebrew Bible and was probably written after the destruction of Jerusalem in 586 BCE. In the text, Obadiah condemns Edom (see note 9 below) for failing to assist Jerusalem in its hour of need.

9. In the ancient period, Edom was the name of the region that extended from the Sinai peninsula in the west to southern tip of the Dead Sea to the Red Sea. According to the Hebrew Bible, the Edomites, enemies of the Israelites, fought King Saul and King David in the decades that spanned the late eleventh and early tenth centuries BCE. Thereafter Edom became a vassal of the Israelite kingdom. By the eighth century BCE Edom had become a dependency of Assyria and later assisted the Babylonians in plundering Jerusalem after the First Temple's destruction in 586 BCE.

10. Nahum the Elkoshite, a minor prophet from Galilee, lived in ancient Palestine in the seventh century BCE. The biblical book attributed to Nahum is essentially a critique of Nineveh. The text was likely written some time between Nineveh's destruction in 612 BCE, which it vividly recounts, and shortly after the conquest of the Egyptian capital of Thebes in 663 BCE, which it also references.

11. According to the Hebrew Bible, Elijah was a prophet in the northern kingdom of Israel who lived during the reign of King Ahab (c. 869–850 BCE). His activity is chronicled in 1 Kings 17:1–2 Kings 2:18. He sought to end the tolerance for cults in Israelite society, particularly the cult of Baalism. Elijah also occupies a special place in Jewish lore and is identified with the several miracles: he supposedly "revived a dead child; divine fire consumed the men who came to arrest him; the Jordan parted to let him through; [and] he was taken to heaven in a flaming chariot." See Robert M. Seltzer, *Jewish People, Jewish Thought: The Jewish Experience in History* (New York: Macmillan, 1980), 78.

12. Sidon originated as an ancient Phoenician coastal city and a key Mediterranean commercial center. It is located south of Beirut in modern-day Lebanon. In the biblical era, Sidon fell successively under the rule of the Assyrian, Babylonian, Egyptian, Greek, and Roman empires. According to 1 Kings 16:31, King Ahab "took as his wife Jezebel daughter of King Ethbaal of the Phoenicians" and thus was the Baal cult introduced into Israelite society. See *The Jewish Study Bible*, ed. Adele Berlin and Marc Zvi Brettler (New York: Oxford University Press, 2004), 711. On the Phoenicians, see also note 15 in chapter 18, "The Myth of Jewish Parasitism," and note 11 in chapter 24, "The Universalism of the Chosen People," in this volume.

13. The First Book of Kings is the last of the four books in the "Former Prophets" section of the Hebrew Bible. It is generally divided into two parts and together they tell the story of Israel and Judah from the decline of King David in the tenth century BCE until the captivity and exile of King Jehoiachin (c. 592–562 BCE).

14. The precise location of Tarshish is unknown. Some scholars believe the biblical narrative refers to a city on the shores of the Red Sea, while others hold it was situated in the Mediterranean basin or the Iberian peninsula.

15. Greenberg appears to be referencing the commentary of Isaac Abravanel (1437–1508), a Portuguese rabbinic sage, who cited the *Mekhilta de-Rabbi Ishmael* (see note 42 in chapter 24, "The Universalism of the Chosen People," in this volume) in his study of

the book of Jonah. Regarding the biblical portion "Bo" (Exod. 10), the *Mekhilta* states Jonah intended to give up his life at sea rather than bring divine wrath upon Israel, for God would see that the gentiles of Nineveh repented while the Jews did not.

16. Jaffa is a port city located south of Tel Aviv in present-day Israel. The city's commercial and naval history dates back to antiquity when it played a significant role as a strategic harbor. The Hebrew Bible mentions Jaffa four times: 2 Chronicles 2:16, Ezra 3:7, Jonah 1:3, and Joshua 19:46.

17. This apparently refers to a commentary by Malbim (the acronym of the Ukrainian rabbinic sage Meir Leibush ben Yehiel Michel Weiser, 1809–79) concerning the biblical phrase "he paid the fare" (Jonah 1:3). Malbim asserts that because the ship on which Jonah sought to flee was not immediately scheduled to set sail, Jonah "paid the fare for a complete contingent of passengers" (which Greenberg translates as "the value of the whole ship") in order that it might depart immediately with as few other people on board as possible.

18. This is apparently a reference to Isaac Abravanel's commentary on Jonah 1:16 (see note 15 above). It seems Greenberg is mistaken about the sequence of events as related by Abravanel, who stresses the idea that after Jonah was thrown overboard and the sea calmed, the sailors vowed to go to Jerusalem, bringing their wives and children with them, offer sacrifices, undertake circumcision, and become Jews.

19. The appellation "God of Abraham, Isaac, and Jacob" originates with Exodus 3:6: "'I am,' He said, 'the God of your father, the God of Abraham, the God of Isaac, and the God of Jacob.'" See Berlin and Brettler, *The Jewish Study Bible*, 110–111. This phrase was later incorporated into the *Amidah* prayer (see note 36 in chapter 13, "Prayer," in this volume) and became a regular feature of traditional Jewish discourse.

20. According to the biblical narrative, this is the second time God commands Jonah to go to Nineveh.

21. Aeschylus (525–456 BCE) was an ancient Greek tragic poet and dramatist who took part in the Greco-Persian Wars (499–449 BCE). More than seventy plays are attributed to him, but only seven have survived intact: *The Persians* (472 BCE), *Seven against Thebes* (467 BCE), *The Suppliants* (463 BCE), and a trilogy titled *The Oresteia* (*Agamemnon*, *The Libation Bearers*, and *The Eumenides*) (458 BCE). He is also generally believed to have written the tragedy *Prometheus Bound* (c. 480–456 BCE). Together with Sophocles and Euripides (see notes 22 and 23 below), Aeschylus was one of the three great tragedians of classical Athens whose work proved foundational to Western theatre.

22. Sophocles (c. 496–406 BCE) was an ancient Greek dramatist and younger rival of Aeschylus. Among Sophocles' innovations to Greek theatre were the addition of a third actor to his plays, painted scenery, and self-contained tragedies rather than trilogies. He is credited with having written over a hundred plays, although only seven survive intact: *Ajax* (c. 450–430 BCE), *Antigone* (c. 441 BCE), *The Women of Trachis* (c. 450–458 BCE), *Oedipus the King* (c. 429 BCE), *Electra* (410 BCE), *Philoctetes* (409 BCE), and *Oedipus at Colonus* (401 BCE).

23. Euripides (c. 480–406 BCE) was an ancient Greek tragic poet who authored over ninety plays, only nineteen of which have survived in complete form. The most important of his extant plays are *Alcestis* (438 BCE), *Medea* (431 BCE), *Hippolytus* (428 BCE), *Andromache* (c. 425 BCE), *Electra* (c. 420 BCE), *Trojan Women* (415 BCE), *Iphigenia in*

Taurus (c. 414 BCE), *Iphigenia in Aulis* (405 BCE), and *Bacche* (405 BCE). In contrast to the work of Aeschylus and Sophocles, Euripides' plays display keen interest in contemporary people and their problems.

24. According to Greek legend, Oedipus was the son of Laius, the king of Thebes, and his wife Jocasta. Sophocles relates the story of Oedipus in the play *Oedipus Rex* (c. 429 BCE). In the latter, Laius is told that his son is destined to kill him and marry Jocasta. Laius attempts to avert fate by sending his son to be raised elsewhere. However, Oedipus unknowingly kills his father in a quarrel and then marries his mother, fulfilling the prophecy.

25. A *golem* (Hebrew and Yiddish for "shapeless mass") is an automaton, especially in human form, unnaturally created through magical means. While a frequent topic in Jewish literature, the term is also used in colloquial Yiddish to mean a foolish person.

26. This quote is from the *Amidah* liturgy (see note 36 in chapter 13, "Prayer," in this volume) used on the holidays of Rosh Hashanah and Yom Kippur. Though the *Amidah* structure is a feature of Jewish worship services generally, its middle section is also altered to represent the basic themes of holidays and festivals, e.g., *Malkhuyot* (kingship), *Zikhronot* (remembrance), and *Shofrot* (rams' horns). See, e.g., *The New Mahzor for Rosh Hashanah and Yom Kippur*, ed. Sidney Greenberg and Jonathan D. Levine (Bridgeport, CT: Media Judaica, 1998), 38.

27. Quoted from the *Neilah* (closing) service, the concluding liturgy of Yom Kippur. The Hebrew sentence reads: "*Atah noten yad lefoshim veminkhah pshutah lekabel shavim*"; see ibid., 773.

28. Quoted from the *Neilah* (closing) service, the concluding liturgy of Yom Kippur. The Hebrew sentence reads: "*Verozeh atah betshuvat reshaim vein atah hafez bemitatam sheneemar: amar elohim hai-ani neum adonai [Yahweh] im ehpoz bemot harashah ki im-beshuv rashah medarko vehayah*"; see ibid., 773–774. The latter combines phrases derived from Isaiah 55:7 and Ezekiel 18:23, 33:11.

Chapter 20

Source: Hayim Greenberg, "*Halakhah* and *Agadah*," in *The Inner Eye: Selected Essays*, vol. 2, ed. Shlomo Katz (New York: Jewish Frontier Association, 1964), 107–118. The Yiddish version of this essay is dated 1943 and appears in Hayim Greenberg, *Yid un velt* (New York: Yidisher Kemfer, 1953), 123–134.

1. Greenberg indicates an earlier version of this essay was published "as an introduction to [Israel Jacob] Schwartz's [1885–1971] Yiddish translation of Bialik's Hebrew essay '*Halakhah* and *Agadah*'" [in *Hebreishe poezye: antologye*, ed. Israel Jacob Schwartz (New York: Yidish Nazionaln Arbeter Farband, 1942)]. See Greenberg, *Yid un welt*, 123.

2. On Haim Nahman Bialik, see note 44 in chapter 1, "The Meaning of Zionism," in this volume.

3. Hebraism, a movement dedicated to the renewal of Hebrew language and literature, arose in Europe in the context of the Haskalah. In the late nineteenth century, Hebraists played a critical role in the rise of Jewish nationalism and Zionism, particularly among eastern European Jewry.

4. Yiddishism was a cultural and linguistic movement that emerged among eastern

European Jews in the latter part of the nineteenth century. Yiddish-speaking Jews from across the social, religious, and political spectrum advocated the perpetuation and preservation of Yiddish culture as a paramount value.

5. The movement for Jewish autonomism developed in eastern Europe in the late nineteenth and early twentieth centuries. Rejecting assimilation and Zionism as answers to the modern Jewish condition, autonomists placed a premium on the notion of Jewish self-rule and the vitality of Yiddish culture. The Russian Jewish historian and political activist Simon Dubnow (1860–1941) articulated an ideological and theoretical intellectual framework for Jewish autonomism.

6. The Yiddish writer Shloyme Zanvl Rappaport (1863–1920), known by the pseudonyms S. Ansky and An-sky, was a popular Russian Jewish author, dramatist, and folklorist. He was active in the Russian socialist movement. His most famous play, *The Dybbuk, or Between Two Worlds* (1914), a seminal Yiddish theatrical work, concerns an evil spirit that possesses a bride on the eve of her wedding.

7. Odessa is a Russian city in Ukraine located on the northwestern shore of the Black Sea. Odessa's Jewish community was founded in 1798 and emerged over time as a major hub of eastern European Jewish culture. In the nineteenth century it was a chief center of both Russo-Jewish assimilation and Jewish literary and nationalist life. The Jewish community of Odessa was obliterated during World War II.

8. Malyi Fontan is a cape located in the city of Odessa that projects into the Gulf of Odessa.

9. In "*Halakhah* and *Agadah* in Jewish History" (1917), Bialik asserts the need for deep knowledge of traditional Jewish sources combined with this-worldly action. His argument weaves together a rich discussion of classical Jewish sources, Western philosophy, and modern Jewish politics. He concludes: "A generation is growing up in an atmosphere of mere phrases and catchwords, and a kind of go-as-you-please Judaism is being created out of the breath of empty words. Our cries are nationalism, revival, literature, creation, Hebrew education, Hebrew thought, Hebrew labor; and all things hang by the gossamer thread of some kind of love—love of the land, love of the language, love of the literature. But what is this love-in-the-air worth? . . . A Judaism all *agadah* is like iron that has been heated but not cooled . . . . Let there be given to us molds in which we can mint our fluid and unformed will into solid coin that will endure. . . . Let us learn to demand more action than speech in the business of life, more *halakhah* than *agadah* in the field of literature." Haim Nahman Bialik, *Revealment and Concealment: Five Essays* (Jerusalem: Ibis, 2000), 86–87.

10. The House of Romanov ruled imperial Russia from 1613 until 1917. At the time of Bialik's remarks, Nicholas II (1868–1918) reigned as tsar. His abdication in 1917 following the Russian Revolution and his execution in 1918 marked the end of the centuries-old family dynasty.

11. Alter Druyanov (1870–1938), a Hebrew author, served as secretary of Odessa's Hibat Zion movement from 1890 to 1905.

12. Sholem Yankev Abramovich (1835–1917), known by the Yiddish pen name Mendele Moykher Sforim (Mendele the Book Seller), was one of the founders of modern Jewish letters. Considered the "grandfather of Yiddish literature," his short stories, novellas,

and translations of biblical psalms and the Pentateuch into Yiddish became foundational texts of the modern Jewish cultural renascence. He also authored the three-volume study *Toldot hatevah* (The Book of Natural History) (1862–73) in Hebrew.

13. Bialik invokes the metaphor of the houses of Hillel and Shammai as a way of poking fun at the differences and disputes that permeated the high-spirited Jewish revolutionary climate at the turn of the nineteenth and twentieth centuries. In the early first century BCE, the rabbinic sages Hillel the Elder (c. 110 BCE–10 CE), who played a seminal role in constructing the Mishnah and Talmud, and Shammai (c. 50 BCE–30 CE) created rival schools of Jewish thought. Though they differed significantly on some matters, they were generally compatible in their views. Their followers, however, sharpened their identities in opposition to each other—the House of Shammai became restrictive; the House of Hillel was more liberal and permissive—and the rivalry between them split the Jewish public arena.

14. Herod the Great (c. 73–74 BCE) was the king of Judea from 37 BCE until his death. Though of Jewish descent, Herod ruled his kingdom through the patronage of Rome. Universally hated by his subjects as a traitor, he destroyed the Hasmonean house and reduced the power of Sanhedrin (see note 50 below). He attempted to generate Jewish support by rebuilding the Holy Temple in Jerusalem; however, this did little to improve his reputation.

15. For example, see B. Eruvin 45a, B. Brakhot 58a, B. Yoma 85b, and B. Sanhedrin 72a.

16. *Tehilim* (Psalms) is the first book of *Ketuvim* (Writings; known in English as Hagiographa), the third and final component of the Hebrew Bible. Psalms contains 150 poetic prayers grouped into five subdivisions, each of which concludes with a benediction of thanksgiving.

17. Solomon ibn Gabirol (c. 1021–58), a highly influential Spanish Jewish poet and neoplatonic philosopher, wrote in Hebrew and Arabic. His ethical treatise *The Improvement of the Moral Qualities* (1045) systematically analyzes man's conception of ethical principles irrespective of religious belief. In *Mekor hayim* (Source of Life), later translated into Latin as the *Fons Vitae* (c. 1050), he discusses the relationship between form and matter. His most famous poem is *Keter malkhut* (The Royal Crown).

18. The Russian poet and prose writer Aleksander Sergeyevich Pushkin's (1799–1837) most famous works include the drama *Boris Gudonov* (1831) and the novel *Eugene Onegin* (1831).

19. Raskolnikov is the name of the protagonist in *Crime and Punishment* (1866), an important novel by the Russian writer Fyodor Dostoyevsky (see note 14 in chapter 8, "Notes on Marxism," in this volume). Possessed of a nihilistic worldview, Raskolnikov commits a heinous murder that results in a profound existential struggle and his alienation from society.

20. In the sixteenth century, Yosef ben Efrayim Karo (1488–1575) wrote several important rabbinic and literary works. He fled the Iberian peninsula owing to the Spanish Inquisition and lived in Edirne, Salonica, and Istanbul before settling in Safed in 1535. His most influential work, the *Shulkhan Arukh* (Prepared Table) (1564), is a comprehensive summation of Jewish practice and emerged as the definitive code of traditional Jewish law.

21. *Modeh ani* (I give thanks) is a prayer recited each morning by traditional Jews upon waking: "I give thanks before you, living and eternal king, for you have mercifully restored my soul within me. Your faithfulness is great."

22. Bialik is referring disdainfully to eastern European Jewish partisans who professed to believe in Zionism but failed to emigrate to Palestine.

23. Greenberg's Russian translation of Bialik's "*Halakhah* and *Agadah* in Jewish History" was published in Soviet Russia in 1920.

24. The Russian novelist and religious philosopher Leo Tolstoy's (1828–1910) "What Is Art?" (1896) explores the relationship of religion, ethics, and moral aesthetics. See also notes 4–5 in chapter 1, "The Meaning of Zionism," in this volume.

25. Maria Andreyeva Gorky (1868–1953), a Russian actress and Communist theatre administrator, was Maxim Gorky's common-law wife.

26. On Maxim Gorky, see note 36 in chapter 1, "The Meaning of Zionism," in this volume.

27. The reference is to Maxim Gorky's "Two Souls" (1915), in which he states: "The Russian seeking-after-God comes from an insufficiency of conviction in the force of reason—from the need of a weak man to find some guiding will outside himself. The turning to mysticism and romantic fantasies is a turning towards stagnation, and is contrary to the interests of a young democracy, poisoning and enfeebling it, giving it a passive attitude towards reality and suggesting doubt in the force of reason. . . . The mind of the ancient east weighs most heavily and murderously on our Russian life and has an influence immeasurably deeper on our psychology than on that of western Europe. . . . We Russians have two souls; one, derived from the wandering Mongol, is that of the dreamer, mystic, idler, believer in fate; the other is the soul of the Slav, which could burn up bravely and clearly, but cannot because of the other." Quoted in Stephen Graham, *Russia in 1916* (New York: Macmillan, 1917), 92–94.

28. See Peter H. Solomon, *Soviet Criminal Justice under Stalin* (Cambridge: Cambridge University Press, 1996), 21–24, especially the issue of "revolutionary consciousness" in the fledgling Soviet court system.

29. The original Yiddish text provides no clue as to the identity of this scholar.

30. Paul the Apostle (c. 5–67 CE), originally a Jew named Saul of Tarsus, is commonly regarded as early Christianity's most significant missionary. The main source of information about his life is the Christian Bible, namely Acts of the Apostles and the Epistles. Paul's conversion to Christianity reportedly occurred on a journey to Damascus, when he was halted by a blinding light and God's voice called out to him. Thereafter, he was known as Paul and with different companions he traveled about the Near East and the Mediterranean basin spreading Christianity, setting up churches, and converting new followers. It is not clear how he died; however, Christian tradition asserts he was persecuted and martyred in Rome by the regime of Roman emperor Nero (c. 37–68 CE).

31. On Ahad Haam, see note 12 in chapter 1, "The Meaning of Zionism," in this volume.

32. The Pharisees were one of two dominant Jewish religious and political sects that arose during the Second Temple period; they were opposed by the Sadducees. The Pharisees emerged as a distinct group around 165 BCE and insisted on the strict observance

of Judaism's doctrines and practices. By the end of the first century CE they represented the religious beliefs and social views of most of Jewish society in ancient Palestine. After the destruction of the Second Temple in 70 CE, the Pharisees' worldview influenced the development of diaspora Jewish traditionalism.

33. *Sotah* (denoting "a woman who has strayed"), derived from the phrase "if any man's wife has gone astray and broken faith with him" (Num. 5:12), is the fifth tractate in the order *Nashim* (Women) of the Mishnah and Talmud. It contains nine chapters and concerns a woman suspected of adultery and the language permitted in testimony and rituals. The text noted here reads: "What is a foolish pietist like?—E.g., a woman is drowning in the river, and he says: 'It is improper for me to look upon her and rescue her'" (B. Sotah 21b).

34. Rabbi Bahya ben Yosef ibn Pakuda (c. 1025), also known as Rabbenu Bahya Hadayan (Hebrew for "our teacher Bahya the judge"), a Jewish philosopher who lived in Zaragosa, Spain, was a student of classical Arabic, Greek, and Roman literature. His ethical treatise *Guide to the Duties of the Heart* (1080) was originally written in Arabic and later translated into Hebrew.

35. Bahya ben Pakuda's *Guide to Duties of the Heart* (1080) distinguishes between "*hovot haevarim*" and "*hovot halev*," Hebrew terms for, respectively, "obligations of the parts of the body" and "obligations of the heart."

36. The source of Greenberg's reference here is uncertain.

37. Rabbi Yehuda Hanasi (135–219 CE) was the patriarch of the Jewish community in second-century Palestine, the nominal head of the Sanhedrin, and the chief redactor of the Mishnah in its final form.

38. Rabbi Elazar ben Pedat (died c. 279 CE) was a second-generation *amora* who emigrated from Babylonia to ancient Palestine. He studied with Rabbi Hanina bar Hama (see note 41 below) and Rabbi Oshaya, a first-generation Palestinian *amora* who lived around 200 CE. He was a disciple of Rabbi Yohanan (see note 42 below), whom he succeeded as head of the Tiberias *yeshivah*.

39. The term "Pharisaic plagues" was used by rabbinic sages in reference to Pharisees who were hypocritical, proud, self-important, and foolish; see, e.g., B. Sotah 22b.

40. In Roman currency, a *denarius* (Latin for "containing ten") (*dinar* in Hebrew) was a small silver coin with a value of ten donkeys. Tractate *Peah* (corner), derived from the phrase "corner of thy field" (Lev. 19:9, 23:22), is the second tractate in Order *Zeraim* (Seeds) of the Mishnah and Talmud. It contains eight chapters pertaining to charitable giving in general, including charity for the poor derived from harvesting fields, vineyards, and orchards.

41. Rabbi Hanina bar Hama (died c. 250 CE), a rabbinic sage whose views are frequently cited in the Babylonian and Jerusalem Talmuds as well as in *midrashim*.

42. Rabbi Yohanan bar Nafkha (died c. 279 CE) was a leading rabbinical scholar. He created the Tiberias *yeshivah*. His teachings are found in both the Babylonian and Jerusalem Talmuds.

43. The precise source of this quotation is unknown; however, the concept is found in B. Sotah 22b.

44. Israel Baal Shem Tov (1669–1761), also known by the acronym the Besht, was

the founder of Hasidism, the Jewish religious and mystical revival movement that first emerged in the Ukraine and swiftly spread to other regions of eastern Europe. His brand of Jewish mysticism gave rise to a new type of spiritual leader called the *zadik* (righteous person) in Hebrew or *rebbe* (teacher) in Yiddish. After the death of Israel Baal Shem Tov, Rabbi Dov Baer Mezhirech (d. 1773) assumed the leadership of the Hasidic movement.

45. Rabbi Eliezer ben Horkenos (Hyrcanus) (c. 40–120 CE), also known in the Talmud as "Rabbi Eliezer" and "Eliezer Hagadol" (Eliezer the Great), was a distinguished disciple of Rabbi Yohanan ben Zakkai (see note 141 in chapter 24, "The Universalism of the Chosen People," in this volume) and later a teacher of Rabbi Akiba (see note 48 below). An eminent *tanna* sage and strict conservative, he established the academy of Lydda (the Greek name of present-day Lod, southeast of Tel Aviv). As a result of his dissent in a dispute concerning purity and impurity in Jewish ritual law, he was accused of heresy by his opponents in the Sanhedrin and excommunicated—a sentence that Rabbi Joshua ben Hananiah revoked after his death (see note 143 in chapter 24, "The Universalism of the Chosen People," in this volume). The exegetical text *Pirkei de-Rabbi Eliezer* (Aramaic for "Chapters of Rabbi Eliezer") bears his name, but the German Jewish scholar Leopold Zunz (see note 65 in chapter 16, "Chosen Peoples," in this volume) demonstrated it was actually written under Islamic rule in the eighth century CE.

46. See *The Talmud Yerushalmi and Graeco-Roman Culture*, vol. 3, ed. Peter Schäfer (Tübingen: J. C. B. Mohr, 2002), 125.

47. Shimon ben Gamliel (Hebrew for "reward of God") (c. 10 BCE–70 CE), also known as Rabban Gamliel and Gamliel the Elder, a leading rabbinic sage of the early first century CE, was a significant *tanna* authority and served as president of the Sanhedrin from 50 to 70 CE. He appears to have been a student of Greek philosophy and natural science. Though inclined to a relatively liberal interpretation of Jewish ritual law, his opinions also stress the importance in upholding the authority of the rabbinic courts and leadership.

48. Rabbi Akiba (Akiva ben Yosef), arguably the most important rabbinic sage of his generation, was a *tanna* who lived in ancient Palestine in the decades that spanned the first and second centuries CE. He played a significant role in systematizing the Mishnah. His approach to hermeneutics and exegetical analysis was critical to the development of the Talmud.

49. Rabbi Tarfon, a mishnaic sage, lived during the period that spanned the destruction of the Second Temple in 70 CE and the failed Bar Kokhba revolt of 135 CE.

50. The Great Sanhedrin of ancient Palestine was a Jewish legal and religious court. It is believed there were two Sanhedrins, one civil and political and the other religious in nature. The Sanhedrins emerged in the period before the destruction of the Second Temple in 70 CE. Along with the patriarchate, this body was abolished by the Roman authorities in c. 425 CE.

51. Tractate *Makot* (Flagellation), derived from the phrase "if the guilty one is to be flogged" (Deut. 25:2), is the fifth tractate in the order *Nezikin* (Damages) of the Mishnah and Talmud. It contains three chapters pertaining to the administration of laws, judicial courts, and punishments.

Chapter 21

Source: Hayim Greenberg, "Bankrupt!" in *The Inner Eye*, vol. 2, ed. Shlomo Katz (New York: Jewish Frontier Association, 1964), 193–202.

1. Greenberg originally delivered this text as an address to a Madison Square Garden audience in New York City on February 12, 1943. A transcript was also published under the title "Bankrupt" in *Der yidisher kemfer* 21:486 (February 12, 1943), 1–3.

2. Casting a sidelong glance at the issue of fratricide, Greenberg is alluding to the Hebrew Bible's suggestion that Cain, who was slain by his brother Abel, was to be avenged sevenfold (Gen. 4:24). On Cain and Abel, see note 2 in chapter 6, "Jew and Arab," in this volume.

3. The status and circumstances of this telegram are unknown. At the time this text was composed, Nazi Germany occupied or controlled much of Europe and was either slaughtering Jews directly or murdering them in camps where they were worked to death.

4. On August 28, 1942, Rabbi Stephen S. Wise (1874–1949), president of the American Jewish Congress, received a telegram—originally transmitted to the US State Department and the British Foreign Office on August 8—from Gerhard Reigner, a Swiss official of the World Jewish Congress. The cable asserted that "in the Fuehrer's Headquarters, a plan has been discussed, and is under consideration, according to which all Jews in countries occupied or controlled by Germany numbering 3½ to 4 million should, after deportation and concentration in the East, be at one blow exterminated, in order to resolve, once and for all the Jewish question in Europe." After noting the potential use of "prussic acid," the cable offered the following caveat: "We transmit this information with all the necessary reservation, as exactitude cannot be confirmed by us. Our informant is reported to have close connexions [*sic*] with the highest German authorities, and his reports are generally reliable. Please inform and consult New York." "New York" was the code word for Wise. This alarming but unconfirmed information languished for twenty-six days in the hands of American and British officials before it reached Wise on Friday, August 28. Next, on Wednesday, September 2, Wise met in Washington with US Undersecretary of State Sumner Welles to discuss the Reigner cable. Welles, who was sympathetic to the plight of European Jewry and later emerged as an important pro-Zionist ally, asked Wise not to publicly reveal the news until it could be fully verified. Thereafter, three months elapsed during which time the Nazi regime murdered hundreds of thousands of Jews. Wise finally broke the story on November 25, 1942, with the blessing of Welles, who told him: "For reasons that you will understand, I cannot give these [facts] to the press, but there is no reason you should not. It might even help if you did."

5. Greenberg is referring to the broad Jewish spectrum of organized opposition in the West to Zionism. In the pre-state era, American Jews who rejected the concept of Jewish sovereignty but supported the continued development of Jewish life in the Yishuv were referred to as "non-Zionists." Meanwhile, those who identified as "anti-Zionists"—either for religious or ideological reasons—flatly opposed all efforts that bolstered the Jewish nationalist cause.

6. At this moment, a stormy debate was underway in American Jewish life about the

advisability, utility, and purpose of perpetuating a special plenary of American Jewry—similar to the American Jewish Congress during World War I (see note 10 below). Only weeks earlier, under the leadership of Henry Monsky (1890–1947), president of the Independent Order of Bnai Brith, an American Jewish Assembly (later renamed the American Jewish Conference) (see note 14 below) had convened in Pittsburgh, Pennsylvania. Monsky proposed to unite American Jewry behind a platform for the rescue of European Jewry, the removal of British restrictions on Jewish immigration to Palestine, and postwar Jewish reconstruction.

7. Orthodox Judaism in North America is a heterogeneous traditionalist religious movement that affirms the divinity of the Hebrew Bible as well as the authority of the homiletic and rabbinic literature produced in the postbiblical and premodern eras. In general, Yosef Karo's *Shulkhan Arukh* (Prepared Table) is a foundational text of Orthodox Judaism (see note 20 in chapter 20, "*Halakhah* and *Agadah,*" in this volume). The numerous Orthodox Jewish subgroups all claim to follow *halakhah* strictly and to observe a set of fixed and unchanging religious practices. In fact, however, Orthodox Jewry is neither unified nor monolithic and, like other branches of Judaism, has evolved over time.

8. Isaac Mayer Wise (see note 11 in chapter 29, "The Future of American Jewry," in this volume) is recognized as the principal founder of the American synagogue movement known as Reform Judaism. In general, the Reform movement posits that Judaism is dynamic and ought to be updated to provide Jews with opportunities for engagement with and participation in the modern world. It views traditional Jewish law as a source of inspiration and the process of selectively emphasizing some aspects of premodern Jewish literature as well as reevaluating and reinterpreting extant Jewish liturgy, rabbinic law, and religious practice to be a legitimate and necessary step in the evolution of contemporary Jewish life and culture.

9. Established in 1906 by affluent American Jews of central European ancestry, the American Jewish Committee was created to defend the rights of Jewish communities around the globe. Though the group originally disparaged Zionism, under New York lawyer Louis Marshall's (1856–1929) leadership it gradually adopted a supportive stance toward the Yishuv in Palestine. In 1929, Marshall and Chaim Weizmann (see note 2 in chapter 2, "Policy and Labor," in this volume) negotiated the expansion of the Jewish Agency so as to include a sizable element of non-Zionist communal leaders and pursue joint fundraising efforts. Despite such cooperation, the AJC remained opposed to the Zionist movement's political aims. Thus, in 1943 it withdrew from the American Jewish Conference when the latter endorsed the creation of a Jewish commonwealth in Palestine. The breach between the AJC and Zionism was not healed until 1947 when the former changed its position and supported the United Nations partition plan.

10. Organized as an independent group in 1922, the American Jewish Congress grew out of a national democratic assembly of American Jewry (called by the same name) convened at the end of World War I. The latter event, which marked the rise of the fledgling American Zionist movement and eastern European Jewish immigrant forces in American Jewish life, emphasized three cardinal issues: minority rights, postwar Jewish reconstruction, and Palestine's development as "a Jewish commonwealth." Following the congress, a

ten-person American Jewish delegation, headed by Julian W. Mack (1866–1943) and including Louis Marshall, Stephen S. Wise, and others, accompanied President Woodrow Wilson to the Paris Peace Conference (see note 5 in chapter 25, "Current Alternatives in Palestine," in this volume). In the 1920s the American Jewish Congress organization (founded by Wise) distinguished itself as a grassroots and pro-Zionist alternative to the American Jewish Committee. In the 1930s it championed a countrywide anti-Nazi economic boycott and fought against British restrictions on Jewish immigration to Palestine.

11. The Independent Order of Bnai Brith (Sons of the covenant), a Jewish fraternal organization founded in New York in 1843, originally modeled itself on the Jewish communal associations characteristic of European Jewry. It swiftly emerged as a regional and then countrywide network of lodges dedicated to social, philanthropic, and political work among American Jews. In response to the notorious Leo Frank case (1913–15), Bnai Brith created the Anti-Defamation League. (In the latter event, Frank, the superintendent of the National Pencil Company in Atlanta, Georgia, was falsely accused of raping and murdering Mary Phagan, a Christian girl employed in the factory. The trial, which showcased regional antisemitism, resulted in Frank's wrongful conviction. Georgia's governor John M. Slaton [1866–1955] commuted Frank's sentence to life imprisonment, assuming he would eventually be proven innocent and set free. Following Slaton's commutation, local riots ensued and white supremacists in Marietta abducted and lynched Frank.) Though formally non-Zionist in the decades that spanned the nineteenth and twentieth centuries, Bnai Brith's support of Jewish communal life in Palestine dated back to the 1860s. After World War I, the organization helped to bolster Zionist settlement throughout the Yishuv. Under Henry Monsky's leadership, Bnai Brith became openly Zionist in its orientation.

12. Founded in 1934 under the leadership of Baruch Charney Vladeck (1886–1938), a prominent American Jewish labor leader, the Jewish Labor Committee represented a broad coalition of left-wing Jewish representatives of the Amalgamated Clothing Workers of America, the Forverts Association, International Ladies' Garment Workers Union, Jewish National Workers' Alliance, Poalei Zion, United Hebrew Trades, and Workmen's Circle (Arbeiter Ring). Among its primary aims was to alert American society to the menace of Nazism and to provide aid to liberal and socialist victims of the Hitler regime. It also sought to educate the general American labor movement about the plight of European Jewry and to raise funds for rescue and relief activity during World War II. Though officially non-Zionist, the JLC gradually moderated its stance and became an overseas partner of the Histadrut trade union in Palestine (and later Israel).

13. In the decades following the American Civil War, a variety of Jewish female social agencies and charitable institutions emerged. In 1893, Hannah G. Solomon (1858–1942) founded the National Council of Jewish Women (NCJW) during a Jewish Women's Congress held as part of the World's Parliament of Religions at the Chicago World's Fair. Thereafter, with the support of social activists Jane Addams (1860–1935) and Lillian Wald (1867–1940), who created, respectively, Chicago's Hull House (1889) and New York's Henry Street Settlement (1893), the NCJW established more than a dozen settlement houses in immigrant neighborhoods across the country, including New York's Clara

De Hirsch Home for Working Girls (1897). In the early decades of the twentieth century, the NCJW emphasized its domestic agenda and worked to improve human welfare through social action and communal service.

14. Greenberg is referring to the first session of the American Jewish Conference, which met in Pittsburgh, Pennsylvania, on January 23–24, 1943, and was attended by seventy-eight representatives of thirty-two major American Jewish organizations. In August 1943, a second meeting of the conference took place in New York City. Following a vigorous debate about a resolution calling for the establishment of a Jewish commonwealth in Palestine, the organization adopted an emphatically pro-Zionist posture. This decision alienated some constituent members, particularly the non-Zionist American Jewish Committee, which subsequently seceded from the conference.

15. Greenberg is likely referring to the American Orthodox group Agudat Israel, established in the United States in the mid-1930s by Rabbi Eliezer Silver (1882–1968), which opposed secular Zionism. The organization's president Jacob Rosenheim (1870–1965) publicly expressed reservations about the American Jewish Conference's pro-Zionist stance.

16. In the late 1930s and early 1940s Stephen S. Wise was arguably American Jewry's preeminent communal leader. Greenberg appears to be singling out Wise and the American Jewish Congress for not having provided unifying leadership of the American Jewish scene in this dark period.

17. On December 8, 1942, President Franklin D. Roosevelt (1882–1945) received a delegation of prominent Jewish community leaders at the White House. The delegates presented FDR with a detailed report of the murder of Europe's Jews and urged "that an American commission be appointed at once to receive and examine all evidence of Nazi barbarities against civilian populations, and to submit that evidence to the bar of public opinion and to the conscience of the world." "Roosevelt Receives Jewish Delegation; Promises Aid to End Nazi Massacres of Jews," *JTA Daily News Bulletin* 9:283 (December 9, 1942), 1, http://pdfs.jta.org/1942/1942-12-09_283.pdf.

18. According to the American media, Roosevelt "gave sympathetic consideration to a proposal of a committee of Jewish organizations in this country, headed by Rabbi Stephen S. Wise, for a United States commission to consider the persecution of the Jews and to act in conjunction with the United Nations in the matter." "Eleven Allies Condemn Nazi War on Jews: United Nations Issue Joint Declaration of Protest on 'Cold-Blooded Extermination,'" *New York Times* (December 18, 1942), 1. Eyewitnesses present at the meeting with the president later reported FDR "did not hesitate to voice his horror." With respect to the issue of Allied retribution against the Nazi regime, he said, "The wheels of the gods grind slowly, but they grind exceedingly small." Quoted in *American Jewish Year Book* 45 (1944): 193–194.

19. The Joint Declaration by Members of the United Nations was issued on December 17, 1942, and signed by the governments of Belgium, Czechoslovakia, Great Britain, Greece, Yugoslavia, Luxembourg, the Netherlands, Norway, Poland, Russia, and the United States and the French Committee of National Liberation. It was announced by British foreign secretary Anthony Eden (see note 20 below).

20. On December 17, 1942, British foreign secretary Anthony Eden (1897–1977) pub-

licly informed the House of Commons of the persecution and mass executions of European Jewry by the Nazi regime. Condemning Nazi Germany's "bestial policy," he described the "conditions of appalling horror and brutality" of Nazi-occupied Europe and asserted that Hitler was implementing his "oft repeated intention to exterminate the Jewish people in Europe." He concluded by reading the Joint Declaration by Members of the United Nations, which stressed the Allies' determination to defeat the Axis powers and pronounced a "solemn resolution to ensure that those responsible for these crimes shall not escape retribution." "Nazi Retribution Widened by Eden: He Warns German People of Responsibility if Cruelties to Jews Are Continued," *New York Times* (December 18, 1942), 10.

21. The Nazis employed this euphemism to refer to areas where European Jews had once lived and from which they were expelled and/or deported and in instances where entire Jewish communities were murdered.

22. The central European region of Galicia (formerly an Austro-Hungarian province) was incorporated into Poland at the conclusion of World War I. In September 1939, when Nazi Germany invaded and conquered Poland, the sizable population of Galician Jewry came under the Hitler regime's direct control. According to a secret report filed by the Nazi SS and police commander responsible for Galicia, mass deportations of the region's Jews began in April 1942, and by June 23, 1943, "all Jewish quarters could be dissolved" with the net result that "the district of Galicia" was now "free of Jews" [*Judenfrei*]. The report also stated that a total of "434,329 Jews had been evacuated up to June 27, 1943," while 21,156 Jews remained in twenty-one camps where many of them would be worked to death or killed outright. See "The Final Report by Katzmann, Commander of the S.S. and Police in the District of Galicia," in *Documents on the Holocaust: Selected Sources on the Destruction of the Jews of Germany and Austria, Poland and the Soviet Union*, ed. Yitzhak Arad, Yisrael Gutman, and Abraham Margaliot (Jerusalem: Yad Vashem, 1981), 335–341.

23. A year earlier, on June 30, 1942, and July 2, 1942, the *New York Times* and *London Daily Telegraph* reported that over one million European Jews had been killed by the Nazis. By February 1943, at the time Greenberg penned this address, unverified and fragmentary data available in the West pushed the total to upward of two million Jewish victims. For example, see the following from the *JTA Daily News Bulletin*: "American Jewry Mourns Today for 2,000,000 Jews Massacred by Nazis in Europe" (December 2, 1942), 1, http://pdfs.jta.org/1942/1942-12-02_277.pdf; "Greatest Calamity in Jewish History, Says Proclamation of Jewish Groups" (December 3, 1942), 1, http://pdfs.jta.org/1942/1942-12-03_278.pdf.

24. It is not clear to whom Greenberg is referring in this instance.

25. In August 1942, a group of American Jewish communal leaders, including representatives of Bnai Brith and the American Jewish Congress, issued a joint statement supporting the Jewish Anti-Fascist Committee in Russia's appeal "for tanks and planes for the Russian army" and "calling for a policy of all-out effort to defeat Hitlerism in 1942 by opening a Western front." Quoted from "Sixty Prominent American Jews Ask for Second Front; Support Moscow Jewish Appeal," *JTA Daily News Bulletin* (August 20, 1942), 2, http://pdfs.jta.org/1942/1942-08–20_192.pdf.

26. Founded in Vilna in 1897, the General Jewish Labor Federation of Lithuania, Poland, and Russia (known as the Bund owing to its Yiddish name, *Algemeyner Yidisher Arbeter Bund in Lite, Poyln un Rusland*) was an eastern European secular Yiddish-speaking Jewish socialist party. In 1898, the Bund helped to establish the Russian Social Democratic Party, and it generally collaborated with the latter (despite political rifts between the Bund and the Bolsheviks). From the outset, the Bund participated in the emerging electoral politics of eastern Europe as a trade union and a political party, and it fought for improvements in working conditions and for popular education. The Bund strongly opposed Zionism, which it considered to be a reactionary force, although it adhered to Yiddishist and autonomist notions of Jewish cultural identity. After the 1905 Revolution, its influence grew and branches were created in other countries outside of eastern Europe including the United States. Following the Russian Civil War (see note 2 in chapter 9, "To a Communist Friend," in this volume), the Bund's branches in the Ukraine and Russia were dissolved and its members merged into the Communist Party. The Polish branch of the Bund was eliminated with the Nazi invasion of eastern Europe in 1939, and although it revived briefly after the war it was forced in 1947 to join the Polish Communist Party. In the United States several Bund activists of eastern European origin played key leadership roles in the Jewish labor movement and the American Socialist Party. In organizational terms, the Bund's American branch never achieved the standing of its eastern European sister movement.

27. See, e.g., "Jewish, Non-Jewish Labor Leaders Protest Execution of Alter, Ehrlich at N.Y. Meeting," *JTA Daily News Bulletin* (March 31, 1943), 3, http://pdfs.jta.org/1943/1943–03–31_075.pdf.

28. See chapter 7, "Revisionism," in this volume.

29. In 1941 Hillel Kook (1915–2001), also known as Peter Bergson, and Benzion Netanyahu (1910–2012) created the Committee for a Jewish Army of Stateless and Palestinian Jews, an activist group that sought to generate support in the United States for the establishment of a Jewish army to fight alongside the Allies. The American and British governments initially rejected the idea. In July 1944, however, the British military created a Jewish Brigade in Palestine with over 5,000 Jewish recruits. The brigade was organized into three infantry units, with the Zionist flag as its official standard.

30. In this period, owing to the efforts of Hillel Kook and Ben Hecht (1894–1964), the Revisionist Party in the United States placed several highly provocative advertisements in major American newspapers. The advertisements are reprinted in David S. Wyman and Rafael Medoff, *A Race against Death: Peter Bergson, America, and the Holocaust* (New York: Free Press, 2002); see plates there between pages 78 and 79.

31. As Greenberg suggests here, the much-anticipated Allied invasion of Europe was still a distant prospect. Indeed, sixteen months elapsed between Greenberg's statement and June 6, 1944, known as D-Day, when over 150,000 Allied troops (half of them American forces) stormed the beaches of Normandy on the coast of northern France in the largest seaborne invasion in history. In the event, codenamed Operation Overlord, the Allies overwhelmed the Nazi forces. D-Day proved to be a major turning point in World War II.

32. See, e.g., "Tortured Jews in Poland Appeal for Retribution against Germans in Allied Countries," *JTA Daily News Bulletin* (March 14, 1943), 1, http://pdfs.jta.org/1943/1943-03-14_060.pdf.

33. The thirty-sixth annual meeting of the American Jewish Committee was held on January 31, 1943 in New York City.

34. See *American Jewish Year Book*, vol. 45 (1944): 212. For the American Jewish Committee's complete statement, see "Statement of Views with Respect to the Present Situation in Jewish Life," in *American Jewish Year Book*, vol. 45 (1944): 608–610.

35. See, e.g., "American Jewish Committee's Statement on Palestine Evokes Zionist Reply," *JTA Daily News Bulletin* (February 17, 1943), 2, http://pdfs.jta.org/1943/1943-02-17_040.pdf.

36. It is unclear who participated in this committee.

37. Stephen S. Wise proposed the American Jewish Congress affiliate with the Interfaith Committee, a national organization he cofounded with the American Protestant leader Henry A. Atkinson. (Atkinson, Reinhold Niebuhr, and other liberal Christian ministers also helped to create the Christian Council on Palestine in 1942.) Subsequently, Conservative rabbi Israel Goldstein (1896–1986), Wise's junior colleague, "led a [rabbinic] delegation that met with the leadership of the Federal Council of Churches" in early January 1943 and discussed "practical steps to rescue Jews trapped in occupied Europe." Israel Goldstein, *My World as a Jew: The Memoirs of Israel Goldstein* (New York: Herzl Press, 1984), 93, 109.

38. This oblique comment likely refers to Israel Goldstein (see note 37 above). In a confidential letter written two days after Greenberg delivered this speech, Goldstein refuted Greenberg's criticism of his participation in American Jewish Congress affairs, charging he did "not ascertain all the facts" and his criticism was "unfair." See letter from Israel Goldstein to Hayim Greenberg, February, 14, 1943, Israel Goldstein Papers, A364/7524, Central Zionist Archives, Jerusalem, Israel. In this period, Conservative rabbi Solomon Goldman (1893–1953) and Reform rabbi James Heller (1892–1971), Goldstein's contemporaries and both visibly active in wartime Zionist and interfaith activity, were also closely associated with Stephen S. Wise and the American Jewish Congress.

39. Full-page advertisements by American citizens of German descent "denouncing Nazi atrocities" appeared in several New York newspapers on December 28, 1942; Goldman, *My World as a Jew*, 109. For example, see the display ad "Christmas Declaration: Men and Women of German Ancestry!": "We, Americans of German descent, raise our voices in denunciation of the Hitler policy of cold-blooded extermination of the Jews of Europe and against the barbarities committed by the Nazis against all other innocent people under their sway," from the *New York Times* (December 28, 1942), 13. A sketch of Jesus wearing a crown of thorns, attributed to the central European Renaissance artist Albrecht Dürer (1471–1528), accompanies the ad.

40. Born in northeastern Poland, Isaac Herzog (1888–1959) emigrated in 1898 to Leeds, England, with his parents and family. He later studied at the Sorbonne in Paris and earned a doctorate at the University of London. Between 1916 and 1919 he was a rabbi in Belfast. From 1922 to 1936, he served as Ireland's chief rabbi. In 1936, he immi-

grated to Palestine, where he succeeded Abraham Isaac Kook (see note 45 in chapter 13, "Prayer," in this volume) as the Yishuv's Ashkenazi chief rabbi, a position he held until his death.

41. See the following items in the *JTA Daily News Bulletin*: "Chief Rabbi Herzog Appeals to Pope to Intercede with Nazis against Deportations of Jews" (August 26, 1942), 3, http://pdfs.jta.org/1942/1942-08-26_197.pdf; "Vatican Assures Chief Rabbi of Palestine of Aid for Jews in Nazi Lands" (February 7, 1943), 1, http://pdfs.jta.org/1943/1943-02-07_031.pdf.

42. American Catholic attitudes to the plight of European Jewry under the Nazi regime varied considerably. At the outset of World War II, most American Catholic leaders and institutions were indifferent to reports of Jewish suffering, which they believed to be wildly exaggerated, and resisted changes in US immigration policy that would have permitted entry to German Jewish refugees. To be sure, many Catholics aligned with Father Charles Coughlin (1891–1979) of Detroit, Michigan, the antisemitic "radio priest" whose weekly broadcasts reached approximately 30 million listeners; his *Social Justice* newspaper had a circulation of 250,000. Coughlin endorsed the Hitler regime's policies, proclaimed the dangers of a worldwide Jewish conspiracy, and denounced the Roosevelt administration as a tool of Wall Street. By contrast, the moderate American Catholic journal *Commonweal*, founded by Michael Williams (1877–1950), warned of the dangers of Catholic indifference to Hitler and Nazi Germany. In a similar vein, Archbishop Wilhelm Mundelein (1872–1939) of Chicago, Cardinal Dennis Dougherty (1865–1951) of Philadelphia, and Cardinal Francis Joseph Spellman (1889–1967) of New York publicly decried the Hitler regime's policies and appealed to the Roosevelt administration to rescue European Jewry. Over time, Amleto Giovanni Cicognani (1883–1973), the Vatican's delegate in Washington, DC, played a critical role in bringing American Jewish concerns to the attention of the Vatican secretary of state Cardinal Luigi Maglione (1877–1944) and Pope Pius XII (Eugenio Maria Giuseppe Giovanni Pacelli, 1876–1958). Among Cicognani's best informed contacts were Stephen S. Wise of the American Jewish Congress and the leaders of the Vaad Hahazalah, notably the American Orthodox rabbis Abraham Kalmanowitz (1891–1964) and Israel Rosenberg (1875–1956) of Brooklyn, NY, Eliezer Silver (1882–1968) of Cincinnati, OH, and Gedaliah Silverstone (1871–1944) of Washington, DC.

43. This appears to be a reference to Nahum Goldmann (1895–1982). In 1936, together with Stephen S. Wise, Goldmann founded the World Jewish Congress. With the outbreak of World War II, Goldmann took up residence in New York City. He spent extended periods of time in Washington, DC, during the war as a representative of the Jewish Agency for Palestine.

44. The American Jewish Congress, acting in concert with the World Jewish Congress and other Jewish organizations, sustained an extensive network of contacts in Latin America. Nahum Goldmann and the American Labor Zionist leader Baruch Zuckerman (1887–1970) were among the organization's prominent emissaries to various Latin American governments and Jewish communities. See the following items in the *JTA Daily News Bulletin*: "Dr. Nahum Goldmann Departs for Latin America" (July 24, 1941), 2, http://

pdfs.jta.org/1941/1941-07-24_188.pdf; "World Jewish Congress Sends Delegate to Central and South America" (April 11, 1943), 4, http://pdfs.jta.org/1943/1943-04-11_084.pdf.

45. Argentina maintained close ties with Nazi Germany—in part, owing to the influence of its sizable German immigrant population—and remained neutral for much of World War II. Meanwhile, throughout the 1930s and 1940s the Argentinian branch of the Nazi Party encouraged local antisemitic activity and supported restrictive immigration legislation aimed at central European Jewish refugees. It is estimated that 20,000–30,000 Jews entered Argentina between 1933 and 1943 by exploiting loopholes in the country's immigration law and using a variety of extralegal means. In time, increasing US pressure prompted Argentina to break relations with Germany and the Axis powers on January 26, 1944. Argentina formally joined the Allied war effort on March 27, 1945.

Chapter 22

Source: Hayim Greenberg, "Concerning Statehood," *Jewish Frontier* 10:5 (May 1943): 23–25.

1. Quoted from a transcribed address by Hayim Greenberg reprinted in *Jewish Frontier* 9:11 (December 1942), 29.

2. Ibid.

3. Lewis Bernstein Namier (1888–1960), a Polish-born Jewish historian, was professor of modern history at the University of Manchester (1931–53) and a Zionist activist. In 1947 he converted to Anglicanism. His major works include *The Structure of Politics at the Accession of George III* (1929), *England in the Age of the American Revolution* (1930), *1848: The Revolution of the Intellectuals* (1946), and the first three volumes of *History of Parliament* (1964).

4. Quoted from Lewis B. Namier, *Conflicts: Studies in Contemporary History* (London: Macmillan, 1942), 163.

5. The Norwegian dramatist and poet Henrik Ibsen (1828–1906) is known for his presentations of natural characters in conflict with their environment and prevailing social customs. Among his most famous works are *Brand* (1866), *Peer Gynt* (1867), *A Doll's House* (1879), *An Enemy of the People* (1882), and *When We Dead Awaken* (1899).

6. Greenberg is apparently referring to a letter from Henrik Ibsen to the Danish Jewish scholar-critic George Morris Cohen Brandes (see note 26 in chapter 3, "East and West," in this volume). See, e.g., *The Correspondence of Henrik Ibsen*, ed. Mary Morison (London: Hodder and Stoughton, 1905), 207–210.

7. The corpus of premodern Jewish literature on the subject of exile is vast. In general, the rabbis of the Talmud asserted that Jewry's exilic status fulfills God's inscrutable plan and should be understood as a sign of divine favor until the messiah appears and Israel is redeemed. See, e.g., B. Sanhedrin 38b.

8. Born in Kishinev in the Pale of Settlement, Mikhail Osipovich Gershenzon (1869–1925), a Russian Jewish scholar of ancient Greek history and literary critic, was an outspoken opponent of Western culture and a champion of the Slavophile movement. Despite tsarist and Soviet anti-Jewish hostility (and irrespective of Gershenzon's antipathy

to the Soviet regime), he became a major figure in Russian letters, serving as president of the Moscow Writers Union and head of the Literary Section of the Soviet Academy of Sciences and Art.

9. On William James, see note 41 in chapter 8, "Notes on Marxism," in this volume.

10. For example, see "Is Life Worth Living?" (1895), in William James, *Pragmatism and Other Writings*, ed. Giles Gunn (New York: Penguin Books, 2000), 219–241.

11. The reference is to the first of the revolutions that took place in Russia in 1917 and brought a provisional government to power, initially under the liberal aristocrat Prince Georgy Yevgenyevich Lvov (1861–1925) and then, after Lvov resigned, under the moderate socialist leader Alexander Kerensky (1881–1970), who was of Jewish ancestry. In October 1917, following months of ineffective governance and social disorder, the Kerensky regime was overthrown by the Bolsheviks under Vladimir Lenin (see note 9 in chapter 6, "Jew and Arab," in this volume), who thereafter established the Soviet dictatorship.

12. According to the Christian Bible, John the Baptist was a forerunner of Jesus who anticipated Jesus' appearance on earth as the messiah. Jesus was supposedly a follower of John and baptized by him. In Christian tradition, John is also identified with the prophecy of Elijah.

13. On Mohandas K. Gandhi, see note 11 in chapter 3, "East and West," and chapter 11, "An Answer to Gandhi," both in this volume.

14. On Baruch Spinoza, see note 50 in chapter 1, "The Meaning of Zionism," in this volume.

15. On Spinoza's argument that civil strife arises from an unequal distribution of land and resources, see Lewis S. Feuer, *Spinoza and the Rise of Liberalism* (New Brunswick, NJ: Transaction Books, 1987), 129–130.

16. Greenberg is referring to the following statement made by Mohandas K. Gandhi: "Zionism in its spiritual sense is a lofty aspiration. By spiritual sense I mean [the Jews] should want to realize the Jerusalem that is within. Zionism meaning reoccupation of Palestine has no attraction for me. I can understand the longing of a Jew to return to Palestine, and he can do so if he can without the help of bayonets, whether his own or those of Britain. In that event he would go to Palestine peacefully and in perfect friendliness with the Arabs. The real Zionism of which I have given you my meaning is the thing to strive for, long for, and die for. Zion lies in one's heart. It is the abode of God. The real Jerusalem is the spiritual Jerusalem. Thus [the Jew] can realize this Zionism in any part of the world." Quoted from "88. 'Interview to *The Jewish Chronicle*,' London (Before October 2, 1931)," reprinted in *The Collected Works of Mahatma Gandhi*, vol. 48 (September 1931–January 1932) (New Delhi: Publications Division, Ministry of Information and Broadcasting, Government of India, 1971), 105–106.

17. On Leo Tolstoy, see note 4 in chapter 1, "The Meaning of Zionism," in this volume.

18. This is apparently a reference to the German Jewish scientist Albert Einstein (see note 3 in chapter 14, "Einstein Discusses Religion," in this volume). On Einstein's complex attitude to Zionism, including his ambivalence about the Yishuv, see Zeev Rosenkranz, *Einstein before Israel: Zionist Icon or Iconoclast?* (Princeton, NJ: Princeton University Press, 2011), 226–228, 256–265.

Chapter 23

Source: Hayim Greenberg, "Notes on the Melting Pot," *Jewish Frontier* 11:4 (April 1944): 26–28.

1. On Karl Kautsky, see note 4 in chapter 17, "Socialism Re-examined," in this volume.

2. Werner Sombart (1863–1941), a German political economist deeply influenced by Karl Marx, was the author of a two-volume work entitled *Modern Capitalism* (1902, 1916). He also wrote three books on the Jews of Europe including *The Jews and Modern Capitalism* (1913) in which he developed an exaggerated theory of the centrality of the Jews in the medieval European economy. The latter caused considerable controversy and provided fodder for antisemitic depictions of the Jews. Sombart himself eventually turned toward German romanticism, becoming an exponent of the authoritarian state and accepting Nazism.

3. In 1883, Karl Kautsky founded the Marxist review *Die Neue Zeit* (The New Times), which he also edited. Published in Zurich, London, Berlin, and Vienna until 1917, it was the official organ of the German Social Democratic Party.

4. On Ahasuerus, see note 58 in chapter 1, "The Meaning of Zionism," in this volume.

5. This excerpt is from Karl Kautsky's treatise *Rasse und Judentum* (Race and Judaism), originally published in German in 1914 and later translated into English and circulated throughout the West. See chapter 12 ("The Last Stages of Judaism") in Karl Kautsky, *Are the Jews a Race?* (New York: International Publishers, 1926), 246–247.

6. On Karl Marx, see note 31 in chapter 1, "The Meaning of Zionism," in this volume.

7. American author Pearl S. Buck (1892–1973) was awarded the Nobel Prize in Literature in 1938. Until 1924 she lived principally in China, where she, her parents, and her first husband were missionaries. She is famous for vivid, compassionate novels about life in China. *The Good Earth* (1931) is considered her most important work.

8. Greenberg is referring to Buck's review of William C. White, *Chinese Jews: A Compilation Relating to the Jews of K'aifeng Fu*, 3 vols. (Toronto: University of Toronto Press, 1942), in which she states: "There was no Jewish problem in China because there the Jews were not hated or discriminated against. So-called 'Jewish qualities' were not there because they did not develop in the easy atmosphere. The Jews were not killed because they ceased to exist as Jews. . . . They became Chinese. Today all that is left of them are a few Jewish names, some relics, a legend or two, the contour of a profile, the seemingly accidental brilliance in an individual mind. It ought to give us food for thought, both Jews and gentiles." See Pearl S. Buck, "Scholars and Travelers," *Asia and the Americas* 43:7 (July 1943): 445.

9. There is evidence that large numbers of Jews settled in China as early as the twelfth century and that sizable Jewish communities existed there well into the thirteenth century, when the Venetian explorer Marco Polo (1254–1324) first recorded their existence in his travel diary. After a long hiatus, significant numbers of Jews again migrated to China in the 1840s when Great Britain obtained control of Hong Kong. In 1937 there were approximately 10,000 Jews living in China. Some 2,000 lived in Shanghai including

native-born Chinese Jews, German Jewish refugees, and immigrants from Russia, India, and Iraq. Between 1938 and 1941 an additional 20,000 German Jewish refugees entered Shanghai. After 1941, the Japanese also deported their Jews to Shanghai, bringing the total number of Jews in China to about 30,000. Most Jews left China after World War II, and many immigrated to North and South America and Israel. A majority of Jews of Russian ancestry, however, including those who had settled in Manchuria and became isolated by the Chinese civil war, were effectively deprived of any option other than the Soviet Union.

10. The American Yiddish daily newspaper *Der forverts* (The Forward) was founded in 1897. In 1902 the Yiddish writer Abe Cahan (1860–1951) became editor-in-chief of the paper, a position which he held for nearly half a century. Under Cahan's leadership the *Forward*—committed to democratic socialism, trade unionism, and the elimination of sweatshops—became a powerful voice for the Jewish labor movement and the most influential Jewish daily in the United States. The paper also emphasized American customs and manners, theatre, arts, literature, and politics. It reached its peak in the 1920s, when the circulation of its local and regional editions as far west as Chicago reached approximately 200,000. After Cahan visited Palestine in 1925, the paper adopted a sympathetic view of Zionism.

11. *Der morgen zhornal* (The Morning Journal) was established in 1901 by the politically conservative and religiously Orthodox publisher Jacob Saferstein (c. 1853–1914). Edited by Peter (Peretz) Wiernik (1865–1936), it was New York City's only morning Yiddish newspaper for many years. It was also unique in its support of the Republican Party in the United States. In 1916 the paper reached a peak circulation of 111,000. During World War I Jacob Fishman (1878–1946) became the paper's editor, and under his direction it adopted a more liberal tone. After World War I the paper's readership steadily declined. In 1928 it merged with the *Yidishe tageblat* (Jewish Daily Paper).

12. *Rahat lukum* (Arabic for "contentment of the throat") refers to a Turkish gel confection made from starch and sugar, often infused with nuts, dates, pistachios and nuts, and flavored with honey, molasses, rosewater, and lemon. Cut from a roll into slices or from a block into cubes, it is a dessert usually served with Turkish coffee.

13. *Tefteli* (Russian for "meatballs"), a dish often prepared with rice, is customarily adapted to different cultural settings by using a variety of meats, spices, and cooking methods.

14. The Greek revolutionary and liberal republican statesman Eleutherios Venizelos (1864–1936) is regarded as the founder of modern Greece. He served as the country's prime minister six times between 1910 and 1933. In 1913, he secured the union of Crete with Greece. He led Greece to victory in the Balkan Wars of 1912–13 and again in World War I on the side of the Allies, resulting in Greece's territorial expansion. In 1924 he established the Greek republic. Thereafter, his anti-royalist and pro-Turkish stance generated political controversy and he was forced to live in exile for extended periods.

15. In the 1930s and 1940s Coca-Cola's marketing strategy emphasized idyllic images of Americans enjoying its product. The artists N. C. Wyeth (1882–1945) and Norman Rockwell (1894–1978) were each hired to produce illustrations with healthy and wholesome looking boys, girls, and young adults drinking bottles of Coke in bucolic settings. The images were widely reproduced and used in magazine ads, billboards, signs, post-

ers, calendars, and household items. See Deborah Solomon, *American Mirror: The Life and Art of Norman Rockwell* (New York: Farrar, Straus and Giroux, 2013), 158. See also Mark Pendergrast, *For God, Country, and Coca-Cola: The Definitive History of the Great American Soft Drink and the Company That Makes It* (New York: Basic Books, 2000), chap. 11.

16. A basilica is a Catholic church that has been granted certain privileges by the Vatican. The basilica originated in antiquity when it was used by the Romans for the purpose of transacting business and legal matters. In the fourth century, Christians began to build edifices for worship modeled on the form of the basilica, including a nave with a semicircular apse, two or four side aisles, a narthex, and a clerestory. These architectural forms became characteristic of Catholic churches throughout Europe.

Chapter 24

Source: The English version of this essay was originally published in three installments: Hayim Greenberg, "The Universalism of the Chosen People," *Jewish Frontier* 12:10 (October 1945): 10–18; *Jewish Frontier* 12:11 (November 1945): 26–34; and *Jewish Frontier* 12:12 (December 1945): 29–37. For the original Yiddish version, published in 1942, see "*Bekhire un bekhore*" (Election and Primogeniture), in Hayim Greenberg, *Yid un velt* (New York: Yidisher Kemfer, 1953), 32–91.

1. On George Bernard Shaw, see note 9 in chapter 8, "Notes on Marxism," in this volume.

2. The Nazi Party had as its goal the creation of a racially homogeneous so-called German "Aryan nation" and viewed "non-Aryans," particularly the Jews, as inferior races who defiled and polluted the German bloodline.

3. The English author and historian H. G. Wells (1866–1946) is best known for his science-fiction works *The Time Machine* (1895), *The Island of Dr. Moreau* (1896), and *The War of the Worlds* (1898). His *Outline of History* (1920) was widely popular and influenced the teaching of Western history in the 1920s and 1930s.

4. Wells used the phrase "gentile fellow-creatures" in a 1939 essay comparing Jewish nationalism and Nazism. He argued that Jews deliberately set themselves apart from gentiles. See H. G. Wells, *Travels of a Republican Radical in Search of Hot Water* (London: Penguin Books, 1939), 56.

5. The Anglican Church, or the Church of England, has been the national church of England since the sixteenth century. It was formed when the English monarch Henry VIII (1491–1547) broke away from the Catholic Church because Pope Clement VII (Giulio di Giuliano de Medici, 1478–1534) would not grant him a divorce.

6. *Kulturkampf*, the German term for "conflict of cultures," derives from the clash in the 1870s and 1880s between the Catholic Church and the German government under Chancellor Otto von Bismarck (1815–98). Bismarck viewed political Catholicism as a threat to a unified German state, and he pursued a series of legislation aimed at intimidating clergy and undermining the Catholic school system. In 1887, fearing the rise of socialism, he rescinded his anti-Catholic measures and reached a modus vivendi with the church.

7. The German phrase "*Blut und Boden*" (Blood and Soil) was a hallmark of Nazi ideology and symbolized the alleged nexus of the German Aryan nation's common bloodline and fatherland. Coined in the late nineteenth century by conservative ultranationalists, the Nazi ideologist Richard Walther Darré (1895–1953) popularized the phrase in *Neuadel aus Blut und Boden* (A New Nobility Based on Blood and Soil) (1930), which proposed a countrywide eugenics policy. Under the Nazi regime, Darré served as Reich Minister of Food and Agriculture (1933–42). The logo of the latter ministry featured the motto "*Blut und Boden*."

8. *The Christian Century*, the flagship publication of mainline American Protestantism, was founded in Chicago in 1884. It is still in print today. Jane Addams (1860–1935), Galen Fisher (1873–1955), and Reinhold Niebuhr (1892–1971) were among its notable contributors in the 1930s and 1940s.

9. According to the Hebrew Bible, Ezra (from the Hebrew for "God helps") (fl. 480–440 BCE) was a priest and a scribe in ancient Israel. Scholars believe the Book of Ezra was written in the fourth and fifth centuries BCE. The narrative, which refers to events that occurred in the fifth century BCE, describes the return of the Judean exiles from Babylonia to ancient Palestine (probably around 459 BCE) and the rebuilding of the Temple in Jerusalem (Ezra 1–6). It credits Ezra with resolving the returnees' legal crises, completing the restoration of the Temple, and reintroducing the Torah in Jerusalem (Ezra 7–10 and Neh. 8).

10. Ezra 9 emphasizes the challenges faced by the returnees upon discovering the prevalence of Jewish-gentile intermarriage in the land. Ezra 10 describes the legal action undertaken by Ezra the priest to resolve the intermarriage crisis. A key passage reads: "Separate yourselves from the people of the land and from the foreign women" (Ezra 10:11); *The Jewish Study Bible*, ed. Adele Berlin and Marc Zvi Brettler (New York: Oxford University Press, 2004), 1686.

11. Tyre, a Phoenician seaport city, was one of the great cities of the ancient world. Built on an island in c. 2800 BCE, it became a hub of the Phoenician mercantile empire that by 1100 BCE included a far-flung colonial network. In the ninth century BCE, Tyrians founded Carthage. In subsequent centuries, Tyre was captured by the Assyrians, Babylonians, Persians, Romans, and Muslims. In 333–332 BCE, during his conquest of the Persian empire, Alexander the Great built a mole connecting the mainland to the island.

12. On Sidon see note 12 in chapter 19, "Go to Nineveh," in this volume.

13. On the Canaanites, see note 14 in chapter 18, "The Myth of Jewish Parasitism," in this volume.

14. *Haazinu* (third-person plural for "Listen"), the first word in Deuteronomy 32, is the name of the Torah portion (Deut. 32:1–52) that is chanted as part of the Sabbath service between the holidays of *Rosh Hashanah* (Jewish New Year) and *Sukkot* (Feast of Tabernacles). *Haazinu* opens with "The Song of Moses" (Deut. 32:1–43), a poem scholars consider a late insertion into the biblical narrative, which reflects on the Israelites' sins, punishment, and the promise of God's redemption.

15. Mount Seir's precise location is unknown. The biblical narrative suggests it formed the southeast border that separated Judah (originally Canaan) from Edom; also the border between southwest Moab and Edom. In modern terms, this equates to the southern tip of

the Dead Sea at the border of Israel and Jordan. See "Map 1: The Land of Israel: Genesis-Deuteronomy," in Berlin and Brettler, *The Jewish Study Bible*.

16. Moab (meaning "from my father") is identified in the Hebrew Bible as Lot's son (Gen. 19:37). According to the biblical narrative, Moab's descendants conquered and inhabited the highlands east of the Dead Sea, from the Arnon River in the north to the Zered River in the south. This area became known as the land of Moab. See "Map 1: The Land of Israel: Genesis-Deuteronomy," in Berlin and Brettler, *The Jewish Study Bible*.

17. The precise location of Ar, a populated region of Moab's kingdom, is unknown. The Hebrew Bible notes it was located near the Arnon River (Num. 21:14–15). Isaiah prophesies the destruction of Ar (Isa. 15:1).

18. On Hillel the Elder, see note 13 in chapter 20, "*Halakhah* and *Agadah*," in this volume. The reference is to a teaching ascribed to Hillel: "That which is hateful to you, do not do to your fellow. That is the whole Torah; the rest is commentary" (B. Shabbat 31a).

19. The Feast of Tabernacles (*Sukkot*), a seven-day Jewish holiday that begins on the fifteenth day of the Hebrew month of Tishrei, commemorates the wandering of the Israelites in the desert following the exodus from Egypt.

20. On Passover, see note 40 in chapter 16, "Chosen Peoples," in this volume.

21. Born in Lithuania, Haim Tchernowitz (1871–1949), known as Rav Zair (Young Rabbi), was a prominent Talmud authority and scholar. In 1897, he founded a *yeshivah* in Odessa that attracted many students from the Russian Jewish intelligentsia including Haim Nahman Bialik (see note 44 in chapter 1, "The Meaning of Zionism," in this volume) and Joseph Klausner (1874–1958), who later became an important historian and professor of Hebrew literature. In 1914, Tchernowitz completed a doctorate at the University of Würzburg. In 1923, at the invitation of Rabbi Stephen S. Wise (see note 4 in chapter 21, "Bankrupt!" in this volume), he immigrated to the United States to become professor of Talmud at the fledgling Jewish Institute of Religion, a liberal pro-Zionist seminary. In 1939, he became the founding editor of the Hebrew monthly *Bizaron* (Stronghold).

22. Haim Tchernowitz's multi-volume work *Toldot hahalakhah* [*The History of the Halakhah*] (New York: Toledoth Ha-Halakhah Publication Committee, 1934) examines the transmission and development of Jewish oral law from its inception to the completion of the Talmud.

23. The Hebrew Bible identifies the "seven nations" as "the Hittites, Girgashites, Amorites, Canaanites, Perizzites, Hivites, and Jebusites" (Gen. 7:1).

24. Though mentioned frequently in the Hebrew Bible, the identity of the Hittites referred to in the biblical text remains a matter of scholarly conjecture. In general, the Bible depicts the Hittites as a distinct group that lived in the mountains outside of Jerusalem (Num. 13:29). Some scholars speculate the Hittites created a powerful federation in Cappadocia c. 1800 BCE, then moved southward through ancient Palestine, and finally came into conflict with Ramses II (c. 1303–1213 BCE) of Egypt. The Hittite kingdom splintered into several neo-Hittite city-states in the late twelfth century BCE.

25. The Girgashites were a tribe that supposedly lived in the area of the Sea of Galilee before being conquered by the Israelites (Josh. 11:1–9, 24:11–13).

26. The Amorites were a nomadic Semitic tribe that dominated Mesopotamia and

ancient Palestine from c. 2000 to 1600 BCE. The Hebrew Bible mentions the Amorites as a specific group defeated by the Israelites (Josh. 11:1–9, 24:11–13). They supposedly lived in the mountains outside of Jerusalem (Num. 13:29) and were eventually enslaved by King Solomon (1 Kgs. 9:20–21).

27. According to the Hebrew Bible, the Perizzites inhabited ancient Palestine before the Israelites and lived in the hill country of Judah (Josh. 17:15). The biblical narrative mentions the Israelite conquest of the Perizzites (Josh. 11:1–9 and 24:11–13) and their enslavement by King Solomon (1 Kgs. 9:20–21).

28. According to the Hebrew Bible, the Hivites lived in the northern region of ancient Palestine (Judg. 3:3) and were one of the seven groups that fell to the Israelite conquest (Josh. 11:1–9 and 24:11–13) and were later enslaved by King Solomon (1 Kgs. 9:20–21). The biblical narrative also relates that a group of Hivites (called the Gibeonites) deceived the prophet Joshua into making a pact with them to prevent their destruction (Josh. 9:3–27).

29. The biblical narrative describes the Jebusites as a Canaanite tribe that dwelled in Jerusalem and the nearby Judean hills (Num. 13:29). They were supposedly one of the seven groups that fell to the Israelite conquest (Josh. 11:1–9, 24:11–13) but could not be driven out of Jerusalem (Josh. 15:63). Though they appear to have been absorbed under Israelite rule (2 Sam. 5:6–7), their descendants were later enslaved by King Solomon (1 Kgs. 9:20–21).

30. Deuteronomy 7:2, which instructs the Israelites to dislodge and defeat the "seven nations," also calls on them to "doom them to destruction: grant them no terms and give them no quarter." See Berlin and Brettler, *The Jewish Study Bible*, 382. However, historical evidence suggests this is not what actually occurred. Rather, Joshua's conquest appears to have been "largely ideological" with many Canaanites communities being won over to "radically new and different religious concepts" rather than physically annihilated. See Jonathan N. Tubb, *Canaanites* (Norman: University of Oklahoma Press, 1998), 109.

31. In the original Hebrew text, this phrase reads: "All the people who were left of the Amorites, Hittites, Perizzites, Hivites, and Jebusites who were not of the Israelite stock." Berlin and Brettler, *The Jewish Study Bible*, 695.

32. It is generally believed that Solomon, the third king of the United Monarchy, ruled ancient Israel from approximately 972 to 931 BCE. His reign was characterized by peace, commercial expansion, and urban development, including the building of the First Temple, on the one hand, and, on the other, extravagance, burdensome taxation, and rising discontent among the northern tribes. Following Solomon's rule, Israelite society split into the northern kingdom of Israel and the southern kingdom of Judah. Rabbinic tradition considers Solomon to be the author of Proverbs, Ecclesiastes, and the Song of Songs.

33. On the Edomites, see note 9 in chapter 19, "Go to Nineveh," in this volume.

34. The citation appears to be an abbreviated form of the biblical text: "You shall not abhor an Edomite, for he is your kinsman. You shall not abhor an Egyptian, for you were a stranger in his land" (Deut. 23:8). See Berlin and Brettler, *The Jewish Study Bible*, 419.

35. According to the Hebrew Bible, the Amalekites were a nomadic people descended from Esau who lived in the Sinai peninsula and the Negev desert. The biblical narrative

describes the Amalekites as the Israelites' perpetual enemies (Exod. 17). In another instance, the text relates that the Amalekites attacked the Israelites during the exodus from Egypt: "Remember what Amalek did to you on your journey, after you left Egypt—how, undeterred by fear of God, he surprised you on the march, when you were famished and weary, and cut down all the stragglers in your rear. . . . Do not forget!" (Deut. 25:17). See Berlin and Brettler, *The Jewish Study Bible*, 423. In time, the name "Amalek" became a metaphor in Jewish tradition for any of the Jewish people's murderous enemies.

36. On Assyria, see note 34 in chapter 13, "Prayer," in this volume.

37. Founded in approximately 2600 BCE on the western bank of the Tigris River (in what is today Iraq), Assur was a religious and political center of the Assyrian Empire. It was also the site of the temple of the god Ashur, Assyria's chief deity.

38. Zephaniah is the name of a minor prophet in the Hebrew Bible. According to the biblical narrative, he was a contemporary of the prophet Jeremiah (c. 626 BCE) and Josiah (c. 648–610 BCE), who reigned as king of Judah from 641 to 610 BCE and fell in a battle with the Egyptians (2 Kgs. 23:29). The Bible relates that Zephaniah denounced the kingdom of Judah for its idolatry and extravagance (Zeph. 1:1–7). He also predicted the return of the Israelites from Babylonian captivity and their salvation (Zeph. 3:11–20).

39. Jeremiah was a major prophet who lived during the seventh and sixth centuries BCE and preached during the reign of King Josiah. He rebuked the Israelites for idolatry (Jer. 11, 13:12–27), openly disagreed with the kingdom of Judah's foreign policy, including resistance to the Babylonian empire (Jer. 38:17–18, 22–23), and called for domestic and religious reform. He was imprisoned but later released by the Babylonians after the fall of Jerusalem in 586 BCE (Jer. 40:2–6). He also prophesied Israel's redemption and salvation (Jer. 33:11).

40. Babylon, a major fortress city, was founded in c. 2350 BCE on the Euphrates River in central Mesopotamia, approximately fifty miles south of present-day Baghdad. As a hub linking the Persian Gulf and the Mediterranean basin, Babylon played a crucial role in the commercial and economic development of the ancient world. In the Hebrew Bible, the Babylonian empire features as a rival power that threatens ancient Israel and ultimately deports the Jews to Babylon between c. 605 and 582 BCE. With the conquest of Babylon in 538 BCE, Cyrus the Great of Persia (c. 600–530 BCE) allowed the Judean exiles to return to the Land of Israel from Babylonian captivity.

41. According to the Hebrew Bible, the ancient city-states of Elam (located in modern-day southern Iraq) were descended from Noah's son Shem. Jeremiah 49 prophesies that Elam was to be dispersed and ultimately redeemed from captivity.

42. The term *mekhilta* (Aramaic for "measure") refers to the rules of scriptural exegesis used in talmudic discourse. Though various texts are known as *mekhiltot* (pl.), the name *Mekhilta* generally refers to a specific compilation of midrashic commentary on the Book of Exodus (known as *Mekhilta de-Rabbi Ishmael*) attributed to Rabbi Ishmael ben Elisha (c. 90–135 CE).

43. *Mekhilta de-Rabbi Ishmael*, Beshalakh 6.

44. On Mount Sinai, see note 46 in chapter 16, "Chosen Peoples," in this volume.

45. *Midrash Eikhah Rabbah* (Interpretation of the Book of Lamentations) is among the oldest extant Jewish homiletic works. It discusses *Eikhah* (literally "how" in Hebrew),

known as Lamentations in English, which appears in *Ketuvim* (Writings). Organized as a series of poems whose initial letters form an alphabetical Hebrew acrostic, *Eikhah* mourns the destruction of Jerusalem in the ancient period.

46. Brakhot (Benedictions) is the first tractate in Order *Zeraim* (Seeds) of the Mishnah and Talmud. It contains nine chapters and concerns the recitation of blessings and prayers.

47. According to the Hebrew Bible, Japheth was one Noah's three sons (Gen. 5:32). He is depicted as the ancestor of various ethnic groups dwelling to the west and north of ancient Israel in the Mediterranean basin (Gen. 10:2–4; 1 Chron. 1:5–7).

48. The Hebrew Bible identifies Shem as Noah's eldest son (Gen. 10:1).

49. Megillah (Scroll) is the tenth tractate in Order *Moed* (Festivals) of the Mishnah and Talmud. It contains four chapters and discusses the significance of the holiday of Purim (see note 216 in chapter 24, "The Universalism of the Chosen People," in this volume), including matters of ritual observance.

50. The *Tanna devei Eliyahu* (Aramaic for "Teachings of the School of Elijah"), a composite homiletic text redacted in the late tenth century CE, is a didactic work that examines the lives and trials of the patriarchs in the Hebrew Bible. It is divided into two parts: Part 1, *Seder Eliyahu Rabbah*, consists of thirty-one chapters; part 2, *Seder Eliyahu Zuta*, consists of fifteen chapters. The text is especially concerned with explaining God's precepts as well as the primacy in Jewish life of prayer, Torah study, and repentance. The work's provenance and authorship is uncertain.

51. See *Tanna Debe Eliyyahu: The Lore of the School of Elijah*, trans. William G. Braude and Israel J. Kapstein (Philadelphia: Jewish Publication Society of America, 1981), 152–153.

52. See *Mekhilta de-Rabbi Ishmael*, Yitro 1:4–5.

53. Shabbat (Sabbath) is the first tractate in Order *Moed* (Festivals) of the Mishnah and Talmud. It contains twenty-four chapters and concerns laws relating to the observance of the Sabbath.

54. Niddah (Excluded) is the seventh tractate in Order *Toharot* (Ritual Purities) of the Mishnah and Talmud. It contains ten chapters and concerns bodily fluids and secretions, women and menstruation, childbirth, and questions of ritual purity.

55. According to the Hebrew Bible, the Temple in ancient Jerusalem included a shrine for the Ark and priestly offerings to God. It served as the primary edifice for the Jews' worship of God until 70 CE. The biblical narrative relates that King Solomon built the First Temple (see note 31 above), which was destroyed in 586 BCE by the Babylonian king Nebuchadnezzar (see note 7 in chapter 19, "Go to Nineveh," in this volume). Cyrus the Great supposedly authorized reconstruction of the temple in 538 BCE and thereafter the Second Temple stood until it was destroyed in 70 CE during the Roman siege of Jerusalem.

56. [Greenberg's footnote:] Prosbul, instituted by Hillel, was a declaration made in court, before the execution of a loan, to the effect that the law of limitation by the entrance of the sabbatical year shall not apply to the loan to be transacted.

57. Yehezkel Kaufmann (1889–1963), an important Jewish philosopher and Hebrew Bible scholar, studied with Haim Tchernowitz (see note 20 above) before completing his

doctorate in 1918 at the University of Berne. In 1920 he emigrated to Palestine. In 1949, he became professor of Bible studies at the Hebrew University of Jerusalem. His first major work, *Golah venekhar* (Exile and Alienation) (1929–32), was published by Haim Nahman Bialik (see note 44 in chapter 1, "The Meaning of Zionism," in this volume). His four-volume magnum opus *Toldot haemunah hayisraelit* (History of the Israelite Religion) (1960) offered a sweeping and innovative approach to the history of Judaism and biblical literature.

58. Yehezkel Kaufmann, *Golah venekhar: mekhkar histori-soziologi besheelat guralo am yisrael meyemei kedem vead hazman hazeh* (Exile and Alienation: A Socio-Historical Study of the Issue of the Fate of the Nation of Israel from Ancient Times to the Present) (Tel Aviv: Dvir, 1929–32), 227.

59. The Russian *mir* system was a form of communal agrarian landholding and limited self-administration sustained by Russian peasants and serfs from the early eighteenth century until the Russian Revolution of 1917. The *mir* assumed responsibility for the upkeep and distribution of arable lands, tax collection, and local commercial undertakings. Though largely inefficient as an economic system, the *mir* satisfied a variety of tsarist Russian provincial and conservative political interests.

60. The Swiss canton system is a confederation of twenty-six member states, each of which is referred to as a "canton." The central political principle of the Swiss Confederation (the official name of the country of Switzerland, with Bern as its de facto capital) is that each canton operates independently insofar as possible and the federal government is restricted to the minimum required for administering the country. Each canton maintains its own local government. The country as a whole is governed by a bicameral legislature comprising the National Council, whose 200 members are elected every four years on a proportional basis, and the Council of States, whose forty-six members (one or two per canton) represent discrete cantons.

61. Gittin (Aramaic for "documents") is the sixth tractate in Order *Nashim* (Women) of the Mishnah and Talmud. It contains nine chapters and primarily concerns the laws of divorce stemming from Deuteronomy 24:1–4.

62. The term *akum*, a Hebrew acronym derived from the phrase "*ovdei kokhavim umazalot*" (worshipper of stars and constellations), is used widely in rabbinic and talmudic literature to identify non-Jews who worship idols. It is also sometimes used as a substitute for the term *goy* (gentile).

63. Philo Judaeus (c. 20 BCE–50 CE), a Hellenized Jewish philosopher who lived in Alexandria, attempted to synthesize Jewish and Greek thought. He asserted Mosaic law to be the foundation of philosophy and believed all beings to have proceeded from and have their unity in the divine Logos. Largely ignored in Jewish tradition, his ideas influenced early Christianity.

64. On Aristotle, see note 2 in chapter 16, "Chosen Peoples," in this volume.

65. See, e.g., Aristotle, *Politics*, Book 1, 1253a, 1254b16–23, 1256b25.

66. On the Sophists, see note 25 in chapter 8, "Notes on Marxism," in this volume.

67. The reference is to a lost didactic political work by Aristotle titled *Huper apoikon* (*Alexander, or On Behalf of Colonists*), which scholars believe Aristotle penned for Alexander the Great to outline the best possible relationship between the city-state (*po-*

lis) and its colonies, including how "appropriate colonists might be chosen and settled in their new home, and how the relationship between the hegemon and the independent *poleis* might work in practice." See Josiah Ober, *Political Dissent in Democratic Athens: Intellectual Critics of Popular Rule* (Princeton, NJ: Princeton University Press, 1998), 348.

68. Alexander the Great (c. 356–323 BCE), one of antiquity's greatest military and romantic figures, reigned as king of Macedon in c. 336–323 BCE. After subduing regional Greek rebellions, he undertook what became the most comprehensive conquest of the ancient world. Between c. 334 and 331 BCE, his victories at the Granicus River, Issus, and Guagamela (Arbela) punctuated his seizure of Asia Minor, peaceful occupation of Egypt, and defeat in 330 BCE of the Persian empire of Daruis III (c. 380–330 BCE). He pursued Darius into Bactria (present-day northern Afghanistan), where the latter was murdered by the satrap Bessus (d. 329 BCE), and advanced to India before his campaign concluded.

69. [Greenberg's footnote:] In this connection we could mention Greek legislation in Pericles' days. It is generally asserted that never in the period of classical antiquity was the democratic ideal so strongly embodied as under Pericles. But it was during that very period that the rule was in effect granting citizenship only to the son of an Athenian man who was a citizen and of an Athenian-born woman. Marriage with non-Athenians was forbidden. [Under Pericles (c. 495–429 BCE), a major Greek statesman, general, and orator, ancient Athens reached its zenith. Athens's golden age began in 448 BCE, after Pericles' aristocratic rival Cimon (c. 510–450 BCE) died and he made peace with Persia, and lasted until the outbreak of the Peloponnesian Wars (431–404 BCE).]

70. The real name of Rabbi Meir Baal Hanes (Illuminator the Miracle Maker), a second-century Jewish sage, who was a disciple of Rabbi Akiba (see note 48 in chapter 20, "*Halakhah* and *Agadah*," in this volume) and member of the Sanhedrin at Usha, may have been Rabbi Nahori or Rabbi Misha. He is sometimes identified in talmudic discourse as "Rabbi Meir." However, according to B. Gittin 4a, owing to political rivalry in the Sanhedrin his contributions to mishnaic discourse were also recorded anonymously. See also note 11 in chapter 27, "Concerning an Israel Constitution," in this volume.

71. Sanhedrin (Assembly) is the fourth tractate in Order *Nezikin* (Damages) of the Mishnah and Talmud. It contains eleven chapters and concerns judges, courts, and judicial procedures.

72. Socrates (see note 56 in chapter 16, "Chosen Peoples," in this volume) and Plato (see note 19 in chapter 9, "To a Communist Friend," in this volume) opposed the Sophists' ideas as superficial and lacking reason and disdained their custom of accepting money from students. In time, the word "sophist" became a pejorative term.

73. The Egyptian pharaoh Akhenaton (c. 1379–1350 BCE), also known as Amenhotep IV, ruled Egypt in c. 1367–1350 BCE. During his reign, he gradually changed the kingdom's religion, introduced the worship of Aten as the supreme deity, and destroyed the temples and images of all other Egyptian gods. Akhenaton's monotheism did not last, however, and after his death the religious practices and worship of the gods antedating his reign were restored.

74. On Sigmund Freud, see note 42 in chapter 8, "Notes on Marxism," in this volume.

75. Greenberg is likely referring to Sigmund Freud's *Moses and Monotheism* (1937). In the latter, Freud upends the Hebrew Bible's account of the Israelites' exodus from Egypt

and offers his own psychoanalytic retelling of the traditional narrative. Freud posits that Moses led a group of Hebrews into exile who rebelled against him, killed him, and united with another monotheistic tribe. Thereafter, Freud suggests, the rebels became remorseful and developed a messianic worldview out of a displaced longing for Moses' return. This archaic memory was presumably transmitted to future generations as part of the Jewish people's cultural inheritance.

76. The pre-Socratics, sixth- and fifth-century BCE Greek philosophers who emerged before Socrates, are generally considered to be Western society's earliest philosophers and scientists. Breaking with the prevailing mythological sensibility of their time, the pre-Socratics created new methods of inquiry that sought to explain nature and the world through rational and critical observation.

77. On Plato, see note 19 in chapter 9, "To a Communist Friend," in this volume.

78. The epic Greek poet Homer (fl. eighth century BCE) is commonly credited as author of two of the oldest extant works of Western literature, *The Iliad* and *The Odyssey*, which were likely composed in the late eighth century BCE. *The Iliad*, set during the Trojan War (c. twelfth or thirteenth century BCE), describes the conflict and struggle between King Agamemnon and the warrior Achilles (see notes 82 and 83 below). *The Odyssey* tells the story of the Greek hero Odysseus's journey home after the fall of Troy.

79. Hesiod (c. 750–650 BCE) was an ancient Greek epic poet. His major works include *The Theogony*, the earliest Greek mythical cosmogony, and *Works and Days*, a didactic text in which the author instructs his irresponsible brother Perses on the art of rural cultivation.

80. See Xenophanes, "Fragments and Commentary," in *The First Philosophers of Greece*, ed. Arthur Fairbanks (London: K. Paul, Trench, Trubner, 1898), 69. Xenophanes, an itinerant Greek poet and philosopher of the late sixth and early fifth centuries BCE, pondered the difference between knowledge and belief, questioned anthropomorphism in Greek mythology, and posited a partial concept of monotheism.

81. On Socrates, see note 56 in chapter 16, "Chosen Peoples," in this volume.

82. Achilles, a Greek mythological hero, is the protagonist of Homer's *Iliad*, wherein he is described as King Agamemnon's greatest soldier in the Trojan War. Post-Homeric legends recount that Achilles' mother Thetis dipped him into the River Styx, which would supposedly make him invulnerable. His foot was not completely submerged in the water, however, and he was later fatally wounded in the heel by an arrow.

83. King Agamemnon of Mycenae (or Argos) is the mythological ruler recounted in Homer's *Iliad* who unites the Greek forces in the Trojan War.

84. In ancient Roman mythology, Jove (also known as "Jupiter") is the supreme deity and king of the gods. He is equivalent to Zeus in Greek mythology.

85. In Greek mythology, Erinyes (pl., Greek for "avengers") are subterranean deities who avenge crimes against the natural order of the universe including crimes against the gods, homicide, undutiful children, and so on. Victims may invoke the curse of Erinys upon their assailants. The Erinyes' wrath can only be assuaged through ritual purification and the performance of a task required for atonement.

86. *The Iliad*, ninth book, verses 86–90.

87. See Adam's response to God in the Hebrew Bible (Gen. 3:12).

88. See the relationship between Cain and God in the Hebrew Bible (Gen. 4:3–9).

89. On Jupiter (Jove), see note 84 above.

90. *The Iliad*, ninth book, verses 270–274.

91. The *Moerae* (Greek for "the fates") are anthropomorphic representations of human destiny in Greek mythology. They are typically depicted as three goddess sisters: Clotho (who spins the thread of human life), Lachesis (who measures the thread), and Atropos (who cuts the thread).

92. In Greek legend, Sarpedon is the son of Zeus, king of the gods. In Homer's *Iliad*, he is depicted as a brave warrior who is slain in the Trojan War by Patroclus.

93. Patroclus is a Greek mythic hero and beloved friend of Achilles. In Homer's *Iliad*, he rallies the Greek forces and pursues the Trojans to the gates of Troy, where he kills Sarpedon. In turn, the Trojan prince Hector kills Patroclus in battle. Achilles subsequently avenges Patroclus's death.

94. Hera, the goddess of women and marriage in Greek mythology, is the vengeful and jealous sister and wife of Zeus, king of the gods.

95. [Greenberg's footnote:] *The Iliad*, fourteenth book, verses 439–461.

96. Greenberg may be alluding to a view espoused by Ludwig Wittgenstein (1889–1951), the Austrian British philosopher of Jewish ancestry: "I cannot bend the happenings of the world to my will; I am completely powerless." See Ludwig Wittgenstein, *Notebooks, 1914–1916*, ed. G. H. von Wright and G. E. M. Anscombe (New York: Harper Brothers, 1961), 73.

97. Zoroaster (known in Greek as "Zarathustra") (c. 628–551 BCE), a Persian religious leader and founder of Zoroastrianism, originally promoted a reformed version of ancient Persian polytheism. Owing to a religious epiphany, Zoroaster broke away from the established belief system and composed the *Yasna haptanghaiti* (Avestan for "Worship in Seven Chapters"), which became the core text of the *Avesta*, Zoroastrianism's collection of sacred literature (see note 7 in chapter 16, "Chosen Peoples," in this volume). Notwithstanding its proto-monotheistic dimensions, Zoroastrianism is rooted in strong dualistic tendencies. According to the *Avesta*, Ormazd (Ahura Mazdah) is chief of the gods of goodness, while Ahriman (Angra Mainyu) is responsible for the gods of evil. An ongoing battle for supremacy between these forces animates the universe, but goodwill eventually triumphs. Zoroastrianism emphasizes the agency of water and fire in its purification rites.

98. Ormazd (also Ahura Mazdah) (Avestan for "wise spirit"), the chief god of Zoroastrianism, is a creative deity and a force for goodness who created the world in order to have a material reality in which to defeat Ahriman.

99. Ahriman (also Angra Mainyu) (Avestan for "destructive spirit") represents evil in Zoroastrianism. Defeated by Ormazd after the world's creation, he lay dormant for 3,000 years before returning and ushering in 3,000 years of renewed conflict that will end when Arihman is finally defeated by Ormazd.

100. On the *Avesta*, see note 7 in chapter 16, "Chosen Peoples," in this volume.

101. On Cyrus the Great, see note 5 in chapter 1, "The Meaning of Zionism," in this volume.

102. In Zoroastrian mythology, Zarvan (Avestan for "old age"), the god of infinite time, is the neutral and remote progenitor of Ormazd and Ahriman.

103. Spenta Armaiti (Avestan for "beneficent devotion"), the daughter and wife of the supreme deity Zarvan, protects the earth and is the goddess of fertility and the dead.

104. Aether (Greek for "incinerate"), a primordial deity in Greek mythology, personifies the celestial air breathed by the Greek gods in contrast to the earth's air breathed by mortals.

105. Mithra (Avestan for "oath") is a Zoroastrian angelic divinity.

106. Gayumart (Avestan for "mortal life"), the first man and ancestor of humankind in Zoroastrianism, plays a key role in Ormazd's battle with Ahriman.

107. [Greenberg's footnote:] Zoroastrianism was unable to defend itself against the invasion of gods from the neighboring countries. Its followers embraced a number of the Semitic gods, proclaiming them the allies of Ormazd in his holy struggle. Anahita, the goddess of springs and streams and all fecundity was, in time, endowed with many of the features of the Babylonian Ishtar and later became the inspiration for temple prostitution. Monotheism eventually captured Persia, not through the further development of the monistic tendencies in Persia's own religion, but through Islam, an offspring of Judaism. The Parsees of India, the only sect in the world today which regards Zoroaster as its prophet, still follow their ancient rituals, and their concept of God is now purely monotheistic.

108. On Maimonides, see note 22 in chapter 4, "Sabbatai Zevi," in this volume.

109. According to Exodus 6:2, *El shadai* is the name by which God was known to Abraham, Isaac, and Jacob.

110. See the discussion of God's name in Moses Maimonides, *The Guide for the Perplexed*, ed. and trans. Michael Friedländer, vol. 1 (London: Trübner, 1885), chap. 63 ("On *Ehyeh*, *Yah*, and *Shaddai*"), 236–241.

111. On Baruch Spinoza, see note 50 in chapter 1, "The Meaning of Zionism," in this volume. In this instance, Greenberg is referring to Spinoza's definition in *Principles of Cartesian Philosophy and Metaphysical Thoughts*: "By *substance* we understand that which, in order to exist, needs only the concurrence of God." He is also alluding to Spinoza's articulation in *Ethics* that "God's existence, like his essence, is an eternal truth." See *Spinoza: Complete Works*, trans. Samuel Shirley, ed. Michael L. Morgan (Indianapolis: Hackett Publishing, 2002), 147, 230.

112. On Jonah see note 1 in chapter 19, "Go to Nineveh," in this volume.

113. On Nineveh see note 4 in chapter 19, "Go to Nineveh," in this volume.

114. The Book of Ruth (c. 950–700 BCE), one of five *megillot* (scrolls) in *Ketuvim* (Writings), the third division of the Hebrew Bible, is traditionally recited in the synagogue during the holiday of Shavuot (Feast of the Weeks). According to the biblical narrative, Ruth, a Moabite woman, refused to desert her Jewish mother-in-law, Naomi, after both women's husbands died. Together they returned to Naomi's home in Bethlehem, where Ruth encountered and married Boaz, a wealthy kinsman. They next experienced a reversal of fortune owing to their fidelity to God and loyalty and commitment to each other. The book concludes by underscoring Ruth's centrality in Jewish tradition as an ancestor of David.

115. According to the Hebrew Bible, David (from the Hebrew "beloved") (c. 1040–970 BCE) was originally a shepherd boy who rose to become the ruler of Judah (c. 1010–1002 BCE) and the second monarch of the united kingdom of Israel (c. 1002–970 BCE).

The biblical narrative celebrates David as one of the Israelites' greatest warriors and rulers as well as for his gifts as a poet and musician. Many biblical psalms are ascribed to him. Under David's reign, the Israelites supposedly transformed from a loose confederation of tribes into a strong nation-state. Jewish tradition prophesies the messiah will be a descendant of the House of David. The Christian Bible maintains that David's lineage proceeds through his son Solomon to a line of kings to Jesus as messiah (Matt. 1:1–17; Luke 3:23–38). Islam considers David a prophet.

116. [Greenberg's footnote:] The blended elements of particularism and universalism and their place in messianic expectations form a fascinating study which cannot be properly dealt with within the framework of this essay. But it should be mentioned, in passing, that according to a remarkable passage in the Talmud, a non-Jew will have a noble place in the "final redemption" (B. Sukkah 52[a]). The sentence "And the Lord showed me four craftsmen" (Zech. 2:3) was interpreted in the name of Rabbi Shimon Hazadik to be a cryptic reference to the four figures destined to play preeminent roles in the drama of the world's redemption: the four "craftsmen" being Messiah ben David, Messiah ben Joseph, the prophet Eliyahu, and the Kohen Zedek—the latter being none other than the same King Melkhizedek of Salem of whom it is told that he brought bread and wine to Abraham as the "priest of the God Most High" and greeted him thus: "Blessed be Abraham of God Most High, Maker of heaven and earth" (Gen. 14:19–20). In his monograph on the Pharisees, Loewe refers to a legend which has it that Abraham was taught the art of almsgiving by King Melkhizedek. [Herbert Martin James Loewe, ed., *Judaism and Christianity: The Contact of Pharasaism with Other Cultures*, vol. 2 (London: Sheldon Press, 1937), 40.]

117. On the Book of Job, see note 57 in chapter 12, "Leon Trotsky," in this volume.

118. Bava Batra (Aramaic for "the last gate") is the third tractate in Order *Nezikin* (Damages) of the Mishnah and Talmud. It contains ten chapters and concerns property law (e.g., real estate, inheritance) and the composition of legal documents.

119. The Hebrew Bible alludes to two locations for Uz, one in or near Aram (in the northern Transjordan area) and the other in or near Edom (see note 9 in chapter 19, "Go to Nineveh," in this volume). Some scholars suggest Uz actually refers to nomadic Arab tribes scattered throughout the region, and this explains why the biblical narrative is not specific. The Book of Job opens with the sentence: "There was a man in the land of Uz named Job" (Job 1:1).

120. The reference is to Eliphaz the Temanite, Bildad the Shuhite, and Zophar the Naamathite (Job 2:11).

121. William Shakespeare's *The Tragedy of Hamlet, Prince of Denmark* (c. 1599–1602) explores the themes of corruption, betrayal, death, indecision, and vengeance.

122. It is useful to note Greenberg wrote this essay in 1945 when, for a brief period, Thailand reverted to the name Siam, the exonym applied to the country until 1939. In 1949, the country (by now a Western-style democratic monarchy) changed its name back to Thailand.

123. Aristotle distinguished between "people either of serious moral stature or of a low sort." See Aristotle, *Poetics*, trans. Joe Sachs (Newburyport, MA: Focus Publishing/R. Pullins, 2006), 1448a, 21.

124. This biblical reference is also frequently translated as "Cushite woman" (Num. 12:1).

125. According to the Hebrew Bible, Aaron, the brother of Moses and his spokesman in Egypt, was the first high priest of the Israelites (Exod. 6:16–20, 7:1–7). Aaron's descendants were high priests and priests.

126. According to the Hebrew Bible, Miriam, the sister of Aaron and Moses, watched over Moses as a baby in the bulrushes (Exod. 2:4) and later led the Israelite women in song at the crossing of the Sea of Reeds (Exod. 15:20–21). She was punished by God for challenging Moses' prophetic authority (Num. 12:1–10) and thereafter disappears from the narrative until the announcement of her death and burial in the wilderness of Zin (Num. 20:1).

127. Haim Tchernowitz, *Toldot hahalakhah*, part 1, 302.

128. According to the Hebrew Bible (Judg. 13–16), Samson (from Hebrew for "man of the sun") the Nazarite, a judge and hero of ancient Israel, owed his strength to a vow he made to God never to cut his hair. Betrayed by Delilah (from Hebrew for "she who weakened"), who shaved his locks, he was abandoned by God and then captured and imprisoned by his enemies, the Philistines. When his hair grew back, he avenged himself by pulling down the Philistine temple and crushing his enemies and himself.

129. Scholars believe the Book of Judges was completed in the sixth century BCE. It is the second book in *Neviim* (Prophets), the second division of the Hebrew Bible, and describes events that supposedly occurred after the death in c. 1380 BCE of Joshua (Hebrew for "Yahweh is salvation"), Moses' successor as leader of the Israelite tribes, and the anointing in c. 1050 BCE of Saul (Hebrew for "prayed for"), the first king of the united Israelite kingdom. The book is not a juridical text, nor is it comprehensive or chronological in scope. In general, the narrative portrays the judges as flawed leaders who deliver the Israelites from oppression, and it serves as a bridge to the establishment of Israel as a united kingdom.

130. Quoted from Samson Raphael Hirsch, *Commentary on the Torah*, trans. Isaac Levy, vol. 1 (London: Judaica Press, 1996), 412.

131. According to the Hebrew Bible, Nehemiah (from the Hebrew for "God is compassionate") was a cupbearer in the court of the Persian king Artaxerxes I (c. 465–424 BCE), from whom he acquired permission to return to Jerusalem and rebuild the city and its fortifications. As the provincial governor of Judah, he spearheaded the repair and rebuilding of the city as well as the Jewish community's purification. Scholars believe the Book of Nehemiah was written in c. 445 BCE and generally consider it part of the unified Ezra-Nehemiah narrative (see also note 9 above).

132. See Ezra 9:1–2 and Nehemiah 13:23–28.

133. [Greenberg's footnote:] Great insight into that period and a keen understanding of the personality of Ezra the Scribe have been shown by the English Protestant historian R. Travers Herford in his meticulous work on the Pharisees.

134. Robert Travers Herford (1860–1950), a British Unitarian minister and scholar of rabbinic literature, devoted his life to researching Judaism in the Second Temple period. He believed Christianity needed what he called ancient Israel's "triumph over paganism" to prevent it from the danger of reverting to pre-monotheistic conceptions of God. See R. Travers Herford, *The Pharisees* (New York: Macmillan, 1924), 229.

135. See, e.g., B. Kidushin 68b; B. Sanhedrin 67a, 90a.

136. This appears to be Greenberg's term.

137. *Bamidbar Rabbah* (Great Numbers) is a classical Jewish homiletic text that contains ancient rabbinic discussions and interpretations of the Book of Numbers.

138. Quoted from the thirteenth blessing of the *Shmoneh Esreh* (Eighteen Benedictions) liturgy. On the latter, also called the *Amidah*, see note 35 in chapter 13, "Prayer," in this volume.

139. In the brief exposition that follows here, Greenberg appears to draw on a rabbinic debate found in B. Brakhot 28a.

140. The Hebrew Bible describes the Ammonites as a tribe descended from Lot (Gen. 19:38) that inhabited the Transjordan region northeast of the Dead Sea. In Deuteronomy 2:19, God commands the Israelites not to harass or enter into battle with the Ammonites while en route to the Promised Land.

141. The academy of higher learning at Yavneh, a city in the southern coastal plan of ancient Palestine (south of present-day Jaffa), was founded by Rabbi Yohanan ben Zakkai (c. 30–90 CE), a disciple of Hillel the Elder and a major *tanna* sage of the Second Temple period. Inclined to pacifism, Ben Zakkai negotiated with Vespasian (c. 9–79 CE), then a Roman general, during the first Jewish-Roman War (66–73 CE), to transfer besieged Jerusalem's rabbinic sages to Yavneh and there establish a center of Jewish learning. After the destruction of the temple, Yavneh functioned as the seat of the Sanhedrin.

142. On Rabbi Shimon ben Gamliel, see note 47 in chapter 20, "*Halakhah* and *Agadah*," in this volume.

143. Rabbi Joshua ben Hananiah, a disciple of Yohanan ben Zakkai and leading *tanna* sage of first half-century CE, was a strong proponent of the teachings of Hillel the Elder. He played a critical role in rabbinic Judaism's transition in the decades that spanned the Second Temple's destruction and its aftermath. He was also one of Rabbi Akiba's teachers (see note 48 in chapter 20, "*Halakhah* and *Agadah*," in this volume).

144. The reign of Sennacherib (c. 705–681 BCE), king of Assyria, was marked by rebellion, warfare, and efforts at imperial expansion. In c. 701 BCE, he defeated the Egyptians and thereafter destroyed the northern kingdom of Israel. He sought to conquer Jerusalem, but instead exacted only tribute. The Hebrew Bible describes Sennacherib's military campaign in 2 Kings 18–19. It is uncertain whether his army was destroyed at this juncture or later. In c. 689 CE, he waged war against Babylonia and destroyed the city of Babylon. He later built a palace at Nineveh. He was murdered, possibly by his sons, one of whom, Esarhaddon (c. 681–669 BCE), succeeded him.

145. *Bereshit Rabbah* (Great Genesis), likely written in the fourth century CE, is a midrashic compilation of ancient rabbinic interpretations concerning the Book of Genesis.

146. Yevamot, in English "levirate marriage" (from the Hebrew word *yavam*, for "husband's brother"), derives its name from Deuteronomy 25:5–10, which obliges a brother to marry the widow of his childless deceased brother. It is the first tractate in Order *Nashim* (Women) of the Mishnah and Talmud. It contains sixteen chapters that examine levirate marriages and laws pertaining to women in general.

147. Shimon ben Lakish (c. 200–275 CE), known as Resh Lakish, was a prominent *amora* sage who lived in ancient Palestine during the period of Roman rule. In talmudic

literature, he is often paired with his brother-in-law and rival Rabbi Yohanan bar Nafha (d. c. 279 CE).

148. Greenberg is referring to an assertion by Resh Lakish in *Tanhuma Lekh Lekha*, a midrashic text concerning Genesis 12:1–17:27: "The proselyte is dearer to God than Israel when it was gathered together at the foot of Mount Sinai. Without the miracles of revelation [i.e., lightning, thunder, sound of the heavenly shofar, etc.], the Jews would not have accepted the Torah. But a proselyte, without seeing a single miracle, has embraced God and accepted the Kingdom of Heaven [of his own free will]. Could anyone love God more than him?" Quoted in Ronald L. Eisenberg, *Essential Figures in the Talmud* (Lanham, MD: Rowman & Littlefield, 2013), 239.

149. *Hagigah* (Festival Offering) is the twelfth and final tractate in Order *Moed* (Festivals) of the Mishnah and Talmud. It concerns the three pilgrimage festivals of Passover, Shavuot, and Sukkot.

150. *Bava Kama* (Aramaic for "the first gate") is the first tractate in Order *Nezikin* (Damages) of the Mishnah and Talmud. It contains ten chapters and concerns damages, torts, compensation, and other civil matters.

151. [Greenberg's footnote:] One of the very few, if not the only limitation of the convert's rights. Since we have already employed several analogies with the America of today to clarify a point, may we be permitted to remind the reader that although the naturalized citizen in this country enjoys the same rights as does the native American, there is one office to which he cannot aspire, that of the president—the "high priest" of the republic.

152. According to the Hebrew Bible, Sisera was a captain in the Canaanite army of King Jabin of Hazor. Under the leadership of Deborah the prophet, Sisera was defeated in battle by the Israelite army commander Barak, and he was subsequently killed by Yael, wife of Heber the Kenite. See Judges 4:4–22.

153. *Menahot* (Aramaic for "grain offerings") is the second tractate in Order *Kodashim* (Holy Things) of the Mishnah and Talmud. It contains thirteen chapters and concerns the sacrificial rules of the Temple with regard to offerings in the Temple of grain, showbread, and drinks.

154. Rabbi Shemayah, a convert to Judaism who became a rabbinic sage, leader of the Pharisees, and president of the Sanhedrin in the first century BCE, was supposedly a descendant of Sennacherib. In talmudic literature, he is paired with Rabbi Avtalyon (B. Pesakhim 66a).

155. Rabbi Avtalyon, who is paired in talmudic literature with Rabbi Shemayah, lived during the first century BCE. He supposedly converted to Judaism (B. Yoma 71b) and rose to become a Pharisee leader and vice president of the Sanhedrin under Shemayah.

156. Yoma (Aramaic for "day") is the fifth tractate in Order *Moed* (Festivals) of the Mishnah and Talmud. It contains eight chapters and describes the Temple services of the high priest on Yom Kippur (Day of Atonement), other regulations involving the observance of Yom Kippur, and the significance generally of atonement.

157. American definitions of racial purity as well as anti-miscegenation codes and laws date back to the colonial era. Before the Civil War (1860–65), most states defined "Negro" as someone of one-eighth African ancestry. In the decades that spanned the turn of

the nineteenth and twentieth centuries, the latter fraction was changed to one-sixteenth, one-thirty-second, and even "any visible admixture of African blood." See "Laws, 1877," in Franklin Johnson, *The Development of State Legislation Concerning the Free Negro* (New York: Arbor Press, 1918), 164. In 1924, Virginia passed the "Racial Integrity Act," which defined race according to the "one-drop rule," created a new state apparatus enforcing racial segregation, and criminalized interracial marriage. The law remained in effect until 1967 when the US Supreme Court overturned it in the landmark case Loving v. Virginia 388 US 1.

158. Born in the city of Carthage in North Africa, Tertullian (c. 150–230), a convert to Christianity, became a significant Latin-writing Christian theologian and early Church Father. He authored numerous Christian apologetic and theological texts, including some of the first expositions of Trinitarianism. In time, he broke away from the mainstream of the church and became a Montanist. His apologetic works include the anti-Jewish polemic *Adversus Iudaeos* (Greek for "Against the Jews"), constructed in the form of a fictional dispute between a Christian and a Jewish proselyte, wherein the former refutes the idea of God's exclusive covenant with Israel.

159. St. Cyprian (c. 200–258 BCE), formerly a trial lawyer and teacher of rhetoric named Thascius, was a convert to Christianity who was influenced by Tertullian's theological writings. In 248 CE, he became bishop of Carthage. Uncompromising in his theological views, including his attitude to paganism and heresy, Cyprian led the early Christians of North Africa during a period of Roman persecution. He was executed by Roman authorities and thereafter became Africa's first bishop-martyr. His writings are reprinted in Jacques-Paul Migne's *Patrologia Latina*, vols. 3–4 (1841–55, 1862–65), an extensive collection of early Latin Christian texts.

160. The Synod at Elvira, a meeting of ecclesiastical authorities held in the southern Spanish city of Elvira (present-day Granada), convened in c. 305–306 CE. Followed in 314 CE by the Synod of Arles and the Synod of Ancyra, the gathering considered moral issues, the influence of paganism on early Christians, and the perceived need to impose order and discipline in the church. It also strengthened the authority of the bishops within the church hierarchy.

161. The provenance of the material quoted here is uncertain. It appears, however, that Greenberg is referring to canon laws 15, 16, and 17 promulgated by the Synod at Elvira. For the original Latin text of the laws, see Charles Joseph von Hefele, *A History of the Christian Councils, from the Original Documents, to the Close of the Council of Nicaea, A.D. 325*, trans. William R. Clark (Edinburgh: T. & T. Clark, 1871), 144.

162. In 306 CE, upon the death of his father Constantius I (c. 250–306 CE), Constantine the Great (c. 272–337 CE) was proclaimed caesar of the western Roman empire. Following the death in 310 of Galerius (c. 260–311 CE), which left four contestants for the imperial office, Constantine and Licinius (c. 262–325 CE) united forces against Maxentius (c. 278–312 CE) and Maximinus II (c. 270–313 CE), whom they defeated in 312 at Milvian. At this juncture, Constantine, who was attracted to Christianity, claimed to see a vision of a flaming cross in the sky heralding his impending victory at the Milivan Bridge. Thereafter, Constantine and Licinus ruled as co-emperors, respectively, in the west and east, and in 313 they proclaimed toleration for Christianity in the Edict of

Milan. In 324, they struggled with each other for control of the empire as a whole. After Licinius was defeated in 324 at the Battle of Chrysopolis, he was executed by Constantine, who now became sole emperor. In 325, Constantine convened the Council of Nicaea, the first ecumenical council representing all of Christendom, and in 330 he moved the empire's capital to Constantinople. Despite Constantine's sympathy to Christianity, he was only baptized on his deathbed. At his death, he divided the empire among his sons, Constantine II (c. 316–340 CE), Constantius II (c. 317–361 CE), and Constans I (c. 323–350 CE), who subsequently warred with each other.

163. Valentinian II (c. 371–392 CE) reigned jointly with his half-brother Gratian (c. 359–383 CE) over the Roman empire until 383 CE when Gratian, betrayed by the Roman general Maximus (c. 335–388 CE), was killed and Maximus usurped his throne. Subsequently, Valentinian was expelled in 387 by Maximus, but restored to power in 388. Though he was never baptized, Valentinian was strongly influenced by St. Ambrose of Milan (c. 340–397 CE) and was sympathetic to early Christianity. His murder is usually attributed to the treachery of the Roman general Flavius Arbogast (d. c. 394 CE).

164. Theodosius I (c. 346–395 CE) was born in Spain and served in the Roman imperial army. Chosen in 379 CE by Gratian to rule the eastern empire as co-emperor, he secured an advantageous peace with the Visigoths. When Valentinian II was deposed in 387, Theodosius invaded Italy, slew Maximus, and restored Valentinian to the throne. He again entered Italy after Valentinian was strangled, presumably by Arbogast, who in 392 installed the puppet rule of Flavius Eugenius (d. c. 394 CE) and defeated the forces of Arbogast and Eugenius in battle. During his reign, Theodosius outlawed paganism and in 382 convened the First Council of Constantinople, an ecumenical gathering that produced the Nicene Creed, a significant liturgical profession of Christian faith.

165. Arcadius (c. 377–408 CE), emperor of the eastern region of the Roman empire in 395–408 CE, was the son and successor of Theodosius I in 395 CE. Possessed of a pious orthodox Christian worldview, he fiercely opposed paganism but was generally a weak ruler.

166. The provenance of this quoted material is unknown. It appears, however, Greenberg is referring to language in the *Theodosian Code*. See "*6.31 Theodosian Code 3.7.2* (Valentinian II, Thedosius, [with Arcadius], 388 CE)," reprinted in *Jewish Life and Thought among Greeks and Romans: Primary Readings*, ed. Louis H. Feldman and Meyer Reinhold (Minneapolis: Augsburg Fortress, 1996), 134–135.

167. Born in Florence, Italy, Maffeo Barberini (1568–1644 CE) was educated by Jesuits, became a classical scholar, and in 1589 earned a doctorate of law from the University of Pisa. Initially a papal legate in the court of King Henry IV (1553–1610) of France, he rose through the church ranks to become a cardinal in 1606. As Pope Urban VIII (1623–44), he used military force to expand the Catholic Church's territory and became a lavish patron of the arts. He also founded the Barberini Library, later part of the Vatican Library.

168. Pope Clement XI (1700–1721), born Giovanni Francesco Albani (1649–1721), was a scholarly theologian. As pope, he first favored Philip V (1683–1746) for the Spanish throne in the War of Spanish Succession (1701–14), but later was forced to recognize Philip's rival, Charles VI (1685–1740) of Habsburg. When the war concluded in 1713,

the ensuing Treaty of Utrecht diminished much of the Vatican's previous authority. He sought to stamp out Jansenism, a dissident French Catholic theological movement, and in the bull *Unigenitus* (1713) he condemned several Jansenist doctrines as heresy.

169. Prospero Lambertini (1675–1758), born in Bologna, was renowned for his learning. He became a cardinal in 1728. As Pope Benedict XIV (1740–58), he actively promoted reforming the education of priests, patronizing art, and advancing scholarship. He sought to protect traditional Catholic rites from the influence of practices followed by converts in China and India in two key papal bulls, *Ex quo singulari* (1742) and *Omnium sollicitudinum* (1744).

170. Ambrogio Damiano Achille Ratti (1857–1939) was an accomplished Italian scholar, librarian, and priest. Before becoming pope, he was legate and then nuncio to Poland and archbishop of Milan. As Pope Pius XI (1922–39), he presided over the formalization in 1929 of the Vatican as a sovereign state. He sought to preserve relations with the world's powers through a series of concordats. Though he condemned fascism and antisemitism, along with Nazism and Communism, he was primarily concerned with the encouragement of religious devotion. In the papal bull *Quadragesimo anno* (1931), recalling Pope Leo XIII's (see note 171 below) plea four decades earlier, he criticized laissez-faire capitalism and urged social reform. In 1937, he issued the encyclical *Mit brennender Sorge* (German for "With burning concern"), which criticized Nazism and defended baptized Jewish converts to Christianity.

171. Italian-born Gioacchino Pecci (1810–1903) studied diplomacy and law as a young man. In 1836, he earned a doctorate in theology. After serving as a prelate to Pope Gregory XVI (1765–1846), he was ordained a priest in 1837. In 1843, he was appointed nuncio to Belgium. Rising through the ranks of the church, in 1878 he became Pope Leo XIII. As pope, he sought to adapt the Catholic Church to the emerging modern world. He issued the encyclical *Immortale Dei* (1885), which charted a course for Catholics to participate as citizens in democratic societies. He later issued *Rerum novarum* (1891), which outlined Catholic social ideals, pointing to the abuses of capitalism, the deficiencies of socialism, and encouraging the creation of trade unions. Addressing intellectual attacks on the church, he embraced the philosophy of St. Thomas Aquinas, and supported the creation of the neo-Thomistic Institute of Philosophy at Louvain. He also opened up the Vatican archives to scholars.

172. The "Westminster Confession of Faith" originated in 1646 as a Calvinist doctrinal statement reflecting the beliefs of the Church of England. In subsequent decades, it was revised and adapted by English Congregationalists, Baptists, and Presbyterians to suit their respective doctrinal sensibilities and cathecisms. Though heavily influenced by Calvinist covenantalism and Puritanism, the Westminster Confession includes dogmatic features common to much of the non-Catholic Christian world. Its vehement anti-Catholic stance is anchored in the assertion that the pope is the antichrist and that the Catholic mass is a form of idolatry. Additionally, heresy is to be punished severely and marriage with non-Christians is expressly forbidden.

173. The Jews were banished from England in 1290 CE by King Edward I (1239–1307 CE). The expulsion decree remained in effect until 1657 when the Lord Protector Oliver Cromwell (1599–1658) permitted the Jews to return.

174. On "9 Will II c.3 (1697): An Act to Prevent Protestants Intermarrying with Papists," see William Edward Hartpole Lecky, *A History of Ireland in the Eighteenth Century*, vol. 1 (London: Longmans, Green and Company, 1892), 387–388.

175. See "12 Geo I c.3 (1725): An Act to Prevent Marriages by Degraded Clergymen and Popish Priests" and "Geo II c.13 (1745): An Act for Annulling all Marriages to Celebrate by Any Popish Priest between Protestant and Protestant, or between Protestant and Papist," ibid., 390–394.

176. In 1772, the rabbinic court of Vilna, fearful of the region's fledgling Hasidic movement, pronounced a *herem* (ban) on all Hasidic Jews. With the approval of Rabbi Elijah ben Shlomo (1720–97), the community's chief sage known as the Gaon of Vilna (an honorific title), all Orthodox Jews, who now assumed the mantle of *Mitnagdim* (opponents), were commanded "to destroy and expunge" the Hasidim and not to intermarry with them. See "The Excommunication of the *Hasidim* (April 1772)," in *The Jew in the Modern World: A Documentary History*, ed. Paul Mendes-Flohr and Jehuda Reinharz, 3rd ed. (New York: Oxford University Press, 2011), 368–369.

177. Hasidim (pious ones) is the term for the followers of Hasidism, the Jewish religious and mystical movement founded by Israel Baal Shem Tov (see note 44 in chapter 20, "*Halakhah* and *Agadah,*" in this volume). Hasidism originated in the Ukraine and swiftly spread to other parts of eastern Europe.

178. The source of this epithet is unknown.

179. "Pharisaic Judaism," also called "Pharisaic-rabbinic Judaism" or "biblical-talmudic Judaism," refers to the prevailing belief systems that cohered as the legal, liturgical, and ritual basis of rabbinic Judaism following the destruction of the Second Temple in 70 CE and which evolved, over time, to become the normative framework of traditional Judaism.

180. Rabbi Ashi (c. 352–427 CE), a prominent *amora* sage and head of the Sura Academy in ancient Babylon, is considered the first redactor of the Babylonian Talmud.

181. Avodah Zarah (Foreign Worship) is the eighth tractate in Order *Nezikin* (Damages) of the Mishnah and Talmud. It contains five chapters and concerns idolatry and the legal framework governing Jewish life in gentile communities.

182. Rabbi Helbo, a third-century CE *amora* sage, studied at the Sura Academy and then emigrated to ancient Palestine.

183. On Herod, see note 14 in chapter 20, "*Halakhah* and *Agadah,*" in this volume.

184. Idumea is the Latin term for Edom (see note 9 in chapter 19, "Go to Nineveh," in this volume).

185. Yohanan Horkenos (John Hyrcanus) (c. 164–104 BCE), a high priest of Judea, reigned as the Hasmonean ethnarch in c. 134–104 BCE. Much of his rule was spent engaged in warfare. In 134, he negotiated a truce with Antiochus VII Sidetes (c. 159–129 BCE) of the Seleucid Empire and thereafter fought with Antiochus against the Parthians. After Antiochus was killed in battle in 129, Horkenos undertook an extended military campaign that resulted in consolidating and expanding his territory as well as achieving complete independence for the Judean state. In the process, he conquered Edom and forced its inhabitants to embrace Judaism. To preserve his autonomy, Horkenos established peaceful relations with the Roman empire and Ptolemaic kingdom. His domestic policies were marked by the separation of civil and religious affairs.

186. On Rabbi Eliezer ben Horkenos, see note 45 in chapter 20, "*Halakhah* and *Agadah*," in this volume.

187. According to Hebrew Bible, the Cutheans inhabited the ancient Babylonian city of Cuthah (today an archeological site in central Iraq), located on the bank of the Upper Euphrates, and converted to Judaism out of fear when attacked by lions. Cuthah is also described as the center of the Mesopotamian cult of the solar deity Nergal, which supposedly spread to Samaria when Cuthean colonists settled there. See 2 Kings 17:24–41. The rabbinic sages of the Talmud debated whether the Cutheans were genuine converts (B. Kidushin 75b) or should be considered idolaters (B. Hullin 6a). In the end, the Cutheans were defined as gentiles and barred from marrying Israelites (B. Ketubot 29a). Traditional rabbinic sources frequently use the terms "Cuthean" and "Samaritan" interchangeably.

188. According to the Hebrew Bible, the Samaritans were an ethnoreligious group descended from the Israelite tribes of Ephraim and Manasseh. After the Israelite conquest of Canaan in c. 1200 BCE, Joshua supposedly allocated the central areas of ancient Palestine to the latter tribes (see Joshua 16, 17:7–10). In time, the region as a whole became known as Samaria. In c. 722 BCE, Samaria was conquered during the Assyrian siege of the northern kingdom of Israel and its inhabitants were deported (1 Chron. 5:26). Thereafter, despite the self-perception of the Samaritan returnees, the Israelite leadership rejected the Samaritans' claims about their Jewish identity and ostracized them (Ezra 4:1–24). Traditional rabbinic sources frequently use the terms "Samaritan" and "Cuthean" interchangeably. A small Samaritan community, with its own language, customs, and rites, continues to exist in Israel today.

189. On Shimon ben Gamliel, see note 47 in chapter 20, "*Halakhah* and *Agadah*," in this volume.

190. Kidushin (Betrothal) is the seventh tractate in Order *Nashim* (Women) of the Mishnah and Talmud. It contains four chapters and concerns matrimonial matters.

191. On Hillel and Shammai, see note 13 in chapter 20, "*Halakhah* and *Agadah*," in this volume.

192. Greenberg is referring to a talmudic discussion about three gentiles who wished to convert to Judaism; see B. Shabbat 31a. Hillel's precept is commonly known as "the golden rule."

193. The Hebrew Bible's Noahide Laws (see note 194 below) derive from Genesis 2:16, 9:9. Jewish tradition interprets the latter in a variety of exegetical discussions. See, e.g., B. Sanhedrin 56a, B. Avodah Zarah 8:4, and *Bereshit Rabbah* 34:8.

194. [Greenberg's footnote:] Noah and his descendants (that is, all mankind) were commanded by God to refrain from: 1) idolatry, 2) adultery and incest, 3) murder, 4) blasphemy, 5) robbery, 6) injustice toward one's neighbor, and 7) eating flesh cut from a live animal ([B.] Sanhedrin [56, 60]). All non-Jews who observe these seven laws will partake of salvation and share in the bliss of the world to come ([B.] Sanhedrin [105]). [The Dutch jurist, philosopher, and theologian] Hugo Grotius [1583–1645], incidentally, makes the Noahide commandments serve as the foundation for his theory of "Natural Law" and for a system of international jurisprudence to be based on it.

195. The phrase *yerei elohim* (ones who fear God) is from Genesis 22:12.

196. On the Baal Shem Tov, see note 44 in chapter 20, "*Halakhah* and *Agadah*," in this volume.

197. Ukrainian-born Rabbi Nahman of Breslov (present-day Wroclaw, Poland) (1772–1811), also known as "Nahman Breslover" and "Nahman from Uman," a great-grandson of the Baal Shem Tov, was the founder of the Breslover Hasidic movement. A charismatic rabbinic leader, he emphasized the importance of private unstructured prayer and silent meditation in Judaism, a concept he called *hitbodedut* (self-seclusion), which was inspired by the noted kabbalist Rabbi Isaac Luria's (1534–72) notion of the *ein sof* (without end), the infinite God who withdraws into himself and leaves only an empty space. In 1798, he traveled to Palestine and visited the Hasidic communities of Safed, Tiberias, and Haifa. Shortly after his return to eastern Europe, he settled in the town of Zlatopol, where he encountered Rabbi Aryeh Leib of Shpola (1725–1811) and the two men became rivals. In 1802, Rabbi Nahman relocated to Breslov (from which the Breslover movement gets its name), and in 1810 he moved to the Ukrainian city of Uman. His legacy is preserved in *Likutei mohoran* (Hebrew acronym for "Collected Teachings of Our Teacher, Rabbi Nahman") (1808–15), a three-volume collection edited by his disciples.

198. Menahem Mendel Morgenstern (1787–1859), also known as the *Kotzker Rebbe* (Yiddish for "Rabbi of Kotzk"), hailed from a traditional Jewish household in Lublin, Poland. Known for his emphasis on intellectual rigor, elitism, and modesty, he favored rationalism and disapproved of Hasidism's ecstatic features. He is considered the forerunner of the Gerrer Hasidic dynasty, founded in the Polish town of Gora Kalwaria (known in Yiddish as "Ger") by his disciple and brother-in-law Rabbi Yizhak Meir Alter (1798–1866). Two important volumes of his teachings, published posthumously, are *Emet veemunah* (Truth and Faith) (1940) and *Amud haemet* (The Pillar of Truth) (1956).

199. Born in Babylon, Eleazer ben Pedat (d. c. 279 CE) was an *amora* sage associated with the academy of Tiberias established by Rabbi Yohanan bar Nafha.

200. *Pesakhim* (Passovers) is the third tractate of Order *Moed* (Festivals) in the Mishnah and the Talmud. It contains ten chapters and primarily concerns the laws for observing the Passover holiday.

201. For example, see Rabbi Moses Maimonides' opinion in the *Mishneh Torah*, "Laws of Prohibited Sexual Relations," 13:1–4.

202. Ananias (Hananya in Hebrew) (c. 15 BCE–30 CE), a Jewish merchant and proselytizer, was reportedly instrumental in the conversion to Judaism of numerous gentile inhabitants of the ancient port city of Charax (located in present-day Kuwait). His most prominent converts supposedly included King Izates I of Adiabene and members of his court (see note 204 below).

203. Born in Jerusalem to a prominent Jewish family, the Roman historian Flavius Josephus (c. 37–100 CE) (originally Yosef ben Matityahu) is considered a chief representative of Hellenistic Jewish culture. During the first Jewish revolt (66–73 CE) in ancient Palestine, he commanded the Jewish rebel forces in the Galilee. In 67 CE, he was captured by Vespasian's (c. 9–79 CE) army, taken hostage, and became an interpreter for the Roman authorities. In 69, Vespasian granted Josephus his freedom. He subsequently defected, was granted Roman citizenship, and served as an interpreter and advisor to Titus (c. 39–81 CE). His works *The Jewish War* (c. 75 CE) and *Antiquities of the Jews* (c. 94 CE)

endure as important albeit partisan sources for understanding Jewish history in the first and second centuries CE.

204. According to classical Jewish sources, notably Josephus and the Talmud, King Izates I (c. 1–55 CE) of Adiabene, a vassal state of the Persian empire, converted to Judaism when he ascended to the throne. Initially, owing to objections from his counselors, including Anianas, who feared Izates might fall into disfavor among his subjects who had not yet adopted Judaism, Izates delayed his circumcision. He was supposedly circumcised in due course. For a useful analysis of this story and its place in the history of Jewish proselytism, see Louis H. Feldman, *Jew and Gentile in the Ancient World: Attitudes and Interactions from Alexander to Justinian* (Princeton, NJ: Princeton University Press, 1993), 328–331.

205. Quoted in Flavius Josephus, *Antiquities of the Jews* (c. 94 CE), 20.41.

206. On Paul, see note 30 in chapter 20, "*Halakhah* and *Agadah*," in this volume.

207. In the first and second centuries CE, even as early Christianity strove to establish an identity and worldview separate from Judaism, it nonetheless considered itself an updated extension of the Abrahamic tradition and the ultimate expression of God's covenant with Moses and the Israelites. There emerged a widespread public debate among Christianity's adherents concerning the preservation, modification, and rejection of various notions, rituals, and practices stemming from Judaism. In addition to the issues of Sabbath observance and dietary laws, the rite of male circumcision proved highly controversial. The Acts of the Apostles records that so-called Jewish Christians pressured new converts to Christianity to sustain the practice, which they considered essential to attaining divine salvation (Acts 15:1). In 49 CE when the Council of Jerusalem (also known as the Apostolic Conference), the first meeting of Christian authorities, convened to discuss and resolve such matters (Acts 15:2–29), Paul, in contrast to the Jewish Christian mindset, argued against the need to sustain traditional Jewish rites (Gal. 3:6–18). His assertion that circumcision was an anachronistic externality signaled an important step in the universalization of Christianity's message. Meanwhile, however, the practice of circumcision persisted, prompting concern about the threat to Christianity of Judaizers and recidivism (see Paul's "Epistle to the Galatians"). In time, the influence of Jewish Christians waned and Christianity as a whole came to regard itself as liberated from Judaism's cultic rites and practices.

208. The concept *kidush hashem* (sanctification of the name) stems from a rabbinic interpretation of the Hebrew Bible's requirements related to the sanctity of God's divine name (e.g., Lev. 22:32; Num. 20:12; Deut. 32:51). In the late Second Temple period, this idea became part of traditional Jewish discourse in reference to persecuted and martyred Jews.

209. The Hebrew Bible identifies Hamor (Hebrew for "donkey") the Hivite as Shekhem's father, from whom Jacob purchased a parcel of land on his return to Canaan from Paddan-aram (Gen. 33:18–19).

210. See *Tanna Debe Eliyyahu*, 27 ("*Ish shalom*"), trans. Braude and Kapstein, 358–359.

211. Ibid.

212. According to the Hebrew Bible, Hamor's son Shekhem is the rapist of Dinah, the daughter of the patriarch Jacob and his first wife, Leah. See Genesis 34.

213. Greenberg is presumably alluding to God's attitude to the vulnerability of converts; see, e.g., Exodus 22:20 and Deuteronomy 23:17.

214. *Shekhinah* (dwelling) refers to God's divine presence in the world. In kabbalistic thought, the term denotes God's feminine dimension.

215. In rabbinic Judaism, the term *ger* refers to a genuine proselyte while *ger toshav* (resident alien) is the term used to describe non-Jews who dwell among the Israelites, adhere to some but not all of the Jewish laws (e.g., disavowal of idolatry), and enjoy many privileges of life in the community. The latter is also referred to as a "proselyte of the gate." Converts through fear are contemptuously called *gerei ariyot* (lion proselytes) in reference to 2 Kings 17:25–26.

216. Some Talmud sages use the Hebrew terms *ger zedek* (righteous proselyte) and *ger emet* (true proselyte), on the one hand, and *ger toshav* (resident proselyte), on the other, to distinguish between converts to Judaism animated, respectively, by pious and utilitarian motives. Converts out of fear are also called *gerei Mordekhai ve-Ester* in reference to Esther ("Hadassah" in Hebrew) and Mordekhai, two key figures in the Hebrew Bible's Book of Esther. In the latter, Esther, the Jewish wife of the Persian king Ahasuerus (presumably Xerxes I, c. 486–465 BCE) and his queen, together with her cousin Mordekhai thwart a plan by the king's wicked vizier, Haman, to exterminate the Jews. The victory of the Jews over Haman is celebrated in the holiday of Purim (Hebrew for "lots"), at which time the Book of Esther is chanted publicly.

217. Rabbi Nehemiah (c. 150 CE), a *tanna* sage, is presumed to be the author of *Mishnat hamidot* (Treatise of Measures), the earliest known Hebrew study of geometry. The work, an examination of the basic unit of measurement in the Hebrew Bible, "seems to have exercised great influence [through the Persian mathematician and astronomer Muhammad ibn Musa al-Khwarizmi (c. 780–850 CE)] on Arabian and indirectly on European mathematical science." See Salo W. Baron, *A Social and Religious History of the Jews: Ancient Times*, vol. 2, 2nd ed. (New York: Columbia University Press, 1952), 307.

218. See Rabbi Eliezer's cautionary statement about a warning in the Torah against the "wronging of a proselyte in thirty-six, or as others say, in forty-six places" (B. Bava Mezia 59b).

219. *Bava Mezia* (Aramaic for "the middle gate") is the second tractate in Order *Nezikin* (Damages) in the Mishnah and Talmud. It contains ten chapters and primarily concerns civil matters, property law, and usury.

220. Rabbi Yossi ben Halafta (c. 135 CE), a *tanna* sage of Babylonian origin, migrated to Usha in the western Galilee, where the Sanhedrin was intermittently located. He was a disciple of Rabbi Akiba and later a mentor of Rabbi Hanasi.

221. The allusion to the war of Gog and Magog derives from the Hebrew Bible, Ezekiel 38–39. The latter articulates an apocalyptic vision of God's victory over the nations that threaten the Israel's existence. The biblical account underscores Israel's salvation and God's supremacy. Some scholars identify Gyges of Lydia (c. 680–652 BCE) in western Anatolia (present-day Turkey) as the historical inspiration for the biblical figure Gog, ruler of the land of Magog.

222. According to the Hebrew Bible, Hagar (from the Hebrew for "flight"), Sarah's Egyptian handmaid, was given by Sarah to the patriarch Abraham as a concubine and be-

came pregnant. Owing to Sarah's jealousy, Hagar fled to the desert where she was saved through divine intervention, and she subsequently returned to bear a son named Ishmael. See Genesis 16.

223. The *Yalkut Shimoni* (Compilation of Simeon) is a thirteenth-century medieval collection of systematic interpretations of verses from the whole of the Hebrew Bible and more than four dozen midrashic works, only some of which remain extant. Like other premodern Jewish pseudepigrapha, the authorship of *Yalkut Shimoni* is a matter of speculation.

224. "*Bo*" (come, go) is the first word of God's command to Moses in Exodus 10:1. It is also the title of the fifteenth (*parashah*) of fifty-four sections (pl., *parashiyot*) of the annual Torah reading cycle. *Bo* (Exod. 10:1–13:16) describes the last three plagues inflicted on Egypt in the Exodus story (locusts, darkness, and slaying of the first-born), the Israelites' departure from Egypt, and the laws for observing the Passover holiday and donning phylacteries (*tefilin*).

225. Saadia Gaon (Saadia ben Yosef al-Fayumi) (c. 882–942 CE), an eminent Egyptian rabbi, philosopher, and scholar, was head of the academy at Sura. He opposed Karaism, the anti-rabbinic literalist movement that flourished in the Islamic world from the tenth to twelfth centuries, and was a chief exponent of the Babylonian *yeshivot*. Regarded as a founder of Judeo-Arabic literature, he translated the Hebrew Bible and other works into Arabic. His *Sefer haemunot vehadeot* (Book of Doctrines and Beliefs) (c. 933), originally published in Arabic, is a defense of rabbinic Judaism and the first systematic treatment of the dogmas of Judaism.

226. This statement appears to be Greenberg's paraphrase of Saadia Gaon's commentary. See, e.g., Saadia ben Yosef Hagaon, *Beliefs and Opinions*, trans. Sam Rosenblatt (New Haven, CT: Yale University Press, 1948), 99–100, 181–182, 241–242, 323–324.

227. On Yehuda ben Shmuel Halevi, see note 62 in chapter 16, "Chosen Peoples," in this volume.

228. Maimonides' statement is quoted at length in Philip Birnbaum, *A Book of Jewish Concepts* (New York: Hebrew Publishing Company, 1964), 133.

229. Ibid., 132.

230. On Henri Bergson, see note 57 in chapter 1, "The Meaning of Zionism," in this volume.

231. Eschatos (from the Greek for "last") is a metaphorical concept integral to many religions signifying the end of the temporal world, humanity's salvation by God, and the start of the messianic age.

232. The phrase "Thou hast chosen us" (*atah bahartanu*) is a central benediction in traditional Jewish liturgy. See Joseph Heinemann, *Prayer in the Talmud: Forms and Patterns*, trans. Richard Sarason (Berlin: De Gruyter, 1977), 31–32, 55.

Chapter 25

Source: Hayim Greenberg, "Current Alternatives in Palestine," *Jewish Frontier* 14:7 (July 1947): 5–12.

1. On the Jewish Agency for Palestine, see note 13 in chapter 10, "Open Letter to the Third International," in this volume.

2. Created in May 1947 at the request of the British government, the UN Special Committee on Palestine (UNSCOP) was charged with investigating the causes of unrest in Palestine and proposing a solution to the Arab-Jewish conflict. UNSCOP representatives traveled to Palestine, where they conducted an investigation and sought to gather testimony from both the Jewish Agency and its Arab counterpart, known as the Arab Higher Committee, as well as local Jewish and Arab groups. The Arab Higher Committee boycotted UNSCOP's efforts and insisted on outright recognition of Palestinian Arab claims on the basis of the UN charter. In September 1947, UNSCOP issued a report which recommended termination of the British mandate and the partition of Palestine into separate Jewish and Arab states.

3. The designation Jewish "National Home" was first employed by the Balfour Declaration in November 1917: "His Majesty's Government view with favour the establishment in Palestine of a national home for the Jewish people, and will use their best endeavours to facilitate the achievement of this object, it being clearly understood that nothing shall be done which may prejudice the civil and religious rights of existing non-Jewish communities in Palestine, or the rights and political status enjoyed by Jews in any other country." While the declaration was a critical turning point in the fortunes of the Zionist movement, the language used by the British was sufficiently vague so as to leave the Yishuv's future status uncertain.

4. On the concept of a bi-nationalism, see the discussion of Brit Shalom in note 10 in chapter 7, "Revisionism," in this volume.

5. On the League of Nations, see note 28 in chapter 11, "An Answer to Gandhi," in this volume.

6. The Charter of the United Nations, the foundational agreement of the United Nations, was signed by fifty-one nations in 1945 following the conclusion of World War II and ratified by the five permanent members of the Security Council (China, France, Great Britain, the Soviet Union, and the United States). Among its provisions, the charter placed all territorial mandates created by the defunct League of Nations under temporary UN custodianship pending future negotiations and agreements.

7. Greenberg is alluding to the conservative and isolationist turn of the United States after World War I, including America's detachment from international affairs and the League of Nations during the interwar period.

8. The United Nations initially comprised only member states that declared war against the Axis Powers by March 1, 1945. The countries Greenberg lists here, including several that fought with the Allies, joined the UN in the mid-1950s.

9. Following World War I, the League of Nations declared South-West Africa, formerly a German colony, to be a mandate territory under the control of the Union of South Africa (the historic predecessor of the present-day Republic of South Africa). For all practical purposes, it remained a British province until 1966 when it became independent and was renamed Namibia.

10. In May 1942 Zionist leaders from North America, Europe, and Palestine, headed by David Ben-Gurion (see note 20 in chapter 27, "Concerning an Israel Constitution," in this volume), chairman of the Jewish Agency for Palestine, and Chaim Weizmann (see note 2 in chapter 2, "Policy and Labor," in this volume), president of the World Zionist Organization, met at New York City's Biltmore Hotel in lieu of a wartime Zionist

congress. The conference, which proved to be mostly symbolic, anticipated the Zionist movement's postwar aims of gaining control over Jewish immigration to Palestine and the eventual founding of a Jewish commonwealth. Although some Biltmore Conference participants cautioned against such demands, including a minority who espoused a bi-nationalist position, Ben-Gurion asserted the need for the mandate to be transferred to the Jewish Agency. In the event, the combative center-left coalition grouped around Ben-Gurion and American Zionist leader Abba Hillel Silver (1893–1963) prevailed. Their vision was embodied in the Biltmore Program, which became the basis for subsequent Zionist claims and public relations efforts.

11. The Biltmore Program is reprinted in *The Jew in the Modern World: A Documentary History*, ed. Paul Mendes-Flohr and Jehuda Reinharz, 3rd ed. (New York: Oxford University Press, 2011), 698–699.

12. The Emirate of Transjordan became a British protectorate after World War I. In 1946, the country gained its independence and was renamed the Hashemite Kingdom of Jordan.

13. The Bantu are native peoples who inhabit much of central, southern, and southeastern Africa. There are several hundred Bantu languages and dialects, including Swahili, Shona, and Zulu. Until the demise in 1994 of South Africa's apartheid regime, the Bantu peoples were exploited and disenfranchised by the dominant white minority.

14. After World War II, the former German, Japanese, and Italian territorial trusteeships (also called "trust territories"), originally established by the League of Nations, fell under the jurisdiction of the Trusteeship Council of the UN. In time, most of the territorial trusteeships gained their independence in the 1950s, 1960s, and 1970s.

15. The Afrikaner military leader and politician Jan Christiaan Smuts (1870–1950), despite his failed leadership in the Second Boer War (1899–1902), came to be known as an advocate of cooperation between the Boers and the British Empire. He was also a proponent of racial segregation and white minority rule in South Africa. Together with Louis Botha (1862–1919), he was instrumental in helping to establish the Union of South Africa. Following World War I, he represented South Africa at the Paris Peace Conference, where he protested the harsh terms imposed by the Allies on Germany. He served as South Africa's prime minister in 1919–24 and 1939–48.

16. After World War I, the Union of South Africa occupied South-West Africa, which it administered as a province. The League of Nations eventually assigned the mandate for South-West Africa to the Union of South Africa. After World War II, when the UN sought to assume responsibility for the mandates previously established by the League, the Union of South Africa refused to make South-West Africa a trust territory because of its intention to annex it.

17. Greenberg wrote this essay against the backdrop of significant pent-up demand for Jewish immigration to Palestine from Europe and the Islamic world. In 1947, the total Jewish population of the Yishuv was approximately 543,000 persons. With the creation of the State of Israel, Jewish immigration skyrocketed: adding 101,821 to the population in 1948, 239,954 in 1949, 170,563 in 1950, and 175,239 in 1951. By 1952, Israel's Jewish population had climbed to nearly 1.5 million, or 89 percent of the country's total inhabitants. See "Appendix 5. Jewish and Non-Jewish Population of Palestine-Israel, 1517–2004"

and "Appendix 7. Immigration to Israel, 1948–2004," in *Israel in the Middle East: Documents and Readings on Society, Politics, and Foreign Relations, Pre-1948 to the Present*, ed. Itamar Rabinovich and Jehuda Reinharz, 2nd ed. (Waltham, MA: Brandeis University Press, 2008), 571, 575.

18. See Article 73 in "Chapter XI: Declaration Regarding Non-Self-Governing Territories," http://www.un.org/en/documents/charter/chapter11.shtml.

19. See Article 76 in "Chapter XII: International Trusteeship System," http://www.un.org/en/documents/charter/chapter12.shtml.

20. Quoted from Article 79 in ibid.

21. The Soviet Union initially boycotted the UN Trusteeship Council because, according to a Soviet delegate, "the trusteeship agreements were not in accord with the [UN] charter, thereby rendering the council unconstitutional; and equal membership in the council made it impossible to adopt 'constructive' resolutions in favor of trust territory inhabitants." Quoted in George Thullen, *Problems of the Trusteeship System: A Study of Political Behavior in the United Nations* (Geneva: Librairie Droz, 1964), 64.

22. Greenberg is referring to three major British initiatives concerning the future of Palestine. First, following clashes in 1936 between Jews and Arabs, a Royal Commission of Inquiry (known as the Peel Commission) conducted an investigation of Palestine and concluded the country should be partitioned into separate Arab and Jewish states. The Zionist movement cautiously favored discussion of the plan, but it was flatly rejected by the Arabs and thereafter rescinded by the British. Second, in response to the ongoing Arab riots (which lasted until 1939) another royal commission, the Palestine Partition Commission (known as the Woodhead Commission), was created in 1938. The commission investigated the cause of violence in Palestine and ultimately decided against partition as impractical. This led the British government to convene the Arab-Jewish Round Table Conference in London (also called the St. James Palace Conference) in 1939 (see note 31 in chapter 11, "An Answer to Gandhi," in this volume) in the hope of reaching a compromise solution with Jewish and Arab representatives, planning Palestine's future administration, and terminating the mandate. The latter did not produce any significant results. Third, in 1946 the Anglo-American Committee of Inquiry, a joint British and American commission, undertook a thorough review of social, economic, and political conditions in Palestine. The committee's recommendations formed the basis of the Morrison-Grady Plan, a strategy for a modified British-sponsored trusteeship. Like the previous initiatives, Arab and Jewish groups rejected the plan.

23. The colonies of Italian East Africa were Eritrea, Somalia, Amhara, Galla-Sidamo, Harar, and Scioa. Italy also controlled Libya and Tunisia in northern Africa.

24. In May 1947 Andrei Gromyko (see note 29 below), the Soviet representative to the UN, announced that although the USSR preferred the creation of a bi-national Arab-Jewish state in Palestine, if both sides were to reject bi-nationalism, then it would support partitioning the country into separate Arab and Jewish states.

25. Greenberg is referring to the confusion that arose in Zionist circles following a comment by David Ben-Gurion in May 1947: "We must not ignore realities. The United Nations will not acquiesce in turning the whole of Palestine into a Jewish state now, and there will perhaps be a need to leave a part of the country under the mandate and a sec-

ond part—where the Jews are settled as well as the barren area—will become a Jewish state." Quoted in *American Jewish Year Book* 49 (1947): 504. Ben-Gurion also stated Zionism ultimately sought to create a Jewish state in all of Palestine. Seven months later, when Ben-Gurion testified before the UN Special Commission on Palestine, he did not repeat the aforementioned equivocal views and instead emphasized the urgent need for Jewish statehood without elaborating on geographic issues.

26. Quoted from Article 22 in "Chapter IV: The General Assembly," http://www.un.org/en/documents/charter/chapter4.shtml.

27. The northern Italian city of Trieste was part of the Austro-Hungarian Empire before Italy annexed it in 1919. It was later claimed by Yugoslavia after World War II, though the Allied Powers disputed the latter's contention. It subsequently became the Free Territory of Trieste in 1947 and was placed under the protection of the UN Security Council. Areas of the city occupied by both Italy and Yugoslavia led to its effective partition, a situation that was made permanent when the Free Territory was terminated in 1975 by the Treaty of Osimo.

28. Danzig is the German name for present-day Gdansk, Poland. A Baltic seaport located on a branch of the Vistula River, the city has a long and complex past. In the premodern era, Polish lords and Teutonic knights frequently fought over the city, and it went through cycles as a Prussian, Polish, or autonomous city-state. It was controlled during much of the nineteenth century by Prussia and Germany. In 1919, following the Paris Peace Conference, it again became a free city, united with Poland, and supervised by a League of Nations high commissioner. In 1935 the local Nazi Party agitated for the reunification of Danzig with Germany, and in 1939 Hitler's vow to "liberate" the city served as his immediate excuse for the Nazi invasion of Poland. During World War II, the city fell to Soviet forces and it was eventually returned to Poland in 1945. Most of the German population was expelled at this time.

29. The Russian diplomat Andrei Andreyevich Gromyko (1909–89), an influential figure in Soviet foreign affairs for much of the twentieth century, served as the USSR's ambassador to the United States (1943–46), chief permanent delegate to the UN (1946–48), chief deputy foreign minister (1949–52), ambassador to Great Britain (1952–53), foreign minister (1957–85), and president (1987–89).

30. On the Swiss Confederation, see note 60 in chapter 24, "The Universalism of the Chosen People," in this volume.

31. Judah L. Magnes (1877–1948) (see also note 27 in chapter 29, "The Future of American Jewry," in this volume) and the Ihud (Unity), a small bi-nationalist Jewish political party formed in 1942 after the Biltmore Conference, proposed the political parity of Jews and Arabs in Palestine regardless of which group was in the majority. Magnes also advocated limiting Jewish immigration to Palestine to the level of the local Arab population and believed in a transitional British trusteeship until a bi-national Palestinian state could be established.

32. On the Peel Commission, see note 22 above.

33. By the time Greenberg penned this essay, he had also analyzed the possibilities and limitations of partition in several other published articles. See, e.g., "Is Zionism Imperialistic?," *Jewish Frontier* 3:1 (January 1936): 11–14; "'Jewish State' Examined," *Jewish*

Frontier 4:8 (August 1937): 4–7; "Partition: The Tragic Minimum," *Jewish Frontier* 5:2 (February 1938): 11–16; "Ten Recommendations: The Anglo-American Committee Report," *Jewish Frontier* 13:5 (May 1946): 3–15.

34. On the debate in the Zionist movement over small- and large-scale Jewish settlement in Palestine, see note 1 in chapter 7, "Revisionism," in this volume.

Chapter 26

Source: Hayim Greenberg, "Patriotism and Plural Loyalties," *Jewish Frontier* 15:10 (October 1948): 11–15.

1. On Diogenes, see note 1 in chapter 1, "The Meaning of Zionism," in this volume.

2. The Greek poet Meleager of Gadara (c. 140–70 BCE) compiled numerous texts and epigrams from the seventh to the third centuries BCE in a collection known as *The Wreath*. Meleager's work was subsequently incorporated into the *Palatine Anthology* of the tenth century CE and spawned the *Greek Anthology*, a collection of classical and Byzantine-era Greek literature edited by ancient and early medieval scholars between the tenth and fourteenth centuries CE.

3. For the original source, see *Anthologia Graeca* 7.417.5–6.

4. On Aristotle, see note 2 in chapter 16, "Chosen Peoples," in this volume.

5. See Aristotle, *Politics*, trans. Benjamin Jowett (Kitchener, ON: Batoche Books, 1999), 158–160.

6. *The Federalist Papers*, a collection of eighty-five political essays authored in 1787–88 by Alexander Hamilton (1755–1804), John Jay (1745–1829), and James Madison (1751–1836), argued in favor of the adoption of the US federal constitution, then under consideration by the Constitutional Convention. Widely published in American newspapers under the name "Publius," the essays helped to secure the Constitution's adoption and came to be regarded as classic works of political theory.

7. See "The Federalist No. 14," in Alexander Hamilton, James Madison, and John Jay, *The Federalist: A Commentary on the Constitution of the United States*, ed. Edward Mead Earle (New York: Modern Library, 1941), 81.

8. Stagira was the birthplace of Aristotle, who was sometimes known as "The Stagyrite."

9. The French writer André Gide (1869–1951) provoked widespread controversy in the 1930s with his spirited defense of homosexuality and support for Communism. He subsequently repudiated the Communist regime after a 1936 visit to the Soviet Union. See André Gide, *Return from the U.S.S.R.* (New York: Alfred A. Knopf, 1937). In 1947 he was awarded the Nobel Prize in Literature.

10. The Dreyfus Affair centered on Captain Alfred Dreyfus (1859–1936), an assimilated French Jew and career military officer, who in 1894 was falsely accused of espionage and convicted of treason. The affair became a *cause célèbre* and a watershed in the history of antisemitism. It stunned many in the West and shook the confidence of Jews in the liberal order. While the evidence did not support the accusations against Dreyfus, the French public generally applauded his conviction and he was imprisoned, where he languished until 1899. In 1906, Dreyfus was fully exonerated following a protracted le-

gal battle, a vigorous public debate championed by Émile Zola (see note 13 below), and an investigation that proved French military officers framed Dreyfus by suppressing and falsifying evidence.

11. Greenberg appears to be paraphrasing Gide's statement in a letter dated January 24, 1898. See *Oeuvres Complètes d'André Gide*, ed. Louis Martin-Chauffier, vol. 2 (Paris: Nouvelle Revue Française, 1932–39, 15 vols.), 486–488.

12. On Anatole France, see note 14 in chapter 14, "Einstein Discusses Religion," in this volume.

13. The French writer Émile Zola (1840–1902), author of the celebrated twenty-volume series *The Rougon-Macquarts: A Natural and Social History of a Family under the Second Empire* (1852–70), in which his characters are generally controlled by heredity and the environment, applied scientific and naturalistic principles in his novels. An ardent anticlerical spokesman and social reformer, in 1898 he championed the cause of Alfred Dreyfus's innocence and risked his career with the publication of "*J'accuse*" on the front page of the Paris newspaper *L'Aurore* (The Dawn). Written as an open letter to the French president, Zola accused the highest levels of the French army of antisemitism and intentional obstruction of justice leading to Dreyfus's wrongful conviction and imprisonment. Zola's jeremiad proved to be a critical turning point in the Dreyfus Affair and led to Dreyfus's eventual vindication.

14. Established in 1802 by Napoleon Bonaparte (1769–1821), the *Légion d'Honneur* is France's highest civil and military decoration.

15. Oliver Cromwell (1599–1658) was a revolutionary English political and military leader who ruled as the virtual dictator of England after it became a commonwealth in 1649. He reigned as First Lord Protector of the Commonwealth from 1653 to 1658.

16. The English poet John Milton (1608–74) is best known for his epic poem about the rebellion of Satan and the story of Adam and Eve, *Paradise Lost* (1667). He was also the author of many political and moral pamphlets, dealing with such topics as censorship by parliament and the morality of divorce. In *The Tenure of Kings and Magistrates* (1649) he claimed that unworthy kings may be put to death. This tract also gained him a spot in Cromwell's government as Latin secretary for foreign affairs.

17. Puritanism was a sixteenth- and seventeenth-century religious movement that sought to reform the Church of England and move it away from the prevailing traditions of Catholicism. While many Puritans emigrated to North America and to other parts of Europe during the seventeenth century, in England Puritanism grew as a political force. After 1661, the Church of England adopted the Clarendon Code, thus enforcing church doctrine countrywide and ostracizing the English Puritans.

18. Charles I (1600–1649), king of England, Scotland, and Ireland of the Tudor House, reigned from 1625 until his execution in 1649. His rule was beset by internal political strife and unsuccessful military ventures. A bitter struggle between the king and the English parliament gave rise to the Puritan Revolution, and Charles responded by governing without parliament from 1629 to 1640. Civil war soon followed. In 1646 Charles I was defeated by the Scottish army and fell into the hands of English revolutionaries led by Oliver Cromwell, after which he was tried, convicted of treason, and beheaded.

19. Quoted from *Select Prose Works of Milton*, ed. J. A. St. John, vol. 2 (London:

J. Hatchard and Son, 1836), xiii. John Milton's *Eikonoklastes* (1649) offers a rationale for the execution of Charles I of England. The book's title, derived from the Greek term for "breaker of icon," is an ironic rejoinder to *Eikon Basilike* (Royal Image), which purported to be Charles I's autobiography but was probably written around the time of the king's execution by the English bishop and Royalist sympathizer John Gaudden (1605–62).

20. The Doukhobors, a Christian sect founded in Russia in the eighteenth century, were persecuted due to their religious objections to militarism and belief that the laws of God are higher than those of any secular state. To flee repression a large number of Doukhorbors immigrated to Canada starting in 1899.

21. The Hutterites, or the Hutterite Brethen, are a body of Christians who practice communism on religious grounds. They base their ideas on those of the Moravian Anabaptists who followed Jacob Hutter (c. 1500–1536), who was burned at the stake. In the nineteenth century, persecution drove them eastward into Russia, and along with the Mennonites a group of them emigrated to the United States in the 1870s.

22. The Mennonites are the descendants of the Dutch and Swiss evangelical Anabaptists of the sixteenth century and, like the Doukhobors, refuse to take up arms due to their religious objections to war and violence. They stress the idea that only believers should be baptized and that people should dress modestly. There are many different branches of the Mennonites, including Amish groups in the United States and other sects in South America, Europe, and Canada.

23. The Quakers, or the Religious Society of Friends, is a Christian religious group that was founded in England in the seventeenth century and spread to North America with English colonization of the New World. Quakers reject the notion that a priest is needed to establish communion between one's soul and God. They are steadfast proponents on non-violence.

24. On Socrates, see note 56 in chapter 16, "Chosen Peoples," in this volume.

25. On Plato, see note 19 in chapter 9, "To a Communist Friend," in this volume.

26. On Sophocles, see note 22 in chapter 19, "Go to Nineveh," in this volume.

27. In Greek mythology, Antigone is the daughter of Oedipus (see note 24 in chapter 19, "Go to Nineveh," in this volume). She was forbidden by Creon (Oedipus's uncle and regent of Thebes after Oedipus's banishment) to bury her brother Polynices, but she defied him. Consequently, Creon buried her alive.

28. In Greek mythology, Polynices is Oedipus's son, the brother of Antigone and Eteocles, and the leader of the "Seven against Thebes," a group of seven Greek heroes who waged war against Eteocles for control of Thebes. In the latter battle, he and Eteocles kill each other.

29. See Sophocles, *The Seven Plays in English Verse*, ed. and trans. Lewis Campbell (London: Oxford University Press, 1906), 4.

30. Ibid., 5.

31. Ibid., 16.

32. This quote can be found in Mark 12:17, Matthew 22:21, and Luke 20:25.

33. The Latin phrase *cuius regio, eius religio* ("whose rule, his religion") was the guiding principle of the Peace of Augsburg (1555), a temporary settlement of conflicts within the Holy Roman Empire that stemmed from the Reformation. Accordingly, dissenters

to a region's prevailing religion were allowed to leave while certain free cities had to accept both Protestants and Catholics. The agreement largely ignored the question of Calvinists and other religious minorities.

34. Thorstein Veblen (1857–1929), an American social scientist who coined the phrase "conspicuous consumption," studied the psychological underpinnings of social institutions and was a founder of institutional economics. Known for his pioneering analyses of business cycles and price systems, his major works include *The Theory of the Leisure Class* (1899) and *The Theory of Business Enterprise* (1904).

35. Thorstein Veblen, *An Inquiry into the Nature of Peace and the Terms of its Perpetuation* (New York: B. W. Huebsch, 1919), 34.

36. Quoted in Theodore Roosevelt, "Yankee Blood versus German Blood; A Speech Delivered at Springfield, Illinois on August 26, 1918," in *New Roosevelt Messages: Speeches, Letters and Magazine Articles Dealing with the War, Before and After, and Other Vital Topics by Theodore Roosevelt*, ed. William Griffith, vol. 3 (New York: Current Literature, 1919), 957.

37. Theodore Roosevelt (1858–1919), twenty-fifth president of the United States (1901–9), championed "100 percent Americanism" and was an outspoken critic of Americans of foreign birth (e.g., German Americans, Irish Americans, Japanese Americans) who sustained strong ethnic-national loyalties to their country of origin. In 1915, Roosevelt asserted: "There is no room in this country for hyphenated Americans. When I refer to hyphenated Americans I do not refer to naturalized Americans. Some of the very best Americans I have ever known were naturalized Americans born abroad. But a hyphenated American is not an American at all." "Roosevelt Bars the Hyphenated," *New York Times* (October 13, 1915), 1.

38. Charles Beard (1874–1948), a prominent American historian, liberal thinker, and founder of the New School for Social research, emphasized the conflict between social and economic interests in American history. Among his most significant works are *An Economic Interpretation of the Constitution of the United States* (1913), *The Economic Basis of Politics* (1923), and *The Rise of American Civilization* (1927). Although an early supporter of President Franklin D. Roosevelt's (1882–1945) New Deal agenda, he later became a vigorous critic of his foreign policy.

39. In 1917 former president Theodore Roosevelt, while campaigning in support of the reelection of New York City's Republican "boy mayor" John P. Mitchel (1879–1918), declaimed, "We ought to decide whether we have got a country or a polyglot boarding house!" "Roosevelt Calls Support of Mayor Duty to Nation," *New York Times* (October 30, 1917), 1. The precise textual source for Greenberg's reference to Beard is unknown. However, as historian Gary Gerstle notes, in the early twentieth century many Progressives, "immersed since youth in the culture of American Protestantism," were disdainful of "the very different heritages of immigrants, especially of those from southern and eastern Europe." They "minced no words" about the desirability of "impress[ing] America's superior Anglo-Saxon mores upon them" and "regarded the dissolution of ethnic cultures and their replacement by a thoroughly American identity as one of Progressivism's most important tasks." Gary Gerstle, "The Protean Character of American Liberalism," *American Historical Review* 99 (October 1994), 1051.

40. French King Louis XIV's (1638–1715) infamous assertion "I am the state" epitomizes the concept of absolute monarchy.

41. At the time Greenberg wrote this essay, Yemen and Saudi Arabia, established in 1918 and 1932, respectively, were absolute monarchies ruled by dynastic tribal families.

42. In 1798, against the backdrop of an undeclared naval war with France and the "XYZ Affair," which caused a rupture in Franco-American relations, the US Congress passed the Alien and Sedition Acts; the legislation was signed into law by President John Adams (1735–1826). The acts empowered the president to expel "dangerous" aliens, provided for the indictment of anyone who might "unlawfully combine or conspire" against the administration, or should write or speak "with the intent to defame" the government, the Congress, or the president. Although the acts expired in 1800–1801, the Alien Enemies Act remains in effect to this day and allows the president to apprehend and deport resident aliens whose home countries are at war with the United States.

43. Quoted in James Truslow Adams, *The Epic of America* (1931; reprint, New Brunswick, NJ: Transaction Publishers, 2012), 134.

44. Passed in 1798 and 1799 in opposition to the Alien and Sedition Acts, the Kentucky and Virginia Resolutions, were written, respectively, by Thomas Jefferson (1743–1826) and James Madison (1751–1836). The resolutions assert the federal government has no right to exercise powers not specifically delegated to it by the US Constitution and, when it does assume such powers, the states have the right to judge the constitutionality of any resulting acts. The resolutions are considered a key expression of the doctrine of states' rights.

45. On the Swiss Confederation, see note 60 in chapter 24, "The Universalism of the Chosen People," in this volume.

46. A southern canton of Switzerland bordering on Italy.

47. The reference is to Conrad Ferdinand Meyer (1825–98), a Swiss poet and novelist, and one of modern German literature's foremost stylists.

48. German for "I am not a sophisticated book; I am a human being with all his contradictions." The phrase is from Conrad Ferdinand Meyer's poem "*Homo Sum*" (Latin for "I Am a Man"), originally published as poem no. 26 in a collection of German verse titled *Huttens letzte Tage* (Hutten's Last Days) (1871). The volume emphasizes themes related to the life of the medieval German knight, poet, and theologian Ulrich von Hutten (1488–1523).

49. Since the days of the Scottish Reformation of 1560, when the Church of Scotland separated from Rome, until the early twentieth century, the various Scotch Presbyterian subgroups withstood consistent British pressure and externally imposed efforts to adopt the standards of and unite with the Church of England. In 1921, the British parliament finally recognized the autonomy of the Church of Scotland and thereafter the branches of Scotch Presbyterianism largely cohered under one rubric.

50. Nancy Astor (1879–1964), an American-born British politician, was a Conservative member of the English parliament from 1919 until 1945. She was known for her support for temperance, women's rights, and efforts to reform child welfare.

51. The French historian and cultural critic Ernest Renan (1823–92) advocated a scientific approach to the study of history, religion, and literature. Among his best-known

works are *Life of Jesus* (1863) and *The Future of Science* (1890). Though generally a tolerant and liberal figure within the context of his time, he nonetheless contributed to late-nineteenth-century European racist and antisemitic discourse.

52. Quoted from a public lecture given by Ernest Renan at the Sorbonne in 1882. See "*Qu'est-ce qu'une nation?*," in *Oeuvres complètes de Ernest Renan*, ed. Henriette Psichari, vol. 1 (Paris: Calmann-Lévy, 1947), 904.

53. Norway was ruled by Denmark until 1814, at which point the country was ceded to Sweden. In 1905, under the leadership of Peter Christian Hersleb Kjerschow Michelson (1857–1925), Norway separated peacefully from Sweden and became an independent nation.

54. Quoted from "For He Is an Englishman," a song from W. S. Gilbert and Arthur Sullivan's comic opera *H. M. S. Pinafore* that celebrates the imperial glory of Great Britain. See W. S. Gilbert, *H. M. S. Pinafore; or, The Lass That Loved a Sailor* (New York: George Munro Publisher, 1883), 9.

55. Winston Churchill (1874–1965), British statesman, soldier, and author, served as prime minister of the United Kingdom in 1940–45 and 1951–55. He is regarded as one of the twentieth century's greatest political and wartime leaders.

56. In June 1940, against the backdrop of France's imminent defeat by Nazi Germany, Winston Churchill supported a stillborn proposal for a "Franco-British Union." For a brief period, the governments of Britain and France considered this idea as an alternative to France's acceptance of an armistice with Germany. In the end, French support for the union proposal faltered. Instead, the French government capitulated to the Nazis, ushering in the wartime regime of Vichy France under Henri Philippe Omer Joseph Pétain (1856–1951).

57. Jehovah's Witnesses (sometimes known, incorrectly, as "Russellites"), a millenarian and nontrinitarian sect of evangelical Christianity, was founded in the United States in 1872 by the restorationist Christian minister Charles Taze Russell (1852–1916). The doctrine of Jehovah's Witnesses centers on an eschatological belief in the second coming of Jesus. The group sustains distinctive communitarian practices, promotes pacifism, and refuses to take oaths to the state.

58. The Irish Free State was established in 1921. In general, Jewish nationalists and Zionists viewed Irish nationalism as a kindred movement.

59. On Yom Kippur (Day of Atonement), see note 2 in chapter 19, "Go to Nineveh," in this volume.

60. See "A Bill Declaring Who Shall Be Deemed Citizens of This Commonwealth," in *The Papers of Thomas Jefferson*, ed. Julian P. Boyd et al., vol. 2 (Princeton, NJ: Princeton University Press, 1950), 476–478.

61. Hersch Lauterpacht (1897–1960), a leading British jurist of eastern European Jewish ancestry, served as a member of the UN International Law Commission (1952–54) and a judge of the International Court of Justice (1955–60).

62. Lauterpacht's *An International Bill of the Rights of Man* (1945), a three-volume philosophical, historical, and legal argument, advocates the creation and enforcement of a proposed "International Bill of the Rights of Man."

63. Quoted from H. Lauterpacht, *An International Bill of the Rights of Man* (New York:

Columbia University Press, 1945), 129. See also the "Expatriation Act of July 27, 1868" (15 Stat. 223), passed by the US Congress as a companion to the Fourteenth Amendment.

64. The Conference for the Codification of International Law, held by the League of Nations in the Hague in March-April 1930, adopted the first "Convention on Certain Questions Relating to the Conflict of Nationality Laws." See League of Nations, Treaty Series, vol. 179, no. 4137, 89.

65. From the Conference for the Codification of International Law, *Acts*, vol. 2, "Minutes of the First Committee," 275; cited in G. H. Hackworth, *Digest of International Law* 3 (1942): 163.

Chapter 27

Source: Hayim Greenberg, "Notes on the Israeli Constitution," *Jewish Frontier* 16:5 (May 1949): 31–38.

1. On the term *Kulturkampf* (German for "conflict of cultures"), see note 6 in chapter 24, "The Universalism of the Chosen People," in this volume.

2. At the request of David Ben-Gurion (see note 20 below), the legal scholar Leo Kohn (see note 3 below) prepared Israel's draft constitution. To this end, Kohn drew on themes and precepts of premodern Jewish law and the modern Western legal tradition. Kohn's document proposed equal rights and full citizenship alike for Jews, Christians, and Moslems, freedom of speech, separation of church and state, recognition of the rights of all religious and ethnic minorities, universal access to social security, health services, and public education, abolition of the death penalty, Hebrew as the national language (with provisions for Arabic speakers in all civic and political institutions), honoring the Jewish Sabbath and Jewish holidays as official days of rest, and so on. It also outlined the operational and structural framework of Israel's parliament. A complete English translation of the text of Kohn's proposed constitution is reprinted in *Jewish Frontier* 16:1 (January 1949): 4–9; see also, immediately following, Leo Kohn, "Observations on the Constitution," 10–20.

3. Leo Kohn (1894–1961), author of Israel's proposed draft constitution and professor of international relations at the Hebrew University of Jerusalem (1953–61), emigrated in 1921 from Frankfurt to Palestine. He served as a legal adviser to the Jewish Agency for Palestine and, after the establishment of the state in 1948, to Israel's foreign ministry.

4. On the Druze Arabs, see note 15 in chapter 3, "East and West," in this volume.

5. On the Amalekites, see note 35 in chapter 24, "The Universalism of the Chosen People," in this volume.

6. On Maimonides, see note 22 in Chapter 4, "Sabbatai Zevi," in this volume.

7. See Maimonides, *Mishneh Torah*, "Laws of Kings," 1:4.

8. Ibid.

9. On the biblical figure Miriam, see note 126 in chapter 24, "The Universalism of the Chosen People," in this volume.

10. According to the Book of Judges (see note 129 in chapter 24, "The Universalism of the Chosen People," in this volume), Deborah, the only female judge in the Hebrew Bible, played a decisive role in the defeat of King Jabin of Canaan and the liberation of

ancient Palestine (Judg. 4). In both the description of the war against Jabin and the subsequent Song of Deborah (Judg. 5), she appears as a national leader.

11. Bruriah, a second-century Jewish sage, is one of the few women quoted in the Talmud. Her husband Rabbi Meir Baal Hanes (see note 70 in chapter 24, "The Universalism of the Chosen People," in this volume) was an important *tanna* authority. In addition to Bruriah's learned insights, she stands out in talmudic discourse for challenging prevailing rabbinic attitudes about matters of ritual purity and repentance.

12. See Maimonides, *Mishneh Torah*, "Laws of Kings," 1:5.

13. Greenberg is referring to the process of Jewish emancipation in Europe in the eighteenth and nineteenth centuries. Against the backdrop of the Enlightenment, many western European regimes and, shortly thereafter, some eastern European regimes opened their societies to greater Jewish civic participation and, in time, citizenship for their Jewish inhabitants. This historic process was gradual and, notwithstanding some common features, varied considerably from country to country. See Robert M. Seltzer, *Jewish People, Jewish Thought: The Jewish Experience in History* (New York: Macmillan, 1980), chap. 11; *The Jew in the Modern World: A Documentary History*, ed. Paul Mendes-Flohr and Jehuda Reinharz, 3rd ed. (New York: Oxford University Press, 2011), chap. 3.

14. Although the biblical narrative justifies the concepts of patriarchy and slavery, Christianity tended to promote sexual egalitarianism from its earliest days. The latter attitude is implicit in the sacraments, particularly in the notions of baptism and the Eucharist. In 585 CE the Council of Macon, meeting in Burgundy, France, discussed the ensoulment of human beings. Although the bishops used the generic Latin term *homo* in their discussions, a myth thereafter arose that the council had declared that women do not have souls. This misrepresentation gained added credence in the medieval era owing to a series of pamphlets and writings that mistranslated and misconstrued the Council of Macon's deliberations. In 1651, Pope Innocent X (Giovanni Battista Pamphili, 1574–1655) publicly refuted the proposition that women do not have souls.

15. In 1878, the first American woman suffrage amendment was proposed in the US Congress; the issue was voted upon and defeated in 1886. Thereafter, the following states adopted woman suffrage: Wyoming (1890), Colorado (1893), Utah (1895), Idaho (1896), Washington (1910), California (1911), Arizona, Kansas, and Oregon (1912), Alaskan Territory (1913), Montana and Nevada (1914), New York, Oklahoma, and South Dakota (1917), and Michigan (1918). Finally, American women gained full voting rights in 1920 with the ratification of the Nineteenth Amendment. In 1928, women in Great Britain gained the right to vote without special qualifications (e.g., being thirty or older, property owners, and/or university graduates).

16. In 1944, women gained partial rights (including the right to vote) in France. In Belgium, the process of woman suffrage unfolded between 1919 and 1948.

17. The First Knesset (1949–51) included three Arab members: Seif el-Din el-Zoubi (1913–86), Amin-Salim Jarjora (1886–1975), and Tawfik Toubi (1922–2011). It also included twelve female members: Rachel Cohen-Kagan (1888–1982), Hasia Drori (1899–1976), Beba Idelson (1895–1975), Fayge Ilanit (1909–2002), Hannah Lamdan (1905–95), Ada Maimon (1893–1973), Golda Meir (1898–1978), Dvorah Netzer (1897–1989),

Shoshana Persitz (1892–1969), Esther Raziel-Naor (1911–2002), Yehudit Simhoni (1902–91), and Genia Tversky (1904–64).

18. During Israel's War of Independence, women served alongside men in combat units. In 1949, the Knesset (with the exception of the religious parties) overwhelmingly voted in favor of compulsory national military service for all Jewish men and women between the ages of eighteen and thirty-eight. Nonetheless, the Israel Defense Forces assumed a gendered division of command and labor.

19. Greenberg is referring to Golda Meir, who served as the country's first minister of labor and housing (1949–56). A native of Russia, Meir immigrated to Milwaukee, Wisconsin, in 1906 with her parents. She joined Poalei Zion in the United States in 1915 and immigrated to Palestine in 1921. She worked as a laborer and eventually joined Kibbutz Merhavyah, but soon left owing to the poor health of her husband, Morris Meyerson (1893–1951). She rose through the ranks of the Histadrut, becoming secretary general of Moezet Hapoalot in 1928 and a member of the World Zionist Organization executive committee in 1934. She also helped found the Palestine labor party Mapai in 1930. Her political role continued to grow in the years leading up to independence, and she became head of the Political Department of the Jewish Agency in 1946. She negotiated with the British regime and King Abdullah I of Jordan (1882–1951) to try to persuade the latter not to participate in the imminent war. During Israel's War of Independence, Meir went to the United States, where she raised over $50 million for the war effort. After Israel was established in 1948, she was appointed ambassador to Moscow. She subsequently became a Knesset member and David Ben-Gurion's minister of labor and housing. Thereafter, she served as foreign minister for ten years, finally becoming prime minister in 1969. She resigned the premiership in 1974 following the calamitous Yom Kippur War (1973), although the investigating Agranat Commission lauded her handling of the crisis.

20. Born in Poland, David Ben-Gurion (1886–1973) joined the Zionist movement as a youth and was active in Russian revolutionary activity. In 1906, he immigrated to Palestine where he became a laborer. In 1908 he joined the Sejera commune in the Lower Galilee and shortly afterward became involved with the Hashomer self-defense group. In 1911 he temporarily relocated to Turkey where he studied law at Istanbul University. During World War I he fought with the Jewish Legion, a British military regiment he helped to organize with other Zionist leaders (see note 11 in chapter 7, "Revisionism," in this volume). In 1920, he was among the founders of the Histadrut and became its secretary general. In 1930, he was a founder of the Palestine labor party Mapai and was elected as its chairman. In 1935, he became chairman of the Jewish Agency for Palestine (see note 14 in chapter 7, "Revisionism," and note 13 in chapter 10, "Open Letter to the Third International," in this volume). Following Israel's War of Independence, he was elected the state's first prime minister (1949–53). In 1955, he returned to government and was reelected prime minister (1955–63). He continued to play an active role in national politics as Israel's elder statesman until retiring in 1970.

21. This is a reference to the following ministers: Haim Moshe Shapira (1902–70), health, immigration, and internal affairs; Yehuda Leib Maimon (1875–1962), religions and war victims; and Yitzhak Meir Levin (1893–1971), welfare.

22. Quoted and translated from David Ben-Gurion, "Speech to the Knesset" (March 8, 1949), *Hayeshivah hashminit shel haknesset harishonah, Divrei haknesset*, n.p.

23. This appears to be a quote from Thomas Aquinas, *Summa Theologica* IIa–IIae, q. 64, a. 2, a. 3. The precise textual source used by Greenberg is unknown. (On Aquinas, see note 22 in chapter 4, "Sabbatai Zevi: The Messiah as Apostate," in this volume.) In this period, Switzerland's use of capital punishment was a topic of controversy in the West.

24. Owing to Leo Kohn's opposition to capital punishment, the death penalty was not included in Israel draft constitution; http://www.jta.org/1948/12/12/archive/u-s-experts-on-international-law-comment-favorably-on-proposed-israeli-constitution.

25. Eleazar ben Azariah, a first-century CE *tanna*, was a contemporary of Rabbi Akiba and Rabbi Tarfon. He served briefly as head of the Sanhedrin.

26. On Rabbi Tarfon, see note 49 in chapter 20, "*Halakhah* and *Agadah,*" in this volume.

27. On Rabbi Akiba, see note 48 in chapter 20, "*Halakhah* and *Agadah,*" in this volume.

28. On Rabbi Shimon ben Gamliel, see note 47 in chapter 20, "*Halakhah* and *Agadah,*" in this volume.

29. See Maimonides, *Mishneh Torah*, "Laws of the Sanhedrin," 15:10–13.

30. Ibid., 2:3.

31. Ibid., 12:4.

32. Ibid., 13:4.

33. On Rav Zair (Haim Tchernowitz), see note 21 in chapter 24, "The Universalism of the Chosen People," in this volume.

34. [Greenberg's footnote:] [Haim Tchernowitz], "On the Question of Religion and State in Israel" (Hebrew), *Bizaron* (Av–Elul 5708/Summer 1948): 297.

35. See Maimonides, *Mishneh Torah*, "Laws of the Sanhedrin," 14:9.

36. The original Hebrew title is Simha Assaf, *Haonshin aharei khatimat hatalmud: khomer letoldot hamishpat haivri* (Jerusalem: Dfus Hapoalim, 1922).

37. Born in Lviv, Ukraine, Simha Assaf (1889–1953), a rabbinic scholar and Jewish historian, immigrated to Palestine in 1921. In 1925 he was appointed professor of rabbinic and Gaonic literature at the Hebrew University of Jerusalem. He represented the Mizrahi religious party in the Vaad Leumi and the World Zionist Organization. He served a rector of the Hebrew University of Jerusalem (1948–50) and in 1948 he was appointed one of the five founding justices of Israel's supreme court.

38. Maimonides, *Mishneh Torah*, "Laws of the Sanhedrin," 17.

39. Ibid., 18–19.

40. On Yom Kippur, see note 2 in chapter 19, "Go to Nineveh," in this volume.

41. Maimonides, *Mishneh Torah*, "Laws of the Sanhedrin," 19.

42. The Puritan justification of flogging as a method of punishment can be traced to William Perkins (1558–1602), the influential Calvinist theologian and Puritan leader, who cited the biblical injunction as follows [*sic*]: "3. To exercise tyranous cruelty in inflicting punishments. Deutr. 25.3. Fourtie stripes shall he cause him to have, and not past, lest if he should exceed, and beate him about that with many stripes, thy brother shou'd appeare despised in thy sight. 2. Corin. 11.24. Of the Jewes I received five times fourtie stripes save one." William Perkins, *A Golden Chaine, or the Description of Theologie* (1591), image 55,

reel position: STC/1638:02, Cambridge University Library, http://eebo.chadwyck.com/search/full_rec?SOURCE=pgimages.cfg&ACTION=ByID&ID=V23203&PAGENO=55. In New England, John Winthrop (1587–1649), the governor of Massachusetts Bay Colony, sanctioned the perpetuation of the practice. See *Winthrop's Journal, "History of New England, 1630–1649,"* ed. James Kendall Hosmer, vol. 2 (New York: Charles Scribner's Sons, 1908), 257–259. The Puritans were "steeped to the core in Hebraism" and "re-enacted the harsh precepts of the primitive Jewish code" as a matter of "religious duty." George Elliott Howard, *A History of Matrimonial Institutions Chiefly in England and the United States*, vol. 2 (Chicago: University of Chicago Press, 1904), 175–179. Apparently, flogging and burning were also used symbolically with respect to heretical texts. In 1754, the *Connecticut Gazette* reported that an offensive publication was sentenced to be "publickly whipt according to Moses' Law, with forty stripes save one, and then burnt"; quoted in Alice Morse Earle, *Curious Punishments of Bygone Days* (Chicago: H. S. Stone, 1896), 69.

43. The "early Massachusetts leaders, at least in attitude, felt their laws were opposed neither to biblical law nor common law, for . . . the common law was founded on the law of God"; William B. Stoebuck, "Reception of English Common Law in the American Colonies," *William and Mary Law Review* 10:2 (1968): 400. As evidence, Stoebuck cites a source indicating "the true Puritan idea of law as the command of God" and the Puritan preference "to go to the original source of law, the Scriptures." Paul Samuel Reinsch, "English Common Law in the Early American Colonies," in *Select Essays in Anglo-American Legal History*, ed. Ernst Freund, William E. Mikell, and John H. Wigmore, vol. 1 (Boston: Little, Brown, 1907–9), 380–381.

44. [Greenberg's footnote:] *Material for the Preparation of a Constitution for the Jewish State on a Religious Basis* (Hebrew), ed. Isaac Lewin (New York: Research Institute for Post-War Problems of Religious Jewry, 1948).

45. On the British mandate for Palestine, see the subsection titled "The Mandate" in chapter 25, "Current Alternatives in Palestine," in this volume, 272.

46. Historically, the Greek Orthodox Church grants divorces only after a formal and rigorous examination of the petitioning parties by an ecclesiastical court. See Timothy Ware, *The Orthodox Church: An Introduction to Eastern Christianity*, 3rd ed. (1963; reprint, London: Penguin Books, 2015), 104, 295, 315; Eileen F. Stuart, *Dissolution and Annulment of Marriage by the Catholic Church* (Sydney: Federation Press, 1994), 82–84.

47. As in the Jewish public arena, the role and authority of Islamic law in Muslim society is a complex issue. Greenberg is intentionally drawing a distinction between traditionalist and modern attitudes to individual rights, property rights, and familial and marital relations.

48. Bahaism is a monotheistic world religion founded in Persia in 1862 when Baháulláh (originally Mirza Hussein Ali Nuri, 1817–92) announced himself a prophet succeeding the Bab ed-Din (Siyyid Ali Mohammed Shirazi, 1819–50), who in 1848 proclaimed himself the successor to Moses, Jesus, and Mohammed. Bahaists believe in the unity of all religions, world peace, equality of men and women, universal education, and modest living.

49. The practice of polygamy in Jewish life gradually disappeared by the early medieval period and was formally banned by European rabbinic authorities in the eleventh

century. Among Jewish communities in the Islamic world, however, where polygamy was a widespread sociocultural phenomenon, the practice persisted into the twentieth century. In 1949, Israel outlawed bigamy and polygamy. Nonetheless, in the early years of the state the practice continued among some Jews from northern Africa, particularly Yemenite Jewish immigrant communities previously isolated from the West for centuries.

50. Greenberg is referring to the Conservative synagogue movement, which did not have a presence in Israel at the time this essay was written. Conservative Judaism, with roots in the central European milieu of modern Jewish philosophical thought, emerged in the United States in the early twentieth century as a new form of traditional Jewish belief and practice. Among its founders were Solomon Schechter (1847–1915), the first president of the Jewish Theological Seminary of America, Israel Friedlaender (1876–1920), Louis Ginzberg (1873–1953), Alexander Marx (1878–1953), and Mordecai M. Kaplan (1881–1983), who later created a splinter movement known as Reconstructionist Judaism. The term "conservative" was intended by the founders to convey the importance of conserving traditional Judaism as a totality while adapting its religious beliefs and practices to modern American society. In contrast to Orthodox Judaism, the Conservative movement does not subscribe to the literality of the Hebrew Bible or the idea that premodern Jewish beliefs and practices have remained valid and binding up to the present. Although Conservative Judaism adopted many innovations characteristic of Reform Judaism (e.g., participation of women, mixed pews, use of the vernacular), it views the Torah as divinely inspired and subscribes to many traditional Ashkenazi beliefs (e.g., centrality of *halakhah*, observance of dietary laws, importance of Hebrew).

51. In 1922 the Conservative rabbinic scholar Mordecai M. Kaplan (1881–1983) founded the Society for the Advancement of Judaism (SAJ) in New York City. The first institutional manifestation of Reconstructionist Judaism, the new SAJ synagogue embodied Kaplan's theological conception of Judaism as an evolving religious tradition. He rejected the notion that the Torah was divinely revealed at Mount Sinai and that *halakhah* is immutable and binding in Jewish religious life. Rather, he posited the necessity of adapting Jewish life and culture to the modern environment. These ideas were later fully developed in Kaplan's *Judaism as a Civilization* (1934). In March 1922 Kaplan conducted the first bat mitzvah in the United States for his daughter Judith (Kaplan) Eisenstein (1909–96). See also note 27 in chapter 29, "The Future of American Jewry," in this volume.

52. Kol Nidrei (Aramaic for "all vows"), the opening prayer that commences the Yom Kippur (Day of Atonement) evening service, is a declaration in which Jewish worshippers ask God to annul all their vows which may not be sustained in the coming year.

53. On Reform Judaism, see note 8 in chapter 21, "Bankrupt!" in this volume.

54. On the Soviet concept of the "revolutionary consciousness of justice," see note 28 in chapter 20, "*Halakhah* and *Agadah*," in this volume.

55. Washington Irving (1783–1859), the American author, historian, and diplomat, lived in Tarrytown, New York, and is best known for his stories "Rip Van Winkle" (1819) and "The Legend of Sleepy Hollow" (1820). He was appointed US minister to Spain (1842–46) by President John Tyler (1790–1862).

56. Greenberg's paraphrase is nearly an exact quote. For the original text, see Wash-

ington Irving, *Diedrich Knickerbocker's A History of New York*, ed. Stanley Williams and Tremaine McDowell (New York: Harcourt, Brace and Company, 1927), 33.

Chapter 28

Source: Hayim Greenberg, "Education in the Diaspora," *Jewish Frontier* 30:2 (March 1963): 18–25. The Yiddish version of this essay, "*Kultur un derzeyung in galut*" (Culture and Education in Exile"), appears in Hayim Greenberg, *Yid un velt* (New York: Yidisher Kemfer, 1953), 330–346.

1. An ecclesiastical ban or rabbinic excommunication.

2. On the *autos-da-fés*, see note 23 in chapter 9, "To a Communist Friend," in this volume.

3. On the Marranos, see note 10 in chapter 9, "To a Communist Friend," in this volume.

4. At the time Greenberg gave this address, the Soviet regime's attitude toward Russian Jewry, which historically lived under uncertain, repressive, and frequently violent antisemitic conditions during tsarist rule, was worsening steadily. Moreover, dramatic changes had taken place in the geographic distribution of the population as a result of World War II. In all, postwar Soviet Jewry numbered approximately two million. Russia's western territories, which formed the Pale of Settlement until the Russian Revolution of 1917, were decimated during the war and the Nazis murdered the vast majority of the region's Jews. Of those Russian Jews who survived, a majority migrated to European Russia and Moscow thereafter became the country's largest Jewish population center, with an estimated 300,000 Jews. Meanwhile, a new concentration of Jewish communities, perhaps as much as a quarter of Soviet Jewry (approximately 500,000 persons), emerged in central Asia. In addition to the Uzbekistan capital of Tashkent, estimated to be the third largest urban Soviet Jewish population, many tens of thousands of Jews gravitated to Almaty, Frunze, Samarkand, Bukhara, and Karaganda. The Jewish population of Birobidzhan in eastern Siberia was estimated at 35,000 to 40,000. Rising anti-Jewish discrimination in the Soviet Union took the form of severe travel restrictions, the elimination of the Jews from the country's academic, cultural, and political institutions, widespread arrests for alleged anti-Soviet activity, deportations, and slave labor. Anti-Zionist and anti-Israel propaganda also became a characteristic feature of official Soviet policy.

5. Before Israel's war for independence in 1948, approximately 800,000 Jews lived in the Arab and Muslim countries of the Middle East. Between 1948 and 1951, when Greenberg gave this address, approximately 260,000 Jews from across the Middle East immigrated to Israel, accounting for roughly 56 percent of the fledgling Jewish state's total population. The Middle East in this period was riven by social and political turmoil, including the rise of Arab nationalist movements, anti-foreign ideologies, religious fanaticism, and xenophobia. A wave of *coups d'états*, royal abdications, and the political assassinations of Jordan's King Abdullah I (1882–1951), Lebanon's prime minister Riad as-Solh (1894–1951), and Iran's prime minister Ali Razmara (1901–51), combined with the emergence of new dictatorships and widespread anti-Jewish sentiment and policies, prompted the mass flight to Israel of many centuries-old Middle Eastern Jewish communities. The

autocratic regimes of Saudi Arabia, Yemen, and Iran were seemingly the only countries unaffected at this juncture by internal crises, convulsions, and revolutions.

6. The Twenty-third World Zionist Congress, held in Jerusalem on August 14–28, 1951, was the first congress to be held in the newly established State of Israel. At the congress a major clash between Israeli and American Zionists came to the fore over the definition of Zionism. The Israeli Zionists insisted on equating Zionism with personal immigration to Israel (*aliyah*), while the majority of American Zionists opposed this conception. See Eliezer Greenberg, "Report of the 23rd World Zionist Congress; Harasses Zionists and Distresses Friends," September 24, 1951, unpublished manuscript, Berman Jewish Policy Archive (http://www.bjpa.org/Publications/downloadFile.cfm?FileID=17937).

7. The "Jerusalem Program" was adopted by the Twenty-third World Zionist Congress in 1951 and subsequently revised in 1953, 1968, and 2004. The original text defines "the task of Zionism" as the "consolidation of the State of Israel, the ingathering of exiles in Erez Israel, and the fostering of the unity of the Jewish people."

8. *Vade mecum* (Latin for "go with me") is equivalent to a reference guide or handbook.

9. Gehenna, a valley south of Jerusalem, is mentioned in the Hebrew Bible as venue of idolatry and cult sacrifices (e.g., 2 Kgs. 23:8–10; Jer. 7:31; 2 Chron. 28:3–4). The term is synonymous in Western culture with "hell."

10. On the *Shulkhan Arukh* (Prepared Table), see note 20 in chapter 20, "*Halakhah* and *Agadah,*" in this volume.

11. In the late 1930s, a Palestine-based cultural and ideological movement known as "Canaanism" (its adherents called themselves "Canaanites") arose in reaction to Zionism and proclaimed Jews everywhere ought to disassociate themselves from Judaism and the concept of Jewish nationalism. Asserting the Land of Israel was actually the Land of Canaan and that the Jews stemmed historically from an ancient Hebrew civilization bound together by Canaanite languages, Canaanism argued the Yishuv's Jewish inhabitants should strive to create a modern non-Jewish Hebrew society. The Polish-born Hebrew poet Yonatan Ratosh (pen name of Uriel [Heilprin] Shelakh, 1908–81) articulated the mission of Canaanism in his "Epistle to Hebrew Youth" (1943).

12. Greenberg is referring to the relationship between Zeev Jabotinsky's right-wing Revisionist Zionist movement and the advocates of Canaanism, including Yonatan Ratosh, who edited the Irgun's official Hebrew publication *Bakherev* (By the Sword).

13. Avraham Kariv (1900–1976), a Hebrew writer, poet, and literary critic born and raised in Lithuania, was educated in eastern Europe in literature, mathematics, and physics. Shortly after World War I, he studied with Haim Nahman Bialik (see note 20 below) and Yosef Klausner (see note 21 in chapter 24, "The Universalism of the Jewish People," in this volume) at the Tarbut Teachers Seminary in Odessa. In 1934, he emigrated to Palestine where he became a teacher and participated actively in the Hebrew press. He proclaimed Hebrew literature to be a cultural mediator in the construction of modern Jewish identity, and he harshly criticized many leading modern Hebrew authors for their dismissal of the significance and value of the diaspora's Jewish literary creativity and potential.

14. The title of Avraham Kariv's collection of essays, *Adaberah veyirvah li* (Hebrew

for "Let me speak, then, and get relief") (Tel Aviv: Am Oved, 1950), is drawn from Job 32:20.

15. Created as an independent nation in 1947, India completed the process in 1950 of ratifying its constitution and establishing itself as a secular democratic republic.

16. Notwithstanding sparse historical data, St. Patrick (c. 390–460), the patron saint of Ireland, is credited with converting the Irish people to Christianity.

17. Aramaic, an English word derived from the biblical Hebrew term *aramit*, is a northwestern Semitic dialect that arose in the ancient period parallel to the Canaanite languages (e.g., Hebrew, Ugaritic, Phoenician) as well as the classical Akkadian and Arabic languages.

18. On Mendele Moykher Sforim, see note 12 in chapter 20, "*Halakhah* and *Agadah,*" in this volume.

19. On Ahad Haam, see note 12 in chapter 1, "The Meaning of Zionism," in this volume.

20. On Haim Nahman Bialik, see note 44 in chapter 1, "The Meaning of Zionism," in this volume.

21. On Sholem Aleichem, see note 24 in chapter 15, "Psychoanalysis and Moral Pessimism," in this volume.

22. Yitzhak Dov Berkovitch (1885–1967), a Yiddish and Hebrew writer and translator, was married to Sholem Aleichem's eldest daughter, Ernestina. Much of his career was devoted to translating and promoting his father-in-law's work. From 1910 to 1913 he served as literary editor of the Zionist weekly *Haolam* (The World). In 1913, he immigrated to the United States where he became a publicist and translated Sholem Aleichem's works into Hebrew. In 1928, he immigrated to Palestine, where he continued to write Hebrew novels and adapted several of Sholem Aleichem's plays for the Habima Theatre.

23. On the tower of Babel, see note 18 in chapter 8, "Notes on Marxism," in this volume.

24. Greenberg is referring to the declarative Hebrew expression "*yehi*" (Hebrew for "let there be"), which appears in Genesis 1:3 ("God said, 'Let there be light,' and there was light").

Chapter 29

Source: Hayim Greenberg, "The Future of American Jewry," in *The Inner Eye: Selected Essays*, vol. 2, ed. Shlomo Katz (New York: Jewish Frontier Association, 1964), 60–76. The Yiddish version of this essay, "*A blik in der zukunft*" (A Glimpse into the Future), appears in Hayim Greenberg, *Yid un velt* (New York: Yidisher Kemfer, 1953), 347–363.

1. The reference is to the Reform, Conservative, and Orthodox branches of American Judaism. See the following in this volume for brief descriptions of each denomination: on Reform Judaism, see note 8 in chapter 21, "Bankrupt!"; on Conservative Judaism, see note 50 in chapter 27, "Concerning an Israel Constitution"; and on Orthodox Judaism, see note 7 in chapter 21, "Bankrupt!"

2. *Tisha Beav* (ninth of Av), an annual fast day observed according to the Hebrew

calendar on the ninth day of the month of Av, commemorates the destruction of the First and Second Temples in Jerusalem, which supposedly occurred on the same date. Over time, *Tisha Beav* also came to be regarded as a day for mourning other tragedies in Jewish history.

3. Long considered Judaism's most sacred site, the Western Wall, also called the Wailing Wall, is located at the base of the Temple Mount in the Old City of Jerusalem. It is believed to be a remnant of the foundation that surrounded the Second Temple in the ancient period.

4. In 1948, during its battle for independence, Israel captured the western area of Jerusalem and Jordan captured the city's eastern area. The latter, largely populated by Muslims and Christians, includes the Temple Mount, the Western Wall, the Al-Aqsa mosque, and the Church of the Holy Sepulcher. The notable exception to the Jordanian conquest was Mount Scopus and the enclave of the Hebrew University, which remained under Israeli control. In the aftermath of the war, Jordan expelled eastern Jerusalem's Jewish residents and destroyed much of the city's Jewish quarter. It also disallowed Jewish worship at the Western Wall. The situation changed abruptly in June 1967 as a result of the Six Day War when Israel captured east Jerusalem. It subsequently granted free access to members of all religions to the city's holy sites.

5. On Jewish society in ancient Palestine under the Roman Empire, see note 14 in chapter 20, "Halakhah and Agadah," and notes 20 and 32 in chapter 10, "Open Letter to the Third International," in this volume.

6. On Edom, see note 9 in chapter 19, "Go to Nineveh," in this volume.

7. In 1654, with the recapture by the Portuguese of Dutch colonies in Brazil, including Pernambuco (Recifé), the local Sephardic Jewish community there disbanded. Not only did the Jews wish to flee from the Inquisition, but they also feared Portuguese retribution for having aided the Dutch in the development of the colonies. Those with means escaped to Amsterdam and London, but a small boatload of twenty-three Jewish refugees eventually landed in Dutch-controlled New Amsterdam aboard the St. Charles. The New Netherland colony was small, with a population of approximately 750 persons. Though technically Dutch subjects, director-general Peter Stuyvesant (see note 8 below) denied the Jews entry, arguing they would defile the New World. Meanwhile, Amsterdam Jewry interceded vigorously on behalf of the St. Charles refugees. They explained the Jewish colonists had shed their blood to defend the Dutch possessions in Brazil, that the French and English allowed Jews in their colonies, and that there were several Jews among the company's "principal shareholders." The utilitarian Dutch calculus stemmed from the directors' overriding concern with the manufacture of raw goods, their consumption, and the quest for Dutch mercantile supremacy over their Western competitors. In the end, the Dutch West India Company permitted the Jews to remain in New Amsterdam and Stuyvesant reluctantly acquiesced. Thus, the Jews gained a foothold in the New World. Within a few years, however, the new New Amsterdam Jewish community was impelled to seek larger opportunities in other parts of the Atlantic Basin, especially in the West Indies, and by the early 1660s it disappeared. See documents 1.01–1.05 in *American Jewish History: A Primary Source Reader*, ed. Gary P. Zola and Marc Dollinger (Lebanon, NH: University Press of New England, 2014), chap. 1.

8. Born in the Netherlands, Peter Stuyvesant (c. 1612–72), a staunch defender of the Dutch Reformed Church, joined the Dutch West India Company in the 1630s. In 1642–44 he directed the company's colony in Curaçao. In 1645 he was appointed director-general of the New Holland colony in North America, a post he held until 1664 when the Dutch ceded most of their territorial holdings on the eastern seaboard to the British.

9. In late 1655, Abraham de Lucena, Salvador Dandrada, and Jacob Cohen submitted a petition for a Jewish burial ground to the New Netherland Council. The request was granted in February 1656. See documents 6:68b and 6:285b in New Netherland Council, *Council Minutes, 1655–1656*, trans. and ed. Charles T. Gehring, vol. 6 (New York: Holland Society of New York, 1995), 68, 229.

10. The precise location of the New Amsterdam Jewish community's original cemetery is unknown. In 1682, however, Congregation Shearith Israel purchased a plot of land for a second cemetery (located in present-day lower Manhattan on St. James Place, opposite Chatham Square) that remained in use until 1828.

11. Isaac Mayer Wise (1819–1900), a native of Bohemia, immigrated to the United States in 1846. Initially, he served as rabbi of Congregation Beth El in Albany, New York, where he introduced a variety of reforms to Jewish religious practice including family pews, the participation of women in the synagogue, and a mixed choir. In 1847 he compiled a new non-Orthodox prayer book titled *Minhag Amerikah* (The American Custom). In 1848 he began agitating for the creation of a national association of liberal Jewish communities and rabbis in the United States. In 1854 he moved to Cincinnati, Ohio, where he became rabbi of the Bnei Yeshurun Congregation and established a national English-language newspaper called *The American Israelite*. In 1873 he founded the Union of American Hebrew Congregations, a new countrywide framework for the emerging movement of Reform Judaism. In 1875 he created Hebrew Union College in Cincinnati to train and ordain Reform rabbis. In 1889 he founded the Central Conference of American Rabbis, the central rabbinic authority of Reform Judaism in the United States.

12. On Reform Judaism, see note 8 in chapter 21, "Bankrupt!" in this volume.

13. Quoted from Isaac M. Wise, *Reminiscences*, ed. and trans. David Philipson (Cincinnati: Leo Wise and Company, 1901), 79.

14. In the decades that spanned the nineteenth and twentieth centuries, a broad spectrum of Jewish ideologies (e.g., Yiddishism, Hebraism, autonomism, Jewish socialism) asserted language and culture were the keys to the continued vitality of diaspora Jewish life.

15. On Maimonides, see note 22 in chapter 4, "Sabbatai Zevi," in this volume.

16. Culling his ideas from a variety of talmudic sources, Moses Maimonides summarized Judaism's key doctrines in a commentary on the Mishnah. He asserted the following "thirteen articles" of Jewish faith: God's existence, unity, incorporeality, and eternity, that God alone is to be worshipped, God's revelation through the Hebrew Bible and prophetic literature, the finality and completeness of the Hebrew Bible, Moses' preeminence in Jewish tradition, God's enduring justice and awareness of human action, the coming of the messiah, and the resurrection of the dead.

17. According to the Hebrew Bible, God destroyed the cities of Sodom and Gomor-

rah, located in the Jordan River plain, possibly near the northern end of the Dead Sea, because of their carnal wickedness (see Gen. 10:19 and Deut. 29:23). Over time, Sodom and Gomorrah became metaphors for vice and deviance.

18. In keeping with the nature of talmudic discourse, Greenberg is here adapting the original biblical narrative to underscore his point about Abraham's piety and capacity to argue with God on behalf of Sodom's inhabitants. According to the biblical narrative it was not Abraham but Lot, Abraham's son, who ventured to Sodom and subsequently fled to Zoar for his safety (see Gen. 18:16–19:29).

19. On H. G. Wells, see note 3 in chapter 24, "The Universalism of the Chosen People," in this volume.

20. See Moshe Davis, "Jewish Religious Life and Institutions in America: A Historical Study," in *The Jews: Their History, Culture, and Religion*, ed. Louis Finkelstein, vol. 1, 2nd ed. (New York: Harper and Brothers, 1955), 354–453. The first edition was published in 1949.

21. Born in Brooklyn, New York, Moshe Davis (1916–96), ordained as a Conservative rabbi and a trained scholar of American Jewish history, was the first American to earn a doctorate at the Hebrew University of Jerusalem. From 1942 to 1959, he taught at the Jewish Theological Seminary of America. In 1959, he immigrated to Israel, where he taught at the Hebrew University and established the Institute of Contemporary Jewry. Among his important works are *Israel: Its Role in Civilization* (1956), which is dedicated to Hayim Greenberg, *The Emergence of Conservative Judaism* (1963), and the volumes produced by America-Holy Land Studies Colloquium (1977–86).

22. In January 1817, Joseph Jonas (1792–1869), a watchmaker who immigrated to the United States from Exeter, England, in October 1816, became the first Jew to settle in Cincinnati. See David Philipson, "The Jewish Pioneers of the Ohio Valley," *Publications of the American Jewish Historical Society* 8 (1900): 44–45.

23. The account in Davis's study reads: "People traveled many miles to view this object of curiosity. One old Quaker woman said to him: 'Art Thou a Jew? Thou art one of God's chosen people. Wilt thou let me examine thee?' As she turned him round about, she remarked, 'Well, thou art no different to other people.'" See Davis, "Jewish Religious Life and Institutions in America," 362.

24. On Friedrich Nietzsche, see note 7 in chapter 6, "Jew and Arab," in this volume.

25. On Orthodox Judaism, see note 7 in chapter 21, "Bankrupt!" in this volume.

26. On Conservative Judaism, see note 50 in chapter 27, "Concerning an Israel Constitution," in this volume.

27. This is likely a reference to Yehoshua Radler-Feldmann (1880–1957), who wrote under the pen name "Rabbi Binyamin." In 1907, after collaborating in London with Yosef Haim Brenner (see note 13 in chapter 18, "The Myth of Jewish Parasitism," in this volume) on *Hameorer* (The Awakener), Radler-Feldmann immigrated to Palestine where he worked as a socialist pioneer, laborer, and teacher. He later became an active leader of the Mizrahi religious Zionist party. In 1925, together with Judah L. Magnes (see note 31 in chapter 25, "Current Alternatives in Palestine," in this volume), Martin Buber (see note 17 in chapter 1, "The Meaning of Zionism," in this volume), and others, he founded Brit Shalom (Covenant of Peace), a Jewish group that advocated establishing a bi-national

Jewish-Arab state in Palestine (see note 10 in chapter 7, "Revisionism," in this volume). Though he broke with Brit Shalom, he remained committed to the goal of Jewish-Arab reconciliation. He published numerous articles about the importance of Judaism to Zionism and the Jewish state.

28. On the so-called Hottentots (Khoikhoi), see note 23 in chapter 10, "Open Letter to the Third International," in this volume.

29. The Zulus are the largest ethnic clan in South Africa and inhabit the lush eastern province of KwaZulu-Natal (formerly Natal). Dominated by European colonial powers for many centuries, the Zulu economy has long been based on subsistence farming and cattle raising.

30. Derived from biblical Hebrew, the term *shmad* literally means "consume" or "destroy" (see Dan. 7:26). Greenberg is referring to the so-called "anti-*shmad* campaign" of Yosef Yitzhak Schneerson (1880–1950), an Orthodox rabbi of eastern European origin and the spiritual leader of the Habad-Lubavitch Hasidic sect, who in 1940 fled wartime Europe and relocated to New York City. Directed by Rabbi Jacob J. Hecht (1924–90), a disciple of Schneerson, the initiative sought to slow or reverse the processes of American Jewish acculturation and secularization by providing free supplementary religious education to Jewish students attending American public schools. In time, the effort expanded and became the "National Committee for Furtherance of Jewish Education."

31. The reference is to a maxim by David "Puddn'head" Wilson, the title character of Mark Twain's novel *Puddn'head Wilson and Those Extraordinary Twins* (Hartford, CT: American Publishing Company, 1894). The original statement reads, "Faith is believing what you know ain't so." See Mark Twain, *Following the Equator: A Journey around the World*, vol. 1 (New York: Harper Brothers, 1906), 132.

32. Originally composed in Arabic as a letter to a student, Moses Maimonides' *The Guide for the Perplexed* (*Morei nevukhim* in Hebrew) is a twelfth-century three-volume compilation that discusses the relationship between Judaism and philosophy. Owing to its Aristotelian orientation, the *Guide* proved to be highly controversial in the Jewish arena; however, it was well received by many Christian thinkers including the philosopher-theologians Thomas Aquinas (1225–74), Meister Eckhart (c. 1260–1327), and Duns Scotus (c. 1266–1308). See also note 22 in chapter 4, "Sabbatai Zevi," in this volume.

33. Greenberg may be referring to the famous biblical phrase "The fool hath said in his heart: 'There is no God'" (Ps. 14:1).

34. In the early 1950s, there were nearly 500 Reform congregations in the United States, 100 more than in the previous decade, while the Conservative movement added more than 150 synagogues in the same period and rose beyond 500 congregations countrywide. (Many of the latter were previously Orthodox and gravitated to Conservatism.) There were more than 700 affiliated Orthodox congregations, but many were inactive and left over from before World War II. A 1950 estimate placed total synagogue membership in the United States at 450,000 families, besides about 250,000 persons who occupied seats in the synagogue on the holidays of Rosh Hashanah and Yom Kippur. Thus, approximately 1.5 million American Jews were synagogally affiliated at the start of the 1950s. As the latter figure increased, the number of denominationally identified congregations grew. An estimated $50–60 million was spent on new synagogue construction,

largely in the suburban districts of major American cities where new Jewish communities arose swiftly. Most new suburban synagogues accommodated not only worship and study but also social functions, sports activities, and recreation.

35. The original phrase in the Hebrew Bible is "*Vekhiti laadonai hamastir panav mebeit yaakov*" ("I will wait for God who is hiding his face from the House of Jacob") (Isa. 8:17).

36. On the eve of the Russian Revolution, Vladimir Lenin (see note 9 in chapter 6, "Jew and Arab," in this volume) coined the phrase "awakening Asia" to describe the spread of communism and the "seething political activity" of China. See "The Awakening of Asia" (1913) in V. I. Lenin, *Collected Works*, trans. George Hanna and ed. Robert Daglish, vol. 19 (Moscow: Progress Publishers, 1977), 85–86.

37. Greenberg is referring to French historian and cultural critic Ernest Renan's *Prière d'un sceptique* (French for "Prayer of a Skeptic"): "*O Seigneur, s'il y a un Seigneur, sauvez mon âme, si j'ai une âme.*" On Renan, see note 51 in chapter 26, "Patriotism and Plural Loyalties," in this volume.

38. This is a reference to the Reform, Conservative, and Orthodox synagogue movements.

39. According to B. Makot 23b, which references a sermon by the talmudic sage Rabbi Simlai (c. third century CE), the Torah contains 613 *mizvot* (commandments or pious deeds). There is no definitive list in this regard and the calculation itself has been the subject of intensive debate among rabbis and students of Jewish religious tradition for centuries.

40. On the *Shulkhan Arukh* (Prepared Table), see note 20 in chapter 20, "*Halakhah* and *Agadah,*" in this volume.

Chapter 30

Source: Hayim Greenberg, "Church and State: Seven Theses," in *The Inner Eye: Selected Essays*, vol. 2, ed. Shlomo Katz (New York: Jewish Frontier Association, 1964), 173–180. Greenberg delivered a modified version of this piece as part of a lecture series held in 1952 by the Seminary Israel Institute of the Jewish Theological Seminary of America, which was jointly sponsored by the Jewish Agency and the World Zionist Organization. See Hayim Greenberg, "Religion and the State in Israel," in *Israel: Its Role in Civilization*, ed. Moshe Davis (New York: Harper and Brothers, 1956), 165–175.

1. Greenberg is referring to the twin Greek and Jewish philosophical conceptions of the human soul as a miniature universe within the individual. In Greek philosophy, dating to the fourth century BCE, the individual is a microcosm or "little world" (from the Greek *micros kosmos*) in which the macrocosm or "universe" (*megas kosmos*) is reflected. Though the origins of this concept are unknown, Socrates (see note 56 in chapter 16, "Chosen Peoples," in this volume), Aristotle (see note 2 in chapter 16, "Chosen Peoples," in this volume), and Plato (see note 19 in chapter 9, "To a Communist Friend," in this volume) employed it in their works. It also "seems to be clearly implied by the teaching of Heraclitus, in so far as he lays it down that both the universe and man are vivified and controlled by the Logos." E. Vernon Arnold, *Roman Stoicism: Being Lectures on the*

History of the Stoic Philosophy with Special Reference to Its Development within the Roman Empire (Cambridge: Cambridge University Press, 1911), 240. Similarly, traditional Jewish sources emphasize the individual's fundamental importance in theological and philosophical terms, e.g., "Whoever destroys a soul, it is considered as if he destroyed an entire world. And whoever saves a life, it is considered as if he saved an entire world." B. Sanhedrin 37a, M. Sanhedrin 4:9.

2. On Sophocles, see note 22 in chapter 19, "Go to Nineveh," in this volume.

3. On Antigone, see note 28 in chapter 27, "Patriotism and Plural Loyalties," in this volume.

4. The Hebrew phrase *melekh malkhei hamlakhim* (king of kings of kings) expresses God's infinite superiority to all earthly rulers. It is used in Sabbath and holiday liturgy.

5. On John Milton, see note 16 in chapter 26, "Patriotism and Plural Loyalties," in this volume.

6. Greenberg is paraphrasing John Milton's statement in *The Second Defense of the English People Against an Anonymous Libel, entitled "The Royal Blood Crying to Heaven for Vengeance on the English Parricides"* (1654): "I did not insult over fallen majesty, as is pretended; I only preferred Queen Truth to King Charles." See John Milton, *Complete Poems and Prose*, ed. Merritt Y. Hughes (1957; reprint, Indianapolis: Hackett Publishing Company, 2003), 832.

7. On the Quakers, see note 23 in chapter 26, "Patriotism and Plural Loyalties," in this volume.

Chapter 31

Source: Hayim Greenberg, "Religious Tolerance," unpublished manuscript, Central Zionist Archives, Jerusalem, Israel, A259/8, n.d.

1. On Heinrich Heine, see note 28 in chapter 1, "The Meaning of Zionism," in this volume.

2. Greenberg is referring to Heine's "Disputation," the third poem in a series titled "Hebrew Melodies" (1850–51). The poem concludes: "'Tell me, what is your opinion? / Which is right, and which the liar? / Will you give your verdict rather / For the rabbi or the friar?' / . . . 'Which is right, I cannot tell you, / But I have a shrewd suspicion / That the rabbi and the monk are / both in stinking bad condition.'" *The Poems of Heine*, trans. Edgar Alfred Bowring (London: George Bell and Sons, 1891), 503. The conclusion portrays "the arrogation of judgment by a representative of power" while the queen's "verdict" is a deliberately "unwarranted closure curiously at odd's with the poem's . . . resolutely critical tenor." Willi Goetschel, "Nightingales Instead of Owls: Heine's Joyous Philosophy," in *A Companion to the Works of Heinrich Heine*, ed. Roger F. Cook (Rochester: Camden House, 2002), 162.

3. The Mormon Church (Church of Jesus Christ of Latter-Day Saints) was founded in 1830 by Joseph Smith (1805–1844). Shortly thereafter, Smith encouraged the practice of private polygamy among his followers. In 1852 the church institutionalized the practice of polygamy. In 1862 the US Congress passed the Morrill Anti-Bigamy Act prohibiting "plural marriage" in the western territories. In 1879 the US Supreme Court upheld

a challenge to the latter legislation. In 1890 the Mormon Church formally abandoned the practice of polygamy.

4. Wilbur Glenn Voliva (1870–1942), an evangelist preacher and head of the Christian Catholic Apostolic Church in Zion, Illinois, advocated a flat earth doctrine and preached against science and evolution.

5. Precisely who Greenberg is referring to in this instance is unclear. However, the promise of physical immortality was characteristic of the followers of Nikolai Sazontovich Ilyin (1809–90), founder of the Russian apocalyptic movement known as the "Jehovists" or "Brotherhood of the Right Hand" (*Desnoe bratstvo*). Il'in was a dualist who believed that Jehovah was the god of the immortals, and Satan the god of the mortals. The New Jerusalem, which was being prepared by beings on another planet, would soon descend, and the immortal followers of Jehovah would live forever—first in the millennial kingdom and then in the new heaven and new earth to be created by Jehovah. See Sergey V. Petrov, "Field Notes: The Jehovists-Il'inites: A Russian Millenarian Movement," *Nova Religio: The Journal of Alternative and Emergent Religions* 9:3 (February 2006): 80–91; Sergei I. Zhuk, *Russia's Lost Reformation: Peasants, Millennialism, and Radical Sects in Southern Russia and Ukraine, 1830–1917* (Baltimore: Johns Hopkins University Press, 2004), 122–132, 185.

6. On John the Baptist, see note 12 in chapter 22, "Concerning Statehood," in this volume. While there is no evidence Nikolai Sazontovich Ilyin (see note 5 above) was considered to be John the Baptist, the Russian Orthodox Church did accuse several sectarian leaders of claiming this distinction. For example, Aleksandr Ivanov Shilov (c. 1713–1800) was often described as John the Baptist because of his close relationship to Kondratii Selivanov (d. 1832), a *Skoptsy* leader (see note 7 below) who claimed to be "the God of Gods and King of Kings." Evlampii Kotelnikov (c. 1775–1855), a captain of the Don Cossacks and the founder of a pietistic, millenarian movement known as the *Dukhonostsy* (Russian for "spirit-bearers"), is also said to have claimed to be John the Baptist. See K. Grass, "II. Other Sects," in *Encyclopaedia of Religion and Ethics*, ed. James Hastings, vol. 11 (New York: Charles Scribner's Sons, 1921), 339–343.

7. The *Skoptsy* (Russian for "self-castrated ones"), a secret Russian Christian sect made up of peasants, believed castration restored humanity to the pristine state it enjoyed before the fall of man in the Garden of Eden (Gen. 2–3). To this end, they practiced the castration of men and the mastectomy of women. Persecuted by the Soviet regime, the sect disappeared by the mid-twentieth century. See Zhuk, *Russia's Lost Reformation*, chap. 2.

8. Greenberg is referring to pre-state Indian society's culture of ostracizing and repressing certain groups based on its caste system. Known as "untouchables" (today called "Dalits"), India's out-of-caste groups historically comprised a sizable segment of the general population and were routinely discriminated against. (See also note 6 in chapter 11, "An Answer to Gandhi," in this volume.) Many Dalits suffered from excessive isolation, oppression, and abuse. Greenberg is also lamenting the plight of Hindu women generally and the Indian funeral practice of *sati* (self-immolation by a woman) according to which a widow immolates herself, typically on her deceased husband's funeral pyre.

9. The central European Lutheran philosopher and dramatist Gotthold Ephraim

Lessing (1729–81), a leading figure of the Enlightenment and German letters, championed intellectual and religious tolerance. His plays and critical essays had a significant impact on German literature.

10. Lessing's *Nathan the Wise* (1754), with its sensitive and affirmative portrayal of a Jewish protagonist—modeled after the central European Jewish philosopher Moses Mendelssohn (see note 54 in chapter 1, "The Meaning of Zionism," in this volume)—emphasized the theme of religious toleration. The play features Nathan as a spokesman for the idealistic strivings of the Enlightenment.

11. The metaphor of the three rings, with roots in Giovanni Boccaccio's *Decameron* (1348–53), suggests the integrity and relative equality of Judaism, Christianity, and Islam.

12. The traditional Jewish prayer known as "*Shemah yisrael*" ("Hear, O Israel"), derived from Deuteronomy 6:4 ("Hear, Israel, the Lord is our God, the Lord is One"), is a cardinal expression of Judaism's monotheistic belief system.

13. Perhaps quoting from memory, Greenberg appears to be inadvertently mixing two talmudic sources in this instance: B. Megillah 3a and B. Bava Kama 82b–83a. The former notes the Land of Israel "quaked" for a distance "four hundred miles by four hundred miles" when the Torah was translated into Aramaic. The latter discusses the Hellenization of Jewish life under the Hasmoneans, reiterates the tale of the land quaking, and argues against Grecian wisdom and the Greek language.

14. Greenberg is referring to the biblical figure Joseph, the eleventh son of the patriarch Jacob. According to the Hebrew Bible, "Israel [Jacob] loved Joseph best of all his sons" (Gen. 37:2).

15. Shimon bar Yohai (often referred to as Rabbi Shimon) was a second-century CE *tanna* sage and a disciple of Rabbi Akiba (see note 48 in chapter 20, "*Halakhah* and *Agadah*," in this volume). The *Mekhilta de-Rabbi Shimon bar Yohai*, an anthology of early rabbinic interpretations of the book of Exodus developed between approximately 70 and 500 CE, is erroneously attributed to Shimon bar Yohai.

16. The precise source of this textual reference is unclear. Greenberg may be paraphrasing elements of tractates "*Sanya*" and "*Pisha*," in the *Mekhilta de-Rabbi Shimon bar Yohai*. See *Mekhilta de-Rabbi Shimon bar Yohai*, trans. and ed. W. David Nelson (Philadelphia: Jewish Publication Society of America, 2006), 2–12.

17. See Salo W. Baron, *A Social and Religious History of the Jews*, 2nd ed., vol. 2 (New York: Columbia University Press, 1952), chap. 12 ("Closing the Ranks"), esp. n. 28, 387–388.

18. On the Noahide laws, see notes 193 and 194 in chapter 24, "The Universalism of the Chosen People," in this volume.

19. On the notion of 613 commandments in the Torah, see note 39 in chapter 29, "The Future of American Jewry," in this volume.

20. Abraham ben Shmuel Abulafia (c. 1240–91), a Sephardic rabbi who founded a branch of ecstatic Jewish mysticism based on contemplation of the Hebrew alphabet, predicted the world's imminent demise. In 1280, moved by a prophetic vision, he journeyed to Rome in an attempt to convert Pope Nicholas III (c. 1210–80) to Judaism. Only the pope's sudden death prevented Abulafia from being burned at the stake. The medieval rabbinate thereafter disavowed Abulafia.

21. For the incident Greenberg describes here, see Matthew 15:21–28 and Mark 7:24–30.

22. Once the capitol of the kingdom of Israel, Samaria was built by Omri (c. 884 BCE) in the early ninth century BCE. In 722 BCE it fell to invading Assyrian forces. It was destroyed in c. 113 BCE by the Hasmonean leader Yohanan Horkenos (see note 185 in chapter 24, "The Universalism of the Chosen People," in this volume) and thereafter rebuilt in c. 27 BCE by Herod the Great (see note 14 in chapter 20, "*Halakhah* and *Agadah,*" in this volume). The city also gave its name to the surrounding region and the Samaritan sect, an offshoot of Judaism that adheres strictly to the Hebrew Bible (see note 188 in chapter 24, "The Universalism of the Chosen People," in this volume).

23. See Matthew 10:5–6.

24. On Paul, see note 30 in chapter 20, "*Halakhah* and *Agadah,*" in this volume.

Glossary of Terms

agadah: Aramaic term that simultaneously connotes "expanding" and "drawing in"; refers to the variegated corpus of non-legal exegetical texts, philosophical statements, folklore, mystical beliefs, and moral discussions codified in the Talmud and Midrash.

Agudat Israel: Hebrew for "Union of Israel," a worldwide organization of Orthodox Jews established in Poland in 1912. Though originally opposed to secular Zionism, the group's rabbinic leadership reconciled with the Jewish Agency for Palestine in 1933, thereby enabling the participation of Agudat Israel in Zionist (and later Israeli) affairs.

aliyah (pl. *aliyot*): Hebrew for "ascent"; a term used to indicate an individual Jewish person's immigration to the Land of Israel or a cohort of people who do so. The First Aliyah is usually dated to 1881–1903; the Second Aliyah, 1903/4–14; the Third Aliyah, 1919–23; the Fourth Aliyah, 1924–28; and the Fifth Aliyah, 1929–39. Each cohort was characterized by distinctive ideological-political views and provenance.

amora (pl., *amoraim*): Aramaic for "spokesmen"; rabbinic scholars active c. 200–500 CE. Their discussions and disputations of Jewish oral law were codified in the Gemara (Aramaic for "learning by tradition"). The latter is also an extended commentary on the Mishnah (Hebrew for "repetition") of Rabbi Judah Hanasi, a second-century CE sage regarded as the chief redactor of Jewish oral tradition. Although the Gemara was intended to expound on the Mishnah, it became a distinctive compilation of information on a variety of subjects. Together, the Gemara and the Mishnah make up the Talmud. The era of the *amoraim* followed that of the *tannaim*.

Ashkenazi Jews: Yiddish-speaking Jews of eastern European ancestry, particularly the lands formerly controlled by tsarist Russia.

dunam: term for one thousand square meters, approximately a quarter of an acre.

Erez Israel (Hebrew), *Erez yisroel* (Yiddish): according to the social, religious, or political context, the term may denote the Land of Israel, the Holy Land, or Palestine.

galut: Hebrew for "exile" (*golus* in Yiddish), term used to describe both spiritual and geographic conditions of Jewish life; often used as a pejorative term.

hagshamah azmit: Hebrew for "self-fulfillment."

hakhsharah (pl., *hakhsharot*): Hebrew for "training," usually in reference to agricultural and/or manual skills required for life in the Jewish colonies of Palestine, including communal values, conversational Hebrew, and self-defense.

halakhah: Hebrew for "the path"; the term used to identify the amalgam of biblical injunctions, rabbinic rulings, and customs that emerged over time to constitute Orthodox Jewish law and historically governed public, private, and ritual Jewish life. Though seemingly fixed, the body of beliefs, rituals, and practices comprising *halakhah* has been reinterpreted and modified over time by different religious authorities in various social and cultural settings.

haluz, haluzah (pl. *haluzim, haluzot*): Hebrew for "pioneer" (masculine, feminine) used to describe the Labor Zionist pioneers in Palestine.

haluziut: Hebrew for "pioneering."

Hashomer Hazair: Hebrew for "The Young Guard," a worldwide Marxist Zionist youth movement established in Vienna in 1916 that stressed class struggle and pioneering settlement in Palestine. It later gave rise to a left-wing Zionist party in Palestine by the same name as well as a framework of communitarian rural settlements.

hasid (pl. *hasidim*): Hebrew for "pious one"; an adherent of Hasidism, a popular eastern European Jewish religious movement inclined to mysticism.

Hasidism: Eastern European Jewish religious movement whose followers embrace the teachings of the Polish rabbi Israel ben Eliezer (c. 1700–1760), known as the Baal Shem Tov or Besht, who opposed intellectualism and stressed emotionalism in prayer and the performance of religious rituals and ceremonies.

Haskalah: Hebrew for "enlightenment"; refers to the movement for spreading modern European culture among the Jews that lasted from roughly 1750 until 1880. The *Haskalah* movement believed that Jewish emancipation required that Jews conform to Europe's non-Jewish host societies and environment and that this could be achieved through modernized and westernized Jewish religion and customs. Among the central figures of the Haskalah were Baruch Spinoza (1632–77), whose biblical criticism heralded a significant shift in Western philosophy; the Prussian Jewish philosopher Moses Mendelssohn (1729–86); Salomon Maimon (1753–1800), a central European Jewish philosopher and proponent of German ethical idealism; and the Russian Jewish thinker Isaac Baer Levinsohn (1788–1860).

Hehaluz: Hebrew for "The Pioneer," a non-partisan political body that emerged after World War I in eastern Europe embracing all factions of the Zionist movement dedicated to *aliyah* (see above) and pioneering values. By the late

1920s, over 40 percent of all Jewish immigrants to Palestine (and 80 percent of kibbutz pioneers) had been trained by Hehaluz. The association ceased to exist after World War II when it was absorbed by the World Zionist Organization, which in turn assumed overall responsibility for the pioneering Zionist youth movements.

Hibat Zion: Hebrew for "Lovers of Zion," a philanthropic, proto-Zionist society that originated in eastern Europe; used interchangeably with the name Hovevei Zion.

Histadrut: a shortened form of Histadrut Haklaklit Shel Haovdim Haivrim Berez Israel, Hebrew for "General Federation of Jewish Workers in the Land of Israel," the umbrella framework of the Labor Zionist movement in Palestine, established in 1920.

Hovevei Zion: see *Hibat Zion*.

Jewish Legion: the military formation of Jewish volunteers in World War I who fought in the British army for the liberation of Palestine from Turkish rule.

Jewish National Fund (JNF): known in Hebrew as Keren Kayemet Leyisrael, founded at the Fifth Zionist Congress in 1901 to further the acquisition of land and development of Jewish colonies in Palestine.

Kabbalah: Hebrew for "receiving," the term used to denote Jewish mysticism, a stream of Jewish esoteric thought emphasizing the presumably concealed dimensions of Judaism in the Hebrew Bible and traditional rabbinic literature. The kabbalistic tradition originated in southern France and the Iberian peninsula in the twelfth and thirteenth centuries CE. The *Zohar* (Hebrew for "splendor"), redacted by the Spanish rabbi Moses de Léon (c. 1250–1305), is the foundational text of Kabbalah. In time, the varieties of kabbalistic ideas spread across the Ottoman empire and throughout much of Europe, where it gave rise to Hasidism (see above).

kaddish: Hebrew for "sanctification," traditional Jewish doxology recited by mourners.

kibbutz (pl. *kibbutzim*): Hebrew term for a cooperative rural settlement in Palestine.

Kupat Holim: Hebrew for the "Workers' Sick Fund," the first Jewish health insurance fund and medical network in Palestine, founded in 1911 by a small group of agricultural laborers and taken over in 1920 by the Histadrut (see above).

kvuzah (pl. *kvuzot*): Hebrew term for a communal rural colony in Palestine.

Labor Zionism: the colonizing movement of socialist Zionist pioneers that created an intricate countrywide network of social, economic, and political institutions which shaped the infrastructure of the Jewish state-in-the-making; comprised a variety of rival factions, each with a different emphasis on Marxism, Hebraism, Yiddish, etc.

Mapai: Hebrew acronym for Mifleget Poalei Erez Israel (Workers Party of the Land of Israel), established in Palestine in 1930; the party dominated Labor Zionism in the mandatory and early state periods.

maskil (pl. *maskilim*): Hebrew for "enlightened [Jew]," referring to an adherent of the Jewish enlightenment movement (see Haskalah above).

Midrash (pl. *midrashim*): Hebrew for the body of homiletic literature created by rabbinic sages that interprets and comments on the Hebrew Bible using exegesis, hermeneutics, and philology.

Mishnah: Hebrew for "repetition," the written record of Jewish oral tradition redacted at the start of the third century CE by Rabbi Yehuda Hanasi. Its sixty-three tractates codifying Jewish law form the basis of the Talmud.

Mizrahi: Hebrew for "eastward," also an acronym for *merkaz ruhani* (spiritual center). In 1902 Rabbi Jacob Reines (1839–1915) established Mizrahi in Vilna as the religious Zionist party within the World Zionist Organization. The group's motto is "The Land of Israel for the people of Israel according to the Torah of Israel."

Moezet Hapoalot: Hebrew for the "Women Workers' Council," established in 1922 as part of the Histadrut (see above); sister organization of Pioneer Women in the United States.

moshav ovdim: Hebrew for "workers' settlement," a rural Jewish colony in Palestine incorporating some cooperative principles.

moshavah (pl. *moshavot*): Hebrew for "plantation village," usually associated with the private landholding Zionist pioneers of the First Aliyah (see *aliyah* above).

pogroms: Russian term for anti-Jewish riots perpetrated by the Christian population against eastern European Jews; widespread in Russia between 1881 and 1921 and generally accompanied by destruction, looting of property, murder, and rape.

rebbe: a Yiddish term, usually refering to a Hasidic rabbi.

Revisionism: established in 1925 by Vladimir (Zeev) Jabotinsky (1880–1940) as a militant faction within the World Zionist Organization (WZO), the Revisionist group rapidly became a right-wing Zionist party. In 1935 the Revisionists seceded from the WZO to form the New Zionist Organization; the group rejoined the WZO following World War II. The Revisionists vehemently opposed the Labor Zionist movement's economic and political agenda.

Sephardi Jews: the term used to identify Ladino-speaking Jews of Iberian ancestry.

shtetl (pl. *shtetlkh*): Yiddish for a small town or village in eastern Europe.

Talmud: the term refers to either of the two works, one compiled in Babylon and the other in Palestine, which contain discussion of Jewish law. Each of these works include the Mishnah along with the Gemara, a commentary on and a supplement to the Mishnah. While both books are important documents, the

Babylonian Talmud is seen as being more authoritative because of its greater length and historical influence over Jews and Judaism.

tanna (pl. *tannaim*): Aramaic for "to teach"; rabbinic sages active in c. 10–220 CE who lived during the era of Roman rule of ancient Palestine. As a cohort, they transmitted Jewish oral tradition to their students. Their teachings were subsequently written down, codified, and became the basis of the Mishnah and Talmud. The era of the *tannaim* was followed by that of the *amoraim* (see above).

Torah: the Hebrew Bible or Pentateuch.

World Zionist Congress: the representative body and highest authority in the World Zionist Organization (see below), created by Theodor Herzl (1860–1904), the father of modern political Zionism. The First Zionist Congress was held in 1897; between 1898 and 1939 the Congress convened every one to two years on twenty-one occasions. Only after World War II did the Twenty-second Zionist Congress convene, thereafter meeting approximately every four years following establishment of the Jewish state.

World Zionist Organization: the political organization established by Theodor Herzl and the World Zionist Congress (see above), responsible for coordinating and implementing the political, financial, and development strategies of the Zionist movement in the diaspora and Palestine.

yeshivah (pl. *yeshivot*): the Hebrew and Yiddish term for a school for advanced talmudic study.

Yishuv: Hebrew term for the Jewish community in Palestine before the creation of the State of Israel in 1948; the "Old Yishuv" refers to the traditional, religiously observant Jewish community established prior to 1881.

zadik: Hebrew for "righteous one," a title given to significant figures and rabbis in traditional Judaism.

Index

Page numbers in italics refer to illustrations